W9-CEU-610

PENGUIN CLASSICS

UNSUNG

MICHELLE D. COMMANDER is associate director and curator of the Lapidus Center for the Historical Analysis of Transatlantic Slavery at the Schomburg Center for Research in Black Culture. A Ford Foundation and Fulbright fellowship recipient, she is the author of *Afro-Atlantic Flight: Speculative Returns and the Black Fantastic* and *Avidly Reads Passages*.

KEVIN YOUNG is currently the director of the Schomburg Center for Research in Black Culture, named a National Historic Landmark in 2017. He is the author of thirteen books of poetry and prose, most recently *Brown* (Knopf, 2018), as featured on *The Daily Show with Trevor Noah*. His nonfiction book *Bunk* (Graywolf Press, 2017) won the Anisfield-Wolf Book Award for Nonfiction, was longlisted for the National Book Award, and was named a *New York Times* Notable Book. He is the editor of nine other volumes, including the anthology *African American Poetry: 250 Years of Struggle & Song*, recently published by Library of America. A member of the American Academy of Arts and Sciences and a Chancellor of the Academy of American Poets, Young is the poetry editor of *The New Yorker* and newly named director of the Smithsonian's National Museum of African American History and Culture.

Hampshire County Public Library
153 West Main Street
Romney, WV 26757

THE SCHOMBURG CENTER FOR RESEARCH IN BLACK CULTURE

Unsung

UNHERALDED NARRATIVES OF AMERICAN SLAVERY & ABOLITION

Foreword by Series Editor
KEVIN YOUNG

Edited with an Introduction by
MICHELLE D. COMMANDER

PENGUIN BOOKS

PENGUIN BOOKS

An imprint of Penguin Random House LLC
penguinrandomhouse.com

First published in the United States of America by Penguin Books 2021

Introduction, suggestions for further reading, headnotes, and compilation
copyright © 2021 by The Schomburg Center for Research in Black Culture
Foreword copyright © 2021 by Kevin Young
Penguin supports copyright. Copyright fuels creativity, encourages diverse voices,
promotes free speech, and creates a vibrant culture. Thank you for buying an authorized
edition of this book and for complying with copyright laws by not reproducing, scanning, or
distributing any part of it in any form without permission. You are supporting writers
and allowing Penguin to continue to publish books for every reader.

The editor wishes to thank Yale University Library, where a scholar recently
found the illustrative 1786 work "An Essay on Slavery, with Justification to Divine
Providence that God Rules over All Things" by Jupiter Hammon, Hillhouse
Family Papers (MS 282). Manuscripts and Archives, Yale University Library.

LIBRARY OF CONGRESS CATALOGING-IN-PUBLICATION DATA
Names: Young, Kevin, 1970– writer of foreword. |
Commander, Michelle D., 1978– editor, writer of introduction. |
Schomburg Center for Research in Black Culture, issuing body.
Title: Unsung: unheralded narratives of American slavery & abolition /
The Schomburg Center for Research in Black Culture; foreword by series
editor Kevin Young; edited with an introduction by Michelle D. Commander.
Other titles: Unheralded narratives of American slavery & abolition
Description: [New York]: Penguin Books, 2021. | Includes bibliographical references.
Identifiers: LCCN 2020042631 (print) | LCCN 2020042632 (ebook) |
ISBN 9780143136088 (paperback) | ISBN 9780525507697 (ebook)
Subjects: LCSH: Slave narratives—United States. | Slaves' writings, American. |
Fugitive slaves—United States—Biography. | African American abolitionists—Biography. |
Abolitionists—United States—Biography. | Slaves—United States—Biography. |
Slavery—United States—History—19th century. | Antislavery movements—United
States—History—19th century. | African Americans—Social conditions—19th century.
Classification: LCC E444 .U57 2021 (print) | LCC E444 (ebook) | DDC
326/.80922 [B]—dc23
LC record available at https://lccn.loc.gov/2020042631
LC ebook record available at https://lccn.loc.gov/2020042632

Printed in the United States of America
1 3 5 7 9 10 8 6 4 2

Set in Sabon LT Pro

Contents

UNSUNG

ACCOUNTS OF SLAVE REBELLION AND INSURRECTION

BLACK ABOLITIONIST VOICES

NARRATIVES OF SLAVERY AND FUGITIVE ESCAPES

ANTISLAVERY POETICS, CHILDREN'S LITERATURE, AND DRAMA

Poetry and Music

Jupiter Hammon, "An Address to the Negroes in the State of New York" (1787); An Evening's Improvement, Shewing the Necessity of Beholding the Lamb of God. To Which Is Added a Dialogue Entitled "The Kind

Children's Literature

Drama

THE DAWN OF FREEDOM

Foreword

Born in Harlem, James Baldwin wrote often of his beginnings here, including his reading "every single book" in the transformative space now known as the Schomburg Center for Research in Black Culture. "I went to the 135th Street library at least three or four times a week, and I read everything here. I mean, every single book in that library," Baldwin wrote. "In some blind and instinctive way, I knew that what was happening in those books was also happening all around me. And I was trying to make a connection between the books and the life I saw and the life I lived." The connection Baldwin made between his life and the lives that the future Schomburg Center contained speaks to the power of the books, history, and culture found there, as well as the center's rich origins.

Part of The New York Public Library from the start, the Schomburg Center was founded in 1925 as the Division of Negro History, Literature, and Prints, recognizing the changing nature of Harlem after the Great Migration. Yet what truly transformed the division found at the 135th Street Branch was the addition of the stellar collection of Afro–Puerto Rican scholar and collector Arturo Alfonso Schomburg the following year. Today the thousands of books, pamphlets, and manuscripts in Arturo Schomburg's initial collection have increased to more than 11 million items that, through new acquisitions, programming, and exhibitions, illuminate the richness of Black history, arts, and experience worldwide.

What has become evident in our recent Mellon Foundation–funded work enriching the catalog of what I call Arturo Schomburg's seed library is that he was not merely a bibliophile or a lover of books but a self-taught scholar, homemade historian, and creator and collector of knowledge. The private collection he assembled was always for public consumption, regularly loaned out to fellow writers, radicals, Prince Hall Masons, and

other seekers of knowledge (and, miraculously, regularly returned). Schomburg's collection bore witness to the travels and
travails of the Black Atlantic, much as he had witnessed firsthand, linking the Caribbean, the broader Americas, Europe,
and Africa. Indeed, Schomburg used the proceeds of the sale of
his collection to The New York Public Library for ten thousand
dollars—a goodly sum in 1926, provided by the Carnegie Corporation—to travel to Spain, the motherland of his native
tongue, in order to collect more books. He carried them back
across the Black Atlantic as the first curator of the Schomburg
Center, serving in the role from 1932 until his death in 1938.

Schomburg may now be thought of as the nexus of an infor-
mal yet important group of Black librarians, bibliographers, educators, and activists who preserved, protected, and provided
access to the rich history of global Black culture—a history that
a teacher once told young Arturo didn't exist. Together with a
number of figures—including Catherine Latimer, the first Black
librarian in The New York Public Library system, who worked
to shape the collections; novelist Nella Larsen, who served as a
children's librarian; and activist Ella Baker and scholar Alain
Locke, who transformed the Schomburg Center with education
programs in the 1930s—Arturo, also known as Arthur, made
the institution a center in all senses of the word. In the year of
its founding, the special issue of *Survey Graphic* edited by
Locke that would later expand into his groundbreaking *New
Negro* anthology, including Schomburg's famous essay "The
Negro Digs Up His Past," said as much: "The branch of the
New York Public Library which stands on the main cross thoroughfare of Harlem, 135th Street, seeks to be what the Carnegie Corporation would call an intelligence center." It is no
accident that the Schomburg Center was founded in the heart
and at the height of the Harlem Renaissance, and it has
served as a beacon for nearly a century, keeping the home lights
burning and helping to make Harlem a global Black cultural
capital.

Today, the Schomburg Center still serves as not only a sanctuary for literature, an intelligence center, and a beacon of
Black brilliance, but also what scholar Vanessa Valdez has
called a liberatory space. Some of this, as Locke noted, is its lo-

cation: the Schomburg Center remains part of the rich cultural corridor of 135th Street, catty-corner from the crucial Speakers Corner, which saw speeches by Marcus Garvey and Malcolm X; situated directly across Lenox Avenue, now renamed Malcolm X Boulevard, from the training, teaching, and tireless practice of doctors and nurses at Harlem Hospital; and sharing the block with the Harlem YMCA, whose neon sign and Aaron Douglas mural often first welcomed those new to town, from Langston Hughes to Ralph Ellison. Countless brilliant scholars, artists, and activists gathered in the Schomburg Center's historic reading room facing 135th Street—including Garvey and Zora Neale Hurston, Countee Cullen and Claude McKay, and, later on, designer Dapper Dan and poet and playwright Sonia Sanchez, iconic figures who still frequently return to the center.

After becoming one of the hubs of the Harlem Renaissance, the Schomburg Center is not only where Baldwin read "every single book" but where saxophone colossus Sonny Rollins remembers spending time—both Harlem-born geniuses journeyed around the world from their start in Harlem, with their archives recently coming back full circle to the Schomburg Center in 2017. Harlem is where Ruby Dee and Ossie Davis met Harry Belafonte, becoming actors and activists together, and where both Ann Petry and Gertrude Hadley Jeannette acted before becoming writers, all in the Schomburg Center's American Negro Theatre, still housed in what is now the courtyard level. Harlem is where filmmaker Oscar Micheaux plotted, filmed, and projected Black life for popular consumption and activist Malcolm X transformed from his troubled beginnings to become our Black Shining Prince. Harlem is where, following in the footsteps of his Garveyite grandfather, Fred "Fab 5 Freddy" Brathwaite makes his home, continuing as a hip-hop pioneer and ambassador—having united downtown and uptown culture and introducing, influencing, and producing many of hip-hop's earliest innovations. All of these artists and activists have become part of the Schomburg Center's broader Home to Harlem initiative, their archives recently returning home to Harlem to live and prosper nearly a hundred years after Schomburg's seed library arrived here.

The "vindicating evidences" that these figures assembled gave birth to the field of Black Studies, advanced adult education, and changed Black theater and film history—all around the intellectual and artistic hub that would become the Schomburg Center for Research in Black Culture.

Today, we at the Schomburg Center have undertaken a new series of books in the spirit of Arturo Schomburg's rich legacy. *Unsung: Unheralded Narratives of American Slavery & Abolition* represents the first in a projected series of volumes edited by the Schomburg Center and published by Penguin Classics. These volumes will consider the full range of the Black lives stewarded at the center, including the history of Black books, liberation, speculation, and imagination.

The center has, in fact, long engaged in a robust publishing program, starting with internal publications charting its holdings and activities in the 1930s, through the revivals and reprints of the 1960s, down to the late 1980s, when we began our most ambitious, concerted publishing effort: the Schomburg Library of Nineteenth-Century Black Women Writers, thirty titles issued in conjunction with Oxford University Press. This groundbreaking series, edited by Henry Louis Gates Jr., helped codify interest in the rich tradition created by African American women, starting with Phillis Wheatley, the first African American to publish a book in the Americas, to essays and romances and serialized novels by Pauline E. Hopkins, Frances E. W. Harper, and others. This also led to an important digital humanities project in 1998, believed to be the first across The New York Public Library, which includes fifty-two published works by Black women. While these print editions are unfortunately out of print, the online resource remains.

As a young writer and student, I fondly remember reading all the Schomburg Black Women Writers volumes I could get my hands on, struck by their sophisticated design and welcoming formats, with texts often reprinted from copies held at the Schomburg Center. While the vast holdings of the Schomburg Center may prove out of reach to a reader less ambitious than Baldwin, here was a compact library one could consume, and I did. The Black Women Writers series rewrote the tale of the past few centuries, correcting the record for those who have willfully forgotten the legacy and urgency of African American women's literature, not to mention of Black print culture, those books, magazines, and pamphlets issued by Black authors and publishers from slavery down to the present day. Today, as series editor of the Penguin Classics series, I am delighted to witness the ways the Schomburg Center will continue to retell the story of Black life, starting with *Unsung*.

The antebellum era remains crucial to understanding our history as a nation and as a people. The oppressive system of that peculiar paradox called American slavery has had its effects on all citizens, especially those whose rights the country regularly denied. The recent global pandemic has only heightened the other, still uncured pandemic of racism that has led to the world's largest civil rights protests in 2020. Slavery wasn't all that long ago—activist and actor Paul Robeson's father grew up enslaved, for instance—and was followed by a century and more of Black Codes, Jim Crow, Jane Crow, and "slavery by another name." Its lingering effects can be felt in everything from extrajudicial violence to police patrols, from unfounded attitudes about Black people to opportunities still denied some four hundred years after our ancestors' arrival on these shores.

But this is looking at it only from the top down. From another angle we see the regular resistance by enslaved African Americans, found in their innumerable daily insurrections, from stolen time and work delays to stealing their very selves away. Such resistance is found not only in outright uprisings such as Nat Turner's but in those forms of radical reading of which Baldwin is an inheritor. As Baldwin said, "You think your pain and your heartbreak are unprecedented in the history of the world, but then you read." Despite the outlawing of Black literacy under slavery, this tradition of radical reading was undertaken and passed down—and might be extended to the writing of tracts (by David Walker and Frederick Douglass), writing down and publishing poems (Phillis Wheatley), composing from memory (George Moses Horton), and inscribing poems on pottery (as with David Drake). Every enslaved person is an abolitionist.

This is the approach behind *Unsung*, which makes use of the compelling collection that's part of the Schomburg Center's Lapidus Center for the Historical Analysis of Transatlantic Slavery. Editor Michelle Commander, curator and associate director of the Lapidus Center, has assembled an anthology that speaks to the subversions found by the enslaved, their steady work in saying who they were and who they weren't. Informed by new scholarship, underexposed stories, and fresh perspectives, *Unsung* manages to go beyond our usual views of enslavement and typically reprinted narratives to offer a look as broad and deep as the Black responses to slavery and the rivers sung of, and crossed, in escaping it. These "unheralded narratives" are stories not always seen, telling the history of enslaved Black people but also speaking of their resistance to an inhumane system in a nation founded on freedom. Black abolition took its roots early in the era, and Commander's expansive editorial approach has yielded an unprecedented volume, featuring rarities and destined-to-be classics, often taken from the more than four hundred tracts, poetry books, and sermons that make up the Lapidus Center collection, telling the story of slavery and abolition across the Atlantic World.

Commander has assembled an anthology that digs up the past but also speaks to the future of the Schomburg Center, sharing its rich holdings with a world that Black people have helped to make. Who knows but that this series too will find its way to a young writer readying to embark on a lifetime of words and radical reading, coming to discover a nation of knowledge, and counting themselves lucky to follow in the legacy of Arturo Schomburg and his namesake Schomburg Center.

KEVIN YOUNG

Introduction

Drawing from the Schomburg Center's rich holdings, including from the strengths of its Lapidus Center for the Historical Analysis of Transatlantic Slavery's collection, *Unsung: Unheralded Narratives of American Slavery & Abolition* presents a series of materials on slavery, rebellion, resistance, and abolitionist protest in the United States that makes the case for recognizing Black people as agents and architects of their own lives and ultimate liberation even as they agitated for emancipation with white abolitionists. *Unsung* takes care to center these stories, particularly focusing on the voices and actions of formerly enslaved Black people and lesser-known abolitionists, not to suggest that antislavery agitation was carried out in wholly racialized silos but rather to demonstrate that from the moment they were captured, enslaved people's resistance propelled what would become an increasingly dynamic and significant series of social, political, and humanist movements across the Atlantic World.

The forced migrations prompted by investments in transatlantic slavery devastated and ripped apart families and communities, brutally killing millions of people of African descent and legalizing the extraction of labor from the survivors who were callously traded, sold, and resold as commodities. The embedded contradictions in America's case, with the founding fathers establishing a nation built on principles of equality, liberty, and democracy on the one hand and its rise dependent on slavery speculation on the other, have led to centuries of political and philosophical conversations and unrest. While slaveholders and vigilantes threatened and attempted to control Black bodily autonomy using a series of inane philosophical, religious, and pseudoscientific justifications, enslaved people and their allies skillfully countered this malevolence via everyday and more formally coordinated types of resistance.

Few known first-person accounts of the Middle Passage exist. Olaudah Equiano's narrative, first published in Britain in 1789, chronicles Equiano and his sister's kidnapping from the safety of their home in the Kingdom of Benin and into the uncertainty of transatlantic slavery, their permanent separation, and Equiano's life through increasingly more brutal forms of slavery as a victim and witness, including his service for slave ship captains and upon British navy vessels. Equiano writes affectingly about the ways that the sensory excesses of the conditions on slave ships exacerbated the captives' feelings of loss, social alienation, and confusion:

> The closeness of the place, and the heat of the climate, added to the number in the ship, which was so crowded that each had scarcely room to turn himself, almost suffocated us. This produced copious perspirations, so that the air soon became unfit for respiration, from a variety of loathsome smells, and brought on a sickness among the slaves, of which many died, thus falling victims to the improvident avarice, as I may call it, of their purchasers. This wretched situation was again aggravated by the galling of the chains, now become insupportable; and the filth of the necessary tubs, into which the children often fell, and were almost suffocated. The shrieks of the women, and the groans of the dying, rendered the whole a scene of horror almost inconceivable (48).

According to the Trans-Atlantic Slave Trade Database, some 12.5 million African captives were plucked from their motherlands and shipped from the coastlines of Africa, through the Middle Passage, and into the New World during the course of the slave trade. Millions of souls perished en route. Ultimately, some 10.7 million African captives survived the harrowing journey and were sold to enslavers across the Americas and the Caribbean. An estimated 388,000 African captives disembarked in what is now the United States. Historian Stephanie Smallwood suggests that the fullness of the lives of Africans pre-captivity was reconfigured by traders and enslavers to that of mere Black "bodies animated only by others' calculated investment in their physical capacities. . . . Along the coast, captives felt the enclosure of prison walls and the weight of iron shackles holding them incarcerated in shore-based trade forts or aboard ships that functioned as floating warehouses as captives were accumulated" (35). On their precarious traversals across the Atlantic Ocean aboard slave ships, the captives were stripped of much of their agency, and their sense of time and place essentially collapsed, as the "experience of motion [was] without discernible direction or destination" (122). Though they spent most of the fateful voyage across the Atlantic chained in the bowels of these vessels, the captives did not remain prone or complacent in their circumstances. Some refused to eat or careened themselves and their children overboard, choosing physical death over uncertain futures. They flew instead toward the surety of spiritual returns to their homelands. In the moments that crew members let down their guards as they exercised the human cargo to keep their investments physically robust, some captives, who realized that they outnumbered the traders and crew, rose up violently in insurrection, setting the course for resistance as the philosophy for subverting and overcoming slavery's most brutal and dehumanizing characteristics. The future to come would be one of spirited slave rebellions and abolitionist revolutions on the ground on plantations across the geographies of the Atlantic World.

THE ART OF ABOLITIONISM

While researching and writing the editorial apparatus for this volume, I was moved by the bravery and artistry of the movement for slavery abolition. It is not as though every narrative or historical fact was new to me as a curator and scholar of slavery and memory. Rather, I continue to find extraordinary the persistence of nineteenth-century antislavery activism by advocates who worked in tandem to defeat racialized slavery using a variety of strategies. In her bold and instructive book *The Slave's Cause: A History of Abolition*, Manisha Sinha stresses, about the significance of what was gained in the struggle for emancipation, "Modern racial slavery was a monstrous hybrid that combined the horrors of an archaic labor system with the rapacious efficiencies of capitalism. Like the slave system they opposed, abolitionists were hybrids, old-fashioned moralizers as well as modern exponents of human rights. It is no coincidence that the brief, incomplete triumph of the abolitionist vision resulted in the greatest expansion of American democracy, and that the demise of abolition went hand in hand with the greatest contraction of democracy" (3). To assert their bodily autonomy and evoke fear among planters, enslaved people skirted what historian Stephanie M. H. Camp refers to as slave plantations' *geography of containment*—the planned restrictive cartographies on and surrounding plantations as well as the means used by enslavers, overseers, and proslavery white citizens to restrain the movements of enslaved Black people—by continuing to resist in overt and covert ways to create *rival geographies* on their plantations, and by working slowly, stealing food and clothing, fighting back, running away, and daring to meet secretly to fellowship with one another and to plan subversive acts.

At the same time, activists attempted to unify across race, gender, class, and other markers of difference. They disagreed, but they pressed on. In the face of violence, intimidation, and even murderous bands of proslavery mobs, abolitionists wrote and signed their names to letters and editorials that demanded prompt reconfigurations of the social order. They held antislavery rallies, fairs, and conventions to educate the masses, strategize, and raise money for the cause. Others traveled widely, delivering stirring speeches and making ardent appeals to lawmakers. Concerned about the younger generation's morality, antislavery educators and activists penned children's books and slavery alphabet primers, and they published columns in antislavery periodicals to advise children of societal ills and the fiery fates that awaited Christian hypocrites who supported slavery or stood by silently. In their minds, the nation's youth had ethical and moral responsibilities to fight for their enslaved brethren's liberty in their contemporary moment and in the future.

For most Black abolitionists, the idea of gradualism—a proposed process whereby enslaved people would be freed in a deliberate, step-by-step manner over the course of a number of years—was an unacceptable compromise. Indeed, appeals for enslaved peoples' liberation were paired with the stipulation that the nation recognize Black people as full citizens who could ex-

ercise their rights immediately. Within and outside of the abolitionist ranks, debates roared over integration, repatriation, and
emigration. Could Black people assimilate safely and successfully in America? Where might Black people best realize the
promises of life, liberty, and the pursuit of happiness? Supported
by American lawmakers, some white citizens who were against
slavery but did not view Black citizenship as practicable, and a
cohort of hopeful Black freepersons, the American Colonization
Society was founded in 1816 to plan and financially support repatriation and colonization schemes to send emancipated people
to Africa and Central and South America as Christian missionaries and as self-appointed governing officials. As highlighted in
the documents included in this anthology, most Black abolitionists deemed such schemes as unacceptable, immoral, and unfeasible for a number of reasons. They cited the American-established
colony of Liberia as the most reprehensible example. The 1847
settlement at Liberia resulted in the deaths of numerous Black
settlers who were not used to the tropical climate and others
who succumbed to illnesses, particularly tropical diseases such
as yellow fever. These settlers brought along Western infectious
diseases, war, land grabs, and other horrors of empire that deci-
mated indigenous populations. Ironically and tragically, their
colonialist postures under the motto "the love of liberty brought
us here" very much imitated the dreadful power dynamics that
marked the institution of slavery.

Other abolitionists tired of the battle within the States
and elected to fight for abolition from places of respite elsewhere, including the large settlement of free Black Americans
and self-liberated individuals in Canada West (Ontario). The
majority, however, demanded their rights in the United States
and were determined to not be moved. The proto-Black nation-
alist and abolitionist David Walker spoke for many when he
exclaimed in his 1829 pamphlet *Walker's Appeal, in Four Articles*, "Let no man of us budge one step, and let slave-holders
come to beat us from our country. America is more our country, than it is the whites—we have enriched it with our *blood
and tears*. The greatest riches in all America have arisen from
our blood and tears:—and will they drive us from our property
and homes, which we have earned with our *blood*? They must

look sharp or this very thing will bring swift destruction upon them" (73). The Fugitive Slave Act of 1850, which not only rendered it legal for enslavers to travel to free states to collect their fugitive enslaved human property but also would likely have the unwitting effect of emboldening crafty kidnappers to capture and sell free Black people into slavery, changed the stakes for those who could not bear the likelihood of how dangerously precarious their lives would become under the new legislation.

In August 1850, graduating senior Lucy Stanton, who had been born free in Ohio in 1831, rose from her seat to give an address before her fellow Oberlin Collegiate Institute graduates, faculty, staff, and attendees. Entitled "A Plea for the Oppressed," Stanton's speech articulated her wish that young women especially understood the weight of the coming federal enactment of the Fugitive Slave Act. With a keen grasp of the nation's history, including the horrific ways that slavery dehumanized both the enslaved and the enslaver, Stanton encouraged her audience to take up the abolitionist cause, as slavery was corrupt and barbaric—it was a system so woefully embedded into America's foundation that the effects of the greed and brutality that sustained it were felt in slave and free states alike. Stanton issued a dire, succinct warning about the wide reach of slavery and the need for abolitionism: "Slavery is the combination of all crime. It is War" (208).

Some seven years later, in August 1857, the prominent abolitionist Frederick Douglass walked onstage in Canandaigua, New York, on the occasion of the twenty-third anniversary of the American Abolition Society, to deliver the speech "West India Emancipation," which outlined with convincing clarity aspects of the fight for slavery abolition in British colonies. Douglass emphatically and effectively drew connections between slavery in various societies, weaving in insight about the United States–based movement's successes and failures, and divisions within the movement, including his own break with moderate white abolitionists who lamented the rise of more aggressive and direct antislavery agitation. As Douglass's speech reached fever pitch, he issued a proclamation about the importance of direct resistance and the changing tenor of the movement. It was a bold articulation, from the movement's most visible Black leader, about the sea change in their abolitionist ranks: a great number of Black activists had begun approaching their reckonings with slavery with the full knowledge that moral suasion—the appeals to religious, humanitarian, and social values—as a strategy had not been as effective as they intended, as far too many U.S. citizens and lawmakers had remained staunchly proslavery or indifferent to the thriving institution:

> If there is no struggle, there is no progress. Those who profess to favor freedom, and yet depreciate agitation, are men who want crops without plowing up the ground. They want rain without thunder and lightning. They want the ocean without the awful roar of its many waters. This struggle may be a moral one; or it may be a physical one; or it may be both moral and physical; but it must be a struggle. Power concedes nothing without a demand. It never did and it never will. Find out just what any people will quietly submit to and you have found out the exact measure of injustice and wrong which will be imposed upon them, and these will continue till they are resisted with either words or blows, or with both. The limits of tyrants are prescribed by the endurance of those whom they oppress (22).

Douglass would know. In his dramatic account of his enslavement and the cruelties suffered by his loved ones, *Narrative of the Life of Frederick Douglass: An American Slave*, Douglass recalls moments of small and extraordinary forms of resistance carried out by himself and his coconspirators. Douglass's use of direct action against his enslavers had actuated his fugitive flight from slavery. They were a series of necessary actions that Douglass rightly viewed as a continuation of Black radicality seen in enslaved people's uprisings and rebellions. He observed about the role of nonviolent and violent methods used to end British slavery, "While one showed that slavery was wrong, the other showed that it was dangerous as well as wrong" (23). From the slave ship to American plantations, ship crews, traders, enslavers, and vigilantes threatened and restricted Black bodily autonomy in a variety of ways. And at every turn, enslaved people participated in everyday and coordinated types of resistance, forged kinship networks, and organized with allied organizations to demand their freedom from the heritable and generational terror of enslavement.

As Walker pointedly declared, Stanton wisely noted, and Douglass's firsthand experiences had shown, the centuries-long "war" inaugurated by chattel slavery required that the majority of Black laypeople and activists remained in the United States. The persistence of slavery prompted them to participate in a range of ever-evolving battles and to agitate in artful, collaborative, and unrelenting ways to defeat the peculiar institution.

COUNTERNARRATIVES AND THE UNSUNG

The Schomburg Center for Research in Black Culture's founder, Arturo Schomburg, stressed, about the importance of rethinking how we conceptualize American history, "The American Negro must remake his past in order to make his future. Though it is orthodox to think of America as the one country where it is unnecessary to have a past, what is a luxury for the nation as a whole becomes a prime social necessity for the Negro. . . . History must restore what slavery took away, for it is the social damage of slavery that the present generations must repair and offset" (670). To this end, *Unsung* features slavery-related items from Arturo Schomburg's seed collection and the Schomburg Center's more recently acquired titles: rare histories and first-person narratives about American slavery that were significant attestants to their own times and most certainly assisted Schomburg's generation in understanding the roots of their contemporary social struggles and triumphs in the early to mid-twentieth century. This volume places documents by well-known abolitionists alongside less-familiar orators and life stories, highlighting overlooked or previously undercelebrated accounts of the everyday lives and activism that were regarded in their own time but are mostly excised from dominant narratives about slavery and its abolition in the United States.

With the long nineteenth century in mind, *Unsung* charts a series of subversive national and international abolitionist moves.

The selected contents herein are unsung and unheralded, though not necessarily forgotten or unknown among scholars of slavery or history enthusiasts. Represented are a range of witnesses, including Eliza Potter, a hairstylist who participates in and listens to conversations between plantation mistresses; orators such as Sarah Mapps Douglass and James Forten Jr., who conveyed impactful messages on the antislavery lecture circuit; the affecting testimonies of formerly enslaved men and women about the dehumanizing properties of the institution as well as the ways that enslaved people loved one another and created spaces of joy despite their circumstances; and antislavery writers' fiction and nonfiction works for young readers to nurture an antislavery future. In the spirit of achieving a fuller view into the struggles involved in any sort of unified protest, for example, this collection also offers a view into how racism and misogyny sometimes seeped through antislavery documents themselves and interpersonally, threatening to irreparably destabilize an otherwise progressive movement. *Unsung* includes excerpts and full reprints of legal and personal accounts of slave rebellion, impactful selections from abolitionist newspapers, and published speeches that circulated and inspired within and outside of the United States, and it uniquely gives insight into five key aspects of American slavery and abolition in its five sections:

1. the ways that enslaved people's coordinated and unplanned acts of resistance across the Atlantic World inspired more formalized antislavery thought and action in the United States;
2. the significant role that women played in the abolitionist cause through their activism, witness bearing, and agitation;
3. the question of Black mobility and debates over integration versus emigration and repatriation, particularly to Canada and West Africa;
4. the art of antislavery protest that were designed to appeal inventively to mass audiences, highlighting known and unheralded slave narratives, poetry, music, and plays; and
5. a select record of antislavery literature for children and

youth, including pamphlets, fiction and nonfiction stories, poetry, and essays that aimed to nurture anti-racist
citizens in the nineteenth century.

Unsung concludes with the promises, successes, and disappointments of the Reconstruction era to signal the limits of liberatory legal statutes in everyday reality and to highlight the
uncertainty of Black freedom in that moment and, with unfortunate echoes, our own. Like any anthology of this size, some
compelling items are lengthy and appear here as thoughtfully
chosen extractions. Regrettably, other fascinating works had to
be left out completely because of space, though in these cases, I
have taken care to select items that articulate critical aspects of
materials that could not be included.

As I write this introduction, we are in the midst of a resur-
gence of public interest in transatlantic slavery. The brutal era
of slavery is our inheritance, and its history is often where we
turn to gain a better understanding of the long, bitter, and ever-
evolving forms of oppression and all that remains in their after-
life. Given the frequent expressions of racist rhetoric, racialized
violence, righteous protests, and debates over slavery-era me-
morialization in the contemporary moment, it is common to
hear utterances in the media and from everyday citizens alike
regarding the state of American progress toward the realization
of a true democracy. In times of social unrest and crisis, we are
wise to look back to determine the paths and missteps that
brought us to those particular junctures—we must take time to
pause, read, reflect, learn, and take reparative actions to attend
to the harm done. My hope is that this volume will serve as a
kind of springboard for readers' journeys into slavery's archives—
that readers will elect to seek out our materials at the Schomburg
Center for Research in Black Culture and/or other repositories
for themselves as they contemplate transatlantic slavery's buried histories and pronounced legacies in the United States and
throughout the Atlantic World.

MICHELLE D. COMMANDER

Suggestions for Further Reading

Baptist, Edward. *The Half Has Never Been Told: Slavery and the Making of American Capitalism.* New York: Basic Books, 2016.

Basker, James G., ed. *American Antislavery Writings: Colonial Beginnings to Emancipation.* New York: Library of America, 2012.

Berlin, Ira. *Many Thousands Gone: The First Two Centuries of Slavery in North America.* Cambridge, MA: Belknap Press, 1998.

Berry, Daina Ramey. *The Price for Their Pound of Flesh: The Value of the Enslaved, from Womb to Grave, in the Building of a Nation.* New York: Beacon Press, 2017.

Blight, David. *Frederick Douglass: Prophet of Freedom.* New York: Simon & Schuster, 2018.

Bordewich, Fergus M. *Bound for Canaan: The Epic Story of the Underground Railroad, America's First Civil Rights Movement.* New York: Amistad, 2006.

Brown, Christopher Leslie. *Moral Capital: Foundations of British Abolitionism.* Williamsburg, VA: Omohundro Institute of Early American History and Culture; Chapel Hill: University of North Carolina Press, 2006.

Brown, Vincent. *Tacky's Revolt: The Story of an Atlantic Slave War.* Cambridge, MA: Belknap Press, 2020.

Camp, Stephanie M. H. *Closer to Freedom: Enslaved Women and Everyday Resistance in the Plantation South.* Chapel Hill: University of North Carolina Press, 2004.

Capshaw, Katharine, and Anna Mae Duane, eds. *Who Writes for Black Children?: African American Children's Literature before 1900.* Minneapolis: University of Minnesota Press, 2017.

Cooper Owens, Deirdre. *Medical Bondage: Race, Gender, and the Origins of American Gynecology.* Athens: University of Georgia Press, 2017.

Dubois, Laurent. *Avengers of the New World: The Story of the Haitian Revolution.* Cambridge, MA: Belknap Press, 2004.

Dunbar, Erica Armstrong. *Never Caught: The Washingtons' Relentless Pursuit of Their Runaway Slave, Ona Judge.* New York: 37Ink/Atria, 2017.

Eltis, David. *The Rise of African Slavery in the Americas*. Cambridge, UK; New York: Cambridge University Press, 2000.

Finley, Cheryl. *Committed to Memory: The Art of the Slave Ship Icon*. Princeton, NJ: Princeton University Press, 2018.

Foner, Eric. *Reconstruction: America's Unfinished Revolution, 1863–1877* (updated edition). New York: Harper Perennial Modern Classics, 2014.

Fuentes, Marisa J. *Dispossessed Lives: Enslaved Women, Violence, and the Archive*. Philadelphia: University of Pennsylvania Press, 2016.

Glymph, Thaviola. *Out of the House of Bondage: The Transformation of the Plantation Household*. Cambridge, UK; New York: Cambridge University Press, 2008.

Gordon-Reed, Annette. *The Hemingses of Monticello: An American Family*. New York: W. W. Norton, 2009.

Hager, Christopher. *Word by Word: Emancipation and the Act of Writing*. Cambridge, MA: Harvard University Press, 2015.

Harris, Leslie M. *In the Shadow of Slavery: African Americans in New York City, 1626–1863*. Chicago: University of Chicago Press, 2003.

Hartman, Saidiya V. *Scenes of Subjection: Terror, Slavery, and Self-Making in Nineteenth-Century America*. New York: Oxford University Press, 1997.

Heywood, Linda M., and John K. Thornton. *Central Africans, Atlantic Creoles, and the Foundation of the Americas, 1585–1660*. New York: Cambridge University Press, 2007.

Horne, Gerald. *The Counter-Revolution of 1776: Slave Resistance and the Origins of the United States of America*. New York: New York University Press, 2014.

Hunter, Tera W. *Bound in Wedlock: Slave and Free Black Marriage in the Nineteenth Century*. Cambridge, MA: Belknap Press, 2017.

Johnson, Walter. *Soul by Soul: Life Inside the Antebellum Slave Market*. Cambridge, MA: Harvard University Press, 1999.

Jones, Martha S. *Birthright Citizens: A History of Race and Rights in Antebellum America*. Cambridge, UK; New York: Cambridge University Press, 2018.

Jones-Rogers, Stephanie E. *They Were Her Property: White Women as Slave Owners in the American South*. New Haven, CT: Yale University Press, 2019.

McInnis, Maurie D. *Slaves Waiting for Sale: Abolitionist Art and the American Slave Trade*. Chicago: University of Chicago Press, 2013.

Miles, Tiya. *Ties That Bind: The Story of an Afro-Cherokee Family in Slavery and Freedom*, 2nd ed. Oakland: University of California Press, 2015.

Mitchell, Mary Niall. *Raising Freedom's Child: Black Children and Visions of the Future after Slavery.* New York: New York University Press, 2008.

Mustakeem, Sowande' M. *Slavery at Sea: Terror, Sex, and Sickness in the Middle Passage.* Urbana: University of Illinois Press, 2016.

Polgar, Paul J. *Standard-Bearers of Equality: America's First Abolition Movement.* Williamsburg, VA: Omohundro Institute of Early American History and Culture; Chapel Hill: University of North Carolina Press, 2019.

Scott, Julius S. *The Common Wind: Afro-American Currents in the Age of the Haitian Revolution.* London: Verso Books, 2018.

Sinha, Manisha. *The Slave's Cause: A History of Abolition.* New Haven, CT: Yale University Press, 2017.

Smallwood, Stephanie. *Saltwater Slavery: A Middle Passage from Africa to American Diaspora.* Cambridge, MA: Harvard University Press, 2008.

Taylor, Amy Murrell. *Embattled Freedom: Journeys through the Civil War's Slave Refugee Camps.* Chapel Hill: University of North Carolina Press, 2020.

White, Deborah Gray. *Ar'n't I a Woman?: Female Slaves in the Plantation South.* New York: W. W. Norton, 1999.

White, Shane, and Graham White. *The Sounds of Slavery: Discovering African American History through Songs, Sermons, and Speech.* Boston: Beacon Press, 2005.

Wilder, Craig Steven. *Ebony and Ivy: Race, Slavery, and the Troubled History of America's Universities.* New York: Bloomsbury Press, 2013.

Wilentz, Sean. *The Rise of American Democracy: Jefferson to Lincoln.* New York: W. W. Norton, 2006.

Unsung

ACCOUNTS OF SLAVE REBELLION AND INSURRECTION

DANIEL HORSMANDEN

In 1741, the British colony of New York was at the height of panic. Fires had raged throughout Manhattan for several weeks, leading lawmakers to question whether depraved members of the enslaved community, recently arrived immigrants, or other agitators were in their midst. In what was eventually deemed to be a certain "Negro plot" in which enslaved people sought vengeance for their condition, authorities rounded up, jailed, and tried two hundred enslaved people and ten white men who were the suspected architects of the terror. Nearly half of the enslaved people were found guilty and either hanged, exiled to plantations outside America, or burned at the stake. Others were summarily tossed into a dungeon beneath city hall, where they were intimidated into "confessing" to their crimes and asked to implicate others in the alleged scheme to burn down the city. Four white defendants were hanged and seven others were pardoned and banned from ever stepping foot in New York. Daniel Horsmanden (1691–1778), the judge who was appointed to investigate the fires and a possibly related robbery, compiled the testimonies, evidence, and a thorough list of those found guilty within this document. It remains unclear whether the "guilty" parties were truly culpable. What is certain is that stories of Black rebellion across the Atlantic World were persistent and increased white paranoia. Enslavers responded to real and imagined conspiracies in increasingly violent ways, as they realized that their prior efforts to tamp down resistance had been futile. Indeed, rebellious enslaved people would go on to fight for their dignity and often attempted to self-liberate, refusing to be held in the bonds of slavery forever.

From *The New-York Conspiracy;*
or, A History of the Negro Plot,
with the Journal of the Proceedings
Against the Conspirators at
New York in the Years 1741–2
(1810)

"Gentlemen of the grand jury,

"It is not without some concern, that I am obliged at this time to be more particular in your charge, than for many preceding terms there hath been occasion. The many frights and terrors which the good people of this city have of late been put into, by repeated and unusual fires, and burning of houses, give us too much room to suspect, that some of them at least, did not proceed from mere chance, or common accidents; but on the contrary, from the premeditated malice and wicked purposes of evil 36 and designing persons; and therefore, it greatly behoves us to use our utmost diligence, by all lawful ways and means, to discover the contrivers and perpetrators of such daring and flagitious undertakings: that, upon conviction, they may receive condign punishment; for although we have the happiness of living under a government which exceeds all others in the excellency of its constitution and laws, yet if those to whom the execution of them (which my lord Coke calls the life and soul of the law) is committed, do not exert themselves in a conscientious discharge of their respective duties, such laws which were intended for a terror to the evil-doer, and a protection to the good, will become a dead letter, and our most excellent constitution turned into anarchy and confusion; every one practising what he listeth, and doing what shall seem good in his own eyes: to prevent which, it is the duty of all grand juries to inquire into the conduct and behaviour of the people in their respective counties; and if, upon examination, they find any to have transgressed the laws of the land, to present them, that so they may by the court be put upon their trial, and then either to be discharged or punished according to their demerits.

"I am told there are several prisoners now in jail, who have been committed by the city magistrates, upon suspicion of having been concerned in some of the late fires; and others, who under pretence of assisting the unhappy sufferers, by saving their goods from the flames, for stealing, or receiving them. This indeed, is adding affliction to the afflicted, and is a very great aggravation of such crime, and therefore deserves a narrow inquiry: that so the exemplary punishment of the guilty (if any such should be so found) may deter others from committing the like villainies; for this kind of stealing, I think, has not been often practised among us.

"*Gentlemen,*

"Arson, or the malicious and voluntary burning, not only a mansion house, but also any other house, and the out buildings, or barns, and stables adjoining thereto, by night or by day, is felony at common law; and if any part of house be burned, the offender is guilty of felony, notwithstanding the fire afterwards be put out, or go out of itself.

"This crime is of so shocking a nature, that if we have any in this city, who, having been guilty thereof, should escape, who can say he is safe, or tell where it will end?

"*Gentlemen,*

"Another Thing which I cannot omit recommending to your 37 serious and diligent inquiry, is to find out and present all such persons who sell rum, and other strong liquor to negroes. It must be obvious to every one, that there are too many of them in this city; who, under pretence of selling what they call a penny dram to a negro, will sell to him as many quarts or gallons of rum, as he can steal money or goods to pay for.

"How this notion of its being lawful to sell a penny dram, or a pennyworth of rum to a slave, without the consent or direction of his master, has prevailed, I know not; but this I am sure of, that there is not only no such law, but that the doing of it is directly contrary to an act of assembly now in force, *for the better regulating of slaves.* The many fatal consequences flowing from this prevailing and wicked practice, are so notorious, and so nearly concern us all, that one would be almost surprised, to think there should be a necessity for a court to recommend a suppressing of such pernicious houses: thus much in particular; now in general.

"My charge, gentlemen, further is, to present all conspiracies, combinations, and other offences, from treasons down to trespasses; and in your inquiries, the oath you, and each of you have just now taken, will, I am persuaded, be your guide, and I pray God to direct and assist you in the discharge of your duty."

Court adjourned until to-morrow morning ten o'clock.

SUPREME COURT.

Wednesday, April 22.

Present, the second justice. The court opened, and adjourned until ten o'clock to-morrow morning.

The grand jury having been informed, that Mary Burton could give them some account concerning the goods stolen from Mr. Hogg's, sent for her this morning, and ordered she should be sworn; the constable returned and acquainted them, that *she said she would not be sworn, nor give evidence;* whereupon they ordered the constable to get a warrant from a magistrate, to bring her before them. The constable was some time gone, but at length returned, and brought her with him; and being asked why she would not be sworn, and give her evidence? she told the grand jury she would not be sworn; and seemed to be under some great uneasiness, or terrible apprehensions; which gave suspicion that she knew something concerning the fires that had lately happened: and being asked a question to that purpose, she gave no answer; which increased the jealousy that she was privy to them; and as it was thought a matter of the utmost concern, the grand jury was very importunate, and used many arguments with her, in public and private, to persuade her to speak the truth, and tell all she knew about it. To this end, the lieutenant governor's proclamation was read to her, promising indemnity, and the reward of one hundred pounds to any person, confederate or not, who should make discovery, &c. She seemed to despise it, nor could the grand jury by any means, either threats or promises, prevail upon her, though they assured her withal, that she should have the protection of the magistrates, and her person be safe and secure from harm; but hitherto all was in vain: therefore the grand jury desired alderman Bancker to commit her; and the constable was charged with her accordingly; but before he had got her to jail, she considered better of it, and resolved to be sworn, and give her evidence in the afternoon.

Accordingly, she being sworn, came before the grand jury; but as they were proceeding to her examination, and before they asked her any questions, she told them she would acquaint them with what she knew relating to the goods stolen from Mr. Hogg's, but would say nothing about the fires.

This expression thus, as it were providentially, slipping from the evidence, much alarmed the grand jury; for, as they naturally concluded, it did by construction amount to an affirmative, that she could give an account of the occasion of the several fires; and therefore, as it highly became those gentlemen in the discharge of their trust, they determined to use their utmost diligence to sift out the discovery, but still she remained inflexible, till at length, having recourse to religious topics, representing to her the heinousness of the crime which she would be guilty of, if she was privy to, and could discover so wicked a design, as the firing houses about our ears; where by not only people's estates would be destroyed, but many persons might lose their lives in the flames: this she would have to answer for at the day of judgment, as much as any person immediately concerned, because she might have prevented this destruction, and would not; so that a most damnable sin would lie at her door; and what need she fear from her divulging it; she was sure of the protection of the magistrates? or the grand jury expressed themselves in words to the same purpose; which arguments at 39 last prevailed, and she gave the following evidence, which however, notwithstanding what had been said, came from her, as if still under some terrible apprehensions or restraints.

Deposition, No. 1.—Mary Burton, being sworn, deposeth,

1. "That Prince[a] and Cæsar[b] brought the things of which they had robbed Mr. Hogg, to her master, John Hughson's house, and that they were handed in through the window, Hughson, his

[a] Mr. Auboyneau's negro.
[b] Vaarck's negro.

wife, and Peggy receiving them, about two or three o'clock on a Sunday morning.[c]

2. "That Cæsar, prince, and Mr. Philipse's negro man (Cuffee) used to meet frequently at her master's house, and that she had heard them (the negroes) talk frequently of burning the fort; and that they would go down to the fly[d] and burn the whole town; and that her master and mistress said, they would aid and assist them as much as they could.

3. "That in their common conversation they used to say, that when all this was done, Cæsar should be governor, and Hughson, her master, should be king.

4. "That Cuffee used to say, that a great many people had too much, and others too little; that his old master had a great deal of money, but that, in a short time, he should have less, and that he (Cuffee) should have more.

5. "That at the same time when the things of which Mr. Hogg was robbed, were brought to her master's house, they brought some indigo and bees wax, which was likewise received by her master and mistress.

6. "That at the meetings of the three aforesaid negroes, Cæsar Prince, and Cuffee, at her master's house, they used to say, in their conversation, that when they set fire to the town, they would do it in the night, and as the white people came to extinguish it, they would kill and destroy them.

7. "That she has known at times, seven or eight guns in her master's house, and some swords, and that she has seen twenty or thirty negroes at one time in her master's house; and that at such large meetings, the three aforesaid negroes, Cuffee, Prince, and Cæsar, were generally present, and most active, and that they used to say, that the other negroes durst not refuse to do what they commanded them, and they were sure that they had a number sufficient to stand by them.

8. "That Hughson (her master) and her mistress used to threaten, that if she, the deponent, ever made mention of the 40 goods stolen from Mr. Hogg, they would poison her; and the negroes swore, if ever she published, or discovered the design of burning the town, they would burn her whenever they met her.

[c]1st March, 1740, 1.
[d]The east end of the city.

9. "That she never saw any white person in company when they talked of burning the town, but her master, her mistress, and Peggy."

This evidence of a conspiracy, not only to burn the city, but also destroy and murder the people, was most astonishing to the grand jury, and that any white people should become so abandoned as to confederate with slaves in such an execrable and detestable purpose, could not but be very amazing to every one that heard it; what could scarce be credited; but that the several fires had been occasioned by some combination of villains, was, at the time of them, naturally to be collected from the manner and circumstances attending them.

The grand jury therefore, as it was a matter of the utmost consequence, thought it necessary to inform the judges concerning it, in order that the most effectual measures might be concerted, for discovering the confederates; and the judges were acquainted with it accordingly.

SUPREME COURT.

Thursday, April 23.

Present, the second and third justices.

The grand jury came into court and were called over.

The foreman desiring that Margaret Sorubiero, alias Kerry, a prisoner might be brought before them, Ordered, that the sheriff do carry the said Margaret Sorubiero, alias Kerry, before the grand jury, and see her safe returned again.

The court adjourned until to-morrow morning, ten o'clock.

This morning the judges summoned all the gentlemen of the law in town, to meet them in the afternoon, in order to consult with them, and determine upon such measures as on the result of their deliberations should be judged most proper to be taken upon this emergency; and Mr. Murray, Mr. Alexander, Mr. Smith, Mr. Chambers, Mr. Nicholls, Mr. Lodge, and Mr. Jamison, met them accordingly; the attorney general being indisposed, could not attend.

It was considered, that though there was an act of the province for trying negroes, as in other colonies, for all manner of offences by the justices, &c. in a summary way; yet as this was a scheme of villainy in which white people were confederated with them, and most probably were the first movers and seducers of the slaves; from the nature of such a conjunction, there was reason to apprehend there was a conspiracy of deeper design and more dangerous contrivance than the slaves themselves were capable of; it was thought a matter that required great secrecy, as well as the utmost diligence, in the conduct of the inquiry concerning it: and upon the whole, it was judged most adviseable, as there was an absolute necessity that a matter of this nature and consequence should be fathomed as soon as possible, that it should be taken under the care of the supreme court; and for that purpose, that application should be made to his honour the lieutenant governor, for an ordinance to enlarge the term for the sitting of that court, which in the ordinary method would determinate on the Tuesday following.

The gentlemen of the law generously and unanimously offered to give their assistance on every trial in their turns, as this was conceived to be a matter that not only affected the city, but the whole province.

Margaret Kerry, commonly called Peggy, committed for Hogg's Robbery, being impeached by Mary Burton, as one of the conspirators, the judges examined her in prison in the evening; they exhorted her to make an ingenuous confession and discovery of what she knew of it, and gave her hopes of their recommendation to the governor for a pardon, if they could be of opinion that she deserved it, assuring her (as the case was) that they had his honour's permission to give hopes of mercy to such criminals as should confess their guilt, and they should think proper to recommend to him as fit and proper objects; but she withstood it, and positively denied that she knew any thing of the matter; and said, that if she should accuse any body of any such thing, she must accuse innocent persons, and wrong her own soul. She had this day been examined by the grand jury, and positively denied knowing any thing about the fires.

SUPREME COURT.

Friday, April 24.

Present, the second and third justices.

The King against Cæsar and Prince, negroes.

The grand jury having found two bills of indictment for felonies, against the prisoners; Mr. Attorney General moved, that they might be brought to the bar, in order to be arraigned.

It was ordered, and they being brought, were arraigned accordingly, and severally pleaded, *not guilty.*

The King against John Hughson, Sarah, his wife, Margaret Sorubiero, alias Kerry.

The grand jury having found a bill of indictment for felony, against the defendants in custody, Mr. Attorney General moved, that they might be brought to the bar in order to be arraigned.

It was ordered, and the prisoners being brought, were arraigned accordingly, and severally pleaded, *not guilty.*

Ordered, that the trials of the two negroes, the Hughsons, and Kerry, do come on tomorrow morning.

Court adjourned till to-morrow morning, nine o'clock.

SUPREME COURT.

Saturday, April 25.

Present, the second justice.

The King against Cæsar and Prince, negroes.

The King against John Hughson, Sarah, his wife, Margaret Kerry.

Ordered, that the prisoners' trials be put off till Tuesday the 28th instant.

Court adjourned till Monday morning, nine o'clock.

SUPREME COURT.

Monday, April 27.

Present, the second justice.

His majesty's ordinance published in court for enlarging the present term to the last Tuesday in May next.

Court adjourned till to-morrow morning, ten o'clock.

SUPREME COURT.

Tuesday, April 28.

Present, the second and third justices.

The King against Cæsar and Prince, negroes.

The King against John Hughson, Sarah, his wife, Margaret Kerry.

Upon motion of Mr. Attorney General, ordered, that the trials of the prisoners in both causes be put off till the first day of May.

Court adjourned till Friday, 1st May, ten o'clock in the morning.

The following letter, dated this day at New-York, was some time afterwards intercepted in New-Jersey, and sent up from a magistrate there to another here.

The original in female Dutch followeth, so much of it as is material to the present purpose.

"Nieu York den 21 April 1741
"Beminde Man Johannis Romme

"Dit is om U bekent te maken dat ik U brief ontfangen heb by de brenger van deze en daer nyt verstaen dat gey van sins ben om weer na huis te komen myn beminde ik versoek van U dat gy het best van U wegh maekt om varder te gaen en niet in Niu Yorck te komen en om U self niet bekent te maken waer gey ben voor John Husen die is van dese dagh zyn tryeli te hebben enook zyn vrou en de mydt is king evidens tegen baye gar en zy het U naemook in kwetze gebrocht en ik ben bang det John Husen en zyn vrou gehangen sall worden by wat ik kan horen en de schout en bombeles soeken voor U over all want Fark neger die houdt zyn woort standen voor jou Brother Lucas is voor een jeure man gekosen en die hoort hoe het is So niet maer maer blyvende U eerwarde vrou Elezabet Romme tot ter doet toe."

Thus translated:

"Beloved Husband John Romme,

"This is to acquaint you that I have received your letter by the bearer hereof and understand out of it that you intend to return 44 home again my dear I desire of you that you make the best of your way to go further and not to come in New-York and not to make yourself known where you are for John Hughson is this day to have his tryal as also his wife and the servant maid is king evidence against both and she has brought your name likewise in question and I am afraid that John Hughson and his wife will be hanged by what I can hear and the sheriff and bumbailiffs seek for you every where Vaarck's negro[e] he keeps his word stedfast for you Brother Lucas is chosen one of the jurymen and he hears how it is So no more but remaining your respectful wife Elezabet Romme even till death."

Superscribed, *for Mr. John Romme* Q D G

SUPREME COURT.

Friday, May 1.

Present, the second and third justices.

The King against Cæsar and Prince, negroes. On trial.

The jury called, and the prisoners making no challenge, the following persons were sworn, viz.

Roger French, John Groesbeek, John Richard, Abraham Kipp, George Witts, John Thurman, Patrick Jackson, Benjamin Moore, William Hamersley, John Lashier, Joshua Sleydall, John Shurmur.

These two negroes were arraigned on two indictments, the

[e]Cæsar.

twenty fourth of April last: the one for their entering the dwelling house of Robert Hogg, of this city, merchant, on the first day of March then last past, with intent then and there to commit some felony; and for feloniously stealing and carrying away then and there the goods and chattels of the said Robert Hogg, of the value of four pounds five shillings sterling, against the form of the statutes in such case made and provided, and against the peace of our sovereign lord the king, his crown and dignity.

The other for their entering the dwelling house of Abraham Meyers Cohen in this city, merchant, on the first day of March. with intent then and there to commit some felony; and for feloniously stealing and carrying away then and there the goods 45 and chattels of the said Abraham Meyers Cohen of the value of five pounds sterling, against the form of the statutes, &c. and against the king's peace, &c.

To each of which indictments they pleaded, *not guilty*.

The attorney general having opened both the indictments, he with Joseph Murray, Esq. of council for the king, proceeded to examine the witnesses, viz.

For the king, Mrs. Hogg, Mrs. Boswell, Christopher Wilson, Rachina Guerin, Mr. Robert Hogg, Mr. Robert Watts, Margaret Sorubiero, alias Kerry, Abraham Meyers Cohen, James Mills, Thomas Wenman, John Moore, Esq. Cornelius Brower, Anthony Ham, Mary Burton.

For the prisoners, Alderman Bancker, Alderman Johnson, John Auboyneau.

The prisoners upon their defence denied the charge against them. And,

The evidence being summed up, which was very strong and full, and the jury charged, they withdrew; and being returned, found them guilty of the indictments.

Ordered, that the trials of the Hughsons and Margaret Kerry, be put off until Wednesday the 6th inst.

Court adjourned until Monday morning, 4th May, at ten o'clock.

Sunday, May 3.

Arthur Price, servant to captain Vincent Pearse, having been committed, upon a charge of stealing out of his master's house several goods belonging to the lieutenant governor, which had been removed thither for safe custody from the fire at the fort; he informed the under-sheriff, that he had had some discourse in the jail with Peggy, which he would communicate to a magistrate: the under-sheriff acquainted one of the judges therewith, and he examined Price in the evening, and the following deposition was taken.

Deposition, No. 1.—Arthur Price being duly sworn, saith,

1. "That about the beginning of last week, Peggy Carey, or Kerry, now in jail, came to the hole in the prison door, in which he is confined, and told him, she was very much afraid of those fellows (meaning the negroes, as he understood) telling or discovering something of her; but, said she, if they do, by God, I will [7] 46 hang them every one; but that she would not *forswear*[e] herself, unless they brought her in. Upon which the deponent asked her, Peggy, how *forswear* yourself? To which she answered, there is fourteen sworn. Upon which he further asked her, what, is it about Mr. Hogg's goods? And she replied, no, by G-d, about the fire. Upon which the deponent said to her, what, Peggy, were you a going to set the town on fire? And she made answer, she was not; but said, by G-d, since I knew of it, they made me swear. Upon which the deponent asked her, was John and his wife in it? (meaning John Hughson and his wife.) And she answered, yes, by G-d, they were both sworn as well as the rest. Then the deponent asked her, if she was not afraid that the negroes would discover her? And she said no; for Prince, Cuff and Cæsar, and Forck's (Vaarck's) negro, were all true-hearted fellows. Then he asked her, if Cæsar was not Forck's negro? And she answered, no, by G-d, it was the other;[f] but what other she meant he did not know.

2. "That yesterday in the afternoon the said Peggy came to him again, and told him, she had no stomach to eat her victuals; for that bitch (meaning Hughson's maid[g] as he understood) has fetched me in, and made me as black as the rest, about the indigo, and Mr. Hogg's goods: but if they did hang the two poor fellows below (meaning Cæsar and Prince, as understood) they (meaning the rest of the negroes) would be revenged on them yet; but if they

[e]What she meant by forswearing herself, will be better guessed at hereafter.
[f]Bastian, alias Tom Peal, also belonging to Vaarck.
[g]Mary Burton.

sent them away, it was another case. Upon which this deponent said to Peggy, I don't doubt but they will endeavour to poison this girl that has sworn, (meaning Hughson's maid.) And Peggy replied, no, by G-d, I don't believe that; but they will be revenged on them some other ways: And she further said to the deponent, for your life and soul of you, you son of a b—h, don't speak a word of what I have told you."

About this time, *i. e.* the beginning of this month, at Hackensack, in New-Jersey, eight miles from this city, the inhabitants of that place were alarmed about an hour before day, and presented with a most melancholy and affrighting scene! no less than seven barns in that neighbourhood were all in flames; and the fire had got such head, that all assistance was in vain; for in a short time they were burnt down to the ground. Two negroes, the one belonging to Derick Van Hoorn, the other to Albert Van Voerheise, 47 were suspected to have been guilty of this fact; the former having been seen coming out of one of the barns with a gun laden, who pretended on his being discovered, that he saw the person who had fired the barns, upon which his master ordered him to fire at him, and the negro thereupon immediately discharged his piece; but no blood was drawn from any mortal that could be discovered. The latter was found at his master's house loading a gun with two bullets, which he had in his hand ready to put in. Upon these and other presumptive circumstances and proofs, both negroes were apprehended, and in a few days tried, convicted, and burnt at a stake: the former confessed he had set fire to three of the barns; the latter would confess nothing; nor would either of them discover that any others were concerned with them in this villainy.

SUPREME COURT.

Monday, May 4.

Present the second and third justices.

The court opened and adjourned till to-morrow afternoon 3 o'clock.

Negro Plot *is an official record prepared by the city of Charleston, South Carolina, to provide an accounting for the attempted slave uprising led by Denmark Vesey in the summer of 1822. One hundred and thirty-one enslaved persons were arrested and tried for their alleged rebellious behaviors. The full report offers a view into the court proceedings, testimonies, and outright confessions given by enslaved people accused of participating in the foiled insurrection, as well as the statements given under oath by enslaved witnesses who testified against the defendants. Of the accused, thirty-seven were exiled from the United States and sold and thirty-five were summarily hanged. The author's voice is not objective in the least, signaling the ruling class's heightened anxiety that such a large act of revolution might be carried out in Charleston and throughout the slaveholding South. The Vesey uprising stoked new fears about enslaved people's craft, thirst for vengeance, and intent to liberate themselves from the chains of slavery. White enslavers' fears that enslaved people would be inspired led to the meting out of severe sentences to punish those found guilty and to warn aspiring rebels of the consequences should they behave similarly.*

From *Negro Plot: An Account of the Late Intended Insurrection Among a Portion of the Blacks of This City*

(1822)

On Thursday the 27th, **DENMARK VESEY,** a free black man, was brought before the Court for trial, Assisted by his Counsel, G. W. CROSS, Esq.

It is perhaps somewhat remarkable, that at this stage of the investigation, although several witnesses had been examined, the *atrocious* guilt of *Denmark Vesey* had not been as yet fully unfolded. From the testimony of most of the witnesses, however, the Court found enough, and amply enough, to warrant the sentence of death, which, on the 28th, they passed on him. But every subsequent step in the progress of the trials of others, lent new confirmation to his overwhelming guilt, and placed him beyond a doubt, on the criminal eminence of having been the individual, in whose bosom the nefarious scheme was first engendered. There is ample reason for believing, that this project was not, with him, of recent origin, for it was said, he had spoken of it for upwards of four years.

These facts of his guilt the journals of the Court will disclose—that no man can be proved to have spoken of or urged the insurrection prior to himself. All the channels of communication and intelligence are traced back to him. His house was the place appointed for the secret meetings of the conspirators, at which he was invariably a leading and influential member; animating and encouraging the timid, by the hopes of prospects of success; removing the scruples of the religious, by the grossest prostitution and perversion of the sacred oracles, and inflaming and confirming the resolute, by all the savage fascinations of blood and booty.

The peculiar circumstances of guilt, which confer a distinction on his case, will be found narrated in the confessions of

Rolla, Monday Gell, Frank and Jesse, in the Appendix. He was
sentenced for execution on the 2d July.*

The Court tried JESSE, the slave of Mr. Thomas Blackwood.
The testimony against *Jesse* was very ample. His activity and
zeal, in promoting the views of Denmark Vesey, in relation to
the plot, were fully proved. He had engaged with Vesey to go

*As Denmark Vesey has occupied so large a place in the conspiracy, a brief no-
tice of him will, perhaps, be not devoid of interest. The following anecdote will
show how near he was to the chance of being distinguished in the bloody events
of San Domingo. During the revolutionary war, Captain Vesey, now an old
resident of this city, commanded a ship that traded between St. Thomas' and
Cape Francais (San Domingo.) He was engaged in supplying the French of that
Island with Slaves. In the year 1781, he took on board at St. Thomas' 390 slaves
and sailed for the Cape; on the passage, he and his officers were struck with the
beauty, alertness and intelligence of a boy about 14 years of age, whom they
made a pet of, by taking him into the cabin, changing his apparel, and calling
him by way of distinction *Telemaque*, (which appellation has since, by gradual
corruption, among the negroes, been changed to *Denmark*, or sometimes *Tel-
mak*.) On the arrival, however, of the ship at the Cape, Captain Vesey, having
no use for the boy, sold him among his other slaves, and returned to St. Thomas'.
On his next voyage to the Cape, he was surprised to learn from his consignee
that Telemaque would be returned on his hands, as the planter, who had purchased him, represented him unsound, and subject to epileptic fits. According
to the custom of trade in that place, the boy was placed in the hands of the
king's physician, who decided that he was unsound, and Captain Vesey was
compelled to take him back, of which he had no occasion to repent, as Denmark proved, for 20 years, a most faithful slave. In 1800, Denmark drew a
prize of $1500 in the East-Bay-Street Lottery, with which he purchased his
freedom from his master, at six hundred dollars, much less than his real value.
From that period to the day of his apprehension he has been working as a carpenter in this city, distinguished for great strength and activity. Among his colour he was always looked up to with awe and respect. His temper was
impetuous and domineering in the extreme, qualfying him for the despotic rule,
of which he was ambitious. All his passions were ungovernable and savage; and,
to his numerous wives and children, he displayed the haughty and capricious
cruelty of an Eastern Bashaw. He had nearly effected his escape, after information had been lodged against him. For three days the town was searched for him
without success. As early as Monday, the 17th, he had concealed himself. It was
not until the night of the 22d of June, during a perfect tempest, that he was
found secreted in the house of one of his wives. It is to the uncommon efforts
and vigilance of Mr. Wesner, and Capt. Dove, of the City Guard, (the latter of
whom seized him) that public justice received its necessary tribute, in the execution of this man. If the party had been one moment later, he would, in all probability, have effected his escape the next day in some outward bound vessel.

out of town on Sunday the 16th, to bring down some negroes from the country, to aid in the rising on that night; and re- marked, to the witnesses, on his way to Hibbens' ferry, "if my father does not assist I will cut off his head." All the particulars in proof against him, he confirmed after receiving his sentence, by his own full and satisfactory Confession, which will be found in the Appendix, marked (H.)

This man excited no small sympathy, not only from the ap- parent sincerity of his contrition, but from the mild and unos- tentatious composure with which he met his fate.

Sentence of death was passed on these six men, on the 28th of June, and they were executed on the 2d of July. With the excep- tion of Jesse and Rolla, they made no disclosures; all of them, with those exceptions, either explicitly or implicitly affirming their innocence. It is much to be lamented that the situation of the Work-House, at this period, precluded, after their sentence, their being separately confined; at least, that Vesey could not have been subjected to the gloom and silence of a solitary cell. He might have been softened, and afforded the most precious con- fessions, as his knowledge and agency in the nefarious scheme very far exceeded the information of others, who, however guilty, seemed but the agents of his will. But these men mutually sup- ported each other, and died obedient to the stern and emphatic injunction of their Comrade (Peter Poyas) "*Do not open your lips! Die silent, as you shall see me do!*" It was, perhaps, *alone*, in Denmark Vesey's power, to have given us the true character, extent and importance of the correspondence, it was afterwards proved, was carried on with certain persons in San Domingo.

On the 1st of July the Court proceeded to the trial of MON- DAY GELL, who, together with CHARLES DRAYTON, had been apprehended; the first, on the 27th of June, and the latter, on the 2d of July.

By referring to the Appendix (D.) & (E.) the nature of the tes- timony against these individuals will be seen. In reference to the case of *Monday Gell* it was established that he had been a very important ringleader, and that his shop, in Meeting-Street, was a place at which many meetings were held; at all of which he was present, lending the most zealous aid, and affording the strongest countenance; and if any confirmation of his guilt should be sought for, it may be found in his own confession in the Appendix (K.) After Monday Gell and Charles Drayton were convicted there appeared to be a pause in our further discoveries, and some prospect of the investigation closing with their execution and that of John Horry, Harry Haig and Gullah Jack, (for the guilt of the latter, see Appendix (D.) (E.) & (F.)

On the 9th of July, however, these five men, where called before the Court to receive sentence, and after it had been pronounced, with the most impressive solemnity, they were withdrawn to a common ward in the Work-House, for half an hour, until separate cells could be provided for them. It was at this moment that *Charles Drayton*, overwhelmed with terror and guilt, went up to *Monday* and reproached him with having induced him to join in a scheme which had placed him in such a miserable and perilous situation. To this appeal Monday, not only confessed his guilt, but observed to Charles—that their present fate was justly and precisely what they had a right to expect, after their detected and defeated project. On which there immediately ensued between them a conversation on the extent of the guilt of others, in which Monday gave Charles the names of many accomplices whom he had not previously known in the plot;—the arrival of the blacksmith to iron the convicts, and the turnkey to convey them to separate cells, interrupted the conversation.

Charles, during the night of the 9th, sent for Mr. Gordon, who has charge of the Work-House, and informed him that he was extremely anxious to see the Intendant, as he had some important disclosures to make. By day-light, on the morning of the 10th, this message was conveyed to the person for whom it was intended, and Charles was visited at sun-rise. He was found, in a state of the most lamentable depression and panic, and he seemed prepared to make the most ample declarations from the fear of death, and the consequences of an *hereafter*, if he went out of the world without revealing all that he knew, in relation to the Conspiracy, in which he had been so active an agent. Before his narrative was received, he was most specially put on his guard, that no promises could be made to him of a reversal of his fate, but that he might rest satisfied, his condition could not be worse by his coming out with a full disclosure of all that he knew. He then stated many particulars, that had come to his own knowledge, proving a much wider diffusion of the plot than, at that period, was imagined; and, after giving up the names of several of his comrades, he mentioned the conversation which had been commenced and broken off, in the common ward of the Work-House, between Monday Gell and himself. As Monday, at this period, did not seem disposed to make any confessions to others, whatever he might be inclined to do to his friend Charles, it was considered important, that the conversation between them, should be renewed, and they were brought together in the same cell, and left for twenty-four hours alone; but some little stratagem was employed, to divert the suspicions of Monday, that Charles was confined with him, merely for the purpose of getting information out of him.

On the morning of the 10th, the Court were convened, and apprized, generally, of these new disclosures, which Charles had made, but as he was still *closeted* with Monday, he could not be examined on that day, the Court adjourned to meet on the 13th; on which day Monday Gell's own confession was heard by them. Between the 10th and 13th, *Charles* and *Monday* were separated (having been respited by His Excellency, the Governor, at the request of the Court) and Charles, on his re-examination afforded much important information, which he had derived from Monday. On Monday's having all this brought to his view, he confessed his own guilt, as well as the truth of the statements which he had made to Charles.*

Cotemporaneously with these communications, PERAULT, be-

Monday Gell is very well known in this city. He is a most excellent harness-maker, and kept his shop in Meeting-street. It would be difficult to name any individual more actively engaged in the plot than himself, or more able to aid Denmark Vesey, from his uncommon sagacity and knowledge. He reads and writes with great and equal facility, and obviously seems to have been the individual who held the pen, at all the meetings. At which he wrote more than one letter to San Domingo, for succors. His own situation afforded no excuse for the effort in which he was engaged, as he enjoyed all the substantial comforts of a free-man; much indulged and trusted by his master, his time and a large proportion of the profits of his labour were at his own disposal. He even kept his master's arms and sometimes his money. Monday is an Ebo, and is now in the prime of life, having been in the country 15 or 20 years.

longing to Mr. Strohecker, was taken up, on the 10th, and on his being closely and judiciously examined by his master, he gave a large mass of intelligence confirming what had been related by Monday and Charles, and supplying several deficiencies in their testimony, more especially that part of it which related to the transmission of *certain* letters to San Domingo. These disclosures, with some further details which were obtained from Harry Haig, (whose confession and subsequent testimony went to implicate a corps of Gullah or Angola negroes, that had been organized under the command of their Chief, Gullah Jack,) gave ample employment for three or four days to the Committee of Vigilance, during which upwards of sixty slaves were apprehended.

It would very much transcend the limits necessarily prescribed to this brief memoir, to go over all the trials that subsequently ensued, on these fresh discoveries. As the most important part of the testimony, adduced on these trials, is to be found in the Appendix, it is deemed altogether, superfluous, to make a special application of it to each of the cases, as this would result in a repetition fatiguing and uninteresting to the reader. It will be sufficient to single out a few of the cases most pregnant in interest, and to remark, that the Court on its reorganization on the 13th, justly estimating the extent of the labour before them, laid down certain rules of discrimination in the guilt of the parties to which they give the most definite precision and perspecuity, by adopting two classes of offence; the first involving a primary and the second a minor degree of guilt. Under the first class, they brought all those who were ringleaders, who had made a declaration of their belonging to the association, and who had been present, aiding and abetting in the contribution of money, arms or ammunition, at Denmark Vesey's, or who were in the constant habit of visiting Monday Gell's shop and Bulkley's farm, for the purpose of obtaining and communicating intelligence of the progress of the conspiracy. Those found guilty in this class, were to be punished with death. Under the second class were arranged those who had merely sent in their adhesion to the ringleaders without ever having attended a meeting at Vesey's, or having been recognized by him as confidential men, or contributed to the purchase of arms or ammunition, or endeavoured to enlist others.

The punishment which awaited those found guilty in this class, was transportation beyond the limits of the United States.*

By reference to the Calendar marked (S) in the Appendix, the names of the prisoners committed will be found, and under a proper column, the mode in which they were disposed of, whether by death, transportation, or discharge, from the insufficiency of testimony. The extent of the evidence adduced, therefore, against each individual, may be inferred with accuracy, by observing the punishment awarded him; as the Court adhered with great and rigid fidelity to these rules, which were in unison both with justice and humanity.

Among the vast number of cases disposed of by the first Court; in a session of nearly six weeks, involving the most intense and unremitting labour, it would be impossible to overlook the case of Jack Pritchard, otherwise called GULLAH JACK. The testimony in the Appendix, of more than one of the witnesses, will establish fully his guilt, and prove the justice of the sentence, by which he was ushered into another world; but no description can accurately convey to others the impression which his trial, defence and appearance made on those who witnessed the workings of his cunning and rude address. Born a conjurer and a physician, in his own country (for in Angola they are matters of inheritance) he practised *these arts* in this country for fifteen years, without its being generally known among the whites. Vesey, who left no engines of power unessayed, seems, in an early stage of his design, to have turned his eye on this Necromancer, aware of his influence with his own countrymen, who are distinguished both for their credulous superstition and clannish sympathies. It does not appear that Jack required much persuasion to induce him to join in a project, which afforded him the most ample opportunities of displaying his peculiar art, whilst it is very obvious that his willingness, to do all that Vesey might require, was in no little degree stimu-

---

*At the meeting of the Court on the morning of the 13th, Mr. James Legare, from feeble health and great exhaustion during its previous sittings, asked, and obtained leave, to withdraw, whereupon Mr. Henry Deas, was summoned by the Magistrates, who took his seat and served until the adjournment of the Court.

lated, by his bitterness and his gall against the whites. Altho' he had been fifteen or twenty years in this country, yet he appeared to be untouched by the influences of civilized life.—If the part which he was to play in this drama, be-spoke that the treacherous and vindictive artifices of war in his own country, existed in unimpaired vigour in his memory, his wildness and vehemence of gesture and the malignant glance with which he eyed the witnesses who appeared against him, all indicated the savage, who indeed had been *caught*, but not *tamed*. It would be both tedious and disgusting to relate the many artifices employed by this miscreant to deceive and cajole his deluded countrymen. Such was their belief in his invulnerability, that his charms and amulets were in request, and he was regarded as a man, who could *only* be harmed but by the *treachery* of his fellows. Even those negroes who were born in this country seem to have spoken of his charmed invincibility with a confidence which looked much like belief. When Jack was dragged forth to the scaffold he seemed conscious that his arts would stand him in little stead, and gave up his spirit without firmness or composure.

The case of TOM RUSSEL, another of the Gullah Band, deserves a brief notice. He was tried some days after Jack, and was executed among the twenty-two Criminals hung on the Lines, on the 26th July. Tom was Jack's *armourer*, and kept his blacksmith's shop on East-Bay. His part in the conspiracy was confined to the making of pikes and spears, which it appears he did on a very approved model. After these weapons were finished, they were held subject to the order of Jack, and by him sent up to Mr. Bulkley's farm,* near the Cross Roads, where handles were provided for them by Polydore Faber, a Gullah, who met his fate on the same scaffold with Tom Russel. This farm was one of the principal rendezvous of the Gullah Band, of which Jack was the Captain.

The trial of LOT FORRESTER, was not without interest, as

*This farm was under the charge of a slave named *Billy*, who became a witness for the state and gave some important details of the meetings of the *Gullahs*. Several of whom were executed on the 26th.

he was the *courier* of the conspiracy, and was proved to have gone out of town, for the purpose of inducing the country negroes to join in the insurrection; his journeys were both south and north of Charleston. His zeal and persevereance in the cause were strongly proved, and there is every reason for believing that the conflagration of the city was confided, by Vesey, to him. Match-rope was found in a situation where he had probably secreted it.—He was hung on the Lines on the 26th of July.

BACCHUS HAMMETT, who was hung, also, on the 26th, did render, and was to have rendered, on the night of the 16th, the most essential aid. Before the latter period he had stolen from his master's store a keg of powder, which was conveyed, first to Vesey's afterwards to Monday Gell's, and lastly to Gullah Jack, to be prepared into cartridges. On the night of the 16th he was to have slept where the arms of the *Neck-Rangers* were deposited, and facilitated their seizure and distribution among Gullah Jack's corps, who were to have carried this post, as well as Mr. *Duquercron's* store, in which there were 500 stands of arms, deposited for sale.

The cases of JACK GLEN, BILLY PALMER, and JACK PURCELL, are distinguished, not by any peculiar atrocity, but for the hypocricy they blended with their crime. Their assent to the plot was distinctly shown, and it was in proof, that Vesey had recognized them all as his men. Jack Glen was a Preacher. Billy Palmer, exceedingly pious, and a communicant at the church of his master; and Jack Purcell no less devout. The case of the latter was not without its pathos, from the deep contrition he expressed before his execution; the distressing interest which his mistress is said to have taken in his fate, and the lamentable delusion under which he laboured, which is more particularly unfolded in his confession, in the Appendix marked (L.)* Jack Glen and Purcell were hung on the Lines. Billy Palmer has been respited by His Excellency, the Governor, until October next, for a commutation of his punishment to banishment beyond the limits of the United States.

---

*This Confession of Purcell's will show, that the evil foretold, from the discussion of the *Missohri Question*, has been, in some degree, realized.

The Court having used the testimony of *Monday Gell, Charles Drayton* and *Harry Haig,* very efficaciously, to the ends of public justice, reconsidered the sentences, which had been passed on them, and instead of death, sentenced them to transportation beyond the limits of the United States.

As a matter of form, *Perault, John Enslow* and *Billy Bulkley,* (who had become witnesses for the state,) were then tried on their own confessions, and sentenced to be transported beyond the limits of the United States. These individuals were important witnesses in all the apprehensions and trials subsequent to the 13th of July.

Perault gave his testimony with great fearlessness and candour, and Enslow with much composure and connexion; the evidence of both, as well indeed as that of most of the witnessess, was much appreciated by the Court, after a severe scrutiny.*

This Court, having disposed of all the cases before them, adjourned on the 26th of July.

At this stage of our investigation we were satisfied that of all the ringleaders in the conspiracy, *William Garner,* (who had effected his escape from the city about the 1st of July) only, remained to be punished. As information had been received of his having travelled towards Columbia, a proclamation was issued by His Excellency, the Governor, for his apprehension, in promotion of the success of which some subsidary steps were taken by private means. On the 2d of August our wishes, relating to Garner, were gratified, by his arrival in town. He had previously been arrested at Columbia, thro' the public spirited efforts of the Indendant of that place and Lieut. Maxcy, who overtook and apprended him at Granby.

On Garner's arrival, a new Court was organized for his trial, and such other cases as might be brought before them, by precisely the same means as those which had been employed on the appointment of the first; and the services of the following gentlemen secured, who were known to possess, deservedly, a large share of the public confidence.

---

*See Enslow's Confession, Appendix (M.)

Magistrates,		*Freeholders.*	

JACOB AXON, and G. M. FURMAN, } Esqrs.	Hon. JOEL R. POINSETT, THOS. R. SMITH, R. Y. HAYNE, } Esqrs. Col. THOMAS ROPER, Col. JOHN GORDON.

This Court adopted the same rules for their government which had been so humanely and dispassionately adopted by the preceding Court, but, as enough had been done for public example, they determined to visit capital punishment on none but ringleaders. The first case they tried was that of WILLIAM GARNER.

Garner's guilt had all the characteristics, which the Court had assigned to the first class of turpitude; it was not only proved that he was actively engaged in recruiting others, but that he was to have led a troop of horse, at the rising, composed of all such of the conspirators as might have appeared in the streets on horseback. And further, that he had made an offer of a command to others in his corps. Four witnesses having sworn positively to his guilt, detailing a variety of particulars, mutually corroborating and supporting each other, he was found guilty and sentenced for execution on the 9th of August, at which period the sentence was carried into effect. This Court having, after a short adjournment, of three or four days, recommenced their session, disposed of twelve cases more, involving a minor degree of guilt, and adjourned finally on the 8th of August.

These trials, together with some private arrangements, made with their owners, in reference to the banishment of several slaves, in cases where their guilt was clear, but not of the first degree, have at length closed the anxious and irksome labours of the corporation, after an examination of little less than two months.

It will be seen, by referring to the Calendar marked (S) that one hundred and thirty-one were committed; thirty-five have suffered death, and thirty-seven have been sentenced to banishment. The most important object to be obtained in uprooting a conspiracy, we have fully accomplished, by bringing to punishment the whole of the ringleaders. Monday Gell, whose knowledge of the plot was, probably, exceeded only by Vesey's, has emphatically stated, that the ringleaders were the first six, who were executed on the 2d of July, to wit: Denmark Vesey, Peter Poyas, Ned Bennett, Rolla, Batteau and Jesse; to which he has since added himself and William Garner, who was executed on the 9th of August.

We, moreover, believe, that all who were active agents (though not ringleaders) in the conspiracy, have expiated their crimes, or are about to do so, by an eternal exile from our shores. It may be mentioned, in confirmation of this belief, that Monday Gell, from memory, made out a list of forty-two names, of those who were in the habit of visiting his shop, for the purpose of combining and confederating in the intended insurrection, whom he called his company; every one of whom have been apprehended, and disposed of. We cannot venture to say, to how many the knowledge of the intended effort, was communicated, who, without signifying their assent, or attending any of the meetings, were yet prepared to profit by events. That there are many who would not have permitted the enterprize to have failed at a *critical moment*, for the want of their co-operation, we have the best reasons for believing.

Before we conclude, some notice of the probable causes of this conspiracy may be expected. As this is a matter of speculation, we shall not speak without reserve. Of the motives of Vesey, we cannot sit in judgment; they have been scanned by a power who can do higher justice than ourselves. But as they are explained by his character and conduct, during the combinations of the plot, they are only to be referred to a malignant hatred of the whites, and inordinate lust of power and booty. Indeed, the belief is altogether justifiable, that his end would have been answered, if, after laying our city in ashes, and moistening its cinders with blood, he could have embarked with a part of the pillage of our banks for San Domingo; leaving a large proportion of his deluded followers to the exterminating desolation of that justice, which would have awaited, in the end, a transient success. His followers were slaves, and for them it would not be so difficult to assign a motive, if it had not been distinctly proved, that without, scarcely an exception, they had no individual hardship to complain of, and were among the most humanely treated negroes in our city. The facilities for

combining and confederating in such a scheme, were amply afforded, by the extreme indulgence and kindness, which charac-
terises the domestic treatment of our slaves. Many slave owners
among us, not satisfied with ministering to the wants of their
domestics, by all the comforts of abundant food, and excellent
clothing, with a misguided benevolence, have not only permitted their instruction, but lent to such efforts their approbation
and applause.

Religious fanaticism has not been without its effect on this
project, and as auxilliary to these sentiments, the secession of a
large body of blacks from the white Methodist Church, with
feelings of irritation and disappointment, formed a hot-bed, in
which the germ might well be expected to spring into life and
vigour. Among the conspirators *a majority* of them belonged to
the *African Church*,* and among those executed were several
who had been Class Leaders. It is, however, due to the late head
of their church (for since the late events the association has
been voluntarily dissolved) and their deacons, to say, that after
the most diligent search and scrutiny, no evidence entitled to
belief, has been discovered against them. A hearsay rumour, in
relation to *Morris Brown*, was traced far enough to end in its
complete falsification.

That the course which certain discussions assumed in Congress were likewise efficacious in producing both discontent
and delusion, is sufficiently apparent. Jack Purcell's confession
in the Appendix, will show to what a purpose Vesey applied
those beautiful propositions of civil and natural freedom, which
were sported with a wanton recklessness of their consequences,
as applied to the condition of a certain portion of our common
country.

It is consoling to every individual, who is proud of the character of his country, in the late unhappy events, to be able to
say, that, within the limits of the City of Charleston, in a period
of great and unprecedented excitement, the laws, without even
one violation, have ruled with uninterrupted sway—that no
cruel vindictive or barbarous modes of punishment have been

---

*An appellation, the seceders assumed after their leaving the white Methodist
Church.

resorted to—that justice has been blended with an enlightened humanity, in according to those who had meted out for us murder, rapine and conflagration, in their most savage forms— trials, which, for the wisdom, impartiality and moderation that governed them, are even superior to those which the ordinary modes of judicature would have afforded ourselves.

With little to fear, and nothing to reproach ourselves we may, without shrinking, submit our conduct to the award of posterity, and ourselves to the protection of the Supreme Ruler of Events.

THOMAS WENTWORTH HIGGINSON

In August 1831, Nat Turner led a band of fugitives from slavery in a bloody, two-day rebellion in Southampton County, Virginia, during which fifty white people were killed. In an ultimate act of retribution for slavery's many horrors, Turner and his men went from home to home, shocking unsuspecting white families and outraging the community. Thomas Wentworth Higginson's recounting of the incident was published some thirty years later and, most compellingly, four months into the Civil War. A passionate abolitionist who was one of John Brown's Secret Six who supported the rebellion strategically and financially, Higginson would later go on to serve as a colonel of the First South Carolina Volunteers (Union)/Thirty-third United States Colored Infantry Regiment. Higginson no doubt understood the Union's fight as a continuation of Turner's and other rebels' violent, nonviolent, covert, and overt acts against slavery. Though other accounts of Turner's life and the moments leading up to the insurrection from the nineteenth century abound, Higginson's narrative stands out in that it takes great care to historicize Turner's life and times and underscore white slaveholders' and slavery sympathizers' many hypocrisies.

From *Nat Turner's Insurrection*
(1861)

Whatever Nat Turner's experiences of slavery might have been, it is certain that his plans were not suddenly adopted, but that he had brooded over them for years. To this day there are traditions among the Virginia slaves of the keen devices of "Prophet

Nat." If he was caught with lime and lamp-black in hand, conning over a half-finished county-map on the barn-door, he was always "planning what to do, if he were blind," or "studying how to get to Mr. Francis's house." When he had called a meeting of slaves, and some poor whites came eavesdropping, the poor whites at once became the subjects for discussion; he incidentally mentioned that the masters had been heard threatening to drive them away; one slave had been ordered to shoot Mr. Jones's pigs, another to tear down Mr. Johnson's fences. The poor whites, Johnson and Jones, ran home to see to their homesteads, and were better friends than ever to Prophet Nat.

He never was a Baptist preacher, though such vocation has often been attributed to him. The impression arose from his having immersed himself, during one of his periods of special enthusiasm, together with a poor white man named Brantley. "About this time," he says in his Confession, "I told these things to a white man, on whom it had a wonderful effect, and he ceased from his wickedness, and was attacked immediately with a cutaneous eruption, and the blood oozed from the pores of his skin, and after praying and fasting nine days he was healed. And the Spirit appeared to me again, and said, as the Saviour had been baptized, so should we be also; and when the white people would not let us be baptized by the Church, we went down into the water together, in the sight of many who reviled us, and were baptized by the Spirit. After this I rejoiced greatly and gave thanks to God."

The religious hallucinations narrated in his Confession seem to have been as genuine as the average of such things, and are very well expressed. It reads quite like Jacob Behmen. He saw white spirits and black spirits contending in the skies, the sun was darkened, the thunder rolled. "And the Holy Ghost was with me, and said, 'Behold me as I stand in the heavens!' And I looked and saw the forms of men in different attitudes. And there were lights in the sky, to which the children of darkness gave other names than what they really were; for they were the lights of the Saviour's hands, stretched forth from east to west, even as they were extended on the cross on Calvary, for the redemption of sinners." He saw drops of blood on the corn: this was Christ's blood, shed for man. He saw on the leaves in the woods letters and numbers and figures of men,—the same symbols which he had seen in the skies. On May 12, 1828, the Holy Spirit appeared to him and proclaimed that the yoke of Jesus must fall on him, and he must fight against the Serpent when the sign appeared. Then came an eclipse of the sun in February, 1831: this was the sign; then he must arise and prepare himself, and slay his enemies with their own weapons; then also the seal was removed from his lips, and then he confided his plans to four associates.

When he came, therefore, to the barbecue on the appointed Sunday, and found, not these four only, but two others, his first question to the intruders was, How they came thither. To this Will answered manfully, that his life was worth no more than the others, and "his liberty was as dear to him." This admitted him to confidence, and as Jack was known to be entirely under Hark's influence, the strangers were no bar to their discussion. Eleven hours they remained there, in anxious consultation: one can imagine those terrible dusky faces, beneath the funereal woods, and amid the flickering of pine-knot torches, preparing that stern revenge whose shuddering echoes should ring through the land so long. Two things were at last decided: to begin their work that night, and to begin it with a massacre so swift and irresistible as to create in a few days more terror than many battles, and so spare the need of future bloodshed. "It was agreed that we should commence at home on that night, and, until we had armed and equipped ourselves and gained sufficient force, neither age nor sex was to be spared: which was invariably adhered to."

John Brown invaded Virginia with nineteen men, and with the avowed resolution to take no life but in self-defence. Nat Turner attacked Virginia from within, with six men, and with the determination to spare no life until his power was established. John Brown intended to pass rapidly through Virginia, and then retreat to the mountains. Nat Turner intended to "conquer Southampton County as the white men did in the Revolution, and then retreat, if necessary, to the Dismal Swamp." Each plan was deliberately matured; each was in its way practicable; but each was defeated by a single false step, as will soon appear.

We must pass over the details of horror, as they occurred

during the next twenty-four hours. Swift and stealthy as Indians, the black men passed from house to house,—not passing, not hesitating, as their terrible work went on. In one thing they were humaner than Indians or than white men fighting against Indians,—there was no gratuitous outrage beyond the death-blow itself, no insult, no mutilation; but in every house they entered, that blow fell on man, woman, and child,—nothing that had a white skin was spared. From every house they took arms and ammunition, and from a few, money; on every plantation they found recruits: those dusky slaves, so obsequious to their master the day before, so prompt to sing and dance before his Northern visitors, were all swift to transform themselves into fiends of retribution now; show them sword or musket and they grasped it, though it were an heirloom from Washington himself. The troop increased from house to house,—first to fifteen, then to forty, then to sixty. Some were armed with muskets, some with axes, some with scythes; some came on their masters' horses. As the numbers increased, they could be divided, and the awful work was carried on more rapidly still. The plan then was for an advanced guard of horsemen to approach each house at a gallop, and surround it till the others came up. Meanwhile what agonies of terror must have taken place within, shared alike by innocent and by guilty! what memories of wrongs inflicted on those dusky creatures, by some,—what innocent participation, by others, in the penance! The outbreak lasted for but forty-eight hours; but during that period fifty-five whites were slain, without the loss of a single slave.

One fear was needless, which to many a husband and father must have intensified the last struggle. These negroes had been systematically brutalized from childhood; they had been allowed no legalized or permanent marriage; they had beheld around them an habitual licentiousness, such as can scarcely exist except in a Slave State; some of them had seen their wives and sisters habitually polluted by the husbands and the brothers of these fair white women who were now absolutely in their power. Yet I have looked through the Virginia newspapers of that time in vain for one charge of an indecent outrage on a woman against these triumphant and terrible slaves. Wherever they went, there went death, and that was all. Compare this with ordinary wars; compare it with the annals of the French Revolution. No one, perhaps, has yet painted the wrongs of the French populace so terribly as Dickens in his "Tale of Two Cities"; yet what man, conversant with slave-biographies, can read that narrative without feeling it weak beside the provocations to which fugitive slaves testify? It is something for human nature that these desperate insurgents revenged such wrongs by death alone. Even that fearful penalty was to be inflicted only till the object was won. It was admitted in the "Richmond Enquirer" of the time, that "indiscriminate massacre was not their intention, after they obtained foothold, and was resorted to in the first instance to strike terror and alarm. Women and children would afterwards have been spared, and men also who ceased to resist."

It is reported by some of the contemporary newspapers, that a portion of this abstinence was the result of deliberate consultation among the insurrectionists; that some of them were resolved on taking the white women for wives, but were overruled by Nat Turner. If so, he is the only American slave-leader of whom we know certainly that he rose above the ordinary level of slave vengeance, and Mrs. Stowe's picture of Dred's purposes is then precisely typical of his. "Whom the Lord saith unto us, 'Smite,' them will we smite. We will not torment them with the scourge and fire, nor defile their women as they have done with ours. But we will slay them utterly, and consume them from off the face of the earth."

When the number of adherents had increased to fifty or sixty, Nat Turner judged it time to strike at the county-seat, Jerusalem. Thither a few white fugitives had already fled, and couriers might thence be despatched for aid to Richmond and Petersburg, unless promptly intercepted. Besides, he could there find arms, ammunition, and money; though they had already obtained, it is dubiously reported, from eight hundred to one thousand dollars. On the way it was necessary to pass the plantation of Mr. Parker, three miles from Jerusalem. Some of the men wished to stop here and enlist some of their friends. Nat Turner objected, as the delay might prove dangerous; he yielded at last, and it proved fatal.

He remained at the gate with six or eight men; thirty or forty went to the house, half a mile distant. They remained too long, and he went alone to hasten them. During his absence a party of eighteen white men came up suddenly, dispersing the small guard left at the gate; and when the main body of slaves emerged from the house, they encountered, for the first time, their armed masters. The blacks halted, the whites advanced cautiously within a hundred yards and fired a volley; on its being returned, they broke into disorder, and hurriedly retreated, leaving some wounded on the ground. The retreating whites were pursued, and were saved only by falling in with another band of fresh men from Jerusalem, with whose aid they turned upon the slaves, who in their turn fell into confusion. Turner, Hark, and about twenty men on horseback retreated in some order; the rest were scattered. The leader still planned to reach Jerusalem by a private way, thus evading pursuit; but at last decided to stop for the night, in the hope of enlisting additional recruits.

During the night the number increased again to forty, and they encamped on Major Ridley's plantation. An alarm took place during the darkness,—whether real or imaginary does not appear,—and the men became scattered again. Proceeding to make fresh enlistments with the daylight, they were resisted at Dr. Blunt's house, where his slaves, under his orders, fired upon them, and this, with a later attack from a party of white men near Captain Harris's, so broke up the whole force that they never reunited. The few who remained together agreed to separate for a few hours to see if anything could be done to revive the insurrection, and meet again that evening at their original rendezvous. But they never reached it.

Sadly came Nat Turner at nightfall into those gloomy woods where forty-eight hours before he had revealed the details of his terrible plot to his companions. At the outset all his plans had succeeded; everything was as he predicted: the slaves had come readily at his call, the masters had proved perfectly defenceless. Had he not been persuaded to pause at Parker's plantation, he would have been master before now of the arms and ammunition at Jerusalem; and with these to aid, and the Dismal Swamp for a refuge, he might have sustained himself indefinitely against his pursuers.

Now the blood was shed, the risk was incurred, his friends

were killed or captured, and all for what? Lasting memories of terror, to be sure, for his oppressors; but on the other hand, hopeless failure for the insurrection, and certain death for him. What a watch he must have kept that night! To that excited imagination, which had always seen spirits in the sky and blood-drops on the corn and hieroglyphic marks on the dry leaves, how full the lonely forest must have been of signs and solemn warnings! Alone with the fox's bark, the rabbit's rustle, and the screech-owl's scream, the self-appointed prophet brooded over his despair. Once creeping to the edge of the wood, he saw men stealthily approach on horseback. He fancied them some of his companions; but before he dared to whisper their ominous names, "Hark" or "Dred,"—for the latter was the name, since famous, of one of his more recent recruits,—he saw them to be white men, and shrank back stealthily beneath his covert.

There he waited two weary days and two melancholy nights,— long enough to satisfy himself that no one would rejoin him, and that the insurrection had hopelessly failed. The determined, desperate spirits who had shared his plans were scattered forever, and longer delay would be destruction for him also. He found a spot which he judged safe, dug a hole under a pile of fence-rails in a field, and lay there for six weeks, only leaving it for a few moments at midnight to obtain water from a neighboring spring. Food he had previously provided, without discovery, from a house near by.

Meanwhile an unbounded variety of rumors went flying through the State. The express which first reached the Governor announced that the militia were retreating before the slaves. An express to Petersburg further fixed the number of militia at three hundred, and of blacks at eight hundred, and invented a convenient shower of rain to explain the dampened ardor of the whites. Later reports described the slaves as making three desperate attempts to cross the bridge over the Nottoway between Cross Keys and Jerusalem, and stated that the leader had been shot in the attempt. Other accounts put the number of negroes at three hundred, all well mounted and armed, with two or three white men as leaders. Their intention was supposed to be to reach the Dismal Swamp, and they must be hemmed in from that side.

Indeed, the most formidable weapon in the hands of slave-insurgents is always this blind panic they create, and the wild exaggerations which follow. The worst being possible, every one takes the worst for granted. Undoubtedly a dozen armed men could have stifled this insurrection, even after it had commenced operations; but it is the fatal weakness of a slaveholding community, that it can never furnish men promptly for such a purpose. "My first intention was," says one of the most intelligent newspaper narrators of the affair, "to have attacked them with thirty or forty men; but those who had families here were strongly opposed to it."

As usual, each man was pinioned to his own hearth-stone. As usual, aid had to be summoned from a distance, and, as usual, the United States troops were the chief reliance. Colonel House, commanding at Fort Monroe, sent at once three companies of artillery under Lieutenant-Colonel Worth, and embarked them on board the steamer Hampton for Suffolk. These were joined by detachments from the United States ships Warren and Natchez, the whole amounting to nearly eight hundred men. Two volunteer companies went from Richmond, four from Petersburg, one from Norfolk, one from Portsmouth, and several from North Carolina. The militia of Norfolk, Nansemond, and Princess Anne Counties, and the United States troops at Old Point Comfort, were ordered to scour the Dismal Swamp, where it was believed that two or three thousand fugitives were preparing to join the insurgents. It was even proposed to send two companies from New York and one from New London to the same point.

When these various forces reached Southampton County, they found all labor paralyzed and whole plantations abandoned. A letter from Jerusalem, dated August 24th, says, "The oldest inhabitant of our county has never experienced such a distressing time as we have had since Sunday night last. . . . Every house, room, and corner in this place is full of women and children, driven from home, who had to take the woods until they could get to this place." "For many miles around their track," says another, "the county is deserted by women and children." Still another writes, "Jerusalem is full of women, most of them from the other side of the river,—about two hundred at Vix's." Then follow descriptions of the sufferings of these persons, many of whom had lain night after night in the woods. But the immediate danger was at an end, the short-lived insurrection was finished, and now the work of vengeance was to begin. In the frank phrase of a North Carolina correspondent,—"The massacre of the whites was over, and the white people had commenced the destruction of the negroes, which was continued after our men got there, from time to time, as they could fall in with them, all day yesterday." A postscript adds, that "passengers by the Fayetteville stage say, that, by the latest accounts, one hundred and twenty negroes had been killed,"—this being little more than one day's work.

These murders were defended as Nat Turner defended his: a fearful blow must be struck. In shuddering at the horrors of the insurrection, we have forgotten the far greater horrors of its suppression.

The newspapers of the day contain many indignant protests against the cruelties which took place. "It is with pain," says a correspondent of the "National Intelligencer," September 7, 1831, "that we speak of another feature of the Southampton Rebellion; for we have been most unwilling to have our sympathies for the sufferers diminished or affected by their misconduct. We allude to the slaughter of many blacks without trial and under circumstances of great barbarity. . . . We met with an individual of intelligence who told us that he himself had killed between ten and fifteen. . . . We [the Richmond troop] witnessed with surprise the sanguinary temper of the population, who evinced a strong disposition to inflict immediate death on every prisoner."

There is a remarkable official document from General Eppes, the officer in command, to be found in the "Richmond Enquirer" for September 6, 1831. It is an indignant denunciation of precisely these outrages; and though he refuses to give details, he supplies their place by epithets: "revolting,"—"inhuman and not to be justified,"—"acts of barbarity and cruelty,"—"acts of atrocity,"—"this course of proceeding dignifies the rebel and the assassin with the sanctity of martyrdom." And he ends by threatening martial law upon all future transgressors. Such general orders are not issued except in rather extreme cases. And in the parallel columns of the newspaper the innocent editor prints equally indignant descriptions of Russian atrocities in Lithuania, where the Poles were engaged in active insurrection, amid profuse sympathy from Virginia.

The truth is, it was a Reign of Terror. Volunteer patrols rode in all directions, visiting plantations. "It was with the greatest difficulty," said General Brodnax before the House of Delegates, "and at the hazard of personal popularity and esteem, that the coolest and most judicious among us could exert an influence sufficient to restrain an indiscriminate slaughter of the blacks who were suspected." A letter from the Rev. G.W. Powell declares, "There are thousands of troops searching in every direction, and many negroes are killed every day: the exact number will never be ascertained." Petition after petition was subsequently presented to the legislature, asking compensation for slaves thus assassinated without trial.

Men were tortured to death, burned, maimed, and subjected to nameless atrocities. The overseers were called on to point out any slaves whom they distrusted, and if any tried to escape, they were shot down. Nay, worse than this. "A party of horsemen started from Richmond with the intention of killing every colored person they saw in Southampton County. They stopped opposite the cabin of a free colored man, who was hoeing in his little field. They called out, 'Is this Southampton County?' He replied, 'Yes, Sir, you have just crossed the line, by yonder tree.'. They shot him dead and rode on." This is from the narrative of the editor of the "Richmond Whig," who was then on duty in the militia, and protested manfully against these outrages. "Some of these scenes," he adds, "are hardly inferior in barbarity to the atrocities of the insurgents."

These were the masters' stories. If even these conceded so much, it would be interesting to hear what the slaves had to report. I am indebted to my honored friend, Lydia Maria Child, for some vivid recollections of this terrible period, as noted down from the lips of an old colored woman, once well known in New York, Charity Bowery. "At the time of the old Prophet Nat," she said, "the colored folks was afraid to pray loud; for the whites threatened to punish 'em dreadfully, if the least noise was heard. The patrols was low drunken whites, and in Nat's time, if they heard any of the colored folks praying or singing a hymn, they would fall upon 'em and abuse 'em, and sometimes kill 'em, afore master or missis could get to 'em. The brightest and best was killed in Nat's time. The whites always suspect such ones. They killed a great many at a place called Duplon. They killed Antonio, a slave of Mr. J. Stanley, whom they shot; then they pointed their guns at him, and told him to confess about the insurrection. He told 'em he didn't know anything about any insurrection. They shot several balls through him, quartered him, and put his head on a pole at the fork of the road leading to the court." (This is no exaggeration, if the Virginia newspapers may be taken as evidence.) "It was there but a short time. He had no trial. They never do. In Nat's time, the patrols would tie up the free colored people, flog 'em, and try to make 'em lie against one another, and often killed them before anybody could interfere. Mr. James Cole, High Sheriff, said, if any of the patrols came on his plantation, he would lose his life in defence of his people. One day he heard a patroller boasting how many niggers he had killed. Mr. Cole said, 'If you don't pack up, as quick as God Almighty will let you, and get out of this town, and never be seen in it again, I'll put you where dogs won't bark at you.' He went off, and wasn't seen in them parts again."

These outrages were not limited to the colored population; but other instances occurred which strikingly remind one of more recent times. An Englishman, named Robinson, was engaged in selling books at Petersburg. An alarm being given, one night, that five hundred blacks were marching towards the town, he stood guard, with others, on the bridge. After the panic had a little subsided, he happened to remark, that "the blacks, as men, were entitled to their freedom, and ought to be emancipated." This led to great excitement, and he was warned to leave town. He took passage in the stage, but the stage was intercepted. He then fled to a friend's house; the house was broken open, and he was dragged forth. The civil authorities, being applied to, refused to interfere. The mob stripped him, gave him a great number of lashes, and sent him on foot, naked, under a hot sun, to Richmond, whence he with difficulty found a passage to New York.

Of the capture or escape of most of that small band who met with Nat Turner in the woods upon the Travis plantation little can now be known. All appear among the list of convicted, except

Henry and Will. General Moore, who occasionally figures as
second in command, in the newspaper narratives of that day,
was probably the Hark or Hercules before mentioned; as no
other of the confederates had belonged to Mrs. Travis, or would
have been likely to bear her previous name of Moore. As usual,
the newspapers state that most, if not all the slaves, were "the
property of kind and indulgent masters." Whether in any case
they were also the sons of those masters is a point ignored; but
from the fact that three out of the seven were at first reported
as being white men by several different witnesses,—the whole
number being correctly given, and the statement therefore probably authentic,—one must suppose that there was an admix-
ture of patrician blood in some of these conspirators.

The subordinate insurgents sought safety as they could. A
free colored man, named Will Artist, shot himself in the woods,
where his hat was found on a stake and his pistol lying by him;
another was found drowned; others were traced to the Dismal
Swamp; others returned to their homes, and tried to conceal
their share in the insurrection, assuring their masters that they
had been forced, against their will, to join,—the usual defence
in such cases. The number shot down at random must, by all
accounts, have amounted to many hundreds, but it is past all
human registration now. The number who had a formal trial,
such as it was, is officially stated at fifty five; of these, seventeen
were convicted and hanged, twelve convicted and transported,
twenty acquitted, and four free colored men sent on for further
trial and finally acquitted. "Not one of those known to be concerned escaped." Of those executed, one only was a woman:
"Lucy, slave of John T. Barrow": that is all her epitaph, shorter
even than that of Wordsworth's more famous Lucy; —but whether
this one was old or young, pure or wicked, lovely or repulsive, oc-
troon or negro, a Cassy, an Emily, or a Topsy, no information appears; she was a woman, she was a slave, and she died.

There is one touching story, in connection with these terrible
retaliations, which rests on good authority, that of the Rev.
M. B. Cox, a Liberian missionary, then in Virginia. In the hunt
which followed the massacre, a slaveholder went into the woods,
accompanied by a faithful slave, who had been the means of
saving his life during the insurrection. When they had reached

a retired place in the forest, the man handed his gun to his master, informing him that he could not live a slave any longer, and requesting him either to free him or shoot him on the spot. The master took the gun, in some trepidation, levelled it at the faithful negro, and shot him through the heart. It is probable that this slaveholder was a Dr. Blunt,—his being the only plantation where the slaves were reported as thus defending their masters. "If this be true," said the "Richmond Enquirer," when it first narrated this instance of loyalty, "great will be the desert of these noble-minded Africans." This "noble-minded African," at least, estimated his own desert at a high standard: he demanded freedom,—and obtained it.

Meanwhile the panic of the whites continued; for, though all others might be disposed of, Nat Turner was still at large. We have positive evidence of the extent of the alarm, although great efforts were afterwards made to represent it as a trifling affair. A distinguished citizen of Virginia wrote three months later to the Hon. W. B. Seabrook of South Carolina,—"From all that has come to my knowledge during and since that affair, I am convinced most fully that every black preacher in the country east of the Blue Ridge was in the secret." "There is much reason to believe," says the Governor's message on December 6th, "that the spirit of insurrection was not confined to Southampton. Many convictions have taken place elsewhere, and some few in distant counties." The withdrawal of the United States troops, after some ten days' service, was a signal for fresh excitement, and an address, numerously signed, was presented to the United States Government, imploring their continued stay. More than three weeks after the first alarm, the Governor sent a supply of arms into Prince William, Fauquier, and Orange Counties. "From examinations which have taken place in other counties," says one of the best newspaper historians of the affair, (in the "Richmond Enquirer" of September 6th,) "I fear that the scheme embraced a wider sphere than I at first supposed." Nat Turner himself, intentionally or otherwise, increased the confusion by denying all knowledge of the North Carolina outbreak, and declaring that he had communicated his plans to his four confederates within six months; while, on the other hand, a slave-girl, sixteen or seventeen years old, belonging to Solomon Parker, testified that she had heard the subject discussed for eighteen months, and that at a meeting held during the previous May some eight or ten had joined the plot.

It is astonishing to discover, by laborious comparison of newspaper files, how vast was the immediate range of these insurrectionary alarms. Every Southern State seems to have borne its harvest of terror. On the Eastern shore of Maryland great alarm was at once manifested, especially in the neighborhood of Easton and Snowhill; and the houses of colored men were searched for arms even in Baltimore. In Delaware, there were similar rumors through Sussex and Dover Counties; there were arrests and executions; and in Somerset County great public meetings were held, to demand additional safeguards. On election-day, in Seaford, Del., some young men, going out to hunt rabbits, discharged their guns in sport; the men being absent, all the women in the vicinity took to flight; the alarm spread like the "Ipswich Fright"; soon Seaford was thronged with armed men; and when the boys returned from hunting, they found cannon drawn out to receive them.

In North Carolina, Raleigh and Fayetteville were put under military defence, and women and children concealed themselves in the swamps for many days. The rebel organization was supposed to include two thousand. Forty-six slaves were imprisoned in Union County, twenty-five in Sampson County, and twenty-three at least in Duplin County, some of whom were executed. The panic also extended into Wayne, New Hanover, and Lenoir Counties. Four men were shot without trial in Wilmington,—Nimrod, Abraham, Prince, and "Dan the Drayman," the latter a man of seventy,—and their heads placed on poles at the four corners of the town. Nearly two months afterwards the trials were still continuing; and at a still later day, the Governor in his proclamation recommended the formation of companies of volunteers in every county.

In South Carolina, General Hayne issued a proclamation "to prove the groundlessness of the existing alarms,"—thus implying that serious alarms existed. In Macon, Georgia, the whole population were roused from their beds at midnight by a report of a large force of armed negroes five miles off. In an hour, every woman and child was deposited in the largest building of the town, and a military force hastily collected in front. The editor of the Macon "Messenger" excused the poor condition of his paper, a few days afterwards, by the absorption of his workmen in patrol duties, and describes "dismay and terror" as the condition of the people, of "all ages and sexes." In Jones, Twiggs, and Monroe Counties, the same alarms were reported; and in one place "several slaves were tied to a tree, while a militia captain hacked at them with his sword."

In Alabama, at Columbus and Fort Mitchell, a rumor was spread of a joint conspiracy of Indians and negroes. At Claiborne the panic was still greater; the slaves were said to be thoroughly organized through that part of the State, and multitudes were imprisoned; the whole alarm being apparently founded on one stray copy of the "Liberator."

In Tennessee, the Shelbyville "Freeman" announced that an insurrectionary plot had just been discovered, barely in time for its defeat, through the treachery of a female slave. In Louisville, Kentucky, a similar organization was discovered or imagined, and arrests were made in consequence. "The papers, from motives of policy, do not notice the disturbance," wrote one correspondent to the Portland "Courier." "Pity us!" he added.

But the greatest bubble burst in Louisiana. Captain Alexander, an English tourist, arriving in New Orleans at the beginning of September, found the whole city in tumult. Handbills had been issued, appealing to the slaves to rise against their masters, saying that all men were born equal, declaring that Hannibal was a black man, and that they also might have great leaders among them. Twelve hundred stand of weapons were said to have been found in a black man's house; five hundred citizens were under arms, and four companies of regulars were ordered to the city, whose barracks Alexander himself visited.

If such were the alarm in New Orleans, the story, of course, lost nothing by transmission to other Slave States. A rumor reached Frankfort, Kentucky, that the slaves already had possession of the coast, both above and below New Orleans. But the most remarkable circumstance is, that all this seems to have been a mere revival of an old terror, once before excited and exploded. The following paragraph had appeared in the Jacksonville (Georgia) "Observer," during the spring previous:—

"FEARFUL DISCOVERY. We were favored, by yesterday's mail, with a letter from New Orleans, of May 1st, in which we find that an important discovery had been made a few days previous in that city. The following is an extract:—'Four days ago, as some planters were digging under ground, they found a square room containing eleven thousand stand of arms and fifteen thousand cartridges, each of the cartridges containing a bullet.' It is said the negroes intended to rise as soon as the sickly season began, and obtain possession of the city by massacring the white population. The same letter states that the mayor had prohibited the opening of Sunday-schools for the instruction of blacks, under a penalty of five hundred dollars for the first offence, and for the second, death."

Such were the terrors that came back from nine other Slave States, as the echo of the voice of Nat Turner; and when it is also known that the subject was at once taken up by the legislatures of other States, where there was no public panic, as in Missouri and Tennessee,—and when, finally, it is added that reports of insurrection had been arriving all that year from Rio Janeiro, Martinique, St. Jago, Antigua, Caraccas, and Tortola, it is easy to see with what prolonged distress the accumulated terror must have weighed down upon Virginia, during the two months that Nat Turner lay hid.

True, there were a thousand men in arms in Southampton County, to inspire security. But the blow had been struck by only seven men before; and unless there were an armed guard in every house, who could tell but any house might at any moment be the scene of new horrors? They might kill or imprison unresisting negroes by day, but could they resist their avengers by night? "The half cannot be told," wrote a lady from another part of Virginia, at this time, "of the distresses of the people. In Southampton County, the scene of the insurrection, the distress beggars description. A gentleman who has been there says that even here, where there has been great alarm, we have no idea of the situation of those in that county. . . . I do not hesitate to believe that many negroes around us would join in a massacre as horrible as that which has taken place, if an opportunity should offer."

Meanwhile the cause of all this terror was made the object of desperate search. On September 17th the Governor offered a reward of five hundred dollars for his capture, and there were other rewards swelling the amount to eleven hundred dollars,— but in vain. No one could track or trap him. On September 30th a minute account of his capture appeared in the newspapers, but it was wholly false. On October 7th there was another, and on October 18th another; yet all without foundation. Worn out by confinement in his little cave, Nat Turner grew more adventurous, and began to move about stealthily by night, afraid to speak to any human being, but hoping to obtain some information that might aid his escape. Returning regularly to his retreat before daybreak, he might possibly have continued this mode of life until pursuit had ceased, had not a dog succeeded where men had failed. The creature accidentally smelt out the provisions hid in the cave, and finally led thither his masters, two negroes, one of whom was named Nelson. On discovering the terrible fugitive, they fled precipitately, when he hastened to retreat in an opposite direction. This was on October 15th, and from this moment the neighborhood was all alive with excitement, and five or six hundred men undertook the pursuit.

It shows a more than Indian adroitness in Nat Turner to have escaped capture any longer. The cave, the arms, the provisions were found; and lying among them the notched stick of this miserable Robinson Crusoe, marked with five weary weeks and six days. But the man was gone. For ten days more he concealed himself among the wheat-stacks on Mr. Francis's plantation, and during this time was reduced almost to despair. Once he decided to surrender himself, and walked by night within two miles of Jerusalem before his purpose failed him. Three times he tried to get out of that neighborhood, but in vain: travelling by day was, of course, out of the question, and by night he found it impossible to elude the patrol. Again and again, therefore, he returned to his hiding-place, and during his whole two months' liberty never went five miles from the Cross Keys. On the 25th of October, he was at last discovered by Mr. Francis, as he was emerging from a stack. A load of buckshot was instantly discharged at him, twelve of which passed through his hat as he fell to the ground. He escaped even then, but his pursuers were rapidly concentrating upon him, and it is perfectly astonishing that he could have eluded them for five days more.

On Sunday, October 30th, a man named Benjamin Phipps, going out for the first time on patrol duty, was passing at noon a clearing in the woods where a number of pine-trees had long since been felled. There was a motion among their boughs; he stopped to watch it; and through a gap in the branches he saw, emerging from a hole in the earth beneath, the face of Nat Turner. Aiming his gun instantly, Phipps called on him to surrender. The fugitive, exhausted with watching and privation, entangled in the branches, armed only with a sword, had nothing to do but to yield; sagaciously reflecting, also, as he afterwards explained, that the woods were full of armed men, and that he had better trust fortune for some later chance of escape, instead of desperately attempting it then. He was correct in the first impression, since there were fifty armed scouts within a circuit of two miles. His insurrection ended where it began; for this spot was only a mile and a half from the house of Joseph Travis.

Torn, emaciated, ragged, "a mere scarecrow," still wearing the hat perforated with buckshot, with his arms bound to his sides, he was driven before the levelled gun to the nearest house, that of a Mr. Edwards. He was confined there that night; but the news had spread so rapidly that within an hour after his arrival a hundred persons had collected, and the excitement became so intense "that it was with difficulty he could be conveyed alive to Jerusalem." The enthusiasm spread instantly through Virginia; Mr. Trezvant, the Jerusalem postmaster, sent notices of it far and near; and Governor Floyd himself wrote a letter to the "Richmond Enquirer" to give official announcement of the momentous capture.

When Nat Turner was asked by Mr. T. R. Gray, the counsel assigned him, whether, although defeated, he still believed in his own Providential mission, he answered, as simply as one who came thirty years after him, "Was not Christ crucified?" In the same spirit, when arraigned before the court, "he answered, 'Not guilty,' saying to his counsel that he did not feel so." But apparently no argument was made in his favor by his counsel, nor were any witnesses called,—he being convicted on the testimony of Levi Waller, and upon his own confession, which was put in by Mr. Gray, and acknowledged by the prisoner before the six justices composing the court, as being "full, free, and voluntary." He was therefore placed in the paradoxical position of conviction by his own confession, under a plea of "Not guilty." The arrest took place on the thirtieth of October, 1831, the confession on the first of November, the trial and conviction on the fifth, and the execution on the following Friday, the eleventh of November, precisely at noon. He met his death with perfect composure, declined addressing the multitude assembled, and told the sheriff in a firm voice that he was ready. Another account says that he "betrayed no emotion, and even hurried the executioner in the performance of his duty." "Not a limb nor a muscle was observed to move. His body, after his death, was given over to the surgeons for dissection."

OSBORNE P. ANDERSON

Osborne P. Anderson (1830–1872) was the sole surviving participant of the white abolitionist John Brown and his compatriots' raid of Harpers Ferry, Virginia. In the preface to the full volume, Anderson describes the necessity of his published testimony as a corrective to the master accounts that proliferated in the aftermath of the failed act of rebellion as well as a subtle warning that more insurrection was imminent: "My own personal experience in it, under the orders of Capt. Brown, on the 16th and 17th of October, 1859, as the only man alive who was at Harper's Ferry during the entire time the unsuccessful groping after these facts, by individuals, impossible to be obtained, except from an actor in the scene and the conviction that the cause of impartial liberty requires this duty at my hands alone have been the motives for writing and circulating the little book herewith presented. I will not, under such circumstances, insult or burden the intelligent with excuses for defects in composition, nor for the attempt to give the facts. A plain, unadorned, truthful story is wanted, and that by one who knows what he says, who is known to have been at the great encounter, and to have labored in shaping the same. My identity as a member of Capt. Brown's company cannot be questioned, successfully, by any in Canada or the United States familiar with John Brown and his plans; as those know his men personally, or by reputation, who enjoyed his confidence sufficiently to know thoroughly his plans. The readers of this narrative will therefore keep steadily in view the main point that they are perusing a story of events which have happened under the eye of the great Captain, or are incidental thereto, and not a compendium of the 'plans' of Capt. Brown; for as his plans were not consummated, and as their fulfillment is committed to the future, no one to whom they are known will recklessly expose all of them to the public gaze."

From *A Voice from Harper's Ferry*
(1861)

Chapter VIII.

COUNCIL MEETINGS—ORDERS GIVEN—
THE CHARGE—ETC.

On Sunday morning, October 16th, Captain Brown arose earlier than usual, and called his men down to worship. He read a
chapter from the Bible, applicable to the condition of the slaves,
and our duty as their brethren, and then offered up a fervent
prayer to God to assist in the liberation of the bondmen in that
slaveholding land. The services were impressive beyond expression. Every man there assembled seemed to respond from the
depths of his soul, and throughout the entire day, a deep solemnity pervaded the place. The old man's usually weighty words
were invested with more than ordinary importance, and the
countenance of every man reflected the momentous thought
that absorbed his attention within.

After breakfast had been despatched, and the roll called by
the Captain, a sentinel was posted outside the door, to warn by
signal if any one should approach, and we listened to prepara-
tory remarks to a council meeting to be held that day. At
10 o'clock, the council was assembled. I was appointed to the
Chair, when matters of importance were considered at length.
After the council adjourned, the Constitution was read for the
benefit of the few who had not before heard it, and the necessary oaths taken. Men who were to hold military positions in
the organization, and who had not received commissions before then, had their commissions filled out by J. H. Kagi, and
gave the required obligations.

In the afternoon, the eleven orders presented in the next

chapter were given by the Captain, and were afterwards carried out in every particular by the officers and men.

In the evening, before setting out to the Ferry, he gave his final charge, in which he said, among other things:—*"And now, gentlemen, let me impress this one thing upon your minds. You all know how dear life is to you, and how dear your life is to your friends. And in remembering that, consider that the lives of others are as dear to them as yours are to you. Do not, therefore, take the life of any one, if you can possibly avoid it; but if it is necessary to take life in order to save your own, then make sure work of it."*

Chapter IX.

THE ELEVEN ORDERS GIVEN BY CAPTAIN BROWN TO HIS MEN BEFORE SETTING OUT FOR THE FERRY.

The orders given by Captain Brown, before departing from the Farm for the Ferry, were:—

1. Captain Owen Brown, F. J. Merriam, and Barclay Coppic to remain at the old house as sentinels, to guard the arms and effects till morning, when they would be joined by some of the men from the Ferry with teams to move all arms and other things to the old school-house before referred to, located about three-quarters of a mile from Harper's Ferry— a place selected a day or two beforehand by the Captain.

2. All hands to make as little noise as possible going to the Ferry, so as not to attract attention till we could get to the bridge; and to keep all arms secreted, so as not to be detected if met by any one.

3. The men were to walk in couples, at some distance apart;

and should any one overtake us, stop him and detain him until the rest of our comrades were out of the road. The same course to be pursued if we were met by any one.

4. That Captains Charles P. Tidd and John E. Cook walk ahead of the wagon in which Captain Brown rode to the Ferry, to tear down the telegraph wires on the Maryland side along the railroad; and to do the same on the Virginia side, after the town should be captured.

5. Captains John H. Kagi and A. D. Stevens were to take the watchman at the Ferry bridge prisoner when the party got there, and to detain him there until the engine house upon the Government grounds should be taken.

6. Captain Watson Brown and Stewart Taylor were to take positions at the Potomac bridge, and hold it till morning. They were to stand on opposite sides, a rod apart, and if any one entered the bridge, they were to let him get in between them. In that case, pikes were to be used, not Sharp's rifles, unless they offered much resistance, and refused to surrender.

7. Captains Oliver Brown and William Thompson were to execute a similar order at the Shenandoah bridge, until morning.

8. Lieutenant Jeremiah Anderson and Adolphus Thompson were to occupy the engine house at first, with the prisoner watchman from the bridge and the watchman belonging to the engine-house yard, until the one on the opposite side of the street and the rifle factory were taken, after which they would be reinforced, to hold that place with the prisoners.

9. Lieutenant Albert Hazlett and Private Edwin Coppie were to hold the Armory opposite the engine house after it had been taken, through the night and until morning, when arrangements would be different.

10. That John H. Kagi, Adjutant General, and John A. Copeland,

(colored,) take positions at the rifle factory through the night, and hold it until further orders.

11. That Colonel A. D. Stevens (the same Captain Stevens who held military position next to Captain Brown) proceed to the country with his men, and after taking certain parties prisoners bring them to the Ferry. In the case of Colonel Lewis Washington, who had arms in his hands, he must, before being secured as a prisoner, deliver them into the hands of Osborne P. Anderson. Anderson being a colored man, and colored men being only *things* in the South, it is proper that the South be taught a lesson upon this point.

John H. Kagi being Adjutant General, was the near adviser of Captain John Brown, and second in position; and had the old gentleman been slain at the Ferry, and Kagi been spared, the command would have devolved upon the latter. But Col. Stevens holding the active military position in the organization second to Captain Brown, when order eleven was given him, had the privilege of choosing his own men to execute it. The selection was made after the capture of the Ferry, and then my duty to receive Colonel Washington's famous arms was assigned me by Captain Brown. The men selected by Col. Stevens to act under his orders during the night were Charles P. Tidd, Osborne P. Anderson, Shields Green, John E. Cook, and Sherrard Lewis Leary. We were to take prisoners, and any slaves who would come, and bring them to the Ferry.

A few days before, Capt. Cook had travelled along the Charlestown turnpike, and collected statistics of the population of slaves and the masters' names. Among the masters whose acquaintance Cook had made, Colonel Washington had received him politely, and had shown him a sword formerly owned by Frederic the Great of Prussia, and presented by him to Genl. Washington, and a pair of horse pistols, formerly owned by General Lafayette, and bequeathed by the old General to Lewis Washington. These were the arms specially referred to in the charge.

At eight o'clock on Sunday evening, Captain Brown said: "Men, get on your arms; we will proceed to the Ferry." His horse and wagon were brought out before the door, and some pikes, a sledge-hammer and crowbar were placed in it. The Captain then put on his old Kansas cap, and said: "Come, boys!" when we marched out of the camp behind him, into the lane leading down the hill to the main road. As we formed the procession line, Owen Brown, Barclay Coppic, and Francis J. Merriam, sentinels left behind to protect the place as before stated, came forward and took leave of us; after which, agreeably to previous orders, and as they were better acquainted with the topography of the Ferry, and to effect the tearing down of the telegraph wires, C. P. Tidd and John E. Cook led the procession. While going to the Ferry, the company marched along as solemnly as a funeral procession, till we got to the bridge. When we entered, we halted, and carried out an order to fasten our cartridge boxes outside of our clothes, when every thing was ready for taking the town.

Chapter X.

THE CAPTURE OF HARPER'S FERRY—
COL. A. D. STEVENS AND PARTY SALLY OUT
TO THE PLANTATIONS—
WHAT WE SAW, HEARD, DID, ETC.

As John H. Kagi and A. D. Stevens entered the bridge, as ordered in the fifth charge, the watchman, being at the other end, came toward them with a lantern in his hand. When up to them, they told him he was their prisoner, and detained him a few minutes, when he asked them to spare his life. They replied, they did not intend to harm him; the object was to free the slaves, and he would have to submit to them for a time, in order that the purpose might be carried out.

Captain Brown now entered the bridge in his wagon, followed by the rest of us, until we reached that part where Kagi and Stevens held their prisoner, when he ordered Watson Brown and Stewart Taylor to take the positions assigned them in order sixth, and the rest of us to proceed to the engine house. We started for the engine house, taking the prisoner along with us. When we neared the gates of the engine-house yard, we found them locked, and the watchman on the inside. He was told to open the gates, but refused, and commenced to cry. The men were then ordered by Captain Brown to open the gates forcibly, which was done, and the watchman taken prisoner. The two prisoners were left in the custody of Jerry Anderson and Adolphus Thompson, and A. D. Stevens arranged the men to take possession of the Armory and rifle factory. About this time, there was apparently much excitement. People were passing back and forth in the town, and before we could do much, we had to take several prisoners. After the prisoners were secured, we passed to the opposite side of the street and took the Armory, and Albert Hazlett and Edwin Coppic were ordered to hold it for the time being.

The capture of the rifle factory was the next work to be done. When we went there, we told the watchman who was outside of the building our business, and asked him to go along with us, as we had come to take possession of the town, and make use of the Armory in carrying out our object. He obeyed the command without hesitation. John H. Kagi and John Copeland were placed in the Armory, and the prisoners taken to the engine house. Following the capture of the Armory, Oliver Brown and William Thompson were ordered to take possession of the bridge leading out of town, across the Shenandoah river, which they immediately did. These places were all taken, and the prisoners secured, without the snap of a gun, or any violence whatever.

The town being taken, Brown, Stevens, and the men who had no post in charge, returned to the engine house, where council was held, after which Captain Stevens, Tidd, Cook, Shields Green, Leary and myself went to the country. On the road, we met some colored men, to whom we made known our purpose, when they immediately agreed to join us. They said they had been long waiting for an opportunity of the kind. Stevens then asked them to go around among the colored people and circulate the news, when each started off in a different direction. The result was that many colored men gathered to the scene of action. The first prisoner taken by us was Colonel Lewis Washington. When we neared his house, Capt. Stevens placed Leary and Shields Green to guard the approaches to the house, the one at the side, the other in front. We then knocked, but no one answering, although females were looking from upper windows, we entered the building and commenced a search for the proprietor. Col. Washington opened his room door, and begged us not to kill him. Capt. Stevens replied, "You are our prisoner," when he stood as if speechless or petrified. Stevens further told him to get ready to go to the Ferry; that he had come to abolish slavery, not to take life but in self-defence, but that he *must* go along. The Colonel replied: "You can have my slaves, if you will let me remain." "No," said the Captain, "you must go along too; so get ready." After saying this, Stevens left the house for a time, and with Green, Leary and Tidd, proceeded to the "Quarters," giving the prisoner in charge of Cook and myself. The male slaves were gathered together in a short time, when horses were tackled to the Colonel's two-horse carriage and four-horse wagon, and both vehicles brought to the front of the house.

During this time, Washington was walking the floor, apparently much excited. When the Captain came in, he went to the sideboard, took out his whiskey, and offered us something to drink, but he was refused. His fire-arms were next demanded, when he brought forth one double-barrelled gun, one small rifle, two horse-pistols and a sword. Nothing else was asked of him. The Colonel cried heartily when he found he must submit, and appeared taken aback when, on delivering up the famous sword formerly presented by Frederic to his illustrious kinsman, George Washington, Capt. Stevens told me to step forward and take it. Washington was secured and placed in his wagon, the women of the family making great outcries, when the party drove forward to Mr. John Allstadt's. After making known our business to him, he went into as great a fever of excitement as Washington had done. We could have his slaves, also, if we would only leave him. This, of course, was contrary to our plans and instructions. He hesitated, puttered around, fumbled and meditated for a long time. At last, seeing no alternative, he got ready, when the slaves were gathered up from about the quarters by their own consent, and all placed in Washington's big wagon and returned to the Ferry.

One old colored lady, at whose house we stopped, a little way from the town, had a good time over the message we took her.

This liberating the slaves was the very thing she had longed for, prayed for, and dreamed about, time and again; and her heart was full of rejoicing over the fulfilment of a prophecy which had been her faith for long years. While we were absent from the Ferry, the train of cars for Baltimore arrived, and was detained. A colored man named Haywood, employed upon it, went from the Wager House up to the entrance to the bridge, where the train stood, to assist with the baggage. He was ordered to stop by the sentinels stationed at the bridge, which he refused to do, but turned to go in an opposite direction, when he was fired upon, and received a mortal wound. Had he stood when ordered, he would not have been harmed. No one knew at the time whether he was white or colored, but his movements were such as to justify the sentinels in shooting him, as he would not stop when commanded. The first firing happened at that time, and the only firing, until after daylight on Monday morning.

Chapter XI.

THE EVENTS OF MONDAY, OCT. 17—ARMING THE SLAVES—TERROR IN THE SLAVEHOLDING CAMP—IMPORTANT LOSSES TO OUR PARTY— THE FATE OF KAGI—PRISONERS ACCUMULATE— WORKMEN AT THE KENNEDY FARM—ETC.

Monday, the 17th of October, was a time of stirring and exciting events. In consequence of the movements of the night before, we were prepared for commotion and tumult, but certainly not for more than we beheld around us. Gray dawn and yet brighter daylight revealed great confusion, and as the sun arose, the panic spread like wild-fire. Men, women and children could be seen leaving their homes in every direction; some seeking refuge among residents, and in quarters further away, others climbing up the hill-sides, and hurrying off in various directions, evidently impelled by a sudden fear, which was plainly visible in their countenances or in their movements.

Capt. Brown was all activity, though I could not help thinking that at times he appeared somewhat puzzled. He ordered Sherrard Lewis Leary, and four slaves, and a free man belonging in the neighborhood, to join John Henry Kagi and John Copeland at the rifle factory, which they immediately did. Kagi, and all except Copeland, were subsequently killed, but not before having communicated with Capt. Brown, as will be set forth further along.

As fast as the workmen came to the building, or persons appeared in the street near the engine house, they were taken prisoners, and directly after sunrise, the detained train was permitted to start for the eastward. After the departure of the train, quietness prevailed for a short time; a number of prisoners were already in the engine house, and of the many colored men living in the neighborhood, who had assembled in the town, a number were armed for the work.

Capt. Brown ordered Capts. Charles P. Tidd, Wm. H. Leeman, John E. Cook, and some fourteen slaves, to take Washington's four-horse wagon, and to join the company under Capt. Owen Brown, consisting of F. J. Merriam and Barclay Coppic, who had been left at the Farm the night previous, to guard the place and the arms. The company, thus reinforced, proceeded, under Owen Brown, to move the arms and goods from the Farm down to the school-house in the mountains, three-fourths of a mile from the Ferry.

Capt. Brown next ordered me to take the pikes out of the wagon in which he rode to the Ferry, and to place them in the hands of the colored men who had come with us from the plantations, and others who had come forward without having had communication with any of our party. It was out of the circumstances connected with the fulfilment of this order, that the false charge against "Anderson" as leader, or "ringleader," of the negroes, grew.

The spectators, about this time, became apparently wild with fright and excitement. The number of prisoners was magnified to hundreds, and the judgment-day could not have presented more terrors, in its awful and certain prospective punishment to the justly condemned for the wicked deeds of a life-time, the chief of which would no doubt be slaveholding, than did Capt. Brown's operations.

The prisoners were also terror-stricken. Some wanted to go home to see their families, as if for the last time. The privilege was granted them, under escort, and they were brought back again. Edwin Coppic, one of the sentinels at the Armory gate, was fired at by one of the citizens, but the ball did not reach him, when one of the insurgents close by put up his rifle, and made the enemy bite the dust.

Among the arms taken from Col. Washington was one double-barrel gun. This weapon was loaded by Leeman with buckshot, and placed in the hands of an elderly slave man, early in the morning. After the cowardly charge upon Coppic, this old man was ordered by Capt. Stevens to arrest a citizen. The old man ordered him to halt, which he refused to do, when instantly the terrible load was discharged into him, and he fell, and expired without a struggle.

After these incidents, time passed away till the arrival of the United States troops, without any further attack upon us. The cowardly Virginians submitted like sheep, without resistance, from that time until the marines came down. Meanwhile, Capt. Brown, who was considering a proposition for release from his prisoners, passed back and forth from the Armory to the bridge, speaking words of comfort and encouragement to his men. "Hold on a little longer, boys," said he, "until I get matters arranged with the prisoners." This tardiness on the part of our brave leader was sensibly felt to be an omen of evil by some us, and was eventually the cause of our defeat. It was no part of the original plan to hold on to the Ferry, or to parley with prisoners; but by so doing, time was afforded to carry the news of its capture to several points, and forces were thrown into the place, which surrounded us.

At eleven o'clock, Capt. Brown despatched William Thompson from the Ferry up to Kennedy Farm, with the news that we had peaceful possession of the town, and with directions to the men to continue on moving the things. He went; but before he could get back, troops had begun to pour in, and the general encounter commenced.

* * *

Chapter XIX.

THE BEHAVIOR OF THE SLAVES—
CAPTAIN BROWN'S OPINION.

Of the various contradictory reports made by slaveholders and their satellites about the time of the Harper's Ferry conflict, none were more untruthful than those relating to the slaves. There was seemingly a studied attempt to enforce the belief that the slaves were cowardly, and that they were really more in favor of Virginia masters and slavery, than of their freedom. As a party who had an intimate knowledge of the conduct of the colored men engaged, I am prepared to make an emphatic denial of the gross imputation against them. They were charged specially with being unreliable, with deserting Captain Brown the first opportunity, and going back to their masters; and with being so indifferent to the work of their salvation from the yoke, as to have to be forced into service by the Captain, contrary to their will.

On the Sunday evening of the outbreak, when we visited the plantations and acquainted the slaves with our purpose to effect their liberation, the greatest enthusiasm was manifested by them—joy and hilarity beamed from every countenance. One old mother, white-haired from age, and borne down with the labors of many years in bonds, when told of the work in hand, replied: "God bless you! God bless you!" She then kissed the party at her house, and requested all to kneel, which we did, and she offered prayer to God for His blessing on the enterprise, and our success. At the slaves' quarters, there was apparently a general jubilee, and they stepped forward manfully, without impressing or coaxing. In one case, only, was there any hesitation. A dark-complexioned freeborn man refused to take up arms. He showed the only want of confidence in the movement, and far less courage than any slave consulted about the plan. In fact, so far as I could learn, the free blacks South are much less reliable than the slaves, and infinitely more fearful. In Washington City, a party of free colored persons offered their services to the Mayor, to aid in suppressing our movement. Of the slaves who followed us to the Ferry, some were sent to help remove stores, and the others were drawn up in a circle around the engine-house, at one time, where they were, by Captain Brown's order, furnished by me with pikes, mostly, and acted as a guard to the prisoners to prevent their escape, which they did.

As in the war of the American Revolution, the first blood shed was a black man's, Crispus Attuck's, so at Harper's Ferry, the first blood shed by our party, after the arrival of the United States troops, was that of a slave. In the begining of the encounter, and before the troops had fairly emerged from the bridge, a slave was shot. I saw him fall. Phil, the slave who died in prison, with fear, as it was reported, was wounded at the Ferry, and died from the effects of it. Of the men shot on the rocks, when Kagi's party were compelled to take to the river, some were slaves, and they suffered death before they would desert their companions, and their bodies fell into the waves beneath. Captain Brown, who was surprised and pleased by the promptitude with which they volunteered, and with their manly bearing at the scene of violence, remarked to me, on that Monday morning, that he was agreeably disappointed in the behavior of the slaves; for he did not expect one out of ten to be willing to fight. The truth of the Harper's Ferry "raid," as it has been called, in regard to the part taken by the slaves, and the aid given by colored men generally, demonstrates clearly: First, that the conduct of the slaves is a strong guarantee of the weakness of the institution, should a favorable opportunity occur; and, secondly, that the colored people, as a body, were well represented by numbers, both in the fight, and in the number who suffered martyrdom afterward.

The first report of the number of "insurrectionists" killed was *seventeen*, which showed that several slaves were killed; for there were only *ten* of the men that belonged to the Kennedy Farm who lost their lives at the Ferry, namely: John Henri Kagi, Jerry Anderson, Watson Brown, Oliver Brown, Stewart Taylor, Adolphus Thompson, William Thompson, William Leeman, all eight whites, and Dangerfield Newby and Sherrard Lewis Leary, both colored. The rest reported dead, according to their own showing, were colored. Captain Brown had but seventeen with him, belonging to the Farm, and when all was over, there were four besides himself taken to Charlestown, prisoners, viz: A. D. Stevens, Edwin Coppic, white; John A. Copeland and Shields Green, colored. It is plain to be seen from this, that there was a proper percentage of colored men killed at the Ferry, and executed at Charlestown. Of those that escaped from the fangs of the human bloodhounds of slavery, there were four whites, and one colored man, myself being the sole colored man of those at the Farm.

That hundreds of slaves were ready, and would have joined in the work, had Captain Brown's sympathies not been aroused in favor of the families of his prisoners, and that a very different result would have been seen, in consequence, there is no question. There was abundant opportunity for him and the party to leave a place in which they held entire sway and possession, before the arrival of the troops. And so cowardly were the slaveholders, proper, that from Colonel Lewis Washington, the descendant of the Father of his Country, General George Washington, they were easily taken prisoners. They had not pluck enough to fight, nor to use the well-loaded arms in their possession, but were concerned rather in keeping a whole skin by parleying, or in spilling cowardly tears, to excite pity, as did Colonel Washington, and in that way escape merited punishment. No, the conduct of the slaves was beyond all praise; and could our brave old Captain have steeled his heart against the entreaties of his captives, or shut up the fountain of his sympathies against their families—could he, for the moment, have forgotten them, in the selfish thought of his own friends and kindred, or, by adhering to the original plan, have left the place, and thus looked forward to the prospective freedom of the slave— hundreds ready and waiting would have been armed before twenty-four hours had elapsed. As it was, even the noble old man's mistakes were productive of great good, the fact of which the future historian will record, without the embarrassment attending its present narration. John Brown did not only capture and hold Harper's Ferry for twenty hours, but he held the whole South. He captured President Buchanan and his Cabinet, convulsed the whole country, killed Governor Wise, and dug the mine and laid the train which will eventually dissolve the union between Freedom and Slavery. The rebound reveals the truth. So let it be!

BLACK
ABOLITIONIST
VOICES

DAVID WALKER

David Walker (1796–1830) was an abolitionist, subscription sales agent, and writer for New York City's Freedom's Journal. His Appeal to the Coloured Citizens of the World was perhaps the most radical antislavery document ever published in the United States.

Walker passionately called for the immediate abolition of slavery and encouraged violent resistance as necessary. Published widely and even said to have been found in garments shipped to clothe enslaved people in the South, the Appeal celebrates Black contributions to American society, rails against religious hypocrites and colonization projects, offers an early philosophy of Black nationalism, and demands that Black people be granted full rights as citizens. Walker's impassioned delivery worried more conservative-minded abolitionists, particularly those who wanted to appear more respectable by appealing to the religious mores and humanitarian leanings of lawmakers and the public. Still, Walker's plea to his brethren, "Let no man of us budge one step, and let slave-holders come to beat us from our country. America is more our country, than it is the whites—we have enriched it with our blood and tears," was well received by many readers, as it matched the sentiments felt by free and enslaved people who were intent on abolishing slavery and forcing lawmakers to codify civil rights for all into the law.

From *Walker's Appeal, in Four Articles; Together with a Preamble, to the Coloured Citizens of the World, but in Particular, and Very Expressly, to Those of the United States of America*

(1829)

APPEAL, &C.

PREAMBLE.

My dearly beloved Brethren and Fellow Citizens.

Having travelled over a considerable portion of these United States, and having, in the course of my travels, taken the most accurate observations of things as they exist—the result of my observations has warranted the full and unshaken conviction, that we, (coloured people of these United States,) are the most degraded, wretched, and abject set of beings that ever lived since the world began; and I pray God that none like us ever may live again until time shall be no more. They tell us of the Israelites in Egypt, the Helots in Sparta, and of the Roman Slaves, which last were made up from almost every nation under heaven, whose sufferings under those ancient and heathen nations, were, in comparison with ours, under this enlightened and Christian nation, no more than a cypher—or, in other words, those heathen nations of antiquity, had but little more among them than the name and form of slavery; while wretchedness and endless miseries were reserved, apparently in a phial, to be poured out upon our fathers, ourselves and our children, by *Christian* Americans!

These positions I shall endeavour, by the help of the Lord, to demonstrate in the course of this *Appeal*, to the satisfaction of the most incredulous mind—and may God Almighty, who is

the Father of our Lord Jesus Christ, open your hearts to understand and believe the truth.

The *causes*, my brethren, which produce our wretchedness
and miseries, are so very numerous and aggravating, that I believe the pen only of a Josephus or a Plutarch, can well enumerate
and explain them. Upon subjects, then, of such incomprehensible
magnitude, so impenetrable, and so notorious, I shall be obliged
to omit a large class of, and content myself with giving you an
exposition of a few of those, which do indeed rage to such an
alarming pitch, that they cannot but be a perpetual source of terror and dismay to every reflecting mind.

I am fully aware, in making this appeal to my much afflicted
and suffering brethren, that I shall not only be assailed by those
whose greatest earthly desires are, to keep us in abject ignorance and wretchedness, and who are of the firm conviction
that Heaven has designed us and our children to be slaves and
beasts of burden to them and their children. I say, I do not only
expect to be held up to the public as an ignorant, impudent and
restless disturber of the public peace, by such avaricious creatures, as well as a mover of insubordination—and perhaps put
in prison or to death, for giving a superficial exposition of our
miseries, and exposing tyrants. But I am persuaded, that many
of my brethren, particularly those who are ignorantly in league
with slave-holders or tyrants, who acquire their daily bread by
the blood and sweat of their more ignorant brethren—and not
a few of those too, who are too ignorant to see an inch beyond
their noses, will rise up and call me cursed—Yea, the jealous
ones among us will perhaps use more abject subtlety, by affirming that this work is not worth perusing, that we are well situated, and there is no use in trying to better our condition, for
we cannot. I will ask one question here.—Can our condition be
any worse?—Can it be more mean and abject? If there are any
changes, will they not be for the better, though they may appear for the worst at first? Can they get us any lower? Where
can they get us? They are afraid to treat us worse, for they
know well, the day they do it they are gone. But against all accusations which may or can be preferred against me, I appeal to
Heaven for my motive in writing—who knows that my object
is, if possible, to awaken in the breasts of my afflicted, degraded

and slumbering brethren, a spirit of inquiry and investigation respecting our miseries and wretchedness in this *Republican Land of Liberty!!!!!!*

The sources from which our miseries are derived, and on which I shall comment, I shall not combine in one, but shall put them under distinct heads and expose them in their turn; in doing which, keeping truth on my side, and not departing from the strictest rules of morality, I shall endeavour to penetrate, search out, and lay them open for your inspection. If you cannot or will not profit by them, I shall have done *my* duty to you, my country and my God.

And as the inhuman system of *slavery*, is the *source* from which most of our miseries proceed, I shall begin with that *curse to nations*, which has spread terror and devastation through so many nations of antiquity, and which is raging to such a pitch at the present day in Spain and in Portugal. It had one tug in England, in France, and in the United States of America; yet the inhabitants thereof, do not learn wisdom, and erase it entirely from their dwellings and from all with whom they have to do. The fact is, the labour of slaves comes so cheap to the avaricious usurpers, and is (as they think) of such great utility to the country where it exists, that those who are actuated by sordid avarice only, overlook the evils, which will as sure as the Lord lives, follow after the good. In fact, they are so happy to keep in ignorance and degradation, and to receive the homage and the labour of the slaves, they forget that God rules in the armies of heaven and among the inhabitants of the earth, having his ears continually open to the cries, tears and groans of his oppressed people; and being a just and holy Being will at one day appear fully in behalf of the oppressed, and arrest the progress of the avaricious oppressors; for although the destruction of the oppressors God may not effect by the oppressed, yet the Lord our God will bring other destructions upon them—for not unfrequently will he cause them to rise up one against another, to be split and divided, and to oppress each other, and sometimes to open hostilities with sword in hand. Some may ask, what is the matter with this united and happy people?—Some say it is the cause of political usurpers, tyrants, oppressors, &c. But has not the Lord an oppressed and suffering people among them? Does the Lord condescend to hear their cries and see their tears in consequence of oppression? Will he let the oppressors rest comfortably and happy always? Will he not cause the very children of the oppressors to rise up against them, and oftimes put them to death? "God works in many ways his wonders to perform."

I will not here speak of the destructions which the Lord brought upon Egypt, in consequence of the oppression and consequent groans of the oppressed—of the hundreds and thousands of Egyptians whom God hurled into the Red Sea for afflicting his people in their land—of the Lord's suffering people in Sparta or Lacedemon, the land of the truly famous Lycurgus—nor have I time to comment upon the cause which produced the fierceness with which Sylla usurped the title, and absolutely acted as dictator of the Roman people—the conspiracy of Cataline—the conspiracy against, and murder of Cæsar in the Senate house—the spirit with which Marc Antony made himself master of the commonwealth—his associating Octavius and Lipidus with himself in power—their dividing the provinces of Rome among themselves—their attack and defeat, on the plains of Phillippi, of the last defenders of their liberty, (Brutus and Cassius)—the tyranny of Tiberius, and from him to the final overthrow of Constantinople by the Turkish Sultan, Mahomed II. A. D. 1453. I say, I shall not take up time to speak of the *causes* which produced so much wretchedness and massacre among those heathen nations, for I am aware that you know too well, that God is just, as well as merciful!—I shall call your attention a few moments to that *Christian* nation, the Spaniards—while I shall leave almost unnoticed, that avaricious and cruel people, the Portuguese, among whom all true hearted Christians and lovers of Jesus Christ, must evidently see the judgments of God displayed. To show the judgments of God upon the Spaniards, I shall occupy but a little time, leaving a plenty of room for the candid and unprejudiced to reflect.

All persons who are acquainted with history, and particularly the Bible, who are not blinded by the God of this world, and are not actuated solely by avarice—who are able to lay aside prejudice long enough to view candidly and impartially, things as they were, are, and probably will be—who are willing to admit that God made man to serve Him *alone*, and that man should have no other Lord or Lords but Himself—that God Almighty is the *sole proprietor* or *master* of the WHOLE human family, and will not on any consideration admit of a colleague, being unwilling to divide his glory with another—and who can dispense with prejudice long enough to admit that we are *men*, notwithstanding our *improminent noses* and *woolly heads*, and believe that we feel for our fathers, mothers, wives and children, as well as the whites do for theirs.—I say, all who are permitted to see and believe these things, can easily recognize the judgments of God among the Spaniards. Though others may lay the cause of the fierceness with which they cut each other's throats, to some other circumstance, yet they who believe that God is a God of justice, will believe that SLAVERY *is the principal cause.*

While the Spaniards are running about upon the field of battle cutting each other's throats, has not the Lord an afflicted and suffering people in the midst of them, whose cries and groans in consequence of oppression are continually pouring into the ears of the God of justice? Would they not cease to cut each other's throats, if they could? But how can they? The very support which they draw from government to aid them in perpetrating such enormities, does it not arise in a great degree from the wretched victims of oppression among them? And yet they are calling for *Peace!—Peace!!* Will any peace be given unto them? Their destruction may indeed be procrastinated awhile, but can it continue long, while they are oppressing the Lord's people? Has He not the hearts of all men in His hand? Will he suffer one part of his creatures to go on oppressing another like brutes always, with impunity? And yet, those avaricious wretches are calling for *Peace!!!!* I declare, it does appear to me, as though some nations think God is asleep, or that he made the Africans for nothing else but to dig their mines and work their farms, or they cannot believe history, sacred or profane. I ask every man who has a heart, and is blessed with the privilege of believing—Is not God a God of justice to *all* his creatures? Do you say he is? Then if he gives peace and tranquillity to tyrants, and permits them to keep our fathers, our mothers, ourselves and our children in eternal ignorance and wretchedness, to support them and their families, would he be to us a God of *justice?* I ask, O ye *Christians!!!* who hold us and our children in the most abject ignorance and degradation, that ever a people were afflicted with since the world began—I say, if God gives you peace and tranquillity, and suffers you thus to go on afflicting us, and our children, who have never given you the least provocation—would he be to us *a God of justice?* If you will allow that we are MEN, who feel for each other, does not the blood of our fathers and of us their children, cry aloud to the Lord of Sabaoth against you, for the cruelties and murders with which you have, and do continue to afflict us. But it is time for me to close my remarks on the suburbs, just to enter more fully into the interior of this system of cruelty and oppression.

ARTICLE I.

Our Wretchedness in Consequence of Slavery.

My beloved brethren:—The Indians of North and of South America—the Greeks—the Irish, subjected under the king of Great Britain—the Jews, that ancient people of the Lord—the inhabitants of the islands of the sea—in fine, all the inhabitants of the earth, (except however, the sons of Africa) are called *men,* and of course are, and ought to be free. But we, (coloured people) and our children are *brutes!!* and of course are, and *ought to be* SLAVES to the American people and their children forever!! to dig their mines and work their farms; and thus go on enriching them, from one generation to another with our *blood* and our *tears!!!!*

I promised in a preceding page to demonstrate to the satisfaction of the most incredulous, that we, (coloured people of these United States of America) are the *most wretched, degraded* and *abject* set of beings that *ever lived* since the world began, and that the white Americans having reduced us to the wretched state of *slavery,* treat us in that condition *more cruel* (they being an enlighted and Christian people,) than any heathen nation did any people whom it had reduced to our condition. These affirmations are so well confirmed in the minds of all unprejudiced men, who have taken the trouble to read histories, that they need no elucidation from me. But to put them beyond all doubt, I refer you in the first place to the children of Jacob, or of Israel in Egypt, under Pharaoh and his people. Some of my brethren do not know who Pharaoh and the Egyptians were—I know it to be a fact, that some of them take the Egyptians to have been a gang of *devils*, not knowing any better, and that they (Egyptians) having got possession of the Lord's people, treated them *nearly* as cruel as *Christian Americans* do us, at the present day. For the information of such, I would only mention that the Egyptians, were Africans or coloured people, such as we are— some of them yellow and others dark—a mixture of Ethiopians and the natives of Egypt—about the same as you see the co- loured people of the United States at the present day.—I say, I call your attention then, to the children of Jacob, while I point out particularly to you his son Joseph, among the rest, in Egypt.

"And Pharaoh, said unto Joseph, 'thou shalt be over my house, and according unto thy word shall all my people be ruled: only in the throne will I be greater than thou.'*

"And Pharaoh said unto Joseph, 'see, I have set thee over all the land of Egypt.'†

"And Pharaoh said unto Joseph, 'I am Pharaoh, and without thee shall no man lift up his hand or foot in all the land of Egypt.'"‡‡

Now I appeal to heaven and to earth, and particularly to the American people themselves, who cease not to declare that our condition is not *hard*, and that we are comparatively satisfied to rest in wretchedness and misery, under them and their children. Not, indeed, to show me a coloured President, a Governor, a Legislator, a Senator, a Mayor, or an Attorney at the Bar.—But to show me a man of colour, who holds the low office of a Con- stable, or one who sits in a Juror Box, even on a case of one of his wretched brethren, throughout this great Republic!!—But let us pass Joseph the son of Israel a little farther in review, as he existed with that heathen nation.

---

*See Genesis, chap. xli.
†xli. 41.
‡‡xli. 44.

"And Pharaoh called Joseph's name Zaphnath-paaneah; and he gave him to wife Asenath the daughter of Potipherah priest of On. And Joseph went out over all the land of Egypt."*

Compare the above, with the American institutions. Do they not institute laws to prohibit us from marrying among the whites? I would wish, candidly, however, before the Lord, to be understood, that I would not give a *pinch of snuff* to be married to any white person I ever saw in all the days of my life. And I do say it, that the black man, or man of colour, who will leave his own colour (provided he can get one, who is good for any thing) and marry a white woman, to be a double slave to her, just because she is *white*, ought to be treated by her as he surely will be, viz: as a NIGER!!!! It is not, indeed, what I care about inter-marriages with the whites, which induced me to pass this subject in review; for the Lord knows, that there is a day coming when they will be glad enough to get into the company of the blacks, notwithstanding, we are, in this generation, levelled by them, almost on a level with the brute creation: and some of us they treat even worse than they do the brutes that perish. I only made this extract to show how much lower we are held, and how much more cruel we are treated by the Americans, than were the children of Jacob, by the Egyptians.—We will notice the sufferings of Israel some further, under *heathen Pharaoh*, compared with ours under the *enlightened Christians of America*.

"And Pharaoh spake unto Joseph, saying, 'thy father and thy brethren are come unto thee:

'The land of Egypt is before thee: in the best of the land make thy father and brethren to dwell; in the land of Goshen let them dwell: and if thou knowest any men of activity among them, then make them rulers over my cattle.'"†

I ask those people who treat us so *well*, Oh! I ask them, where is the most barren spot of land which they have given unto us? Israel had the most fertile land in all Egypt. Need I mention the very notorious fact, that I have known a poor man of colour, who laboured night and day, to acquire a little money, and having

---

*xli. 45.
†See Genesis, chap. xlvii, 5, 6.

acquired it, he vested it in a small piece of land, and got him a house erected thereon, and having paid for the whole, he moved his family into it, where he was suffered to remain but nine months, when he was cheated out of his property by a white man, and driven out of door! And is not this the case generally? Can a man of colour buy a piece of land and keep it peaceably? Will not some white man try to get it from him, even if it is in a *mud hole*? I need not comment any farther on a subject, which all, both black and white, will readily admit. But I must, really, observe that in this very city, when a man of colour dies, if he owned any real estate it most generally falls into the hands of some white person. The wife and children of the deceased may weep and lament if they please, but the estate will be kept snug enough by its white possessor.

But to prove farther that the condition of the Israelites was better under the Egyptians than ours is under the whites. I call upon the professing Christians, I call upon the philanthropist, I call upon the very tyrant himself, to show me a page of history, either sacred or profane, on which a verse can be found, which maintains, that the Egyptians heaped the *insupportable insult* upon the children of Israel, by telling them that they were not of the *human family*. Can the whites deny this charge? Have they not, after having reduced us to the deplorable condition of slaves under their feet, held us up as descending originally from the tribes of *Monkeys* or *Orang-Outangs*? O! my God! I appeal to every man of feeling—is not this insupportable? Is it not heaping the most gross insult upon our miseries, because they have got us under their feet and we cannot help ourselves? Oh! pity us we pray thee, Lord Jesus, Master.—Has Mr. Jefferson declared to the world, that we are inferior to the whites, both in the endowments of our bodies and of minds? It is indeed surprising, that a man of such great learning, combined with such excellent natural parts, should speak so of a set of men in chains. I do not know what to compare it to, unless, like putting one wild deer in an iron cage, where it will be secured, and hold another by the side of the same, then let it go, and expect the one in the cage to run as fast as the one at liberty. So far, my brethren, were the Egyptians from heaping these insults upon their slaves, that Pharoah's daughter took Moses, a son of Israel for her own, as will appear by the following.

"And Pharoah's daughter said unto her, [Moses' mother] 'take this child away, and nurse it for me, and I will pay thee thy wages.' And the woman took the child [Moses] and nursed it.

"And the child grew, and she brought him unto Pharoah's daughter and he became her son. And she called his name Moses: and she said because 'I drew him out of the water.'"*

In all probability, Moses would have become Prince Regent to the throne, and no doubt, in process of time but he would have been seated on the throne of Egypt. But he had rather suffer shame, with the people of God, than to enjoy pleasures with that wicked people for a season. O! that the coloured people were long since of Moses' excellent disposition, instead of courting favour with, and telling news and lies to our *natural enemies*, against each other—aiding them to keep their hellish chains of slavery upon us. Would we not long before this time, have been respectable men, instead of such wretched victims of oppression as we are? Would they be able to drag our mothers, our fathers, our wives, our children and ourselves, around the world in chains and hand-cuffs as they do, to dig up gold and silver for them and theirs? This question, my brethren, I leave for you to digest; and may God Almighty force it home to your hearts. Remember that unless you are united, keeping your tongues within your teeth, you will be afraid to trust your secrets to each other, and thus perpetuate our miseries under the *Christians!!!!!*

Remember, also to lay humble at the feet of our Lord and Master Jesus Christ, with prayers and fastings. Let our enemies go on with their butcheries, and at once fill up their cup. Never make an attempt to gain our freedom or *natural right*, from under our cruel oppressors and murderers, until you see your way clear†—when that hour arrives and you move, be not afraid

---

*Exodus, chap. ii. 9, 10.

†It is not to be understood here, that I mean for us to wait until God shall take us by the hair of our heads and drag us out of abject wretchedness and slavery, nor do I mean to convey the idea for us to wait until our enemies shall make preparations, and call us to seize those preparations, take it away from them, and put every thing before us to death, in order to gain our freedom which God

or dismayed; for be you assured that Jesus Christ the King of heaven and of earth who is the God of justice and of armies, will surely go before you. And those enemies who have for hundreds of years stolen our *rights*, and kept us ignorant of Him and His divine worship, he will remove. Millions of whom, are this day, so ignorant and avaricious, that they cannot conceive how God can have an attribute of justice, and show mercy to us because it pleased Him to make us black—which colour, Mr. Jefferson calls unfortunate!!!!!! As though we are not as thankful to our God, for having made us as it pleased himself, as they, (the whites,) are for having made them white. They think because they hold us in their infernal chains of slavery, that we wish to be white, or of their color—but they are dreadfully deceived—we wish to be just as it pleased our Creator to have made us, and no avaricious and unmerciful wretches, have any business to make slaves of, or hold us in slavery. How would they like for us to make slaves of, and hold them in cruel slavery, and murder them as they do us?—But is Mr. Jefferson's assertions true? viz. "that it is unfortunate for us that our Creator has been pleased to make us *black*." We will not take his say so, for the fact. The world will have an opportunity to see whether it is unfortunate for us, that our Creator *has made us* darker than the *whites*.

Fear not the number and education of our *enemies*, against whom we shall have to contend for our lawful right; guaranteed to us by our Maker; for why should we be afraid, when God is, and will continue, (if we continue humble) to be on our side?

The man who would not fight under our Lord and Master Jesus Christ, in the glorious and heavenly cause of freedom and of God—to be delivered from the most wretched, abject and servile slavery, that ever a people was afflicted with since the foundation of the world, to the present day—ought to be kept

---

has given us. For you must remember that we are men as well as they. God has been pleased to give us two eyes, two hands, two feet, and some sense in our heads as well as they. They have no more right to hold us in slavery than we have to hold them, we have just as much right, in the sight of God, to hold them and their children in slavery and wretchedness, as they have to hold us, and no more.

with all of his children or family, in slavery, or in chains, to be butchered by his *cruel enemies*.

I saw a paragraph, a few years since, in a South Carolina paper, which, speaking of the barbarity of the Turks, it said: "The Turks are the most barbarous people in the world—they treat the Greeks more like *brutes* than human beings." And in the same paper was an advertisement, which said: "Eight well built Virgina and Maryland *Negro fellows* and four *wenches* will positively be *sold* this day, *to the highest bidder!*" And what astonished me still more was, to see in this same *humane* paper!! the cuts of three men, with clubs and budgets on their backs, and an advertisement offering a considerable sum of money for their apprehension and delivery. I declare, it is really so amusing to hear the Southerners and Westerners of this country talk about *barbarity*, that it is positively enough to make a man *smile*.

The sufferings of the Helots among the Spartans, were somewhat severe, it is true, but to say that theirs, were as severe as ours among the Americans, I do most strenuously deny—for instance, can any man show me an article on a page of ancient history which specifies, that, the Spartans chained, and handcuffed the Helots, and dragged them from their wives and children, children from their parents, mothers from their suckling babes, wives from their husbands, driving them from one end of the country to the other? Notice the Spartans were heathens, who lived long before our Divine Master made his appearance in the flesh. Can Christian Americans deny these barbarous cruelties? Have you not, Americans, having subjected us under you, added to these miseries, by insulting us in telling us to our face, because we are helpless, that we are not of the human family? I ask you, O! Americans, I ask you, in the name of the Lord, can you deny these charges? Some perhaps may deny, by saying, that they never thought or said that we were not men. But do not actions speak louder than words?—have they not made provisions for the Greeks, and Irish? Nations who have never done the least thing for them, while *we*, who have enriched their country with our blood and tears—have dug up gold and silver for them and their children, from generation to generation, and are in more miseries than any other people under heaven, are not seen, but by comparatively, a handful of the American people? There are indeed, more ways to kill a dog, besides choking it to death with butter. Further—The Spartans or Lacedemonians, had some frivolous pretext, for enslaving the Helots, for they (Helots) while being free inhabitants of Sparta, stirred up an intestine commotion, and were, by the Spartans subdued, and made prisoners of war. Consequently they and their children were condemned to perpetual slavery.*

I have been for years troubling the pages of historians, to find out what our fathers have done to the *white Christians of America*, to merit such condign punishment as they have inflicted on them, and do continue to inflict on us their children. But I must aver, that my researches have hitherto been to no effect. I have therefore, come to the immoveable conclusion, that they (Americans) have, and do continue to punish us for nothing else, but for enriching them and their country. For I cannot conceive of any thing else. Nor will I ever believe otherwise, until the Lord shall convince me.

The world knows, that slavery as it existed among the Romans, (which was the primary cause of their destruction) was, comparatively speaking, no more than a *cypher*, when compared with ours under the Americans. Indeed I should not have noticed the Roman slaves, had not the very learned and penetrating Mr. Jefferson said, "when a master was murdered, all his slaves in the same house, or within hearing, were condemned to death."†—Here let me ask Mr. Jefferson, (but he is gone to answer at the bar of God, for the deeds done in his body while living,) I therefore ask the whole American people, had I not rather die, or be put to death, than to be a slave to any tyrant, who takes not only my own, but my wife and children's lives by the inches? Yea, would I meet death with avidity far! far!! in preference to such *servile submission* to the murderous hands of tyrants. Mr. Jefferson's very severe remarks on us have been so extensively argued upon by men whose attainments in literature, I shall never be able to reach, that I would not have

*See Dr. Goldsmith's History of Greece—page 9. See also, Plutarch's Lives. The Helots subdued by Agis, king of *Sparta*.
†See his Notes on Virginia, page 210.

meddled with it, were it not to solicit each of my brethren, who has the spirit of a man, to buy a copy of Mr. Jefferson's "Notes on Virginia," and put it in the hand of his son. For let no one of us suppose that the refutations which have been written by our white friends are enough—they are *whites*—we are *blacks*. We, and the world wish to see the charges of Mr. Jefferson refuted by the blacks *themselves*, according to their chance; for we must remember that what the whites have written respecting this subject, is other men's labours, and did not emanate from the blacks. I know well, that there are some talents and learning among the coloured people of this country, which we have not a chance to develope, in consequence of oppression; but our oppression ought not to hinder us from acquiring all we can. For we will have a chance to develope them by and by. God will not suffer us, always to be oppressed. Our sufferings will come to an *end*, in spite of all the Americans this side of *eternity*. Then we will want all the learning and talents among ourselves, and perhaps more, to govern ourselves.—"Every dog must have its day," the American's is coming to an end.

But let us review Mr. Jefferson's remarks respecting us some further. Comparing our miserable fathers, with the learned philosophers of Greece, he says: "Yet notwithstanding these and other discouraging circumstances among the Romans, their slaves were often their rarest artist. They excelled too, in science, insomuch as to be usually employed as tutors to their master's children; Epictetus, Terence and Phædrus, were slaves,—but they were of the race of whites. It is not their *condition* then, but *nature*, which has produced the distinction."* See this, my brethren!! Do you believe that this assertion is swallowed by millions of the whites? Do you know that Mr. Jefferson was one of as great characters as ever lived among the whites? See his writings for the world, and public labours for the United States of America. Do you believe that the assertions of such a man, will pass away into oblivion unobserved by this people and the world? If you do you are much mistaken—See how the American people treat us— have we souls in our bodies? Are we men who have any spirits at all? I know that there are many

*See his Notes on Virginia, page 211.

swell-bellied fellows among us, whose greatest object is to fill their stomachs. Such I do not mean—I am after those who know and feel, that we are MEN, as well as other people; to them, I say, that unless we try to refute Mr. Jefferson's arguments respecting us, we will only establish them.

But the slaves among the Romans. Every body who has read history, knows, that as soon as a slave among the Romans obtained his freedom, he could rise to the greatest eminence in the State, and there was no law instituted to hinder a slave from buying his freedom. Have not the Americans instituted laws to hinder us from obtaining our freedom? Do any deny this charge? Read the laws of Virginia, North Carolina, &c. Further: have not the Americans instituted laws to prohibit a man of colour from obtaining and holding any office whatever, under the government of the United States of America? Now, Mr. Jefferson tells us, that our condition is not so hard, as the slaves were under the Romans!!!!!!

It is time for me to bring this article to a close. But before I close it, I must observe to my brethren that at the close of the first Revolution in this country, with Great Britain, there were but thirteen States in the Union, now there are twenty-four, most of which are slave-holding States, and the whites are dragging us around in chains and in handcuffs, to their new States and Territories to work their mines and farms, to enrich them and their children—and millions of them believing firmly that we being a little darker than they, were made by our Creator to be an inheritance to them and their children for ever—the same as a parcel of *brutes*.

Are we MEN!!—I ask you, O my brethren! are we MEN? Did our Creator make us to be slaves to dust and ashes like ourselves? Are they not dying worms as well as we? Have they not to make their appearance before the tribunal of Heaven, to answer for the deeds done in the body, as well as we? Have we any other Master but Jesus Christ alone? Is he not their Master as well as ours?—What right then, have we to obey and call any other Master, but Himself? How we could be so *submissive* to a gang of men, whom we cannot tell whether they are *as good* as ourselves or not, I never could conceive. However, this is shut up with the Lord, and we cannot precisely tell—but I declare, we judge men by their works.

The whites have always been an unjust, jealous, unmerciful, avaricious and blood-thirsty set of beings, always seeking after power and authority.—We view them all over the confederacy of Greece, where they were first known to be any thing, (in consequence of education) we see them there, cutting each other's throats—trying to subject each other to wretchedness and misery—to effect which, they used all kinds of deceitful, unfair, and unmerciful means. We view them next in Rome, where the spirit of tyranny and deceit raged still higher. We view them in Gaul, Spain, and in Britain.—In fine, we view them all over Europe, together with what were scattered about in Asia and Africa, as heathens, and we see them acting more like devils than accountable men. But some may ask, did not the blacks of Africa, and the mulattoes of Asia, go on in the same way as did the whites of Europe. I answer, no—they never were half so avaricious, deceitful and unmerciful as the whites, according to their knowledge.

But we will leave the whites or Europeans as heathens, and take a view of them as Christians, in which capacity we see them as cruel, if not more so than ever. In fact, take them as a body, they are ten times more cruel, avaricious and unmerciful than ever they were; for while they were heathens, they were bad enough it is true, but it is positively a fact that they were not quite so audacious as to go and take vessel loads of men, women and children, and in cold blood, and through devilishness, throw them into the sea, and murder them in all kind of ways. While they were heathens, they were too ignorant for such barbarity. But being Christians, enlightened and sensible, they are completely prepared for such hellish cruelties. Now suppose God were to give them more sense, what would they do? If it were possible, would they not *dethrone* Jehovah and seat themselves upon his throne? I therefore, in the name and fear of the Lord God of Heaven and of earth, divested of prejudice either on the side of my colour or that of the whites, advance my suspicion of them, whether they are *as good by nature* as we are or not. Their actions, since they were known as a people, have been the reverse, I do indeed suspect them, but this, as I before oberved, is shut up with the Lord, we cannot exactly tell, it will be proved in succeeding generations.—The whites have had the essence of the gospel as it was preached by my master and his apostles—the Ethiopians have not, who are to have it in its meridian splendor—the Lord will give it to them to their satisfaction. I hope and pray my God, that they will make good use of it, that it may be well with them.*

ˈIt is my solemn belief, that if ever the world becomes Christianized, (which must certainly take place before long) it will be through the means, under God of the *Blacks*, who are now held in wretchedness, and degradation, by the white *Christians* of the world, who before they learn to do justice to us before our Maker—and be reconciled to us, and reconcile us to them, and by that means have clear consciencies before God and man.—Send out Missionaries to convert the Heathens, many of whom after they cease to worship gods, which neither see nor hear, become ten times more the children of Hell, then ever they were, why what is the reason? Why the reason is obvious, they must learn to do justice at home, before they go into distant lands, to display their charity, Christianity, and benevolence; when they learn to do justice, God will accept their offering, (no man may think that I am against Missionaries for I am not, my object is to see justice done at home, before we go to convert the Heathens.)

SARAH MAPPS DOUGLASS

Sarah Mapps Douglass (1806–1882) was born into a free abolitionist family in Philadelphia, Pennsylvania. An educator, lecturer, and writer, Douglass helped cofound the Female Literary Society and the biracial Philadelphia Female Anti-Slavery Society, which championed self-improvement and total abolition, respectively. In this speech before the Female Literary Society, Douglass implores its members to turn their intellectual and religious attention to the matter of slavery, as a unified commitment to abolition would "elevate the character of my wronged and neglected race."

"Anti-Slavery Speech Before the Female Literary Society of Philadelphia," *The Liberator*
(1832)

SARAH MAPPS DOUGLASS URGES SUPPORT FOR THE ANTISLAVERY CAUSE

My Friends—My Sisters:
How important is the occasion for which we have assembled ourselves together this evening, to hold a feast, to feed our never-dying minds, to excite each other to deeds of mercy, words of peace; to stir up in the bosom of each, gratitude to God for his increasing goodness, and feeling of deep sympathy for our brethren and sisters, who are in this land of christian light and liberty held in bondage the most cruel and degrading—to make their cause our own!

An English writer has said, "We must feel deeply before we can act rightly; from that absorbing, heart-rendering compassion for ourselves springs a deeper sympathy for others, and from a sense of our weakness and our own upbraidings arises a disposition to be indulgent, to forbear, to forgive." This is my experience. One short year ago, how different were my feelings on the subject of slavery! It is true, the wail of the captive sometimes came to my ear in the midst of my happiness, and caused my heart to bleed for his wrongs; but, alas! the impression was as evanescent as the early cloud and morning dew. I had formed a little world of my own, and cared not to move beyond its precincts. But how was the scene changed when I beheld the oppressor lurking on the border of my own peaceful home! I saw his iron hand stretched forth to seize me as his prey, and the cause of the slave became my own. I started up, and with one mighty effort threw from me the lethargy which had covered me as a mantle for years; and determined, by the help of the Almighty, to use every exertion in my power to elevate the character of my wronged and neglected race. One year ago, I detested the slaveholder; now I can pity and pray for him. Has not this been your experience, my sisters? Have you not felt as I have felt upon this thrilling subject? My heart assures me some of you have.

And now, my sisters, I would earnestly and affectionately press upon you the necessity of placing your whole dependence on God; poor, weak, finite creatures as we are, we can do nothing for ourselves. He is all powerful; He is waiting to be gracious to us as a people. Do you feel your inability to do good? Come to Him who giveth liberally and upbraideth not; bring your wrongs and fears to Him, as you would to a tender parent—He will sympathise with you. I know from blessed, heart-cheering experience the excellency of having a God to trust to in seasons of trial and conflict. What but this can support us should the pestilence which has devastated Asia be born to us by the summer breezes? What but this can uphold our fainting footsteps in the swellings of Jordan? It is the only thing worth living for—the only thing that can disarm death of his sting. I am earnestly solicitous that each of us may adopt this language:

"I have no hope in man, but much in God— Much in the rock of ages."

In conclusion, I would respectfully recommend that our mental feast should commence by reading a portion of the Holy

Scriptures. A pause should proceed the reading for supplication. It is my wish that the reading and conversation should be altogether directed to the subject of slavery. The refreshment which may be offered to you for the body, will be of the most simple kind, that you may feel for those who have nothing to refresh body and mind.

MARIA STEWART

Maria Stewart (1803–1879) was a teacher, lecturer, abolitionist, and proponent of women's rights who worked closely with the radical activist David Walker. Stewart's speeches often contained sharp critiques of slavery and America's hypocrisy regarding democracy and freedom, which were well received, if a tad unusual for a woman to speak in such a forthright, public manner during the nineteenth century. In her 1833 speech "Address Delivered at the African Masonic Hall, Boston," Stewart vigorously declared about colonization and repatriation projects that sought to relocate Black people outside America: "The unfriendly whites first drove the native American from his much loved home. Then they stole our fathers from their peaceful and quiet dwellings, and brought them hither, and made bond-men and bond-women of them and their little ones; they have obliged our brethren to labor, kept them in utter ignorance, nourished them in vice, and raised them in degradation; and now that we have enriched their soil, and filled their coffers, they say that we are not capable of becoming like white men, and that we never can rise to respectability in this country. They would drive us to a strange land. But before I go, the bayonet shall pierce me through. African rights and liberty is a subject that ought to fire the breast of every free man of color in these United States, and excite in his bosom a lively, deep, decided and heartfelt interest." In the selected speeches here, Stewart builds her arguments using traditional Christian beliefs about familial hierarchies, and challenges free Black men in particular to do more to lead Black people toward freedom and upward mobility.

From *Productions of Mrs. Maria W. Stewart Presented to the First African Baptist Church & Society, of the City of Boston*

(1835)

LECTURE.

DELIVERED AT THE FRANKLIN HALL, BOSTON, SEPTEMBER 21, 1832.

Why sit ye here and die? If we say we will go to a foreign land, the famine and the pestilence are there, and there we shall die. If we sit here, we shall die. Come, let us plead our cause before the whites. If they save us alive, we shall live; and if they kill us, we shall but die.

Methinks I heard a spiritual interrogation—"Who shall go forward and take off the reproach that is cast upon the people of color? Shall it be a woman?" And my heart made this reply: "If it is Thy will, be it even so, Lord Jesus!"

I have heard much respecting the horrors of slavery; but may heaven forbid that the generality of my color throughout these United States should experience any more of its horrors than to be a servant of servants, or hewers of wood and drawers of water! Tell us no more of Southern slavery; for, with few exceptions, although I may be very erroneous in my opinion, yet I consider our condition but little better than that. Yet, after all, methinks there are no chains so galling as the chains of ignorance—no fetters so binding as those that bind the soul, and exclude it from the vast field of usefulness and scientific knowledge. O, had I received the advantages of early education, my idea would, ere now, have expanded far and wide; but, alas! I possess nothing but moral capability—no teaching but the teaching of the Holy Spirit.

I have asked several individuals of my sex, who transact business for themselves, if, providing our girls were to give them the most satisfactory references, they would not be willing to grant them an equal opportunity with others? Their reply has been: For their own part, they had no objection; but as it was not the custom, were they to take them into their employ, they would be in danger of losing the public patronage.

And such is the powerful force of prejudice. Let our girls possess what amiable qualities of soul they may; let their characters be fair and spotless as innocence itself; let their natural taste and ingenuity be what they may, it is impossible for scarce an individual of them to rise above the condition of servants. Ah! why is this cruel and unfeeling distinction? Is it merely because God has made our complexion to vary? If it be, O shame to soft, relenting humanity! "Tell it not in Gath! publish it not in the streets of Askelon!" Yet, after all, methinks were the American free people of color to turn their attention more assiduously to moral worth and intellectual improvements, this would be the result: Prejudice would gradually diminish, and the whites would be compelled to say, unloose those fetters!

> Though black their skins as shades of night,
> Their hearts are pure, their souls are white.

Few white persons of either sex, who are calculated for anything else, are willing to spend their lives and bury their talents in performing mean, servile labor. And such is the horrible idea that I entertain respecting a life of servitude, that if I conceived of there being no possibility of my rising above the condition of a servant, I would gladly hail death as a welcome messenger. O, horrible idea, indeed, to possess noble souls, aspiring after high and honorable acquirements, yet confined by the chains of ignorance and poverty to lives of continual drudgery and toil. Neither do I know of any who have enriched themselves by spending their lives as house-domestics, washing windows, shaking carpets, brushing boots, or tending upon gentlemen's tables. I can but die for expressing my sentiments; and I am as willing to die by the sword as the pestilence; for I am a true-born American; your blood flows in my veins, and your spirit fires my breast.

I observed a piece in the *Liberator* a few months since, stating that the colonizationists had published a work respecting us, asserting that we were lazy and idle. I confute them on that point. Take us generally as a people, we are neither lazy nor idle; and considering how little we have to excite or stimulate us, I am almost astonished that there are so many industrious and ambitious ones to be found: although I acknowledge, with extreme sorrow, that there are some who never were and never will be serviceable to society. And have you not a similar class among yourselves?

Again. It was asserted that we were a "ragged set, crying for liberty." I reply to it: The whites have so long and so loudly proclaimed the theme of equal rights and privileges, that our souls have caught the flame also, ragged as we are. As far as our merit deserves, we feel a common desire to rise above the condition of servants and drudges. I have learned, by bitter experience, that continual hard labor deadens the energies of the soul, and benumbs the faculties of the mind; the ideas become confined, the mind barren, and, like the scorching sands of Arabia, produces nothing; or, like the uncultivated soil, brings forth thorns and thistles.

Again. Continual hard labor irritates our tempers and sours our dispositions; the whole system becomes worn out with toil and fatigue; nature herself becomes almost exhausted, and we care but little whether we live or die. It is true, that the free people of color throughout these United States are neither bought nor sold, nor under the lash of the cruel driver. Many obtain a comfortable support; but few, if any, have an opportunity of becoming rich and independent; and the employments we must pursue are as unprofitable to us as the spider's web or the floating bubbles that vanish into air. As servants, we are respected; but let us presume to aspire any higher, our employer regards us no longer. And were it not that the King Eternal has declared that Ethiopia shall stretch forth her hands unto God, I should indeed despair.

I do not consider it derogatory, my friends, for persons to live out to service. There are many whose inclination leads them to aspire no higher; and I would highly commend the performance of almost anything for an honest livelihood; but where constitutional strength is wanting, labor of this kind, in its mildest form, is painful; and, doubtless, many are the prayers that have ascended to heaven from Afric's daughters for strength to perform their work. O, many are the tears that have been shed for the want of that strength! Most of our color have dragged out a miserable existence of servitude from the cradle to the grave. And what literary acquirements can be made, or useful knowledge derived, from either maps, books, or charts, by those who continually drudge from Monday morning until Sunday noon? O, ye fairer sisters, whose hands are never soiled, whose nerves and muscles are never strained, go learn by experience! Had we had the opportunity that you have had to improve our moral and mental faculties, what would have hindered our intellects from being as bright, and our manners from being as dignified, as yours? Had it been our lot to have been nursed in the lap of affluence and ease, and to have basked beneath the smiles and sunshine of fortune, should we not have naturally supposed that we were never made to toil? And why are not our forms as delicate and our constitutions as slender as yours? Is not the workmanship as curious and complete? Have pity upon us, have pity upon us, O ye who have hearts to feel for other's woes; for the hand of God has touched us. Owing to the disadvantages under which we labor, there are many flowers among us that are

"—born to bloom unseen,
And waste their fragrance on the desert air."

My beloved brethren, as Christ has died in vain for those who will not accept of offered mercy, so will it be vain for the advocates of freedom to spend their breath in our behalf, unless with united hearts and souls you make some mighty efforts to raise your sons and daughters from the horrible state of servitude and degradation in which they are placed. It is upon you that woman depends; she can do but little beside using her influence; and it is for her sake and yours that I have come forward and made myself a hissing and a reproach among the people; for I am also one of the wretched and miserable daughters of the descendants of Africa. Do you ask: "Why are you wretched and miserable?" I reply: Look at many of the most worthy and interesting of us doomed to spend our lives in gentlemen's kitchens. Look at our young men—smart, active and energetic, with souls filled with ambitious fire; if they look forward, alas! what are their prospects? They can be nothing but the humblest laborer, on account of their dark complexion; hence many of them lose their ambition, and become worthless. Look at our middle-aged men, clad in their rusty plaids and coats. In winter, every cent they earn goes to buy their wood and pay their rent; their poor wives also toil beyond their strength, to help support their families. Look at our aged sires, whose heads are whitened with the frosts of seventy winters, with their old wood-saws on their backs. Alas, what keeps us so? Prejudice, ignorance, and poverty. But ah! methinks our oppression is soon to come to an end; yea, before the Majesty of heaven our groans and cries have reached the ears of the Lord of Sabaoth. As the prayers and tears of Christians will avail the finally impenitent nothing, neither will the prayers and tears of the friends of humanity avail us anything unless we possess a spirit of virtuous emulation within our breasts. Did the pilgrims, when they first landed on these shores, quietly compose themselves, and say: "The Britons have all the money and all the power, and we must continue their servants forever?" Did they sluggishly sigh, and say: "Our lot is hard; the Indians own the soil, and we cannot cultivate it?" No; they first made powerful efforts to raise themselves, and then God raised up those illustrious patriots, WASHINGTON and LAFAYETTE, to assist and defend them. And, my brethren, have you made a powerful effort? Have you prayed the Legislature for mercy's sake to grant you all the rights and privileges of free citizens, that your daughters may rise to that degree of respectability which true merit deserves, and your sons above the servile situations which most of them fill?

* * *

AN ADDRESS.

DELIVERED AT THE AFRICAN MASONIC HALL, BOSTON, FEBRUARY 27, 1833.

African rights and liberty is a subject that ought to fire the breast of every free man of color in these United States, and excite in his bosom a lively, deep, decided, and heart-felt interest. When I cast my eyes on the long list of illustrious names that are enrolled on the bright annals of fame among the whites, I turn my eyes within and ask my thoughts, "Where are the names of *our* illustrious ones?" It must certainly have been for the want of energy on the part of the free people of color that they have been long willing to bear the yoke of oppression. It must have been the want of ambition and force that has given the whites occasion to say that our natural abilities are not as good, and our capacities by nature inferior to theirs. They boldly assert that did we possess a natural independence of soul, and feel a love for liberty within our breasts, some one of our sable race, long before this, would have testified it, notwithstanding the disadvantages under which we labor. We have made ourselves appear altogether unqualified to speak in our own defense, and are therefore looked upon as objects of pity and commiseration. We have been imposed upon, insulted, and derided on every side; and now, if we complain, it is considered as the height of impertinence. We have suffered ourselves to be considered as dastards, cowards, mean, faint-hearted wretches; and on this account (not because of our complexion) many despise us, and would gladly spurn us from their presence.

These things have fired my soul with a holy indignation, and compelled me thus to come forward and endeavor to turn their attention to knowledge and improvement, for knowledge is power. I would ask, is it blindness of mind or stupidity of soul or the want of education that has caused our men who are sixty or seventy years of age never to let their voices be heard nor their hands be raised in behalf of their color? Or has it been for fear of offending the whites? If it has, O ye fearful ones, throw off your fearfulness and come forth, in the name of the Lord and in the strength of the God of Justice, and make yourselves useful and active members in society; for they admire a noble and patriotic spirit in others, and should they not admire it in us? If you are men, convince them that you possess the spirit of men: and as your day so shall your strength be. Have the sons of Africa no souls? Feel they no ambitious desires? Shall the chains of ignorance forever confine them? Shall the insipid appellation of "clever negroes" or "good creatures" any longer content them? Where can we find among ourselves the man of science, or a philosopher, or an able statesman, or a counsellor at law? Show me our fearless and brave, our noble and gallant ones. Where are our lecturers on natural history and our critics in useful knowledge? There may be a few such men among us, but they are rare. It is true, our fathers bled and died in the revolutionary war, and others fought bravely, under the command of Jackson, in defense of liberty. But where is the man that has distinguished himself in these modern days by acting wholly in the defense of African rights and liberty? There was one; although he sleeps, his memory lives.

I am sensible that there are many highly intelligent gentlemen of color in these United States in the force of whose arguments, doubtless, I should discover my inferiority; but if they are blessed with wit and talent, friends and fortune, why have they not made themselves men of eminence by striving to take all the reproach that is cast upon the people of color, and in endeavoring to alleviate the woes of their brethren in bondage? Talk, without effort, is nothing. You are abundantly capable, gentlemen, of making yourselves men of distinction; and this gross neglect on your part causes my blood to boil within me. Here is the grand cause which hinders the rise and progress of the people of color. It is the want of laudable ambition and requisite courage.

Individuals have been distinguished according to their genius and talents ever since the first formation of man, and will continue to be while the world stands. The different grades rise to honor and respectability as their merits may deserve. History informs us that we sprung from one of the most learned nations of the whole earth; from the seat, if not the parent of science; yes, poor, despised Africa was once the resort of sages and legislators of other nations, was esteemed the school of learning, and the most illustrious men of Greece flocked thither for instruction. But it was our gross sins and abominations that provoked the Almighty to frown thus heavily upon us and give our glory unto others. Sin and prodigality have caused the downfall of nations, kings, and emperors; and were it not that God in wrath remembers mercy, we might indeed despair; but a promise is left us: "Ethiopia shall again stretch forth her hands unto God."

But it is no use for us to boast that we sprung from this learned and enlightened nation, for this day a thick mist of moral gloom hangs over millions of our race. Our condition as a people has been low for hundreds of years, and it will continue to be so, unless, by true piety and virtue, we strive to regain that which we have lost. White Americans, by their prudence, economy, and exertions, have sprung up and become one of the most flourishing nations in the world, distinguished for their knowledge of the arts and sciences, for their polite literature. While our minds are vacant and starving for want of knowledge, theirs are filled to overflowing. Most of our color have been taught to stand in fear of the white man from their earliest infancy, to work as soon as they could walk, and to call "master" before they scarce could lisp the name of *mother*. Continual fear and laborious servitude have in some degree lessened in us that natural force and energy which belong to man; or else, in defiance of opposition, our men, before this, would have nobly and boldly contended for their rights. But give the man of color an equal opportunity with the white from the cradle to manhood, and from manhood to the grave, and you would discover the dignified statesman, the man of science, and the philosopher. But there is no such opportunity for the sons of Africa, and I fear that our powerful ones are fully determined that there never shall be. Forbid, ye Powers on high, that it should any longer be said that our men possess no force. O ye sons of Africa, when will your voices be heard in our legislative halls, in defiance of your enemies, contending for equal rights and liberty? How can you, when you reflect from what you have fallen, refrain from crying mightily unto God, to turn away from us the fierceness of his anger, and remember our transgressions against us no more forever. But a God of infinite purity will not regard the prayers of those who hold religion in one hand, and prejudice, sin, and pollution in the other; he will not regard the prayers of self-righteousness and hypocrisy. Is it possible, I exclaim, that for the want of knowledge we have labored for hundreds of years to support others, and been content to receive what they chose to give us in return? Cast your eyes about, look as far as you can see; all, all is owned by the lordly white, except here and there a lowly dwelling which the man of color, midst deprivations, fraud, and opposition has been scarce able to procure. Like King Solomon, who put neither nail nor hammer to the temple, yet received the praise; so also have the white Americans gained themselves a name, like the names of the great men that are in the earth, while in reality we have been their principal foundation and support. We have pursued the shadow, they have obtained the substance; we have performed the labor, they have received the profits; we have planted the vines, they have eaten the fruits of them.

I would implore our men, and especially our rising youth, to flee from the gambling board and the dance-hall; for we are poor, and have no money to throw away. I do not consider dancing as criminal in itself, but it is astonishing to me that our young men are so blind to their own interest and the future welfare of their children as to spend their hard earnings for this frivolous amusement; for it has been carried on among us to such an unbecoming extent that it has become absolutely disgusting. "Faithful are the wounds of a friend, but the kisses of an enemy are deceitful." Had those men among us, who have had an opportunity, turned their attention as assiduously to mental and moral improvement as they have to gambling and dancing, I might have remained quietly at home and they stood contending in my place. These polite accomplishments will never enroll your names on the bright annals of fame who admire the belle void of intellectual knowledge, or applaud the dandy that talks largely on politics, without striving to assist his fellow in the revolution, when the nerves and muscles of every other man forced him into the field of action. You have a right to rejoice, and to let your hearts cheer you in the days of your youth; yet remember that for all these things God will bring you into judgment. Then, O ye sons of Africa, turn your mind from these perishable objects, and contend for the cause of God and the rights of man. Form yourselves into temperance societies. There are temperate men among you; then why will you any longer neglect to strive, by your example, to suppress vice in all its abhorrent forms? You have been told repeatedly of the glorious results arising from temperance, and can you bear to see the whites arising in honor and respectability without endeavoring to grasp after that honor and respectability also?

But I forbear. Let our money, instead of being thrown away as heretofore, be appropriated for schools and seminaries of learning for our children and youth. We ought to follow the example of the whites in this respect. Nothing would raise our respectability, add to our peace and happiness, and reflect so much honor upon us, as to be ourselves the promoters of temperance, and the supporters, as far as we are able, of useful and scientific knowledge. The rays of light and knowledge have been hid from our view; we have been taught to consider ourselves as scarce superior to the brute creation; and have performed the most laborious part of American drudgery. Had we as a people received one-half the early advantages the whites have received, I would defy the Government of these United States to deprive us any longer of our rights.

I am informed that the agent of the Colonization Society has recently formed an association of young men for the purpose of influencing those of us to go to Liberia who may feel disposed. The colonizationists are blind to their own interest, for should the nations of the earth make war with America, they would find their forces much weakened by our absence; or should we remain here, can our "brave soldiers" and "fellow-citizens," as they were termed in time of calamity, condescend to defend the rights of the whites and be again deprived of their own, or sent to Liberia in return? Or, if the colonizationists are the real friends to Africa, let them expend the money which they collect, in erecting a college to educate her injured sons in this land of gospel, light, and liberty; for it would be most thankfully received on our part, and convince us of the truth of their professions, and save time, expense, and anxiety. Let them place before us noble objects worthy of pursuit, and see if we prove ourselves to be those unambitious negroes they term us. But, ah, bethinks their hearts are so frozen toward us they had rather their money should be sunk in the ocean than to administer it to our relief; and I fear, if they dared, like Pharaoh, king of Egypt, they would order every male child among us to be drowned. But the most high God is still as able to subdue the lofty pride of these white Americans as He was the heart of that ancient rebel. They say, though we are looked upon as *things*. yet we sprang from a scientific people. Had our men the requisite force and energy they would soon convince them by their efforts, both in public and private, that they were men. or things in the shape of men. Well may the colonizationists laugh us to scorn for our negligence, well may they cry: "Shame to the sons of Africa." As the burden of the Israelites was too great for Moses to bear, so also is our burden too great for our noble advocate to bear. You must feel interested, my brethren, in what he undertakes. and hold up his hands by your good works. or in spite of himself his soul will become discouraged and his heart will die within him; for he has, as it were, the strong bulls of Bashan to contend with.

It is of no use for us to wait any longer for a generation of well educated men to arise. We have slumbered and slept too long already; the day is far spent; the night of death approaches; and you have sound sense and good judgment sufficient to begin with, if you feel disposed to make a right use of it. Let every man of color throughout the United States, who possesses the spirit and principles of a man, sign a petition to Congress to abolish slavery in the District of Columbia, and grant you the rights and privileges of common free citizens; for if you had had faith as a grain of mustard seed, long before this the mountains of prejudice might have been removed. We are all sensible that the Anti-Slavery Society has taken hold of the arm of our whole population, in order to raise them out of the mire. Now all we have to do is, by a spirit of virtuous ambition, to strive to raise ourselves; and I am happy to have it in my power thus publicly to say that the colored inhabitants of this city, in some respects, are beginning to improve. Had the free people of color in these United States nobly and boldly contended for their rights, and showed a natural genius and talent, although not so brilliant as some; had they held up, encouraged and patronized each other,

nothing could have hindered us from being a thriving and flourishing people. There has been a fault among us. The reason why
our distinguished men have not made themselves more influential, is because they fear that the strong current of opposition
through which they must pass would cause their downfall and
prove their overthrow. And what gives rise to this opposition?
Envy. And what has it amounted to? Nothing. And who are the
cause of it? Our whited sepulchres, who want to be great, and
don't know how; who love to be called of men "Rabbi, Rabbi;"
who put on false sanctity, and humble themselves to their brethren for the sake of acquiring the highest place in the synagogue
and the uppermost seat at the feast. You, dearly beloved, who
are the genuine followers of our Lord Jesus Christ—the salt of
the earth, and the light of the world—are not so culpable. As I
told you in the very first of my writing, I tell you again, I am but
as a drop in the bucket—as one particle of the small dust of the
earth. God will surely raise up those among us who will plead
the cause of virtue and the pure principles of morality more eloquently than I am able to do.

It appears to me that America has become like the great City
of Babylon, for she has boasted in her heart: "I sit a queen, and
am no widow, and shall see no sorrow!" She is, indeed, a seller
of slaves and the souls of men; she has made the Africans drunk
with the wine of her fornication; she has put them completely
beneath her feet, and she means to keep them there; her right
hand supports the reins of government and her left hand the
wheel of power, and she is determined not to let go her grasp.
But many powerful sons and daughters of Africa will shortly
arise, who will put down vice and immorality among us, and
declare by Him that sitteth upon the throne that they will have
their rights; and if refused, I am afraid they will spread horror
and devastation around. I believe that the oppression of injured
Africa has come up before the Majesty of Heaven; and when
our cries shall have reached the ears of the Most High, it will
be a tremendous day for the people of this land; for strong is the
arm of the Lord God Almighty. Life has almost lost its charms
for me; death has lost its sting, and the grave its terrors; and at
times I have a strong desire to depart and dwell with Christ,
which is far better. Let me entreat my white brethren to awake

and save our sons from dissipation and our daughters from ruin. Lend the hand of assistance to feeble merit; plead the cause of virtue among our sable race; so shall our curses upon you be turned into blessings; and though you should endeavor to drive us from these shores, still we will cling to you the more firmly; nor will we attempt to rise above you; we will presume to be called your equals only.

The unfriendly whites first drove the native American from his much loved home. Then they stole our fathers from their peaceful and quiet dwellings, and brought them hither, and made bond-men and bond-women of them and their little ones. They have obliged our brethren to labor; kept them in utter ignorance; nourished them in vice, and raised them in degradation; and now that we have enriched their soil, and filled their coffers, they say that we are not capable of becoming like white men, and that we never can rise to respectability in this country. They would drive us to a strange land. But before I go, the bayonet shall pierce me through. African rights and liberty is a subject that ought to fire the breast of every free man of color in these United States, and excite in his bosom a lively, deep, decided, and heartfelt interest.

JAMES FORTEN JR.

*Born in Philadelphia, Pennsylvania, James Forten Jr. (1813–?)
was the son of James and Charlotte Forten, wealthy Black
business owners, abolitionists, and proponents of civil rights.
His father fought in the Revolutionary War and later fi-
nanced and wrote for William Lloyd Garrison's abolitionist
newspaper* The Liberator. *From an early age, Forten Jr. followed closely in his father's footsteps, writing for* The Liberator *and taking up membership in the Young Men's
Anti-Slavery Society and the American Moral Reform Society. The Forten family was adamant that total liberation
was necessary and that colonization schemes that shuttled
Black Americans to Africa, the Caribbean, and other lo-
cales were unfeasible. Black Americans, in their estimation,
had a birthright in the United States and deserved to be recognized as full citizens in their own land. In this powerful
speech delivered before the Ladies' Anti-Slavery Society of
Philadelphia in 1836, Forten Jr. compels abolitionist women
to remember their moral duty as Christians and Americans
to keep up the righteous fight. He encourages them to hold
on, despite the odds against them: "To falter now, would be
to surrender your pure and unsullied principles into the
hands of a vicious and perverted portion of the community, who are anxiously waiting to see you grow weak and
faint-hearted; you would be casting the whole spirit and genius of patriotism into that polluted current just described.
To falter now would retard the glorious day of emancipation which is now dawning, for years, perhaps for ever. But
why should you pause?"*

"An Address Delivered Before the Ladies' Anti-Slavery Society of Philadelphia, on the Evening of the 14th of April, 1836"

(1836)

AN ADDRESS, &C.

LADIES—There is nothing that could more forcibly induce me to express my humble sentiments at all times, than an entire consciousness that it is the duty of every individual who would wish to see the foul curse of slavery swept for ever from the land—who wishes to become one amongst the undaunted advocates of the oppressed—who wishes to deal justly and love mercy. In a word, it is my indispensable duty, in view of the wretched, the helpless, the friendless condition of my countrymen in chains, to raise my voice, feeble though it be, in their behalf; to plead for the restoration of their inalienable rights. As to the character of the ANTI-SLAVERY SOCIETY, it requires but one glance from an impartial eye, to discover the purity of its motives—the great strength of its moral energies; its high and benevolent—its holy and life giving principles. These are the foundations, the very architecture of Abolition, and prove its sovereignty. In fact, all associated bodies which have for their great aim the destruction of tyranny, and the moral and intellectual improvement of mankind, have been, and ever will be, considered as bearing a decided superiority over all others. And how well may this Association, before which I now have the honour to appear, be deemed one of that description; and still more is its superiority increased from a knowledge of the truth that it is composed entirely of your sex. It stands aloof from the storms of passion and political tumult, exhibiting in its extended and Christian views a disposition to produce an immediate reformation of the heart and soul. Never before has there been a subject brought into the arena of public investigation, so fraught with humanity—so alive to the best interest of our country—so dear to all those for whose benefit it was intended, as the one which now calls you together. How varied and abundant—how eloquent and soul-thrilling have been the arguments advanced in its defence, by the greatest and best of the land; and yet, so boundless is the theme—so inexhaustible the fountain, that even the infant may be heard lisping a prayer for the redemption of the perishing captive.

LADIES—The task you are called upon to perform is certainly of vital importance. Great is the responsibility which this association imposes upon you; however, I need scarcely remind you of it, feeling confident that long before this you have made a practical and familiar acquaintance with all its bearings, and with every sentence contained in your society's sacred declaration; ever remembering that in it is concentrated one of the noblest objects that ever animated the breast of a highly favoured people—*the immediate and unconditional abolition of Slavery.* It is the acknowledgment of a broad principle like this, and recommending it to a prejudiced public, who have been all along accustomed to reason upon the dangerous doctrine of gradualism, viewing it as the only safe and efficient remedy for this monstrous evil which has brought about such an excitement, and convulsed our country from North to South; an excitement which I have every reason to believe will prove a powerful engine towards the furtherance of your noble cause. As to this opposition now arrayed against you, terrible as it appears, it is no more than what you might anticipate; it is a fate which, in this age of iniquity, must inevitably follow such a change as your society proposes to effect. For what else is to be expected for a measure the tendency of which is to check the tide of corruption—to make narrower the limits of tyrannical power—to unite *liberty* and *law*—to save the body of the oppressed from the blood-stained lash of the oppressor—and to secure a greater respect and obedience to Him who wills the happiness of all mankind, and who endowed them with life, and liberty, as conducive to that happiness? What else, I repeat, can be expected but opposition, at a time like this, when brute force reigns supreme: when ministers of the Gospel, commissioned to spread the light of Christianity among all nations are overleap-

ing the pale of the church, forsaking the holy path, and sowing
the seeds of discord where they should plant the "olive branch
of peace." When liberty has dwindled into a mere shadow, its
vitality being lost, shrouded in darkness, swallowed up as it
were in the eternal dumbness of the grave. This, my friends, is
the present situation of things, and warns you that the desperate struggle has commenced between *freedom* and *despotism*—
light and *darkness*. This is the hour you are called upon to
move with a bold and fearless step; there must be no lukewarm-
ness, no shrinking from the pointed finger of scorn, or the contemptuous vociferation of the enemy; no withholding your aid,
or concealing your mighty influence behind the screen of timid-
ity; no receding from the foothold you have already gained. To
falter now, would be to surrender your pure and unsullied principles into the hands of a vicious and perverted portion of the
community, who are anxiously waiting to see you grow weak
and faint-hearted; you would be casting the whole spirit and
genius of patriotism into that polluted current just described.
To falter now would retard the glorious day of emancipation
which is now dawning, for years, perhaps for ever. But why
should you pause? It is true that public opinion is bitter against
you, and exercises a powerful influence over the minds of many;
it is also true that you are frustrated in nearly every attempt to
procure a place to hold your meetings, and the hue and cry is
raised, "Down with the incendiaries—hang all who dare to
open their mouths in vindication of equal rights;" still, this
would be no excuse for a dereliction of duty; you are not bound
to follow public opinion constantly and lose sight of the demands of justice; for it is plain to be seen that public opinion,
in its present state, is greatly at fault; it affixes the seal of condemnation upon you without giving you an opportunity to be
fairly heard; therefore I think the obligation ought to cease, and
you pursue a more natural course by looking to your own
thoughts and feelings as a guide, and not to the words of others. Again—in order to promote your antislavery principles you
should make it the topic of your conversation amidst your acquaintances, in every family circle, and in the shades of private
life. Be assured that by acting thus, hundreds will rise up to
your aid.

I will now claim your indulgence for a few moments while I make some remarks on the subject of natural rights. It certainly is one of great magnitude. I will not, however, enter into an extensive discussion of its various branches; but would earnestly suggest it for the future consideration of our friends. Of what incalculable value must these rights be to those who possess them unrestricted? And yet they were intended for all—high and low—rich and poor—of whatever clime or complexion. They were spoke into existence along with the world; and although the establishment of legal authority was unknown to us, and there "subsisted not a vestige of civil government any where, still they would belong to man." Or, if we who form this present assembly were, by some sudden and unknown cause, thrown upon a desolate spot in the remotest corner of the Globe, we would, from the very first moment, be entitled to these rights—the right to the produce of our own labour, to our limbs, life, liberty and property—perfect rights, not human institutions, but Divine ordinations. Now, with these facts before you, the question should arise, whether all your fellow creatures are in the full enjoyment of these rights. If you look to the South, you will see how they are violated—how outrage, oppression and wrong has blighted them—how man, (corrupted worm of the earth) forgetting his accountability to God, suffering passion and avarice to dethrone reason, has torn them from his fellow man. Yes, the poor slave is deprived of these rights—these great essentials to man's happiness—these bountiful gifts of nature—he does not possess even as much freedom "as the beasts that perish." My friends, reflect for a moment upon what constitutes natural rights; analyze them, search deep into their component parts, and then ask yourselves if slavery recognises any of them? Why, every rational being who has bestowed one thought upon the inhuman traffic must come to the conclusion that it does not. Again, look on the other side of the picture— turn your eyes to your own city, and behold that class of American citizens with whom I am identified; see them borne down by the weight of innumerable persecutions, their situation but little better than the millions of their brethren now suffering under the galling yoke of servitude; they are nearly stripped of their rights. The remorseless hand of prejudice—the despoiler

of our rights—our inveterate foe, whose birth place is the neth-
ermost pit—year after year wages an ignoble warfare against
us. If we are arrested on suspicion of having stolen our own
bodies, and run away with them, so few are the advocates we
have at the Bar of Justice, that the pleadings of humanity are
silenced, and we too frequently consigned to hopeless bondage.
If our property be destroyed by a cowardly and ruffian mob,
our persons maltreated and our limbs broken, the hand of charity is scarcely extended to the sufferer; seldom do we find that
redress shown to us which would be fully bestowed upon any
other class of people similarly situated. The omnipotent Being
said, "Let there be light." Is it permitted to shine brightly around
our path? No. Where is that all-powerful light of knowledge?
Where are the academies thrown open for our reception, that
we may come in and quench our parched lips at the fountain of
Literature? With but few exceptions there are none; even the
doors of the sanctuary, devoted to all that is sacred, are closed
against us. And is this fair—is it noble—is it generous—is it
patriotic—is it consistent with the professions of our republican
principles? Was it ever intended that man should lift his rebel
hand against the natural rights of his brother, and try to uproot
them from his breast? That he should thus tamper with the works
of nature?—should thus presumptuously exercise his own will
in defiance of the benevolent and comprehensive wisdom of Providence? My friends, ought not the united efforts of every Christian to be aimed at the destruction of this persecution, which, like
a universal pall, overspreads our prospects? Is not the call imperative? What have we done to merit this abuse? Have we usurped
the authorities of the land? No. Are we out-laws—cut-throats?
No. Are we not men, in common with other men; fully capable
of appreciating the inestimable worth of these rights, which are
our own? True, we are told by our enemies that we are inferior
to them in intellect—our mental faculties being of the lowest
order—that we stand but one degree above the brute creation;
these are assertions without a shadow of proof; they tie our feet
and seal our mouths, and then exclaim, "see how superior we
are to these people!" They have no authority for crushing us to
the ground, therefore we will not cease to urge our case, calmly
and dispassionately. We are stimulated to act thus by the instinct

of our natures. There is nothing that our enemies can bring against us but the colour of our skin; and is this not a mean, pitiful objection to the elevation of any one? Oh! what a shameful prejudice. If this is to be our judge, if the uncertain and wavering shades of colour are to decide whether we shall be entitled to rights in common with our fellow citizens, (which is all we ask,) if mercy and compassion is to be disregarded, and beneficence utterly annihilated, no longer to strengthen, guide and ennoble the hearts of men, then has our country's grandeur fallen— then has she sunk into a state which would have disgraced the dark ages, when civilization was unknown, and man had not yet begun to do homage to the potency of mind. We claim our rights, then, not as a mere boon, for that would be doing violence to that honest pride which is always found pervading the breast and flowing through every vein of conscious innocence, but we claim them as rights guaranteed by the living God— natural, indefeasible rights.

There is another point to which I would draw your notice. The recent scenes in Congress are a specimen of the evil times we live in, the corrupted atmosphere we breathe. There, behold the Constitution of the United States—our national compact, the great organ of national sentiment, perjured, immolated upon the altar of expediency there; the right to petition, the right of free discussion, the freedom of speech, the freedom of the press—rights which should be the pride and boast of a republic, are trampled under foot, scoffed at by statesmen and senators, and the gag and Lynch law held up as a a model of the glorious march of *Virtue, Liberty* and *Independence;* as the dearest gift that a noble and dignified people could transfer to posterity; why posterity would spurn such a legacy as coming from heathens, and not from their Christian forefathers. The demands of the South are growing every day more extravagant, insolent and imperative. As an evidence of this, I have only to refer you to the report and resolutions adopted in the Legislature of South Carolina, published in the 9th number of the Liberator. I allude to the report of the Joint Committee of Federal Relations, on so much of Gov. M'Duffie's message as relates to the institution of domestic slavery, and the proceedings of the Abolitionists in the non-slaveholding states. It ought to be extensively read, for I think it would be the means of arousing many to a sense of the danger which threatens their own liberties. I will read a few of the resolutions offered by Mr. Hamilton, chairman of that most grave and reverend committee.

"*Resolved*, That the formation of Abolition Societies, and the acts and doings of certain fanatics calling themselves Abolitionists, in the non-slaveholding states of this confederacy, are in direct violation of the obligations of the compact of Union, dissocial and incendiary in the extreme.

"*Resolved*, That the Legislature of South Carolina, having every confidence in the justice and friendship of the non slaveholding states, announces to her co-states her confident expectations, and she earnestly requests that the governments of these states will promptly and effectually suppress all those associations within their respective limits, purporting to be Abolition Societies; and that they will make it highly penal, to print, publish and distribute newspapers, pamphlets, tracts, and pictorial representations, calculated and having an obvious tendency to excite the slaves of the southern states to insurrection and revolt.

"*Resolved*, In order that a salutary negative may be put on the mischievous and unfounded assumption of some of the Abolitionists—the non-slaveholding states are requested to disclaim, by legislative declaration, all right, either on the part of themselves or the government of the United States, to interfere in any manner with domestic slavery, either in the states or in the territories where it exists."

Was ever a request so modest? There never was a request more unreasonable, more abominable—evincing in its tone the greatest insult that could be offered to a free and independent people. But what do the majority of the citizens in the North about the matter? Why, I regret to have it in my power to say, that, with few exceptions, they are yielding to this daring presumption of the South; tamely acquiescing without venturing even as much as a word in reply. They ask of them to relinquish the sacred and legitimate right to think and act as they please. Freemen are, in one sense, threatened with slavery; the chains are shaken in their faces, and yet they appear unwilling to resist them as becomes freemen. Such votaries are they at the shrine of mammon that they have not courage enough to join the standard of patriotism which their fathers reared, and with the dignity of a free and unshackled people, repel with scorn, this unheard of infringement upon their dearest rights—this death-blow to their own liberties. My friends, do you ask why I thus speak? It is because I love America; it is my native land; because I feel as one should feel who sees destruction, like a corroding cancer, eating into the very heart of his country, and would make one struggle to save her;—because I love the stars and stripes, emblems of our National Flag—and long to see the day when not a slave shall be found resting under its shadow; when it shall play with the winds pure and unstained by the blood of "captive millions."

Again, the South most earnestly and respectfully solicits the North to let the question of Slavery alone, and leave it to their bountiful honesty and humanity to settle. Why, honesty, I fear, has fled from the South, long ago; sincerity has fallen asleep there; pity has hidden herself; justice cannot find the way; helper is not at home; charity lies dangerously ill; benevolence is under arrest; faith is nearly extinguished; truth has long since been buried, and conscience is nailed on the wall. Now, do you think it would be better to leave it to the bountiful honesty and humanity of the South to settle? No, no. Only yield to them in this one particular and they will find you vulnerable in every other. I can tell you, my hearers, if the North once sinks into profound silence on this momentous subject, you may then bid farewell to peace, order and reform; then the condition of your fellow creatures in the southern section of our country will never be ameliorated; then may the poor slave look upon his weighty chains, and exclaim, in the agony of his heart, "To these am I immutably doomed; the glimmering rays of hope are lost to me for ever; robbed of all that is dear to man, I stand a monument of my country's ingratitude. A *husband*, yet separated from the dearest tie which binds me to this earth. A *father*, yet compelled to stifle the feelings of a father, and witness a helpless offspring torn by a savage hand from its mother's fond embrace, no longer to call her by that endearing title. A wretched slave, I look upon the departing brightness of the setting sun, and when her glorious light revists the morn, these clanking irons tell me I am that slave still;

still am I to linger out a life of ignominious servitude, till death shall unloose these heavy bars—unfetter my body and soul."

Will not the wrath of offended Heaven visit my guilty brethren? My friends, this is no chimera of the imagination, but it is the reality; and I beseech you to consider it as such. Cease not to do as you are now doing, notwithstanding the invidious frowns that may be cast upon your efforts; regard not these—for bear in mind that the future prosperity of the nation rests upon the successful labours of the Abolitionists; this is as certain as that there is a God above. Recollect you have this distinction—you have brought down upon your heads the anger of many foes for that good which you seek to do your country; you are insulted and sneered at because you feel for the proscribed, the defence-less, the down-trodden; you are despised because you would raise them in the scale of beings; you are charged as coming out to the world with the Bible in one hand and a firebrand in the other. May you never be ashamed of that firebrand. It is a holy fire, kindled from every page of that sacred chronicle.

You are called fanatics. Well, what if you are? Ought you to shrink from this name? God forbid. There is an eloquence in such fanaticism, for it whispers hope to the slave; there is sanctity in it, for it contains the consecrated spirit of religion; it is the fanaticism of a Benezet, a Rush, a Franklin, a Jay; the same that animated and inspired the heart of the writer of the Declaration of Independence. Then flinch not from your high duty; continue to warn the South of the awful volcano they are recklessly sleeping over; and bid them remember, too, that the drops of blood which trickle down the lacerated back of the slave, will not sink into the barren soil. No, they will rise to the common God of nature and humanity, and cry aloud for vengeance on his destroyer's head. Bid them think of this, that they may see from what quarter the terrible tempest will come; not from the breakings out of insurrections, so much dreaded, but for which men are indebted to the imagery of their minds more than to fact; not from the fanatics, or the publication of their papers, calculated to spread desolation and blood, and sever the Union, as is now basely asserted, but it will come from Him who has declared "Vengeance is mine, and I will repay."

You are not aiming to injure your southern brethren, but to

benefit them; to save them from the impending storm. You are
not seeking the destruction of the Union; but to render it still
stronger; to link it together in one universal chain of *Justice*,
and *Love*, and *Freedom*. The Faith you have embraced teaches
you to live in bonds of charity with all mankind. It is not by the
force of arms that Abolitionists expect to remove one of the
greatest curses that ever afflicted or disgraced humanity; but by
the majesty of moral power. Oh! how callous, how completely
destitute of feeling, must that person be, who can think of the
wrongs done to the innocent and unoffending captive, and not
drop one tear of pity—who can look upon slavery and not
shudder at its inhuman barbarities? It is a withering blight to
the country in which it exists—a deadly poison to the soil on
which it is suffered to breathe—and to satiate the cravings of its
appetite, it feeds, like a vulture, upon the vitals of its victims.
But it is in vain that I attempt to draw a proper likeness of its
horrors; it is far beyond the reach of my abilities to describe to
you the endless atrocities which characterize the system. Well
was it said by Thomas Jefferson, that "God has no attribute
which can take sides with such oppression." See what gigantic
force is concentrated in these few words—God has no attribute
which can take sides with such oppression.

Ladies—I feel that I should have confined my remarks more
particularly to your society, and not have extended them to the
whole field of Abolition. Pardon me for the digression.

I rejoice to see you engaged in this mighty cause; it befits you;
it is your province; your aid and influence is greatly to be desired in this hour of peril; it never was, never can be insignificant. Examine the records of history, and you will find that
woman has been called upon in the severest trials of public
emergency. That your efforts will stimulate the men to renewed
exertion I have not the slightest doubt; for, in general, the pride
of man's heart is such, that while he is willing to grant unto
woman exclusively, many conspicuous and dignified privileges,
he at the same time feels an innate disposition to check the
modest ardour of her zeal and ambition, and revolts at the idea
of her managing the reigns of improvement. Therefore, you have
only to be constantly exhibiting some new proof of your interest in the cause of the oppressed, and shame, if not duty, will

urge our sex on the march. It has often been said by anti-abolitionists that the females have no right to interfere with the question of slavery, or petition for its overthrow; that they had better be at home attending to their domestic affairs, &c. What a gross error—what an anti-christian spirit this bespeaks. Were not the holy commands, "Remember them that are in bonds, as bound with them," and "Do unto others as ye would they should do unto you," intended for woman to obey as well as man? Most assuredly they were. But from whom does this attack upon your rights come? Not, I am confident, from the respectable portion of our citizens, but invariably from men alienated by avarice and self-importance from that courtesy and respect which is due to your sex on all occasions; such "men of property and standing" as mingled with the rank breath, and maniac spirit, of the mob at Boston; men (I am sorry to say) like the Representative from Virginia, Mr. Wise, who, lost to all shame, openly declared you to be devils incarnate. And for what? Why, because the ladies in the several states north of the Potomac, in the magnitude of their philanthropy, with hearts filled with mercy, choose to raise their voices in behalf of the suffering and the dumb—because they choose to exercise their legal privileges, and offer their time and talents as a sacrifice, in order that the District of Columbia may be freed, and washed clean from the stains of blood, cruelty and crime. It is for acting thus that you received so refined a compliment. Truly, some of our great men at the South are hand and hand in iniquity; they are men after the heart of the tyrant Nero, who wished that all the Romans had but one neck that he might destroy them all at a single blow. This is just the position in which these Nero's of a modern mould would like to place all who dare to utter one syllable against the sin of slavery,—that is if they had the power.

But, Ladies, I verily believe that the time is fast approaching when thought, feeling and action, the three principal elements of public opinion, will be so revolutionized as to turn the scale in your favour; when the prejudice and contumely of your foes will be held in the utmost contempt by an enlightened community. You have already been the means of awakening hundreds from the deep slumber into which they had fallen; they have arisen, and put on the armour of righteousness, and gone forth to battle. Yours is the cause of Truth, and must prevail over error; it is the cause of sympathy, and therefore it calls aloud for the aid of woman.

> "Sympathy is woman's attribute,
> By that she has reign'd—by that she will reign."

Yours is the cause of Christianity; for it pleads that the mental and physical powers of millions may not be wasted—buried for ever in ruins; that virtue may not be sacrificed at the altar of lasciviousness; making the South but one vast gulf of infamy; that the affections of a parent may not be sundered; that hearts may not be broken; that souls, bearing the impress of the Deity—the proof of their celestial origin and eternal duration—may not be lost. It is for all these you plead, and you must be victorious; never was there a contest commenced on more hallowed principles. Yes, my friends, from the height of your holy cause, as from a mountain, I see already rising the new glory and grandeur of regenerated—FREE—America! And on the corner stone of that mighty fabric, posterity shall read your names. But if there be the shadow of a doubt still remaining in the breasts of any one present as to your success, I would beg them to cast their eyes across the broad bosom of the Atlantic, and call to mind the scenes which transpired a short time since. (There shone the influence of woman!) Call to mind the 1st of August, a day never to be forgotten by the real philanthropist; when *Justice*, mantled in renovated splendour, with an arm nerved to action—her brow lighted up by a ray from Heaven, mounted on the car of *Freedom*, betook her way to the spot where *Slavery* was stalking over the land, making fearful ravages among human beings. There, the "lust of gain, had made the fiercest and fellest exhibition of its hardihood." There, Justice looked, on the one hand, to the "prosperity of the lordly oppressor, wrung from the sufferings of a captive and subjugated people;" and on the other, to the "tears and untold agony of the hundreds beneath him." There, was heard the sighs and stifled groans of the once happy and gay; hopes blighted in the bud. There, cruelty had wrought untimely furrows upon the check of youth. She saw all this; but the supplicating cry of mercy did not fall unheeded upon her ear. No. She smote the monster in the height of his power; link after link fell from the massive chain, and *eight hundred thousand human beings sprang into life again.*

It was WOMAN who guided that car! It was woman who prompted Justice to the work. Then commenced the glorious Jubilee; then the eye, once dim, was seen radiant with joy—

> "Caste and proscription cease,
>   The Bondsman wakes to Liberty; he sleeps in peace.
>   Read the great charter on his brow:
>   'I am a MAN, a BROTHER, now.'"

Ladies, ought not this to be enough to induce you to persevere? I am sure you are just as capable as your sisters of England; let me entreat you, then, to be for ever on the watch; let your motto be—*onward*. Oh! forget not the thrilling appeals of that Christian missionary, GEORGE THOMPSON; he whose brilliant talents and matchless eloquence illumined all they touched; he who left his native land, and appeared among you like a guiding star, shedding rays of peace and good will to all mankind; his voice still may be heard, and bids you onward. A voice speaks from the sainted ashes of WILBERFORCE, and bids you onward. A voice from our GARRISON of Liberty is wafted to your ears on every eastern breeze; it speaks in tones of thunder, and bids you onward—onward. Then, pause not—tremble not—God is with you; you contend for the privilege of "breaking the bonds and letting the oppressed go free." Obey the commands of the Bible—upon this rock hang all your hopes—and in the darkest and most perilous hour of your enterprise, your fortitude will not forsake you; and, remembering under what influences you have reared the Banner of Universal Freedom, your enemies will be constrained to admit that no power on earth can ever oppose the ARM OF OMNIPOTENCE.

LUCY STANTON

An educator and abolitionist, Lucy Stanton (1831–1910) was born free in Ohio. As the president of the Ladies' Literary Society at Oberlin Collegiate Institute, Stanton delivered the speech "A Plea for the Oppressed" at her graduation with the hopes of encouraging her fellow women graduates to understand the gravity of the looming enactment of the Fugitive Slave Act. She implored her cohort to battle mightily to end the complicated institution of slavery, as "Slavery is the combination of all crime. It is War."

"A Plea for the Oppressed"
(1850)

When I forget you, Oh my people, may my tongue cleave to the roof of my mouth, and may my right hand forget her cunning! Dark hover the clouds. The Anti-Slavery pulse beats faintly. The right of suffrage is denied. The colored man is still crushed by the weight of oppression. He may possess talents of the highest order, yet for him is no path of fame or distinction opened. He can never hope to attain those privileges while his brethren remain enslaved. Since, therefore, the freedom of the slave and the gaining of our rights, social and political, are inseparably connected, let all the friends of humanity plead for those who may not plead their own cause.

Reformers, ye who have labored long to convince man that happiness is found alone in doing good to others, that humanity is a unit, that he who injures one individual wrongs the race;— that to love one's neighbor as one's self is the sum of human virtue—ye that advocate the great principles of Temperance, Peace, and Moral Reform will you not raise your voice in behalf of these stricken ones!—will you not plead the cause of the Slave?

Slavery is the combination of all crime. It is War.

Those who rob their fellow-men of home, of liberty, of education, of life, are really at war against them as though they cleft them down upon the bloody field. It is intemperance; for there is an intoxication when the fierce passions rage in man's breast, more fearful than the madness of the drunkard, which if let loose upon the moral universe would sweep away everything pure and holy, leaving but the wreck of man's nobler nature. Such passions does Slavery foster—yea, they are a part of herself. It is full of pollution. Know you not that to a slave, virtue is a sin counted worthy of death? That many, true to the light within, notwithstanding the attempts to shut out the truth, feeling that a consciousness of purity is dearer than life, have nobly died? Their blood crieth to God, a witness against the oppressor.

Statesmen, you who have bent at ambition's shrine, who would leave your names on the page of history, to be venerated by coming generations as among those of the great and good, will you advocate the cause of the down-trodden, remembering that the spirit of liberty is abroad in the land? The precious seed is sown in the heart of the people, and though the fruit does not appear, the germ is there, and the harvest will yet be gathered. Truly is this an age of reform. The world is going on, not indeed keeping pace with the rapid tread of its leaders, but none the less progressing. As the people take a step in one reform, the way is prepared for another. Now while other evils in man's social and political condition are being remedied, think you that Slavery can stand the searching test—an enlightened people's sense of justice? Then speak the truth boldly; fear not loss of property or station. It is a higher honor to embalm your name in the hearts of a grateful people than to contend for the paltry honors of party preferment.

Woman, I turn to thee. Is it not thy mission to visit the poor? to shed the tear of sympathy? to relieve the wants of the suffering? Where wilt thou find objects more needing sympathy than among the slaves!

Mother, hast thou a precious gem in thy charge, like those that make up the Savior's jewels? Has thy heart, trembling with its unutterable joyousness, bent before the throne of the Giver with the prayer that thy child might be found in his courts? Thou hast seen the dawning of intelligence in its bright eye, and watched with interest the unfolding of its powers. Its gentle, winning ways have doubly endeared it to thee. Death breathes upon the flower, and it is gone. Now thou canst feel for the slave-mother who has bent with the same interest over her child, whose heart is entwined around it even more firmly than thine own around thine, for to her it is the only ray of joy in a dreary world. She returns weary and sick at heart from the labors of the field; the child's beaming smile of welcome half banishes the misery of her lot. Would she not die for it? Ye who know the depths of a mother's love, answer! Hark! Strange footsteps are near her dwelling! The door is thrown rudely open! Her master says—"There is the woman!" She comprehends it all—she is sold! From her trembling lips escape the words—"my child!" She throws herself at the feet of those merciless men, and pleads permission to keep her babe, but in vain. What is she more than any other slave, that she should be permitted this favor? They are separated.

Sister, have you ever had a kind and loving brother? How often would he lay aside his book to relieve you from some difficulty? How have you hung upon the words of wisdom that he has uttered? How earnestly have you studied that you might stand his companion—his equal. You saw him suddenly stricken by the destroyer. Oh! How your heart ached!

There was a slave-girl who had a brother kind and noble as your own. He had scarcely any advantages: yet stealthily would he draw an old volume from his pocket, and through the long night would pore over its contents. His soul thirsted for knowledge. He yearned for freedom, but free-soil was far away. That sister might not go, he staid with her. They say that slaves do not feel for or love each other; I fear that there are few brothers with a pale face who would have stood that test. For her he tamed the fire of his eye, toiled for that which profited him not, and labored so industriously that the overseer had no apology for applying the lash to his back. Time passed on: that brother stood in his manhood's prime as tenderly kind and as dearly beloved as ever. That sister was insulted;—the lash was applied to her quivering back; her brother rushed to save her! He tore away the fastenings which bound her to the whipping post, he held her on his arm—she was safe. She looked up, encountered the ferocious gaze of the overseer, heard the report of a pistol, and felt the heart's blood of a brother gushing over her. But we draw the veil.

Mother, sister, by thy own deep sorrow of heart; by the sympathy of thy woman's nature, plead for the downtrodden of thy own, of every land. Instill the principles of love, of common brotherhood, in the nursery, in the social circle. Let these be the prayer of thy life.

Christians, you whose souls are filled with love for your fellow men, whose prayer to the Lord is, "Oh! that I may see thy salvation among the children of men!" Does the battle wax warm? dost thou faint with the burden and heat of the day? Yet a little longer; the arm of the Lord is mighty to save those who trust in him. Truth and right must prevail. The bondsman shall go free. Look to the future! Hark! the shout of joy gushes from the heart of earth's freed millions! It rushes upward. The angels on heaven's outward battlements catch the sound on their golden lyres, and send it thrilling through the echoing arches of the upper world. How sweet, how majestic, from those starry isles float those deep inspiring sounds over the ocean of space! Softened and mellowed they reach earth, filing the soul with harmony, and breathing of God—of love—and of universal freedom.

MARY ANN SHADD CARY

Born free in Wilmington, Delaware, Mary Ann Shadd Cary (1823–1893) was an abolitionist, teacher, and lawyer who championed emigration to Canada West (Ontario) as a safe and rational option for free Black people and runaways who were making their way through the Underground Railroad. The Fugitive Slave Act of 1850 made Black life in the United States even more precarious than it had been previously, as it unwittingly encouraged kidnappers to set their sights on snatching and selling free Black people into slavery. Cary and her brother fled to Windsor, Ontario, Canada, that very year to escape that looming terror. In A Plea for Emigration, *Cary presents her case for Black settlement in Canada, noting the social, educational, agricultural, and racial benefits and drawbacks of Canada. She argues that Canada is uniquely fit for Black Americans over similar settlements in Mexico, South America, and Africa.*

From *A Plea for Emigration; or, Notes of Canada West*
(1852)

SETTLEMENTS,—DAWN,—ELGIN,— INSTITUTION,—FUGITIVE HOME.

Much has been said of the Canada colored settlements, and fears have been expressed by many, that by encouraging exclusive settlements, the attempt to identify colored men with degraded men of like color in the States would result, and as a consequence, estrangement, suspicion, and distrust would be induced. Such would inevitably be the result, and will be, shall they determine to have entirely proscriptive settlements. Those in existence, so far as I have been able to get at facts, do not exclude whites from their vicinity; but that settlements may not be established of that character, is not so certain. Dawn, on the Suydenham river, Elgin, or King's Settlement, as it is called, situated about ten miles from Chatham, are settlements in which there are regulations in regard to morals, the purchase of lands, etc., bearing only on the colored people; but whites are not excluded because of dislike. When purchase was made of the lands, many white families were residents,—at least, locations were not selected in which none resided. At first, a few sold out, fearing that such neighbors might not be agreeable; others, and they the majority, concluded to remain, and the result attests their superior judgment. Instead of an increase of vice, prejudice, improvidence, laziness, or a lack of energy, that many feared would characterize them, the infrequency of violations of law among so many, is unprecedented; due attention to moral and intellectual culture has been given; the former prejudices on the part of the whites, has given place to a perfect reciprocity of religious and social intercommunication. Schools are patronized equally; the gospel is common, and hospitality is shared alike by all. The school for the settlers, at Elgin, is so far superior to the one established for white children, that the latter was discontinued, and, as before said, all send together, and visit in common the Presbyterian church, there established. So of Dawn; that settlement is exceedingly flourishing, and the moral influence it exerts is good, though, owing to some recent arrangements, regulations designed to further promote its importance are being made. Land has increased in value in those settlements. Property that was worth but little, from the superior culture given by colored persons over the method before practiced, and the increasing desires for country homes, is held much higher. Another fact that is worth a passing notice, is, that a spirit of competition is alive in their vicinity. Efforts are now put forth to produce more to the acre, and to have the land and tenements present a tidy appearance. That others than those designed to be benefitted by the organization, should be, is not reasonable, else might persons, not members of a society justly claim equal benefits with members. If Irishmen should subscribe to certain regulations on purchasing land, no neighboring landholders could rightfully share with them in the result of that organization. But prejudice would not be the cause of exclusion. So it is of those two settlements; it cannot be said of them, that they are caste institutions, so long as they do not express hostility to the whites; but the question of their necessity in the premises may be raised, and often is, by the settlers in Canada as well as in the States. The "Institution" is a settlement under the direction of the A. M. E. Church; it contains, at present, two hundred acres, and is sold out in ten acre farms, at one dollar and fifty cents per acre, or one shilling less than cost. They have recently opened a school, and there is a log meeting house in an unfinished state, also a burying ground. There are about fifteen families settled on the land, most of whom have cleared away a few trees, but it is not in a very prosperous condition, owing, it is said, to bad management of agents—a result to be looked for when a want of knowledge characterise them. This "Institution" bids fair to be one nucleus around which caste settlements will cluster in Canada.

The Refugees' Home is the last of the settlements of which I may speak in this place. How many others are in contemplation I do not know, though I heard of at least two others. This Society is designed to appropriate fifty thousand acres of land for fugitives from slavery, *only*, but at present the agents have in possession two hundred acres, situated about eight miles from Windsor, in the western district. The plan is to sell farms of twenty-five acres, that is, to give five acres to actual settlers, with the privilege of buying the adjoining twenty acres, at the market value—one-third of the purchase money constitutes a fund for school and other purposes; and ten years are given to pay for the twenty acres, but no interest may accumulate. This society may now be considered in operation, as they have made a purchase, though, as yet, no one has settled thereon, and the results to be looked for from it, from the extent of the field of operations, will have an important bearing on the colored people who are now settled in Canada, or who may emigrate thither. The friends of the society, actuated by benevolent feelings towards victims of American oppression and the odious Fugitive Law, are sanguine as to the success of the measure, but not so universal is the opinion in its favor, even among those designed to be benefitted; in fact, all the objections raised against previously existing settlements, hold good against these, with the additional ones of greater magnitude. It is well known that the Fugitive Bill makes insecure every northern colored man,—those *free* are alike at the risk of being sent south,—consequently, many persons, always free, will leave the United States, and settle in Canada, and other countries, who would have remained had not that law been enacted. In pro-slavery communities, or where colonization influence prevails, they would leave at a sacrifice; they arrive in Canada destitute, in consequence, but may not settle on the land of the Refugees' Home, from the accident of nominal freedom, when it is well known that even slaves south, from the disgrace attending manual labor when performed by whites, have opportunities, in a pecuniary way, that colored men have not in some sections north. Again, the policy of slaveholders has been to create a contempt for *free* people in the bosom of their slaves, and pretty effectually have they succeeded. Their journey to Canada for liberty has not rooted out that prejudice, quite, and reference to a man's birth, as free or slave, is generally made by colored persons, should he not be as prosperous as his better helped fugitive brethren. Thus, discord among members of the same family, is engendered; a breach made, that the exclusive use, by fugitives of the society lands is not likely to mend. Again, the society, with its funds, is looked upon in the light of a powerful rival, standing in the way of poor *free* men, with its ready cash, for its lands will not all be government purchases; neither does it contemplate large blocks, exclusively, but, as in the first purchase, land, wherever found, and in small parcels also. From the exclusive nature of the many settlements, (as fugitive homes,) when it shall be known for what use it is wanted, individual holders will not sell but for more than the real value, thus embarrassing poor men who would have bought on time, and as an able purchaser from government, the society must have a first choice. The objections in common with other settlements, are: the individual supervision of resident agents, and the premium indirectly offered for good behavior. "We are free men," say they who advocate independent effort, "we, as other subjects, are amenable to British laws; we wish to observe and appropriate to ourselves, *ourselves*, whatever of good there is in the society around us, and by our individual efforts, to attain to a respectable position, as do the many foreigners who land on the Canada shores, as poor in purse as we were; and we do not want agents to beg for us." The accompanying are articles in the Constitution:

Article 2. The object of this society shall be to obtain permanent homes for the refugees in Canada, and to promote their moral, social, physical, intellectual, and political elevation.

Article 11. This society shall not deed lands to any but actual settlers, who are refugees from southern slavery, and who are the owners of no land.

Article 12. All lands purchased by this society, shall be divided into twenty-five acre lots, or as near as possible, and at least one-tenth of the purchase price of which shall be paid down by actual settlers before possession is given, and the balance to be paid in equal annual instalments.

Article 13. One-third of all money paid in for land by settlers, shall be used for educational purposes, for the benefit of said settlers' children, and the other two-thirds for the purchase of more lands for the same object, while chattel slavery exists in the United States.

BY-LAWS.

No person shall receive more than five acres of land from this society, at less than cost.

Article 4. No person shall be allowed to remove any timber from said land until they have first made payment thereon.

These are the articles of most importance, and, as will be seen, they contemplate more than fifty thousand acres continual purchases, till slavery shall cease; and other terms, as will be seen by Art. 13 of Con., and Art. 4, By-Laws, than most fugitives just from slavery can comply with, (as destitute women with families, old men, and single women,) until after partial familiarity with their adopted country. This, say many colored Canadians, begins not to benefit until a man has proven his ability to act without aid, and is fit for political equality by his own industry, that money will get for him at any time.

POLITICAL RIGHTS—ELECTION LAW—OATH—CURRENCY.

There is no legal discrimination whatever effecting colored emigrants in Canada, nor from any cause whatever are their privileges sought to be abridged. On taking proper measures, the most ample redress can be obtained. The following "abstracts of acts," bearing equally on all, and observed fully by colored men qualified, will give an idea of the measures given them:*

"The qualifications of voters at municipal elections in townships, are freeholders and householders of the township or ward, entered on the roll for rateable real property, in their own right or that of their wives, as proprietors or tenants, and resident at the time in the township or ward."

"In towns, freeholders and householders for rateable real property in their own names or that of their wives, as proprietors or tenants to the amount of £5 per annum or upwards, resident at the time in the ward. The property qualification of town voters may consist partly of freehold and partly of leasehold."

In villages it is £3 and upwards, with freehold or leasehold; in cities £8.

The laws regulating elections, and relating to electors, are not similar in the two Canadas; but colored persons are not affected by them more than others.

"No person shall be entitled to vote at county elections, who has not vested in him, by legal title, real property in said county of the clear yearly value of forty-four shillings and five pence and one farthing, currency. Title to be in fee simple or freehold under tenure of free and common soccage, or in *fief* in *rature*, or in *franc allen*, or derived from the Governor and Council of the late Province of Quebec, or Act of Parliament. Qualificatiori, to be effective, requires actual and uninterrupted possession on

*Scobies' Canadian Almanac for 1852.

the part of the elector, or that he should have been in receipt of the rents and profits of said property for his own use and benefit at least six months before the date of the writ of election. But the title will be good without such anterior possession, if the property shall have come by inheritance, devise, marriage or contract of marriage, and also if the deed or patent from the Crown on which he holds to claim such estate in Upper Canada, have been registered three calendar months before the date of the writ of election. In Lower Canada, possession of the property under a written promise of sale registered, if not a notarial deed, for twelve months before the election, to be sufficient title to vote. In Upper Canada, a conveyance to wife after marriage must have been registered three calendar months, or husband have been in possession of property six months before election."

"Only British subjects of the full age of twenty-one are allowed to vote. Electors may remove objection by producing certificate, or by taking the oath."

These contain no proscriptive provisions, and there are none. Colored men comply with these provisions and vote in the administration of affairs. There is no difference made whatever; and even in the slight matter of taking the census it is impossible to get at the exact number of whites or colored, as they are not designated as such. There is, it is true, petty jealousy manifested at times by individuals, which is made use of by the designing; but impartiality and strict justice characterise proceedings at law, and the bearing of the laws. The oath, as prescribed by law, is as follows:

"I, A. B., do sincerely promise and swear, that I will bear faithful and true allegiance to Her Majesty Queen Victoria, as lawful Sovereign of the United Kingdom of Great Britian and Ireland, and of this Province of Canada, dependent on and belonging to the said United Kingdom, and that I will defend her to the uttermost of my power against all traitors, conspiracies and attempts whatever which shall be made against Her Person, Crown and Dignity, and that I will do my utmost endeavor to disclose and make known to Her Majesty, Her Heirs and Successors all treasons and traitorous conspiracies and attempts which I shall know to be against Her or any of them, and all this I do swear without any equivocation, mental evasion, or secret reservation, and, renouncing all pardons and dispensations from persons whatever, to the contrary. So help me God."

"The Deputy Returning Officer may administer oath of allegiance to persons who, according to provisions of any Act of Parliament, shall become, on taking such oath, entitled to the privileges of British birth in the Province."

"Persons knowing themselves not to be qualified, voting at elections, incur penalty of £10; and on action brought, the burden of proof shall be on the defendant. Such votes null and void."

"The qualifications of Municipal Councillors are as follows :— Township Councillor must be a freeholder or householder of the township or ward, * * * as proprietor or tenant rated on the roll, in case of a freeholder for £100 or upwards; householder for £200 or upwards: Village Councillor, in case of a freeholder, for £10 or upwards; a householder for £20 and upwards: Town Councillor, in case of a freeholder £20 per annum; if a householder to the amount of £40 and upwards. The property qualification of Town Councillors may be partly freehold and partly leasehold."

A tenant voter in town or city must have occupied by actual residence, as a separate tenant, a dwelling house or houses for twelve months, of the yearly value of £11 2s. 1½d. currency, and have paid a year's rent, or that amount of money for the twelve months immediately preceding the date of election writ. A person holding only a shop or place of business, but not actually residing therein, is not entitled to vote. And a voter having changed his residence within the town during the year, does not affect his right to vote, but must vote in the ward in which he resides on the day.

THE THIRTY THOUSAND COLORED FREEMEN OF CANADA.

The colored subjects of her Majesty in the Canadas are, in the general, in good circumstances, that is, there are few cases of

positive destitution to be found among those permanently settled. They are settled promiscuously in cities, towns, villages,
and the farming districts, and no equal number of colored men
in the States, north or south, can produce more freeholders.
They are settled on, and own portions of the best farming lands
in the province, and own much valuable property in the several
cities, etc. There is, of course, a difference in the relative prosperity and deportment in different sections, but a respect for,
and observance of the laws, is conceded to them by all; indeed,
much indifference on the part of whites has given place to genuine sympathy, and the active abolitionists and liberal men of the
country, look upon that element in their character as affording
ground for hope of a bright future for them, and as evidence
that their sympathy for the *free* man is not misplaced, as more
than compensation for their own exertions for those yet in
bonds. I have said, there is but little actual poverty among
them. They are engaged in the different trades and other manual occupations. They have a paper conducted by the Rev.
Henry Bibb, and other able men, white and colored, are laboring among them, and in view of the protection afforded, there
is no good reason why they should not prosper. After the passage of the fugitive law, the sudden emigration of several thousand in a few months, destitute as they necessarily were, from
having, in many instances, to leave behind them all they possessed, made not a little suffering for a brief period, (only
among them,) and the report of *their* condition had an injurious
bearing upon all the colored settlers. Clothing, provisions, and
other articles were sent them, but often so disposed of, or appropriated, as not to benefit those for whom intended. Distrust
of agents, indiscriminately, and altogether but little real good
has followed from the charity. The sensible men among them,
seeing the bad results from a general character for poverty and
degradation, have not been slow to express their disapproba-
tion in the social circle, in meetings, and through the public papers. The following extracts express fully the sentiments of
nine-tenths of the colored men of Canada; they think they are
fully able to live without begging. There are others (very ignorant people,) who think differently, as there will be in all com-

munities, though they are in the minority. There are those, also, and they are a respectable minority, (in point of numbers,) who are in favor of distinctive churches and schools, and of being entirely to themselves; they will come in for especial notice, but first, let us hear the people of Buxton and other places:

"If facts would bear out the statements made, the fugitives would have little to choose between slavery on one side of the line, and starvation on the other; but we rejoice that he is not reduced to the alternative. The man who is willing to work need not suffer, and unless a man supports himself he will neither be independent nor respectable in any country." * * * "The cry that has been often raised, that we could not support ourselves, is a foul slander, got up by our enemies, and circulated both on this and the other side of the line, to our prejudice. Having lived many years in Canada, we hesitate not to say that all who are able and willing to work, can make a good living." * * * It is time the truth should be known concerning the relief that has been sent to the "suffering fugitives in Canada," and to what extent it has been applied. The boxes of clothing and barrels of provisions which have been sent in, from time to time, by the praiseworthy, but misguided zeal of friends in the United States, has been employed to support the idle, who are too lazy to work, and who form but a small portion of the colored population in Canada. There are upwards of thirty thousand colored persons in Canada West, and not more than three thousand of them have ever received aid, and not more than half of them required it had they been willing to work. We do not think it right that twenty-seven thousand colored persons, who are supporting themselves by their own industry, should lie under the disgrace of being called public beggars, when they receive nothing, and don't want anything. * * We wish the people of the United States to know that there is one portion of Canada West where the colored people are self-supporting, and they wish them to send neither petticoat nor pantaloons to the county of Kent. * * * The few cases of real want which arise from sickness or old age, can, with a trifling effort, be relieved here, without making it a pretext for a system of wholesale begging in the United States."

EDWARD R. GRANTS, ⎫
SAMUEL WICKHAM,   ⎬ Committee.
ROBERT HARRIS.   ⎭

"As to the state of things in Toronto and in Hamilton, I can say, from actual observation, that extreme suffering is scarcely known among the black people, while some who are far from being as industrious and deserving as they ought to be, receive aid to which they would hardly seem entitled."—*S. R. Ward's Letter to the Voice of the Fugitive.*

Notwithstanding the prosperity and liberal sentiment of the majority, there is yet a great deal of ignorance, bigotry, prejudice, and idleness. There are those who are only interested in education so far as the establishment of separate schools, churches, &c., tend to make broad the line of separation they wish to make between them and the whites; and they are active to increase their numbers, and to perpetuate, in the minds of the newly arrived emigrant or refugee, prejudices, originating in slavery, and as strong and objectionable in their manifestations as those entertained by whites towards them. Every casual remark by whites is tortured into a decided and effective negro hate. The expressions of an individual are made to infer the existence of prejudice on the part of the whites, and partiality by the administrators of public affairs. The recently arrived fugitives, unacquainted with the true state of things, is "*completely convinced*" by the noisy philippic against all the "white folks," and all colored ones who think differently from them, and he is thus prepared to aid demagogues in preventing the adoption of proper measures for the spread of education and general intelligence, to maintain an ascendency over the inferior minds around them, and to make the way of the missionary a path of thorns. Among that portion, generally, may those be found, who by their indolent habits, tend to give point to what of prejudice is lingering in the minds of the whites; and it is to be feared that they may take some misguided step now, the consequences of which will entail evil on the many who will hereafter settle in Canada. The only ground of hope is in the native good sense of those who are now making use of the same instrumentalities for improvement as are the whites around them.

THE FRENCH AND FOREIGN POPULATION.

The population of Canada consists of English, Scotch, French, Irish and Americans; and, including colored persons, numbers about 1,582,000. Of the whites, the French are in the majority, but the increasing emigration of Irish, Scotch, English and other Europeans, is fast bringing about an equality in point of numbers that will be felt in political circles. In Canada West the French are in the minority.

The disposition of the people generally towards colored emigrants, that is, so far as the opinions of old settlers may be taken, and my own observation may be allowed, is as friendly as could be looked for under the circumstances. The Yankees, in the country and in the States adjoining, leave no opportunity unimproved to embitter their minds against them. The result is, in some sections, a contemptible sort of prejudice, which, among English, is powerless beyond the individual entertaining it—not even affecting *his circle*. This grows out of the constitution of English society, in which people are not obliged to think as others do. There is more independent thought and free expression than among Americans. The affinity between the Yankees and French is strong; said to grow out of similar intentions with respect to political affairs: and they express most hostility, but it is not of a complexional character only, as that serves as a mark to identify men of a different policy. Leaving out Yankees—having but little practical experience of colored people—they, (the French,) are pre-disposed, from the influence alluded to, to deal roughly with them; but in the main benevolence and a sense of justice are elements in their character. They are not averse to truth. There is a prevailing hostility to chattel slavery, and an honest representation of the colored people: their aims and progressive character, backed by uniform good conduct on their part, would in a very short time destroy every vestige of prejudice in the Province.

"The public mind literally thirsts for the truth, and honest listeners, and anxious inquirers will travel many miles, crowd our country chapels, and remain for hours eagerly and patiently seeking the light. * * * * Let the ignorance now prevalent on the subject of slavery be met by fair and full discussion, and open and thorough investigation, and the apathy and prejudice now existing will soon disappear."—*S. R. Ward.*

Colored persons have been refused entertainment in taverns, (invariably of an inferior class,) and on some boats distinction is made; but in all cases, it is that kind of distinction that is made between poor foreigners and other passengers, on the cars and steamboats of the Northern States. There are the emigrant train and the forward deck in the United States. In Canada, colored persons, holding the same relation to the Canadians, are in some cases treated similarly. It is an easy matter to make out a case of prejudice in any country. We naturally look for it, and the conduct of many is calculated to cause unpleasant treatment, and to make it difficult for well-mannered persons to get comfortable accommodations. There is a medium between servility and presumption, that recommends itself to all persons of common sense, of whatever rank or complexion; and if colored people would avoid the two extremes, there would be but few cases of prejudices to complain of in Canada. In cases in which tavern keepers and other public characters persist in refusing to entertain them, they can, in common with the traveling public generally, get redress at law.

Persons emigrating to Canada, need not hope to find the general state of society as it is in the States. There is as in the old country, a strong class feeling—lines are as completely drawn between the different classes, and aristocracy in the Canadas is the same in its manifestations as aristocracy in England, Scotland and elsewhere. There is no approach to Southern chivalry, nor the sensitive democracy prevalent at the North; but there is an aristocracy of birth, not of skin, as with Americans. In the ordinary arrangements of society from wealthy and titled immigrants and visitors from the mother country, down through the intermediate circles to Yankees and Indians, it appears to have been settled by common consent, that one class should not "see any trouble over another;" but the common ground on which all honest and respectable men meet, is that of innate hatred of American Slavery.

RECAPITULATION.

The conclusion arrived at in respect to Canada, by an impartial person, is, that no settled country in America offers stronger inducements to colored people. The climate is healthy, and they enjoy as good health as other settlers, or as the natives; the soil is of the first quality; the laws of the country give to them, at first, the same protection and privileges as to other persons not born subjects; and after compliance with Acts of Parliament affecting them, as taking oath, &c., they may enjoy full "privileges of British birth in the Province." The general tone of society is healthy; vice is discountenanced, and infractions of the law promptly punished; and, added to this, there is an increasing anti-slavery sentiment, and a progressive system of religion.

MARTIN ROBISON DELANY

A journalist, physician, and abolitionist, Martin Delany (1812–1885) was born free in Charles Town, Virginia. For years, Delany maintained an interest in emigrating to West Africa and was concerned with the liberation and uplift of Black people. A friend and colleague to Frederick Douglass, Delany helped Douglass found the important abolitionist newspaper the North Star *in Rochester, New York, in 1847. The* North Star *centered the voices of Black abolitionists and allowed those with more radical views to make their cases without fear of editorial censorship. In 1850, Delany and two other Black American men were accepted to Harvard Medical School. Within two weeks of their matriculation, all three men were expelled from campus due to racist complaints about their presence. Delany came to the conclusion that there was no future to be had in the United States and that Black nationalism was the political ideology through which all Black people would get free. After spending several years in Canada, Delany returned to the United States to serve in the Civil War and to work for the Freedmen's Bureau in South Carolina during Reconstruction.*

From *The Condition, Elevation, Emigration, and Destiny of the Colored People of the United States, Politically Considered* (1852)

COMPARATIVE CONDITION OF THE COLORED PEOPLE OF THE UNITED STATES.

The United States, untrue to her trust and unfaithful to her professed principles of republican equality, has also pursued a policy of political degradation to a large portion of her native born countrymen, and that class is the Colored People. Denied an equality not only of political, but of natural rights, in common with the rest of our fellow citizens, there is no species of degradation to which we are not subject.

Reduced to abject slavery is not enough, the very thought of which should awaken every sensibility of our common nature; but those of their descendants who are freeman even in the non-slaveholding States, occupy the very same position politically, religiously, civilly and socially, (with but few exceptions,) as the bondman occupies in the slave States.

In those States, the bondman is disfranchised, and for the most part so are we. He is denied all civil, religious, and social privileges, except such as he gets by mere sufferance, and so are we. They have no part nor lot in the government of the country, neither have we. They are ruled and governed without representation, existing as mere nonentities among the citizens, and excrescences on the body politic—a mere dreg in community, and so are we. Where then is our political superiority to the enslaved? none, neither are we superior in any other relation to society, except that we are defacto masters of ourselves and joint rulers of our own domestic household, while the bondman's self is claimed by another, and his relation to his family denied him. What the unfortunate classes are in Europe, such are we in the United States, which is folly to deny, insanity not to understand, blindness not to see, and surely now full time that our eyes were opened to these startling truths, which for ages have stared us full in the face.

It is time that we had become politicians, we mean, to understand the political economy and domestic policy of nations; that we had become as well as moral theorists, also the practical demonstrators of equal rights and self-government. Except we do, it is idle to talk about rights, it is mere chattering for the sake of being seen and heard—like the slave, saying something because his so called "master" said it, and saying just what he told him to say. Have we not now sufficient intelligence among us to understand our true position, to realise our actual condition, and determine for ourselves what is best to be done? If we have not now, we never shall have, and should at once cease prating about our equality, capacity, and all that.

Twenty years ago, when the writer was a youth, his young and yet uncultivated mind was aroused, and his tender heart made to leap with anxiety in anticipation of the promises then held out by the prime movers in the cause of our elevation.

In 1830 the most intelligent and leading spirits among the colored men in the United States, such as James Forten, Robert Douglass, I. Bowers, A. D. Shadd, John Peek, Joseph Cassey, and John B. Vashon of Pennsylvania; John T. Hilton, Nathaniel and Thomas Paul, and James G. Barbodoes of Massachusetts; Henry Sipkins, Thomas Hamilton, Thomas L. Jennings, Thomas Downing, Samuel E. Cornish, and others of New York; R. Cooley and others of Maryland, and representatives from other States which cannot now be recollected, the data not being at hand, assembled in the city of Philadelphia, in the capacity of a National Convention, to "devise ways and means for the bettering of our condition." These Conventions determined to assemble annually, much talent, ability, and energy of character being displayed; when in 1831 at a sitting of the Convention in September, from their previous pamphlet reports, much interest having been created throughout the country, they were favored by the presence of a number of whites, some of whom were able and distinguished men, such as Rev. R. R. Gurley, Arthur Tappan, Elliot Cresson, John Rankin, Simeon Jocelyn and others, among them William Lloyd Garrison, then quite a young man, all of whom were staunch and ardent Colonizationists, young Garrison at that time, doing his mightiest in his favorite work.

Among other great projects of interest brought before the convention at a previous sitting, was that of the expedieney of a general emigration, as far as it was practicable, of the colored people to the British Provinces of North America. Another was that of raising sufficient means for the establishment and erection of a College for the proper education of the colored youth. These gentlemen long accustomed to observation and reflection on the condition of their people, saw at once, that there must necessarily be means used adequate to the end to be attained— that end being an unqualified equality with the ruling class of their fellow citizens. He saw that as a class, the colored people of the country were ignorant, degraded and oppressed, by far the greater portion of them being abject slaves in the South, the

very condition of whom was almost enough, under the circumstances, to blast the remotest hope of success, and those who
were freemen, whether in the South or North, occupied a subservient, servile, and menial position, considering it a favor to
get into the service of the whites, and do their degrading offices.
That the difference between the whites and themselves, consisted
in the superior advantages of the one over the other, in point of
attainments. That if a knowledge of the arts and sciences, the
mechanical occupations, the industrial occupations, as farming,
commerce, and all the various business enterprises, and learned
professions were necessary for the superior position occupied
by their rulers, it was also necessary for them. And very reasonably too, the first suggestion which occurred to them was, the
advantages of a location, then the necessity of a qualification.
They reasoned with themselves, that all distinctive differences
made among men on account of their origin, is wicked, unrigh-
teous, and cruel, and never shall receive countenance in any
shape from us, therefore, the first acts of the measures entered
into by them, was to protest, solemnly protest, against every
unjust measure and policy in the country, having for its object
the proscription of the colored people, whether state, national,
municipal, social, civil, or religious.

But being far-sighted, reflecting, discerning men, they took a
political view of the subject, and determined for the good of
their people to be governed in their policy according to the facts
as they presented themselves. In taking a glance at Europe, they
discovered there, however unjustly, as we have shown in another part of this pamphlet, that there are and have been numerous classes proscribed and oppressed, and it was not for
them to cut short their wise deliberations, and arrest their proceedings in contention, as to the cause, whether on account of
language, the color of eyes, hair, skin, or their origin of country—
because all this is contrary to reason, a contradiction to common sense, at war with nature herself, and at variance with
facts as they stare us every day in the face, among all nations,
in every country—this being made the pretext as a matter of
policy alone—a fact worthy of observation, that wherever the
objects of oppression are the most easily distinguished by any
peculiar or general characteristics, these people are the more

easily oppressed, because the war of oppression is the more easily waged against them. This is the case with the modern Jews
and many other people who have strongly-marked, peculiar, or
distinguishing characteristics. This arises in this wise. The policy of all those who proscribe any people, induces them to select as the objects of proscription, those who differed as much
as possible, in some particulars, from themselves. This is to ensure the greater success, because it engenders the greater prejudice, or in other words, elicits less interest on the part of the
oppressing class, in their favor. This fact is well understood in
national conflicts, as the soldier or civilian, who is distinguished
by his dress, mustache, or any other peculiar appendage, would
certainly prove himself a madman, if he did not take the pre-
caution to change his dress, remove his mustache, and conceal as
much as possible his peculiar characteristics, to give him access
among the repelling party. This is mere policy, nature having
nothing to do with it. Still, it is a fact, a great truth well worthy of
remark, and as such we adduce it for the benefit of those of our
readers, unaccustomed to an enquiry into the policy of nations.

In view of these truths, our fathers and leaders in our elevation, discovered that as a policy, we the colored people were
selected as the subordinate class in this country, not on account
of any actual or supposed inferiority on their part, but simply
because, in view of all the circumstances of the case, they were
the very best class that could be selected. They would have as
readily had any other class as subordinates in the country, as the
colored people, but the condition of society *at the time*, would
not admit of it. In the struggle for American Independence,
there were among those who performed the most distinguished
parts, the most common-place peasantry of the Provinces. English, Danish, Irish, Scotch, and others, were among those whose
names blazoned forth as heroes in the American Revolution. But
a single reflection will convince us, that no course of policy
could have induced the proscription of the parentage and relatives of such men as Benjamin Franklin the printer, Roger Sher-
man the cobbler, the tinkers, and others of the signers of the
Declaration of Independence. But as they were determined to
have a subservient class, it will readily be conceived, that according to the state of society at the time, the better policy on

their part was, to select some class, who from their political position—however much they may have contributed their aid as we certainly did, in the general struggle for liberty by force of arms—who had the least claims upon them, or who had the *least chance*, or was the *least potent* in urging their claims. This class of course was the colored people and Indians.

The Indians who in the early settlement of the continent, before an African captive had ever been introduced thereon, were reduced to the most abject slavery, toiling day and night in the mines, under the relentless hands of heartless Spanish taskmasters, but being a race of people raised to the sports of fishing, the chase, and of war, were wholly unaccustomed to labor, and therefore sunk under the insupportable weight, two millions and a half having fallen victims to the cruelty of oppression and toil suddenly placed upon their shoulders. And it was only this that prevented their farther enslavement as a class, after the provinces were absolved from the British Crown. It is true that their general enslavement took place on the islands and in the mining districts of South America, where indeed, the Europeans continued to enslave them, until a comparatively recent period; still, the design, the feeling, and inclination from policy, was the same to do so here, in this section of the continent.

Nor was it until their influence became too great, by the political position occupied by their brethren in the new republic, that the German and Irish peasantry ceased to be sold as slaves for a term of years fixed by law, for the repayment of their passage-money, the descendants of these classes of people for a long time being held as inferiors, in the estimation of the ruling class, and it was not until they assumed the rights and privileges guaranteed to them by the established policy of the country, among the leading spirits of whom were their relatives, that the policy towards them was discovered to be a bad one, and accordingly changed. Nor was it, as is frequently very erroneously asserted, by colored as well as white persons, that it was on account of hatred to the African, or in other words, on account of hatred to his color, that the African was selected as the subject of oppression in this country. This is sheer nonsense; being based on policy and nothing else, as shown in another place. The Indians, who being the most foreign to the sympathies of the Europeans on this continent, were selected in the first place, who, being unable to withstand the hardships, gave way before them.

But the African race had long been known to Europeans, in all ages of the world's history, as a long-lived, hardy race, subject to toil and labor of various kinds, subsisting mainly by traffic, trade, and industry, and consequently being as foreign to the sympathies of the invaders of the continent as the Indians, they were selected, captured, brought here as a laboring class, and as a matter of policy held as such. Nor was the absurd idea of natural inferiority of the African ever dreamed of, until recently adduced by the slave-holders and their abettors, in justification of their policy. This, with contemptuous indignation, we fling back into their face, as a scorpion to a vulture. And so did our patriots and leaders in the cause of regeneration know better, and never for a moment yielded to the base doctrine. But they had discovered the great fact, that a cruel policy was pursued towards our people, and that they possessed distinctive characteristics which made them the objects of proscription. These characteristics being strongly marked in the colored people, as in the Indians, by color, character of hair and so on, made them the more easily distinguished from other Americans, and the policies more effectually urged against us. For this reason they introduced the subject of emigration to Canada, and a proper institution for the education of the youth.

At this important juncture of their proceedings, the afore named white gentlemen were introduced to the notice of the Convention, and after gaining permission to speak, expressed their gratification and surprise at the qualification and talent manifested by different members of the Convention, all expressing their determination to give the cause of the colored people more serious reflection. Mr. Garrison, the youngest of them all, and none the less honest on account of his youthfulness, being but 26 years of age at the time, (1831) expressed his determination to change his course of policy at once, and espouse the cause of the elevation of the colored people here in their own country. We are not at present well advised upon this point, it now having escaped our memory, but we are under the impression that Mr. Jocelyn also, at once changed his policy.

During the winter of 1832, Mr. Garrison issued his "Thoughts on African Colonization," and near about the same time or shortly after, issued the first number of the "Liberator," in both of which, his full convictions of the enormity of American slavery, and the wickedness of their policy towards the colored people, were fully expressed. At the sitting of the Convention in this year, a number, perhaps all of these gentlemen were present, and those who had denounced the Colonization scheme, and espoused the cause of the elevation of the colored people in this country, or the Anti Slavery cause, as it was now termed, expressed themselves openly and without reserve.

Sensible of the high-handed injustice done to the colored people in the United States, and the mischief likely to emanate from the unchristian proceedings of the deceptious Colonization scheme, like all honest hearted penitents, with the ardor only known to new converts, they entreated the Convention, whatever they did, not to entertain for a moment, the idea of recommending emigration to their people, nor the establishment of separate institutions of learning. They earnestly contended, and doubtless honestly meaning what they said, that they (the whites) had been our oppressors and injurers, they had obstructed our progress to the high positions of civilization, and now, it was their bounden duty to make full amends for the injuries thus inflicted on an unoffending people. They exhorted the Convention to cease; as they had laid on the burden, they would also take it off; as they had obstructed our pathway, they would remove the hindrance. In a word, as they had oppressed and trampled down the colored people, they would now elevate them. These suggestions and promises, good enough to be sure, after they were made, were accepted by the Convention—though some gentlemen were still in favor of the first project as the best policy, Mr. A. D. Shadd of West Chester, Pa., as we learn from himself, being one among that number—ran through the country like wild-fire, no one thinking, and if he thought, daring to speak above his breath of going any where out of certain prescribed limits, or of sending a child to school, if it should but have the name of "colored" attached to it, without the risk of being termed a "traitor" to the cause of his people, or an enemy to the Anti Slavery cause.

At this important point in the history of our efforts, the colored men stopped suddenly, and with their hands thrust deep in their breeches-pockets, and their mouths gaping open, stood gazing with astonishment, wonder, and surprise, at the stupendous moral colossal statues of our Anti-Slavery friends and brethren, who in the heat and zeal of honest hearts, from a desire to make atonement for the many wrongs inflicted, promised a great deal more than they have ever been able half to fulfill, in thrice the period in which they expected it. And in this, we have no fault to find with our Anti-Slavery friends, and here wish it to be understood, that we are not laying any thing to their charge as blame, neither do we desire for a moment to reflect on them, because we heartily believe that all that they did at the time, they did with the purest and best of motives, and further believe that they now are, as they then were, the truest friends we have among the whites in this country. And hope, and desire, and request, that our people should always look upon *true* anti-slavery people, Abolitionists we mean, as their friends, until they have just cause for acting otherwise. It is true, that the Anti-Slavery, like all good causes, has produced some recreants, but the cause itself is no more to be blamed for that, than Christianity is for the malconduct of any professing hypocrite, nor the society of Friends, for the conduct of a broad-brimmed hat and shad-belly coated horse-thief, because he spoke *thee* and *thou* before stealing the horse. But what is our condition even amidst our Anti-Slavery friends? And here, as our sole intention is to contribute to the elevation of our people, we must be permitted to express our opinion freely, without being thought uncharitable.

In the first place, we should look at the objects for which the Anti-Slavery cause was commenced, and the promises or inducements it held out at the commencement. It should be borne in mind, that Anti-Slavery took its rise among *colored men*, just at the time they were introducing their greatest projects for their own elevation, and that our Anti-Slavery brethren were converts of the colored men, in behalf of their elevation. Of course, it would be expected that being baptized into the new doctrines, their faith would induce them to embrace the principles therein contained, with the strictest possible adherence.

The cause of dissatisfaction with our former condition, was, that we were proscribed, debarred, and shut out from every respectable position, occupying the places of inferiors and menials.

It was expected that Anti-Slavery, according to its professions, would extend to colored persons, as far as in the power of its adherents, those advantages nowhere else to be obtained among white men. That colored boys would get situations in their shops and stores, and every other advantage tending to elevate them as far as possible, would be extended to them. At least, it was expected, that in Anti-Slavery establishments, colored men would have the preference. Because, there was no other ostensible object in view, in the commencement of the Anti-Slavery enterprise, than the *elevation* of the *colored man*, by facilitating his efforts in attaining to equality with the white man. It was urged, and it was true, that the colored people were susceptible of all that the whites were, and all that was required was to give them a fair opportunity, and they would prove their capacity. That it was unjust, wicked, and cruel, the result of an unnatural prejudice, that debarred them from places of respectability, and that public opinion could and should be corrected upon this subject. That it was only necessary to make a sacrifice of feeling, and an innovation on the customs of society, to establish a different order of things,—that as Anti-Slavery men, they were willing to make these sacrifices, and determined to take the colored man by the hand, making common cause with him in affliction, and bear a part of the odium heaped upon him. That his cause was the cause of God—that "In as much as ye did it not unto the least of these my little ones, ye did it not unto me," and that as Anti-Slavery men, they would "do right if the heavens fell." Thus, was the cause espoused, and thus did we expect much. But in all this, we were doomed to disappointment, sad, sad disappointment. Instead of realising what we had hoped for, we find ourselves occupying the very same position in relation to our Anti-Slavery friends, as we do in relation to the pro-slavery part of the community—a mere secondary, underling position, in all our relations to them, and any thing more than this, is not a matter of course affair—it comes not by established anti-slavery custom or right, but like that which emanates from the proslavery portion of the community, by mere sufferance.

It is true, that the "Liberator" office, in Boston, has got Elijah Smith, a colored youth, at the cases—the "Standard," in New York, a young colored man, and the "Freeman," in Philadelphia, William Still, another, in the publication office, as "packing clerk;" yet these are but three out of the hosts that fill these offices in their various departments, all occupying places that could have been, and as we once thought, would have been, easily enough, occupied by colored men. Indeed, we can have no other idea about anti-slavery in this country, than that the legitimate persons to fill any and every position about an anti-slavery establishment are colored persons. Nor will it do to argue in extenuation, that white men are as justly entitled to them as colored men; because white men do not from *necessity* become anti-slavery men in order to get situations; they being white men, may occupy any position they are capable of filling—in a word, their chances are endless, every avenue in the country being opened to them. They do not therefore become abolitionists, for the sake of employment—at least, it is not the song that anti-slavery sung, in the first love of the new faith, proclaimed by its disciples.

And if it be urged that colored men are incapable as yet to fill these positions, all that we have to say is, that the cause has fallen far short; almost equivalent to a failure, of a tithe, of what it promised to do in half the period of its existence, to this time, if it have not as yet, now a period of twenty years, raised up colored men enough, to fill the offices within its patronage. We think it is not unkind to say, if it had been half as faithful to itself, as it should have been—its professed principles we mean; it could have reared and tutored from childhood, colored men enough by this time, for its own especial purpose. These we know could have been easily obtained, because colored people in general, are favorable to the anti-slavery cause, and wherever there is an adverse manifestation, it arises from sheer ignorance; and we have now but comparatively few such among us. There is one thing certain, that no colored person, except such as would reject education altogether, would be adverse to putting their child with an anti-slavery person, for educational advantages. This then, could have been done. But it has not been done, and let the cause of it be whatever it may, and let whoever may be to blame, we are willing to let all that pass, and extend to our anti-slavery brethren the right-hand of fellowship, bidding them God-speed in the propagation of good and wholesome sentiments—for whether they are practically carried out or not, the professions are in themselves all right and good. Like Christianity, the principles are holy and of divine origin. And we believe, if ever a man started right, with pure and holy motives, Mr. Garrison did; and that, had he the power of making the cause what it should be, it would all be right, and there never would have been any cause for the remarks we have made, though in kindness, and with the purest of motives. We are nevertheless, still occupying a miserable position in the community, wherever we live; and what we most desire is, to draw the attention of our people to this fact, and point out what, in our opinion, we conceive to be a proper remedy.

AMERICAN COLONIZATION.

When we speak of colonization, we wish distinctly to be understood, as speaking of the "American Colonization Society"—or that which is under its influence—commenced in Richmond, Virginia, in 1817, under the influence of Mr. Henry Clay of Ky., Judge Bushrod Washington of Va., and other Southern slaveholders, having for their express object, as their speeches and doings all justify us in asserting in good faith, the removal of the free colored people from the land of their birth, for the security of the slaves, as property to the slave propagandists.

This scheme had no sooner been propagated, than the old and leading colored men of Philadelphia, Pa., with Richard Allen, James Forten, and others at their head, true to their trust and the cause of their brethren, summoned the colored people together, and then and there, in language and with voices pointed and loud, protested against the scheme as an outrage, having no other object in view, than the benefit of the slaveholding interests of the country, and that as freemen, they would never prove recreant to the cause of their brethren in bondage, by leaving them without hope of redemption from their chains. This determination of the colored patriots of Philadelphia was published in full, authentically, and circulated throughout the length and breadth of the country by the papers of the day. The colored people every where received the news, and at once endorsed with heart and soul, the doings of the Anti-Colonization Meeting of colored freemen. From that time forth, the colored people generally have had no sympathy with the colonization scheme, nor confidence in its leaders, looking upon them all, as arrant hypocrites, seeking every opportunity to deceive them. In a word, the monster was crippled in its infancy, and has never as yet recovered from the stroke. It is true, that like its ancient sire, that was "more subtile than all the beasts of the field," it has inherited a large portion of his most prominent characteristic—an idiosyncrasy with the animal— that enables him to entwine himself into the greater part of the Church and other institutions of the country, which having once entered there, leaves his venom, which put such a spell on the conductors of those institutions, that it is only on condition that a colored person consents to go to the neighborhood of his kindred brother monster the boa, that he may find admission in the one or the other. We look upon the American Colonization Society as one of the most arrant enemies of the colored man, ever seeking to discomfit him, and envying him of every privilege that he may enjoy. We believe it to be anti-Christian in its character, and misanthropic in its pretended sympathies. Because if this were not the case, men could not be found professing morality and Christianity—as to our astonishment we have found them—who unhesitatingly say, "I know it is right"—that is in itself—"to do" so and so, "and I am willing and ready to do it, but only on condition, that you go to Africa." Indeed, a highly talented clergyman, informed us in November last (three months ago) in the city of Philadelphia, that he was present when the Rev. Doctor J. P. Durbin, late President of Dickinson College, called on Rev. Mr. P. of B., to consult him about going to Liberia, to take charge of the literary department of an University in contemplation, when the following conversation ensued: Mr. P.—"Doctor, I have as much and more than I can do here, in educating the youth of our own country, and preparing them for usefulness here at home." Dr. D.—"Yes, but do as you may, you can never be elevated here." Mr. P.—"Doctor, do you not believe that the religion of our blessed Redeemer Jesus Christ, has morality, humanity, philanthropy, and justice enough in it to elevate us, and enable us to obtain our rights in this our own country?" Dr. D.—"No, indeed, sir, I do not, and if you depend upon that, your hopes are vain!" Mr. P.—Turning to Doctor Durbin, looking him solemnly, though affectionately in the face, remarked—"Well, Doctor Durbin, we both profess to be ministers of Christ; but dearly as I love the cause of my Redeemer, if for a moment, I could entertain the opinion you do about Christianity, I would not serve him another hour!" We do not know, as we were not advised, that the Rev. doctor added in fine,—"Well, you may quit now, for all your serving him will not avail against the power of the god (hydra) of Colonization." Will any one doubt for a single moment, the justice of our strictures on colonization, after reading the conversation between the Rev. Dr. Durbin and the colored clergyman? Surely not. We can therefore make no account of it, but that of setting it down as being the worst enemy of the colored people.

Recently, there has been a strained effort in the city of New York on the part of the Rev. J. B. Pinney and others, of the leading white colonizationists, to get up a movement among some poor pitiable colored men—we say pitiable, for certainly the colored persons who are at this period capable of loaning themselves to the enemies of their race, against the best interest of all that we hold sacred to that race, are pitiable in the lowest extreme, far beneath the dignity of an enemy, and therefore, we pass them by with the simple remark, that this is the hobby that colonization is riding all over the country, as the "tremendous" access of colored people to their cause within the last twelve months. We should make another remark here perhaps, in jus tification of governor Pinney's New York allies—that is, report says, that in the short space of some three or five months, one of his confidants, benefited himself to the "reckoning" of from eleven to fifteen hundred dollars, or "such a matter, "while others were benefited in sums "pretty considerable" but of a less "reckoning." Well, we do not know after all, that they may not have quite as good a right, to pocket part of the spoils of this "grab game," as any body else. However, they are of little consequence, as the ever watchful eye of those excellent gentlemen and faithful guardians of their people's rights—the *Committee of Thirteen*, consisting of Messrs. John J. Zuille, *Chairman*, T. Joiner White, Philip A. Bell, *Secretaries*, Robert Hamilton, George T. Downing, Jeremiah Powers, John T. Raymond, Wm. Burnett, James McCuen Smith, Ezekiel Dias, Junius C. Morel, Thomas Downing, and Wm. J. Wilson, have properly chastised this pet-slave of Mr. Pinney, and made it "know its place," by keeping within the bounds of its master's enclosure.

In expressing our honest conviction of the designedly injurious character of the Colonization Society, we should do violence to our own sense of individual justice, if we did not express the belief, that there are some honest hearted men, who not having seen things in the proper light, favor that scheme, simply as a means of elevating the colored people. Such persons, so soon as they become convinced of their error, immediately change their policy, and advocate the elevation of the colored people, anywhere and everywhere, in common with other men. Of such were the early abolitionists as before stated; and the great and good Dr. F. J. Lemoyne, Gerrit Smith, and Rev. Charles Avery, and a host of others, who were Colonizationists, before espousing the cause of our elevation, here at home, and nothing but an honorable sense of justice, induces us to make these exceptions, as there are many good persons within our knowledge, whom we believe to be well wishers of the colored people, who may favor colonization.* But the animal itself is the same "hydra-headed monster," let whomsoever may fancy

---

*Benjamin Coates, Esq., a merehant of Philadelphia, we believe to be an honest hearted man, and real friend of the colored people, and a true, though as yet, rather undecided philanthropist. Mr. Coates, to our knowledge, has supported three or four papers published by colored men, for the elevation of colored people in the United States, and given, as he continues to do, considerable sums to their support. We have recently learned from himself, that, though he still advocates Colonization, simply as a means of elevating the colored race of the United States, that he has *left* the Colonization Society, and prefers seeing colored people located on this continent, to going to Liberia, or elsewhere off of it—though his zeal for the enlightenment of Africa, is unabated, as every good man's should be; and we are satisfied, that Mr. Coates is neither well understood, nor rightly appreciated by the friends of our cause. One thing we do know, that he left the Colonization Society, because he could not conscientiously subscribe to its measures.

to pet it. A serpent is a serpent, and none the less a viper, because nestled in the bosom of an honest hearted man. This the colored people must bear in mind, and keep clear of the hideous thing, lest its venom may be tost upon them. But why deem any argument necessary to show the unrighteousness of colonization? Its very origin as before shown—the source from whence it sprung, being the offspring of slavery—is in itself, sufficient to blast it in the estimation of every colored person in the United States, who has sufficient intelligence to comprehend it.

We dismiss this part of the subject, and proceed to consider the mode and means of our elevation in the United States.

JAMES W. C. PENNINGTON

*James W. C. Pennington (1807–1870) was an abolitionist,
pastor, and writer who escaped slavery in Maryland, fleeing to Pennsylvania, where he was taken care of and taught
by members of the Quaker community. Pennington later
moved to Long Island, New York, where he worked as a
blacksmith and continued his education. Pennington was
the first Black person to attend courses at Yale University,
where he could not enroll officially because of strict racial
codes. Yale's administrators instead allowed him to sit in
on divinity courses for three years. Afterward, Pennington
served as an ordained minister at churches across the United
States and later completed tours on the antislavery lecture
circuit in England. Pennington published his personal narrative of slavery,* The Fugitive Blacksmith, *in 1834 and a history of Black Americans entitled* A Text Book of the Origin
and History of the Colored People *in 1841. In recognition of
his fervent abolitionist organizing, the Connecticut Anti-
Slavery Society appointed Pennington as a delegate for the
World Anti-Slavery Conference in 1843. In his speech "The
Reasonableness of the Abolition of Slavery at the South,"
Pennington builds a historical argument against naysayers
who believed that abolishing slavery in the United States
was impossible. Using a comparative lens to demonstrate
how enslaved people and activists were able to compel the
eradication of slavery in other nations, Pennington asserts
"with the Bible and the Declaration of Independence for
our weapons, we will make a bold push" in the struggle for
abolition.*

From *The Reasonableness of the Abolition of Slavery at the South, a Legitimate Inference from the Success of British Emancipation. An Address, Delivered at Hartford, Connecticut, on the First of August, 1856*

(1856)

REIGN OF TERROR.

In 1769, occurred the Somerset case. James Somerset was taken by his master, Charles Stewart, from Jamaica to London, and having absconded, he was seized and carried by force on board of a vessel, with intent to transport him back to the island.*

This case was tested on this question, *whether a slave by coming into England became free.* It was argued three times by Glynn, Davy, Hargrave, and Mansfield, and twice decided against them. The third time the decision was that *"as soon as any slave touched English soil he became free whether baptized or not!"*

This decision was in 1772, and was gained after a struggle of forty-three years.

*Since the 'Address' was in type we have seen a biographical memoir of Granville Sharp, in which a different version is given of the 'Somerset case,' which we subjoin. "A negro, named Somerset, who had been brought by his master, from the West Indies, and turned into the streets, in consequence of illness, was placed by Mr. Sharp in Bartholomew's Hospital, and on his restoration to health, established by his benefactor in a comfortable situation. His former master on ascertaining this, thought proper to seize him, and commit him to prison as a runaway slave, when Mr. Sharp brought the case before the Lord Mayor, who decided in favor of the slave's freedom. His inhuman master, however, grasping him by the collar, and attempting to detain him, Mr. Sharp commenced an action against the former, in the Court of King's Bench; and the result was, by a decision of the twelve judges, that slavery could not exist in Great Britain."

Having now driven slavery from the metropolis, the spirit of abolitionism began to look out upon slavery and the slave-trade with indomitable energy.

The year of 1785 presents us with another matter of interest. A voice came forth from the university of Cambridge, which has sounded long and loud even to this day.

The vice-chancellor, Dr. Peckhard, gave out for prize essays the question, *"An liceat invitas in servitutem dare?"* "Is it right to make slaves of others against their will?"

Thomas Clarkson was a competitor for the prize, and while treating the question as a literary one, he was led so deeply into its moral character, that while he obtained the prize, he established his own convictions in favor of the rights of the slave.

Two years after this, in 1787, we have the formation of the committee to promote the abolition of the slave-trade, with Mr. Wilberforce for its parliamentary head, and Mr. Clarkson for agent.

And now commenced the struggle which ended in the abolition of the slave-trade in 1807.

This glance is important, as it shows how the abolitionists prepared themselves, step by step, to attack slavery in the colonies. For forty-three years they battled slavery in the metropolis; thirty-five years they wrestled with the slave-trade, and thirty-one years conflict had they with slavery in the colonies, making one hundred and nine years from the adverse decision of Talbot, to the memorable first of August, 1838.

Symptoms of parturition exhibited themselves in 1834, but emancipation was not fully developed until 1838, when the experiment attained its full growth by the abolition of the apprenticeship system.

1. THE CHARACTER OF OUR EVENT.

In looking at the character of this event, we must notice the precise point at issue during the controversy pending its discussion.

It was a question as to the right or wrong of slavery. They began, continued and ended with this question, Is slavery right, or is it wrong? The abolitionists, of course, took the ground that it was wrong, and they made progress just in proportion as they proved to the sober views of the community, that their position was correct.

This was the identical question discussed by Mr. Clarkson in his essay. It has been found even in the most corrupt ages of the world, that when a question is placed fairly before the moral vision of men, it will seldom fail to be decided according to its true character.

The British abolitionists understood this, and they were ever vigilant to guide their question to its true issue. They displayed their talents and energy in collecting and arranging their anti-slavery facts so as to carry the question home to the moral feelings of the nation.

The West India emancipation was a response to the question which they had faithfully and skillfully pressed home; a response too in the negative.

Their opponents had sought at various times, and by various means, to throw a shade of contempt upon them. It was said that they were men of one idea, and of one song, and that that one idea and one song had grown threadbare upon their lips; a stereotyped saying that has been taken from the vile vocabulary of those transatlantic abusers of good men, to fix on abolitionists of our own day and country.

But though it is difficult to conceive how a man with any tolerable share of intellect can have less than *two* IDEAS, at least, yet if we were driven to the alternative, we would much rather have *one* good idea of humanity, and live and die vindicating that, than to have ten thousand of cruelty and blood, such as fill a slaveholder's mind.

Yes, let it be one IDEA; and let it, like the mustard in our Saviour's parable, be the smallest of all seed; only let it be carefully sown, though in tears, as well as scorn and ignominy; and let it be carefully cultivated, and in due time the birds of the air may have a jubilee in its branches, while the care-worn prisoner may shade himself beneath it.

One idea! Would you not know, Mr. caviler, that no idea of human liberty can be fruitless or prove abortive? Not an argument used by the British abolitionists for the half century next preceding the event we are this day commemorating, had failed of its object, but had established itself immovably in the moral convictions of the nation. As evidence of this, when just previous to 1834, they made a bold push for the issue, the question was so well understood by the men, women and children of the nation, and its character was so well appreciated, that their opponents could not slide in a false issue, nor could they divert the minds of the people from the true and proper point, "Is it right to make slaves of others against their will? Is it right to continue men in slavery who have lost their liberty by no crime of their own?"

As the question came up for adjudication, the ground was disputed inch by inch, and the abolitionists did not stop to ask who had a vested property in the slave, whether king, royal dukes, lords or commoners. Nor did they stay to ask who had been silly enough to set his death-palsied hand to an instrument leaving the estate of his widow and children vested in the bones and blood of God's poor. They did not regard the argument predicated upon the fact that slavery bore "the date of days of older times," nor yet the objection that it was sanctified by legislation.

They condemned slavery in all its length and its breadth—in its total character. They pushed their arguments to the throne, and they spoke in thunder-tones to the parliament, DECLARING, that the enslavement of men is a monstrous crime, which endangers the very existence of a nation, by exposing it to the wrath of heaven; that freedom is the slave's birth right; that the only way to do him justice is to set him free immediately and unconditionally; that the slave's ignorance which has been entailed upon him by slavery, is no argument for delaying his emancipation; that whatever preparation he may need for freedom, can not be made while in a state of slavery. And moreover, that as the best way to fit a man for slavery is to place him in a state of slavery, so the best way to fit a man for freedom is to lay upon him the responsibility of acting the part of a free man.

THE APPRENTICESHIP SYSTEM, with the twenty millions of pounds sterling, was no part of the plan of British abolitionists. They were political expedients of the government to appease the planters.

The abolitionists accepted the apprenticeship system rather than delay their success, and the twenty millions, to show that they had no ill-will toward the planters. When they came out with a long and mournful face, pleading ruin and bankruptcy, the abolitionists were willing to let them succeed in begging the twenty millions as a boon of pecuniary salvation. But when the abolitionists found that the apprenticeship system did not work well, they treated it as David treated Saul's armor, they put it off.

Taking a suggestion from the wise course of Antigua and Bermuda, which dispensed with the apprenticeship system on the first of August, 1834, the abolitionists began a new campaign, and gained a new victory. The plan of apprenticeship was to have extended to the first of August, 1840, but they cut it short by two years. God wrought wonderfully.

II. THE MAGNITUDE OF OUR EVENT.

In speaking of the magnitude of the event we commemorate, we shall do well to advert to the geographical locality of its birthplace. That grand string of islands lying partly in the Atlantic ocean, and partly in the Caribbean sea, constituting the great islanded pathway between the northern and southern hemispheres of the western continent; belting the shore from Florida, the great toe of the United States, down to the neck and shoulders of South America, were selected, in the wisdom of God, to be the theater of this moral drama; and the varied character of these islands,—of their inhabitants,—relative location, their distance from the mother country, and their adjacency as a whole, to the United States, where the strength and struggle of the battle of liberty was next to be fought, all fitted them to give greater importance to the event than would have attended it had it taken place in some one solitary state.

Again, the number of subjects in this drama are to be taken into the account in estimating its magnitude.

The world had seen no similar event upon so large a scale, since the exit of the Jews out of Egypt.

The world had seen thirty thousand Hottentots emancipated

at Cape Colony; we have seen eighty-five thousand set free at
Guadaloupe, and six hundred thousand at St. Domingo. But as
the first two instances bear no resemblance to the one we are des-
canting on, in point of numbers, so the last bears none in some
important respects, for those men put off the chains, to put on
the knapsack:—they laid down the hoe, to take up the musket.

THE MORAL MAGNITUDE is what most intensely ad-
dresses itself to the sympathies of the philanthropist. Eight hundred thousand divided into at least one hundred thousand
families, each with a united head of a father and a mother,
whose hearts were full of affections; hearts that had suffered
cruelties untold by mortal tongue.

But on this auspicious day, the arms of the father and mother
were unshackled, to embrace each the other, and their children.

It was a convocation of families, a jubilee of their united
members; and there was a long and loud chorus of music, in
which the melodious voice of the mother, and thrill lisping of
the child, were happily mingled with the deeper intonations
of the father.

What a change thus came over their prospects! The music of
the cart-whip is swept away; the clanking of the chain is heard
no more, nor the cry of the brokenhearted. These and kindred
horrors belong to by-gone days, and a record of them, will not,
in future, disgrace the page of history.

Chapels were now open, but no arsenals; ministers of the
gospel had enough to do, but it was a holiday for military officers and magistrates.

III. GOD WORKS WONDERFULLY IN
THE TENDENCY OF THIS EVENT.

This event having come down to us through a train of other significant incidents, affording indisputable and satisfactory evidence of the approbation of God, and indubitable proof of the
complete success of our coadjutors, the British abolitionists, we
may hail it as another bright chapter of proof-texts to which we
may refer the American objector.

If the stubborn adherent to, and advocate of slavery wishes to know what we mean by immediate emancipation, we ask him to read this chapter.

If he talks bloodshed and murder, we ask him to read this chapter, and tell how much blood he finds in it. Nay did not this event blot out the blood which had stained the land before? Murder or homicide may have been the result of slavery, but never of emancipation. Does he talk about the slaves not being capable of taking care of themselves? We only ask him to review and study this chapter, and see how much pauperism it has inflicted upon Great Britain. We can but rejoice in the happy results of this benevolent achievement, as affording the most satisfactory proof that not only did no ill consequences follow West Indian emancipation, but that it led to a vast amount of good; and that it therefore presents the best argument why it should take place in this our land.

Nor can we be driven from the proud estimate we place upon this striking event by the caviling exceptions taken to the political motives of Great Britain.

It is neither my province nor my object to defend the motives of Great Britain. A nation of such eminence, and possessing such an amount of political and judicial wisdom, together with the experience of nearly a thousand years, is abundantly competent to the task of defending herself.

But as it has pleased God to honor her before all the nations, as the instrument to accomplish this great event, we may congratulate her upon the success of her abolition measure, while the powerful and even dangerous combination of the West India interest, or rather prejudice was against it, and while the political prayers of France, Denmark, Sweden, Spain, Portugal, Holland, and our own United States, were mingling in unhallowed unison to the god of slavery (if it has any) for its failure.

No, the truth is, all this shows that the event was a Godsend; we care not what the motives of Great Britain were; and we may add that the more British duplicity our opponents can sift out of it, the more they establish God's agency in our behalf, and better would emancipation be for them too, if they had the good sense to see it; but the scales may some day fall from their eyes, and then they will perhaps give us credit for the truth of our prophecy.

This great experiment, as it is called, is now upon the wings of the universal winds that waft the merchant and the missionary-ship away to distant lands, and as the news is thus spread, it bespeaks the gradual but certain approach of ultimate success to the cause of human liberty in every land.

Let no abolitionist in our land be ashamed of his name, or afraid of his acts. Many years ago Thomas Clarkson began his labors in the cause of emancipation, and like his fellow-laborers in the same holy enterprise, his motives were impugned, and his life endangered. With the thrilling vivacity of an old man made young by the inspiration of his theme, he related to us some years ago, the circumstance of the attempt to throw him off the dock at Liverpool, while he was engaged in collecting facts to expose the slave-trade. "But," said he, "I think myself to have been called to suffer such reproach, and happy am I that I have been spared to see this cause crowned with such abundant success. The slave in my own country is free, and I am now watching the progress of the cause in your country and the world; I can do but little more; I am an old man. But the cause has so far advanced, and is in such good hands, that I feel perfectly willing to leave the stage. It must prevail."

Tyrants, look on and prepare to resign your long abused power. Whoever had more power over a slave than the British slaveholder? Not even Nero himself. He was fortified by royal patronage, wealth and nobility. Dukes, lords and commoners were his partners in the commerce of blood. The British lion, with horrid teeth and claws, was his ally; the ships of the royal navy, and the regiments of the imperial army were his defense. God wrought wonderfully, and he resigned. But oh, he says, I am ruined. He goes grumbling about, with long face and droning voice, "I am ruined; my West India interests are destroyed."

What does he mean? He can't sit quite so easy in his easy chair. He can't find those hogsheads of sugar which used to fill that coffer with sovereigns. His wine money gone; his horse-race money; his coach and four money; his traveling money.

What slave in ours or any other country need despair of liberty since the British slave has gone free! His case was a desperate one; literally imprisoned in the sea, dark waters were the boundary of his habitation of sorrow. No free States or Canadas bounded him on either side, to which he could fly.

But God, who ordained that the isles should wait for his law, enforced that law in due season. That law came on the auspicious first of August, 1838; and then broke forth from the islands in the sea the triumphal song,—"Sound the loud timbrel over India's dark sea; Jehovah hath triumphed, his people are free!"

The law came, and it restored the bondman his body; his body that was marked, bruised and lacerated; but it *was* his body, dear to him still, as was the body of his oppressor to *him*, whose skin had never been broken by the scratch of a pin. The law came, and the bondman received back his soul; his soul long benighted and vexed, but it was still his soul, possessed of its own immortality, an immortality of which the cart-whip and other instruments of torture, plied with deadly effect to the body that enshrined it, could not divest it.

And here is an eternal truth that is destined to beat away every refuge of lies that can be brought by the ingenuity of critics, tyrants and cavilers, to support slavery. When you have made of man a slave by a seven-fold process of selling, bartering and chaining, and garnished him with that rough and bloody brush, the cart-whip, and set him to the full by blowing into the eyes of his mind cloud after cloud of moral darkness, his own immortality still remains. Subtract from him what you *can*, immortality still remains; and this is a weapon in the bosom of the slave which is more terrible and terrifying to the slaveholder than the thunder of triumphal artillery in the ears of a retreating army. At every stripe of the cart-whip there is a plaintive shriek which betokens the inwardly dwelling immortality of the soul.

The law of 1838 came, and the bondman received back his wife, his children, his Bible, his Sabbath, his sanctuary.

Oh, what moral sublimity is here, when the law spoke with such stern eloquence to the tyrant, in regard to the personal liberty and rights of the slave, and the mandate was, *"give them, give them back!"* and when the man of chains and stripes came forth, and reached out his hand to receive the precious trust!

How was he to act? How did he act? How has he acted since? How is he acting to-day?

Echo, songs of praise; echo, ye sacred chapels; echo, school houses; echo, ye railroads of beautiful cottages; ye villages, VICTORIA and WILBERFORCE; echo, ye colored magistrates, lawyers, merchants, members of assembly, governors and secretaries, and still the echo comes, how are they acting? Look over and see. Then let us make a bold push, for our day is hard by. We devote this day to rejoice with the West India freedman. When it has passed, we will go down again like "good Samaritans," and put our shoulder close by the American slave, and make, we say, a bold push for *his* day. With the Bible and the Declaration of Independence for our weapons, we will make a bold push, for the day begins. In the course of events, it dawns. The fruitful womb of time is already pregnant with another heir, and *that* heir is ours. The last was born yonder, but the next shall be born here. They tell us that slavery is here, and that it must remain; and that it is useless to discuss it. So say the public men with private motives. They say that however desirable it may be that slavery should be abolished, it can not be done. IT IS IMPOSSIBLE. So said the British slaveholder. We lay down as a general truth, that what is desirable is possible with God; is possible unto us, with His aid. *Upon this basis, what have we to do in order to success?* Why, to concentrate our energies upon this desirable object. Let our means harmonize with the moral government of God. Let our plans harmonize with His wisdom. Let our action harmonize with the perceptible economy of Providence. And what becomes of the impossibility? It is annihilated.

Founded in 1859 by the New York–based journalist Thomas Hamilton, the Anglo-African Magazine *was a publication dedicated to the political, social, scientific, and literary perspectives of Black Americans and African-descended people from around the globe. The selections here are from the January 1860 issue. Rather than postulate solely about the best course of action to abolish slavery, both authors boldly ruminate on the aftermath of liberation: Would white supremacy end or be reconfigured? What might the future hold for Black people in the United States?*

Selections from the
Anglo-African Magazine
(January 1860)

WHAT SHALL WE DO WITH THE WHITE PEOPLE?

BY ETHIOP.

This is a grave question, and gravely will we attempt to consider it. But before entering upon the discussion, a brief outline of the rise and career of this people in this country may be necessary.

For many centuries now have they been on this continent; and for many years have they had entire rule and sway; yet they are to-day no nearer the solution of the problem, *"are they fit for self-government"*—than they were at the commencement of their career. Discontent and disaffection have marked every footstep, and the word *"failure"* is to-day written on every door-post.

They came over to this country in the first instance in small numbers, and forth-with began upon a course of wrong doing. The Aborigines were the first victims of their cupidity. They took advantage of them in every conceivable manner. They robbed them of their lands, plundered their wigwams, burned their villages, and murdered their wives and children. This may seem over-drawn; for in some instances small purchases of lands were made; but this was merely for the sake of foothold—a kind of entering-wedge; and when once gained, the work of ravage and devastation would commence. Thus, step by step they advanced, until now they have almost the entire possession of the continent.

One would naturally conclude, that with such a condition of things, this people would be content, that a condition seemingly so favorable, would ensure some sort of quietude, some substantial peace. Not so this people. Restless, grasping, unsatiated, they are ever on the lookout for not what is, or ought to be theirs, but for what they can get. Like a band of sailors (call them by what name you please), who, after having appropriated all the rich treasures of a merchantman, make the captain, crew and passengers walk the plank, so these white people insist not merely in having country and government and everything else therein, but that rightful owners shall vacate and tread the plank in the bargain. Twice they have quarreled with, stripped off, and fought the mother who gave them origin and nursed them till they were grown; and once have they most unmercifully beaten their weaker and more pacific neighbor; and then despoiled him of a large portion of his lands, and are now tormented with longings after the balance.

If we go back to an earlier page in their history, we find them stealing and appropriating what? Why, men, women and children from abroad and consigning them to a perpetual bondage; them and their children, and their childrens' children forever. This infamous business they continued unmolested for over a century; but for some reasons, certainly not from any convictions of wrong they abandoned the practice; only however, as it has subsequently appeared to fasten the chains tighter and to press harder the hereditary victims they so cruelly hold in bondage. It is but just to add, that the internal slave trade, is, to-day, more actively carried on than was ever the foreign trade by this people, and, too, with great pecuniary advantages, which, with them, is sufficient for a full justification of the business.

Let us turn our attention to another page of their history. Prior to their broil with the English people in Europe, they framed a form of government, which to all human appearance promised well. It seemed to contain all the elements of success. Its foundation had the look of solidity and its frame work, that of strength and durability. "*We hold these truths to be self-evident, that all men are created free and equal; and endowed with certain and inalienable rights; among which are life, liberty, and the pursuits of happiness.*"

This grand, this lofty, this truthful language constituted its four corner stones; and the civilized world naturally enough looked for a noble and lasting superstructure to be built thereon. The great masses of the old world sighed and hoped for it: and the *Crowns* trembled and feared because of it. Both clearly expected the rearing high up in its topmost lattice a beacon light that would lead to a new era among the governments of the world; but both have been disappointed.

Disaffection and discontent came almost simultaneously with the bud and the blossom, and ere the first summer fruits, confusion and division had entire sway. From thence forth have they gone on, amidst the jar and confusion of tongues, until we stand, to-day, a most perfect Babel; out-rivalling in every respect that ancient one so summarily disposed of by the Great Disposer himself.

Scarce three-fourths of a century has passed away since the basis of the government was laid, and we find the foremost of their leaders earnestly and laboriously engaged in pulling out the foundation stones thereof and anathematizing them as "glittering generalities;" gross blunders, untempered mortar, &c., &c. Dissolution and overthrow are the war-whoop of the entire *corps* of their leaders; not one of whom, but would, were it in his power, pull down the pillars of the Republic over his own head. Such is the unbridled sway the vilest of passions have over them.

If, in our scrutiny, we pass down to the present, we shall find increased discontent and disruption. Looking at this people in the light of their present existing institutions, what do we behold? Strife, confusion and disaffection. If we peruse their journals, which constitute the true index of the general mind, without exception we find nothing but grumblings, murmurings and moanings over the sad state things are in; coupled with a war of words, gross language and shameful vituperation.—These make up the sum of all you find therein. If we go into the Halls of Legislation, which are the exponents of the will of this peo-ple, we shall discover that fearful quarrels, brutal fights, cow-ardly assassinations, bludgeons, knives and pistols, are the chief arguments used, the weighty bills passed, the grave laws made; the burthen of the legislation accomplished; True, there are other arguments offered, other bills passed, and other codes en-acted; but these play but a secondary part, and fall as dead weights at the feet of the people. In these little or no interest is taken. They afford the people no satisfaction: they bring them no content, no happiness.

If we ascend to the Judicial Chamber, we shall find there op-erations in process, producing the same unsatisfactory results to this people. We shall find there instead of laws, wicked codes; for justice we find injustice; for truth, falsehood; for right, wrong; and these perversions insisted on and enforced to the very letter. They reverse there the very principle of law, so that in doubtful cases, or where the interpretation may favour right or wrong, justice or injustice, humanity or inhumanity; they give wrong, injustice and inhumanity the benefit of the doubt. And moreover, that these worst of codes, may be enforced and recognized as law, and this perversion of principles swelled and digested the worst and most unprincipled of men—*men with-out scruple* and without conscience, are selected to do their work, and faithfully do they execute their task. "The people," say they, "must be made to conquer their prejudices and accept these proceedings."

If we go to the pulpits we behold the same unsatisfactory state of things. We find these places filled with men who, to do them credit, we firmly believe, try to preach the gospel of Christ but fail in the attempt. The fault is not so much their's as the system under which they have been reared. A system under which, instead of proclaiming the everlasting gospel of Christ, they are compelled to look after their bread, or places of preferment. Instead of uttering the truths that Christ's system teaches and applying them to the hearts and consciences of men, and bringing them to bear upon their daily life and practice, we find them wholly absorbed in cutting and trimming theological garments to suit their various patrons. Though, notwithstanding all this, manifestations of dissatisfaction may be traced through all their clerical performances. How can it be otherwise. They feel that something is wrong, that a screw is somewhere loose in the general machinery of society. Standing by, they dare not bind what they find loosed, and they dare not loosen what they find bound.

They stand a powerless, self-condemned body, and call up all our pity, and we can scarcely mingle with it any tincture of bitterness. The congregations who gather round these pulpits make God's word of none effect. No love, no humility, such as Christ taught, is there. They build costly and gorgeous temples, and worshiping instead the Great God therein they turn them into engines, for generating prejudice and bitter hate against the oppressed, the outcast, and the lowly, thus making God's word a contempt, and their own conduct a wonder to angels.

If we look into their social state, we shall discover but strife, bitterness, and distraction. Not those honest and frank differences of opinion that beget and strengthen sound opinion, but low petty captiousness and cowardly vindictiveness, everywhere pervade. On looking over the country as a whole, we see section divided against section, and clan pitted against clan, and each cheered on by fierce leaders and noisy demagogues on the one side; while compromises and harmony and quiet are sued for on the other by men who are denounced as fogies and fossils by the general voice of the whole people. If we take locality after locality, we shall find the same state of turmoil and confusion. Hand raised against hand, and frown meeting frown. Everywhere is the exclamation sounding "Am I my brother's keeper!!" Everywhere is written the sentence "What have I to do with thee!" It would seem as if this people ancw had builded a tower of Babel, and that a confusion of ideas infinitely more disintegrating than a confusion of tongues, had begun the work of separation and isolation,—their first step in the downward path of barbarism, just as truly as "*E Pluribus Unum*" was their first step to progress and civilization.

Go with us over the plains of Kansas, and witness there the recent death struggle between sections of this people for the supremacy of wrong over right. Go stand by the grave mounds made there by that fierce struggle; or returning go through the guilded palaces and gorgeous streets, and then through the low sickening hovels of the metropolis of the country; or go with us even to cold philosophical New England, even industrious intellectual Massachusetts, and wander about the factories there; and above all, go with us to the regions of the sunny South, where, without shadow of law, they torture men to their death, outrage women gather up their own little children as calves for the slaughter, and sell them to the highest bidder. Witness all this, and tell us if these things of this people are not true?

The manifold blessings, physical and intellectual, with which God and nature have crowned them in granting them a country so manifestly fitted for the development of a people—a people especially of their peculiar bent and endowments, stand out in wonderful contrast with their conduct, their course, their abuse of the great priveledges so kindly bestowed upon them. Climate the finest in the world, soil the most fertile, topographical facilities the best conceivable; resources greater than that of any other part of the globe, and facilities for their development beyond that of any other country extant; with just enough difficulties—(no more)—to develop in addition, their genius in overcoming the same. These all have been theirs. Everything that nature could bestow and art devise has been placed at their hands, and yet the blight of discord disruption and disunion, has, like a Simoon settled down upon this people.

What then shall we Anglo-Africans do with these white people? "*What shall we do with them?*" It may seem strange, that a people so crushed and trodden upon; so insignificant as the Anglo-Africans, should even ask the question "what shall we do with the whites?" Indeed, the question may seem presumptuous, quizzical ridiculous; but the truth is, that these white people themselves, through their Press and Legislative Halls, in their pulpits, and on their Rostrums, so constantly talk of nothing but us black people, and have apparently got so far beyond every thing else, that it would seem that their very instincts regard us as in a measure able to settle and make quiet there restlessness, and hence they have actually forced upon us the question which is, the title of this article. It has indeed become a serious question with us: What shall we do with the white people?

We have, perhaps, been too modest, else we would have raised the question before; and might, it may be, ere this, have found its proper solution. Let us endeavor to compensate for past neglect by an earnest endeavor to settle this important question. But before proceeding to the answer we find another and equally vital question forcing itself in our way, which demanding a moments attention, viz: What is the cause of all this discontent, this unquiet state, this distress? This answer we think may be found in this, viz: *a long continued, extensive, and almost complete system of wrong-doing.* Like a man who commences the life of a pick-pocket and changes not his way, becomes not only an adept in the profession, but a hardened offender, and reaps the bitter fruits in the end thereof, so also this people. They commenced with the plunder of the Indian, theft of the African, followed by the grossest wrongs upon the Africo-American, and broils with their neighbors without, and stripes among themselves within, the fruits of which are thorough disaffection and agitation.

But another and equally important question forces itself upon us, viz: whither are this people tending? If permitted in their course; if no restraining hand arrest them, who does not forsee that the goal at which they will ultimately arrive will be sure and certain barbarism. Already do we hear it proclaimed through their *presses* that if other hands than their own are not compelled to labour for them, want and starvation will stalk abroad through the land; blood will flow through the streets like water from the fountain, and repine follow in its train. That where now they have thrift and plenty, dirth will abound, the thorn and the thistle and the deadly brier will spring up and grow, and the more deadly serpent will hiss and nestle therein, that the harvest will be passed and ended, the summer over and gone, and the voice of the turtle be no more heard in the land.

And, indeed, this picture which is not ours but theirs, seems to be not an exaggeration, no fancy sketch, but a reality; for already do we find them grappling each other by the throat for opinion sake—opinions, the result of honest convictions of right and truth. In a large portion of the country already no man among them can express honest truth, without risk of life while everywhere will the hiss of contempt follow him, and the finger of scorn point toward him if he venture upon it. Honesty and truth, unless they be of a certain character, are at discount among this people, and like Rachel for her children go weeping through the land; while dishonesty and falsehood, if of a certain character, stalk boldly forth with the laugh and the joy of demons, and exclaiming, 'we have triumphed! we have triumphed!!"

And verily they have triumphed; and in that triumph and what else we have instanced, who does not see that this people are on the direct road to barbarism.

What then shall we Anglo-Africans do with them? How save them and the country from their sure and impending fate? What agencies shall we put forth to arrest so direful a calamity? These are indeed serious questions, and reviewed in the light of earnestness demand, if possible, immediate solution.

This people must be saved; quiet and harmony must be restored. Plans for the removal of these white people, as all such schemes are—such for example as these people have themselves laid for the removal of others out of their midst—would be wrong in conception, and prove abortive in attempt; nor ought it be desirable on our part were it even possible to forcibly remove them. It is their right to stay, only they have no right to jeopard the interest or the peace of the country if permitted to remain. God, in his all wise purpose, has reserved this fair land for other, and higher and nobler purposes than a theatre for the exhibition of prejudices, bitter hates, fierce strifes, dissentions, oppressions, frauds. On the contrary, it was so to speak, reserved for centuries, like a sealed book, and then thrown open just when needed by the *Great Author himself* that men of every tongue, and clime and hue, should gather thereon, and perfect their development.

So long as we have entertained the belief that this people would ultimately approach toward this point, we have silently bowed without remonstrance or even murmur. We have labored long and faithfully with little or no remuneration, we have been patient, under every trial, and enduring under every burthen placed upon us or self-imposed, that these people might redeem themselves, that they might retrieve their past errors and return to a sense of right. Pressed and circumscribed by them, we have been disposed to make the best of our way; narrow as the space we have as yet been enabled to acquire for our labours, we have been content. But the white people, on the other hand are not content. We find even under depressing circumstances room enough for us in this country, they the white people and they alone, find its boundaries too circumscribed for their greedy grasp. Possessing acres by the millions, yet they would elbow us and all others off of what we possess, to give them room for what they cannot occupy. We want this country, say they, for ourselves, and ourselves alone. What right have they but that of might, to put forth such a cool assumption? Who are these people that they come forth in the light of the Nineteenth century, and, too, after creating the agitation and confusion which now effervesce the entire nation and demand the whole country for themselves and their posterity.

Seriously do we hope, that if the peace of the country is to be so continuously disturbed that they would withdraw. We have arrived at a period when they could easily be spared. We have ceded to these people energy and force of character, and we may add one other characteristic, viz: a roving, *unsettled, restless* disposition. They are in inclination if not habit, marauders.

It may be, unless we shall find some other effective means of adjusting existing difficulties, that from this point we may have some hope for their Exodus.

We give them also high credit for their material progress. Who knows, but that some day, when, after they shall have fulfilled their mission, carried arts and sciences to their highest point, they will make way for a milder and more genial race, or become so blended in it, as to lose their own peculiar and objectionable characteristics? In any case, in view of the existing state of things around us, let our constant thought be, *what for the best good of all shall we do with the White people?*

* * *

THE ANGLO-AFRICAN
AND THE FUTURE.

BY WILLIAM H. HALL, OF CALIFORNIA.

A review of the past and present condition of the social world proves, beyond a doubt, that the human family are yet to attain a grander attitude than ever before. No earthly power can resist the rapid march of intelligence, wealth, and progress, which now distinguish every enlightened movement; all errors, prejudices, and false dogmas must recede before its advancing strides; and level all differences among the brotherhood of men, by its culminating glory. While the affairs of mankind are to be controlled and dispensed by the several and distinct *races* in proportion to their capacity, none may hope to win individual eminence or collective greatness, unless by a display of force and character essential to the occasion. The Anglo-Africans, unlike the migratory bands of other countries who, forgetful of the many reminiscences of home, become contented in any land, have nobler aspirations and higher claims in the future upon the law and justice of their country, than to be moved as mere machines to others' dictation; they will not vote unless they understand that the exercise of such an inestimable privilege will benefit the happiness of society, and conduce to the perpetuity of a wise and beneficent government; they will scorn false evidence in a conflict between right and wrong, because the precepts of religion, and the fidelity of nature, enjoin otherwise; these manifestations of the superior force of mind over the materiality of matter, must make its impression, and convince the dominant authority that all immunities should be divided alone among those responsible for their actions. The 19th century has produced many startling revolutions, which have amazed the learned, induced some to think, and confounded the illiterate, annihilated space and time, lessened the drudgeries of life, and almost transcended the sublime laws of nature; yet the triumphs of genius have not solved its problems, the object of the Creator in diffusing the countless millions of his children in widely different circumstances, varied climates, and unlimited distances of separation; some rich and swaying power, clothed with liberty and its benignant advantages; while others poor and suffering the depravities of misfortune. The primary cause, the unequal disparity, has not been accounted for—who can study the reflex of time, and cull examples from the recorded pages of antiquity, denoting the many changes of dynasties, the reverses of men, and not to be able to divine the unmistakable solution, why the motives of oppression seem inexhaustible.

The lessons of experience are unfolding mighty results, they are pregnant with interest; every moment that flies, every hour that passes, and every morn that beams the light of day, afford hope and encouragement to the coming generation to press forward.

The "Anglo-African and the Future," a period of bliss and promise! it enchains meditation, divests reflection of its gloom and solitude, intoxicates all thought, and enchants the imagination with contemplative beauties and wonders unseen and not realized. The hidden and untrodden future it foreshadows, a time almost beyond comprehension; of things which are to take place, and innumerable changes that will be made, showing a greater number of equals than inferiors of full age and rank, all ready to fulfill their endless variety of duties—the works of art, the emanations of the brain, the touch and grace of the pencil, the mold and finish of the sculptor, the achievements of learning, the inspiration of poetry, and the charms of eloquence, will not be ascribed to any one race more than another; all will vie upon equal merits for the highest niche in the temple of fame; the Anglo-African, against all opposing difficulties, will have a tremendous work to perform, to meet the exigency of the future and assume the elevating conditions which the improved state of society will impose upon him.

Throughout the civilized world the acquirement of knowledge has been the incentive of men's ambition; but here, in progressive America, the general laws of philosophy, the wonders

of science, and the abstruse doctrines of theology are made subservient to the accumulation of money; so powerful is the sway
of this necessary evil that it warps the understanding, corrupts
the conscience, corrodes affection, friendship, and patriotism,
and turns the very virtues of congeniality into perverseness; its
seductive allurements check impartial legislation, penetrates
the privacy of Executive prerogatives, and guides the destiny of
legal authority. In such an age and struggling under such diverse circumstances, the Anglo-African, now only nominally
recognized, will be forced to gain the control of that element
which accomplishes so much, and without which all things
languish and decay; are they prepared to sacrifice their accustomed ease of living, to enter the wilderness amid bleak winds
and storms, to hew towering trees, to engage the sterile and
rugged earth, with her huge boulders and uncounted rocks,
which may consume years of toil before labor will be rewarded;
in order to build cities, rear churches and school-houses so that
home may be happy in the success of free institutions; it is here
where mankind will become ennobled, minds embellished,
blood nourished, bones and muscles strengthened, in the children who are growing to maturity, to combat the degradation
which poverty exercises to her discipline.

Among the prominent features that will charactarize the future, will be the respective grades that men will occupy in society; position must be attained at all hazards, whatever class
embraces menial pursuits to the exclusion of all other employments, must remain in a state of vassalage, and a consequent
inferiority; equal advantages flow through the sources of equal
motives and respect; that a race of people inured for hundreds of
years to perform the meanest duties of life, can, at one bound,
imitate the controlling class in the intricacies of commerce, the
perplexities of professions, and the civilizing influences of education, none will pretend to maintain; but that the *fathers* and
mothers—the pupils of the school of time—have a most sacred
obligation in preparing the rising child for all the conditions that
may be entailed, is clearly apparent and expedient.

The future to the Anglo-African resembles the genial drops
of the dew to the sprouting vegetation; there is a self-respect to
one another deficient which must be changed, the rank weeds

must be torn from the soil, so that fragrant flowers may bud and perfume the surrounding air. The young babe in the cradle, when it commences its lispings, should be taught the grand idea of the natural equality of the human family, that all distinctions ensue from the impress of intellect and native power, and wherever its mark is discerned, whether enveloped under the fair skin of the Anglo-American or the swarthy, repulsive countenance of the African, it is none the less a gem to the votaries of letters; the rare and priceless gifts of nature are an inheritance seldom enjoyed, but are composed of qualities which will only command its intrinsic value in the time which is to come.

H. FORD DOUGLAS

Hezekiah Ford Douglas (1831–1865) escaped slavery in Virginia at the age of fifteen and eventually settled in Illinois. As he learned more about the abolitionist movement, Douglas became an active participant and agitator via his compelling antislavery oration at state conventions and local gatherings. Though Douglas remained a proponent of the abolitionist cause and took part in debates and various campaigns, he soon began to question the feasibility of true liberation for Black people in the United States. Douglas's politics shifted to an antislavery emigrationism; that is, he believed that the institution of slavery should be eradicated and that Black people would have a better chance at life if they settled outside the United States, especially in Canada. In this speech from July 4, 1860, Douglas levels pointed, controversial critiques of the Republican Party and Abraham Lincoln, questioning Lincoln's devotion to abolition and the extent of his support for social and political equality for all.

"I Do Not Believe in the Antislavery of Abraham Lincoln," *The Liberator* (1860)

MR. PRESIDENT, LADIES AND GENTLEMEN: I hope that my friends will not do me the injustice to suppose for a single moment that I have any connection either by blood or politically, with Stephen Arnold Douglas, of Chicago. I am somewhat proud of the name of Douglas. It was once, in the history of dear old Scotia, a tower of strength on the side of free principles; and so firmly did they oppose the usurpations of royal power, that, on one of the kings of Scotland coming to the throne, he issued an edict, expelling from his realm every man who bore that hated name; and I cannot account for the signal departure from the ancient and hereditary principles by one who bears that name, upon any other theory than that of bastard blood.

There are a great many people in this country who seem to be in love with Stephen A. Douglas, and to regard him as a great statesman. It seems to me that there are certain elements necessary to true statesmanship. In the first place, a statesman must have a heart—that is one of the essential elements of statesmanship. Now, who supposes that Stephen A. Douglas has a heart? I cannot account for the existence of so mean a man as Douglas on any other theory than that of the transmigration of souls. It was held by one of the old philosophers of Greece that when a man died, somebody was born, and that the soul of the dead entered the body of the newborn; but when Douglas was born, nobody happened to die! But, ladies and gentlemen, I had no intention of making these remarks. We are here for the purpose of celebrating the Fourth of July. Eighty-four years ago today, this nation had its birth. We stand, today, a governmental prodigy, surpassing, in our extraordinary growth, any of the states of ancient or modern times. But nations who seek success amid the possibilities of the future are not measured by the accumulation of wealth or by the breadth of territorial domain; for down beneath the glittering splendor which the jeweled hand of Croesus has lifted up to intoxicate the gaze of the unthinking multitude, there will be found a silent and resistless influence working its way beneath the surface of society and shaping the destiny of men.

When John Adams wrote that this would always be a day of bonfires and rejoicing, he did not foresee the evils which half a century would bring, when his own son, standing in his place amid the legislators of the Republic, would shame posterity into a brave indifference to its empty ceremonies. John Quincy Adams said, twenty years ago, that "the preservation, propagation and perpetuation of slavery is the vital animating spirit of the national government," and this truth is not less apparent today. Every department of our national life—the President's chair, the Senate of the United States, the Supreme Court, and the American pulpit—is occupied and controlled by the dark spirit of American slavery. We have four parties in this country that have marshaled themselves on the highway of American politics, asking for the votes of the American people to place them in possession of the government. We have what is called the Union party, led by Mr. Bell of Tennessee; we have what is called the Democratic party, led by Stephen A. Douglas, of Illinois; we have the party called the Seceders, or the Slave-Code Democrats, led by John C. Breckinridge, of Kentucky and then we have the Republican party, led by Abraham Lincoln, of Illinois. All of these parties ask for your support, because they profess to represent some principle. So far as the principles of freedom and the hopes of the black man are concerned, all these parties are barren and unfruitful; neither of them seeks to lift the Negro out of his fetters and rescue this day from odium and disgrace.

Take Abraham Lincoln. I want to know if any man can tell me the difference between the antislavery of Abraham Lincoln and the antislavery of the old Whig party or the antislavery of Henry Clay? Why, there is no difference between them. Abraham Lincoln is simply a Henry Clay Whig, and he believes just as Henry Clay believed in regard to this question. And Henry Clay was just as odious to the antislavery cause and antislavery men as ever was John C. Calhoun. In fact, he did as much to perpetuate Negro slavery in this country as any other man who has ever lived. Henry Clay once said "That is property which the law declares to be property," and that "two hundred years of legislation have sanctioned and sanctified property in slaves." Wherever Henry Clay is today in the universe of God, that atheistic lie is with him, with all its tormenting memories.

I know Abraham Lincoln, and I know something about his antislavery. I know the Republicans do not like this kind of talk, because, while they are willing to steal our thunder, they are unwilling to submit to the conditions imposed upon that party that assumes to be antislavery. They say that they cannot go as fast as you antislavery men go in this matter; that they cannot afford to be uncompromisingly honest, or so radical as you Garrisonians; that they want to take time; that they want to do the work gradually. They say, "We must not be in too great a hurry to overthrow slavery; at least, we must take half a loaf, we cannot get the whole." Now, my friends, I believe that the very best way to overthrow slavery in this country is to occupy the highest possible antislavery ground. Washington Irving tells a story of a Dutchman who wanted to jump over a ditch, and he went back three miles in order to get a good start, and when he got up to the ditch he had to sit down on the wrong side to get his breath. So it is with these political parties; they are compelled, they say, when they get up to the ditch of slavery, to stop and take breath.

I do not believe in the antislavery of Abraham Lincoln, because he is on the side of this slave power of which I am speaking, that has possession of the federal government. What does he propose to do? Simply to let the people and the territories regulate their domestic institutions in their own way. In the great debate between Lincoln and Douglas in Illinois, when he was interrogated as to whether he was in favor of the admission of more slave states in the Union, he said, that so long as we owned the territories, he did not see any other way of doing than to admit those states when they made application, with or without slavery.

Now, that is Douglas's doctrine; it is stealing the thunder of Stephen A. Douglas. In regard to the repeal of the Fugitive Slave Law, Abraham Lincoln occupies the same position that the old Whig party occupied in 1852. They asserted then, in their platform, that they were not in favor of the repeal of that law, and that they would do nothing to lessen its efficiency. What did he say at Freeport Why, that the South was entitled to a Fugitive Slave Law; and although he thought the law could be modified a little, yet, he said, if he was in Congress, he would have it done in such a way as not to lessen its efficiency! Here, then, is Abraham Lincoln in favor of carrying out that infamous Fugitive Slave Law, that not only strikes down the liberty of every black man in the United States, but virtually the liberty of every white man as well; for, under that law, there is not a man in this presence who might not be arrested today upon the simple testimony of one man, and, after an ex parte trial, hurried off to slavery and to chains. Habeas corpus, trial by jury—those great bulwarks of freedom, reared by the blood and unspeakable woe of your English ancestors, amidst the conflicts of a thousand years—are struck down by this law; and the man whose name is inscribed upon the Presidential banner of the Republican party is in favor of keeping it upon the statute book!

Not only would I arraign Mr. Lincoln in regard to that law, for his proslavery character and principles, but when he was a member of the House of Representatives, in 1849, on the tenth day of January, he went through the District of Columbia and consulted the prominent proslavery men and slaveholders of the District, and then went into the House of Representatives and introduced, on his own responsibility, a fugitive-slave law for the District of Columbia. It is well known that the law of 1793 did not apply to the District, and it was necessary, in order that slaveholders might catch their slaves who sought safety under the shadow of the Capitol, that a special law should be passed for the District of Columbia; and so Mr. Lincoln went down deeper into the proslavery pool than ever Mr. Mason of Virginia did in the Fugitive Slave Law of 1850. Here, then, is the man who asks for your votes and for the votes of the antislavery people of New England; who, on his own responsibility, without any temptation whatever, introduced into the District of Columbia a fugitive-slave law! That is a fact for the consideration of antislavery men. Then, there is another item which I want to bring out in this connection. I am a colored man; I am an American citizen, and I think that I am entitled to exercise the elective franchise. I am about twenty-eight years old, and I would like to vote very much. I think I am old enough to vote, and I think that, if I had a vote to give, I should know enough to place it on the side of freedom. No party, it seems to me, is entitled to the sympathy of antislavery men, unless that party is willing to extend to the black man all the rights of a citizen. I care nothing about that antislavery which wants to make the territories free, while it is unwilling to extend to me, as a man, in the free states, all the rights of a man. In the state of Illinois, where I live—my adopted state—I have been laboring to make it a place fit for a decent man to live in. In that state, we have a code of black laws that would disgrace any Barbary State, or any uncivilized people in the far-off islands of the sea. Men of my complexion are not allowed to testify in a court of justice where a white man is a party. If a white man happens to owe me anything, unless I can prove it by the testimony of a white man, I cannot collect the debt. Now, two years ago, I went through the state of Illinois for the purpose of getting signers to a petition asking the legislature to repeal the "Testimony Law," so as to permit colored men to testify against white men. I went to prominent Republicans, and among others, to Abraham Lincoln and Lyman Trumbull, and neither of them dared to sign that petition, to give me the right to testify in a court of justice! In the state of Illinois, they tax the colored people for every conceivable purpose. They tax the Negro's property to support schools for the education of the white man's children, but the colored people are not permitted to enjoy any of the benefits resulting from that taxation. We are compelled to impose upon ourselves additional taxes in order to educate our children. The state lays its iron hand upon the Negro, holds him down, and puts the other hand into his pocket and steals his hard earnings, to educate the children of white men; and if we sent our children to school, Abraham Lincoln would kick them out, in the name of Republicanism and antislavery! I have, then, something to say against the antislavery character of the Republican party. Not only are the Republicans of Illinois on the side of slavery, and against the rights of the Negro but even some of the prominent Republicans of Massachusetts are not acceptable to antislavery men in that regard. In the Senate of the United States, some of your Senators from the New England states take special pains to make concessions to the slave power, by saying that they are not in favor of bringing about Negro equality; just as Abraham Lincoln did down in Ohio two years ago. When he went there to stump that state, the colored people were agitating the question of suffrage in that state. The *Ohio Statesman,* a paper published in Columbus, asserted, on the morning of the day that Mr. Lincoln made his speech, that he was in favor of Negro equality; and Mr. Lincoln took pains at that time to deny the allegation, by saying that he was not in favor of bringing about the equality of the Negro race; that he did not believe in making them voters, in placing them in the jury box, or in ever bringing about the political equality of the races. He said that so long as they lived here, there must be an inferior and superior position, and that he was, as much as anybody else, in favor of assigning to white men the superior position.

There is a good deal of talk in this country about the superiority of the white race. We often hear, from this very platform, praise of the Saxon race. Now, I want to put this question to those who deny the equal manhood of the Negro: What peculiar trait of character do the white men of this country possess, as a mark of superiority, either morally or mentally, that is not also manifested by the black man, under similar circumstances? You may take down the white and black part of the social and political structure, stone by stone, and in all the relations of life, where the exercise of his moral and intellectual functions is not restricted by positive law, or by the arbitrary restraints of society, you will find the Negro the equal of the white man in all the elements of head and heart. Of course, no one pretends that all men are mentally equal, or morally equal, any more than we do that all men are of the same weight, or equal in physical endowments. Here in this country, under the most favorable circumstances, we have idiots and fools, some in the lunatic asylum, and others, in the high places of government, who essay to be statesmen, who ought to be there. You say to the German, the Hungarian, the Irishman, as soon as he lands here, "Go out on the highway of the world's progress, and compete with me, if you can, in the race for empire and dominion." You throw no fetters upon that ever-restless sea of energies that chafes our shores, saying, "Thus far shalt thou go, but no further." No, with all that magnanimity which must be ever-present in the true soul, you say to the foreigner, whose liberty has been cloven down upon some disastrous European battlefield, whose fortune has been wrecked and lost amid the storms of adversity abroad, "Come here and better your condition, if you can!" I remember that a few years ago, when a Hungarian refugee—not an American citizen; he had only declared his intention to become one—was arrested in the harbor of Smyrna, for an offense against the Austrian government, Captain Ingraham, of the American warship *St. Louis*, demanded, in the name of the federal government, his instant release, and under the cover of her guns, the shackles of Austrian bondage melted from his limbs, and Martin Kozta walked the deck of that vessel a free man, as proud of his adopted country as we were of the gallant deed. That poor Hungarian, in the hour of his misfortune, could look at the American flag as it gleamed in the sunlight of the Austrian sky, and as he looked at its stars, that symbolized a constellation of republican states, he could feel all the poetic inspiration of Halleck when he sang,

> Flag of the seas! on Ocean's wave
> Thy stars shall glitter o'er the brave!
> When death, careering on the gale,
> Sweeps darkly 'round the bellied sail,
> And frighted waves rush wildly back
> Before the broadside's reeling rack,
> The dying wanderer of the sea,
> Shall look at once to heaven and thee,
> And smile to see thy splendors fly,
> In triumph o'er his closing eye.

But no colored man can feel any of this inspiration. We are denied all participation in the government; we remember that the flag only covers us as slaves, and that our liberties are only respected and our rights only secured to us, when, escaping from the beak of the American eagle, we can nestle in the shaggy mane of the British lion; and feeling this, we can feel no inspiration when we look at the American flag. But I was speaking in reference to the gratuitous concessions of some of our Republican leaders. Some three or four months ago a bill was under consideration in the Senate of the United States for the purpose of establishing a school for the education of free colored children in the District of Columbia. The matter created some discussion in the Senate, and, under the lash of Senator Mason, and other slave-drivers of the South, your own Senator, Mr. Wilson caved in on this question and admitted, in the presence of the Senate, and with all Massachusetts to read his words, that the Negro was inferior. Now, I do not believe that the Negro is inferior. Man's ability wholly depends upon surrounding circumstances. You may take all of those races that have risen from the lowest estate of degradation to the highest eminence of intellectual and moral splendor, and you will discover that no race has ever yet been able, by any internal power and will of its own, to lift itself into respectability, without contact with other civilized tribes. Rome served as the scaffolding for the erection of the tribes of

Western Europe into that huge political constellation whose drumbeats follow the sun round the world. When Julius Caesar landed in Britain, he found the ancestors of this boasted English race a miserable set of barbarians, bowing down to stocks and stones, and painting their bodies in fantastic colors. They were carried to Rome by the soldiers of Caesar and sold in the streets for five dollars; and so thoroughly brutalized were they that Cicero, the great Roman orator, said that the meanest slaves in Rome came from Great Britain; and, writing to his friend Atticus, he advised him not to buy the worthless wretches. Emerson says that it took many generations to trim and comb and perfume the first boatload of Norse pirates into royal highnesses and most noble knights of the garter; and yet, every spark and ornament of regal splendor dates back to the twenty thousand thieves that landed at Hastings. You will find, after that, I think, that there is no truth in the assertion that the Negro is inferior. The men who justify slavery upon the assumed inferiority of the Negro race, are very slow to admit these facts. They are just as tardy in admitting that the remains of ancient grandeur, which have been exhumed from beneath the accumulated dust of forty centuries, were wrought by the ingenuity and skill of the Negro race, ere the Saxon was known in history. We are informed that the scepter of the world passed from the colored to the white race at the fall of Babylon. I know ethnological writers tell us we do not look like the Egyptian. They dig up an Egyptian mummy that has been dead and buried three thousand years, that once tripped "the light fantastic toe" amid the gilded halls of the Pharaohs, over whose grave the storms of thirty or forty centuries have swept, and because it doesn't look just like a Mississippi Negro of today, set it down that there is a difference in species between them! I admit that centuries of oppression, under a vertical sun, may have worked marvelous changes not only in the physical, but in the intellectual characteristics of the race—I know it has. All other races are permitted to travel over the wild field of history and pluck the flowers that blossom there, to glean up the heroes, philosophers, sages and poets, and put them into a galaxy of brilliant genius and claim all the credit to themselves; but if a black man attempts to do so, he is met at the threshold by the objection, "You have no ancestry behind you." Now, friends, I am proud of the Negro race, and I thank God today that there does not course in my veins a single drop of Saxon blood. The blood that I boast was immortalized in Scotland's song and story at a time when the Saxon was wearing an iron collar, with the name of his Norman master written thereon. There was never such a subjugated race in the world as were the Saxons in the days of William the Conqueror. So thoroughly humbled and degraded were they, that Macaulay says it was considered as disgraceful for a Norman to marry a Saxon as it is now for a white person to marry a negro. I am proud of the Negro race. I think that Negro looks just as well on paper and sounds just as sweetly to the ear as Saxon; and I believe that by education, by wealth, by religion, the Negro may make that name as honorable as ever was that of Saxon, while the Saxon, by the practice of the opposite vices, may drag himself down as low as the Negro. I believe that man, like certain productions of the vegetable kingdom, will grow better in some soils than in others. God has given us a goodly land in which to build up an empire of thought; it ought also to be an empire of freedom. The anti-slavery men of the country intend to make this truly 'the land of the free and the home of the brave,' by coming to such meetings as these on gala days. When Boston conservatism goes down to the Music Hall to air itself in Everett's lying eulogy, we mean to come here and criticise the various political parties, in order to rescue this day from priestly cant and from political mockery. Oh, no, friends; we colored men may well feel proud of our ancestors. Why, we were held in very high esteem by the ancient Greeks. There is a Grecian fable that we descended from the gods. Virgil says that Jupiter, in his aerial chariot, sailing through the skies, went so near the sun that it burnt his face black; and on that hypothesis they account for the existence of the colored race! The father of Grecian poetry, standing away back in the gray dawn of history, has struck some noble lines from his lyre, in praise of our ancestors of the sunny clime.

> The sire of Gods, and all the ethereal train
> On the warm limits of the farthest main,
> Now mix with mortals, nor disdain to grace
> The feast of Ethiopia's blameless race.

Friends, I have no idea that those men who talk about the inferiority of the Negro race really believe it. They think it is absolutely necessary, for the success of their party, to cater to the dark spirit of slavery. But, after all, I say that the Negro is a man, and has all the elements of manhood, like other men; and by the way, I think that, in this country, he has the highest element of manhood. Certainly he has developed here its highest element. I do not believe that the highest element of manhood is the ability to fight. If he is the noblest man who can do the most fighting, then you ought to elect John C. Heenan, the 'Benecia Boy,' as President of the United States. If muscle is evidence of the highest manhood, you will find any of the 'short boys' of New York, any of the 'plug-uglies' and ugly plugs of Tammany Hall, better qualified to be President of the United States than Abraham Lincoln. The negro is emphatically a Christian man; patient under long suffering, as ready to forgive an injury as the Saxon is to inflict one; he would rather 'bear the ills he has, than fly to others that he knows not of.' You may dwarf his manhood by the iron of bondage, you may dry up the fountain of his intellectual life, but you can never destroy his faith in God, and the ultimate triumph of His almighty purpose. Over a sea of blood and tears, he catches, in every lull of the midnight storm that breaks around him, the small voice that bids him 'Hope on, hope ever!' He constitutes the very oxygen of civilization, potent in that arterial action that imparts life and health to the permanent and successful achievements of the human race. Therefore, I do not like these gratuitous admissions on the part of men who go to Congress from New England with an antislavery purpose in their hearts.

But, my friends, I must bring my remarks to a close; and I say, that in view of the fact that the influence of slavery is dominant in every department of the government, I would rather curse than bless the hour that marked the fatal epoch in American history, when we threw off the yoke of a decent despotism, to become, in turn, the slaves of a mean and arrogant democracy.

NARRATIVES OF
SLAVERY AND
FUGITIVE ESCAPES

JAMES ALBERT UKAWSAW GRONNIOSAW

James Albert Ukawsaw Gronniosaw (1705–1775) was born in the kingdom of Borno (present-day Chad and Nigeria). Gronniosaw was kidnapped at the age of fifteen and sold into slavery first in the Barbados to an American enslaver and then again to an enslaver from the British American colony of New Jersey. The first narrative of slavery published in England, Gronniosaw's account, scribed by an amanuensis, lacks the political, antislavery tone that is typical of later titles in the genre. In fact, Gronniosaw's articulated longings for home and family are not belabored; neither are his criticisms of the institution of slavery. Gronniosaw's spiritual path takes precedence, including his acceptance of the Christian doctrine that has both undergirded and rationalized slavery as a positive good that inspired the ways that his enslaver expects Gronniosaw to comport himself as human property and as a racial subordinate in society. After his enslaver's death, Gronniosaw was emancipated and his life was marked by misfortune and abject poverty, though he experiences moments of joy in his family, economic stability, and social acceptance when he serves in the Royal Navy during the Seven Years' War. Gronniosaw remained in England, which he erroneously imagined would be a kind of religious utopia, only to experience great hardship as he attempted to establish a life there.

From *A Narrative of the Most Remarkable Particulars in the Life of James Albert Ukawsaw Gronniosaw, an African Prince, as Related by Himself*

(1772)

I was born in the city BOURNOU; my mother was the eldest daughter of the reigning King there, of which BOURNOU is the chief city. I was the youngest of six children, and particularly loved by my mother, and my grand-father almost doated on me.

I had, from my infancy, a curious turn of mind; was more grave and reserved in my disposition than either of my brothers and sisters. I often teazed them with questions they could not answer: for which reason they disliked me, as they supposed that I was either foolish, or insane. 'Twas certain that I was, at times, very unhappy in myself: it being strongly impressed on my mind that there was some GREAT MAN of power which resided above the sun, moon and stars, the objects of our worship. My dear indulgent mother would bear more with me than any of my friends beside.—I often raised my hand to heaven, and asked her who lived there? was much dissatisfied when she told me the sun, moon and stars, being persuaded, in my own mind, that there must be some SUPERIOR POWER.—I was frequently lost in wonder at the works of the Creation: was afraid and uneasy and restless, but could not tell for what. I wanted to be informed of things that no person could tell me; and was always dissatisfied.—These wonderful impressions begun in my childhood, and followed me continually 'till I left my parents, which affords me matter of admiration and thankfulness.

To this moment I grew more and more uneasy every day, in so much that one saturday, (which is the day on which we keep our sabbath) I laboured under anxieties and fears that cannot be expressed; and, what is more extraordinary, I could not give a reason for it.—I rose, as our custom is, about three o'clock, (as we are oblig'd to be at our place of worship an hour before the sun rise) we say nothing in our worship, but continue on our knees with our hands held up, observing a strict silence 'till the sun is at a certain height, which I suppose to be about 10 or 11 o'clock in England: when, at a certain sign made by the priest, we get up (our duty being over) and disperse to our different houses.—Our place of meeting is under a large palm tree; we divide ourselves into many congregations; as it is impossible for the same tree to cover the inhabitants of the whole City, though they are extremely large, high and majestic; the beauty and usefulness of them are not to be described; they supply the inhabitants of the country with meat, drink and clothes;* the body of the palm tree is very large; at a certain season of the year they tap it, and bring vessels to receive the wine, of which they draw great quantities, the quality of which is very delicious: the leaves of this tree are of a silky nature; they are large and soft; when they are dried and pulled to pieces it has much the same appearance as the English flax, and the inhabitants of BOURNOU manufacture it for cloathing &c. This tree likewise produces a plant or substance which has the appearance of a cabbage, and very like it, in taste almost the same: it grows between the branches. Also the palm tree produces a nut, something like a cocoa, which contains a kernel, in which is a large quantity of milk, very pleasant to the taste: the shell is of a hard substance, and of a very beautiful appearance, and serves for basons, bowls, &c.

I hope this digression will be forgiven.—I was going to observe that after the duty of our Sabbath was over (on the day in which I was more distressed and afflicted than ever) we were all on our way home as usual, when a remarkable black cloud arose and covered the sun; then followed very heavy rain and thunder more dreadful than ever I had heard: the heav'ns roared, and the earth trembled at it: I was highly affected and cast down; in so much that I wept sadly, and could not follow my relations and friends home.—I was obliged to stop and felt

---

'It is a generally received opinion, in *England*, that the natives of *Africa* go entirely unclothed; but this supposition is very unjust: they have a kind of dress so as to appear decent, though it is very slight and thin.

as if my legs were tied, they seemed to shake under me: so I stood still, being in great fear of the MAN of POWER that I was persuaded in myself, lived above. One of my young companions (who entertained a particular friendship for me and I for him) came back to see for me: he asked me why I stood still in such very hard rain? I only said to him that my legs were weak, and I could not come faster: he was much affected to see me cry, and took me by the hand, and said he would lead me home, which he did. My mother was greatly alarmed at my tarrying out in such terrible weather; she asked me many questions, such as what I did so for, and if I was well? My dear mother says I, pray tell me who is the great MAN of POWER that makes the thunder? She said, there was no power but the sun, moon and stars; that they made all our country.—I then enquired how all our people came? She answered me, from one another; and so carried me to many generations back.—Then says I, who made the *First Man*? and who made the first Cow, and the first Lyon, and where does the fly come from, as no one can make him? My mother seemed in great trouble; she was apprehensive that my senses were impaired, or that I was foolish. My father came in, and seeing her in grief asked the cause, but when she related our conversation to him, he was exceedingly angry with me, and told me he would punish me severely if ever I was so troublesome again; so that I resolved never to say any thing more to him. But I grew very unhappy in myself; my relations and acquaintance endeavoured by all the means they could think on, to divert me, by taking me to ride upon goats, (which is much the custom of our country) and to shoot with a bow and arrow; but I experienced no satisfaction at all in any of these things; nor could I be easy by any means whatever: my parents were very unhappy to see me so dejected and melancholy.

About this time there came a merchant from the *Gold Coast* (the third city in GUINEA) he traded with the inhabitants of our country in ivory &c. he took great notice of my unhappy situation, and enquired into the cause; he expressed vast concern for me, and said, if my parents would part with me for a little while, and let him take me home with him, it would be of more service to me than any thing they could do for me.—He told me that if I would go with him I should see houses with wings to them walk upon the water, and should also see the white folks; and that he had many sons of my age, which should be my companions; and he added to all this that he would bring me safe back again soon.—I was highly pleased with the account of this strange place, and was very desirous of going.—I seemed sensible of a secret impulse upon my mind which I could not resist that seemed to tell me I must go. When my dear mother saw that I was willing to leave them, she spoke to my father and grandfather and the rest of my relations, who all agreed that I should accompany the merchant to the Gold Coast. I was the more willing as my brothers and sisters despised me, and looked on me with contempt on the account of my unhappy disposition; and even my servants slighted me, and disregarded all I said to them. I had one sister who was always exceeding fond of me, and I loved her entirely; her name was L O G W Y, she was quite white, and fair, with fine light hair though my father and mother were black.—I was truly concerned to leave my beloved sister, and she cry'd most sadly to part with me, wringing her hands, and discovered every sign of grief that can be imagined. Indeed if I could have known when I left my friends and country that I should never return to them again my misery on that occasion would have been inexpressible. All my relations were sorry to part with me; my dear mother came with me upon a camel more than three hundred miles, the first of our journey lay chiefly through woods: at night we secured ourselves from the wild beasts by making fires all around us; we and our camels kept within the circle, or we must have been torn to pieces by the Lyons, and other wild creatures, that roared terribly as soon as night came on, and continued to do so 'till morning.— There can be little said in favour of the country through which we passed; only a valley of marble that we came through which is unspeakably beautiful.—On each side of this valley are exceedingly high and almost inaccessible mountains—Some of these pieces of marble are of prodigious length and breadth but of different sizes and colour, and shaped in a variety of forms, in a wonderful manner.—It is most of it veined with gold mixed with striking and beautiful colours; so that when the sun darts upon it, it is as pleasing a sight as can be imagined.—The merchant that brought me from B O U R N O U, was in partnership with another gentleman who accompanied us; he was very un-willing that he should take me from home, as, he said, he fore-saw many difficulties that would attend my going with them.—He endeavoured to prevail on the merchant to throw me into a very deep pit that was in the valley, but he refused to listen to him, and said, he was resolved to take care of me: but the other was greatly dissatisfied; and when we came to a river, which we were obliged to pass through, he purpos'd throwing me in and drowning me; but the Merchant would not consent to it, so that I was preserv'd.

We travel'd 'till about four o'clock every day, and then began to make preparations for night, by cutting down large quanti-ties of wood, to make fires to preserve us from the wild beasts.—I had a very unhappy and discontented journey, being in continual fear that the people I was with would murder me. I often reflected with extreme regret on the kind friends I had left, and the idea of my dear mother frequently drew tears from my eyes.—I cannot recollect how long we were in going from BOURNOU to the GOLD COAST; but as there is no shipping nearer to BORNOU than that City, it was tedious in travelling so far by land, being upwards of a thousand miles.—I was heartily rejoic'd when we arriv'd at the end of our journey: I now vainly imagin'd that all my troubles and inquietudes would terminate here; but could I have looked into futurity, I should have perceiv'd that I had much more to suffer than I had before experienc'd, and that they had as yet but barely commenc'd.

I was now more than a thousand miles from home, without a friend or any means to procure one. Soon after I came to the merchant's house I heard the drums beat remarkably loud, and the trumpets blow—the persons accustom'd to this employ, are oblig'd to go upon a very high structure appointed for that pur-pose, that the sound might be heard at a great distance: They are higher than the steeples are in England. I was mightily pleas'd with sounds so entirely new to me, and was very inquisitive to know the cause of this rejoicing, and ask'd many questions con-cerning it: I was answer'd that it was meant as a compliment to me, because I was Grandson to the King of BOURNOU.

This account gave me a secret pleasure; but I was not suffer'd long to enjoy this satisfaction, for in the evening of the same day, two of the merchant's sons (boys about my own age) came running to me, and told me, that the next day I was to die, for the King intended to behead me.—I reply'd that I was sure it could not be true, for that I came there to play with them, and to see houses walk upon the water with wings to them, and the white folks; but I was soon inform'd that their King imagined that I was sent by my father as a spy, and would make such discoveries at my return home that would enable them to make war with the greater advantage to ourselves; and for these reasons he had resolved I should never return to my native country.—When I heard this I suffered misery that cannot be described.—I wished a thousand times that I had never left my friends and country.— But still the ALMIGHTY was pleased to work miracles for me.

The morning I was to die, I was washed and all my gold ornaments made bright and shining, and then carried to the palace, where the King was to behead me himself (as is the custom of the place).—He was seated upon a throne at the top of an exceeding large yard, or court, which you must go through to enter the palace, it is as wide and spacious as a large field in England.—I had a lane of lifeguards to go through.—I guessed it to be about three hundred paces.

I was conducted by my friend, the merchant, about half way up; then he durst proceed no further: I went up to the KING alone—I went with an undaunted courage, and it pleased GOD to melt the heart of the King, who sat with his scymitar in his hand ready to behead me; yet, being himself so affected, he dropped it out of his hand, and took me upon his knee and wept over me. I put my right hand round his neck, and prest him to my heart.—He sat me down and blest me; and added that he would not kill me, and that I should not go home, but be sold, for a slave, so then I was conducted back again to the merchant's house.

The next day he took me on board a French brig; but the Captain did not chuse to buy me: he said I was too small; so the merchant took me home with him again.

The partner, whom I have spoken of as my enemy, was very angry to see me return, and again purposed putting an end to my life; for he represented to the other, that I should bring them into troubles and difficulties, and that I was so little that no person would buy me.

The merchant's resolution began to waver, and I was indeed afraid that I should be put to death: but however he said he would try me once more.

A few days after a Dutch ship came into the harbour, and they carried me on board, in hopes that the Captain would purchase me.—As they went, I heard them agree, that, if they could not sell me *then*, they would throw me overboard.—I was in extreme agonies when I heard this; and as soon as ever I saw the Dutch Captain, I ran to him, and put my arms round him, and said, "father, save me." (for I knew that if he did not buy me, I should be treated very ill, or, possibly, murdered) And though he did not understand my language, yet it pleased the ALMIGHTY to influence him in my behalf, and he bought me *for two yards of check*, which is of more value *there*, than in England.

When I left my dear mother I had a large quantity of gold about me, as is the custom of our country, it was made into rings, and they were linked into one another, and formed into a kind of chain, and so put round my neck, and arms and legs, and a large piece hanging at one ear almost in the shape of a pear. I found all this troublesome, and was glad when my new Master took it from me—I was now washed, and clothed in the Dutch or English manner.—My master grew very fond of me, and I loved him exceedingly. I watched every look, was always ready when he wanted me, and endeavoured to convince him, by every action, that my only pleasure was to serve him well.— I have since thought that he must have been a serious man. His actions corresponded very well with such a character.—He used to read prayers in public to the ship's crew every Sabbath day; and when first I saw him read, I was never so surprised in my whole life as when I saw the book talk to my master; for I thought it did, as I observed him to look upon it, and move his lips.—I wished it would do so to me.—As soon as my master had done reading I follow'd him to the place where he put the book, being mightily delighted with it, and when nobody saw me, I open'd it and put my ear down close upon it, in great hope that it wou'd say something to me; but was very sorry and greatly disappointed when I found it would not speak, this thought immediately presented itself to me, that every body and every thing despis'd me because I was black.

I was exceedingly sea-sick at first; but when I became more accustom'd to the sea, it wore off.—My master's ship was bound for Barbadoes. When we came there, he thought fit to speak of me to several gentlemen of his acquaintance, and one of them exprest a particular desire to see me.—He had a great mind to buy me; but the Captain could not immediately be prevail'd on to part with me; but however, as the gentleman seem'd very solicitous, he at length let me go, and I was sold for fifty dollars (*four and sixpenny-pieces in English*). My new master's name was Vanhorn, a young Gentleman; his home was in New-England in the City of New-York; to which place he took me with him. He dress'd me in his livery, and was very good to me. My chief business was to wait at table, and tea, and clean knives, and I had a very easy place; but the servants us'd to curse and swear surprizingly; which I learnt faster than any thing, 'twas almost the first English I could speak. If any of them affronted me, I was sure to call upon God to damn them immediately; but I was broke of it all at once, occasioned by the correction of an old black servant that liv'd in the family—One day I had just clean'd the knives for dinner, when one of the maids took one to cut bread and butter with; I was very angry with her, and called upon God to damn her; when this old black man told me I must not say so. I ask'd him why? He replied there was a wicked man call'd the Devil, that liv'd in hell, and would take all that said these words, and put them in the fire and burn them.—This terrified me greatly, and I was entirely broke of swearing.—Soon after this, as I was placing the china for tea, my mistress came into the room just as the maid had been cleaning it; the girl had unfortunately sprinkled the wainscot with the mop; at which my mistress was angry; the girl very foolishly answer'd her again, which made her worse, and she call'd upon God to damn her.—I was vastly concern'd to hear this, as she was a fine young lady, and very good to me, insomuch that I could not help speaking to her, "Madam, says I, you must not say so," Why, says she? Because there is a black man call'd the Devil that lives in hell, and he will put you in the fire and burn you, and I shall be very sorry for that. Who told you this replied my lady? Old Ned, says I. Very well was all her answer; but she told my master of it, and he order'd that old Ned should be tyed up and whipp'd, and was never suffer'd to come into the kitchen with the rest of the servants afterwards.—My mistress was not angry with me, but rather diverted with my simplicity and, by way of talk, She repeated what I had said, to many of her acquaintance that visited her; among the rest, Mr. Freelandhouse, a very gracious, good Minister, heard it, and he took a great deal of notice of me, and desired my master to part with me to him. He would not hear of it at first, but, being greatly persuaded, he let me go, and Mr. Freelandhouse gave £50. for me.—He took me home with him, and made me kneel down, and put my two hands together, and pray'd for me, and every night and morning he did the same.—I could not make out what it was for, nor the meaning of it, nor what they spoke to when they talk'd—I thought it comical, but I lik'd it very well.—After I had been a little while with my new master I grew more familiar, and ask'd him the meaning of prayer: (I could hardly speak english to be understood) he took great pains with me, and made me understand that he pray'd to God, who liv'd in Heaven; that He was my Father and BEST Friend.— I told him that this must be a mistake; that *my* father liv'd at BOURNOU, and I wanted very much to see him, and likewise my dear mother, and sister, and I wish'd he would be so good as to send me home to them; and I added, all I could think of to induce him to convey me back. I appeared in great trouble, and my good master was so much affected that the tears ran down his face. He told me that God was a GREAT and GOOD SPIRIT, that He created all the world, and every person and thing in it, in Ethiopia, Africa, and America, and every where. I was delighted when I heard this: There, says I, I always thought so when I liv'd at home! Now if I had wings like an Eagle I would fly to tell my dear mother that God is greater than the sun, moon, and stars; and that they were made by Him.

I was exceedingly pleas'd with this information of my master's, because it corresponded so well with my own opinion; I thought now if I could but get home, I should be wiser than all my country-folks, my grandfather, or father, or mother, or any of them—But though I was somewhat enlighten'd by this information of my master's, yet, I had no other knowledge of God but that He was a GOOD SPIRIT, and created every body, and every thing—I never was sensible in myself, nor had any one ever told me, that He would punish the wicked, and love the just. I was only glad that I had been told there was a God because I had always thought so.

My dear kind master grew very fond of me, as was his Lady; she put me to School, but I was uneasy at that, and did not like to go; but my master and mistress requested me to learn in the gentlest terms, and persuaded me to attend my school without any anger at all; that, at last, I came to like it better, and learnt to read pretty well. My schoolmaster was a good man, his name was Vanosdore, and very indulgent to me.—I was in this state when, one Sunday, I heard my master preach from these words out of the Revelations, chap. i. v. 7. *"Behold, He cometh in the clouds and every eye shall see him and they that pierc'd Him."* These words affected me excessively; I was in great agonies because I thought my master directed them to me only; and, I fancied, that he observ'd me with unusual earnestness—I was farther confirm'd in this belief as I look'd round the church, and could see no one person beside myself in such grief and distress as I was; I began to think that my master hated me, and was very desirous to go home, to my own country; for I thought that if God did come (as he said) He would be sure to be most angry with *me*, as I did not know what He was, nor had ever heard of him before.

I went home in great trouble, but said nothing to any body.— I was somewhat afraid of my master; I thought he disliked me.—The next text I heard him preach from was, Heb. xii. 14. *"follow peace with all men, and holiness, without which no man shall see the LORD."* he preached the law so severely, that it made me tremble.—he said, that GOD would judge the whole world; ETHIOPIA, ASIA, and AFRICA, and every where.—I was now excessively perplexed, and undetermined what to do; as I had now reason to believe my situation would be equally bad to go, as to stay.—I kept these thoughts to myself, and said nothing to any person whatever.

I should have complained to my good mistress of this great trouble of mind, but she had been a little strange to me for several days before this happened, occasioned by a story told of me by one of the maids. The servants were all jealous, and envied me the regard, and favour shewn me by my master and mistress; and the Devil being always ready, and diligent in wickedness, had influenced this girl, to make a lye on me.—This happened about hay-harvest, and one day when I was unloading the waggon to put the hay into the barn, she watched an opportunity, in my absence, to take the fork out of the stick, and hide it: when I came again to my work, and could not find it, I was a good deal vexed, but I concluded it was dropt somewhere among the hay; so I went and bought another with my own money: when the girl saw that I had another, she was so malicious that she told my mistress I was very unfaithful, and not the person she took me for; and that she knew, I had, without my master's permission, order'd many things in his name, that he must pay for; and as a proof of my carelessness produc'd the fork she had taken out of the stick, and said, she had found it out of doors—My Lady, not knowing the truth of these things, was a little shy to me, till she mention'd it, and then I soon cleared myself, and convinc'd her that these accusations were false.

I continued in a most unhappy state for many days. My good mistress insisted on knowing what was the matter. When I made known my situation she gave me John Bunyan on the holy war, to read; I found his experience similar to my own, which gave me reason to suppose he must be a bad man; as I was convinc'd of my own corrupt nature, and the misery of my own heart: and as he acknowledg'd that he was likewise in the same condition, I experienc'd no relief at all in reading his work, but rather the reverse.—I took the book to my lady, and inform'd her I did not like it at all, it was concerning a wicked man as bad as myself; and I did not chuse to read it, and I desir'd her to give me another, wrote by a better man that was holy and without sin.—She assur'd me that John Bunyan was a good man, but she could not convince me; I thought him to be too much like myself to be upright, as his experience seem'd to answer with my own.

I am very sensible that nothing but the great power and unspeakable mercies of the Lord could relieve my soul from the heavy burden it laboured under at that time.—A few days after my master gave me Baxter's *Call to the unconverted*. This was no relief to me neither; on the contrary it occasioned as much distress in me as the other had before done, *as it* invited all to come to *Christ* and I found myself so wicked and miserable that I could not come—This consideration threw me into agonies that cannot be described; insomuch that I even attempted to put an end to my life—I took one of the large case-knives, and went into the stable with an intent to destroy myself; and as I endeavoured with all my strength to force the knife into my side, it bent double. I was instantly struck with horror at the thought of my own rashness, and my conscience told me that had I succeeded in this attempt I should probably have gone to hell.

I could find no relief, nor the least shadow of comfort; the extreme distress of my mind so affected my health that I continued very ill for three Days, and Nights; and would admit of no means to be taken for my recovery, though my lady was very kind, and sent many things to me; but I rejected every means of relief and wished to die—I would not go into my own bed, but lay in the stable upon straw—I felt all the horrors of a troubled conscience, so hard to be born, and saw all the vengeance of God ready to overtake me—I was sensible that there was no way for me to be saved unless I came to *Christ*, and I could not come to Him: I thought that it was impossible He should receive such a sinner as me.

The last night that I continued in this place, in the midst of my distress these words were brought home upon my mind, "*Behold the Lamb of God.*" I was something comforted at this, and began to grow easier and wished for day that I might find these words in my bible—I rose very early the following morning, and went to my school-master, Mr. Vanosdore, and communicated the situation of my mind to him; he was greatly rejoiced to find me enquiring the way to Zion, and blessed the Lord who had worked so wonderfully for me a poor heathen.— I was more familiar with this good gentleman than with my master, or any other person; and found myself more at liberty to talk to him: he encouraged me greatly, and prayed with me frequently, and I was always benefited by his discourse.

About a quarter of a mile from my Master's house stood a large remarkably fine Oak-tree, in the midst of a wood; I often used to be employed there in cutting down trees, (a work I was very fond of) I seldom failed going to this place every day; sometimes twice a day if I could be spared. It was the highest pleasure I ever experienced to set under this Oak; for there I used to pour out all my complaints to the LORD: and when I had any particular grievance I used to go there, and talk to the tree, and tell my sorrows, as if it had been to a friend.

Here I often lamented my own wicked heart, and undone state; and found more comfort and consolation than I ever was sensible of before.—Whenever I was treated with ridicule or contempt, I used to come here and find peace. I now began to relish the book my Master gave me, Baxter's *Call to the unconverted*, and took great delight in it. I was always glad to be employ'd in cutting wood, 'twas a great part of my business, and I follow'd it with delight, as I was then quite alone and my heart lifted up to GOD, and I was enabled to pray continually; and blessed for ever be his Holy Name, he faithfully answer'd my prayers. I can never be thankful enough to Almighty GOD for the many comfortable opportunities I experienced there.

HENRY BROWN

Via the subversive planning with free Black people and abo-
litionists, Henry Brown (1816–1897) escaped slavery by
shipping himself in a wooden crate from Richmond, Vir-
ginia, to Philadelphia, Pennsylvania. Brown's published
narrative gives an overview of his life in and after slavery,
detailing his love and longings for his family, describing
with clarity the horrific treatment from which he was flee-
ing, and offering an account for just how he was able to
carry out his escape. It is a fascinating tale of how one man's
determination and craft prompted a multiracial coalition of
antislavery-minded laypeople and abolitionists to put their
own reputations and freedom on the line to actuate the lib-
erty of others. In the early periods of his freedom, Brown
created and performed in a traveling antislavery panorama
and served as an abolitionist orator, recounting his unlikely
life story before setting the words to print in 1849. In an ef-
fort to subvert the Fugitive Slave Act of 1850, Brown moved
to England, where he took on the cause of American aboli-
tion and worked as a performer and magician for nearly
three decades.

From *Narrative of Henry Box Brown,*
Who Escaped from Slavery Enclosed in
a Box 3 Feet Long and 2 Feet Wide

(1849)

It was on a pleasant morning, in the month of August, 1848,
that I left my wife and three children safely at our little home,
and proceeded to my allotted labor. The sun shone brightly as
he commenced his daily task, and as I gazed upon his early rays,
emitting their golden light upon the rich fields adjacent to the

city, and glancing across the abode of my wife and family, and
as I beheld the numerous companies of slaves, hieing their way
to their daily labors, and reflected upon the difference between
their lot and mine, I felt that, although I was a slave, there were
many alleviations to my cup of sorrow. It was true, that the
greater portion of my earnings was taken from me, by the un-
scrupulous hands of my dishonest master,—that I was entirely
at his mercy, and might at any hour be snatched from what
sources of joy were open to me—that he might, if he chose, extend his robber hand, and demand a still larger portion of my
earnings,—and above all, that intellectual privileges were entirely denied me; but as I imprinted a parting kiss upon the lips
of my faithful wife, and pressed to my bosom the little darling
cherubs, who followed me saying, in their childish accents, "Father, come back soon," I felt that life was not all a blank to me;
that there were some pure joys yet my portion. O, how my heart
would have been riven with unutterable anguish, if I had then
realized the awful calamity which was about to burst upon my
unprotected head! Reader, are you a husband, and can you listen to my sad story, without being moved to cease all your connection with that stern power, which stretched out its piratical
arm, and basely robbed me of all dear to me on earth!

The sun had traced his way to mid-heaven, and the hour for
the laborers to turn from their tasks, and to seek refreshment
for their toil-worn frames,—and when I should take my prattling children on my knee,—was fast approaching; but there
burst upon me a sound so dreadful, and so sudden, that the
shock well nigh overwhelmed me. It was as if the heavens themselves had fallen upon me, and the everlasting hills of God's
erecting, like an avalanche, had come rolling over my head!
And what was it? "Your wife and smiling babes are gone; in
prison they are locked, and to-morrow's sun will see them far
away from you, on their way to the distant South!" Pardon the
utterance of my feelings here, reader, for surely a man may feel,
when all that he prizes on earth is, at one fell stroke, swept
from his reach! O God, if there is a moment when vengeance
from thy righteous throne should be hurled upon guilty man,
and hot thunderbolts of wrath, should burst upon his wicked
head, it surely is at such a time as this! And this is Slavery;

its certain, necessary and constituent part. Without this terrific pillar to its demon walls, it falls to the ground, as a bridge sinks, when its buttresses are swept from under it by the rushing floods. This is Slavery. No kind master's indulgent care can guard his chosen slave, his petted chattel, however fond he may profess to be of such a piece of property, from so fearful a calamity. My master treated me as kindly as he could, and retain me in slavery; but did that keep me from experiencing this terrible deprivation? The sequel will show you even his care for me. What could I do? I had left my fond wife and prattling children, as happy as slaves could expect to be; as I was not anticipating their loss, for the pious man who bought them last, had, as you recollect, received a sum of money from me, under the promise of not selling them. My first impulse, of course, was to rush to the jail, and behold my family once more, before our final separation. I started for this infernal place, but had not proceeded a great distance, before I met a gentleman, who stopped me, and beholding my anguish of heart, as depicted on my countenance, inquired of me what the trouble was with me. I told him as I best could, when he advised me not to go to the jail, for the man who had sold my wife, had told my master some falsehoods about me, and had induced him to give orders to the jailor to seize me, and confine me in prison, if I should appear there. He said I would undoubtedly be sold separate from my wife, and he thought I had better not go there. I then persuaded a young man of my acquaintance to go to the prison, and sent by him, to my wife, some money and a message in reference to the cause of my failure to visit her. It seems that it would have been useless for me to have ventured there, for as soon as this young man arrived, and inquired for my wife, he was seized and put in prison,—the jailor mistaking him for me; but when he discovered his mistake, he was very angry, and vented his rage upon the innocent youth, by kicking him out of prison. I then repaired to my Christian master, and three several times, during the ensuing twenty-four hours, did I beseech and entreat him to purchase my wife; but no tears of mine made the least impression upon his obdurate heart. I laid my case before him, and reminded him of the faithfulness with which I had served him, and of my utmost endeavors to please him, but this *kind* master—recollect reader—utterly refused to advance a small portion of the $5,000 I had paid him, in order to relieve my sufferings; and he was a member, in good and regular standing, of an Episcopal church in Richmond! His reply to me was worthy of the morality of Slavery, and shows just how much religion, the kindest and most pious of Southern slaveholders have. "*You can get another wife,*" said he; but I told him the Bible said, "What God has joined together, let not man put asunder," and that I did not want any other wife but my own lawful one, whom I loved so much. At the mention of this passage of Scripture, he drove me from his house, saying, he did not wish to hear that!

I now endeavored to persuade two gentlemen of my acquaintance, to buy my wife; but they told me they did not think it was right to hold slaves, or else they would gladly assist me, for they sincerely pitied me, and advised me to go to my master again; but I knew this would be useless. My agony was now complete. She with whom I had travelled the journey of life, for the space of twelve years, with three little pledges of domestic affection, must now be forever separated from me—I must remain alone and desolate. O God, shall my wife and children never more greet my sight, with their cheerful looks and happy smiles? Far, far away, in Carolina's swamps are they now, toiling beneath the scorching rays of the hot sun, with no husband's voice to soothe the hardships of my wife's lot, and no father's kind look to gladden the heart of my disconsolate little ones.*

I call upon you, Sons of the North, if your blood has not lost its bright color of liberty, and is not turned to the blackened gore which surrounds the slaveholder's polluted hearts, to arise in your might, and demand the liberation of the slaves. If you do not, at the day of final account, I shall bear witness against you, as well as against the slaveholders themselves, as the cause of my and my brethren's bereavement. Think you, at that dread hour, you can escape the scrutinizing look of the Judge of all

*I would here state, that Mr. Brown is endeavoring to raise money to purchase his family. Twelve hundred dollars being the sum demanded for them. Any person wishing to assist him in this laudable purpose, can enclose donations to him, directing No. 21 Cornhill, Boston.

the earth, as he "maketh inquisition for the blood of the inno-
cents?" Oh, no; but equally with the Southern slaveholders, will
your character be condemned by the Ruler of the universe.

The next day, I stationed myself by the side of the road, along
which the slaves, amounting to three hundred and fifty, were to
pass. The purchaser of my wife was a *Methodist* minister, who
was about starting for North Carolina. Pretty soon five waggon-
loads of little children passed, and looking at the foremost one,
what should I see but a little child, pointing its tiny hand towards me, exclaiming, "There's my father; I knew he would
come and bid me good-bye." It was my eldest child! Soon the
gang approached in which my wife was chained. I looked, and
beheld her familiar face; but O, reader, that glance of agony!
may God spare me ever again enduring the excruciating horror
of that moment! She passed, and came near to where I stood. I
seized hold of her hand, *intending* to bid her farewell; but
words failed me; the gift of utterance had fled, and I remained
speechless. I followed her for some distance, with her hand
grasped in mine, as if to save her from her fate, but I could not
speak, and I was obliged to turn away in silence.

This is not an imaginary scene, reader; it is not a fiction, but
an every-day reality at the South; and all I can say more to you,
in reference to it is, that if you will not, after being made acquainted with these facts, consecrate your all to the slaves' release from bondage, you are utterly unworthy the name of a
man, and should go and hide yourself, in some impenetrable
cave, where no eye can behold your demon form.

One more scene occurs in the tragical history of my life, before the curtain drops, and I retire from the stage of observation, as far as past events are concerned; not, however, to shrink
from public gaze, as if ashamed of my perilous adventures, or to
retire into private life, lest the bloodhounds of the South should
scent my steps, and start in pursuit of their missing property.
No, reader, for as long as three millions of my countrymen pine
in cruel bondage, on Virginia's exhausted soil, and in Carolina's
pestilential rice swamps; in the cane-breaks of Georgia, and on
the the cotton fields of Louisiana and Mississippi, and in the in-
salubrious climate of Texas; as well as suffer under the slave-
driver's cruel lash, all over the almost God-forsaken South; I

shall never refuse to advocate their claims to your sympathy, whenever a fitting occasion occurs to speak in their behalf.

But you are eager to learn the particulars of my journey from freedom to liberty. The first thing that occurred to me, after the cruel separation of my wife and children from me, and I had recovered my senses, so as to know how to act, was, thoughts of freeing myself from slavery's iron yoke. I had suffered enough under its heavy weight, and I determined I would endure it no longer; and those reasons which often deter the slave from attempting to escape, no longer existed in reference to me, for my family were gone, and slavery now had no mitigating circumstances, to lessen the bitterness of its cup of woe. It is true, as my master had told me, that I could "get another wife;" but no man, excepting a brute below the human species, would have proposed such a step to a person in my circumstances; and as I was not such a degraded being, I did not dream of so conducting. Marriage was not a thing of personal convenience with me, to be cast aside as a worthless garment, whenever the slaveholder's will required it; but it was a sacred institution binding upon me, as long as the God who had "joined us together," refrained from untying the nuptial knot. What! leave the wife of my bosom for another! and while my heart was leaping from its abode, to pour its strong affections upon the kindred soul of my devoted partner, could I receive a stranger, another person to my embrace, as if the ties of love existed only in the presence of the object loved! Then, indeed, should I have been a traitor to that God, who had linked our hearts together in fond affection, and cemented our union, by so many additional cords, twining around our hearts; as a tree and an arbor are held together by the clinging of the tendrils of the adhering vine, which winds itself about them so closely. Slavery, and slavery abettors, seize hold of these tender scions, and cut and prune them away from both tree and arbor, as remorselessly as a gardener cuts down the briars and thorns which disturb the growth of his fair plants; but all humane, and every virtuous man, must instinctively recoil from such transactions, as they would from soul murder, or from the commission of some enormous deed of villany.

Reader, in the light of these scenes you may behold, as in a glass, your true character. Refined and delicate you may pretend to be, and may pass yourself off as a pure and virtuous person; but if you refuse to exert yourself for the overthrow of a system, which thus tramples human affection under its bloody feet, and demands of its crushed victims, the sacrifice of all that is noble, virtuous and pure, upon its smoking altars; you may rest assured, that if the balances of *purity* were extended before you, He who "searcheth the hearts, and trieth the reins," would say to you, as your character underwent his searching scrutiny, "Thou art weighed in the balance and found wanting."

I went to Mr. Allen, and requested of him permission to refrain from labor for a short time, in consequence of a disabled finger; but he refused to grant me this permission, on the ground that my hand was not lame enough to justify him in so doing. Nothing daunted by this rebuff, I took some oil of vitriol, intending to pour a few drops upon my finger, to make it sufficiently sore, to disable me from work, which I succeeded in, beyond my wishes; for in my hurry, a larger quantity than it was my purpose to apply to my finger, found its way there, and my finger was soon eaten through to the bone. The overseer then was obliged to allow me to absent myself from business, for it was impossible for me to work in that situation. But I did not waste my precious furlough in idle mourning over my fate. I armed myself with determined energy, for action, and in the words of one of old, in the name of God, "I leaped over a wall, and run through a troop" of difficulties. After searching for assistance for some time, I at length was so fortunate as to find a friend, who promised to assist me, for one half the money I had about me, which was one hundred and sixty-six dollars. I gave him eighty-six, and he was to do his best in forwarding my scheme. Long did we remain together, attempting to devise ways and means to carry me away from the land of separation of families, of whips and thumbscrews, and auction blocks; but as often as a plan was suggested by my friend, there would appear some difficulty in the way of its accomplishment. Perhaps it may not be best to mention what these plans were, as some unfortunate slaves may thereby be prevented from availing themselves of these methods of escape.

At length, after praying earnestly to Him, who seeth afar off, for assistance, in my difficulty, suddenly, as if from above, there darted into my mind these words, "Go and get a box, and put yourself in it." I pondered the words over in my mind. "Get a box?" thought I; "what can this mean?" But I was "not disobedient unto the heavenly vision," and I determined to put into practice this direction, as I considered it, from my heavenly Father.* I went to the depot, and there noticed the size of the largest boxes, which commonly were sent by the cars, and returned with their dimensions. I then repaired to a carpenter, and induced him to make me a box of such a description as I wished, informing him of the use I intended to make of it. He assured me I could not live in it; but as it was dear liberty I was in pursuit of, I thought it best to make the trial.

When the box was finished, I carried it, and placed it before my friend, who had promised to assist me, who asked me if that was to "put my clothes in?" I replied that it was not, but to "*put Henry Brown in!*" He was astonished at my temerity; but I insisted upon his placing me in it, and nailing me up, and he finally consented.

After corresponding with a friend in Philadelphia, arrangements were made for my departure, and I took my place in this narrow prison, with a mind full of uncertainty as to the result. It was a critical period of my life, I can assure you, reader; but if you have never been deprived of your liberty, as I was, you cannot realize the power of that hope of freedom, which was to me indeed, "an anchor to the soul, both sure and steadfast."

I laid me down in my darkened home of three feet by two, and like one about to be guillotined, resigned myself to my fate. My friend was to accompany me, but he failed to do so; and contented himself with sending a telegraph message to his correspondent in Philadelphia, that such a box was on its way to his care.

I took with me a bladder filled with water to bathe my neck with, in case of too great heat; and with no access to the fresh air, excepting three small gimblet holes, I started on my perilous cruise. I was first carried to the express office, the box being

*Reader, smile not at the above idea, for if there is a God of love, we must believe that he suggests steps to those who apply to him in times of trouble, by which they can be delivered from their difficulty. I firmly believe this doctrine, and know it to be true from frequent experience. C. S.

placed on its end, so that I started with my head downwards, although the box was directed, "this side up with care." From the express office, I was carried to the depot, and from thence tumbled roughly into the baggage car, where I *happened* to fall "right side up," but no thanks to my transporters. But after a while the cars stopped, and I was put aboard a steamboat, *and placed on my head*. In this dreadful position, I remained the space of an hour and a half, it seemed to me, when I began to feel of my eyes and head, and found to my dismay, that my eyes were almost swollen out of their sockets, and the veins on my temple seemed ready to burst. I made no noise however, determining to obtain "*victory or death*," but endured the terrible pain, as well as I could, sustained under the whole by the thoughts of sweet liberty. About half an hour afterwards, I attempted again to lift my hands to my face, but I found I was not able to move them. A cold sweat now covered me from head to foot. Death seemed my inevitable fate, and every moment I expected to feel the blood flowing over me, which had burst from my veins. One half hour longer and my sufferings would have ended in that fate, which I preferred to slavery; but I lifted up my heart to God in prayer, believing that he would yet deliver me, when to my joy, I overheard two men say, "We have been here *two* hours and have travelled twenty miles, now let us sit down, and rest ourselves." They suited the action to the word, and turned the box over, containing my soul and body, thus delivering me from the power of the grim messenger of death, who a few moments previously, had aimed his fatal shaft at my head, and had placed his icy hands on my throbbing heart. One of these men inquired of the other, what he supposed that box contained, to which his comrade replied, that he guessed it was the mail. "Yes," thought I, "it is a *male*, indeed, although not the *mail* of the United States."

Soon after this fortunate event, we arrived at Washington, where I was thrown from the wagon, and again as my luck would have it, fell on my head. I was then rolled down a declivity, until I reached the platform from which the cars were to start. During this short but rapid journey, my neck came very near being dislocated, as I felt it crack, as if it had snapped asunder. Pretty soon, I heard some one say, "there is no room for this box, it will have to remain behind." I then again applied to the Lord, my help in all my difficulties, and in a few minutes I heard a gentleman direct the hands to place it aboard, as "it came with the mail and must go on with it." I was then tumbled into the car, my head downwards again, as I seemed to be destined to escape on my head; a sign probably, of the opinion of American people respecting such bold adventurers as myself; that our heads should be held downwards, whenever we attempt to benefit ourselves. Not the only instance of this propensity, on the part of the American people, towards the colored race. We had not proceeded far, however, before more baggage was placed in the car, at a stopping place, and I was again turned to my proper position. No farther difficulty occurred until my arrival at Philadelphia. I reached this place at three o'clock in the morning, and remained in the depot until six o'clock, A. M., at which time, a waggon drove up, and a person inquired for a box directed to such a place, "right side up." I was soon placed on this waggon, and carried to the house of my friend's correspondent, where quite a number of persons were waiting to receive me. They appeared to be some afraid to open the box at first, but at length one of them rapped upon it, and with a trembling voice, asked, "Is all right within?" to which I replied, "All right." The joy of these friends was excessive, and like the ancient Jews, who repaired to the rebuilding of Jerusalem, each one seized hold of some tool, and commenced opening my grave. At length the cover was removed, and I arose, and shook myself from the lethargy into which I had fallen; but exhausted nature proved too much for my frame, and I swooned away.

After my recovery from this fainting fit, the first impulse of my soul, as I looked around, and beheld my friends, and was told that I was safe, was to break out in a song of deliverance, and praise to the most high God, whose arm had been so signally manifest in my escape. Great God, was I a freeman! Had I indeed succeeded in effecting my escape from the human wolves of Slavery? O what extastic joy thrilled through every nerve and fibre of my system! My labor was accomplished, my warfare was ended, and I stood erect before my equal fellow men, no longer a crouching slave, forever at the look and nod of a whimsical and tyrannical slave-owner. Long had seemed my journey, and terribly hazardous had been my attempt to gain my birth-right; but it all seemed a comparatively light price to pay for the precious boon of *Liberty*. O ye, who know not the value of this "pearl of great price," by having been all your life shut out from its life-giving presence; learn of how much importance its possession is regarded, by the panting fugitive, as he traces his way through the labyrinths of snares, placed between him and the object of his fond desires! Sympathize with the three millions of crushed and mangled ones who this day pine in cruel bondage, and arouse yourself to action in their behalf! This you will do, if you are not traitors to your God and to humanity. Aid not in placing in high offices, *baby-stealers and women-whippers*; and if these wicked men, all covered with the clotted gore of their mangled victims, come among you, scorn the idea of bowing in homage to them, whatever may be the character of their claims to your regard. No matter, if they are called presidents of your nation, still utterly refuse to honor them; which *you will most certainly do*, if you are true to the Slave!

After remaining a short time in Philadelphia, it was thought expedient that I should proceed to Massachusetts, and accordingly funds sufficient to carry me there, were raised by some anti-slavery friends, and I proceeded to Boston. After remaining a short time in that city, I concluded to go to New Bedford, in which place I remained a few weeks, under the care of Mr. Joseph Rickerston of that place, who treated me very kindly. At length hearing of a large anti-slavery meeting to be held in Boston, I left New Bedford, and found myself again in that city, so famous for its devotion to liberty in the days of the American revolution; and here, in the presence of several thousand people, did I first relate in public, the story of my sufferings, since which time I have repeated my simple tale in different parts of Massachusetts, and in the State of Maine.

I now stand before you as a free man, but since my arrival among you, I have been informed that your laws require that I should still be held as a slave; and that if my master should espy me in any nook or corner of the free states, according to the constitution of the United States, he could secure me and carry me back into Slavery; so that I am confident I am not safe, even here, if what I have heard concerning your laws is true. I cannot imagine why you should uphold such strange laws. I have been told that every time a man goes to the polls and votes, he virtually swears to sustain them, frightful as they are. It seems to me to be a hard case, for a man to endure what I have endured in effecting my escape, and then to be continually exposed to be seized by my master, and carried back into that horrid pit from which I have escaped. I have been told, however, that the people here would not allow me to be thus returned, that they would break their own laws in my behalf, which seems quite curious to me; for why should you make laws, and swear to uphold them, and then break them? I do not understand much about laws, to be sure, as the law of my master is the one I have been subject to all my life, but some how, it looks a little singular to me, that wise people should be obliged to break their own laws, or else do a very wicked act. I have been told that there are twice as many voters at the North as there are at the South, and much more wealth, as well as other things of importance, which makes me study much, why the Northern people live under such laws. If I was one of them, and had any influence among them, it appears to me, I should advocate the overthrow of such laws, and the establishment of better ones in their room. Many people tell me besides, that if the slaves should rise up, and do as they did in Nat Turner's time, endeavor to fight their way to freedom, that the Northern people are pledged to shoot them down, and keep them in subjection to their masters. Now I cannot understand this, for almost all the people tell me, that they "are opposed to Slavery," and yet they swear to prevent the slaves from obtaining their liberty! If these things could be made clear to my mind, I should be glad; but a fog hangs over my eyes at present in reference to this matter.

I now wish to introduce to your hearing, a friend of mine, who will tell you more about these things than I can, until I have had more time to examine this curious subject. What he shall have to say to you, may not be as interesting as the account of my sufferings, but if you really wish to help my brethren in bondage, you will not be unwilling to hear what he may say to you, in reference to the way to abolish slavery, as you cannot be opposed to my sufferings, unless you are willing to exert yourselves for the overthrow of the cruel system which caused them.

BENJAMIN DREW

*In the preface to his important collection of narratives from
self-liberated individuals who escaped slavery in the United
States, the American journalist Benjamin Drew (1812–
1903) notes that most Canadians possessed little to no insight about the community of more than thirty thousand
Black American refugees who lived in Canada West. Drew
found that the refugees' "enemies, the supporters of slavery,
have represented them as 'indolent, vicious, and debased;
suffering and starving, because they have no kind masters to
do the thinking for them, and to urge them to the necessary
labor, which their own laziness and want of forecast, lead
them to avoid.' Some of their friends, anxious to obtain aid
for the comparatively few in number, (perhaps three thousand in all,) who have actually stood in need of assistance,
have not, in all cases, been sufficiently discriminating in their
statements: old settlers and new, the rich and the poor, the
good and the bad, have suffered alike from imputations of
poverty and starvation—misfortunes, which, if resulting
from idleness, are akin to crimes. Still another set of men,
selfish in purpose, have, while pretending to act for the fugitives, found a way to the purses of the sympathetic, and appropriated to their own use, funds intended for supposititious
sufferers." Accompanied by interlocutors, Drew traveled
throughout Canada West to record the voices of these fugitives from slavery, properly historicize the circumstances
that compelled their migration to Canada, and to report
on the condition of the more impoverished and vulnerable
among the inhabitants and their ongoing needs.*

From *A North-Side View of Slavery.*
The Refugee; or, The Narratives of Fugitive Slaves in Canada, Related by Themselves
(1856)

WINDSOR.

Windsor, at the terminus of the Great Western Railway, is in the township of Sandwich. It was incorporated January 1, 1854, with a population of 1000 souls. It is now estimated to contain one thousand four hundred inhabitants. There are settled in various parts of the village fifty families of colored people, some of whom entertain as boarders a number of fugitives from bondage. Assuming an average of five in a family, the colored population may be set down at two hundred and fifty. The general appearance of these is very much in their favor. There are many good mechanics among them: nearly all have comfortable homes, and some occupy very neat and handsome houses of their own.

Appearances indicate that the inhabitants of Windsor will unite in supporting good schools for the rising generation, without distinction of color. Where separate schools exist, the advantage in respect to buildings and teachers is for the most part on the side of the whites; and unless the separate schools are abolished, there is reason to fear that the progress of the colored people in education will be very much retarded in the greater part of the province. Mrs. Mary E. Bibb, widow of the late lamented Henry Bibb, Esq., has devoted herself to teaching a private school in Windsor, and with good success. During the last spring term, she had an attendance of forty-six pupils, seven of whom were white children.

A gentleman of Windsor who has long taken a deep interest in the welfare of the African race, is of opinion that immigrants who have been engaged in agricultural pursuits in Pennsylvania

and other free States are more industrous and "more to be depended upon than those who come into Canada directly from a
state of slavery." The same gentleman assured me that the best
and most dexterous blacksmith he had ever known was a refugee: he had not such tools as he wanted, nor would take good
ones on credit, for fear he might not be able to pay: yet he
would make or mend various utensils, while other smiths could
not. He is now at Buxton.

While in Windsor, I was repeatedly informed by those who
have the best means of knowing, that "there is no need of raising money to aid the colored people here, unless for a day or
two when a fugitive family first comes in. Women get half a
dollar for washing, and it is difficult to hire them at that."

A circumstance which fell under my notice in this township
of Sandwich,* reminds me of what I might with propriety have
said in referring to other parts of the province, that it is fortunate for some conscience-stricken slaveholders, that Canada affords a refuge for a certain class of their household victims—their
slavewives, or slave-children, or both. If it be a crime to assist
slaves in reaching a land of freedom, it is not a crime of which
those terrible fellows, the northern abolitionists, alone are
guilty. Slaveholders may pour contempt on the names and the
deeds of northern philanthropists: but these have no slanderous
epithets to hurl back upon the southerner, who snatches his
children and the mother of his children from the threatening
hammer of the auctioneer, and hurriedly and tearfully starts
them for the North with the parting injunction, "Stop not short
of Canada!" We rejoice with him that England offers a place of
refuge where his wife and his offspring may be free. Yet, of any
head of such a family, a northern fanatic might be prompted
to ask, Is this course honorable and manly? Do not these children need *both* parents to look after their interests? and does
not this slave-wife, ignorant and among strangers in a strange
land, need your presence, your counsel, your direction? He that
provideth not for his own household is worse than an infidel,
and almost as bad as an abolitionist: but your family are in arrears

*See the narrative of J. C. Brown, Chatham.

for board, and are quartered upon the charity of persons who are themselves poor refugees.

Mr. David Cooper, who lives on the lands of the Industrial Institution, has furnished a statement which will be found below, showing the position of affairs where he resides.

REFUGEES' HOME.

At about nine miles from Windsor, in the townships of Sandwich and Madison, the Refugees' Home Society have made a purchase of nearly two thousand acres of land, on which reside some twenty families, each on a farm of twenty-five acres. Forty 25 acre lots have been taken up. A school is maintained there three fourths of the year.

Mr. Henry Bibb, who was himself a fugitive from the house of bondage, originated the idea of establishing a society which should "aim to purchase thirty thousand acres of government land somewhere in the most suitable sections of Canada where it can be obtained for the homeless refugees from American slavery to settle upon." This was soon after the passage of the fugitive slave bill.

The society was organized and a constitution adopted in August, 1852. The object of the society is declared to be "to assist the refugees from American slavery to obtain permanent homes, and to promote their social, moral, physical, and intellectual elevation." The society propose to purchase of the Canadian government, fifty thousand acres of land, at a cost of one hundred thousand dollars. Money for the purchase is obtained in part by contributions; and one half the moneys received for the sale of lands is devoted to the purchase of other lands. The other moiety of moneys received is to be devoted to the support of schools.

By the constitution adopted in 1852, it appears that each family of actual settlers receives twenty-five acres of land, five of which they receive free of cost, provided they shall, within three years from the time of occupancy, clear and cultivate the same. "For the remaining twenty acres, they shall pay the primary cost in nine equal payments, free of use, for which they shall receive deeds." This article may be varied to favor the aged, etc. "This Society shall give deeds to none but landless refugees from American slavery." "No person receiving land by gift or purchase from the Society shall have power to transfer the same under fifteen years from the time of the purchase or gift." "All lands becoming vacated by the removal or extinction of families, shall revert to the Executive Committee."

Here, too, as in Buxton, the claims of temperance are kept fully in view. A by-law provides that "No house shall be used for manufacturing or vending intoxicating liquors on any lot received from this Society."

The Refugees' Home Society, its officers and agents, possess the entire confidence of the American public: at least of that portion which sympathizes with the wandering outcasts from the United States. It will be seen by some of the testimonials which follow, that some dissatisfaction exists among the settlers: having its origin doubtless, in some misapprehension or mistake. Still, I have not felt at liberty to depart from my original plan—that so far as the limits of a single volume may extend, the colored people of Canada might express their own opinions, and tell their own story of their slavery in the past, their present condition, and their future prospects.

The second report of the Canada Anti-Slavery Society (for 1853), remarks: "There is doubtless a better state of things amongst the fugitives, than existed at the time when such a plan was proposed. The panic produced by the fugitive law, having subsided, the poor refugees have had more time allowed them to prepare for the change, and in consequence, their wants have been diminished. The true principle is now to assume that every man, unless disabled by sickness, can support himself and his family after he has obtained steady employment. All that able-bodied men and women require, is a fair chance, friendly advice, and a little encouragement, perhaps a little assistance at first. Those who are really willing to work, can procure employment in a short time after their arrival, so that what is specially needed, is such associations of friends at the different places where fugitives land, as will interest themselves in the colored man, put him in the way of finding employment, and extend to him such encouragement in the way of grants of land or otherwise, as his altered circumstances may require. In some places, fully to accomplish this, aid from abroad may be necessary, though in most places local charity will, we think, prove sufficient."

A True Band has been organized by the residents of the Home, and other persons in the vicinity.

THOMAS JONES.

I was a slave in Kentucky, and made my escape five years ago, at the age of thirty. The usage in Kentucky on the front part of the State is pretty good,—back, it is rather tight.

I came here without any thing. I had no money or aid of any kind. I went right into the bush chopping wood. I brought my lady with me, and we were married on the way at Bloomingsburg in Fayette Co. I have one child. With what I earned by hard licks, I bought land and have built me a frame-house. I now follow plastering and any thing I can find to do. I am worth three or four thousand dollars, and pay about thirty dollars a year tax.

If a man have aid furnished him, he does not have so much satisfaction in what he has,—he feels dependent and beholden, and does not make out so well. I have seen this, ever since I have been here,—the bad effects of this giving. I have seen men waiting, doing nothing, expecting something to come over to them. Besides, it makes a division among the colored people. The industrious are against it, the other class favor it; and so they fall out. My opinion is, that the fugitive on the road, should be assisted, but not after he gets here. If people have money to give, they had better give it to those who suffer in trying to help them here. For those who come sick, or actually stand in need, there is a society here among ourselves to take care of them.

In regard to aid from societies on the other side, there are many who know that money is raised for the poor travelling fugitive, and they take advantage of it: free people of color from the States come over pretending to be fugitives, who never were fugitives. They come in a miserable condition, often drinking men, worthless, to get the money that is raised. I have known six or seven such cases.

The colored people are doing very well. They are poor, some of them, but are all able to have enough to cat and wear, and they have comfortable homes, with few exceptions,—and some of these are in a way to have them. Some few don't seem to care whether they have good houses or not, as is the case among all people.

In the Refugees' Home they are not doing very well. Land was to be sold to the refugees at cost, giving them five acres, and they to buy twenty. Some dissatisfaction exists because there has been an advance made of four shillings an acre for surveying, although the land had been surveyed once. The refugees all refused to pay it. They were to clear up the five acres in three years. They have altered the constitution bringing it down to two years. Some had not been on three years, but went with that understanding. Alterations were made, too, enlarging the size of the houses. One of them has left the lands in consequence, and more talk of doing so. They doubt about getting deeds, and they begin to think 't is a humbug. The restrictions in regard to liquor, and not selling under so many years, nor the power to will his property to his friends, only to his children, if he have any, make them dissatisfied. They want to do as they please. If they want to exchange and get a bigger place, they want to do it without being cramped.

In addition, the men who have settled there, have been a bother to the society. As they were dependent, smart men would not go, and it has been occupied by men who expected aid from the other side.

The colored men must rely on their own two hands, or they'll never be any thing.

The colored people are temperate and moral.

WILLIAM S. EDWARDS.

I was born in Springfield, Ohio. My mother was, to the best of my belief, a free-woman. While I was a little child, a man claimed my mother as a slave woman whom he had lost seven years before, and took both her and me into Kentucky,—as I have been told to Burlington. He took us to Louisville to sell us, and there 't was proved that she was not his, but another man's slave; that other man took us back to Burlington. Here was another dispute, and another man examined, and found more marks than the other, and proved that she belonged to him. After passing through several hands she was sold, and I have not seen her since, nor do I know where she is. I have heard that when she was sold, it was left her, to take me with her into slavery, or remain there and be free. She chose to let me remain. I stayed with the family until, at thirteen, I was put to the trade of a tobacconist: remained until twenty-one. Then I did not dare to talk about freedom. I dared not name it,—I still stayed working at the business. After a while, hearing some talking about my rights, I questioned as closely as I could, but not to awaken distrust.

When I was about twenty-five, we had a dispute about a holiday, and then I first claimed my rights to his teeth, telling him that I was free. He said I must stay two years more. A man offered to lend me two hundred dollars, to buy my time: he refused. I then hired to another man, paying my claimant twenty dollars a month, for a year and five months.

I kept on inquiring, until I found the man who first carried me into Kentucky. He told me a very straight story,—that he had found the woman whom he had lost in New Orleans—she having been absent from him fifteen years and six months, having been in New Orleans all that time. I searched the records at the Recorder's office, but there was nothing on the books,—the whole being a rascally scheme, therefore they took no account of it on the books. The clerk said there surely was no trial or transaction in the court; if there had been, it would have been on record. But the man who brought me said there was a trial; he acknowledged that neither me nor my mother ever belonged to him; that it was a mistake.

Another man went with me to search, but found no scratch of a pen from ten years back to forty. I then got a white man to go to the persons who pretended to own me, and he told me, in their presence, that if a man were half white and born free, he ought to be free; and you are all of that. My boss said that I would be free after a time—that he never meant to keep me over time. He probably meant my time as long as I lived,—as a master told his slave once, "When you die, I'll give you your papers." He said I could n't pass without papers: he went with me, saying to get papers, and then he would not, but said I must stay a while longer before I could get them; that he could not give them to me just yet. Things went on in this way two or three months, until I was nearly twenty-seven years old. At length my mistress's son, by her consent, gave me free papers. I went to Ohio: then came into Canada, and settled down in Chatham.

I have five children. One goes to school; we are not able to send all on account of the price partly, as we have to pay fifty cents a quarter for each child, at the public school. I went into Chatham with nothing, and I want the children some in the family.

I have seen many things practised in slavery which are too horrible to name.

MRS. COLMAN FREEMAN.

I am a native of North Carolina. I was born free, and lived with my father and mother. My father was a quadroon—my mother a mulatto. My father fought the British in the Revolution. His brother was drafted, but being sick, my father volunteered to take his place, and was in the army seven years. When he returned his brother was dead. He did not get a pension until three years before he died, not knowing that he was entitled to one, until, on some abuse from white men, he went into court, and the lawyer said, "Will you suffer injustice to be done to this white-headed old man, who has faced the cannon's mouth, fighting for our liberties; who has maintained himself and family without drawing a penny from the government?"

When colored persons had their meetings in the groves, white men would stand with their whips where they were coming out, to examine for passes, and those who had passes would go free,—the others would break and run, like cattle with hornets after them. I have seen them run into the river. I remember one time, I was going with my brother, and saw them at the meeting, trying to get away from the patrollers. I could not help shedding tears to see the distress they were in. They ran into the river, and tried to get away. Said I to my brother, "What are they running so into the river for?" He hunched me, and said, "Do n't you see the patrollers?" This was because they wanted to hear preaching, and learn a little about Almighty God that made them. They were not allowed to meet without patrollers.

I knew a slave named Adam who experienced religion, and wanted to be baptized. Saturday night the overseer told him he should not be baptized. He went to his mistress, and she gave him a pass for the purpose. Next day, I went down to the shore of the mill-pond to see the baptizing. Just as Adam was ready to go into the water, the overseer rode up, and cried out, "Adam! Adam! if you get baptized, I will give you a hundred lashes to-morrow morning!" Adam said, "I have but two masters to serve, my earthly and my heavenly master, and I can mind nobody else." I know that overseer very well; —— ——his name was: I was standing right by him. Then he forbade Mr. L—— from baptizing him. Mr. L.: "If there is a God I will baptize Adam; if not, I will not baptize him." The overseer stood up in his stirrups, and cursed so that he frightened all the people on the beach: his eyes glowed like two lighted candles. As soon as Adam came out of the water, he ran for home to get protection from his mistress. She prevented the overseer from punishing him.

I came away from North Carolina in consequence of persecution. There was a rebellion among the slaves in Virginia, under Nat Turner, near where I was. A doctor near me had his mother and brothers and sisters, except two, killed in that rebellion. The white people that had no slaves would have killed the colored, but their masters put them in jail to protect them from the white people, and from fears they had themselves of being killed. They came to my mother's, and threatened us—they searched for guns and ammunition: that was the first time I was ever silenced by a white man. One of them put his pistol to my breast, and said, "If you open your head, I'll kill you in a minute!" I had told my mother to hush, as she was inquiring what their conduct meant. We were as ignorant of the rebellion as they had been. Then I made up my mind not to remain in that country. We had to stay a while to sell our crop: but I would not go to church there any more.

I lived in Ohio ten years, as I was married there,—but I would about as lief live in the slave States as in Ohio. In the slave States I had protection sometimes, from people that knew me—none in Ohio. I understand the laws are better in Ohio now than they were then. In the slave States I had no part in the laws: the laws were all against the colored men: they allowed us no schools nor learning. If we got learning, we stole it.

We live here honestly and comfortably. We entertain many poor strangers.

BEN BLACKBURN.

I was born in Maysville, Ky. I got here last Tuesday evening, and spent the Fourth of July in Canada. I felt as big and free as any man could feel, and I worked part of the day for my own benefit: I guess my master's time is out. Seventeen came away in the same gang that I did.

WILLIAM L. HUMBERT.

I am from the city of Charleston, S. C., and have been in various parts of South Carolina and Georgia. I used to run in a steamboat from Savannah to Charleston.

I left Charleston in September, 1853. I lived in the free States some months, but finally left on account of the Fugitive Slave Bill. This was a law of tyranny, and I had to come to Canada to avoid the ten dollar commissioner. I would rather die than go back,—that's a settled point with me—not on account of ill-treatment of the person; but I could not stand the idea of being held by another man as a chattel. Slavery itself is cruel enough, without regard to the hardships which slaves in general have to undergo.

I do not believe that any slaveholder under the canopy of heaven can see God's face; that is, if I read the Bible right. Slaveholding is against all reason. All men are from the same mother dust, and one can have no right to hold another as a chattel. I know three or four preachers of the gospel who hold slaves. As the minister goes, the congregation goes. The ministers preach to please the people, and not in the fear of God. I never knew but one exception there. I have seen a minister hand the sacrament to the deacons to give the slaves, and, before the slaves had time to get home, living a great distance from church, have seen one of the same deacons, acting as patrol, flog one of the brother members within two hours of his administering the sacrament to him, because he met the slave in the road without a passport, beyond the time allowed him to go home. My opinion of slavery is not a bit different now from what it was then: I always hated it from childhood. I looked on the conduct of the deacon with a feeling of revenge. I thought that a man who would administer the sacrament to a brother church-member, and flog him before he got home, ought not to live.

DAVID COOPER.

There was an institution started here in Sandwich about six years ago, called the Industrial Institution.

LYDIA ADAMS.

[Mrs. A. lives in a very comfortable log-house on the road from Windsor to the Refugees' Home.]

I am seventy or eighty years old. I was from Fairfax county, old Virginia. I was married and had three children when I left there for Wood county, where I lived twenty years: thence to Missouri, removing with my master's family. One by one they sent four of my children away from me, and sent them to the South: and four of my grandchildren all to the South but one. My oldest son, Daniel—then Sarah—all gone. "It's no use to cry about it," said one of the young women, "she's got to go." That's what she said when Esther went away. Esther's husband is here now, almost crazy about her: they took her and sold her away from him. They were all Methodist people—great Methodists—all belonged to the church. My master died—he left no testimony whether he was willing to go or not. . . . I have been in Canada about one year, and like it as far as I have seen.

I've been wanting to be free ever since I was a little child. I said to them I didn't believe God ever meant me to be a slave, if my skin was black—at any rate not all my lifetime: why not have it as in old times, seven years' servants? Master would say, "No, you were made to wait on white people: what was niggers made for?—why, just to wait on us all."

I am afraid the slaveholders will go to a bad place—I am really afraid they will. I do n't think any slaveholder can get to the kingdom.

J. F. WHITE.

I have served twenty-five years as a slave; born in Virginia, and brought up, or rather whipped up, in Kentucky. I have lived in Canada two years—I have bought one hundred acres of land in Sandwich, suitable to raise any kind of grain.

I want you to tell the people of the United States, that as far as begging for fugitives is concerned, that we are amply able to take care of ourselves: we have done it, and can do it. We want none to beg for us; let them give to the fugitive on his way, and to those who are assisting him on his way. Money has been raised—an immense quantity of it too, but we don't get it—indeed, we do n't want it. We have a society here to take care of our brothers when they get here, and we can do it without assistance. If people send things through pure motives to the suffering, we thank them for their intentions,—still, there is no need of their doing even that.

LEONARD HARROD.

I was born and bred in Georgetown, D. C., where I had a wife and two children. About six o'clock one morning, I was taken suddenly from my wife; she knew no more where I had gone than the hen knows where the hawk carries her children. Fifteen hundred miles I wore iron on my wrist, chained in a gang from Georgetown to Port Gibson. There I was sold and put to receive and pack cotton, etc., for six years. Then I was sold to Nashville, Tenn., one year; then to New Orleans fifteen years; then I took up my bed and walked for Canada. I have been in Canada nearly two years. I was poor—as low down as a man could be who is not underground. It was in winter,—my wife was in a delicate situation,—and we had nothing for bedclothes at night but what we had worn through the day. We suffered all the winter for things we left on the way, which were never sent us. My wife is now under the doctor's care in consequence.

I have hired a place to work on, and have bought two acres of land.

A man can get more information in Canada about slavery, than he can in the South. There I would have told you to ask master, because I would have been afraid to trust a white man: I would have been afraid that you would tell my master. Many a time my master has told me things to try me. Among others, he said he thought of moving up to Cincinnati, and asked me if I did not want to go. I would tell him, "No! I do n't want to go to none of your *free* countries!" Then he'd laugh,—but I did want to come—surely I did. A colored man tells the truth here,—there he is afraid to.

THOMAS H. JONES

Written with the author's goal of raising enough money to purchase his son's freedom, the personal narrative of Thomas H. Jones (1806–?) is penned in an unabashed fashion: he uses the "Uncle Tom" name from Harriet Beecher Stowe's Uncle Tom's Cabin's *beloved, if controversial, eponymous character to attract the attention of potential book buyers. Told in the style of similar propagandistic antislavery texts of its time,* Experience and Personal Narrative of Uncle Tom Jones *describes the hardships he experienced under slavery, family separations, violence, and physical abuse by enslavers and other white people, Jones's desire to be educated, as well as the events leading up to his escape. Jones also underscores the hypocrisy of proslavery white people, as he grapples with his embrace of religion while suffering at the hands of a cruel, supposedly Christian enslaver whose brutality is relentless and belies Jones's understanding of biblical teachings. A second feature of the volume, a fictional narrative about a protagonist named Wild Tom, serves as a kind of speculative foray into the darker side: a Tom who is not tamed by Christianity but who is tempted to be as vengeful and rebellious as the institution of slavery is barbaric and dehumanizing.*

From *Experience and Personal Narrative of Uncle Tom Jones; Who Was for Forty Years a Slave. Also the Surprising Adventures of Wild Tom, of the Island Retreat, a Fugitive Negro from South Carolina* (c. 1850s)

I was born a slave. My recollections of early life are associated with poverty, suffering and shame. I was made to feel, in my boyhood's first experience, that I was inferior and degraded, and that I must pass through life in a dependent and suffering condition. The experience of forty-three years, which were passed by me in slavery, was one of dark fears and darker realities. John Hawes was my first master. He lived in Hanover County, N.C., between the Black and South Rivers, and was the owner of a large plantation called Hawes' Plantation. He had over fifty slaves. I remained with my parents nine years. They were both slaves, owned by John Hawes. They had six children, Richard, Alexander, Charles, Sarah, myself, and John. I remember well that dear old cabin, with its clay floor and mud chimney, in which, for nine years, I enjoyed the presence and love of my wretched parents.

Father and mother tried to make it a happy place for their dear children. *They* worked late into the night many and many a time to get a little simple furniture for their home and the home of their children; and they spent many hours of willing toil to stop up the chinks between the logs of their poor hut, that they and their children might be protected from the storm and the cold. I can testify, from my own painful experience, to the deep and fond affection which the slave cherishes in his heart for his home and its dear ones. We have no other tie to link us to the human family, but our fervent love for those who are *with* us and of us in relations of sympathy and devotedness, in wrongs and wretchedness. My dear parents were conscious of the desperate and incurable woe of their position and destiny; and of the lot of inevitable suffering in store for their beloved children. They talked about our coming misery, and they lifted up their voices and wept aloud, as they spoke of our being torn from them and sold off to the dreaded slave trader, perhaps never to see them or hear from them a word of fond love. I am a father, and I have had the same feelings of unspeakable anguish, as I have looked upon my precious babes, and have thought of the ignorance, degradation and woe which they must endure as slaves. The great God, who knoweth all the secrets of the earth, and He only, knows the bitter sorrow I now feel when I think of my four dear children who are slaves, torn from me and consigned to hopeless servitude by the iron hand of ruthless wrong. I love those children with all a father's fondness.

Mr. Hawes was a very severe and cruel master. He kept no overseer, but managed his own slaves with the help of Enoch, his oldest son. To the men he gave one pair of shoes, one blanket, one hat, and five yards of coarse, home-spun cotton. To the women a corresponding outfit, and enough to make one frock for each of the children. The slaves were obliged to make up their own clothes, after the severe labor of the plantation had been performed. Any other clothing, beyond this yearly supply, which they might need, the slaves were compelled to get by extra work, or do without.

The supply of food given out to slaves, was one peck of corn a week, or some equivalent, and nothing besides. They must grind their own corn, after the work of the day was performed, at a mill which stood on the plantation. We had to eat our coarse bread without meat, or butter, or milk. Severe labor alone gave us an appetite for our scanty and unpalatable fare. Many of the slaves were so hungry after their excessive toil, that they were compelled to steal food in addition to this allowance.

During the planting and harvest season, we had to work early and late. The men and women were called at three o'clock in the morning, and were worked on the plantation till it was dark at night. After that they must prepare their food for supper and for the breakfast of the next day, and attend to other duties of their own dear homes. Parents would often have to work for their children at home, after each day's protracted toil, till the middle of the night, and then snatch a few hours' sleep, to get strength for the heavy burdens of the next day.

In the month of November, and through the winter season, the men and women worked in the fields, clearing up new land, chopping and burning bushes, burning tar kilns, and digging ditches. They worked together, poorly clad, and suffering from the bitter cold and wet of those winter months. Women, wives and mothers, daughters and sisters, on that plantation, were compelled to toil on cold, stormy days in the open field, while the piercing wind and driving storm benumbed their limbs, and almost froze the tears that came forth out of their cold and desolate hearts. Little boys, and girls, too, worked and cried, toting brush to the fires, husking the corn, watching the stock, and running out errands for master and mistress, for their three sons, Enoch, Edward and John, and constantly receiving from them scoldings and beatings as their reward.

Thus passed nine years of my life; years of suffering, the shuddering memory of which is deeply fixed in my heart.

These nine years of wretchedness passed, and a change came for me. My master sold me to Mr. Jones of Washington, N.C., distant forty-five miles from Hawes' plantation. Mr. Jones sent his slave driver, a colored man, named Abraham, to conduct me to my new home in Washington. I was at home with my mother when he came. He looked in at the door, and called to me, "Tom, you must go with me." His looks were ugly and his voice was savage. I was very much afraid, and began to cry, holding on to my mother's clothes and begging her to protect me, and not let the man take me away. Mother wept bitterly, and, in the midst of her loud sobbings, cried out in broken words, "I can't save you, Tommy; master has sold you, you must go." She threw her arms around me, and while the hot tears fell on my face, she strained me to her heart. There she held me, sobbing and mourning, till the brutal Abraham came in, snatched me away, hurried me out of the house where I was born, my only home, and tore me away from the dear mother who loved me as no other friend could do. She followed him, imploring a moment's delay and weeping aloud, to the road, where he turned around, and striking at her with his heavy cow hide, fiercely ordered her to stop bawling, and go back into the house.

Thus was I snatched from the presence of my loving parents, and from the true affection of the dear ones of home. For thirteen weary years did my heart turn in its yearnings to that precious home. And then, at the age of twenty-two, I was permitted to revisit my early home. I found it all desolate; the family all broken up; father was sold and gone; Richard, Alexander, Charles, Sarah, and John were sold and gone. Mother prematurely old, heart-broken, utterly desolate, weak and dying, alone remained. I saw her, and wept once more on her bosom. I went back to my chains with a deeper woe in my heart than I had ever felt before. There was but one thought of joy in my wretched consciousness, and that was, that my kind and precious mother would soon be at rest in the grave. And then, too, I remember, I mused with deep earnestness on death, as the only friend the poor slave had. And I wished that I, too, might lie down by my mother's side, and die with her in her loving embrace.

I should have related, that one of the earliest scenes of painful memory associated with my opening years of suffering is connected with a severe whipping which my master inflicted on my sister Sarah. He tied her up, having compelled her to strip herself entirely naked in the smoke-house, and gave her a terrible whipping,—at least so it seemed to my young heart, as I heard her scream, and stood by my mother, who was wringing her hands in an agony of grief at the cruelties which her tender child was enduring. I do not know what my sister had done for which she was then whipped; but I remember that her body was marked and scarred for weeks after that terrible scourging, and that our parents always after *seemed* to hold their breath when they spoke of it. Sarah was the last of the family who was sold; and my poor mother never looked up after this final act of cruelty was accomplished. I think of my only sister now; and often try to imagine *where* she is, and *how* she fares in this cruel land of slavery. And, Oh, my God, how dark and wretched are these pictures! Can I think of that poor sister without a sorrow too great for utterance?

My journey to Wilmington with the heartless Abraham was a very sad one. We walked all the way. I was afraid of my savage companion; and yet, my heart felt so desolate, and my longings for sympathy so intense, that I was impelled to turn to my cruel guide for relief. He was striding along in stern gloom and silence, too fast for my young feet to keep pace; and I began to feel that I *must* stop and rest. It was bitter cold, too, and I was poorly clad to bear the keen air of a January day. My limbs were weary with travel and stiff with cold. I could not go on at the rate I had done, and so I turned to my guide, and begged him to take me into some hut and let me rest and get warm. He cursed me, and told me to keep silence and come along, or he would warm me with the cow-hide. Oh, I thought how cruel and hopeless my lot! Would that I could fall down here and die. And I did fall down. We had just passed through a soft, wet place, and it seemed then to me that I was frozen. And I fell down on my dark, cold way, unable to proceed. I was then carried into a slave's cabin and allowed to warm and rest. It was nearly midnight when I arrived with my conductor at my place of exile and suffering. And certainly no heart could be more entirely wretched than I was when I threw my weary, aching body on my cold hard bed.

The next morning I was called into the presence of Mr. Jones, my new master, and my work was assigned to me. I was to take care of the old gray horse, kept for the use of the family when they wished to ride out, to fetch water from the spring to the house, to go on errands to my master's store, to clean the boots and shoes belonging to the white members of the family and to the white visiters, to sweep the rooms, and to bring wood from the wharf on my head for the fires at the house and store. From the first dawn of the day till ten and eleven, and sometimes twelve at night, I could hardly find one moment's time for rest. And, Oh, how the memory of that year of constant toil and weariness is imprinted on my heart, an impression of appalling sorrow. My dreams are still haunted with the agony of that year. I had just been torn from my home; my yearning heart was deprived of the sweet sympathy of those to whose memory I then clung, and to whom my heart still turns with irrepressible and unotterable longings. I was torn from them and put into a circle of cold, selfish and cruel hearts, and put then to perform labors too great for my young strength. And yet I lived through that year, just as the slave lives on through weary years of suffering, on which no ray or light shines, save that which hope of a better, happier future gives even to the desolate bondman. I lived through it, with all its darkness and sorrow. That year I received my first whipping. I had failed one day to finish my allotted task. It seemed to me that I had done my best; but, somehow, that day, thoughts of home came so fresh and tender into my mind, and, along with these thoughts, a sense of my utter hopeless desolation came in and took such a strong hold of my heart, that I sank down a helpless, heart-broken child. My tasks for that day were neglected. The next morning my master made me strip off my shirt, and then whipped me with the cowhide till the blood ran trickling down upon the floor. My master was very profane, and, with dreadful oaths, he assured me that there was only one way for me to avoid a repetition

of this terrible discipline, and that was, to do my tasks every
day, sick or well.

And so this year went by, and my duties were changed, and
my lot was made a little easier. The cook, Fanny, died, and I
was put into her place. I still had to get wood and keep the fires
in the house, and, after the work of cooking, setting the table,
clearing away and washing the dishes, there was always something to be done for my mistress. I got but little time to rest; but
I got enough to eat, which I had not done the year before. I was
by the comfortable fire, a good part of the cold winter weather,
instead of being exposed to the cold and wet, without warm
clothing, as I had been the year before, and my labor was not so
hard the second year as it had been the first.

My mistress complained of me at length, that I was not so
obedient as I ought to be, and so I was taken from the house
into the the store. My business there was to open and sweep out
the store in the morning, and get all the things ready for the accommodation of customers who might come in during the day.
Then I had to bring out and deliver all heavy articles that might
be called for during the day, such as salt, large quantities of
which were sold in the store; ship stores, grain, &c., &c. I had
also to hold myself ready to run on any errand my master or his
clerk, David Cogdell, might wish to send me on. While Cogdell
remained in the store, I enjoyed a *gleam* of happiness. He was
very kind to me, never giving me a cross word or a sour look;
always ready to show me how to do anything which I did not
understand, and to perform little acts of kindness to me. But
his kindness and generosity to the poor slaves was very offen-
sive to my master and to other slave-holders; and so, at length,
Mr. Jones turned him off, though he was compelled to acknowledge, at the same time, that he was the most trustworthy
and valuable assistant he had ever had in his store.

After my master dismissed Mr. C., he tried to get along with
me alone in the store. He kept the books and waited upon the
most genteel of his customers, leaving me to do the rest of the
work. This went on six months, when he declared that he could
not bear this confinement any longer; and so he got a white boy
to come and enter as clerk, to stay till he was of age. James

Dixon was a poor boy, about my own age, and when he came into the store, could hardly read or write. He was accordingly engaged a part of each day with his books and writing. I saw him studying, and asked him to let me see his book. When he felt in a good humor, James was very kind and obliging. The great trouble with him was, that his fits of ill-humor were much more frequent than his times of good feeling. It happened, however, that he was on good terms with himself when I asked him to show me his book, and so he let me take it, and look at it, and he answered very kindly many questions which I asked him about books and schools and learning. He told me that he was trying to get learning enough to fit him to do a good business for himself after he should get through with Mr. Jones. He told me that a man who had learning would always find friends, and get along very well in the world without having to work hard, while those who had no learning would have no friends and be compelled to work very hard for a poor living all their days. This was all new to me, and furnished me topics for wondering thought for days afterwards. The result of my meditations was, that an intense, burning desire to learn to read and write took possession of my mind, occupying me wholly in waking hours, and stirring up earnest thoughts in my soul even when I slept. The question, which then took hold of my whole consciousness was, how can I get a book to begin? James told me that a spelling-book was the first one necessary in getting learning. So I contrived how I might obtain a spelling-book. At length, after much study, I hit upon this plan: I cleaned the boots of a Mr. David Smith, Jr., who carried on the printing business, in Wilmington, and edited the Cape Fear Recorder. He had always appeared to me to be a very kind man. I thought I would get him to aid me in procuring a spelling-book. So I went one morning, with a beating heart, into his office, and asked him to sell me a spelling-book. He looked at me in silence, and with close attention, for some time, and asked me what I wanted. I told him I wanted to learn to read. He shook his head, and replied, "No, Thomas, it would not answer for me to sell you a book to learn out of; *you* will only get yourself into trouble if you attempt it; and I advise you to get that foolish notion out of your head as quickly as you can."

David's brother, Peter Smith, kept a book and stationery store under the printing-office, and I next applied to him for a book, determined to persevere till I obtained this coveted treasure. He asked me the same question that his brother David had done, and with the same searching, suspicious look. By my previous repulse I had discovered that I could not get a spelling-book, if I told what I wanted to do with it, and so I told a lie, in order to get it. I answered, that I wanted it for a white boy, naming one that lived at my master's, and that he had given me the money to get it with, and had asked me to call at the store and buy it. The book was then handed out to me, the money taken in return, and I left. feeling very rich with my long desired treasure. I got out of the store, and, looking round to see that no one observed me, I hid my book in my bosom, and hurried on to my work, conscious that a new era in my life was opening upon me through the possession of this book. That consciousness at once awakened new thoughts, purposes and hopes, a new life, and act, in my experience. My mind was excited. The words spoken by James Dixon of the great advantages of learning, made me intensely anxious to learn. I was a slave; and I knew that the whole community was in league to keep the poor slave in ignorance and chains. Yet I longed to be free, and to be able to move the minds of other men by my thoughts. It seemed to me now, that, if I could learn to read and write, this learning might—nay, I really thought it would, point out to me the way to freedom, influence, and real, secure happiness. So I hurried on to my master's store, and, watching my opportunity to do it safe from curious eyes, I hid my book with the utmost care, under some liquor barrels in the smokehouse. The first opportunity I improved to examine my book. I looked it over with the most intent eagerness, turned over its leaves, and tried to discover what the new and strange characters which I saw in its pages might mean. But I found it a vain endeavor. I could understand a picture, and from it make out a story of immediate interest to my mind. But I could not associate any thought or fact with these crooked letters with which my primmer was filled. So the next day I sought a favorable moment, and asked James to tell me where a scholar must begin in order to learn to read, and how. He laughed at my ignorance, and, taking his spelling-book, shewed me the alphabet in large and small letters on the same page. I asked him the name of the first letter, pointing it out, he told me A; so of the next, and so on through the alphabet. I managed to remember A and B, and I studied and looked out the same letters in many other parts of the book. And so I fixed in a tenacious memory the names of the two first letters of the alphabet. But I found I could not get on without help, and so I applied to James again to show me the letters and tell me their names. This time he suspected me of trying to learn to read myself, and he plied me with questions till he ascertained that I was, in good earnest, entering upon an effort to get knowledge. At this discovery, he manifested a good deal of indignation. He told me, in scorn, that it was not for such as *me* to try to improve, that *I* was a *slave*, and that it was not proper for *me* to learn to read. He threatened to tell my master, and at length, by his hard language, my anger was fully aroused, and I answered taunt with taunt. He called me a poor, miserable nigger; and I called him a poor, ignorant white servant boy. While we were engaged in loud and angry words, of mutual defiance and scorn, my master came into the store. Mr. Jones had never given me a whipping since the time I have already described, during my first year of toil, want and suffering in his service. But he had now caught me in the unpardonable offence of giving saucy language to a white boy, and one, too, who was in his employ. Without stopping to make any enquiries, he took down the cow-hide, and gave me a severe whipping. He told me never to talk back to a white man on pain of flogging. I suppose this law or custom is universal at the south. And I suppose it is thought necessary to enforce this habit of obsequious submission on the part of the colored people to the whites, in order to maintain their supremacy over the poor, outraged slaves.

I will mention, in this connection, as illustrative of this cruel custom, an incident which I saw just before I ran away from my chains. A little colored boy was carrying along through Wilmington a basket of food. His name was Ben, and he belonged to Mrs. Runkin, a widow lady. A little mischievous white boy, just about Ben's age and size, met him, and purposely overturned the little fellow's basket, and scattered his load in the mud. Ben, in return for this wanton act called him some hard name, when the white boy clinched him to throw him down with the scattered fragments upon his basket in the mud. Ben resisted and threw down the white boy, proving to be the stronger of the two. Tom Myers, a young lawer of Wilmington, saw the contest, and immediately rushing out, seized little Ben, and dragged him into the store opposite the place of battle. He sent out to a saddler's shop, procured a cow-hide, and gave the little fellow a tremendous flogging, for the daring crime of resisting a white boy who had wantonly invaded his rights. Is it any wonder that the spirit of self-respect of the poor, ignorant slave is broken down by such treatment of unsparing and persevering cruelty?

I was now repulsed by James, so that I could hope for no assistance from him in learning to read. But I could not go on alone. I must get some one to aid me in starting, or give up the effort to learn. This I could not bear to do. I longed to be able to read, and so I cast about me to see what I should do next. I thought of a kind boy at the bake-house, near my own age. I thought he would help me, and so I went to him, showed my book, and asked him to teach me the letters. He told their names, and went over the whole alphabet with me three times. By this assistance, I learned a few more of the letters, so that I could remember them afterwards when I sat down alone and tried to call them over. I could now pick out and name five or six of the letters in any part of the book. I felt then that I was getting along, and the consciousness that I was making progress, though slow and painful, was joy and hope to my sorrowing heart, such as I had never felt before. I could not with safety go to the bake-honse, as there I was exposed to detection by the sudden entrance of customers or idlers. I wanted to get a teacher who would give me a little aid each day, and I now set about securing this object. As kind Providence would have it, I easily succeeded, and on this wise: A little boy, Hiram Bricket, ten years old, or about that age, came along by the store one day, on his way home from school, while my master was gone home to dinner, and James was in the front part of the store. I beckoned to Hiram to come round to the back door; and with him I made a bargain to meet me each day at noon, when I was allowed a little while to get my dinner, and to give me instruction in reading. I was to give him six cents a week. I met him the next day at his father's stable, the place agreed upon for our daily meeting; and, going into one of the stables, the noble little Hiram gave me a thorough lesson in the alphabet. I learned it nearly all at that time, with what study I could give it by stealth during the day and night. And then again I felt lifted up and happy.

I was permitted to enjoy these advantages, however, but a short time. A black boy, belonging to Hiram's father, one day discovered our meeting and what we were doing. He told his master of it, and Hiram was at once forbidden this employment. I had then got along so that I was reading and spelling in words of two syllables. My noble little teacher was very patient and faithful with me, and my days were passing away in very great happiness under the consciousness that I was learning to read. I felt at night, as I went to my rest, that I was really beginning to be a *man*, preparing myself for a condition in life better and higher and happier than could belong to the ignorant *slave*. And in this blessed feeling I found, waking and sleeping, a most precious happiness.

After I was deprived of my kind little teacher, I plodded on the best way I could by myself, and in this way I got into words of five syllables. I got some little time to study by daylight in the morning, before any of my master's family had risen. I got a moment's opportunity also at noon, and sometimes at night. During the day, I was in the back store a good deal, and whenever I thought I could have five minutes to myself, I would take my book and try to learn a little in reading and spelling. If I heard James, or master Jones, or ainy customer coming in, I would drop my book among the barrels, and pretend to be very busy shovelling the salt or doing some other work. Several times I came very near being detected. My master suspected something, because I was so still in the back room, and a number of times he came very slyly to see what I was about. But at such times I was always so fortunate as to hear his tread or to see his shadow on the wall in time to hide away my book.

When I had got along to words of five syllables, I went to see a free colored friend, Ned Cowen, whom I knew I could trust. I told him I was trying to learn to read, and asked him to help me a little. He said he did not dare to give me any instruction, but he heard me read a few words, and then told me I should learn if I would only persevere as nobly as I had done thus far. I told him *how* I had got along, and what difficulties I had met with. He encouraged me, and spoke very kindly of my efforts to improve my condition by getting learning. He told me I had got along far enough to get another book, in which I could learn to write the letters, as well as to read. He told me where and how to procure this book. I followed his directions, and obtained another spelling-book at Worcester's store, in Wilmington. Jacob showed me a little about writing. He set me a copy, first of straight marks. I now got me a box, which I could hide under my bed, I some ink, pens, and a bit of candle. So, when I went to bed, I puled my box out from under my cot, turned it up on end, and began my first attempt at writing. I worked away till my candle was burned out, and then lay down to sleep. Jacob next set me a copy, which he called pot-hooks; then, the letters of the alphabet. These letters were also in my new spelling-book, and according to Jacob's directions, I set them before me for a copy, and wrote on these exercises till I could form all the letters and call them by name. One evening I wrote out my name in large letters,—**THOMAS JONES.** This I carried to Jacob, in a great excitement of happiness, and he warmly commended me for my perseverance and diligence.

About this time, I was at the store early one morning, and, thinking I was safe from all danger for a few minutes, had seated myself in the back store, on one of the barrels, to study in my precious spelling-book. While I was absorbed in this happy enterprize, my master came in, much earlier than usual, and I did not hear him. He came directly into the back store. I saw his shadow on the wall, just in time to throw my book over in among the barrels, before he could see what it was, although he saw that I had thrown something quickly away. His suspicion was aroused. He said that I had been stealing something out of the store, and he fiercely ordered me to get what I threw away just as he was coming in at the door. Without a moment's hesitation, I determined to save my precious book and my future opportunities to learn out of it. I knew if my book was discovered, that all was lost, and I felt prepared for any hazard or suffering rather than give up my book and my hopes of improvement. So I replied at once to his question, that I had not thrown anything away; that I had not stolen anything from the store; that I did not have anything in my hands which I could throw away when he came in. My master declared, in a high passion, that I was lying, and ordered me to begin and roll away the barrels. This I did; but managed to keep the book slipping along so that he could not see it, as he stood in the door-way. He charged me again with stealing and throwing something away, and I again denied the charge. In a great rage, he then got down his long, heavy cow-hide, and ordered me to strip off my jacket and shirt, saying, with an oath, "I will make you tell me what it was you had when I came in." I stripped myself, and came forward, according to his directions, at the same time denying his charge with great earnestness of tone, and look, and manner. He cut me on my naked back, perhaps thirty times, with great severity, making the blood flow freely. He then stopped, and asked me what I had thrown away as he came in. I answered again that I had thrown nothing away. He swore terribly; said he was certain I was lying, and declared that he would kill me, if I did not tell him the truth. He whipped me the second time with greater severity, and at greater length than before. He then repeated his question, and I answered again as before. I was determined to die, if I could possibly bear the pain, rather than give up my dear book. He whipped me the third time, with the same result as before, and then, seizing hold of my shoulders, turned me round, as though he would inflict on my quivering flesh still another scourging; but he saw the deep gashes he had already made, and the blood already flowing under his cruel infliction; and his stern purpose failed him. He said, "Why, Tom, I didn't think I had cut you so bad," and, saying that, he stopped, and told me to put on my shirt again. I did as he bade me, although my coarse shirt touching my raw back put me to a cruel pain. He then went out, and I got my book and hid it safely away before he came in again. When I went to the house, my wounds had dried, and I was in an agony of pain. My mistress told the servant girl, Rachel, to help me off with my shirt, and to wash my wounds for me, and put on to them some sweet oil. The shirt was dried to my back, so that it could not be got off without tearing off some of the skin with it. The pain, upon doing this, was greater even than I had endured from my cruel whipping. After Rachel had got my shirt off, my mistress asked me what I had done for which my master had whipped me so severely. I told her he had accused me of stealing when I had not, and then had whipped me to make me own it.

While Rachel was putting on the sweet oil, my master came in, and I could hear mistress scolding him for giving me such an inhuman beating, when I had done nothing. He said in reply, that Tom was an obstinate liar, and that was the reason why he had whipped me.

But I got well of my mangled back, and my book was still left. This was my best, my constant friend. With great eagerness, I snatched every moment I could get, morning, noon, and night, for study. I had begun to read; and, Oh, how I loved to study, and to dwell on the thoughts which I gained from my reading. About this time, I read a piece in my book about God. It said that "God, who sees and knows all our thoughts, loves the good and makes them happy; while he is angry with the bad, and will punish them for all their sins." This made me feel very unhappy, because I was sure that I was not good in the sight of God. I thought about this, and couldn't get it out of my mind a single hour. So I went to James Galley, a colored man, who exhorted the slaves sometimes on Sunday, and told him my trouble, asking, "what shall I do?" He told me about Jesus, and told me I must pray the Lord to forgive me and help me to be good and happy. So I went home, and went down cellar and prayed, but I found no relief, no comfort for my unhappy mind. I felt so bad, that I could not even study my book. My master saw that I looked very unhappy, and he asked me what ailed me. I did not dare now to tell a lie, for I wanted to be good, that I might be happy. So I told master just how it was with me; and then he swore terribly at me, and said he would whip me if I did not give over praying. He said there was no heaven and no hell, and that Christians were all hypocrites, and that there was nothing after this life, and that he would not permit me to go moping round, praying and going to the meetings. I told him I could not help praying; and then he cursed me in a great passion, and declared that he would whip me if he knew of my going on any more in that foolish way. The next night I was to a meeting, which was led by Jack Cammon, a free colored man, and a class leader in the Methodist Church. I was so much overcome by my feelings, that I staid very late. They prayed for me, but I did not yet find any relief; I was still very unhappy. The next morning, my master came in, and asked me if I went the night before to the meeting. I told him the truth. He said, "didn't I tell you I would whip you if you went nigh these meetings, and didn't I tell you to stop this foolish praying." I told him he did, and if he would, why, he might whip me, but still I could not stop praying, because I wanted to be good, that I might be happy and go to heaven. This reply made my master very angry. With many bitter oaths, he said he had promised me a whipping, and now he should be as good as his word. And so he was. He whipped me, and then forbade, with bitter threatenings, my praying any more, and especially my going again to meeting. This was Friday morning. I continued to pray for comfort and peace. The next Sunday I went to meeting. The minister preached a sermon on being born again, from the words of Jesus to Nicodemus. All this only deepened my trouble of mind. I returned home very unhappy. Collins, a free man of color, was at the meeting, and told my master that I was there. So, on Monday morning my master whipped me again, and once more forbade my going to meetings and praying. The next Sunday there was a class meeting, led by Binney Pennison, a colored free man. I asked my master, towards night, if I might go out. I told him I did not feel well. I wanted to go to the class meeting. Without asking me where I was going, he said I might go. I went to the class. I staid very late, and was so overcome by my feelings, that I could not go home that night. So they carried me to Joseph Jones's cabin, a slave of Mr. Jones. Joseph talked and, prayed with me nearly all night. In the morning I went home as soon as it was light, and, for fear of master, I asked Nancy, one of the slaves, to go up into mistress's room and get the store key for me, that I might go and open the store. My master told her to go back and tell me to come up. I obeyed with many fears.

My master asked me where I had been the night before. I told
him the whole truth. He cursed me again, and said he should
whip me for my obstinate disobedience; and he declared that he
would kill me if I did not promise to obey him. He refused to
listen to my mistress, who was a professor, and who tried to in-
tercede for me. And, just as soon as he had finished threatening
me with what he would do, he ordered me to take the key and
go and open the store. When he came into the store that morning, two of his neighbors, Julius Dumbiven, and McCauslin,
came in too. He called me up, and asked me again where I staid
last night. I told him with his boy, Joseph. He said he knew that
was a lie; and he immediately sent off for Joseph to confirm his
suspicious. He ordered me to strip off my clothes, and, as I did
so, he took down the cow-hide heavy and stiff with blood which
he had before drawn from my body with that cruel weapon,
and which was congealed upon it. Dumbiven professed to be a
Christian, and he now came forward and earnestly interceded
for me, but to no purpose, and then he left. McCauslin asked
my master, if he did not know, that a slave was worth more
money after he became pious than he was before. And why
then, he said, should you forbid Tom going to meetings and
praying? He replied, that religion was all a damned mockery,
and he was not going to have any of his slaves praying and
whining round about their souls. McCauslin then left. Joseph
came and told the same story about the night before that I had
done; and then he began to beg master not to whip me. He
cursed him and drove him off. He then whipped me with great
severity, inflicting terrible pain at every blow upon my quivering body, which was still very tender from recent lacerations.
My suffering was so great, that it seemed to me I should die. He
paused at length, and asked me would I mind him and stop
praying. I told him I could not promise him not to pray any
more, for I felt that I must and should pray as long as I lived.
"Well, then, Tom," he said, "I swear that I will whip you to
death." I told him I could not help myself, if he was determined
to kill me, but that I must pray while I lived. He then began to
whip me the second time, but soon stopped, threw down the
bloody cow-hide, and told me to go wash myself in the river,
just back of the store, and then dress myself, and if I was deter-

mined to be a fool, why, I must be one. My mistress now interceded earnestly for me with my cruel master. The next Sabbath
was love feast, and I felt very anxious to join in that feast. This
I could not do without a paper from my master, and so I asked
mistress to help me. She advised me to be patient, and said she
would help me all she could. Master refused to give any paper,
and so I could not join the lovein feast the next day.

On the next Friday evening, I went to the prayer meeting.
Jack Cammon was there, and opened the meeting with prayer.
Then Binney Pennison gave out the sweet hymn, which begins
in these words:

> "Come ye sinners poor and needy,
>   Weak and wounded, sick and sore."

I felt that it all applied most sweetly to my condition, and I said
in my heart, I will come now to Jesus, and trust in him. So
when those who felt anxious were requested to come forward
and kneel within the altar for prayer, I came and knelt down.
While Jacob Cammon was praying for me, and for those who
knelt by my side, my burden of sorrow, which had so long
weighed me down, was removed. I felt the glory of God's ove
warming my heart, and making me very happy. I shouted aloud
for joy, and tried to tell all my poor slave brothers and sisters,
who were in the house, what a dear Savior I had found, and
how happy I felt in his precious love. Binney Pennison asked me
if I could forgive my master. I told him I could, and did, and that
I could pray God to forgive him, too, and make him a good man.
He asked me if I could tell my master of the change in my feelings. I told him I should tell him in the morning. "And what," he
asked, "will you do if he whips you still for praying and going to
meeting?" I said I will ask Jesus to help me to bear the pain, and
to forgive my master for being so wicked. He then said, "Well,
then, Brother Jones, I believe that you are a Christian."

A good many of us went from the meeting to a brother's
cabin, where we began to express our joy in happy songs. The
palace of General Dudley was only a little way off, and he soon
sent over a slave with orders to stop our noise, or he would send
the patrolers upon us. We then stopped our singing, and spent

the remainder of the night in talking, rejoicing, and praying. It was a night of very great happiness to me. The contrast between my feelings then, and for many weeks previous, was very great. Now all was bright and joyous in my relations towards my precious Savior. I felt certain that Jesus was my Savior, and, in this blessed assurance, a flood of glory and joy filled my happy soul. But this sweet night passed away, and, as the morning came, I felt that I must go home, and bear the slave's heavy cross. I went, and told my mistress the blessed change in my feelings. She promised me what aid she could give me with my master, and enjoined upon me to be patient and very faithful to his interest, and, in this way, I should at length wear out his opposition to my praying and going to meeting.

I went down to the store in a very happy state of mind. I told James my feelings. He called me a fool, and said master would be sure to whip me. I told him I hoped I should be able to bear it, and to forgive master for his cruelty to me. Master came down, talked with me a while, and told me that he should whip me because I had disobeyed him in staying out all night. He had told me he should whip me if ever I do so, and he should make every promise good. So I began to take off my clothes. He called me a crazy fool, and told me to keep my clothes on, till he told me to take them off. He whipped me over my jacket; but I enjoyed so much peace of mind, that I scarcely felt the cow-hide. This was the last whipping that Mr. Jones inflicted upon me.

I was then nearly eighteen years old. I waited and begged for a paper to join the Church six months before I could get it. But all this time I was cheerful, as far as a slave can be, and evry-earnest to do all I could for my master and mistress. I was resolved to convince them that I was happier and better for being a Christian; and my master at last acknowledged that he could not find any fault with my conduct, and that it was impossible to find a more faithful slave than I was to him. And so, at last, he gave me a paper to Ben English, the leader of the colored members, and I joined the love feast, and was taken into the Church on trial for six months. I was put into Billy Cochran's class. At the expiration of six months, I was received into the Church in full fellowship, Quaker Davis' class. I remained there three years. My master was so much kinder after this time than he had ever been before; and I was allowed some more time to myself than I had been before. I pursued my studies as far as I could, but I soon found the utter impossibility of carrying on my studies as I wished to do. I was a slave, and all avenues to real improvement I found guarded with jealous care and cruel tenacity against the despised and desolated bondman.

I still felt a longing desire to improve, to be free, but the conviction was getting hold of my soul, that I was only struggling in vain when seeking to elevate myself into a manly and happy position. And now my mind was fast sinking into despair. I could read and write, and often enjoyed much happiness in poring over the very few books I could obtain; and especially, at times, I found great peace in reading my old, worn Testament. But I wanted now that hope which had filled my mind with such joy when I first began to learn to read. I found much happiness in prayer. But here, also, my mind labored in sadness and darkness much of the time.

About this time, my master was taken sick. On Sunday, he was prostrated by mortal pains; and, on Friday the same week, he died. He left fifteen slaves. I was purchased by Owen Holmes for $435,00. I was then in my twenty-third year. I had just passed through the darkest season of despairing agony that I had yet known. This came upon me in consequence of the visit, which I have already described, to my dear old desolate home. About this time, too, I entered into a new and distinct period of life, which I will unfold in another chapter. I will close this period of sorrow and shame with a few lines of touching interest to my mind.

> Who shall avenge the slave? I stood and cried;
> The earth, the earth, the echoing sea replied.
> I turned me to the cean, but each wave
> Declined to be the avenger of the slave.
> Who *shall* avenge the slave? my species cried;
> The winds, the flood, the lightning of the sky.
> I turned to these, from them one echo ran,
> The *right* avenger of the slave is man.
> Man was my fellow; in *his* sight I stood,

Wept and besought him by the voice of blood.
Sternly he looked, as proud on earth he trod,
Then said, the avenger of the slave is GOD.
I looked in prayer towards Heaven, a while 'twas still,
And then, methought, God's voice replied, I WILL.

ELIZA POTTER

A freeborn woman of mixed heritage, Eliza Potter (1820–1893) traveled widely in the United States and Europe, working as a beautician for prominent white women. A rare look into the musings, greed, mental illness, and abuse of members of the upper echelons, including women enslavers, A Hairdresser's Experience in High Life *uniquely features Potter's bold voice and observational wit as she closely traverses race and class lines in an "avocation [that] calls me into the upper classes of society almost exclusively; and there reign as many elements of misery as the world can produce. No one need go into alleys to hunt up wretchedness; they can find it in perfection among the rich and fashionable of every land and nation."*

From *A Hairdresser's Experience in High Life*
(1859)

I knew a gentleman who was cashier to one of the largest banks in New Orleans who married a colored woman. He got a physician to transfer some of her blood into his veins and then went to the court and swore he had colored blood in him. A gentleman of high position from Pennsylvania, having gone down South bought him a housekeeper; as soon as she became the mistress of the house, she became hard to please. One morning she went in the kitchen to command the cook, who answered her impudently; the lady flew to the gentleman, who gave her a note for the woman to take to the calaboose, saying, give the bearer thirty-nine lashes. The mistress, afraid the servant would not get the lashes, took the note herself; after reading it the officers took hold of her and cut her back almost to pieces;

she, running home furious, showed the gentleman her back, he flew to the calaboose with pistol and bowie knife, but for fear of being arrested, did not use them.

During my visits to New Orleans every winter, I saw many amusing and affecting scenes, one of which was the following: A servant went to New Orleans as nurse, a gentleman of high standing married her, he bought two slaves, one of whom was a very old woman, and, as every bond woman does, she treated this old woman very severely, made her get up at four o'clock and work about the house, and then do a day's work; if she did not bring her day's earning every evening, let her get it or not, although she was a woman of fifty years of age, she was severely punished. The old woman went to a colored woman to get work, and as it is not the custom for free people to give work to slaves, she told her she had no work; one day she went again to this free colored woman, and finding no person at home, she sat in a corner and cried; when the woman came in she asked her what was the matter; she told her if she did not bring home the money she would be whipped. The woman questioned her closely about who she belonged to, who she knew in Virginia, and how many children she had, and then asked her what marks her children had, and all about herself. She found this poor old woman was her own mother, whom she had not seen for thirty-five years. She flew to embrace her when the poor mother cried and screamed for joy until she gathered the people round her for squares. It was just the hour when business men went to their business, but not many of them went to business that day, for I never saw men in my life show such sympathy and feeling as they did on that occasion; every gentleman was eager to purchase and liberate her if the daughter had not been able to have done so; notwithstanding the woman was well off and able to purchase her mother, fives, tens, and twenties were given to the poor old woman to the amount, almost, of the sum required.

The gentleman, seeing the sympathies of the people, asked a moderate price for her, but the lady, whose anger was aroused, would not give her up on any reasonable terms; but at length she was compelled to take for her a moderate price, or nothing, as there was so much excitement going on. Just at that time a few children were coming by from market, and they ran up to her, with five and ten cent pieces, saying, here, Aunty, this will help to buy you, making the scene more affecting.

People congregate at the St. Charles from all the different parts of the United States, and during the season many come from the different countries of Europe. I have known ladies to be six months preparing, and no expense or pains spared, when coming to this place. They are more particular at this hotel than any I know of in the Western or Southern countries; for instance, every two weeks they have a soiree, to which the ladies are entitled to five tickets, and can invite any gentleman they wish; even the gentlemen that board there are not invited, unless there are ladies who are acquainted with them. The more gentlemen a lady knows the greater belle she is. I have seen seven or eight hundred people there at one time, all of whom came to enjoy themselves, and well they succeeded. One afternoon and evening, I had to dress twenty-five heads; and indeed, it was very amusing to hear the different places they were going to; some going to the St. Charles Theater, some to French Opera, some to Placide's Theater, some to soirees, some to public balls and some to private ones.

One week I thought I would see how many queer things would come under my notice; in the first place there was a charming couple from Boston, passing as brother and sister, but when it was found they were not related, they were quietly asked "out." Next day the lady wished me to comb her, and be with her as much as I could, although she seemed to be in great distress. Every day she, together with a gentleman, would take a carriage and leave the hotel for a drive. For a day or two, she seemed more and more troubled and would pace the floor and wring her hands in the greatest distress; once, on entering her room, I found her in deep thought, and, not noticing me, she looked up to heaven and said, "Oh, if I should fail," three or four times. That afternoon she got me to help her on with a double set of clothing, and, taking a bonnet under her shawl, she went away at her usual time. The next morning there was a great stir about a lady from the St. Charles, who had brought a set of clothing and put on her husband, who was in prison, and both made their escape. I learned they were from Baton Rouge; the report was that he had forged a bill.

In a day or two came off one of the grand soirees, and it happened that an actress got an invitation, through the intimacy of
a lady's husband. This raised a general row—some saying she
ought not to be there, and some again saying she should be—
the gentlemen taking a decided stand, and saying whoever the
ladies, who are regular boarders, invited, should be admitted.
The next day, trying to make my way through the ladies' private door, I was interrupted by the door-tender, who told me
hair-dressers were not allowed to pass through that door, that
they must go through the public door; I turned in and gave the
boy a good shaking, and went my way, much to the amusement
of the ladies and the mortification of the man; there were several ladies of our Queen City there to enjoy the sport. I went in
a room where there was a lady who had recently come from
France, and found her perfectly furious—nearly foaming with
rage and anger; she told me there was a lady who slandered her.
It so happened that a certain lady in the opposite hotel saw a
gentleman in this lady's room, and she saw the lady dressed in
her morning wrapper, which she mistook for a night gown; she
came over and told a lady in the hotel of the circumstance. This
lady was catholic and of Irish descent, and kept the money of
both males and females of the different servants, and this was
the reason given for the appearance of the gentleman in the
room; this raised a general stir. The lady the report was raised
against was a grass widow and a very smart woman, and she
plead her own case, so that nothing could be proved; then
she got several lawyers and commenced a suit for her character;
the lady who made the accusation was an officer's wife and the
officer had to sign a libel or pay heavily. I told my associate
hair-dresser that I had promised to notice for a week or so, and
I noticed what had happened for two or three weeks, and I was
perfectly tired out, as there was nothing but quarreling and
fussing, more than I ever noticed in the hotel before.

That season passed away and I returned to the city. There
had been many cases of yellow fever in the hotel, but it was
thoroughly purified and was filling up with visitors, amongst
them was the family of Zachary Taylor; it was during the trial
of Gen. Taylor in Mexico, and great excitement prevailed all
over the Union. While every one in the hotel was worried and

troubled, the family did not at all look alarmed, and a gentleman one day asked Gen. Taylor's daughter whether she did not
feel worried about her father, she said, "Oh, no, Pa means and
does what is right, and God will protect him." His daughters
and neices reigned belles for weeks. Quiet was restored, no
more quarreling or fussing, and I never in all the days of my
life, saw so many matches made, for truly, it was the greatest
market that had been seen in many seasons. The first thing
asked when a lady came there was, "are there any rich planters
or other rich men here," if there are the next saying is, "make
me pretty." I will tell you of a circumstance that occurred at
this time.

There was a young lady and her aunt, who got acquainted
with a middle aged man who dressed very elegantly, went every
night to the Theater and Opera, and was called a very rich
man; he, however, was but an overseer of the plantation and
property of a gentleman who was at that time in France. The
young lady and her aunt went to work to win the gentleman,
thinking it was a good match, and the gentleman striving to
win the young lady, because he thought it would be very agreeable to have the aunt's money, as she was rich; he took them to
what he called his plantation, and both aunt and niece thought
it a very good market. The young lady came to me and said,
"Oh, Iangy, I am engaged to be married, and I want you to devote your time to me for two or three weeks." I told here not to
be too fast, as all is not gold that glitters, for I knew the gentleman was not what he seemed to be, but as her mind was made
up it was not for me to say more. I myself spent some two hundred dollars buying little things, to say nothing of the aunt
spending fifteen hundred dollars for the wedding. They were
married, and he took her to the plantation and she enjoyed
wealth to her satisfaction for some time: when the real owner of
the plantation came home, he had married and brought his
bride with him to settle up his affairs. The overseer's wife was
very indignant at the privileges the gentleman and his bride
took, thinking all was hers; but her husband said, never mind,
she might make a short visit to her aunt till they would leave.
When she got there she found her aunt was also engaged, and
she got married during her stay. The aunt's husband got tired of

the niece's long visit—so she left and returned home; when she got there she found that the plantation was sold, and her husband was overseer of a neighboring plantation, when she, in a rage, kicked up a row, and went back to her aunt's. So this young lady lost her husband, and all his supposed riches, by her duplicity.

There is no true knowledge to be had of the wealth of the South; for, on some of the plantations on the coast they live very sparing—indeed, some of the slaves have no hats on, and others are scarcely half clad, and that of the coarse stuff that goods are packed in. Such families as these make the greatest show at the opera-house, in winter, in New Orleans, while, during the spring and summer, they barely have enough to sustain nature in themselves and slaves. Their slaves have nothing provided for them to either eat, drink or wear; they work hard all the day, and at night they plunder what they can from some of the rich plantations. If they are not caught, they are smart; and if they are, they are punished. On every New Year they have to sell a servant to support the balance the rest of the year.

While combing one of my ladies, she said, "Oh, langy, papa is going to buy a housekeeper to-day—there is one to be sold down stairs in the rotunda, and he is going to buy her.

I hurried through my work to get my usual stand to observe how matters got along with this gentleman, who said he was so good to his slaves. There was a very fine, bright mulatto put up to the highest bidder; this gentleman bid for her, but there was another bid against him, and they put the girl up to one thousand dollars. The girl then declared this man need not bid any higher, as she would never serve him; but he said he was determined to have her, and made some threats what he would do. She said she did not like his looks, and that she had been raised by a lady, and always led a virtuous life; and, as there was an understanding between her owner and the seller, that she should not be sold to any one she did not like, the sale was put off till the next day.

On the father of these young ladies going up to them, they said, from what they had heard of the woman, they wished him to buy her, even should he pay twelve hundred for her. The next day the girl was sent up for the young ladies to see. On talking to her a little, they liked her so well they told their father to buy her should it take two thousand; however, he got her for twelve hundred. She was very much pleased with her young mistresses and master, bundled up with a good grace, and went with them.

I did not see her again for some four years, when one day, as I was combing some ladies in the Burnet House, in this city, I heard her voice, and knew it. On going out in the hall I found her there, with a friend of her master, who had sent her up here to be emancipated.

I asked her how she got along, and how she liked the young ladies; she was warm in praise of them, and said she had the first cross word to hear from any one of them. These young ladies were cousins to a lady who married a trader in Nashville, Tenn. They often used to ask me about this lady, and I frequently remarked that it was a wonder to me how a refined lady, as she seemed to be, could marry such a degraded trader. I was not then aware that they were connections.

This lady and her sister visited the St. Charles nearly every season, literally loaded with diamonds. All the fortune-hunters ran after her, as her husband, when he died, left her some millions of dollars; and these seekers-of-wealth cared but little how the money was made, though there were many ladies there who would not associate with her owing to her lowering herself by marrying such a man. I have known him bring, from Nashville and Virginia, the largest droves of slaves that were brought into the market; he has often taken a fine child from a poor-looking woman, and given it to a fine-looking woman, who had a delicate child of her own, to sell together, and given her little one to the other. Again, he would make a woman marry a man, let her like him or not, should a gentleman come along who wished to have a man and wife. Anything to make money.

As the weather was getting warm, and the ladies leaving very fast, I determined, what I had not seen in past years, I would see now; so I went to the highest circles, then to the lowest; to the free people, and to slave people; and every-where it was proper for a woman to go. I could not but notice, in some of the wealthy families, where there were but three or four in a family, and five or six servants, these were well treated; again, in other places, where there were nine or ten in a family, and but one or two servants to do the work for the whole, those poor creatures had to get up at four o'clock in the morning, and not see bed again, probably, till one or two the next morning.

These poor creatures are worked to death, and, when worn out and good for nothing, all at once a charitable feeling rises up in the master's breast, and he gives them free papers, puts them on the cars, and sends them off to Cincinnati. This I can testify to, as I have one in my house now, in her fifty second year, perfectly helpless, afflicted with rheumatism, and not able to more than limp around. From her appearance, she has been a hard-working and faithful servant. Her master one day took a charitable notion, came home and asked her if she would not like to go to Cincinnati. She told him she would go any place to get her freedom. He started the poor old soul off, with fifteen dollars in her pocket, to a strange place, where she knew no one. Had she not fallen in with friends, she might have been sent to jail, or the pest-house, where there are several at this time from the South and other slave States, who have been very charitably dealt with, and given their freedom. This poor old creature was knocked about from post to pillar, till at length I stumbled over her, and she is with me now. Her master is a captain on one of the most elegant steamers that float on the Southern waters.

I sometimes think it strange how so many of these creatures fall into my hands; but I can tell you how one woman and child, from New Orleans, fell into my hands, and I was very glad to let her fall out.

There was a gentleman, from New Orleans, at Saratoga. From his appearance and conversation, and that of his lady, I thought them New England people; his name was W———. They begun a conversation with me on slavery, which is, with me, a very exciting topic, and I would much rather hold a conversation on any other subject; but, being dragged into it, I did not fail to express my opinion. He showed how well some slaves were treated, and I showed how badly others are treated. I told him there was one blasting thing to slavery—how a man good to his slaves may die, and the slaves fall into the hands of very cruel masters, and can not help themselves; their situation is a great deal worse than those that have had bad masters, and fall into the hands of good ones. He then said slaves could not take care of themselves. I replied, they could if they had a chance: as a good slave would make a good citizen, and a bad slave a bad one; but give them a chance. He said he had a woman he would gladly give her freedom, if she could do anything for herself to make a living. I told him if she was a respectable woman I would give her a trade. His wife then spoke up, and said the woman was whiter than herself, and was very smart. I told them to send her to me.

Some eighteen months passed away, and I got a letter, saying they would send the girl and her child, though, in the first place, they had not said anything about a child. She came, and with her a child some three years old; and no one would think there was one drop of African blood in either of their veins. The woman had evidently been badly raised, as she was very profane in her speech, and they must have been glad to get rid of her on account of her temper. She stayed with me a few weeks, and my husband would not allow me to have her about the house any longer.

I took her child and put it in the Orphan Asylum, and got her a good situation in a family where she would be well taken care of; but her language and conversation were such they would not have her about the house. It was now easy to be seen why her former owners wished to get rid of her—she was so white they could not sell her, and her language was so bad they could not keep her; so they determined to impose her on our so-called picayune State.

These are the kind usually emancipated, either those who are too bad to keep, or too old to be made any longer useful.

CHARLES BALL

Charles Ball (1780–?) was born into slavery on a tobacco plantation in Maryland. In his autobiographical accounts, Ball describes a precarious life, one that often separated him from kith and kin and caused him to suffer from the sociopathic tendencies of enslavers. Ball planned and executed escapes from slavery several times over the course of his life. During one period of fugitivity, he served in the War of 1812's Battles of St. Leonard Creek and Bladensburg. Ball's narrative of slavery is full of imagination, suffering, and adventure. It is a fateful story of a man who is marked as a slave yet determinedly attempts to assert his bodily autonomy through flight.

From *Fifty Years in Chains; or, The Life of an American Slave*

(1860)

Chapter I.

SEPARATED FROM MY MOTHER.

My story is a true one, and I shall tell it in a simple style. It will be merely a recital of my life as a slave in the Southern States of the Union—a description of negro slavery in the "model Republic."

My grandfather was brought from Africa and sold as a slave in Calvert county, in Maryland. I never understood the name of the ship in which he was imported, nor the name of the planter who bought him on his arrival, but at the time I knew him he was a slave in a family called Maud, who resided near Leonard-town. My father was a slave in a family named Hauty, living near the same place. My mother was the slave of a tobacco planter, who died when I was about four years old. My mother had several children, and they were sold upon master's death to separate purchasers. She was sold, my father told me, to a Georgia trader. I, of all her children, was the only one left in Maryland. When sold I was naked, never having had on clothes in my life, but my new master gave me a child's frock, belonging to one of his own children. After he had purchased me, he dressed me in this garment, took me before him on his horse, and started home; but my poor mother, when she saw me leaving her for the last time, ran after me, took me down from the horse, clasped me in her arms, and wept loudly and bitterly over me. My master seemed to pity her, and endeavored to soothe her distress by telling her that he would be a good master to me, and that I should not want anything. She then, still holding me in her arms, walked along the road beside the horse as he moved slowly, and earnestly and imploringly besought my master to buy her and the rest of her children, and not permit them to be carried away by the negro buyers; but whilst thus entreating him to save her and her family, the slave-driver, who had first bought her, came running in pursuit of her with a raw-hide in his hand. When he overtook us, he told her he was her master now, and ordered her to give that little negro to its owner, and come back with him.

My mother then turned to him and cried, "Oh, master, do not take me from my child!" Without making any reply, he gave her two or three heavy blows on the shoulders with his raw-hide, snatched me from her arms, handed me to my master, and seizing her by one arm, dragged her back towards the place of sale. My master then quickened the pace of his horse; and as we advanced, the cries of my poor parent became more and more indistinct—at length they died away in the distance, and I never again heard the voice of my poor mother. Young as I was, the horrors of that day sank deeply into my heart, and even at this time, though half a century has elapsed, the terrors of the scene return with painful vividness upon my memory. Frightened at the sight of the cruelties inflicted upon my poor mother, I forgot

my own sorrows at parting from her and clung to my new master, as an angel and a saviour, when compared with the hardened fiend into whose power she had fallen. She had been a
kind and good mother to me; had warmed me in her bosom in
the cold nights of winter; and had often divided the scanty pittance of food allowed her by her mistress, between my brothers, and sisters, and me, and gone supperless to bed herself.
Whatever victuals she could obtain beyond the coarse food,
salt fish and corn bread, allowed to slaves on the Patuxent and
Potomac rivers, she carefully distributed among her children,
and treated us with all the tenderness which her own miserable
condition would permit. I have no doubt that she was chained
and driven to Carolina, and toiled out the residue of a forlorn
and famished existence in the rice swamps, or indigo fields of
the South.

My father never recovered from the effects of the shock,
which this sudden and overwhelming ruin of his family gave
him. He had formerly been of a gay, social temper, and when he
came to see us on a Saturday night, he always brought us some
little present, such as the means of a poor slave would allow—
apples, melons, sweet potatoes, or, if he could procure nothing
else, a little parched corn, which tasted better in our cabin, because he had brought it.

He spent the greater part of the time, which his master permitted him to pass with us, in relating such stories as he had
learned from his companions, or in singing the rude songs common amongst the slaves of Maryland and Virginia. After this
time I never heard him laugh heartily, or sing a song. He became gloomy and morose in his temper, to all but me; and spent
nearly all his leisure time with my grandfather, who claimed
kindred with some royal family in Africa, and had been a great
warrior in his native country. The master of my father was a
hard, penurious man, and so exceedingly avaricious, that he
scarcely allowed himself the common conveniences of life. A
stranger to sensibility, he was incapable of tracing the change in
the temper and deportment of my father, to its true cause; but
attributed it to a sullen discontent with his condition as a slave,
and a desire to abandon his service, and seek his liberty by escaping to some of the free States. To prevent the perpetration of

this suspected crime of *running away from slavery*, the old man resolved to sell my father to a southern slave-dealer, and accordingly applied to one of those men, who was at that time in Calvert, to become the purchaser. The price was agreed on, but, as my father was a very strong, active, and resolute man, it was deemed unsafe for the Georgian to attempt to seize him, even with the aid of others, in the day-time, when he was at work, as it was known he carried upon his person a large knife. It was therefore determined to secure him by stratagem, and for this purpose, a farmer in the neighborhood, who was made privy to the plan, alleged that he had lost a pig, which must have been stolen by some one, and that he suspected my father to be the thief. A constable was employed to arrest him, but as he was afraid to undertake the business alone, he called on his way, at the house of the master of my grandfather, to procure assistance from the overseer of the plantation. When he arrived at the house, the overseer was at the barn, and thither he repaired to make his application. At the end of the barn was the coach-house, and as the day was cool, to avoid the wind which was high, the two walked to the side of the coach-house to talk over the matter, and settle their plan of operations. It so happened that my grandfather, whose business it was to keep the coach in good condition, was at work at this time, rubbing the plated handles of the doors, and brightening the other metallic parts of the vehicle. Hearing the voice of the overseer without, he suspended his work, and listening attentively, became a party to their councils. They agreed that they would delay the execution of their project until the next day, as it was then late. They supposed they would have no difficulty in apprehending their intended victim, as, knowing himself innocent of the theft, he would readily consent to go with the constable to a justice of the peace, to have the charge examined. That night, however, about midnight, my grandfather silently repaired to the cabin of my father, a distance of about three miles, aroused him from his sleep, made him acquainted with the extent of his danger, gave him a bottle of cider and a small bag of parched corn, and then enjoined him to fly from the destination which awaited him. In the morning the Georgian could not find his newly purchased slave, who was never seen or heard of in Maryland from that day.

After the flight of my father, my grandfather was the only person left in Maryland with whom I could claim kindred. He was an old man, nearly eighty years old, he said, and he manifested all the fondness for me that I could expect from one so old. He was feeble, and his master required but little work from him. He always expressed contempt for his fellow-slaves, for when young, he was an African of rank in his native land. He had a small cabin of his own, with half an acre of ground attached to it, which he cultivated on his own account, and from which he drew a large share of his sustenance. He had singular religious notions—never going to meeting or caring for the preachers he could, if he would, occasionally hear. He retained his native traditions respecting the Deity and hereafter. It is not strange that he believed the religion of his oppressors to be the invention of designing men, for the text oftenest quoted in his hearing was, "Servants, be obedient to your masters."

The name of the man who purchased me at the vendue, and became my master, was John Cox; but he was generally called Jack Cox. He was a man of kindly feelings towards his family, and treated his slaves, of whom he had several besides me, with humanity. He permitted my grandfather to visit me as often as he pleased, and allowed him sometimes to carry me to his own cabin, which stood in a lonely place, at the head of a deep hollow, almost surrounded by a thicket of cedar trees, which had grown up in a worn out and abandoned tobacco field. My master gave me better clothes than the little slaves of my age generally received in Calvert, and often told me that he intended to make me his waiter, and that if I behaved well I should become his overseer in time. These stations of waiter and overseer appeared to me to be the highest points of honor and greatness in the whole world, and had not circumstances frustrated my master's plans, as well as my own views, I should probably have been living at this time in a cabin on the corner of some tobacco plantation.

Fortune had decreed otherwise. When I was about twelve years old, my master, Jack Cox, died of a disease which had long confined him to the house. I was sorry for the death of my master, who had always been kind to me; and I soon discovered that I had good cause to regret his departure from this world. He had several children at the time of his death, who were all young; the oldest being about my own age. The father of my late master, who was still living, became administrator of his estate, and took possession of his property, and amongst the rest, of myself. This old gentleman treated me with the greatest severity, and compelled me to work very hard on his plantation for several years, until I suppose I must have been near or quite twenty years of age. As I was always very obedient, and ready to execute all his orders, I did not receive much whipping, but suffered greatly for want of sufficient and proper food. My master allowed his slaves a peck of corn, each, per week, throughout the year; and this we had to grind into meal in a hand-mill for ourselves. We had a tolerable supply of meat for a short time, about the month of December, when he killed his hogs. After that season we had meat once a week, unless bacon became scarce, which very often happened, in which case we had no meat at all. However, as we fortunately lived near both the Patuxent river and the Chesapeake Bay, we had abundance of fish in the spring, and as long as the fishing season continued. After that period, each slave received, in addition to his allowance of corn, one salt herring every day.

My master gave me one pair of shoes, one pair of stockings, one hat, one jacket of coarse cloth, two coarse shirts, and two pair of trowsers, yearly. He allowed me no other clothes. In the winter time I often suffered very much from the cold; as I had to drive the team of oxen which hauled the tobacco to market, and frequently did not get home until late at night, the distance being considerable, and my cattle traveled very slow.

One Saturday evening, when I came home from the corn field, my master told me that he had hired me out for a year at the city of Washington, and that I would have to live at the Navy Yard.

On the New Year's day following, which happened about two weeks afterwards, my master set forward for Washington, on horseback, and ordered me to accompany him on foot. It was night when we arrived at the Navy Yard, and everything appeared very strange to me.

I was told by a gentleman who had epaulets on his shoulders, that I must go on board a large ship, which lay in the river. He at the same time told a boy to show me the way. This ship proved to be a frigate, and I was told that I had been brought there to cook for the people belonging to her. In the course of a few days the duties of my station became quite familiar to me; and in the enjoyment of a profusion of excellent provisions, I felt very happy. I strove by all means to please the officers and gentlemen who came on board, and in this I soon found my account. One gave me a half-worn coat, another an old shirt, and a third, a cast off waistcoat and pantaloons. Some presented me with small sums of money, and in this way I soon found myself well clothed, and with more than a dollar in my pocket. My duties, though constant, were not burthersome, and I was permitted to spend Sunday afternoon in my own way. I generally went up into the city to see the new and splendid buildings; often walked as far as Georgetown, and made many new acquaintances among the slaves, and frequently saw large numbers of people of my color chained together in long trains, and driven off towards the South. At that time the slave-trade was not regarded with so much indignation and disgust, as it is now. It was a rare thing to hear of a person of color running away, and escaping altogether from his master: my father being the only one within my knowledge, who had, before this time, obtained his liberty in this manner, in Calvert county; and, as before stated, I never heard what became of him after his flight.

I remained on board the frigate, and about the Navy Yard, two years, and was quite satisfied with my lot, until about three months before the expiration of this period, when it so happened that a schooner, loaded with iron and other materials for the use of the yard, arrived from Philadelphia. She came and lay close by the frigate, to discharge her cargo, and amongst her crew I observed a black man, with whom, in the course of a day or two, I became acquainted. He told me he was free, and lived in Philadelphia, where he kept a house of entertainment for sailors, which, he said, was attended to in his absence by his wife.

His description of Philadelphia, and of the liberty enjoyed there by the black people, so charmed my imagination that I determined to devise some plan of escaping from the frigate, and making my way to the North. I communicated my designs to my new friend, who promised to give me his aid. We agreed that the night before the schooner should sail, I was to be concealed in the hold, amongst a parcel of loose tobacco, which, he said, the captain had undertaken to carry to Philadelphia. The sailing of the schooner was delayed longer than we expected; and, finally, her captain purchased a cargo of flour in Georgetown, and sailed for the West Indies. Whilst I was anxiously awaiting some other opportunity of making my way to Philadelphia, (the idea of crossing the country to the western part of Pennsylvania, never entered my mind,) New Year's day came, and with it came my old master from Calvert, accompanied by a gentleman named Gibson, to whom, he said, he had sold me, and to whom he delivered me over in the Navy Yard. We all three set out that same evening for Calvert, and reached the residence of my new master the next day. Here, I was informed, that I had become the subject of a law-suit. My new master claimed me under his purchase from old Mr. Cox; and another gentleman of the neighborhood, named Levin Ballard, had bought me of the children of my former master, Jack Cox. This suit continued in the courts of Calvert county more than two years; but was finally decided in favor of him who had bought me of the children.

I went home with my master, Mr. Gibson, who was a farmer, and with whom I lived three years. Soon after I came to live with Mr. Gibson, I married a girl of color named Judah, the slave of a gentleman by the name of Symmes, who resided in the same neighborhood. I was at the house of Mr. Symmes every week; and became as well acquainted with him and his family, as I was with my master.

Mr. Symmes also married a wife about the time I did. The lady whom he married lived near Philadelphia, and when she first came to Maryland, she refused to be served by a black chambermaid, but employed a white girl, the daughter of a poor man, who lived near. The lady was reported to be very wealthy, and brought a large trunk full of plate and other valuable articles. This trunk was so heavy that I could scarcely carry it, and it impressed my mind with the idea of great riches in the owner, at that time. After some time Mrs. Symmes dismissed her white chambermaid and placed my wife in that situation, which I regarded as a fortunate circumstance, as it insured her good food, and at least one good suit of clothes.

The Symmes' family was one of the most ancient in Maryland, and had been a long time resident in Calvert county. The grounds had been laid out, and all the improvements projected about the family abode, in a style of much magnificence, according to the custom of the old aristocrary of Maryland and Virginia.

Appendant to the domicile, and at no great distance from the house, was a family vault, built of brick, in which reposed the occupants of the estate, who had lived there for many previous generations. This vault had not been opened or entered for fifteen years previous to the time of which I speak; but it so happened, that at this period, a young man, a distant relation of the family, died, having requested on his death-bed, that he might be buried in this family resting place. When I came on Saturday evening to see my wife and child, Mr. Symmes desired me, as I was older than any of his black men, to take an iron pick and go and open the vault, which I accordingly did, by cutting away the mortar, and removing a few bricks from one side of the building; but I could not remove more than three or four bricks before I was obliged, by the horrid effluvia which issued at the aperture, to retire. It was the most deadly and sickening scent that I have ever smelled, and I could not return to complete the work until after the sun had risen the next day, when I pulled down so much of one of the side walls, as to permit persons to walk in upright. I then went in alone, and examined this house of the dead, and surely no picture could more strongly and vividly depict the emptiness of all earthly vanity, and the nothingness of human pride. Dispersed over the floor lay the fragments of more than twenty human skeletons, each in the place where it had been deposited by the idle tenderness of surviving friends. In some cases nothing remained but the hair and the larger bones, whilst in several the form of the coffin was yet visible, with all the bones resting in their proper places. One coffin, the sides of which were yet standing, the lid only having decayed and partly fallen in, so as to disclose the contents of this narrow cell, presented a peculiarly moving spectacle. Upon the centre of the lid was a large silver plate, and the head and foot were adorned with silver stars.—The nails which had united the parts of the coffin had also silver heads. Within lay the skeletons of a mother and her infant child, in slumbers only to be broken by the peal of the last trumpet. The bones of the infant lay upon the breast of the mother, where the hands of affection had shrouded them. The ribs of the parent had fallen down, and rested on the back bone. Many gold rings were about the bones of the fingers. Brilliant ear-rings lay beneath where the ears had been; and a glittering gold chain encircled the ghastly and haggard vetebræ of a once beautiful neck. The shroud and flesh had disappeared, but the hair of the mother appeared strong and fresh. Even the silken locks of the infant were still preserved. Behold the end of youth and beauty, and of all that is lovely in life! The coffin was so much decayed that it could not be removed. A thick and dismal vapor hung embodied from the roof and walls of this chamal house, in appearance somewhat like a mass of dark cobwebs; but which was impalpable to the touch, and when stirred by the hand vanished away. On the second day we deposited with his kindred, the corpse of the young man, and at night I again carefully closed up the breach which I had made in the walls of this dwelling-place of the dead.

WILLIAM CRAFT

In 1848, William Craft (1824–1900) and his wife, Ellen (1826–1891), successfully plotted their escape from slavery in Macon, Georgia, by first obtaining passes from their owners to travel freely for a few days around Christmastime. By dressing the biracial Ellen in men's clothing, cutting her hair, and fashioning her with glasses, Ellen was able to pass as an older white man. William and Ellen made their way through the South and northward to Philadelphia, where they were assisted by abolitionists, and to Boston via train, staying in hotels along the way. Their fugitive flight was a harrowing journey, one prompted by the want of freedom and the Crafts' determination to make liberty a possibility for others. Welcomed into Boston's prominent Black community, William and Ellen became active abolitionist speakers and agitators, giving witness to life under slavery and speaking forthrightly about the ways that the institution dehumanized and violated enslaved people. After the passage of the Fugitive Slave Act of 1850, the Crafts' former enslaver attempted to locate them using bounty hunters, a frightful prospect that prompted them to move from safe house to safe house in the Boston area until they were able to escape again—this time to Liverpool, England. The Crafts continued to fight for American abolition abroad by delivering lectures and speeches about their escape. They published their well-received narrative in 1860. A decade later, the Crafts returned to Georgia and established an agricultural school for newly freed young people.

From *Running a Thousand Miles for Freedom; or, The Escape of William and Ellen Craft from Slavery*
(1860)

My wife was torn from her mother's embrace in childhood, and taken to a distant part of the country. She had seen so many other children separated from their parents in this cruel manner, that the mere thought of her ever becoming the mother of a child, to linger out a miserable existence under the wretched system of American slavery, appeared to fill her very soul with horror; and as she had taken what I felt to be an important view of her condition, I did not, at first, press the marriage, but agreed to assist her in trying to devise some plan by which we might escape from our unhappy condition, and then be married.

We thought of plan after plan, but they all seemed crowed with insurmountable difficulties. We knew it was unlawful for any public conveyance to take us as passengers, without our master's consent. We were also perfectly aware of the startling fact, that had we left without this consent the professional slave-hunters would have soon had their ferocious bloodhounds baying on our track, and in a short time we should have been dragged back to slavery, not to fill the more favourable situations which we had just left, but to be separated for life, and put to the very meanest and most laborious drudgery; or else have been tortured to death as examples, in order to strike terror into the hearts of others, and thereby prevent them from even attempting to escape from their cruel taskmasters. It is a fact worthy of remark, that nothing seems to give the slaveholders so much pleasure as the catching and torturing of fugitives. They had much rather take the keen and poisonous lash, and with it cut their poor trembling victims to atoms, than allow one of them to escape to a free country, and expose the infamous system from which he fled.

The greatest excitement prevails at a slave-hunt. The slaveholders and their hired ruffians appear to take more pleasure in this inhuman pursuit than English sportsmen do in chasing a fox or a stag. Therefore, knowing what we should have been compelled to suffer, if caught and taken back, we were more than anxious to hit upon a plan that would lead us safely to a land of liberty.

But, after puzzling our brains for years, we were reluctantly driven to the sad conclusion, that it was almost impossible to escape from slavery in Georgia, and travel 1,000 miles across the slave States. We therefore resolved to get the consent of our owners, be married, settle down in slavery, and endeavour to make ourselves as comfortable as possible under that system; but at the same time ever to keep our dim eyes steadily fixed upon the glimmering hope of liberty, and earnestly pray God mercifully to assist us to escape from our unjust thraldom.

We were married, and prayed and toiled on till December, 1848, at which time (as I have stated) a plan suggested itself that proved quite successful, and in eight days after it was first thought of we were free from the horrible trammels of slavery, and glorifying God who had brought us safely out of a land of bondage.

Knowing that slaveholders have the privilege of taking their slaves to any part of the country they think proper, it occurred to me that, as my wife was nearly white, I might get her to disguise herself as an invalid gentleman, and assume to be my master, while I could attend as his slave, and that in this manner we might effect our escape. After I thought of the plan, I suggested it to my wife, but at first she shrank from the idea. She thought it was almost impossible for her to assume that disguise, and travel a distance of 1,000 miles across the slave States. However, on the other hand, she also thought of her condition. She saw that the laws under which we lived did not recognize her to be a woman, but a mere chattel, to be bought and sold, or otherwise dealt with as her owner might see fit. Therefore the more she contemplated her helpless condition, the more anxious she was to escape from it. So she said, "I think it is almost too much for us to undertake; however, I feel that God is on our side, and with his assistance, notwithstanding all the difficulties, we shall be able to succeed. Therefore, if you will purchase the disguise, I will try to carry out the plan."

But after I concluded to purchase the disguise, I was afraid to go to any one to ask him to sell me the articles. It is unlawful in Georgia for a white man to trade with slaves without the master's consent. But, notwithstanding this, many persons will sell a slave any article that he can get the money to buy. Not that they sympathize with the slave, but merely because his testimony is not admitted in court against a free white person.

Therefore, with little difficulty I went to different parts of the town, at odd times, and purchased things piece by piece, (except the trowsers which she found necessary to make,) and took them home to the house where my wife resided. She being a ladies' maid, and a favourite slave in the family, was allowed a little room to herself; and amongst other pieces of furniture which I had made in my overtime, was a chest of drawers; so when I took the articles home, she locked them up carefully in these drawers. No one about the premises knew that she had anything of the kind. So when we fancied we had everything ready the time was fixed for the flight. But we knew it would not do to start off without first getting our master's consent to be away for a few days. Had we left without this, they would soon have had us back into slavery, and probably we should never have got another fair opportunity of even attempting to escape.

Some of the best slaveholders will sometimes give their favourite slaves a few days' holiday at Christmas time; so, after no little amount of perseverance on my wife's part, she obtained a pass from her mistress, allowing her to be away for a few days. The cabinet-maker with whom I worked gave me a similar paper, but said that he needed my services very much, and wished me to return as soon as the time granted was up. I thanked him kindly; but somehow I have not been able to make it convenient to return yet; and, as the free air of good old England agrees so well with my wife and our dear little ones, as well as with myself, it is not at all likely we shall return at present to the "peculiar institution" of chains and stripes.

On reaching my wife's cottage she handed me her pass, and I showed mine, but at that time neither of us were able to read them. It is not only unlawful for slaves to be taught to read, but in some of the States there are heavy penalties attached, such as fines and imprisonment, which will be vigorously enforced upon any one who is humane enough to violate the so-called law.

The following case will serve to show how persons are treated in the most enlightened slaveholding community.

"INDICTMENT.

COMMONWEALTH OF VIRGINIA, } *In the Circuit Court*
NORFOLK COUNTY, *ss.*

The Grand Jurors empannelled and sworn to inquire of offences committed in the body of the said County on their oath present, that Margaret Douglass, being an evil disposed person, not having the fear of God before her eyes, but moved and instigated by the devil, wickedly, maliciously, and feloniously, on the fourth day of July, in the year of our Lord one thousand eight hundred and fifty-four, at Norfolk, in said County, did teach a certain black girl named Kate to read in the Bible, to the great displeasure of Almighty God, to the pernicious example of others in like case offending, contrary to the form of the statute in such case made and provided, and against the peace and dignity of the Commonwealth of Virginia.

"VICTOR VAGABOND, *Prosecuting Attorney.*"

"On this indictment Mrs. Douglass was arraigned as a necessary matter of form, tried, found guilty of course; and Judge Scalawag, before whom she was tried, having consulted with Dr. Adams, ordered the sheriff to place Mrs. Douglass in the prisoner's box, when he addressed her as follows: 'Margaret Douglass, stand up. You are guilty of one of the vilest crimes that ever disgraced society; and the jury have found you so. You have taught a slave girl to read in the Bible. No enlightened society can exist where such offences go unpunished. The Court, in your case, do not feel for you one solitary ray of sympathy, and they will inflict on you the utmost penalty of the law. In any other civilized country you would have paid the forfeit of your crime with your life, and the Court have only to regret that such is not the law in this country. The sentence for your offence is, that you be imprisoned one month in the county jail, and that you pay the costs of this prosecution. Sheriff, remove the prisoner to jail.' On the publication of these proceedings, the Doctors of Divinity preached each a sermon on the necessity of obeying the laws; the *New York Observer* noticed with much pious gladness a revival of religion on Dr. Smith's plantation in Georgia, among his slaves; while the *Journal of Commerce* commended this political preaching of the Doctors of Divinity because it favoured slavery. Let us do nothing to offend our Southern brethren."

However, at first, we were highly delighted at the idea of having gained permission to be absent for a few days; but when the thought flashed across my wife's mind, that it was customary for travellers to register their names in the visitors' book at hotels, as well as in the clearance or Custom-house book at Charleston, South Carolina—it made our spirits droop within us.

So, while sitting in our little room upon the verge of despair, all at once my wife raised her head, and with a smile upon her face, which was a moment before bathed in tears, said, "I think I have it!" I asked what it was. She said, "I think I can make a poultice and bind up my right hand in a sling, and with propriety ask the officers to register my name for me." I thought that would do.

It then occurred to her that the smoothness of her face might betray her; so she decided to make another poultice, and put it in a white handkerchief to be worn under the chin, up the cheeks, and to tie over the head. This nearly hid the expression of the countenance, as well as the beardless chin.

The poultice is left off in the engraving, because the likeness could not have been taken well with it on.

My wife, knowing that she would be thrown a good deal into the company of gentlemen, fancied that she could get on better if she had something to go over the eyes; so I went to a shop and bought a pair of green spectacles. This was in the evening.

We sat up all night discussing the plan, and making preparations. Just before the time arrived, in the morning, for us to leave, I cut off my wife's hair square at the back of the head, and got her to dress in the disguise and stand out on the floor. I found that she made a most respectable looking gentleman.

My wife had no ambition whatever to assume this disguise, and would not have done so had it been possible to have obtained our liberty by more simple means; but we knew it was not customary in the South for ladies to travel with male servants; and therefore, notwithstanding my wife's fair complexion, it would have been a very difficult task for her to have come off as a free white lady, with me as her slave; in fact, her not being able to write would have made this quite impossible. We knew that no public conveyance would take us, or any other slave, as a passenger, without our master's consent. This consent could never be obtained to pass into a free State. My wife's being muffled in the poultices, &c., furnished a plausible excuse for avoiding general conversation, of which most Yankee travellers are passionately fond.

There are a large number of free negroes residing in the southern States; but in Georgia (and I believe in all the slave States,) every coloured person's complexion is *primâ facie* evidence of his being a slave; and the lowest villain in the country, should he be a white man, has the legal power to arrest, and question, in the most inquisitorial and insulting manner, any coloured person, male or female, that he may find at large, particularly at night and on Sundays, without a written pass, signed by the master or some one in authority; or stamped free papers, certifying that the person is the rightful owner of himself.

If the coloured person refuses to answer questions put to him, he may be beaten, and his defending himself against this attack makes him an outlaw, and if he be killed on the spot, the murderer will be exempted from all blame; but after the coloured person has answered the questions put to him, in a most humble and pointed manner, he may then be taken to prison; and should it turn out, after further examination, that he was caught where he had no permission or legal right to be, and that he has not given what they term a satisfactory account of himself, the master will have to pay a fine. On his refusing to do this, the poor slave may be legally and severely flogged by public officers. Should the prisoner prove to be a free man, he is most likely to be both whipped and fined.

The great majority of slaveholders hate this class of persons with a hatred that can only be equalled by the condemned spirits of the infernal regions. They have no mercy upon, nor sympathy for, any negro whom they cannot enslave. They say that

God made the black man to be a slave for the white, and act as though they really believed that all free persons of colour are in open rebellion to a direct command from heaven, and that they (the whites) are God's chosen agents to pour out upon them unlimited vengeance. For instance, a Bill has been introduced in the Tennessee Legislature to prevent free negroes from travelling on the railroads in that State. It has passed the first reading. The bill provides that the President who shall permit a free negro to travel on any road within the jurisdiction of the State under his supervision shall pay a fine of 500 dollars; any conductor permitting a violation of the Act shall pay 250 dollars; provided such free negro is not under the control of a free white citizen of Tennessee, who will vouch for the character of said free negro in a penal bond of one thousand dollars. The State of Arkansas has passed a law to banish all free negroes from its bounds, and it came into effect on the 1st day of January, 1860. Every free negro found there after that date will be liable to be sold into slavery, the crime of freedom being unpardonable. The Missouri Senate has before it a bill providing that all free negroes above the age of eighteen years who shall be found in the State after September, 1860, shall be sold into slavery; and that all such negroes as shall enter the State after September, 1861, and remain there twenty-four hours, shall also be sold into slavery for ever. Mississippi, Kentucky, and Georgia, and in fact, I believe, all the slave States, are legislating in the same manner. Thus the slaveholders make it almost impossible for free persons of colour to get out of the slave States, in order that they may sell them into slavery if they don't go. If no white persons travelled upon railroads except those who could get some one to vouch for their character in a penal bond of one thousand dollars, the railroad companies would soon go to the "wall." Such mean legislation is too low for comment; therefore I leave the villanous acts to speak for themselves.

But the Dred Scott decision is the crowning act of infamous Yankee legislation. The Supreme Court, the highest tribunal of the Republic, composed of nine Judge Jeffries's, chosen both from the free and slave States, has decided that no coloured person, or persons of African extraction, can ever become a citizen of the United States, or have any rights which white men are bound to respect. That is to say, in the opinion of this Court, robbery, rape, and murder are not crimes when committed by a white upon a coloured person.

Judges who will sneak from their high and honourable position down into the lowest depths of human depravity, and scrape up a decision like this, are wholly unworthy the confidence of any people. I believe such men would, if they had the power, and were it to their temporal interest, sell their country's independence, and barter away every man's birthright for a mess of pottage. Well may Thomas Campbell say—

> United States, your banner wears,
>   Two emblems,—one of fame;
> Alas, the other that it bears
>   Reminds us of your shame!
> The white man's liberty in types
>   Stands blazoned by your stars;
> But what's the meaning of your stripes?
>   They mean your Negro-scars.

When the time had arrived for us to start, we blew out the lights, knelt down, and prayed to our Heavenly Father mercifully to assist us, as he did his people of old, to escape from cruel bondage; and we shall ever feel that God heard and answered our prayer. Had we not been sustained by a kind, and I sometimes think special, providence, we could never have overcome the mountainous difficulties which I am now about to describe.

After this we rose and stood for a few moments in breathless silence,—we were afraid that some one might have been about the cottage listening and watching our movements. So I took my wife by the hand, stepped softly to the door, raised the latch, drew it open, and peeped out. Though there were trees all around the house, yet the foliage scarcely moved; in fact, everything appeared to be as still as death. I then whispered to my wife, "Come my dear, let us make a desperate leap for liberty!" But poor thing, she shrank back, in a state of trepidation. I turned and asked what was the matter; she made no reply, but burst into violent sobs, and threw her head upon my breast. This appeared to touch my very heart, it caused me to enter into her feelings more fully than ever. We both saw the many mountainous difficulties that rose one after the other before our view, and knew far too well what our sad fate would have been, were we caught and forced back into our slavish den. Therefore on my wife's fully realizing the solemn fact that we had to take our lives, as it were, in our hands, and contest every inch of the thousand miles of slave territory over which we had to pass, it made her heart almost sink within her, and, had I known them at that time, I would have repeated the following encouraging lines, which may not be out of place here—

> "The hill, though high, I covet to ascend,
>   The *difficulty will not me offend;*
>   For I perceive the way to life lies here:
>   Come, pluck up heart, let's neither faint nor fear;
>   Better, though difficult, the right way to go,—
>   Than wrong, though easy, where the end is woe."

However, the sobbing was soon over, and after a few moments of silent prayer she recovered her self-possession, and said, "Come, William, it is getting late, so now let us venture upon our perilous journey."

We then opened the door, and stepped as softly out as "moonlight upon the water." I locked the door with my own key, which I now have before me, and tiptoed across the yard into the street. I say tiptoed, because we were like persons near a tottering avalanche, afraid to move, or even breathe freely, for fear the sleeping tyrants should be aroused, and come down upon us with double vengeance, for daring to attempt to escape in the manner which we contemplated.

We shook hands, said farewell, and started in different directions for the railway station. I took the nearest possible way to the train, for fear I should be recognized by some one, and got into the negro car in which I knew I should have to ride; but my *master* (as I will now call my wife) took a longer way round, and only arrived there with the bulk of the passengers. He obtained a ticket for himself and one for his slave to Savannah, the first port, which was about two hundred miles off. My master then had the luggage stowed away, and stepped into one of the best carriages.

But just before the train moved off I peeped through the window, and, to my great astonishment, I saw the cabinet-maker with whom I had worked so long, on the platform. He stepped up to the ticket-seller, and asked some question, and then commenced looking rapidly through the passengers, and into the carriages. Fully believing that we were caught, I shrank into a corner, turned my face from the door, and expected in a moment to be dragged out. The cabinet-maker looked into my master's carriage, but did not know him in his new attire, and, as God would have it, before he reached mine the bell rang, and the train moved off.

I have heard since that the cabinet-maker had a presentiment that we were about to "make tracks for parts unknown;" but, not seeing me, his suspicions vanished, until he received the startling intelligence that we had arrived safely in a free State.

As soon as the train had left the platform, my master looked round in the carriage, and was terror-stricken to find a Mr. Cray—an old friend of my wife's master, who dined with the family the day before, and knew my wife from childhood— sitting on the same seat.

The doors of the American railway carriages are at the ends. The passengers walk up the aisle, and take seats on either side; and as my master was engaged in looking out of the window, he did not see who came in.

HIRAM MATTISON

Born in Columbia, South Carolina, and later sold to enslavers in Mobile, Alabama, and New Orleans, Louisiana, Louisa Picquet (1828–1896) worked with Hiram Mattison (1811–1868), an abolitionist minister, to write and publish her autobiography. Picquet was aware that her heartwrenching autobiography would serve two main purposes: (1) equip her with adequate funds to purchase her mother's freedom, which she achieved in 1860; and (2) offer evidence of the specific horrors that women faced in bondage, lending even more credence to the abolitionist cause. Written as a conversation more so than a story with a fully developed narrative arc, The Octoroon recounts generations of sexual assault, concubinage, and trauma experienced by Picquet, her mother, and other mixed-race women in their community. Piquet bravely offers a view into the deep moral corruption that plagued white enslavers and the South.

From *Louisa Picquet, the Octoroon; or, Inside Views of Southern Domestic Life*
(1861)

A WHITE SLAVE LOVE ADVENTURE.

"While I was living in Mobile, a gentleman there owned a colored man that was more white than I am. He was about my age. He had no beard; just a young man, might have been nineteen or twenty. His master was not married, but had a girl belong to him, a very light girl he bought from Charleston; he bought her for himself, though he kept her boarding out.

"This colored man I spoke of used to drive out when his master's sisters wanted to go out. They often came to Mr. English's with them, and right the bell. There I met him often at the door before I knew he was colored, and when he found out I was colored, he was always very polite, and say, 'Good morning, miss,' and ask if the ladies was in. Then, after he got acquainted, he used to come and see me Sundays. He wanted me to marry him, and I liked him very well, and would have had him if he had not run off."

Q.—"How came he to run off?"

A.—"You see Mr. ——* kept that girl, but never go where she was; but, whenever he want to see her he send for her to the office. And this young man who wanted me had to go always and tell that girl, and go with her to the office, whenever his master wanted him to.

"Then this man had another waitman, one was perfectly white, and the other jet black; and the black one got jealous of the other one, and thought his master thought more of his other servant, the white one. (He did think more of him.) So the two had a falling out; and, to seek revenge, the dark one told the master he see something which he did not see—that the other one was out walking with this girl. He knew [that is, the black one] that his master would whip him [the light one] for that, when he would not whip him for any thing else. That night his master had not sent for her, and, of course, he thought it might be true.

"Then he ask T—— about it, and he denied it, but the owner believed it. Then he whipped him awfully, soon as he came to the office that morning; and sent for the girl, and whipped her, and sent her off to New Orleans.

"Then the partner of this man, he spoke to T—— afterward, and told him he would go away. He was an Englishman, or Scotchman. He came out that way—was not raised there. He never would own a slave. He felt sorry that T—— was whipped so, and told him he would go away. His first excuse was he had no money, and the next was on account of being acquainted with me. Then the man inquire what kind of looking girl I was, and told him if I was white as he represented there would be no

---

*Mrs. P. dare not have *any* of these names published, as all the parties are still living.

difficulty at all about getting away, and he would let him have money for both of us to go away.

"Then he told me what this gentleman said to him, and that he had the money from this gentleman, and wanted me to go away with him. Well, I knew that he could neither read nor write, and was afraid that we would be caught, and so I dare not go. We had about two hours' talk then, but when he found out I would not go, he said he must go; he had the money, and all his arrangements made. That's the last I saw of him. I suppose T—— left that night. 'Twas not very long after that I went to Mr. Bachelor's to live, and we were all sold."

We shall hear of this fugitive T—— again, further on in our narrative.

INTRIGUES OF A MARRIED "SOUTHERN GENTLEMAN."

Q.—"Did Mr. Cook always treat *you* well, as to any insults?"

A.—"No. After we went to Mobile, I went to Mr. Bachelor's, after I was at Mr. English's, and Mr. Cook was boarding there. I was a little girl, not fourteen years old. One day Mr. Cook told me I must come to his room that night, and take care of him. He said he was sick, and he want me and another slave girl to come to his room and take care of him. In the afternoon he went to his room, and said he was sick. I was afraid to go there that night, and I told Mrs. Bachelor what Mr. Cook said to me. Then she whispered with her sister, Mrs. Simpson, and then told me I need not go. She said she would go up and see Mr. Cook, and have some one else go and take care of him. Then I went up after Mrs. Bachelor, not to let him see me, and listen to the door. Mrs. Bachelor went in and ask him how he done. She said, 'I heard you was sick, and I thought I would come up and see if there was any thing serious.' He groaned, and seemed to get worse than ever—told how bad he felt about his head, and one thing an'other. Then her reply was, that she would have some water put on to bathe his feet, and some mustard, and have one of the boys come up and take care of him. She went right on in that way, without his asking, and smooth it off in that way, so as not to let on that she thought any thing, at the same time clearing me.

"Then he thanked her very kindly. So she went down, and had the water sent up. Then, pretty soon, he sent down by the boy, to tell me to bring up some more *mustard*. Then Mrs. Bachelor, she understood it, and *she* took up the mustard herself. Then the boy stay with him all night, and just about daylight he come down. When he come down he come to the room (you see, I slept in Mrs. Bachelor's room)—he call me and says, 'Your massa, Henry, says you must take him up a fresh pitcher of water;' and Mrs. Bachelor told him to go and take it up himself; that I was busy.

Q.—"Were you hired to Mrs. Bachelor then?"

A.—"I don't know. I was workin' there; it might have been in part for his board, for aught I know. Mrs. Bachelor kept boarding-house. She was Scotch; came from Scotland."

Q.—"Well, what happened next?"

A.—"I didn't go up till breakfast-time. At breakfast-time I had to take his breakfast up to his room, on a waiter. He had not got up yet—I take the waiter up to the bed. Well, him thinking that all the boarders gone down, talk rather louder than he would if he'd a thought they were there. The door was open wide enough for a person to come in.

"Then he order me, in a sort of commanding way (I don't want to tell what he said), and told me to shut the door. At the same time he was kind a raising up out of the bed; then I began to cry; but before I had time to shut the door, a gentleman walk out of another room close by, picking his nails, and looking in the room as he passed on. Then Mr. Cook turned it off very cute. He said, 'What you stand there crying for, you dam' fool? Go 'long down stairs, and get me some more salt.' Same time he had not taste his breakfast, to see whether he want any salt, or not. That was to blind with that gentleman, because he see me there crying, or heard me, or something. Then I was very glad to get out to get the salt, but still I knew I should have to come back again, and it would not be much better. Then I went down to get the salt, and Mrs. Bachelor caught my looks, and spoke and said, 'Louisa, one of the boys will take that salt up, I want you a minute.' Then I thought she was the best friend I had in the world. She had such a nice way of turning off things. Then I didn't go up till that day, some time. He did not come down, but call out of the window for me to bring him up a pitcher of water. Then I brought the water up, and he want to know why I did not come up with the salt. I told him the reason, that Mrs. Bachelor said she wanted me, and sent it up by one of the boys. Then he said he wanted me to understand that I belong to him, and not to Mrs. Bachelor—that when he called, or wanted me, I was not to consult with Mrs. Bachelor, or any person else.

"Then he told me I must come up in his room that night; if I didn't he'd give me hell in the mornin'. Then I promised him I would, for I was afraid to say any thing else. Then he forbid me sayin' any thing to Mrs. Bachelor about what he said to me—you see there where he got me. Then I came to conclusion he could not do any thing but whip me—he could not kill me for it; an' I made up my mind to take the whippin'. So I didn't go that night.

"Then in the mornin' he want to know why I didn't come up, and I told him I forget it. Then he said, I don't believe you forgot it; but if you forget that, I won't forget what I told you. So he whip me, so that I won't forget another time."

Q.—"Well, how did he whip you?"

A.—"With the cowhide."

Q.—"Around your shoulders, or how?"

A.—"That day he did."

Q.—"How were you dressed—with thin clothes, or how?"

A.—"Oh, very thin; with low-neck'd dress. In the summertime we never wore but two pieces—only the one under, and the blue homespun over. It is a striped cloth they make in Georgia just for the colored people. All the time he was whippin' me I kept sayin' I forgot it, and promisin' I would come another time."

Q.—"Did he whip you hard, so as to raise marks?"

A.—"Oh yes. He never whip me in his life but what he leave the mark on, I was dressed so thin. He kept asking me, all the time he was whippin' me, if I intended to mind him. Of course I told him I would, because I was gettin' a whippin'. At the same time, I did not mean to go to his room; but only did it so that he would stop whippin' me. He want to know what I was afraid of—if I could not sleep as well there as anywhere else? Of course I told him, yes, sir; and that I wan't afraid of any thing. At the same time, I was afraid of him; but I wouldn't tell him. Then he let me go. Then, as luck would have it, he got playin' cards with some gentleman after dinner, about two or three o'clock, and never stop all night; so I thought from appearance of things in the mornin'. They were playin' and drinkin' together all night; so I did not go to his room till mornin'. I had my excuse all made up—because he had company, and I was waitin', and got to sleep. At the same time I didn't intend, and expect to take another whippin' in the mornin'.

"Then, in the mornin', I went up to call him to breakfast; and, as I knock at the door to call him, to tell him that breakfast was ready, he told me to come in. He came to the door, and I smelt his breath, and see from the way he spoke to me that he had been drinkin'. He told me to come in, that he had somethin' for me. At the same time, he took hold of my hand, and kind a pull me, and put a whole handful of half-dollars in my hand. Then I knew he was drunk, but it surprise me so that I didn't know what to think. At the same time, he was holdin' on to me, and askin' me if I would come back. I told him, yes. But I thought he was so drunk he would forget, and so I have all that money. I never had any money but copper and five cents before; and, of course, my hand full of half-dollars looked to me like a fortune. I thought he had got it that night playin' cards. I went on, then, down stairs; and in the afternoon, when he got a little sober, he ask me what I done with that money. First I ask him, what money? I thought he would forget it, and didn't let on that I knew any thing about it. Then he said, that money I let you have this mornin'. Then I knew he had not forgot.

"Then, you see, I had seen a flowered muslin dress in the store several times, and I take a fancy to it; I thought it look beautiful. It was perfectly white, with a little pink leaf all over it. So I went to the store, and ask the man what's the price of it. Then he told me, but I could not reckon it, so I lay the money out, and told him to give just as many yards as I had half-dollars. Then he told me that would be too large a pattern for me; but I told him, no, I wanted a nice full dress. That was the largest pattern I ever had afore, or since. Then I told Mr. Cook I put the money away, and could not find it. I had sense enough to know he would not dare tell any one that he gave me the money, and would hardly dare to whip me for it. Then he say no more about it, only he told me to come up there that night. He said he want to see some more about that money; he didn't believe I lost it. Then I told Mrs. Bachelor that I guess I'd have to go up stairs that night; and ask her what I should do. She was the best friend I had; but she could not interfere no more, because if she did he'd know that I told her. Then she said she had no patience with him—he was the meanest man she ever saw. She abused him then a great deal, before her sister and before me. Then she said, the best plan would be to keep out of his way, and if he called me, not to answer. I was to keep in her room that evening as much as possible.

"Well, about tea-time he wanted water. That was sent up. Then he wanted to know where I was; he wanted a button sewed on his wristband. Then Mrs. Bachelor sent him word that, if he could not find me, to send the shirt down, and her sister, or one of the girls, would put a button on for him, if he was in a hurry. The shirt came down, and the button was sewed on. I suppose he just took the button off for an excuse. Then, when they went up with the shirt, he sent word down that, when I came, I must come up and get his boots and black them. He did not care about waitin' so long for them in the mornin'. He thought I'd give out somewhere. Then, about bedtime, he call one of the boys to know if they told me about the boots; and they said they hadn't seen me. I was all the time in Mrs. Bachelor's room, but none of them knew it. I sewed the button on, but he didn't know it. Then he pretended to be mad because I was gone out at night, and she excuse me, and said, perhaps I had gone out with some children, and got to playin', and didn't know it was so late. He was mad; and told her his wife never allowed me to go out nights, and she must not; and allowed he would give me a floggin' for it. He said I knew better than to go out. He thought I was out; or, perhaps, he thought it was a trick to keep me from him, and that made him so mad.

"In the mornin' he came down, and want to know where I was. You see, I'd made up my mind to take the whippin'. I knew he would not kill me, and I'd get over it the same as I had before. So I told him I was down stairs asleep.

"Then he came to me in the ironin'-room, down stairs, where

I was, and whip me with the cowhide, naked, so I 'spect I'll take some of the marks with me to the grave. One of them I know I will." [Here Mrs. P. declines explaining further how he whipped her, though she had told our hostess where this was written; but it is too horrible and indelicate to be read in a civilized country.] Mrs. P. then proceeds, "He was very bad, and whipped me awfully. That was the worst whippin' I ever had."

Q.—"Did he cut through your skin?"

A.—"Oh yes; in a good many places. I don't believe he could whip me much worse, if I struck his wife or children; and I didn't do any thing. He pretended it was because I was out, but I knew what it was for When he came out of the room, after he had whipped me, he said, to make Mrs. Bachelor believe, 'I'll be bound she won't go out another time without permission.' Then, when he was whippin' me so awfully, I made up my mind 'twas of no use, and I'd go, and not be whipped any more; and told him so. I saw he was bent on it, and I could not get Mrs. Bachelor to protect me any more. Then he went away, and that was the last I ever saw him. That very day, about noon, we was taken by the sheriff, and was all sold the next mornin'. I tell you I was glad when I heard I was taken off to be sold, because of what I escape; but I jump out of the fryin'-pan into the fire. Mrs. Bachelor said it was a good thing, when I went away."

Q.—"Where was Mrs. Cook all this time?"

A.—"She was up the country, in Georgia, with a sister of hers. When he failed in Georgia, he sent her up to her sister. I suppose she was willing to do it; she must have understood it."

Q.—"How many children had she?"

A.—"I could not tell; they had a lot of them. I know I been nursin' all my life up to that time."

THE FAMILY SOLD AT AUCTION— LOUISA BOUGHT BY A "NEW ORLEANS GENTLEMAN," AND WHAT CAME OF IT.

Q.—"How did you say you come to be sold?"

A.—"Well, you see, Mr. Cook made great parties, and go off to watering-places, and get in debt, and had to break up [fail], and then he took us to Mobile, and hired the most of us out, so the men he owe should not find us, and sell us for the debt. Then, after a while, the sheriff came from Georgia after Mr. Cook's debts, and found us all, and took us to auction, and sold us. My mother and brother was sold to Texas, and I was sold to New Orleans."

Q.—"How old were you, then?"

A.—"Well, I don't know exactly, but the auctioneer said I wasn't quite fourteen. I didn't know myself."

Q.—"How old was your brother?"

A.—"I suppose he was about two months old. He was little bit of baby."

Q.—"Where were you sold?"

A.—"In the city of Mobile."

Q.—"In a yard? In the city?"

A.—"No. They put all the men in one room, and all the women in another; and then whoever want to buy come and examine, and ask you whole lot of questions. They began to take the clothes off of me, and a gentleman said they needn't do that, and told them to take me out. He said he knew I was a virtuous girl, and he'd buy me, anyhow. He didn't strip me; only just under my shoulders."

Q.—"Were there any others there white like you?"

A.—"Oh yes, plenty of them. There was only Lucy of our lot, but others!"

Q.—"Were others stripped and examined?"

A.—"Well, not quite naked, but just same."

Q.—"You say the gentleman told them to 'take you out.' What did he mean by that?"

A.—"Why, take me out of the *room* where the women and girls were kept; where they examine them—out where the auctioneer sold us."

Q.—"Where was that? In the street, or in a yard?"

A.—"At the market, where the block is?"

Q.—"What block?"

A.—"My! don't you know? The stand, where we have to get up?"

Q.—"Did *you* get up on the stand?"

A.—"Why, of course; we all have to get up to be seen."

Q.—"What else do you remember about it?"

A.—"Well, they first begin at upward of six hundred for me, and then some bid fifty more, and some twenty-five more, and that way."

Q.—"Do you remember any thing the auctioneer said about you when he sold you?"

A.—"Well, he said he could not recommend me for any thing else only that I was a good-lookin' girl, and a good nurse, and kind and affectionate to children; but I was never used to any hard work. He told them they could see that. My hair was quite short, and the auctioneer spoke about it, but said, 'You see it good quality, and give it a little time, it will grow out again. You see Mr. Cook had my hair cut off. My hair grew fast, and look so much better than Mr. Cook's daughter, and he fancy I had better hair than his daughter, and so he had it cut off to make a difference."

Q.—"Well, how did they sell you and your mother? that is, which was sold first?"

A.—"Mother was put up the first of our folks. She was sold for splendid cook, and Mr. Horton, from Texas, bought her and the baby, my brother. Then Henry, the carriage driver, was put up, and Mr. Horton bought him, and then two field-hands, Jim and Mary. The women there tend mills and drive ox wagons, and plough, just like men. Then I was sold next. Mr. Horton run me up to fourteen hundred dollars. He wanted I should go with my mother. Then some one said 'fifty.' Then Mr. Williams allowed that he did not care what they bid, he was going to have me anyhow. Then he bid fifteen hundred. Mr. Horton said 'twas no use to bid any more, and I was sold to Mr. Williams. I went right to New Orleans then."

Q.—"Who was Mr. Williams?"

A.—"I didn't know then, only he lived in New Orleans. Him and his wife had parted, some way—he had three children, boys. When I was going away I heard some one cryin', and prayin' the Lord to go with her only daughter, and protect me. I felt pretty bad then, but hadn't no time only to say good-bye. I wanted to go back and get the dress I bought with the half-dollars, I thought a good deal of that; but Mr. Williams would not let me go back and get it. He said he'd get me plenty of nice dresses. Then I thought mother could cut it up and make dresses for my brother, the baby. I knew she could not wear it; and I had a thought, too, that she'd have it to remember me."

Q.—"It seems like a dream, don't it?"

A.—"No; it seems fresh in my memory when I think of it— no longer than yesterday. Mother was right on her knees, with her hands up, prayin' to the Lord for me. She didn't care who saw her: the people all lookin' at her. I often thought her prayers followed me, for I never could forget her. Whenever I wanted any thing real bad after that, my mother was always sure to appear to me in a dream that night, and have plenty to give me, always."

Q.—"Have you never seen her since?"

A.—"No, never since that time. I went to New Orleans, and she went to Texas. So I understood."

Q.—"Well, how was it with you after Mr. Williams bought you?"

A.—"Well, he took me right away to New Orleans."

Q.—"How did you go?"

A.—"In a boat, down the river. Mr. Williams told me what he bought me for, soon as we started for New Orleans. He said he was getting old, and when he saw me he thought he'd buy me, and end his days with me. He said if I behave myself he'd treat me well: but, if not, he'd whip me almost to death."

Q.—"How old was he?"

A.—"He was over forty; I guess pretty near fifty. He was gray headed. That's the reason he was always so jealous. He never let me go out anywhere."

Q.—"Did you never go to church?"

A.—"No, sir; I never darken a church door from the time he bought me till after he died. I used to ask him to let me go to church. He would accuse me of some object, and said there was more rascality done there than anywhere else. He'd sometimes say, 'Go on, I guess you've made your arrangements; go on, I'll catch up with you.' But I never dare go once."

Q.—"Had you any children while in New Orleans?"

A.—"Yes; I had four."

Q.—"Who was their father?"

A.—"Mr. Williams."

Q.—"Was it known that he was living with you?"

A.—"Every body knew I was housekeeper, but he never let on that he was the father of my children. I did all the work in his house—nobody there but me and the children."

Q.—"What children?"

A.—"My children and his. You see he had three sons."

Q.—"How old were his children when you went there?"

A.—"I guess the youngest was nine years old. When he had company, gentlemen folks, he took them to the hotel. He never have no gentlemen company home. Sometimes he would come and knock, if he stay out later than usual time; and if I did not let him in in a minute, when I would be asleep, he'd come in and take the light, and look under the bed, and in the wardrobe, and all over, and then ask me why I did not let him in sooner. I did not know what it meant till I learnt his ways."

Q.—"Were your children mulattoes?"

A.—"No, sir! They were all white. They look just like him. The neighbors all see that. After a while he got so disagreeable that I told him, one day, I wished he would sell me, or 'put me in his pocket'—that's the way we say—because I had no peace at all. I rather die than live in that way. Then he got awful mad, and said nothin' but death should separate us; and, if I run off, he'd blow my brains out. Then I thought, if that be the way, all I could do was just to pray for him to die."

Q.—"Where did you learn to pray?"

A.—"I first begin to pray when I was in Georgia, about whippin'—that the Lord would make them forget it, and not whip me: and it seems if when I pray I did not get so hard whippin'."

INSIDE VIEWS OF ANOTHER SOUTHERN FAMILY.

Q.—"Did you feel that you were doing right in living, as you did, with Mr. Williams?"

A.—"No; when I was a little girl in Georgia the madame, Mrs. Cook, used to read the Bible, and explain it to us. One night she read the commandments about stealin', and committin' adultery. They made a great impression on my mind. I knew what stealin' was, but I did not know what adultery was. Then

I asked her the meanin'. She did not want to answer for a good while. I suppose I was so small she hated to tell me, but I kept on askin'. Then she said, 'You see *Lucy*, how many children she's got?' I told her yes. Then she said she did not know the father of any of them children, and said when folks had children that way they must be married like *she* (Mrs. Cook) was to her husband. It was adultery to stay with any one without bein' married—that was the meanin' of it."

Q.—"Who was this Lucy?"

A.—"She was a seamstress in Mrs. Cook's family."

Q.—"What was her color?"

A.—"Right white—light hair and blue eyes. All her children were right white."

Q.—"And was *she* a slave?"

A.—"Yes, sir."

Q.—"How many children had she?"

A.—"Five or six in Georgia, and one after she went to Mobile."

Q.—"And had she no husband?"

A.—"No, sir; never had a husband in her life."

Q.—"Do not the slave women usually have husbands, or those they call their husbands?"

A.—"Yes, sir; some of them do; but some of them do not. They can't have any husbands, because their masters have them all the time."

Q.—"How did you say it was with Lucy?"

A.—"She sew in the house all day, and then go to her room, off, at night."

Q.—"What became of her?"

A.—"Well, she was sold the day I was, in Mobile, and got free after a while; and each of the white men bought his child. Mr. Moore bought his, and Mr. Hale bought his; and then the others, that their fathers would not own, her relations bought and set free."

Q.—"Who do you mean by her relations?"

A.—"Why Lucy's sister Judy, and Mr. ——*, who kept her. I

---

*We have the name, but Mrs. P. dare not have it published, as the parties are still living, and she fears they might shoot her.

tell you how he did: He bought Elcy, Lucy's sister, first, and lived with her till she died. He had her learn to read and write, and taught her music, and done first rate by her. Then, when Elcy died, he bought her sister, Judy, and is livin' with her yet. Then, when they heard that Lucy was sold, all her sisters and brothers unite, sent on and bought her, and set her free."

HARPER TWELVETREES

A London-based business owner and abolitionist, Harper Twelvetrees (1823–1881) edited the narrative of John Anderson, a self-liberated fugitive from slavery in Missouri. After Anderson is sold away from his wife and child and forced to marry another woman, he elects to flee his circumstances instead and heads northward to freedom. Along the way, Anderson is detected by an enslaver, and, rather than acquiesce, he fights back by stabbing the man to death. Anderson eventually arrives in Windsor, Canada West, where a robust community of former enslaved people have settled. Anderson never feels truly safe, however, as he left a dead man on his path to liberty. Anderson's anxiety prompts him to travel throughout Canada for years before he is captured and arrested, pending extradition to the United States for murder. After the Canadian government acquits him, deeming Anderson's fateful action "justifiable," Anderson settles in London, where Twelvetrees and other abolitionists support him financially and educationally before sponsoring his repatriation to Liberia with the prominent Black abolitionist minister and missionary Alexander Crummell.

From *The Story of the Life of John Anderson, the Fugitive Slave*
(1863)

ANDERSON'S ESCAPE FROM SLAVERY.—
DESPERATE STRUGGLE FOR LIFE AND LIBERTY.

Leaves the Plantation.—Bids farewell to his Wife and Child.—
Encounters Diggs, a Slaveholder.—"Give me Liberty, or give me
Death."—Wounds his Adversary and Flies—Perilous Journey
through the Woods.—Reaches the State of Illinois.—Hospitality of
an English Settler.—Proceeds to Chicago.

As Anderson's master insisted that he should follow the practice usual among plantation slaves, he at once proceeded to
carry out his resolution to bid Mr. McDonald and slavery,
"good bye." He chose a Sunday at the latter end of September
(having been but six or seven weeks in his new position) for his
departure. The day seemed favourable for his project, as his
master had been summoned from home to attend a church
meeting, called to investigate a charge brought against a religious slaveholder of *whipping a slave to death!* To aid him in
his flight he borrowed one of his master's mules, and two hours
before daybreak made fast his blankets on the back of the mule,
took a rope, some twenty feet long, to be of use in making a
raft, and helping himself to a bridle, started for a ferry on the
Missouri river. This river was about thirty-five miles from the
point of starting. Here he tried to induce the ferryman to give
him a passage across, but being unable to produce a pass was
compelled to retire. He betook himself to the wood and lay till
night, when he returned to the river, and was about to seize a
boat that was lying on the bank, when some one appearing, he
was obliged a second time to retreat into the woods. About two
hours before sun-rise he ventured again to the river side, and

was fortunate enough to find a skiff upon the bank, but without oars. Furnishing himself with a piece of bark for a paddle, he launched the boat and succeeded in reaching the opposite bank, where he landed and drew up the skiff. This was the first time he had ever been in a boat. He immediately started for Fayette, the residence of his father-in-law. It was yet dark. Fayette was about six miles away, but he was fortunate enough to get a lift part of the way by a stage.

To Lewis Tomlin, Anderson made known his intention of making his way to Canada, and his determination to surrender his life rather than be captured in his attempt to gain his liberty. His father-in-law did not attempt to dissuade him from his purpose, and offered him a pistol for the defence of his person, which, however, he declined, saying he had a dirk knife which he thought would be sufficient for his purpose. He next visited his wife, with whom he had a brief and affecting interview; and after caressing his infant child, bade both farewell, and hastened forth upon an unknown path to the soil whose touch gives freedom to the slave. He returned to Fayette to the roof of his father-in-law, and bidding him also adieu, pursued his journey.

We now come to Anderson's encounter with the man whom he is charged, under the laws of Missouri, with "wilfully, maliciously, and feloniously stabbing and killing."

About noon on Tuesday (the third day of his departure from McDonald's plantation), Anderson, while pursuing his journey to the North, passed a field belonging to one Seneca T. P. Diggs, who was at the time engaged in superintending the drying of tobacco. Diggs demanded of him who he was, where he was going, and whether he had the necessary pass. It should be known that, according to the law of the State of Missouri, any Negro, found more than twenty miles from the plantation of his master without a pass, may be arrested, and that the person taking him back is entitled to a reward of five dollars and mileage, at the rate of ten cents or fivepence per mile.

Anderson confessed to being without a pass, but represented that he had legitimate business in that direction, and that he was bound on that business to a certain place. Diggs told him to accompany him to the house, saying he would give him some dinner and then shew him the way. This offer Anderson de-

clined, upon which Diggs expressed his belief that Anderson
was a runaway, and that he should be restored to his owner.
Upon this Anderson immediately started; Diggs calling to three
of his Negroes, saying, "Catch that runaway, and I will give
you the reward." Diggs also pursued, having at the time an axe
in his hand, which he threw at Anderson, but without hitting
him. After about an hour's pursuit, Anderson fled into the woods,
followed by the Negroes, whose number had been increased to
half-a-dozen. When they had hunted Anderson for two or three
hours they were joined by Diggs, who encouraged his slaves to
seize the fugitive, and at last issued an order that they should
take him dead or alive. Anderson had repeatedly shown his
dirk knife, and declared that he would not be taken alive. He
was now exhausted, and Diggs was able to come up with him,
brandishing at the time a club; the Negroes, also, were near and
armed, each with a similar weapon. Anderson's sole hope of escape now lay in the use of his knife. With this he struck a blow
at Diggs and retired from the spot; but hearing him repeat his
order that the slaves should take him dead or alive, and fearing
that he had not inflicted sufficient injury to prevent pursuit, he
returned and again struck Diggs, and effectually disarmed him.
The Negroes followed for a short distance, but being advised
by Anderson to go back and say they could not take him, they
retired and left him to himself.

Anderson, the same night returned to his wife and informed
her of what had transpired. She said that a rumour had reached
her master's plantation of some old slaveholder having been
struck by a Negro with a knife, and exhorted him at once to
make his way out of the State with all possible speed. She was
much frightened when informed that her husband was the man
who had committed the act of which she had already heard.
After receiving a shirt or two from his wife, he again started for
the land of true liberty, and has seen neither wife, nor child, nor
his birthplace since.

Anderson commenced his distant and perilous journey with
only a dollar and-a-half in his pocket. His travelling was, for
the most part, performed during the night, and what rest he got
he took, where he thought himself most secure, in the day time.
He was often greatly in want of food, and for days together had

to subsist upon what fell in his way—corn, hazel nuts, paw-paws, or raw potatoes. He had several narrow escapes from being captured. On one occasion, while resting himself by the wayside, a man on horseback rode up, and, charging him with being a fugitive slave, would have made him a prisoner, but he fled into a neighbouring field, and succeeded in concealing him-self amongst some tall Indian corn. In the evening he ventured again into the public road, and observing a fire in the wood not far distant, and imagining that some of his own people might be engaged husking corn, he drew near the spot, and discov-ered, just in time to avoid the trap that had been set for him, that the fire had been kindled by the man from whose clutches he had escaped during the day. His enemy had adopted this method of decoying him into his ambush.

Under the provocation of extreme hunger, Anderson was sometimes impelled to levy contributions upon the eatable property of those whose dwellings lay in his way. Creeping into the back kitchen of a farm house, he filled one of his pockets with salt, and from a farm yard at another place he helped him-self to three chickens, and having pulled their necks, retired into the woods to regale himself upon their flesh. He speedily deprived two of them of their feathers and roasted them; but in the midst of his repast, though not until he had nearly picked the bones of both birds, he was alarmed by the sounds of ap-proaching footsteps, when, suspecting that the owner of the chickens was in pursuit, he hastily decamped, carrying the un-cooked chicken with him, which was his entire supply of food during the next two days. He crossed the Mississippi as he had done the Missouri, by using a boat which he found on the bank. It was now Saturday night, and he had been just a fortnight ab-sent from the plantation of McDonald, and had gained the free State of Illinois. Knowing, however, that successful attempts had been made to recover fugitives in that State, he did not feel secure, and therefore resolved to observe the same circumspec-tion he had practised in Missouri.

On the following day providence directed his footsteps to the threshold of an English settler, who gave him a cordial recep-tion, and offered him a night's lodging. Before putting him to bed, his host furnished him with a good supper. Anderson's mind was afterwards greatly disturbed, and his apprehensions excited, by seeing a gun in his lodging room, which he thought might be kept for the purpose of overcoming runaway subjects like himself. His weariness, however, soon got the better of his fears, and after a long and sound sleep he rose much refreshed. Before breakfast his kind entertainer supplied him with a razor, and he was enabled to indulge in the luxury of a shave. In addition to a substantial breakfast, the good-hearted Englishman filled his pockets with apples and bread, and he departed on his way well rested, well cleansed, well fed, and well supplied. After several adventures, some of them of a critical nature, during the day and the night that succeeded, Anderson again ventured to present himself at the door of a white man's dwelling. Here he got a breakfast, and purchased a loaf of bread of the housewife. The farmer undertook to direct him, and went forth with him under pretence of doing so. They had not proceeded far, however, when Anderson perceived that the man was leading him back towards the house, through a field in which two of his sons were working. Fearful that he was about to be betrayed, Anderson took to flight, and soon left the farmer and his sons far behind him.

At the end of two days he struck a branch of the Illinois river, which he crossed, and after proceeding some distance, came to a railway track, with the use of which he was acquainted. He kept by this track until he arrived within a short distance of Bloomington.

After various adventures he overtook some teams which were on the way to a place called Rock Island, and being permitted to mount one of them he reached the town that evening. The next day he hired himself to a barber, though quite ignorant of the art of shaving any one besides himself, but stayed with him only two days, and then started for Chicago, his fare being paid by a society of abolitionists. In Chicago, Anderson lived for three weeks with another barber, and then left for Windsor, Upper Canada, where he safely arrived.

ANDERSON BENEATH THE BRITISH FLAG.

Arrives at Windsor, Upper Canada.—His first employment as a
Free man.—Discovers a plot to get him back to slavery.—Changes
his name and residence.—For five years remains unmolested.

Anderson reached Windsor in the month of September, 1853, and obtained employment as a labourer on the Great Western Railway of Canada, on that part of the line lying between Windsor and Chatham, and was paid at the rate of about seven shillings per day; his work consisted in laying "ties" for the rails, and the job lasted six or seven weeks. During the month of October, he got a friend to write two letters to his wife in Missouri, one of which he sent to the care of Tomlin, his wife's father, and the other to a free coloured man, of the name of Allen, following the trade of a shoemaker, in the town of Fayette; the information in both letters was the same—to the effect that he had got safely to Detroit. When he had finished his job upon the railway, he returned to Windsor; with his earnings he purchased himself some clothes and entered the institution of Mr. William Bibb—a fugitive slave, who had established a school—resolving to devote one half of his time to his education, and the other half to manual labour, and thus be able to support himself and attend school at the same time. He found in a lady of the name of Evelyn a very kind friend; she was a widow, and obtained her living by teaching. This lady sent for Anderson to inform him that a letter had arrived in Windsor, stating that his wife and children had reached Detroit, and were waiting for him. Mrs. Evelyn read the letter to him, and told him it was her belief that it had been sent to decoy him across the river into the State of Michigan, and that if he crossed he would, in all probability, be seized and carried to Missouri. Mrs. Evelyn advised him to leave the institution, to remove to Chatham, and the better to avoid detection, to assume another name. He acted according to this counsel; and making up a small bundle of clothes, and leaving his trunk under the care of a Mrs. Jackson, immediately started for Chatham, which place

was sixty or seventy miles from Windsor; he avoided the high
road, and walked as far as Belle River, where he took the railway cars for Chatham. This change of residence took place in
the second or third week of April, 1854. In Chatham he took
another name. In Missouri he had always been called Jack, in
Windsor he went by the name of John Anderson, but in Chatham he became James Hamilton. This was the name of a coloured man—like himself, a fugitive—who resided in the town,
and who was old enough to pass for his father. In Chatham,
Anderson went to wood chopping, by the "cord," for which he
was paid at the rate of three and sixpence per cord, and he
could do on an average two cords a day. He had not been many
weeks in Chatham before a rumour spread among the coloured
people of the place, that certain parties were on the look-out for
him, and that a reward had been offered for his apprehension.
The report alarmed him, and he deemed it advisable to go to a
lawyer, and tell him in what way he had made his escape from
slavery, and at the same time, take his advice as to the course he
should pursue. Having related to him all the facts of the case,
the lawyer told him he had better leave the neighbourhood, and
again change his name, for though his enemies might not be
able to "get him," they might give him a "heap of trouble."

It is difficult in the absence of reliable information, to furnish
any connected account of the proceedings of Anderson during
the five following years of his residence in Canada. He has
stated that he travelled from place to place, and pursued various employments, until having learned the trade of a mason
and plasterer, he settled down in the town of Caledonia, where
he became the owner of a house. With this brief notice of his
first six years of freedom, we proceed to record those events in
his history, which excited so much public attention, and made
his name so widely known.

ANDERSON'S ARREST, AND THE DIPLOMATIC
CORRESPONDENCE THEREON.

*Anderson's confidence is betrayed.—He is arrested, and afterwards
released.—He is arrested a second time, and after some weeks
confinement discharged.—He is a third time arrested, and is
committed to the County Jail.—His rendition is demanded.—
Diplomatic correspondence.*

About the commencement of the year 1860, Anderson was imprudent enough to mention, in confidence, to a person of the
name of Wynne, with whom he was at the time on terms of intimate friendship, the facts connected with his escape from slavery,
including his encounter with Diggs. Wynne, in retaliation for
some offence given him by Anderson, reported what he had
heard to a Justice of the Peace of the name of Mathews; who,
upon the information thus furnished, caused the fugitive to be
arrested. It is believed that he (Mathews) further communicated
the fact of Anderson's capture to the friends of the deceased
Diggs. After several weeks' imprisonment—no witnesses appearing, Anderson was released. But on the 30th of April, and only
three days after his discharge, he was again arrested on the information of a man of the name of Gunning—a detective police officer, and professional slave-catcher, who came over from Detroit,
in the State of Michigan, and deposed on oath, that he "verily
believed Anderson had wilfully, deliberately, and maliciously
murdered Diggs, on the 28th of September, 1853."

After some additional weeks imprisonment, Anderson was
again set at liberty through the interposition of legal aid; but
the man Gunning did not abandon his intention of procuring
his extradition. Accordingly on his return to the United States,
Gunning applied himself to the obtaining of evidence from Missouri in support of his original charge, and returning with witnesses, Anderson was once more arrested, and brought up for
examination. The case was gone into on the 27th of September,
when there appeared as witnesses, against him, William C. Baker,
of Howard Country, Missouri; also, two sons of the deceased

Diggs; also a lawyer of the name of Holliday; also a constable of the name of Hazlehurst, and finally, a slave called Phil. The evidence of these witnesses having been taken, Anderson was committed to the common jail of Brantford, "to be there safely kept, until he should be delivered by due course of law." The warrant was dated the 28th of September, and was signed by Mathews and two other Justices of the Peace.

There appears to have been an immediate application by Anderson's prosecutors to Washington, as on the 2nd of October, the Secretary of State, General Cass, addressed a letter to the British Minister, requesting her Majesty's government to issue the necessary warrant to "deliver up the person of John Anderson, otherwise called Jack, a man of colour, charged with the commission of murder in the State of Missouri." There was an important omission in this official requisition. John Anderson was described simply as *a coloured man* and not as a *slave;* and therefore, a piece of property. This omission might have been attended with serious if not fatal consequences, as the proceedings, both at the British Embassy at Washington, and at the Foreign and Colonial offices in London, were based upon the presumption that Anderson was a free man, and that he was charged with the crime of murder in the capacity of a free man. At a later date, April 8th, 1861, Lord Lyons, in a despatched to Lord John Russell, says,— "When I despatched the requisition for the surrender, to Canada, I was not aware that John Anderson had been a slave, or that there were any peculiar circumstances in the case."

Lord Lyons, on receiving the requisition of General Cass, transmitted it to the Foreign office in London, and on the 22nd of October, 1860, Lord John Russell requested the Secretary of State for the Colonies "to take the necessary steps for complying with the application should there be no objection thereto." Accordingly, on the 27th of October, a despatch from the Colonial office, and a letter from the Foreign office, went out to Canada, instructing Sir Edmund Head "to take such measures as were authorized by the laws of Canada, for the extradition to the authorities of the State of Missouri, of the person of John Anderson, otherwise called Jack, charged with the commission of murder in that State."

ELIZABETH KECKLEY

Elizabeth Keckley (1818–1907) was born into slavery in Virginia, where she experienced an array of foul treatment, including brutal whippings and sexual assault. A talented seamstress, Keckley saved enough money to purchase her and her son's freedom, and they moved to Washington, DC, where she quickly found success as a sought-after dressmaker for the city's political elite and became a close confidante of First Lady Mary Todd Lincoln. Behind the Scenes is a narrative of slavery that also offers glimpses of Black life in the nation's capital as well as the private lives of President Abraham Lincoln and his family. Keckley's connections with wealthy clients helped her establish the Ladies' Freedmen and Soldiers' Relief Association, which supported contraband enslaved people during the Civil War. Though Keckley presents the Lincolns positively in the narrative, she was ultimately derided for breaking Victorian mores of privacy and discretion, leading her to lose most of her dedicated clients. Despite the controversy over its publication, Keckley's narrative remains an insightful story of a determined woman whose craft and enterprise lifts her family out of the bonds of slavery.

From *Behind the Scenes; or, Thirty Years a Slave, and Four Years in the White House*
(1868)

Chapter VII.

WASHINGTON IN 1862–3.

In the summer of 1862, freedmen began to flock into Washington from Maryland and Virginia. They came with a great hope in their hearts, and with all their worldly goods on their backs.

Fresh from the bonds of slavery, fresh from the benighted regions of the plantation, they came to the Capital looking for liberty, and many of them not knowing it when they found it. Many good friends reached forth kind hands, but the North is not warm and impulsive. For one kind word spoken, two harsh ones were uttered; there was something repelling in the atmosphere, and the bright joyous dreams of freedom to the slave faded—were sadly altered, in the presence of that stern, practical mother, reality. Instead of flowery paths, days of perpetual sunshine, and bowers hanging with golden fruit, the road was rugged and full of thorns, the sunshine was eclipsed by shadows, and the mute appeals for help too often were answered by cold neglect. Poor dusky children of slavery, men and women of my own race—the transition from slavery to freedom was too sudden for you! The bright dreams were too rudely dispelled; you were not prepared for the new life that opened before you, and the great masses of the North learned to look upon your helplessness with indifference—learned to speak of you as an idle, dependent race. Reason should have prompted kinder thoughts. Charity is ever kind.

One fair summer evening I was walking the streets of Washington, accompanied by a friend, when a band of music was heard in the distance. We wondered what it could mean, and curiosity prompted us to find out its meaning. We quickened our steps, and discovered that it came from the house of Mrs. Farnham. The yard was brilliantly lighted, ladies and gentlemen were moving about, and the band was playing some of its sweetest airs. We approached the sentinel on duty at the gate, and asked what was going on. He told us that it was a festival given for the benefit of the sick and wounded soldiers in the city. This suggested an idea to me. If the white people can give festivals to raise funds for the relief of suffering soldiers, why should not the well-to-do colored people go to work to do something for the benefit of the suffering blacks? I could not rest. The thought was ever present with me, and the next Sunday I made a suggestion in the colored church, that a society of colored people be formed to labor for the benefit of the unfortunate freedmen. The idea proved popular, and in two weeks "the Contraband Relief Association" was organized, with forty working members.

In September of 1862, Mrs. Lincoln left Washington for New York, and requested me to follow her in a few days, and join her at the Metropolitan Hotel. I was glad of the opportunity to do so, for I thought that in New York I would be able to do something in the interests of our society. Armed with credentials, I took the train for New York, and went to the Metropolitan, where Mrs. Lincoln had secured accommodations for me. The next morning I told Mrs. Lincoln of my project; and she immediately headed my list with a subscription of $200. I circulated among the colored people, and got them thoroughly interested in the subject, when I was called to Boston by Mrs. Lincoln, who wished to visit her son Robert, attending college in that city. I met Mr. Wendell Phillips, and other Boston philanthropists, who gave me all the assistance in their power. We held a mass meeting at the Colored Baptist Church, Rev. Mr. Grimes, in Boston, raised a sum of money, and organized there a branch society. The society was organized by Mrs. Grimes, wife of the pastor, assisted by Mrs. Martin, wife of Rev. Stella Martin. This branch of the main society, during the war, was able to send us over eighty large boxes of goods, contributed exclusively by the colored people of Boston. Returning to New York, we held a successful meeting at the Shiloh Church, Rev. Henry Highland Garnet, pastor. The Metropolitan Hotel, at that time as now, employed colored help. I suggested the object of my mission to Robert Thompson, Steward of the Hotel, who immediately raised quite a sum of money among the dining-room waiters. Mr. Frederick Douglass contributed $200, besides lecturing for us. Other prominent colored men sent in liberal contributions. From England* a large quantity of stores was received. Mrs. Lincoln made frequent contributions, as also did the President. In 1863 I was re-elected President of the Association, which office I continue to hold.

For two years after Willie's death the White House was the

---

*The Sheffield Anti-Slavery Society of England contributed through Mr. Frederick Douglass, to the Freedmen's Relief Association, $24.00; Aberdeen Ladies' Society, $40.00; Anti-Slavery Society of Edinburgh, Scotland, $48.00; Friends at Bristol, England, $176.00; Birmingham Negro's Friend Society, $50.00. Also received through Mr. Charles R. Douglass, from the Birmingham Society, $33.00.

scene of no fashionable display. The memory of the dead boy was duly respected. In some things Mrs. Lincoln was an altered woman. Sometimes, when in her room, with no one present but myself, the mere mention of Willie's name would excite her emotion, and any trifling memento that recalled him would move her to tears. She could not bear to look upon his picture; and after his death she never crossed the threshold of the Guest's Room in which he died, or the Green Room in which he was embalmed. There was something supernatural in her dread of these things, and something that she could not explain. Tad's nature was the opposite of Willie's, and he was always regarded as his father's favorite child. His black eyes fairly sparkled with mischief.

The war progressed, fair fields had been stained with blood, thousands of brave men had fallen, and thousands of eyes were weeping for the fallen at home. There were desolate hearthstones in the South as well as in the North, and as the people of my race watched the sanguinary struggle, the ebb and flow of the tide of battle, they lifted their faces Zionward, as if they hoped to catch a glimpse of the Promised Land beyond the sulphureous clouds of smoke which shifted now and then but to reveal ghastly rows of new-made graves. Sometimes the very life of the nation seemed to tremble with the fierce shock of arms. In 1863 the Confederates were flushed with victory, and sometimes it looked as if the proud flag of the Union, the glorious old Stars and Stripes, must yield half its nationality to the tri-barred flag that floated grandly over long columns of gray. These were sad, anxious days to Mr. Lincoln, and those who saw the man in privacy only could tell how much he suffered. One day he came into the room where I was fitting a dress on Mrs. Lincoln. His step was slow and heavy, and his face sad. Like a tired child he threw himself upon a sofa, and shaded his eyes with his hands. He was a complete picture of dejection. Mrs. Lincoln, observing his troubled look, asked:

"Where have you been, father?"

"To the War Department," was the brief, almost sullen answer.

"Any news?"

"Yes, plenty of news, but no good news. It is dark, dark everywhere."

He reached forth one of his long arms, and took a small Bible from a stand near the head of the sofa, opened the pages of the holy book, and soon was absorbed in reading them. A quarter of an hour passed, and on glancing at the sofa the face of the President seemed more cheerful. The dejected look was gone, and the countenance was lighted up with new resolution and hope. The change was so marked that I could not but wonder at it, and wonder led to the desire to know what book of the Bible afforded so much comfort to the reader. Making the search for a missing article an excuse, I walked gently around the sofa, and looking into the open book, I discovered that Mr. Lincoln was reading that divine comforter, Job. He read with Christian eagerness, and the courage and hope that he derived from the inspired pages made him a new man. I almost imagined that I could hear the Lord speaking to him from out the whirlwind of battle: "Gird up thy loins now like a man: I will demand of thee, and declare thou unto me." What a sublime picture was this! A ruler of a mighty nation going to the pages of the Bible with simple Christian earnestness for comfort and courage, and finding both in the darkest hours of a nation's calamity. Ponder it, O ye scoffers at God's Holy Word, and then hang your heads for very shame!

Frequent letters were received warning Mr. Lincoln of assassination, but he never gave a second thought to the mysterious warnings. The letters, however, sorely troubled his wife. She seemed to read impending danger in every rustling leaf, in every whisper of the wind.

"Where are you going now, father?" she would say to him, as she observed him putting on his overshoes and shawl.

"I am going over to the War Department, mother, to try and learn some news."

"But, father, you should not go out alone. You know you are surrounded with danger."

"All imagination. What does any one want to harm me for? Don't worry about me, mother, as if I were a little child, for no one is going to molest me;" and with a confident, unsuspecting air he would close the door behind him, descend the stairs, and pass out to his lonely walk.

For weeks, when trouble was anticipated, friends of the President would sleep in the White House to guard him from danger.

Robert would come home every few months, bringing new joy to the family circle. He was very anxious to quit school and enter the army, but the move was sternly opposed by his mother.

"We have lost one son, and his loss is as much as I can bear, without being called upon to make another sacrifice," she would say, when the subject was under discussion.

"But many a poor mother has given up all her sons," mildly suggested Mr. Lincoln, "and our son is not more dear to us than the sons of other people are to their mothers."

"That may be; but I cannot bear to have Robert exposed to danger. His services are not required in the field, and the sacrifice would be a needless one."

"The services of every man who loves his country are required in this war. You should take a liberal instead of a selfish view of the question, mother."

Argument at last prevailed, and permission was granted Robert to enter the army. With the rank of Captain and A. D. C. he went to the field, and remained in the army till the close of the war.

I well recollect a little incident that gave me a clearer insight into Robert's character. He was at home at the time the Tom Thumb combination was at Washington. The marriage of little Hop-o'-my-thumb—Charles Stratton—to Miss Warren created no little excitement in the world, and the people of Washington participated in the general curiosity. Some of Mrs. Lincoln's friends made her believe that it was the duty of Mrs. Lincoln to show some attention to the remarkable dwarfs. Tom Thumb had been caressed by royalty in the Old World, and why should not the wife of the President of his native country smile upon him also? Verily, duty is one of the greatest bugbears in life. A hasty reception was arranged, and cards of invitation issued. I had dressed Mrs. Lincoln, and she was ready to go below and receive her guests, when Robert entered his mother's room.

"You are at leisure this afternoon, are you not, Robert?"

"Yes, mother."

"Of course, then, you will dress and come down-stairs."

"No, mother, I do not propose to assist in entertaining Tom Thumb. My notions of duty, perhaps, are somewhat different from yours."

Robert had a lofty soul, and he could not stoop to all of the follies and absurdities of the ephemeral current of fashionable life.

Mrs. Lincoln's love for her husband sometimes prompted her to act very strangely. She was extremely jealous of him, and if a lady desired to court her displeasure, she could select no surer way to do it than to pay marked attention to the President. These little jealous freaks often were a source of perplexity to Mr. Lincoln. If it was a reception for which they were dressing, he would come into her room to conduct her down-stairs, and while pulling on his gloves ask, with a merry twinkle in his eyes:

"Well, mother, who must I talk with to-night—shall it be Mrs. D.?"

"That deceitful woman! No, you shall not listen to her flattery."

"Well, then, what do you say to Miss C.? She is too young and handsome to practise deceit."

"Young and handsome, you call her! You should not judge beauty for me. No, she is in league with Mrs. D., and you shall not talk with her."

"Well, mother, I must talk with some one. Is there any one that you do not object to?" trying to button his glove, with a mock expression of gravity.

"I don't know as it is necessary that you should talk to anybody in particular. You know well enough, Mr. Lincoln, that I do not approve of your flirtations with silly women, just as if you were a beardless boy, fresh from school."

"But, mother, I insist that I must talk with somebody. I can't stand around like a simpleton, and say nothing. If you will not tell me who I may talk with, please tell me who I may *not* talk with."

"There is Mrs. D. and Miss C. in particular. I detest them both. Mrs. B. also will come around you, but you need not listen to her flattery. These are the ones in particular."

"Very well, mother; now that we have settled the question to your satisfaction, we will go down-stairs;" and always with stately dignity, he proffered his arm and led the way.

WILLIAM STILL

William Still (1821–1902) was born to formerly enslaved parents in New Jersey. As an adult, Still relocated to Philadelphia, Pennsylvania, where he became a prominent businessman, writer, abolitionist, and active participant in the city's Vigilance Committee and the Pennsylvania Anti-Slavery Society. Still, perhaps inspired by his father's ability to purchase his own freedom and his mother's courage in taking two fugitive passages with children in tow, was a dedicated conductor of the Underground Railroad and assisted in the care for untold numbers of fugitives from slavery. Drawn from his larger compilation of official records: letters and other documentation that reveal the deliberate, covert strategizing carried out by abolitionists and enslaved people alike, narratives of hairbreadth escapes, and the conditions from which self-liberated people were fleeing, the selections here focus on the courageous escapes of Cordelia Loney, a woman in her fifties who had suffered many abuses over the course of her life, including having her children sold away, and the teenager Ann(a) Maria Weems, who dressed in men's clothing to escape and join family members who had fled successfully before her turn at flight.

Selections from
The Underground Railroad (1872)

A SLAVE GIRL'S NARRATIVE.

Cordelia Loney, Slave of Mrs. Joseph Cahell (Widow of the Late Hon. Joseph Cahell, of Va.), of Fredericksburg, Va.— Cordelia's Escape from Her Mistress in Philadelphia.

Rarely did the peculiar institution present the relations of mistress and maid-servant in a light so apparently favorable as in the case of Mrs. Joseph Cahell (widow of the late Hon. Jos Cahell, of Va.), and her slave, Cordelia. The Vigilance Committee's first knowledge of either of these memorable personages was brought about in the following manner.

About the 30th of March, in the year 1859, a member of the Vigilance Committee was notified by a colored servant, living at a fashionable boarding-house on Chestnut street that a lady with a slave woman from Fredericksburg, Va., was boarding at said house, and, that said slave woman desired to receive counsel and aid from the Committee, as she was anxious to secure her freedom, before her mistress returned to the South. On further consultation about the matter, a suitable hour was named for the meeting of the Committee and the Slave at the above named boarding-house. Finding that the woman was thoroughly reliable, the Committee told her "that two modes of deliverance were open before her. One was to take her trunk and all her clothing and quietly retire." The other was to "sue out a writ of habeas corpus, and bring the mistress before the Court, where she would be required, under the laws of Pennsylvania, to show cause why she restrained this woman of her freedom." Cordelia concluded to adopt the former expedient, provided the Committee would protect her. Without hesitation the Committee answered her, that to the extent of their ability, she should have their aid with pleasure, without delay. Consequently a member of the Committee was directed to be on hand at a given hour that evening, as Cordelia would certainly be ready to leave her mistress to take care of herself. Thus, at the appointed hour, Cordelia, very deliberately, accompanied the Committee away from her "kind hearted old mistress."

In the quiet and security of the Vigilance Committee Room, Cordelia related substantially the following brief story touching her relationship as a slave to Mrs. Joseph Cahell. In this case, as with thousands and tens of thousands of others, as the old adage fitly expresses it, "All is not gold that glitters." Under this apparently pious and noble-minded lady, it will be seen, that Cordelia had known naught but misery and sorrow.

Mrs. Cahell, having engaged board for a month at a fashionable private boarding-house on Chestnut street, took an early opportunity to caution Cordelia against going into the streets, and against having anything to say or do with "free niggers in particular"; withal, she appeared unusually kind, so much so, that before retiring to bed in the evening, she would call Cordelia to her chamber, and by her side would take her Prayer-book and Bible, and go through the forms of devotional service. She stood very high both as a church communicant and a lady in society.

For a fortnight it seemed as though her prayers were to be answered, for Cordelia apparently bore herself as submissively as ever, and Madame received calls and accepted invitations from some of the *elite* of the city, without suspecting any intention on the part of Cordelia to escape. But Cordelia could not forget how her children had all been sold by her mistress!

Cordelia was about fifty-seven years of age, with about an equal proportion of colored and white blood in her veins; very neat, respectful and prepossessing in manner.

From her birth to the hour of her escape she had worn the yoke under Mrs. C., as her most efficient and reliable maid-servant. She had been at her mistress' beck and call as seamstress, dressing-maid, nurse in the sickroom, etc., etc., under circumstances that might appear to the casual observer uncommonly favorable for a slave. Indeed, on his first interview with her, the Committee man was so forcibly impressed with the belief, that her condition in Virginia had been favorable, that he hesitated to ask her if she did not desire her liberty. A few moments' conversation with her, however, convinced him of her good sense and decision of purpose with regard to this matter. For, in answer to the first question he put to her, she answered, that "As many creature comforts and religious privileges as she had been the recipient of under her 'kind mistress,' still she 'wanted to be free,' and 'was bound to leave,' that she had been 'treated very cruelly;' that her children had 'all been sold away' from her; that she had been threatened with sale herself 'on the first insult,'" etc.

She was willing to take the entire responsibility of taking care of herself. On the suggestion of a friend, before leaving her mistress, she was disposed to sue for her freedom, but, upon a reconsideration of the matter, she chose rather to accept the hospitality of the Underground Rail Road, and leave in a quiet way and go to Canada, where she would be free indeed. Accordingly she left her mistress and was soon a free woman.

The following sad experience she related calmly, in the presence of several friends, an evening or two after she left her mistress:

Two sons and two daughters had been sold from her by her mistress, within the last three years, since the death of her master. Three of her children had been sold to the Richmond market and the other in Nelson county.

Paulina was the first sold, two years ago last May. Nat was the next; he was sold to Abram Warrick, of Richmond. Paulina was sold before it was named to her mother that it had entered her mistress's mind to dispose of her. Nancy, from infancy, had been in poor health. Nevertheless, she had been obliged to take her place in the field with the rest of the slaves, of more rugged constitution, until she had passed her twentieth year, and had become a mother. Under these circumstances, the overseer and his wife complained to the mistress that her health was really too bad for a field hand and begged that she might be taken where her duties would be less oppressive. Accordingly, she was withdrawn from the field, and was set to spinning and weaving. When too sick to work her mistress invariably took the ground, that "nothing was the matter," notwithstanding the fact, that her family physician, Dr. Ellsom, had pronounced her "quite weakly and sick."

In an angry mood one day, Mrs. Cahell declared she would cure her; and again sent her to the field, "with orders to the overseer, to whip her every day, and make her work or kill her." Again the overseer said it was "no use to try, for her health would not stand it," and she was forthwith returned. The mistress then concluded to sell her.

One Sabbath evening a nephew of hers, who resided in New Orleans, happened to be on a visit to his aunt, when it occurred to her, that she had "better get Nancy off if possible." Accordingly, Nancy was called in for examination. Being dressed in her "Sunday best" and "before a poor candle-light," she appeared to good advantage; and the nephew concluded to start with her on the following Tuesday morning. However, the next morning, he happened to see her by the light of the sun, and in her working garments, which satisfied him that he had been grossly deceived; that she would barely live to reach New Orleans; he positively refused to carry out the previous evening's contract, thus leaving her in the hands of her mistress, with the advice, that she should "doctor her up."

The mistress, not disposed to be defeated, obviated the difficulty by selecting a little boy, made a lot of the two, and thus made it an inducement to a purchaser to buy the sick woman; the boy and the woman brought $700.

In the sale of her children, Cordelia was as little regarded as if she had been a cow.

"I felt wretched," she said, with emphasis, "when I heard that Nancy had been sold," which was not until after she had been removed. "But," she continued, "I was not at liberty to make my grief known to a single white soul. I wept and couldn't help it." But remembering that she was liable, "on the first insult," to be sold herself, she sought no sympathy from her mistress, whom she describes as "a woman who shows as little kindness towards her servants as any woman in the States of America. She neither likes to feed nor clothe well."

With regard to flogging, however, in days past, she had been up to the mark. "A many a slap and blow" had Cordelia received since she arrived at womanhood, directly from the madam's own hand.

One day smarting under cruel treatment, she appealed to her mistress in the following strain: "I stood by your mother in all her sickness and nursed her till she died!" "I waited on your niece, night and day for months, till she died." "I waited upon your husband all my life—in his sickness especially, and shrouded him in death, etc., yet I am treated cruelly." It was of no avail.

Her mistress, at one time, was the owner of about five hundred slaves, but within the last few years she had greatly lessened the number by sales.

She stood very high as a lady, and was a member of the Episcopal Church.

To punish Cordelia, on several occasions, she had been sent to one of the plantations to work as a field hand. Fortunately, however, she found the overseers more compassionate than her mistress, though she received no particular favors from any of them.

Asking her to name the overseers, etc., she did so. The first was "Marks, a thin-visaged, poor-looking man, great for swearing." The second was "Gilbert Brower, a very rash, portly man." The third was "Buck Young, a stout man, and very sharp." The fourth was "Lynn Powell, a tall man with red whiskers, very contrary and spiteful." There was also a fifth one, but his name was lost.

Thus Cordelia's experience, though chiefly confined to the "great house," extended occasionally over the corn and tobacco fields, among the overseers and field hands generally. But under no circumstances could she find it in her heart to be thankful for the privileges of Slavery.

After leaving her mistress she learned, with no little degree of pleasure, that a perplexed state of things existed at the boarding-house; that her mistress was seriously puzzled to imagine how she would get her shoes and stockings on and off; how she would get her head combed, get dressed, be attended to in sickness, etc., as she (Cordelia), had been compelled to discharge these offices all her life.

Most of the boarders, being slave-holders, naturally sympathized in her affliction; and some of them went so far as to offer a reward to some of the colored servants to gain a knowledge of her whereabouts. Some charged the servants with having a hand in her leaving, but all agreed that "she had left a very kind and indulgent mistress," and had acted very foolishly in running out of Slavery into Freedom.

A certain Doctor of Divinity, the pastor of an Episcopal church in this city and a friend of the mistress, hearing of her distress, by request or voluntarily, undertook to find out Cordelia's place of seclusion. Hailing on the street a certain colored man with a familiar face, who he thought knew nearly all the colored people about town, he related to him the predicament of his lady friend from the South, remarked how kindly she had always treated her servants, signified that Cordelia would rue the change, and be left to suffer among the "miserable blacks down town," that she would not be able to take care of herself; quoted Scripture justifying Slavery, and finally suggested that he (the colored man) would be doing a duty and a kindness to the fugitive by using his influence to "find her and prevail upon her to return."

It so happened that the colored man thus addressed, was Thomas Dorsey, the well-known fashionable caterer of Philadelphia, who had had the experience of quite a number of years as a slave at the South,—had himself once been pursued as a fugitive, and having, by his industry in the condition of Freedom, acquired a handsome estate, he felt entirely qualified to reply to the reverend gentleman, which he did, though in not very respectful phrases, telling him that Cordelia had as good a right to her liberty as he had, or her mistress either; that God had never intended one man to be the slave of another; that it was all false about the slaves being better off than the free colored people; that he would find as many "poor, miserably degraded," of his own color "down-town," as among the "degraded blacks"; and concluded by telling him that he would "rather give her a hundred dollars to help her off, than to do aught to make known her whereabouts, if he knew ever so much about her."

What further steps were taken by the discomfited divine, the mistress, or her boarding-house sympathizers, the Committee was not informed.

But with regard to Cordelia: she took her departure for Canada, in the midst of the Daniel Webster (fugitive) trial, with the hope of being permitted to enjoy the remainder of her life in Freedom and peace. Being a member of the Baptist Church, and professing to be a Christian, she was persuaded that, by industry and assistance of the Lord, a way would be opened to the seeker of Freedom even in a strange land and among strangers.

This story appeared in part in the N. Y. *Evening Post*, having been furnished by the writer, without his name to it. It is certainly none the less interesting now, as it may be read in the light of Universal Emancipation.

* * *

"FLEEING GIRL OF FIFTEEN," IN MALE ATTIRE.

Professors H. and T. Offer Their Services—Captains B. Also Are Enlisted—Slave-Trader Grasping Tightly His Prey, but She Is Rescued—Long Conflict, but Great Triumph— Arrival on Thanksgiving Day, Nov. 25, 1855.

It was the business of the Vigilance Committee, as it was clearly understood by the friends of the Slave, to assist all needy fugitives, who might in any way manage to reach Philadelphia, but, for various reasons, not to send agents South to incite slaves to run away, or to assist them in so doing. Sometimes, however, this rule could not altogether be conformed to. Cases, in some instances, would appeal so loudly and forcibly to humanity, civilization, and Christianity, that it would really seem as if the very stones would cry out, unless something was done. As an illustration of this point, the story of the young girl, which is now to be related, will afford the most striking proof. At the same time it may be seen how much anxiety, care, hazard, delay and material aid, were required in order to effect the deliverance of some who were in close places, and difficult of access. It will be necessary to present a considerable amount of correspondence in this case, to bring to light the hidden mysteries of this narrative. The first letter, in explanation, is the following:

LETTER FROM J. BIGELOW, ESQ.

WASHINGTON, D. C., June 27, 1854.

MR. WM. STILL—*Dear Sir*:—I have to thank you for the prompt answer you had the kindness to give to my note of 22d inst. Having found a correspondence so quick and easy, and withal so very flattering, I address you again more fully.

The liberal appropriation for *transportation* has been made chiefly on account of a female child of ten or eleven years old, for whose purchase I have been authorized to offer $700 (refused), and for whose sister I have paid $1,600, and some $1,000 for their mother, &c.

This child sleeps in the same apartment with its master and mistress, which adds to the difficulty of removal. She is some ten or twelve miles from the city, so that really the chief hazard will be in bringing her safely to town, and in secreting her until a few days of *storm* shall have abated. All this, I think, is now provided for with entire safety.

The child has two cousins in the immediate vicinity; a young man of some twenty-two years of age, and his sister, of perhaps

seventeen—*both Slaves*, but bright and clear-headed as anybody. The young man I have seen often—the services of *both*
seem indispensable to the main object suggested; but having
once rendered the service, they cannot, and ought not return to
Slavery. They look for *freedom* as the reward of what they shall
now do.

Out of the $300, cheerfully offered for the whole enterprise,
I must pay some reasonable sum for transportation to the city
and sustenance while here. It cannot be much; for the balance,
I shall give a draft, which will be *promptly paid* on their arrival
in New York.

If I have been understood to offer the whole $300, *it shall be
paid*, though I have meant as above stated. Among the various
ways that have been suggested, has been that of taking *all of
them* into the cars here; that, I think, will be found impracti-
cable. I find so much vigilance at the depot, that I would not
deem it safe, though in any kind of carriage they might leave in
safety at any time.

All the rest I leave to the experience and sagacity of the gentleman who maps out the enterprise.

Now I will thank you to reply to this and let me know that it
reaches you in safety, and is not put in a careless place, whereby I
may be endangered; and state also, whether all my propositions
are understood and acceptable, and whether, (pretty quickly after
I shall inform you that *all things are ready*), the gentleman will
make his appearance?

I live alone. My office and bed-room, &c., are at the corner
of E. and 7th streets, opposite the east end of the General Post
Office, where any one may call upon me.

It would, of course, be imprudent, that this letter, or any
other *written* particulars, be in his pockets for fear of accident.

Yours very respectfully,
J. BIGELOW.

While this letter clearly brought to light the situation of
things, its author, however, had scarcely begun to conceive of
the numberless difficulties which stood in the way of success

before the work could be accomplished. The information which Mr. Bigelow's letter contained of the painful situation of this young girl was submitted to different parties who could be trusted, with a view of finding a person who might possess sufficient courage to undertake to bring her away. Amongst those consulted were two or three captains who had on former occasions done good service in the cause. One of these captains was known in Underground Rail-Road circles as the "powder boy."* He was willing to undertake the work, and immediately concluded to make a visit to Washington, to see how the "land lay." Accordingly in company with another Underground Rail Road captain, he reported himself one day to Mr. Bigelow with as much assurance as if he were on an errand for an office under the government. The impression made on Mr. Bigelow's mind may be seen from the following letter; it may also be seen that he was fully alive to the necessity of precautionary measures.

SECOND LETTER FROM
LAWYER BIGELOW.

WASHINGTON, D. C., September 9th, 1855.

MR. WM. STILL, DEAR SIR:—I strongly hope the little matter of business so long pending and about which I have written you so many times, will take a move now. I have the promise that the merchandize shall be delivered in this city to-night. Like so many other promises, this also may prove a failure, though I have reason to believe that it will not. I shall, however, know before I mail this note. In case the goods arrive here I shall hope to see your long-talked of "Professional gentleman" in Washington, as soon as possible. He will find me by the enclosed card, which shall be a satisfactory introduction for him. You have never given me his name, nor am I anxious to

*He had been engaged at different times in carrying powder in his boat from a powder magazine, and from this circumstance, was familiarly called the "Powder Boy."

know it. But on a pleasant visit made last fall to friend Wm. Wright, in Adams Co., I suppose I accidentally learned it to be a certain Dr. H—. Well, let him come.

I had an interesting call a week ago from two gentlemen, masters of vessels, and brothers, one of whom, I understand, you know as the "powder boy." I had a little light freight for them; but not finding enough other freight to ballast their craft, they went down the river looking for wheat, and promising to return soon. I hope to see them often.

I hope this may find you returned from your northern trip,[*] as your time proposed was out two or three days ago.

I hope if the whole particulars of Jane Johnson's case[†] are printed, you will send me the copy as proposed.

I forwarded some of her things to Boston a few days ago, and had I known its importance in court, I could have sent you one or two witnesses who would prove that her freedom was intended by her before she left Washington, and that a man was *engaged* here to go on to Philadelphia the same day with her to give notice there of her case, though I think he failed to do so. It was beyond all question her purpose, *before leaving Washington and provable too*, that if Wheeler should make her a free woman by taking her to a free state *"to use it rather."*

Tuesday, 11th September. The attempt was made on Sunday to forward the merchandize, but failed through no fault of any of the parties that I now know of. It will be repeated soon, and you shall know the result.

"Whorra for Judge Kane." I feel so indignant at the man, that it is not easy to write the foregoing sentence, and yet who is helping our cause like Kane and Douglas, not forgetting Stringfellow. I hope soon to know that this reaches you in safety.

It often happens that light freight would be offered to Captain B., but the owners cannot by possibility *advance* the amount of freight. I wish it were possible in some such extreme

---

[*]Mr. Bigelow's correspondent had been on a visit to the fugitives to Canada.
[†]Jane Johnson of the Passmore Williamson Slave Case.

cases, that after advancing *all they have*, some public fund should be found to pay the balance or at least lend it.

[I wish here to caution you against the supposition that I would do any act, or say a word towards helping servants to escape. Although I hate slavery so much, I keep my hands clear of any such wicked or illegal act.]

Yours, very truly,
J. B.

Will you recollect, hereafter, that in any of my future letters, in which I may use [ ] whatever words may be within the brackets are intended to have no signification whatever to you, only to blind the eyes of the uninitiated. You will find an example at the close of my letter.

Up to this time the chances seemed favorable of procuring the ready services of either of the above mentioned captains who visited Lawyer Bigelow for the removal of the merchandize to Philadelphia, providing the shipping master could have it in readiness to suit their convenience. But as these captains had a number of engagements at Richmond, Petersburg, &c., it was not deemed altogether safe to rely upon either of them, consequently in order to be prepared in case of an emergency, the matter was laid before two professional gentlemen who were each occupying chairs in one of the medical colleges of Philadelphia. They were known to be true friends of the slave, and had possessed withal some experience in Underground Rail Road matters. Either of these professors was willing to undertake the operation, provided arrangements could be completed in time to be carried out during the vacation. In this hopeful, although painfully indefinite position the matter remained for more than a year; but the correspondence and anxiety increased, and with them disappointments and difficulties multiplied. The hope of Freedom, however, buoyed up the heart of the young slave girl during the long months of anxious waiting and daily expectation for the hour of deliverance to come. Equally true and faithful also did Mr. Bigelow prove to the last;

but at times he had some painfully dark seasons to encounter, as may be seen from the subjoined letter:

WASHINGTON, D. C., October 6th, 1855.

MR. STILL, DEAR SIR:—I regret exceedingly to learn by your favor of 4th instant, that all things are not ready. Although I cannot speak of any immediate and positive danger. [*Yet it is well known that the city is full of incendiaries.*]

Perhaps you are aware that any colored citizen is liable at any hour of day or night without any show of authority to have his house ransacked by constables, and if others do it and commit the most outrageous depredations none but white witnesses can convict them. Such outrages are always common here, and no kind of property exposed to colored protection only, can be considered safe. [I don't say that *much liberty* should not be given to constables on account of numerous runaways, but it don't always work for good.] Before advertising they go round and offer rewards to sharp colored men of perhaps *one or two hundred dollars*, to betray runaways, and having discovered their hiding-place, seize them and then cheat their informers out of the money.

[*Although a law abiding man,*] I am anxious in this case of *innocence* to raise no conflict or suspicion. [*Be sure that the manumission is full and legal.*] And as I am *powerless* without your aid, *I pray you* don't lose a moment in giving me relief. The idea of waiting yet for weeks seems dreadful; do reduce it to days if possible, and give me notice of the *earliest possible time.*

The property is not yet advertised, but will be, [and if we delay too long, may be sold and lost.]

It was a great misunderstanding, though not your fault, that so much delay would be necessary. [I repeat again that I must have the thing done legally, therefore, please get a good lawyer to draw up the deed of manumission.]

Yours Truly,
J. BIGELOW.

Great was the anxiety felt in Washington. It is certainly not too much to say, that an equal amount of anxiety existed in Philadelphia respecting the safety of the merchandise. At this juncture Mr. Bigelow had come to the conclusion that it was no longer safe to write over his own name, but that he would do well to henceforth adopt the name of the renowned Quaker, Wm. Penn, (he was worthy of it) as in the case of the following letter.

WASHINGTON, D. C., November 10th, 1855.

DEAR SIR:—Doctor T. presented my card last night about half past eight which I instantly recognized. I, however, soon became suspicious, and afterwards confounded, to find the doctor using your name and the well known names of Mr. McK. and Mr. W. and yet, neither he nor I, could conjecture the object of his visit.

The doctor is agreeable and sensible, and doubtless a true-hearted man. He seemed to see the whole matter as I did, and was embarrassed. He had nothing to propose, no information to give of the "P. Boy," or of any substitute, and seemed to want no particular information from me concerning my anxieties and perils, though I stated them to him, but found him as powerless as myself to give me relief. I had an agreeable interview with the doctor till after ten, when he left, intending to take the cars at six, as I suppose he did do, this morning.

This morning after eight, I got your letter of the 9th, but it gives me but little enlightenment or satisfaction. You simply say that the doctor is a *true man*, which I cannot doubt, that you thought it best we should have an interview, and that you supposed I would meet the expenses. You informed me also that the "P. Boy" left for Richmond, on Friday, the 2d, to be gone *the length of time named in your last*, I must infer that to be *ten days* though in your last *you assured me* that the "P. Boy" would certainly start for *this place* (not Richmond) in two or three days, though the difficulty about freight might cause delay, and the whole enterprise might not be accomplished under ten days, &c., &c. That time having elapsed and I having agreed to an extra fifty dollars to ensure promptness. I have scarcely left my office since, except for my hasty meals, awaiting his arrival. You now inform me he has gone to Richmond, to be gone ten days, which will expire to-morrow, but you do not say he will return here or to Phila., or where, at the expiration of that time, and Dr. T. could tell me nothing whatever about him. Had he been able to tell me that this *best plan*, which I have so long rested upon, would fail, or was abandoned, I could then understand it, but he says no such thing, and you say, as you have twice before said, "ten days more."

Now, my dear sir, after this recapitulation, can you not see that I have reason for great embarrassment? I have given assurances, both here and in New York, founded on your assurances to me, and caused my friends in the latter place great anxiety, so much that I have had no way to explain my own letters but by sending your last two to Mr. Tappan.

I cannot doubt, I do not, but that you wish to help me, and the cause too, for which both of us have made many and large sacrifices with no hope of reward in this world. If in this case I have been very urgent since September Dr. T. can give you some of my reasons, they have not been selfish.

The whole matter is in a nutshell. Can I, in your opinion, depend on the "P. Boy," and when?

If he promises to come here next trip, will he come, or go to Richmond? This I think is the best way. Can I depend on it?

Dr. T. promised to write me some explanation and give some advice, and at first I thought to await his letter, but on second thought concluded to tell you how I feel, as I have done.

Will you answer my questions with some explicitness, and without delay?

I forgot to inquire of Dr. T. who is the head of your Vigilance Committee, whom I may address concerning other and further operations?

> Yours very truly,
> WM. PENN.

P. S. I ought to say, that I have no doubt but there were good reasons for the P. Boy's going to Richmond instead of W.; *but what can they be?*

Whilst there are a score of other interesting letters, bearing on this case, the above must suffice, to give at least, an idea of the perplexities and dangers attending its early history. Having accomplished this end, a more encouraging and pleasant phase of the transaction may now be introduced. Here the difficulties, at least very many of them, vanish, yet in one respect, the danger became most imminent. The following letter shows that the girl had been successfully rescued from her master, and that a reward of five hundred dollars had been offered for her.

WASHINGTON, D. C., October 12, 1855.

MR. WM. STILL:—AS YOU PICK UP ALL THE NEWS THAT IS STIRRING, I CONTRIBUTE A FEW SCRAPS TO YOUR STOCK, GOING TO SHOW THAT THE POOR SLAVE-HOLDERS HAVE THEIR TROUBLES AS WELL AS OTHER PEOPLE.

FOUR HEAVY LOSSES ON ONE SMALL SCRAP CUT FROM A SINGLE NUMBER OF THE "SUN!" HOW VEXATIOUS! HOW PROVOKING! ON THE OTHER HAND, THINK OF THE POOR, TIMID, BREATHLESS, FLYING CHILD OF FIFTEEN! FIVE HUNDRED DOLLARS REWARD! OH, FOR SUCCOR! TO WHOM IN ALL THIS WIDE LAND OF FREEDOM SHALL SHE FLEE AND FIND SAFETY? ALAS!—ALAS!—THE LAW POINTS TO NO ONE!

IS SHE STILL RUNNING WITH BLEEDING FEET?* OR HIDES SHE IN SOME COLD CAVE, TO REST AND STARVE? "$500 REWARD." YOURS, FOR THE WEAK AND THE POOR. PERISH THE REWARD.

J. B.

Having thus succeeded in getting possession of, and secreting this fleeing child of fifteen, as best they could, in Washington, all concerned were compelled to "possess their souls in patience," until the storm had passed. Meanwhile, the "child of fifteen" was christened "Joe Wright," and dressed in male attire to prepare for traveling as a lad. As no opportunity had hitherto presented itself, whereby to prepare the "package" for

*At the time this letter was written, she was then under Mr. B.'s protection in Washington, and had to be so kept for six weeks. His question, therefore, "is she still running with bleeding feet," etc., was simply a precautionary step to blind any who might perchance investigate the matter.

shipment, from Washington, neither the "powder boy" nor Dr. T.,* was prepared to attend to the removal, at this critical moment. The emergency of the case, however, cried loudly for aid. The other professional gentleman (Dr. H.), was now appealed to, but his engagements in the college forbade his absence before about Thanksgiving day, which was then six weeks off. This fact was communicated to Washington, and it being the only resource left, the time named was necessarily acquiesced in. In the interim, "Joe" was to perfect herself in the art of wearing pantaloons, and all other male rig. Soon the days and weeks slid by, although at first the time for waiting seemed long, when, according to promise, Dr. H. was in Washington, with his horse and buggy prepared for duty. The impressions made by Dr. H., on William Penn's mind, at his first interview, will doubtless be interesting to all concerned, as may be seen in the following letter:

WASHINGTON, D. C., November 26, 1855.

MY DEAR SIR:—A recent letter from my friend, probably has led you to expect this from me. He was delighted to receive yours of the 23d, stating that the boy was *all right.* He found the "Prof. gentleman" a *perfect gentleman;* cool, quiet, thoughtful, and *perfectly competent to execute his undertaking.* At the first three minutes of their interview, he felt assured that all would be right. He, and all concerned, give you and that gentleman sincere thanks for what you have done. May the blessings of Him, who cares for the poor, be on your heads.

The especial object of this, is to inform you that there is a half dozen or so of packages here, *pressing for transportation;* twice or thrice that number are also pressing, but less so than the others. Their aggregate means will average, say, $10 each; besides these, we know of a few, say three or four, *able and smart,* but utterly destitute, and kept so purposely by their oppressors. For all these, we feel deeply interested; $10 each would

---

*Dr. T. was one of the professional gentlemen alluded to above, who had expressed a willingness to act as an agent in the matter.

not be enough for the "powder boy." Is there any fund from which a pittance could be spared to help these poor creatures? I don't doubt but that they would honestly repay a small loan as soon as they could earn it. I know full well, that if you begin with such cases, there is no boundary at which you can stop. For years, one half at least, of my friend's time here has been gratuitously given to cases of distress among this class. He never expects or desires to do less; he literally has the *poor always with him*. He knows that it is so with you also, therefore, he only states the case, being especially anxious for at least those to whom I have referred.

I think a small lot of hard coal might always be sold here *from the vessel* at a profit. Would not a like lot of Cumberland coal always sell in Philadelphia?

My friend would be very glad to see the powder boy here again, and if he brings coal, there are those here, who would try to help him sell.

Reply to your regular correspondent as usual.

WM. PENN.

By the presence of the Dr., confidence having been reassured that all would be right, as well as by the "inner light," William Penn experienced a great sense of relief. Everything having been duly arranged, the doctor's horse and carriage stood waiting before the White House (William Penn preferred this place as a starting point, rather than before his own office door). It being understood that "Joe" was to act as coachman in passing out of Washington, at this moment he was called for, and in the most polite and natural manner, with the fleetness of a young deer, he jumped into the carriage, took the reins and whip, whilst the doctor and William Penn were cordially shaking hands and bidding adieu. This done, the order was given to Joe, "drive on." Joe bravely obeyed. The faithful horse trotted off willingly, and the doctor sat in his carriage as composed as though he had succeeded in procuring an honorable and lucrative office from the White House, and was returning home to tell his wife the good news. The doctor had some knowledge of the roads, also

some acquaintances in Maryland, through which State he had
to travel; therefore, after leaving the suburbs of Washington,
the doctor took the reins in his own hands, as he felt that he
was more experienced as a driver than his young coachman. He
was also mindful of the fact, that before reaching Pennsylvania,
his faithful beast would need feeding several times, and that
they consequently would be obligated to pass one or two nights
at least in Maryland, either at a tavern or farm-house.

In reflecting upon the matter, it occurred to the doctor, that
in earlier days, he had been quite intimately acquainted with a
farmer and his family (who were slave-holders), in Maryland,
and that he would about reach their house at the end of the first
day's journey. He concluded that he could do no better than to
renew his acquaintance with his old friends on this occasion.
After a very successful day's travel, night came on, and the doctor was safely at the farmer's door with his carriage and waiter
boy; the doctor was readily recognized by the farmer and his
family, who seemed glad to see him; indeed, they made quite a
"fuss" over him. As a matter of strategy, the doctor made quite
a "fuss" over them in return; nevertheless, he did not fail to assume airs of importance, which were calculated to lead them to
think that he had grown older and wiser than when they knew
him in his younger days. In casually referring to the manner of
his traveling, he alluded to the fact, that he was not very well,
and as it had been a considerable length of time since he had
been through that part of the country, he thought that the drive
would do him good, and especially the sight of old familiar
places and people. The farmer and his family felt themselves
exceedingly honored by the visit from the distinguished doctor,
and manifested a marked willingness to spare no pains to render his night's lodging in every way comfortable.

The Dr. being an educated and intelligent gentleman, well
posted on other questions besides medicine, could freely talk
about farming in all its branches, and "niggers" too, in an emergency, so the evening passed off pleasantly with the Dr. in the
parlor, and "Joe" in the kitchen. The Dr., however, had given
"Joe" precept upon precept, "here a little, and there a little," as
to how he should act in the presence of master white people, or

slave colored people, and thus he was prepared to act his part with due exactness. Before the evening grew late, the Dr., fearing some accident, intimated, that he was feeling a "little languid," and therefore thought that he had better "retire." Furthermore he added, that he was "liable to vertigo," when not quite well, and for this reason he must have his boy "Joe" sleep in the room with him. "Simply give him a bed quilt and he will fare well enough in one corner of the room," said the Dr. The proposal was readily acceded to, and carried into effect by the accommodating host. The Dr. was soon in bed, sleeping soundly, and "Joe," in his new coat and pants, wrapped up in the bed quilt, in a corner of the room quite comfortably.

The next morning the Dr. arose at as early an hour as was prudent for a gentleman of his position, and feeling refreshed, partook of a good breakfast, and was ready, with his boy, "Joe," to prosecute their journey. Face, eyes, hope, and steps, were set as flint, Pennsylvania-ward. What time the following day or night they crossed Mason and Dixon's line is not recorded on the Underground Rail Road books, but at four o'clock on Thanksgiving Day, the Dr. safely landed the "fleeing girl of fifteen" at the residence of the writer in Philadelphia. On delivering up his charge, the Dr. simply remarked to the writer's wife, "I wish to leave this young lad with you a short while, and I will call and see further about him." Without further explanation, he stepped into his carriage and hurried away, evidently anxious to report himself to his wife, in order to relieve her mind of a great weight of anxiety on his account. The writer, who happened to be absent from home when the Dr. called, returned soon afterwards. "The Dr. has been here" (he was the family physician), "and left this 'young lad,' and said, that he would call again and see about him," said Mrs. S. The "young lad" was sitting quite composedly in the dining-room, with his cap on. The writer turned to him and inquired, "I suppose you are the person that the Dr. went to Washington after, are you not?" "No," said "Joe." "Where are you from then?" was the next question. "From York, sir." "From York? Why then did the Dr. bring you here?" was the next query, "the Dr. went expressly to Washington after a young girl, who was to be brought away dressed up as a boy, and I took you to be the person." Without replying "the lad" arose and walked out of the house. The querist, somewhat mystified, followed him, and then when the two were alone, "the lad" said, "I am the one of the Dr. went after." After congratulating her, the writer asked why she had said, that she was not from Washington, but from York. She explained, that the Dr. had strictly charged her not to own to any person, except the writer, that she was from Washington, but from York. As there were persons present (wife, hired girl, and a fugitive woman), when the questions were put to her, she felt that it would be a violation of her pledge to answer in the affirmative. Before this examination, neither of the individuals present for a moment entertained the slightest doubt but that she was a "lad," so well had she acted her part in every particular. She was dressed in a new suit, which fitted her quite nicely, and with her unusual amount of common sense, she appeared to be in no respect lacking. To send off a prize so rare and remarkable, as she was, without affording some of the stockholders and managers of the Road the pleasure of seeing her, was not to be thought of. In addition to the Vigilance Committee, quite a number of persons were invited to see her, and were greatly astonished. Indeed it was difficult to realize, that she was not a boy, even after becoming acquainted with the facts in the case.

The following is an exact account of this case, as taken from the Underground Rail Road records:

"THANKSGIVING DAY, Nov., 1855.

Arrived, Ann Maria Weems, *alias* 'Joe Wright,' *alias* 'Ellen Capron,' from Washington, through the aid of Dr. H. She is about fifteen years of age, bright mulatto, well grown, smart and good-looking. For the last three years, or about that length of time, she has been owned by Charles M. Price, a negro trader, of Rockville, Maryland. Mr. P. was given to 'intemperance,' to a very great extent, and gross 'profanity.' He buys and sells many slaves in the course of the year. 'His wife is cross and peevish.' She used to take great pleasure in 'torturing' one 'little slave boy.' He was the son of his master (and was owned by him); this was the chief cause of the mistress' spite."

Ann Maria had always desired her freedom from childhood, and although not thirteen, when first advised to escape, she received the suggestion without hesitation, and ever after that time waited almost daily, for more than two years, the chance to flee. Her friends were, of course, to aid her, and make arrangements for her escape. Her owner, fearing that she might escape, for a long time compelled her to sleep in the chamber with "her master and mistress;" indeed she was so kept until about three weeks before she fled. She left her parents living in Washington. Three of her brothers had been sold South from their parents. Her mother had been purchased for $1,000, and one of her sisters for $1,600 for freedom. Before Ann Maria was thirteen years of age $700 was offered for her by a friend, who desired to procure her freedom, but the offer was promptly refused, as were succeeding ones repeatedly made. The only chance of procuring her freedom, depended upon getting her away on the Underground Rail Road. She was neatly attired in male habiliments, and in that manner came all the way from Washington. After passing two or three days with her new friends in Philadelphia, she was sent on (in male attire) to Lewis Tappan, of New York, who had likewise been deeply interested in her case from the beginning, and who held himself ready, as was understood, to cash a draft for three hundred dollars to compensate the man who might risk his own liberty in bringing her on from Washington. After having arrived safely in New York, she found a home and kind friends in the family of the Rev. A. N. Freeman, and received quite an ovation characteristic of an Underground Rail Road.

After having received many tokens of esteem and kindness from the friends of the slave in New York and Brooklyn, she was carefully forwarded on to Canada, to be educated at the "Buxton Settlement."

An interesting letter, however, from the mother of Ann Maria, conveying the intelligence of her late great struggle and anxiety in laboring to free her last child from Slavery is too important to be omitted, and hence is inserted in connection with this narrative.

LETTER FROM THE MOTHER.

WASHINGTON, D. C., September 19th, 1857.

WM. STILL, ESQ., Philadelphia, Pa. SIR:—I have just sent for my son Augustus, in Alabama. I have sent eleven hundred dollars which pays for his body and some thirty dollars to pay his fare to Washington. I borrowed one hundred and eighty dollars to make out the eleven hundred dollars. I was not very successful in Syracuse. I collected only twelve dollars, and in Rochester only two dollars. I did not know that the season was so unpropitious. The wealthy had all gone to the springs. They must have returned by this time. I hope you will exert yourself and help me get a part of the money I owe, at least. I am obliged to pay it by the 12th of next month. I was unwell when I returned through Philadelphia, or I should have called. I had been from home five weeks.

My son Augustus is the last of the family in Slavery. I feel rejoiced that he is soon to be free and with me, and of course feel the greatest solicitude about raising the one hundred and eighty dollars I have borrowed of a kind friend, or who has borrowed it for me at bank. I hope and pray you will help me as far as possible. Tell Mr. Douglass to remember me, and if he can, to interest his friends for me.

You will recollect that five hundred dollars of our money was taken to buy the sister of Henry H. Garnett's wife. Had I been able to command this I should not be necessitated to ask the favors and indulgences I do.

I am expecting daily the return of Augustus, and may Heaven grant him a safe deliverance and smile propitiously upon you and all kind friends who have aided in his return to me.

Be pleased to remember me to friends, and accept yourself the blessing and prayers of your dear friend,

EARRO WEEMS.

P. S. Direct your letter to E. L. Stevens, in Duff Green's Row, Capital Hill, Washington, D. C.

E. W.

That William Penn who worked so faithfully for two years for the deliverance of Ann Maria may not appear to have been devoting all his time and sympathy towards this single object it seems expedient that two or three additional letters, proposing certain grand Underground Rail Road plans, should have a place here. For this purpose, therefore, the following letters are subjoined.

LETTERS FROM WILLIAM PENN.

WASHINGTON, D. C., Oct. 3, 1854.

DEAR SIR:—I address you to-day chiefly at the suggestion of the Lady who will hand you my letter, and who is a resident of your city.

After stating to you, that the case about which I have previously written, remains just as it was when I wrote last—full of difficulty—I thought I would call your attention to another enterprise; it is this: to find a man with a large heart for doing good to the oppressed, who will come to Washington to live, and who will *walk out to Penn'a., or a part of the way there, once or twice a week*. He will find parties who will *pay him for doing so*. Parties of say, two, three, five or so, who will pay him *at least* $5 each, for the privilege of following him, but *will never speak to him*; but will keep just in sight of him and obey any sign he may give; say, he takes off his hat and scratches his head as a sign for them to go to some barn or wood to rest, &c. No living being shall be found to say he ever spoke to them. A white man would be best, and then even parties led out by him could not, if they would, testify to any *understanding* or anything else against a white man. I think he might make a good living at it. Can it not be done?

If one or two safe stopping-places could be found on the way—such as a barn or shed, they could walk quite safely all night and then sleep all day—about two, or *easily* three nights would convey them to a place of safety. The traveler might be a peddler or huckster, with an old horse and cart, and bring us in eggs and butter if he pleases.

Let him once plan out his route, and he might then take ten or a dozen at a time, and they are often able and willing to pay $10 a piece.

I have a hard case now on hand; a brother and sister 23 to 25 years old, whose mother lives in your city. They are cruelly treated; they want to go, they *ought* to go; but they are utterly destitute. Can nothing be done for such cases? If you can think of anything let me know it. I suppose you know me?

WASHINGTON, D. C., April 3, 1856.

DEAR SIR:—I sent you the recent law of Virginia, under which all vessels are to be searched for fugitives within the waters of that State.

It was long ago suggested by a sagacious friend, that the "powder boy" might find a better port in the Chesapeake bay, or in the Patuxent river to communicate with this vicinity, than by entering the Potomac river, even were there no such law.

Suppose he opens a trade with some place south-west of Annapolis, 25 or 30 miles from here, or less. He might carry wood, oysters, &c., and all his customers from this vicinity might travel in *that direction* without any of the suspicions that might attend their journeyings *towards this city.* In this way, doubtless, a good business might be carried on without interruption or competition, and provided the plan was conducted without affecting the inhabitants along that shore, no suspicion would arise as to the manner or magnitude of his business operations. How does this strike you? What does the "powder boy" think of it?

I heretofore intimated a *pressing necessity* on the part of several females—they are variously situated—two have children, say a couple each; some have none—of the latter, one can raise $50, another, say 30 or 40 dollars—another who was gazetted last August (a copy sent you), can raise, through her friends, 20 or 30 dollars, &c., &c. None of these can walk so far or so fast as scores of *men* that are constantly leaving. I cannot shake off my anxiety for these poor creatures. Can you think of anything

for any of these? Address your other correspondent in answer
to this at your leisure.

Yours,
Wm. Penn.

P. S.—April 3d. Since writing the above, I have received yours
of 31st. I am rejoiced to hear that business is so successful and
prosperous—may it continue till *the article* shall cease to be
merchandize.

I spoke in my last letter of the departure of a "few friends." I
have since heard of their good health in Penn'a. Probably you
may have seen them.

In reference to the expedition of which you think you can
"hold out some little encouragement," I will barely remark,
that I shall be glad, if it is undertaken, to have all the notice of
the *time and manner* that is possible, so as to make ready.

A friend of mine says, anthracite coal will always pay here
from Philadelphia, and thinks a small vessel might run often—
that she never would be searched in the Potomac, unless she
went outside.

You advise caution towards Mr. P. I am precisely of your
opinion about him, that he is a "queer stick," and while I advised him carefully in reference to his own undertakings, I took
no counsel of him concerning mine.

Yours,
W. P.

Washington, D. C., April 23d, 1856.

Dear Sir:—I have to thank you for your last two encouraging letters of 31st of March and 7th April. I have seen nothing in the papers to interest you, and having bad health and a
press of other engagements, I have neglected to write you.

Enclosed is a list of persons referred to in my last letter, all
most anxious to travel—all meritorious. In some of these I feel
an especial interest for what they have done to help others in
distress.

I suggest for yours and the "powder boy's" consideration the
following plan: that he shall take in coal for Washington and

come directly here—sell his coal and go to Georgetown for freight, and *wait* for it. If any fancy articles are sent on board, *I understand he has a place* to put them in, and *if he has* I suggest that he lies still, still waiting for freight till the first anxiety is over. Vessels that have *just left* are the ones that will be inquired after, and perhaps chased. If he lays still a day or two all suspicion will be prevented. If there shall be occasion to refer to any of them hereafter, it may be by their numbers in the list.

The family—5 to 11—will be missed and inquired after soon and urgently; 12 and 13 will also be soon missed, but *none of the others.*

JACOB STROYER

The son of an enslaved man from Sierra Leone and an enslaved woman whose family had labored on plantations in South Carolina for several generations, Jacob Stroyer (1849–1908) was born in slavery in Eastover, South Carolina. Stroyer's narrative is a rare look into the lives of enslaved people in rural South Carolina that offers a critique of the hostile, sociopathic, and avaricious tendencies of nearly every white person of authority: enslavers, overseers, slave drivers, and plantation mistresses. Stroyer recalls his secret endeavors to teach himself to read, a skill that serves him well while he is in bondage and during his years of formal education after emancipation. During the Civil War, Stroyer and other enslaved men and boys were sent to the South Carolina Lowcountry to Sullivan's Island and Fort Sumter to "repair forts, build batteries, mount guns, and arrange them. While the men were engaged at such work, the boys of my age, namely, thirteen, and some older, waited on officers and carried water for the men at work, and in general acted as messengers between different points on the island." With no strong remaining family ties due to deaths and family separations, Stroyer moved to Worcester, Massachusetts, where he attended the Worcester Academy and later became an ordained African Methodist Episcopal minister in Salem.

From *My Life in the South*
(1885)

Chapter I.

My father was born in Sierra Leone, Africa. Of his parents and his brothers and sisters, I know nothing; I only remember that it was said that his father's name was Moncoso, and his mother's

Mongomo, which names are known only among the native Africans. He was brought from Africa when but a boy, and sold to old Colonel Dick Singleton, who owned a great many plantations in South Carolina, and when the old colonel divided his property among his children, father fell to his second son, Col. M. R. Singleton.

Mother was never sold, but her parents were; they were owned by one Mr. Crough, who sold them and the rest of the slaves, with the plantation, to Col. Dick Singleton, and mother was born on that place. I was born on this extensive plantation twenty-eight miles southeast of Columbia, South Carolina, in the year 1849. I belonged to Col. M. R. Singleton, and was held in slavery up to the time of the emancipation proclamation issued by President Lincoln.

THE CHILDREN.

My father had fifteen children: four boys and three girls by his first wife, and eight by his second. Their names were as follows: of the boys,—Tony, Aszerine, Duke and Dezine; of the girls,—Violet, Priscilla, and Lydia. Those of his second wife were as follows: Footy, Embrus, Caleb, Mitchell, Cuffey and Jacob; and of the girls, Catherine and Retta.

SAND-HILL DAYS.

Col. M. R. Singleton was like many other rich slave owners in the South, who had summer seats four, six or eight miles from the plantation, where they carried the little negro boys and girls while they were too small to work.

Our summer seat, or the sand-hill, as the slaves used to call it, was four miles from the plantation. Among the four hundred and sixty-five slaves owned by the Colonel, there were a great many children. If my readers had visited Col. Singleton's plantation the last of May or the first of June in the days of slavery, they would have seen three or four large plantation wagons loaded with little negroes of both sexes, of various complexions

and conditions, who were being carried to this summer residence, and among them they would have found the author of
this little work, in his sand-hill days.

My readers would naturally ask, how many seasons these
children were taken to the summer seats? I answer, until, in the
judgment of the overseer, they were large enough to work; then
they were kept at the plantation. How were they fed? There
were three or four women who were too old to work on the
plantation, who were sent as nurses at the summer seat with the
children; they did the cooking. The way in which these old
women cooked for 80, and sometimes 150 children, in my sand-
hill days, was this,—they had two or three large pots, which
held about a bushel each, in which they used to cook corn-flour,
stirred with large wooden paddles. The food was dealt out with
the paddles into each child's little wooden tray or tin pail,
which was furnished by the parents according to their ability.

With this corn flour, which the slaves called mush, each child
used to get a gill of sour milk, brought daily from the plantation in a large wooden pail on the head of a boy or man. We
children used to like the sour milk, or hard clabber as it was
called by the slaves; but that seldom changed diet, namely the
mush, was hated worse than medicine. Our hatred was increased against the mush from the fact that they used to give us
molasses to eat with it instead of clabber. The hateful mixture
made us anxious for Sundays to come, when our mothers, fathers,
sisters and brothers would bring something from the plantation, which, however poor, we considered very nice, compared
with what we had during the week days. Among the many desirable things our parents brought us, the most delightful was
cow pease, rice, and a piece of bacon, cooked together; the
mixture was called by the slaves "hopping John."

THE STORY OF GILBERT.

A few large boys were sent yearly to the sand-hill among the
smaller ones, as guides for them. At the time to which I am referring, there was one by the name of Gilbert, who used to go

around with the smaller boys in the woods to gather bushes and sticks for the old women to cook our food with.

Gilbert was a cruel boy. He used to strip his little fellow ne-groes while in the woods, and whip them two or three times a week, so that their backs were all scarred, and threatened them with severer punishment if they told it; this state of things had been going on for quite a while. As I was a favorite of Gilbert, I always had managed to escape a whipping, with the promise of keeping the secret of the punishment of the rest, which I did, not so much that I was afraid of Gilbert, as because I always was inclined to mind my own business. But finally, one day Gil-bert said to me, "Jake," as he used to call me, "you am a good boy, but I'm gwine to wip you some to-day, as I wip dem 'toder' boys." Of course I was required to strip off my only garment, which was an Osnaburg linen shirt, worn by both sexes of the negro children in the summer. As I stood trembling before my merciless superior, who had a switch in his hand, thousands of thoughts went through my little mind as to how to get rid of the whipping. I finally fell upon a plan which I hoped would save me from a punishment that was near at hand. There were some carpenters in the woods, some distance from us, hewing tim-ber; they were far away, but it was a clear morning, so we could hear their voices and the sound of the axes. Having resolved in my mind what I would do, I commenced reluctantly to take off my shirt, and at the same time pleading with Gilbert, who paid no attention to my prayer, but said, "Jake, I is gwine to wip you to-day as I did dem toder boys." Having satisfied myself that no mercy was to be found with Gilbert, I drew my shirt off and threw it over his head, and bounded forward on a run in the direction of the sound of the carpenters. By the time he got from the entanglement of my garment, I had quite a little start of him; between my starting point and the place where the car-penters were at work, I jumped over some bushes five or six feet high. Gilbert soon gained upon me, and sometimes touched me with his hands, but as I had on nothing for him to hold to, he could not take hold of me. As I began to come in sight of the carpenters, Gilbert begged me not to go to them, for he knew that it would be bad for him, but as that was not a time for me to listen to his entreaties, I moved on faster. As I got near to the carpenters, one of them ran and met me into whose, arms I jumped. The man into whose arms I ran, was Uncle Benjamin, my mother's uncle. As he clasped me in his arms, he said, "Bres de Lo, my son, wat is de matter." But I was so exhausted that it was quite a while before I could tell him my trouble; when recovered from my breathless condition, I told him that Gilbert had been in the habit of stripping the boys and whipping them two or three times a week, when we went into the woods, and threatened them with greater punishment if they told it. I said he had never whipped me before, but I was cautioned to keep the secret which I did up to this time; but he said he was going to whip me this morning, so I threw my shirt over his head and ran here for protection. Gilbert did not follow me after I got in sight of the carpenters, but sneaked away. Of course my body was all bruised and scratched up by the bushes. Acting as a guide for Uncle Benjamin, I took him to where I left my garment.

At this time the children were scattered around in the woods, waiting for what the trouble would bring; they all were gathered up and taken to the sand-hill house, examined, and it was found, as I have stated, that their backs were all scarred up. Gilbert was brought to trial, severely whipped, and they made him beg all the children to pardon him for his treatment to them. But he never was allowed to go into the woods with the rest of the children during that season. My sand-hill associates always thanked me for the course I took, which saved them and myself from further punishment by him.

Chapter II.—Sketches.

THE SALE OF MY TWO SISTERS.

I have stated that my father had fifteen children; four boys and three girls by his first wife, and six boys and two girls by his second. Their names are as follows: Toney, Aszerine, Duke and Dezine; of the girls, Violet, Priscilla and Lydia; those of the second wife as follows: Footy, Embrus, Caleb, Mitchell, Cuffee, and Jacob, who is the author, and the girls Catherine and Retta.

As I have said, old Col. Dick Singleton had two sons and two daughters, and each had a plantation. Their names were John, Matt, Marianna and Angelico; they were very agreeable together, so that if one wanted negro help from another's plantation he or she could have it, especially in cotton picking time.

John Singleton had a place about twenty miles from master's, who used to send him slaves to pick cotton. At one time my master, Col. M. R. Singleton sent my two sisters, Violet and Priscilla, to his brother John, and while they were there they married two of the men on his place; by mutual consent master allowed them to remain on his brother's place. But sometime after this, John Singleton had some of his property destroyed by water as is often the case in the South at the time of May freshets, what is known in the North as high tides.

One of these freshets swept away John Singleton's slave houses, his barns with horses, mules and cows; these caused his death by a broken heart, and owing a great deal of money, his slaves had to be sold. A Mr. Manning bought a portion of them and Charles Login the rest; these two men were known as the greatest slave traders in the South, my sisters were among the number that Mr. Manning bought.

He was to take them into the state of Louisiana for sale, but some of the men did not want to go with him, and he put those in prison until he was ready to start. My sisters' husbands were among the prisoners in the Sumterville Jail, which was about twenty-five or thirty miles across the river from master's place. Those who did not show any unwillingness to go were allowed to visit their relatives and friends for the last time. So my sisters with the rest of their unfortunate companions came to master's place to visit us. When the day came for them to leave, some, who seemed to have been willing to go at first, refused, and were handcuffed together and guarded on their way to the cars by white men. The women and children were driven to the depot in crowds, like so many cattle, and the sight of them caused great excitement among master's negroes. Imagine a mass of uneducated people shedding tears and yelling at the tops of their voices in anguish and grief.

The victims were to take the cars from a station called Clarkson turnout, which was about four miles from master's place. The excitement was so great that the overseer and driver could not control the relatives and friends of those that were going away, as a large crowd of both old and young went down to the depot to see them off. Louisiana was considered by the slaves as a place of slaughter, so those who were going did not expect to see their friends again. While passing along, many of the negroes left their master's fields and joined us as we marched to the cars; some were yelling and wringing their hands, while others were singing little hymns that they were accustomed to for the consolation of those that were going away, such as,

> "When we all meet in heaven,
> There is no parting there;
> When we all meet in heaven,
> There is parting no more."

We arrived at the depot and had to wait for the cars to bring the others from the Sumterville Jail, but they soon came in sight, and when the noise of the cars died away we heard wailing and shrieks from those in the cars. While some were weeping, others were fiddling, picking banjo, and dancing as they used to do in their cabins on the plantations. Those who were so merry, had very bad masters, and even though they stood a chance of being sold to one as bad or even worse, yet they were glad to be rid of the one they knew.

While the cars were at the depot, a large crowd of white people gathered, and were laughing and talking about the prospect of negro traffic; but when the cars began to start and the conductor cried out, "all who are going on this train must get on board without delay," the colored people cried out with one voice as though the heavens and earth were coming together, and it was so pitiful, that those hard hearted white men who had been accustomed to driving slaves all their lives, shed tears like children. As the cars moved away we heard the weeping and wailing from the slaves, as far as human voice could be heard; and from that time to the present I have neither seen nor heard from my two sisters, nor any of those who left Clarkson depot on that memorable day.

THE WAY THE SLAVES LIVED.

Most of the cabins in the time of slavery were built so as to contain two families; some had partitions while others had none. When there were no partitions, each family would fit up its own part as it could; sometimes they got old boards and nailed them up, stuffing the cracks with old rags; when they could not get boards they hung up old clothes. When the family increased, the children all slept together, both boys and girls, until either got married, then a part of another cabin was assigned to the one that was married, but the rest would have to remain with their mother and father as they did when children, unless they could get with some of their relatives or friends who had small families, or when they were sold; but of course the rules of modesty were held in some degree by the slaves, while it could not be expected that they could entertain the highest degree of it, on account of their condition. A portion of the time the young men slept in the apartment known as the kitchen and the young women slept in the room with their mother and father. The two families had to use one fireplace. One, who was accustomed to the way in which the slaves lived in their cabins, could tell as soon as they entered whether they were friendly or not, for when they did not agree the fires of the two families did not meet on the hearth, but there was a vacancy between them, that was a sign of disagreement. In a case of this kind when either of the families stole a hog, cow or sheep from the master, he had to carry it to some of his friends for fear of being betrayed by the other family. On one occasion a man, who lived with one unfriendly, stole a hog, killed it, and carried some of the meat home. He was seen by some one of the other family who reported him to the overseer and he gave the man a severe whipping. Sometime after, this man who was betrayed, thought he would get even with his enemy; so about two months after, he killed another hog, and after eating a part of it, stole into the apartment of the other and hid a portion of the meat among the old clothes. Then he told the overseer that he saw the man go out late that night and he did not come home until the next morning; when he came, he called his wife to the window and she took something in, but he did not know what it was, but if the overseer would go there right away he would find it. The overseer went and searched and found the meat, so the man was whipped. He told the overseer that the other man put it in his apartment while the family were away, but the overseer told him that every man must be responsible for his own apartment.

No doubt you would like to know how the slaves could sleep in their cabins in summer, when it was so very warm. When it was too warm for them to sleep comfortably, they all slept under trees until it grew too cool, which would be along in the month of October. Then they took up their beds and walked.

BETHANY VENEY

Bethany Veney (1813–1916) was born enslaved in the Shenandoah Valley of Virginia. Veney's parents passed away early in her childhood, and she was resold to new enslavers a few times. Because of slavery's irreverent calculus, whereby enslavers' financial stability was valued more than the lives and kinship connections forged between enslaved people, Veney's testimony is one of perpetual heartbreak. She loses her parents, children, and two husbands during the course of her enslavement and experiences and witnesses appalling abuses. Veney maintains that she was able to overcome slavery's cruelties through her firm commitment to her Christian faith. In one final transaction, Veney and one of her sons are purchased by G. J. Adams, a Providence, Rhode Island–based antislavery businessman who frees them. Veney works for the Adams family until the start of the Civil War, when she moves to Worcester, Massachusetts, and takes care of injured Union soldiers. Veney later travels back to Virginia several times, reuniting with and settling sixteen of her family members with her in Massachusetts.

From *The Narrative of Bethany Veney, a Slave Woman* (1889)

AUNT BETTY'S STORY.

Chapter I.

*Childhood—First Lessons in Morality—
First Lesson in the Art of Entertaining.*

I have but little recollection of my very early life. My mother and her five children were owned by one James Fletcher, Pass Run, town of Luray, Page County, Virginia. Of my father I know nothing.

The first thing I remember with any distinctness was when, about seven years old, I was, with other children, knocking apples from a tree, when we were surprised by my young mistress, Miss Nasenath Fletcher, calling to us, in a loud and threatening tone, demanding what we were doing. Without waiting for reply, she told us to follow her; and, as she led the way down to a blackberry pasture not far off, she endeavored, in a very solemn manner, to impress us with the importance of always telling the truth. "If asked a question," she said, "we must answer directly, yes or no." I asked her "what we must say if asked something which we did not know." She answered, "Why, you must say you don't know, of course." I said, "I shall say, 'Maybe 'tis, and maybe 'tain't.'" I remember well how the children laughed at this; and then Miss Nasenath went on to tell us that *some time* all this world that we saw would be burned up,— that the moon would be turned into blood, the stars would fall out of the sky, and everything would melt away with a great heat, and that everybody, *every little child* that had told a lie, would be cast into a lake of fire and brimstone, and would burn there for ever and ever, and, what was more, though they should burn for ever and ever, they would never be burned up.

I was dreadfully frightened; and, as soon as I could get away, I ran to my mammy, and, repeating what mistress had said, begged to know if it could be true. To my great sorrow, she confirmed it all, but added what Miss Nasenath had failed to do; namely, that those who told the truth and were good would always have everything they should want. It seemed to me then there was nothing so good as molasses and sugar; and I eagerly asked, "Shall I have all the molasses and sugar I want, if I tell the truth?" "Yes," she replied, "*if you are good*; but remember, if you tell lies, you will be burned in the lake that burns for ever and ever."

This made a very strong impression upon me. I can never forget my mammy's manner at the time. I believed every word she said, and from that day to this I have never doubted its truth.

Though my conception of what constituted the truth was very dim, my fear of what should befall me, if I were to tell a lie, was very great. Still, I was only a young child, and could not, long at a time, be very unhappy.

My old master, who at times was inclined to be jolly, had a way of entertaining his friends by my singing and dancing. Supper over, he would call me into his room, and, giving me to understand what he wanted of me, I would, with all manner of grotesque grimaces, gestures, and positions, dance and sing:—

> "Where are you going, Jim?
> Where are you going, Sam?
> To get a proper larning,
> To jump Jim Crow."

or

> "David the king was grievit and worrit,
> He went to his chamber—
> His chamber and weppit;
> And, as he went, he weppit and said,
> 'O my son, O my son!
> Would to God I had died
> For thee, O Absalom,
> My son, my son,'"—

and many other similar songs, of the meaning of which I had of course no idea, and I have since thought neither he nor his friends could have had any more than I.

Chapter II.

Bereavement—Change of Master and Home—
Unjust Demands—Punishment Escaped.

The next thing I recall as being of any particular importance to me was the death of my mother, and, soon after, that of Master Fletcher. I must have been about nine years old at that time.

Master's children consisted of five daughters and two sons.

As usual in such cases, an inventory was taken of his property (all of which nearly was in slaves), and, being apportioned in shares, lots were drawn, and, as might chance, we fell to our several masters and mistresses.

My sister Matilda and myself were drawn by the eldest daughter, Miss Lucy. My grandmother had begged hard to be reckoned with me, but she and Uncle Peter fell to Miss Nasenath; but as after a time she married David Kibbler, and Miss Lucy went to live with them, taking her human property with her, to wait on her, and also to work for Mr. Kibbler, we were brought together again. In the mean time, I was put out with an old woman, who gave me my food and clothes for whatever work I could do for her. She was kind to me, as I then counted kindness, never whipping me or starving me; but it was not what a free-born white child would have found comforting or needful.

Going into the family of David Kibbler as I did with my mistress, I was really under his direction and subject to his control, almost as much as if he and not Miss Lucy had owned me.

Master Kibbler was a Dutchman,—a man of most violent temper, ready to fight anything or anybody who resisted his authority or in any way crossed his path. His one redeeming quality was his love for his horses and dogs. These must be fed before his servants, and their comfort and health always considered. He was a blacksmith by trade, and would have me hold his irons while he worked them. I was awkward one day, and he struck me with a nail-rod, making me so lame my mistress noticed it, and asked Matilda what was the matter with me; and, when she was told, she was greatly troubled, and as I suppose spoke to Kibbler about it, for he called me to him, and bade me go a long way off into a field, and, as he said, *cut some sprouts there*. But he very soon followed me, and, cutting a rod, beat me severely, and then told me to "go again and tell my mistress that he had hit me with a nail-rod, if I wanted to."

Poor Miss Lucy! She was kind and tender-hearted. She often said she hated slavery, and wanted nothing to do with it; but she could see no way out of it.

It will give a clearer idea of the kind of a man Kibbler was, and the way I grew to manage with him, if I tell here a circumstance that happened after I had grown much older and stronger. I had been in the field a good ways from the house, helping him to haul logs. Our work was done, and he had mounted the team to go home, and the bars were let down for him to pass out, when a drove of hogs ran in to get the clover that was growing in a part of the field. He called to me to drive out the hogs. I clapped my hands together, and shouted, "Shoo! shoo!" This frightened the horses, and Kibbler was unable to control them; and, rushing through the gateway, the team hit the side post, tearing it up from its place. Of course, all this made him very angry; and, of course, I was to blame for it all. As soon as he could hold the horses, he turned, and shouted to me to drive out the hogs, set the post into the ground, and get back to the house by the time he did, or he would whip me so I would remember it.

A big boy who had been hauling the logs with us now helped me drive out the hogs and plant the post. We hurried with all our might, and then tried to run home; but, by the time we got out of the woods, we saw master so far ahead of us I knew it was no use to try, and I said I would risk the whipping and not run any longer. So, when we came up to the house, master was sitting in his chair by the window; and, as I passed into the room near him, he handed me his jack-knife, and said, "Now, girl, go cut me a good hickory,—a good one, mind you; for, if I have to cut it myself, I'll get a hard one, you may be sure." I took the knife, passed through the kitchen to the back door, just beside which was a little shelf where the pails of water just filled from the spring were standing. I laid the knife on the shelf, and passed out the door, and ran for the woods and the mountain. By the time I reached the woods, it began to rain, and poured fearfully all the night. I crowded my head under the alder bushes, while my shoulders and body were dripping wet. All night I crouched in this way; and, when morning came, I was afraid to show myself, and all day kept concealed by the trees and bushes as best I could. As night came on, I was very hungry, having eaten nothing for more than thirty-six hours; and so I decided to go down the mountain where old Kibbler, my master's father, lived, knowing that he would give me something to satisfy my hunger. As I drew nigh the house, the dogs barked; and I was afraid to encounter them, and so laid out all night on the side of the hill. In the morning,—it was Sunday,—I ventured near the house;

and the old man, seeing me, came out and gave me "How-dye," and asked how the home folks were. I told him I had not seen them since Friday, and added the reason for my running away, to which he listened, and then said, "Well, what are you going to do about it?" I said, "Won't you, Masser Kibbler, go home with me, and tell Masser David he mustn't whip me?"

I don't know how I dared to say this, for to his own slaves he was a hard, ugly man; but he gave me something to eat, then went home with me, and, after repeating my story to Master David, asked him if that was true, and added, "Then you have no right to whip her." And that was the end of it.

I must go back here to my mistress and her wish not to hold slaves. A gentleman from Ohio was visiting in the neighborhood; and Miss Lucy, knowing he was from a free State, asked him if he would not take me North with him. He very readily consented, promising to do the best he could for me; but, when Master David and others heard about it, they said it was a foolish thing to do, for this man would very likely sell me before he left the South, and put the money into his own pocket, and I should find myself worse off than ever. It was true that many Northern men came South very bitter in their opposition to slavery, and after a little while came to be the hardest and most cruel slaveholders.

I have sometimes tried to picture what my life might have been could I have been set free at that age; and I have imagined myself with a young girl's ambition, working hard and carefully saving my earnings, then getting a little home with garden, where I could plant the kind of things I had known in the South, then bringing my sisters and brothers to share with me these blessings of freedom. But I had yet to know far deeper sorrows before I could have any of this glad experience.

Miss Lucy now told me, if I would be contented and stay quietly where I was, and not be married, she would, when her nephew Noe came to be of age, give me my freedom. Instead of this, however, I was told soon after that she had made her will, bequeathing me already to this nephew. I was never sure this was true. Her kindness to me and my love for her made it always seem impossible.

Chapter III.

Religious Experiences.

I come now to a phase in my experience which aroused the impressions made upon me so long before in the blackberry pasture.

At Powell's Fort, not far from where I now lived, was the Mount Asa school-house, where the different religious denominations held their meetings. My master's brother, Jerry Kibbler, and his sister Sally had been to a camp-meeting, and got "religion." They came home determined their religion should help others; and, through their influence, this little school-house had been fitted up with pulpit and seats, and now there was to be a series of revival meetings held there. I had never been to any kind of a meeting since I was a little girl, and then my mistress had sometimes taken me along for company.

At this time, Miss Ellen Mills was spinning wool at Mr. Jonathan Grandstaff's; and one night, as it was growing dusk, she came down to master's, to see if some of the family would go to meeting with her. No one cared to go; and Miss Lucy, turning to me, said: "There is Betty. Take Betty. She will be company for you." So I went. The minister was preaching when we entered; and I have no recollection of anything he said in his sermon, but, when he took his seat, he sang the hymn,—

> "Then let this feeble body fail,
>   Or let it faint or die,
>   My soul shall quit this mournful vale,
>   And soar to worlds on high,
>   Shall join those distant saints,
>   And find its long-sought rest."

It was a hymn of many verses (I afterwards got an old woman to teach them to me); and there was such tenderness in his voice and such solemnity in his manner that I was greatly affected. When the singing was over, he moved about among the congregation; and, coming close to me, he said, "Girl, don't you want religion? don't you want to be happy when you die?" Then he asked me to promise him that, when I got home, I would go upon my knees and ask God to give me the witness that I was his. I made him no answer; but, as soon as I reached home and was alone, I knelt down, and in my feeble and ignorant way begged to be saved. From that day to this, I have been praying and trying to do as I thought my heavenly Master has required of me; and I think I have had the witness of the Spirit.

So, night after night, I went to the little school-house, and had many precious seasons. Master Jerry and Miss Sally were very kind to me, and tried to show me the way to be a Christian.

But there came a time when Master David said he was not going to have me running to meeting all the time any longer. He had decided to send me up to old Mr. Levers, two miles away, there to stay until I should get over my "religious fever," as he called it. Accordingly, I went as directed; but, when it came night, I asked if I might go down to Mount Asa school-house for meeting. The old man said: "Yes. You can go; and, as it is so far away, you need not come back here till morning. But go home, and stay with the children, as you always do, and have the care of them." I couldn't understand it, but I went; and, when in the morning Kibbler saw me, he scolded, and sent me off to Levers again. Every night, old Mr. Levers would tell me I could go; and I did, till, in the middle of the meeting one night, Master Kibbler came up to me, and, taking me by the arm, carried me out, scolding and fuming, declaring that old Webster (the minister) was a liar, and that for himself he didn't want such a "whoopin' and hollerin' religion," and, if that was the way to heaven, he didn't "want to go there." After this, my conscience troubled me very much about going. Mr. Levers would tell me to go; but I knew that Master David had forbidden me to do so. One night, I started out, and, as I came to a persimmon-tree, I felt moved to go down on my knees and ask the Lord to help me, and make Master David willing. In a few minutes, I felt very happy. I wanted to remain on my knees, and wished I could walk on them till I could come before Master David. I tried to do so, and was almost surprised to find I could get along so well. At last, I reached the piazza, and was able to enter the room, where I saw him sitting; and, as I did so, I said,

"O Master, *may* I go to meeting?" He saw my position; and, as if "rent by the Spirit," he cried out: "Well, I'll go to the devil if you ain't *my match!* Yes: go to meeting, and stay there."

After this, I had no trouble from this cause. When I was to be taken into the church, I asked him if he was willing, and he said: "I don't care. If that's your way of getting to heaven, I don't care. I only wish you were all there." So I was baptized, and have been trying, in my poor way ever since to serve the Lord.

Chapter IV.

Courtship and Marriage—A Slaveholder's Idea of Its Requirements—Separation.

Year after year rolled on. Master Jonas Mannyfield lived seven miles from us, on the other side of the Blue Ridge; and he owned a likely young fellow called Jerry. We had always known each other, and now he wanted to marry me. Our masters were both willing; and there was nothing to hinder, except that there was no minister about there to marry us. "No matter for that," Kibbler said to Jerry. "If you want Bett, and she wants you, that's the whole of it." But I didn't think so. I said, "No: never till somebody comes along who can marry us." So it happened, one day, there was a colored man—a pedler, with his cart—on the road, and Jerry brought him in, and said he was ready to be minister for us. He asked us a few questions, which we answered in a satisfactory manner, and then he declared us husband and wife. I did not want him to make us promise that we would always be true to each other, forsaking all others, as the white people do in their marriage service, because I knew that at any time our masters could compel us to break such a promise; and I had never forgotten the lesson learned, so many years before, in the blackberry pasture.

So Jerry and I were happy as, under all the circumstances, we could well be. When he asked his master's consent to our marriage, he told him he had had thoughts of removing to Missouri, in which case he should take him with him, and we would have to be separated; but, if he chose to run the risk, he had nothing to say. Jerry did not think there was any danger, and we were not dissuaded; for hearts that love are much the same in bond or free, in white or black.

Eight or ten months passed on, when one night my brother Stephen, who lived on the Blue Ridge, near Master Mannyfield, came to see me, and, as we talked of many things, he spoke of Jerry in a way that instantly roused my suspicion. I said: "Tell me what is the matter? I know there is something. Is Jerry dead? Is he sold? Tell me what it is." I saw he dreaded to speak, and that frightened me the more.

At last, he said: "'Tis no use, Betty. You have got to know it. Old Look-a-here's people are all in jail for debt." "Old Look-a-here" was the nickname by which Mannyfield was known by the colored people far and near, because he had a way of saying, when he was about to whip one of his slaves, "Now look-a-here, you black rascal," or "you black wench."

The next day was Saturday, and I hurried to complete my task in the corn-field, and then asked my master if I could go to see Jerry. He objected at first, but at last gave me a pass to see my brother, and be gone until Monday morning.

The sun might have been two hours high when I started; but, before I was half over the mountain, night had closed round me its deepest gloom. The vivid flashes of lightning made the carriage path plain at times, and then I could not see a step before me; and the rolling thunder added to my fear and dread. I was dripping wet when, about nine o'clock, I reached the house. It had been my plan to get Stephen to go on with me to Jerry's mother's, and stay the night there; but his mistress, who was sister to my Miss Lucy, declared we must not go on in the storm, and, giving me supper, brought bedding, that I might lie on the kitchen floor and rest me there. In the morning, after a good breakfast, she started us off, with a bag of biscuits to eat by the way. Jerry's mother was glad to go with us; and we hurried along to Jerry, in jail at Little Washington, where he with his fellow-slaves was confined, like sheep or oxen, shut up in stalls, to be sold to pay their owner's debts.

Jerry saw us, as we came along the road, through the prison bars; and the jailer allowed us to talk together there, not, however, without a witness to all we might say. We had committed no offence against God or man. Jerry had not; and yet, like base criminals, we were denied even the consolation of privacy. This was a necessary part of the system of American slavery. Neither wife nor mother could intervene to soften its rigors one jot.

Several months passed, and Mannyfield was still unable to redeem his property; and they were at last put up at auction, and sold to the highest bidder. Frank White, a slave-trader, bought the entire lot, and proceeded at once to make up a gang for the Southern market.

Arrangements were made to start Friday morning; and on Thursday afternoon, chained together, the gang were taken across the stream, and encamped on its banks. White then went to Jerry, and, taking the handcuffs from his wrists, told him to go and stay the night with his wife, and see if he could persuade her to go with him. If he could, he would buy her, and so they need not be separated. He would pass that way in the morning, and see. Of course, Jerry was only too glad to come; and, at first, I thought I would go with him. Then came the consciousness that this inducement was only a sham, and that, once exposed for sale in a Southern market, the bidder with the largest sum of money would be our purchaser singly quite as surely as together; and, if separated, what would I do in a strange land? No: I would not go. It was far better for me to stay where, for miles and miles, I knew every one, and every one knew me. Then came the wish to secrete ourselves together in the mountains, or elsewhere, till White should be gone; but, to do this, detection was sure. Then we remembered that White had trusted us, in letting him come to me, and we felt ashamed, for a moment, as if we had tried to cheat; but what *right* had White to carry him away, or even to own him at all? Our poor, ignorant reasoning found it hard to understand his rights or our own; and we at last decided that, as soon as it was light, Jerry should take to the mountains, and, when White was surely gone, either I would join him there, and we would make for the North together, or he would come back, go to White's mother, who lived a few miles distant, and tell her he would work for her and obey her, but he would never go South to be worked to death in the rice-swamps or cotton-fields.

We talked late into the night; and at last, in the silence and dread, worn out with sorrow and fear, my head on his shoulder, we both dropped asleep.

Daylight was upon us when we waked. The sad consciousness of our condition, and our utter helplessness, overpowered us. I opened the door, and there was my mistress, with pail in hand, going to the spring for water. "Oh, what shall I do? Where shall I go?" cried Jerry, as he saw her. "Have no fear," I said. "Go right along. I know mistress will never betray you." And, with a bound, he was over the fence, into the fields, and off to the mountains.

In a very short time, White and his poor, doomed company came along, and called for Jerry. I had taken my pail to milk the cows; and, seeing me, he sung out, "Woman, where is Jerry, I say?" "I don't know where Jerry is," I answered. Then, turning to Kibbler, who, hearing the outcry, now came out, he said, "You told me that woman wouldn't lie; and you know well enough she is lying now, when she says she don't know where that—rascal is." Kibbler answered very slowly and thoughtfully, "I never knowed her to lie; but may be this time,—may be this time." White then turned to me, and said, "I took off his handcuffs, and let him go to you, and you had no business to serve me so."

It was true I did not know where Jerry was at that time. We had agreed that we would meet that night near the blacksmith's old shop, on the other side of the run; and that was all I knew of his whereabouts, though he had not been gone long enough to be far away. It was true he had trusted us, and I felt very badly; but what else *could* we have done? Kind reader, *what* think you?

I then told him that Jerry had said he was willing to work, and would go to his mother's and serve her, but *never*, if he could help it, would he be carried South.

Then White tried to bargain with Kibbler for my purchase, saying he would give any price he should name for me, because he knew I would then find Jerry. But it was no use. Kibbler had a kind spot in his heart, and would not consent to let me go. So the slave-trader moved on with his human cattle.

Five miles on the road lived David McCoy, another slave-trader. When White reached his house, it was agreed by them that, if McCoy could find Jerry within two days, he should bring him on, and they would meet at Stanton, Va.

Chapter V.

Meeting—A Last Interview—Separation.

The place where I was to meet Jerry was, as I have said, across the run, in a corn-field, near the blacksmith's shop, the time Friday night.

It had rained hard all day, and the stream was swollen, and pouring and rushing at a fearful rate. I waited till everybody was in bed and asleep, when I lighted my pine knot, and started for the Pass. It was still raining, and the night was very dark. Only by my torch could I see a step before me; and, when I attempted to wade in, as I did in many different places, I found it was no use. I should surely be drowned if I persisted. So, disappointed and grieved, I gave up and went home. The next morning I was able to get over on horseback to milk the cows, but I neither heard nor saw anything of Jerry.

Saturday night came. I knew well that, if not caught by White, Jerry would be round. At last, every one was in bed, and all was still. I waited and listened. I listened and waited. Then I heard his step at the door. I hurriedly opened it, and he came in. His clothes were still damp and stiff from the rain of yesterday. He was frightened and uneasy. He had been hiding around in different places, constantly fearing detection. He had seen me from behind the old blacksmith's shop when I had tried the night before, with my pine knot, to ford the stream; and he was glad, he said, when he saw me go back, for he knew I should be carried down by the current and be drowned, if I had persisted. I went to my mistress's bedroom, and asked her if I might go to the cellar. She knew at once what I meant, and whispered softly,

"Betty, has Jerry come?" then, without waiting for reply, added, "get him some milk and light bread and butter." I was not long in doing so; and the poor fellow ate like one famishing. Then he wanted to know all that had happened, and what White had said when he found he was gone. We talked a long time, and tried to devise some plans for our mutual safety and possible escape from slavery altogether; but, every way we looked, the path was beset with danger and exposure. We were both utterly disheartened. But sleep came at last and, for the time being, relieved us of our fears.

In the morning, which was Sunday, we had our breakfast together, and, as the hours passed, began to feel a little comforted. After dinner, we walked out to the field and strolled about for some time; and, when ready to go back to the house, we each took an armful of fodder along for the horses. As we laid it down and turned to go into the house, David McCoy rode up on horseback. He saw Jerry at once, and called him to come to the fence. The excitement of the last days—the fasting and the fear—had completely cowed and broken whatever of manhood, or even of brute courage, a slave might by any possibility be presumed at any time to be possessed of, and the last remains of these qualities in poor Jerry were gone. He mutely obeyed; and when, with an oath, McCoy commanded him to mount the horse behind him, he mutely seated himself there. McCoy then called to me to go to the house and bring Jerry's clothes. "Never,"—I screamed back to him,—"never, not to save your miserable life." But Jerry said: "O Betty, 'tis no use. We can't help it." I knew this was so. I stifled my anger and my grief, brought his little bundle, into which I tucked a testament and catechism some one had given me, and shook hands "good-by" with him. So we *parted forever*, in this world.

OCTAVIA V. ROGERS ALBERT

In this collection, Octavia V. Rogers Albert (1824–1889) presents a series of conversations that she arranged with formerly enslaved people about their experiences living under the brutality and dehumanization of slavery. Formerly enslaved herself, Albert attended Atlanta University after the Civil War and became an educator and social activist. Upon reading numerous narratives of slavery, Albert felt as though the intricacies of the institution itself, such as the perpetual suffering, the glimmers of joy and hope, as well as the mundane aspects of its horror, had not been recorded fully. She determinedly elected to center the voices of enslaved people to offer a better understanding of how slavery impacted their lives during and after their bondage. Albert's personal observations are weaved throughout the narrative and work to highlight the hypocrisy of white Christians whose direct involvement or relative silence about slavery rendered the institution viable and enormously profitable for centuries.

From *The House of Bondage; or, Charlotte Brooks and Other Slaves* (1891)

Chapter III.

AUNT CHARLOTTE'S FRIENDS.

Death of Aunt Charlotte's children—Jane Lee's master leaves the neighborhood—Nellie Johnson tries to escape to her old Virginia home.

"Aunt Charlotte, what became of your baby? were you blest to raise it?"

"No; my poor child died when it was two years old. Old marster's son was the father of my child."

"Did its father help to take care of it?"

"Why, no; he never noticed my child."

"Did you have any more children?"

"Yes; but they all died."

"Why could you not rear any of them?"

"La, me, child! they died for want of attention. I used to leave them alone half of the time. Sometimes old mistress would have some one to mind them till they got so they could walk, but after that they would have to paddle for themselves. I was glad the Lord took them, for I knowed they were better off with my blessed Jesus than with me."

Poor Charlotte Brooks! I can never forget how her eyes were filled with tears when she would speak of all her children: "Gone, and no one to care for me!" Sometimes she failed to come and see me (for she always visited me when she was able; never missed a day, unless she was sick, during the two years I lived near her). She was in poor health, and had no one to help her in her old age, when she really needed help. She had spent her life working hard for her masters, and after giving all of her youthful days to them was turned upon this cold, unfriendly world with nothing. She left her master's plantation with two blankets, and was several days on the road walking to get to the town of ——, and, having become so exhausted, dropped them by the way-side. She said when she arrived at her destination she had nothing but the clothes she had on her back. She was then old and feeble.

I remember she used to come and beg me to save the stale coffee for her, saying she had not eaten any thing all day. Notwithstanding all of her poverty she was always rejoicing in the love of God. I asked her once whether she felt lonely in this unfriendly world.

She answered, "No, my dear; how can a child of God feel lonesome? My heavenly Father took care of me in slave-time. He led me all the way along, and now he has set me free, and I am free both in soul and body."

She said, "I heard a preacher say once since I got free, 'Not a foot of land do I possess, not a cottage in the wilderness.' Just so it is with me; sometimes I don't have bread to eat; but I tell you, my soul is always feasting on my dear Jesus. Nobody knows what it is to taste of Jesus but them that has been washed by him. Many years ago, my white folks did not want me even to pray, and would whip me for praying, saying it was foolishness for me to pray. But the more old marster whipped me the more I'd pray. Sometimes he'd put me in jail; but, la, me! it did not stop me from praying. I'd kneel down on the jail floor and pray often, and nearly all day Sundays. I'd fall asleep sometimes praying. Old marster would come and call me about sundown. He would always call out loud before he got to the jail to let me know he was coming. I could always tell his walk. I tell you, I used to feel rested and good when he let me out. He let me go so I could always be ready to go to work on Monday morning. One Sunday night, just as I got to my door, Aunt Jane met me. I was just coming from the jail, too. I knowed Aunt Jane was coming to hold prayer-meeting, and I hurried. If old marster heard us he would put me in jail the next Sunday morning; but, child, that did not stop me; I was always ready for the prayer-meeting. I told Aunt Jane I had been in jail all day, and it was a happy day in jail, too.

"Aunt Jane's white folks was not so hard on her as mine was. They did not let her go off at night, but she would slip away and come and lead prayer-meeting at my house. She always brought her Bible and hymn-book. She read to us that night something like this: 'I know my Redeemer lives.'"

I said to her, "O, yes, Aunt Charlotte; I remember it very well. It is in the book of Job, nineteenth chapter, twenty-fifth verse."

"Well, it has been so long since I heard it read. Wont you get the Bible and please read it for me?"

"With much pleasure I'll read it to you. Here it is: 'For I know that my Redeemer liveth, and that he shall stand at the latter day upon the earth: and though after my skin worms destroy this body, yet in my flesh shall I see God: whom I shall see for myself, and mine eyes shall behold, and not another; though my reins be consumed within me.' I've read three verses of that chapter for you."

"Thank you, too, for it. O, how it makes me think of them happy times in the canefield I used to have! I do wish I could read. I long to read the Bible and hymn-book. When I was in Virginia I used to study some. I learned my A, B, C, and begun to spell some in my blue-back spelling-book. I could spell 'ba-ker' and 'sha-dy,' and all along there in the spelling-book; but after I came to Louisiana I forgot every thing."

I said, "You have no hope of learning, now that you are free, although you are at liberty to do as you please?"

"No, my child; I can't see how to thread my needle now. I have given all my young days to the white folks. My eye-sight is gone. Nothing for me to do but to wait till my Jesus comes."

"Aunt Charlotte, what became of Jane Lee?"

"Well, about five or six years before the war her marster moved 'way off to Texas, and I never saw her any more. We all cried when she left us. We felt lost, because we had nobody to lead us in our little meetings. After a while I begun to lead, and then some of the others would lead. Aunt Jane caused many of our people to get religion on our place. Where she lived the black folks were all Catholic, and she could not do much with them. I tell you, them Catholic people loved them beads and crosses they used to pray to. The last time Aunt Jane was with us she told us her white people was going to move, and she might never see us any more in this world; but she said, 'Char-lotte, promise me you will meet me in heaven.' And then she turned around to all the others in the little cabin that night and asked them all to promise to meet her there. We all promised to fight on till death. La, me! such crying there in that little cabin that night! Aunt Jane cried, and we cried too. It was past mid-night when we all parted. Aunt Jane had about two miles to go after she left our place that night. She lived about two miles from our plantation.

"Aunt Jane said that when she came out here a pretty woman was brought here with her by the name of Nellie Johnson. Nel-lie was sold to a mighty bad man. She tried to run away to her old Virginia home, but the white men caught her and brought her back. Aunt Jane told me Nellie was almost white, and had pretty, long, straight hair. When they got her back they made her wear men's pants for one year. They made her work in the field in that way. She said they put deer-horns on her head to punish her, with bells on them. Aunt Jane said once while she was passing on the levee she saw Nellie working with the men on the Mississippi River, and she had men's clothes on then. The white folks used to have the levee worked on often before the war. They were afraid the levees would cave in."

Chapter IV.

CRUEL MASTERS.

Nellie Johnson is barbarously treated—Sam Wilson living in the swamps of Louisiana—Richard's wife living on another plantation—His master refuses to allow him to visit her— He is caught by the patrollers and beaten almost to death.

"Aunt Jane loved Nellie, although Nellie was no kin to her, and she used to talk very often to me about her white people using her so bad. She said once that a baby was born to Nellie on the road when she was coming in the speculator's drove, and the speculator gave the child away to a white woman near by where they camped that night. The speculator said they could not take care of the child on the road, and told Nellie it was better to let the white woman have the child."

"Poor Nellie! I reckon she was trying to go back to see her child when she was caught by the white barbarous creatures, who evidently were without human nature."

"Yes, I think so too," said Aunt Charlotte, "for blood is thicker than water. The white people thought in slave-time we poor darkies had no soul, and they separated us like dogs. So many poor colored people are dead from grieving at the separation of their children that was sold away from them."

"Aunt Jane said Nellie's owner was *so* bad! She said they had a man named Sam Wilson; he stayed one half of his time in the swamp. His master used to get after him to whip him, but Sam would not let his marster beat him. He would run off and stayed in the woods two and three months at a time. The white folks would set the dogs behind him, but Sam could not be caught by the dogs. The colored people said Sam greased his feet with rabbit-grease, and that kept the dogs from him. Aunt Jane said to me that she did not know what Sam used, but it looked like Sam could go off and stay as long as he wanted when the white folks got after him."

Aunt Charlotte said to me, "I tell you, my child, nobody could get me to run away in those Louisiana swamps. Death is but death, and I just thought if I'd run off in those swamps I'd die. I used to hear old people say it was just as well to die with fever as with ague; and that is what I thought. Aunt Jane said Sam was from Louisiana, and was a Catholic. She said she did not know what sort of religion Sam's was, to let people dance and work all day Sunday. She used to try to get Sam to come to her prayer-meetings, but she could not get him inside the door when they was praying and singing. She said Sam used to laugh at them, and call our religion ''Merican Niggers' religion.'"

"Aunt Charlotte, how many of you all used to carry on prayer-meeting after Aunt Jane left?"

"Well, let me count; we had Mary, Lena, Annie, Ann, Sarah, Nancy, and Martha—seven sisters and four brethren, Billy, Green, Jones, and Richard. La, me! what a good time we all used to have in my cabin on that plantation! I think of them good, happy times we used to have now since freedom, and wish I could see all of them once more. I tell you, child, religion is good anywhere—at the plow-handle, at the hoe-handle, any-where. If you are filled with the love of my Jesus you are happy. Why, the best times I ever had was when I first got religion, and when old marster would put me in that old jail-house on his plantation all day Sunday.

"Richard used to be mighty faithful to his prayer-meeting, but old marster begun to be mighty mean to him. His wife lived on another plantation, and marster told Richard he had to give up that wife and take a woman on our place. Richard told old marster he did not want any other woman; he said he loved his wife and could never love any other woman. His wife was named Betty. I believe Richard would die for Betty. Sometimes Richard would slip off and go to see Betty, and marster told the patrollers every time they caught Richard on the plantation where Betty lived to beat him half to death. The patrollers had caught Richard many times, and had beat him mighty bad. So one night

Richard heard the dogs coming in the woods near his wife's house, and he jumped out of his wife's window, and he went for dear life or death through the woods. He said he had to always pass over the bayou to go to his wife, but that night the patrollers were so hot behind him that he lost his way. He had a skiff he always went over in, but he forgot about the skiff when they were after him. Richard said he just took off every piece of clothes he had on and tied them around his neck and swam across the bayou. He lost his hat, and went without any all day in the field. Richard said when he got to the bayou he was wet with sweat, and it was one of the coldest nights he had ever felt in Louisiana. He said he had about two miles to go after he got over the bayou, and when he got across he just slipped on his clothes he had around his neck, and ran every step of the way to his own plantation. Sometimes they would catch Richard and drive four stakes in the ground, and they would tie his feet and hands to each one and beat him half to death. I tell you, sometimes he could not work. Marster did not care, for he had told Richard to take some of our women for a wife, but Richard would not do it. Richard loved Betty, and he would die for her."

"Did you say Richard was a Christian, Aunt Charlotte?"

"Yes; he used to pray and sing with us, many, many times, all the hymns Aunt Jane sung to us. I remember Richard used to sing:

> "'In the valley, in the valley,
>   There's a mighty cry to
> Jesus in the valley;
>   So weary, so tired, Lord, I wish
> I was in heaven, hallelu.'"

Aunt Charlotte said: "Poor Richard! I reckon he is dead now. When the Yankees came he was one of the first ones to leave our place, and I never heard from him any more. I reckon if he is dead he is resting at last in heaven. O, he had so many trials in this cold, unfriendly world! But he never give up praying and trusting in the Lord. Sometimes when we all would be hoeing the cane we did not go home to dinner, but we had our victuals in a basket, and we ate under a shade-tree. When it was hot marster used to let us have one hour and a half at twelve o'clock.

Then we used to have good times under the shade-trees. We used to talk of Aunt Jane Lee, and we would sing some of her hymns till we all would go to sleep."

* * *

Chapter XI.

PRISON HORRORS.

Uncle John taking lessons—Andersonville horrors—Blood-hounds—Silas bitten by blood-hounds and eaten by buzzards.

Uncle John always made it a habit to stop in on Saturday evenings. He was a steward of his church, and as he could not read very well he said he had made up his mind to study and try to learn more. He wanted to learn to read the Bible and hymn-book, anyhow, he said. He had to lead prayer-meeting in his church very often, and he said it would do him so much good if he could only read his Bible and hymn-book; so he employed me to teach him. I must confess Uncle John was pretty hard to teach. His mind was blunted, no doubt, and, having to work hard every day, and old and feeble as he was, I did not expect much of him. He decided that the first thing I must do was to read a chapter in the Bible, and also to read a hymn, saying he wanted to get them "by heart." His favorite hymns were: "Show pity, Lord," "How firm a foundation," "Must I be to judgment brought?" and "Try us, O God."

He would say: "La, Mrs. A., if I only had these good times in my young days! But I tell you, ma'am, I am glad I'm blest to see freedom! How many of my poor people died in slave-time and never knowed nothing but hard work all their life-time! I know," he said, "my poor Nancy is dead, and buried some-where in Georgia. She worked hard all of her life-time, for the white folks never knowed what rest was. Sometimes I dream of all of my people I left in Georgia. It seems I can see my mammy in my sleep, and she comes right up beside my bed and talks with me sometimes. I know she is in heaven, for she used to be always talking about heaven when I was with her."

I said: "It would afford you so much joy to see your children once more; I reckon they are still living."

He said: "Yes, ma'am; I reckon if they is still living they is all married; but the white folks was so bad in slave-time I expect they all is dead. They used to run black people down with Nigger-hounds, and would let the dogs bite them all over."

"Yes, Uncle John; your wife spent several hours not long ago telling of a poor woman that lived there near her plantation who was caught by the dogs, and she said the last she saw of the woman she was bleeding from dog-bites."

"Yes, ma'am; the white folks was bad here in Louisiana, but I think they was worse in Georgia for blood-hounds."

"Why, Uncle John," I said, "it looks as if allowing the dogs to bite them would bring on hydrophobia, and thereby cause a great many deaths among the slaves?"

"Yes; they did die often; but I always thought they died from being worked to death. Why, ma'am, I have seen poor colored men bleeding and dying from dog-bites. Once right in Georgia I saw a man where he crawled 'way off from his plantation and died under a shade-tree. Madam, that poor man had iron around his feet when we found him, and the buzzards had almost eaten his body up. I knowed the poor man; his name was Silas. He had run away and was caught by the dogs one morning, and his marster came up to him while he was fighting with the dogs, and Silas give one dog a blow and almost killed him. The hound was one of the best ones his marster had. Madam, Silas's marster got off of his horse right there where they caught him and beat Silas with his pistol all over for nothing because he would not let the dog bite him. He made the dogs bite Silas all over his body. The dogs bit him under the throat. When he got Silas home he put him in irons, but Silas could not walk. Silas was almost dead when his marster put the irons on him."

Uncle John said: "Poor Silas! I will never forget how I went out one Sunday morning and found him laying dead under that big oak-tree. He had a wife and six or seven children. He lived on one of the plantations in Georgia. We used to go to church on Sundays together. O, how he used to love that hymn, 'How firm a foundation!' He knowed every word of it by heart," said Uncle John. "We used to hear the white people sing it at church."

I asked Uncle John if Silas's master allowed him to attend church, and he said:

"Why, yes, ma'am; he used to let his slaves go to church on Sunday, and he went too; but that did not keep our white people from beating us through the week. They took sacrament in the morning, and we colored people took it in the evening."

"You were never allowed to take the sacrament with your masters?"

"No, ma'am; we been always separated here, and I reckon when we get up yonder in glory they will want to be separated," said Uncle John.

"No; there is no separation in glory. We read in the third chapter of Galatians, twenty-sixth to twenty-eighth verses: 'For ye are all the children of God by faith in Christ Jesus. For as many of you as have been baptized into Christ have put on Christ. There is neither Jew nor Greek, there is neither bond nor free, there is neither male nor female: for ye are all one in Christ Jesus.' Thus you see and hear what the Bible says: 'We are all one.'

> "'God is faithful; he will never
> Break his covenant sealed in blood;
> Signed when our Redeemer died;
> Sealed when he was glorified.'"

HENRY CLAY BRUCE

Some thirty years after the Civil War, Henry Clay Bruce (1836–1902) published a set of reflections on his time in slavery in Missouri. In the preface to the volume, Bruce suggests that his narrative is a measured account, one that seeks to demonstrate that enslavers held different temperaments with regard to the treatment of their human property, and that there were class designations—good and bad—within each race. Bruce reflects on what he views as the curious decision of poor white people to remain mired in poverty when they had the possibility of freely escaping what Bruce refers to as the "quasi-slavery" of their Southern lives that forecasted the lives of many of their descendants who, in the late nineteenth century, continued to be hateful, murderous individuals whose sense of worth and power came with the tormenting of Black communities. Bruce writes about the loyalty and determination of Black people even through the uncertainty of their lives under white supremacy: "But though they were robbed of the reward of their labor, though they have been denied their common rights, though they have been discriminated against in every walk of life and in favor of every breed of foreign anarchist and socialist, though they have been made to feel the measured hate of the poor white man's venom, yet through it all they have been true; true to the country they owe (?) so little, true to the flag that denies them protection, true to the government that practically disowns them, true to their honor, fidelity and loyalty, the birthrights of superior blood."

From *The New Man:*
Twenty-Nine Years a Slave,
Twenty-Nine Years a Free Man (1895)

Chapter II.

Early in the spring of 1847, we reached the Perkinson farm in Virginia, where we found our master, whom we had not seen for nearly three years, and his son Willie, as he was then called, with hired slaves cultivating the old farm. My older brothers, James and Calvin, were at once hired to Mr. Hawkins, a brick-maker, at Farmville, Prince Edward County, Virginia.

In as much as it was not the custom in that state to put slaves at work in the field before they had reached thirteen years of age, I, being less, was allowed to eat play and grow, and I think the happiest days of my boyhood were spent here. There were seven or eight boys about my age belonging to Mrs. Perkinson, living less than a mile distant on adjoining farms, who also enjoyed the same privileges, and there were four or five hounds which we could take out rabbit hunting when we wished to do so. It was grand sport to see five or six hounds in line on a trail and to hear the sweet music of these trained fox hounds. To us, at least, it was sweet music. We roamed over the neighboring lands hunting and often catching rabbits, which we brought home. During the fishing season we often went angling in the creeks that meandered through these lands to the millpond which furnished the water for the mill near by, which was run by Uncle Radford, an old trustworthy slave belonging to Mrs. Prudence Perkinson. He was the lone miller, and ground wheat and corn for the entire neighborhood.

There were several orchards of very fine fruit on these farms. We were allowed to enjoy the apples, peaches, cherries and plums, to our heart's content. Besides, there were large quantities of wild berries and nuts, especially chinquapins. When we had nothing else to do in the way of enjoyment we played the game of "shinney"—a game that gave great pleasure to us all. I was playmate and guardian for Willie Perkinson, and in addition to this I had a standing duty to perform, which was to drive up three cows every afternoon. At this time Willie was old enough to attend the school which was about two miles away, and I had to go with him in the forenoon and return for him in the afternoon. He usually went with me after the cows.

I had been taught the alphabet while in Missouri and could spell "baker," "lady," "shady," and such words of two syllables, and Willie took great pride in teaching me his lessons of each day from his books, as I had none and my mother had no money to buy any for me. This continued for about a year before the boy's aunt, Mrs. Prudence Perkinson, who had cared for Willie while we were in Missouri, found it out, and I assure you, dear reader, she raised a great row with our master about it. She insisted that it was a crime to teach a Negro to read, and that it would spoil him, but our owner seemed not to care anything about it and did nothing to stop it, for afterward I frequently had him correct my spelling. In after years I learned that he was glad that his Negroes could read, especially the Bible, but he was opposed to their being taught writing.

But my good time ended when I was put to the plow in the Spring of 1848. The land was hilly and rocky. I, being of light weight, could not hold the plow steadily in the ground, however hard I tried. My master was my trainer and slapped my jaws several times for that which I could not prevent. I knew then as well as I know now, that this was unjust punishment. But after the breaking season and planting the crop of corn and tobacco was over, I was given a lighter single horse plow and enjoyed the change and the work. Compared with some of his neighbors, our master was not a hard man on his slaves, because we enjoyed many privileges that other slaves did not have. Some slave owners did not feed well, causing their slaves to steal chickens, hogs and sheep from them or from other owners. Bacon and bread with an occassional meal of beef was the feed through the entire year; but our master gave us all we could eat, together with such vegetables as were raised on the farm. My mother was the cook for the families, white and black, and of course I fared well as to food.

Willie Perkinson had become as one of us and regarded my mother as his mother. He played with the colored boys from the time he got home from school till bedtime, and again in the morning till time to go to school, and every Saturday and Sunday. Having learned to spell I kept it up, and took lessons from Willie as often as I could. My younger brother, B. K. Bruce (now Ex-Senator) had succeeded me as playmate and guardian of Willie, and being also anxious to learn, soon caught up with me, and by Willie's aid went ahead of me and has held his place during all the years since.

Mrs. Prudence Perkinson and her son Lemuel, lived about one mile from our place, and they owned about fifty field hands, as they were called. They also had an overseer or negro-driver whose pay consisted of a certain percentage of the crop.

The larger the crop the larger his share would be, and having no money interest in the slaves he drove them night and day without mercy. This overseer was a mean and cruel man and would, if not checked by her, whip some one every day. Lemuel Perkinson, was a man who spent his time in pleasure seeking, such as fox-hunting, fishing, horse racing and other sports, and was away from home a great deal, so much so that he paid little attention to the management of the farm. It was left to the care of his mother and the overseer. Mrs. Sarah Perkinson, wife of Lemuel Perkinson, was a dear good woman and was beloved by all her slaves as long as I knew her, and I am informed that she is living now and is still beloved by her ex-slaves. Mrs. Prudence Perkinson would not allow her overseer to whip a grown slave without her consent, because I have known of cases where the overseer was about to whip a slave when he would break loose and run to his old mistress. If it was a bad case she would punish the slave by taking off her slipper and slapping his jaws with it. They were quite willing to take that rather than be punished by the overseer who would often have them take off the shirt to be whipped on their bare backs.

Mrs. Prudence Perkinson was a kind hearted woman, but when angry and under the excitement of the moment would order a servant whipped, but before the overseer could carry it out would change her mind. I recall a case where her cook, Annica, had sauced her and refused to stop talking when told to do so. She sent for the overseer to come to the Great House to whip her (Annica). He came and called her out; she refused to obey. He then pulled her outside and struck her two licks with his whip, when her "old mistress" promptly stopped him and abused him, and drove him out of the Great House yard for his brutality. She went to Annica, spoke kindly to her and asked her if she was hurt.

I write of this as I saw it. I can recall only one or two instances where our master whipped a grown person, but when he had it to do or felt that it should be done, he did it well.

Our owner had one serious weakness which was very objectionable to us, and one in which he was the exception and not the rule of the master class. It was this: He would associate with "poor white trash," would often invite them to dine with him, and the habit remained with him during his entire life.

There lived near our farm two poor white men, better known at the South as "poor white trash," named John Flippen and Sam Hawkins. These men were too lazy to do steady work and made their living by doing chores for the rich and killing hawks and crows at so much a piece, for the owner of the land on which they were destroyed. These men would watch us and report to our master everything they saw us do that was a violation of rules. I recall one instance in which I was whipped on account of a lie told by Sam Hawkins. The facts in the case are as follows: I was sent one Saturday afternoon to Major Price's place after some garden seed and was cautioned not to ride the mare hard, and I did not therefore take her out of a walk or a very slow trot as it was not to my interest to do otherwise, for the distance was but two miles and if I came back before sundown I would have to go into the field to work again. I got back about sundown, but had met Sam Hawkins on the road as I went, and he was at our house when I returned. He was invited to supper, and while at the table told my master that I had the mare in a gallop when he met me. Coffee was very costly at that time, too high for the "poor white trash;" none but the rich could afford it, and the only chance these poor whites had to get a cup of coffee was when so invited. It was always a God-send to them, not only the good meal, but the honor of dining with the "BIG BUGS." Being illiterate their conversation could not exceed what they had seen and heard, and to please their masters, for such they were to these poor whites almost as much as to their slaves, they told everything they had seen the slaves do, and oftener more.

After supper that evening my master sent for me. When I came, he had a switch in his hand and proceeded to explain why he was going to whip me. I pleaded innocence and posi-tively disputed the charge. At this he then became angry and whipped me. When he stopped he said it was not so much for the fast riding that he had punished me as it was for disputing a white man's word. Fool that I was then, for I would not have received any more whipping at that time, but knowing that I was not guilty I said so again and he immediately flogged me again. When he stopped he asked me in a loud tone of voice, "Will you have the impudence to dispute a white man's word again?" My answer was "No sir." That was the last whipping he ever gave me, and that on account of the lie told by a poor white man. But I lived not only to dispute the word of these poor whites in their presence, but in after years abused and threatened to punish them for tress-passing upon his lands.

Other ex-slaves can relate many such cases as the Hawkins' case and such instances, in my opinion, have been the cause of the intense hatred of slaves against the poor whites of the South, and I believe that from such troubles originates the term "poor white trash." In many ways this unfortunate class of Southern people had but a few more privileges than the slaves. True, they were free, could go where they pleased without a "pass," but they could not, with impunity, dispute the word of the rich in anything, and obeyed their masters as did the slaves. It has been stated by many writers, and I accept it as true, that the Eman-cipation Proclamation issued by President Lincoln, not only freed the slaves, but the poor whites of the South as well, for they occupied a condition nearly approaching that of slavery.

They were nominally free, but that freedom was greatly re-stricted on account of the prejudice against them as a class. They were often employed by the ruling class to do small jobs of work and while so engaged were not allowed, even to eat with them at the same table, neither could they in any way associate or intermarry with the upper classes. Of course this unfortunate class of people had a vote, but it was always cast just as the master class directed, and not as the voter desired, if he had a desire. I recall very clearly the fact, that at each County, State or National election the poor white people were hauled to the voting places in wagons belonging to the aristocratic class. They also furnished a prepared ballot for each man and woe unto that poor white man who failed to vote that ticket or come when sent for. Each one of the master class kept a strict lookout for every poor white man in his neighborhood and on election days sent his wagons and brought each one of these voters to the polls.

When the war of the Rebellion broke out this class of men constituted the rank and file of the Confederate army and rendered good service for their masters, who had only to speak a kind word to them when they would take the oath and obediently march to the front, officered by the aristocratic class. These poor people contributed their full share to the death roll of the Southern Army.

True to his low instinct, the poor white man is represented at the South as the enemy of the Colored people to-day, just as he was before the war, and is still as illiterate as he was then. He is not far enough up the scale to see the advantage of education, and will not send his children to school, nor allow the Colored child to go, if it is in his power to prevent it. It is this class who burn the school houses in the Southland to-day. The aristocracy and the Colored people of the South would get along splendidly, were it not for these poor whites, who are the leaders in all the disorders, lynchings and the like. The South will be the garden spot, the cradle of liberty, the haven of America, when the typical poor whites of that section shall have died off, removed, or become educated, and not till then.

ANTISLAVERY POETICS, CHILDREN'S LITERATURE, AND DRAMA

Poetry and Music

JUPITER HAMMON

Jupiter Hammon (1711–1806) was born into slavery in Lloyd Neck, Long Island, New York. Encouraged by his enslavers to attend school, Hammon thrived as a scholar and served as a trusted bookkeeper for his owners. Hammon later became a preacher, poet, and essayist, and is widely held as the first published African American poet. Hammon's poems concern Christian morality and/or the relation between master and slave and underscore Hammon's spiritual conversion to the traditionalist Calvinist faith. Hammon's speech "An Address to the Negroes in the State of New York" demonstrates his support of gradual abolition, though his openly articulated politics remain tepid and grounded in Christian morality. Hammon seemingly viewed accommodation to slavery as God's will, though it can certainly be argued that his verse in "The Kind Master and Dutiful Servant" is coded with a subversive critique of slavery and his understanding of final judgment. In 2011, the Hammon scholar Cedrick May uncovered an unpublished poem by Hammon in the Yale University archives entitled "An Essay on Slavery" that gives insight into Hammon's inner feelings about the injustices of slavery that, perhaps, his enslaver rejected, Hammon never attempted to publish for fear of harm, or Hammon had changed his perspectives about.

"An Address to the Negroes in the State of New York" (1787); An Evening's Improvement, Shewing the Necessity of Beholding the Lamb of God. To Which Is Added a Dialogue Entitled "The Kind Master and Dutiful Servant" (1790); and "An Essay on Slavery, with Justification to Divine Providence, That God Rules over All Things" (1786)

"Of a truth I perceive that God is no respecter of persons: But in every Nation, he that feareth him and worketh righteousness, is accepted with him."

Acts x. 34, 35.

"AN ADDRESS TO THE NEGROES IN THE STATE OF NEW YORK" (1787)

To the Members of the African Society in the city of New York Gentlemen,

I take the liberty to dedicate an address to my poor brethren to you. If you think it is likely to do good among them, I do not doubt but you will take it under your care. You have discovered so much kindness and good will to those you thought were oppressed, and had no helper, that I am sure you will not despise what I have wrote, if you judge it will be of any service to them. I have nothing to add, but only to wish that "the blessing of many ready to perish, may come upon you."

I am Gentlemen, Your Servant,
Jupiter Hammon

To the Public:

An Address to the Negroes of the State of New York

When I am writing to you with a design to say something to you for your good, and with a view to promote your happiness, I can with truth and sincerity join with the apostle Paul, when speaking of his own nation the Jews, and say, "That I have great heaviness and continual sorrow in my heart for my brethren, my kinsmen according to the flesh." Yes my dear brethren, when I think of you, which is very often, and of the poor, despised and miserable state you are in, as to the things of this world, and when I think of your ignorance and stupidity, and the great wickedness of the most of you, I am pained to the heart. It is at times, almost too much for human nature to bear, and I am obliged to turn my thoughts from the subject or endeavour to still my mind, by considering that it is permitted thus to be, by that God who governs all things, who seteth up one and pulleth down another. While I have been thinking on this subject, I have frequently had great struggles in my own mind, and have been at a loss to know what to do. I have wanted exceedingly to say something to you, to call upon you with the tenderness of a father and friend, and to give you the last, and I may say, dying advice, of an old man, who wishes our best good in this world, and in the world to come. But while I have had such desires, a sense of my own ignorance, and unfitness to teach others, has frequently discouraged me from attempting to say any thing to you; yet when I thought of your situation, I could not rest easy. When I was at Hartford in Connecticut, where I lived during the war, I published several pieces which were well received, not only by those of my own colour, but by a number of the white people, who thought they might do good among their servants. This is one consideration, among others, that emboldens me now to publish what I have written to you. Another is, I think you will be more likely to listen to what is said, when you know it comes from a negro, one of your own nation and colour, and therefore can have no interest in deceiving you, or in saying any thing to you, but what he really thinks is your interest and duty to comply with. My age, I think, gives me some right to speak to you, and reason to expect you will hearken to my advice. I am now upwards of sev-

enty years old, and cannot expect, though I am well, and able
to do almost any kind of business, to live much longer. I have
passed the common bounds set for man, and must soon go the
way of all the earth. I have had more experience in the world
than the most of you, and I have seen a great deal of the vanity,
and wickedness of it. I have great reason to be thankful that my
lot has been so much better than most slaves have had. I suppose I have had more advantages and privileges than most of
you, who are slaves have ever known, and I believe more than
many white people have enjoyed, for which I desire to bless
God, and pray that he may bless those who have given them to
me. I do not, my dear friends, say these things about myself to
make you think that I am wiser or better than others; but that
you might hearken, without prejudice, to what I have to say to
you on the following particulars.

1st. Respecting obedience to masters. Now whether it is right,
and lawful, in the Sight of God, for them to make slaves of us
or not, I am certain that while we are slaves, it is our duty to
obey our masters, in all their lawful commands, and mind them
unless we are bid to do that which we know to be sin, or forbidden in God's word. The apostle Paul says, "Servants be obedient to them that are your masters according to the flesh, with
fear and trembling in singleness in your heart as unto Christ:
Not with eye service, as men pleasers, but as the servants of
Christ doing the will of God from the heart: With good will
doing service to the Lord, and not to men: Knowing that whatever thing a man doeth the same shall he receive of the Lord,
whether he be bond or free."—Here is a plain command of God
for us to obey our masters. It may seem hard for us, if we think
our masters wrong in holding us slaves, to obey in all things,
but who of us dare dispute with God! He has commanded us to
obey, and we ought to do it cheerfully, and freely. This should
be done by us, not only because God commands, but because
our own peace and comfort depend upon it. As we depend upon
our masters, for what we eat and drink and wear, and for all our
comfortable things in this world, we cannot be happy, unless
we please them. This we cannot do without obeying them

freely, without muttering or finding fault. If a servant strives to please his master and studies and takes pains to do it, I believe there are but few masters who would use such a servant cruelly. Good servants frequently make good masters. If your master is really hard, unreasonable and cruel, there is no way so likely for you to convince him of it, as always to obey his commands, and try to serve him, and take care of his interest, and try to promote it all in your power. If you are proud and stubborn and always finding fault, your master will think the fault lies wholly on your side, but if you are humble, and meek, and bear all things patiently, your master may think he is wrong, if he does not, his neighbors will be apt to see it, and will befriend you, and try to alter his conduct. If this does not do, you must cry to him, who has the hearts of all men in his hands, and turneth them as the rivers of waters are turned.

2d: The particular I would mention is honesty and faithfulness. You must suffer me now to deal plainly with you, my dear brethren, for I do not mean to flatter, or omit speaking the truth, whether it is for you or against you. How many of you are there who allow yourselves in stealing from your masters. It is very wicked for you not to take care of your masters goods, but how much worse is it to pilfer and steal from them, whenever you think you shall not be found out. This you must know is very wicked and provoking to God. There are none of you so ignorant, but that you must know that this is wrong. Though you may try to excuse yourselves, by saying that your masters are unjust to you, and though you may try to quiet your consciences in this way, yet if you are honest in owning the truth you must think it is as wicked, and on some accounts more wicked to steal from your masters, than from others.

We cannot certainly, have any excuse either for taking any thing that belongs to our masters without their leave, or for being unfaithful in their business. It is our duty to be faithful, not with eye service as men please. We have no right to stay when we are sent on errands, any longer than to do the business we were sent upon. All the time spent idly, is spent wickedly, and is unfaithfulness to our masters. In these things I must say, that I

think many of you are guilty. I know that many of you endeavor
to excuse yourselves, and say that you have nothing that you can
call your own, and that you are under great temptations to be
unfaithful and take from your masters. But this will not do, God
will certainly punish you for stealing and for being unfaithful.
All that we have to mind is our own duty. If God has put us in
bad circumstances that is not our fault and he will not punish us
for it. If any are wicked in keeping us so, we cannot help it, they
must answer to God for it. Nothing will serve as an excuse to us
for not doing our duty. The same God will judge both them and
us. Pray then my dear friends, fear to offend in this way, but be
faithful to God, to your masters, and to your own souls.

The next thing I would mention, and warn you against, IS
profaneness. This you know is forbidden by God. Christ tells
us, "swear not at all," and again it is said "thou shalt not take
the name of the Lord thy God in vain, for the Lord will not
hold him guiltless, that taketh his name in vain." Now though
the great God has forbidden it, yet how dreadfully profane are
many, and I don't know but I may say the most of you? How
common is it to hear you take the terrible and awful name of
the great God in vain?—To swear by it, and by Jesus Christ, his
Son—How common is it to hear you wish damnation to your
companions, and to your own souls and to sport with in the
name of Heaven and Hell, as if there were no such places for
you to hope for, or to fear. Oh my friends, be warned to forsake
this dreadful sin of profaneness. Pray my dear friends, believe
and realize, that there is a God—that he is great and terrible
beyond what you can think—that he keeps you in life every
moment—and that he can send you to that awful Hell, that you
laugh at, in an instant, and confine you there for ever, and that
he will certainly do it, if you do not repent. You certainly do
not believe, that there is a God, or that there is a Heaven or
Hell, or you would never trifle with them. It would make you
shudder, if you heard others do it, if you believe them as much,
as you believe any thing you see with your bodily eyes.

I have heard some learned and good men say, that the heathen, and all that worshiped false Gods, never spoke lightly or
irreverently of their Gods, they never took their names in vain,

or jested with those things which they held sacred. Now why should the true God, who made all things, be treated worse in this respect, than those false Gods, that were made of wood and stone, I believe it is because Satan tempts men to do it, He tried to make them love their false Gods, and to speak well of them, but he wishes to have men think lightly of the true God, to take his holy name in vain, and to scoff at, and make a jest of all things that are really good. You may think that Satan has not power to do so much, and have so great influence on the minds of men: But the scripture says, "he goeth about like a roaring Lion, seeking whom he may devour—That he is the prince of the power of the air—and that he rules in the hearts of the children of disobedience,—and that wicked men are led captive by him, to do his will." All those of you who are pro-fane, are serving the Devil. You are doing what he tempts and desires you to do. If you could see him with your bodily eyes, would you like to make an agreement with him, to serve him, and do as he bid you. I believe most of you would be shocked at this, but you may be certain that all of you who allow your-selves in this sin, are as really serving him, and to just as good purpose, as if you met him, and promised to dishonor God, and serve him with all your might. Do you believe this? It is true whether you believe it or not. Some of you to excuse yourselves, may plead the example of others, and say that you hear a great many white-people, who know more, than such poor ignorant negroes, as you are, and some who are rich and great gentle-men, swear, and talk profanely; and some of you may say this of your masters, and say no more than is true. But all this is not a sufficient excuse for you. You know that murder is wicked. If you saw your master kill a man, do you suppose this would be any excuse for you, if you should commit the same crime? You must know it would not; nor will your hearing him curse and swear, and take the name of God in vain, or any other man, be he ever so great or rich, excuse you. God is greater than all other beings, and him we are bound to obey. To him we must give an account for every idle word that we speak. He will bring us all, rich and poor, white and black, to his judgment seat. If we are found among those who feared his name, and trembled at his word, we shall be called good and faithful servants. Our slavery will be at an end, and though ever so mean, low, and despited in this world, we shall sit with God in his kingdom as Kings and Priests, and rejoice forever, and ever. Do not then, my dear friends, take God's holy name in vain, or speak profanely in any way. Let not the example of others lead you into the sin, but reverence and fear that great and fearful name, the Lord our God. I might now caution you against other sins to which you are exposed; but as I meant only to mention those you were exposed to, more than others, by your being slaves, I will conclude what I have to say to you, by advising you to become religious, and to make religion the great business of your lives.

Now I acknowledge that liberty is a great thing, and worth seeking for, if we can get it honestly, and by our good conduct, prevail on our masters to set us free: Though for my own part I do not wish to be free, yet I should be glad, if others, especially the young negroes were to be free, for many of us, who are grown up slaves, and have always had masters to take care of us, should hardly know how to take care of ourselves; and it may be more for our own comfort to remain as we are. That liberty is a great thing we may know from our own feelings, and we may likewise Judge so from the conduct of the white-people, in the late war. How much money has been spent, and how many lives has been lost, to defend their liberty. I must say that I have hoped that God would open their eyes, when they were so much engaged for liberty, to think of the state of the poor blacks, and to pity us. He has done it in some measure, and has raised us up many friends, for which we have reason to be thankful, and to hope in his mercy. What may be done further, he only knows, for known unto God are all his ways from the beginning. But this my dear brethren IS by no means, the greatest thing we have to be concerned about. Getting our liberty in this world, is nothing to our having the liberty of the children of God. Now the Bible tells us that we are all by nature, sinners, that we are slaves to sin and Satan, and that unless we are converted, or born again, we must be miserable forever. Christ says, except a man be born again, he cannot see the kingdom of God, and all that do not see the kingdom of God, must be in the kingdom of darkness.

There are but two places where all go after death, white and
black, rich and poor; those places are Heaven and Hell. Heaven
is a place made for those, who are born again, and who love
God, and it is a place where they will be happy for ever. Hell IS
a place made for those who hate God, and are his enemies, and
where they will be miserable to all eternity. Now you may think
you are not enemies to God, and do not hate him: But if your
heart has not been changed, and you have not become true
Christians, you certainly are enemies to God, and have been
opposed to him ever since you were born. Many of you, I suppose, never think of this, and are almost as ignorant as the
beasts that perish. Those of you who can read I must beg you to
read the Bible, and whenever you can get time, study the Bible,
and if you can get no other time, spare some of your time from
sleep, and learn what the mind and will of God is. But what
shall I say to them who cannot read. This lay with great weight
on my mind, when I thought of writing to my poor brethren,
but I hope that those who can read will take pity on them and
read what I have to say to them. In hopes of this I will beg of
you to spare no pains in trying to learn to read. If you are once
engaged you may learn. Let all the time you can get be spent in
trying to learn to read. Get those who can read to learn you,
but remember, that what you learn for, is to read the Bible. If
there was no Bible, it would be no matter whether you could
read or not. Reading other books would do you no good. But
the Bible is the word of God, and tells you what you must do to
please God; it tells you how you may escape misery, and be
happy for ever. If you see most people neglect the Bible, and
many that can read never look into it, let it not harden you and
make you think lightly of it, and that it is a book of no worth.
All those who are really good, love the Bible, and meditate on
it day and night. In the Bible God has told us every thing it is
necessary we should know, in order to be happy here and hereafter. The Bible is a revelation of the mind and will of God to
men. Therein we may learn, what God is. That he made all
things by the power of his word; and that he made all things for
his own glory, and not for our glory. That he is over all, and
above all his creatures, and more above them that we can think
or conceive—that they can do nothing without him—that he

upholds them all, and will over-rule all things for his own glory. In the Bible likewise we are told what man is. That he was at first made holy, in the image of God, that he fell from that state of holiness, and became an enemy to God, and that since the fall, all the imaginations of the thoughts of his heart, are evil and only evil, and that continually. That the carnal mind is not subject to the law of God, neither indeed can be. And that all mankind, were under the wrath, and curse of God, and must have been for ever miserable, if they had been left to suffer what their sins deserved. It tells us that God, to save some of mankind, sent his Son into this world to die, in the room and stead of sinners, and that now God can save from eternal misery, all that believe in his Son, and take him for their saviour, and that all are called upon to repent, and believe in Jesus Christ. It tells us that those who do repent, and believe, and are friends to Christ, shall have many trials and sufferings in this world, but that they shall be happy forever, after death, and reign with Christ to all eternity. The Bible tells us that this world is a place of trial, and that there is no other time or place for us to alter, but in this life. If we are Christians when we die, we shall awake to the resurrection of life; if not, we shall awake to the resurrection of damnation. It tells us, we must all live in Heaven or Hell, be happy or miserable, and that without end. The Bible does not tell us of but two places, for all to go to. There is no place for innocent folks, that are not Christians. There is no place for ignorant folks, that did not know how to be Christians. What I mean is, that there is no place besides Heaven and Hell. These two places, will receive all mankind, for Christ says, there are but two sorts, he that is not with me is against me, and he that gathereth not with me, scattereth abroad.—The Bible likewise tells us that this world, and all things in it shall be burnt up—and that "God has appointed a day in which he will judge the world, and that he will bring every secret thing whether it be good or bad into judgment that which is done in secret shall be declared on the house top." I do not know, nor do I think any can tell, but that the day of judgment may last a thousand years. God could tell the state of all his creatures in a moment, but then every thing that every one has done, through his whole life is to be told, before the whole world of angels, and men. There, Oh how solemn is the thought! You, and I, must stand, and hear every thing we have thought or done, however secret, however wicked and vile, told before all the men and women that ever have been, or ever will be, and before all the angels, good and bad.

Now my dear friends seeing the Bible is the word of God, and every thing in it is true, and it reveals such awful and glorious things, what can be more important than that you should learn to read it; and when you have learned to read, that you should study it day and night. There are some things very encouraging in God's word for such ignorant creatures as we are; for God hath not chosen the rich of this world. Not many rich, not many noble are called, but God hath chosen the weak things of this world, and things which are not, to confound the things that are: And when the great and the rich refused coming to the gospel feast, the servant was told, to go into the highways, and hedges, and compel those poor creatures that he found there to come in. Now my brethren it seems to me, that there are no people that ought to attend to the hope of happiness in another world so much as we do. Most of us are cut off from comfort and happiness here in this world, and can expect nothing from It. Now seeing this is the case, why should we not take care to be happy after death. Why should we spend our whole lives in sinning against God: And be miserable in this world, and in the world to come. If we do thus, we shall certainly be the greatest fools. We shall be slaves here, and slaves forever. We cannot plead so great temptations to neglect religion as others. Riches and honours which drown the greater part of mankind, who have the gospel, in perdition, can be little or no temptations to us.

We live so little time in this world that it is no matter how wretched and miserable we are, if it prepares us for heaven. What is forty, fifty, or sixty years, when compared to eternity. When thousands and millions of years have rolled away, this eternity will be no nigher coming to an end. Oh how glorious is an eternal life of happiness! And how dreadful, an eternity of misery. Those of us who have had religious masters, and have been taught to read the Bible, and have been brought by their example and teaching to a sense of divine things, how happy shall we be to meet them in heaven, where we shall join them in praising God forever. But if any of us have had such masters, and yet have lived and died wicked, how will it add to our misery to think of Our folly. If any of us, who have wicked and profane masters should become religious, how will our estates be changed in another world. Oh my friends, let me entreat of you to think on these things, and to live as if you believed them to be true. If you become Christians you will have reason to bless God forever, that you have been brought into a land where you have heard the gospel, though you have been slaves. If we should ever get to Heaven, we shall find nobody to reproach us for being black, or for being slaves. Let me beg of you my dear African brethren, to think very little of your bondage in this life, for your thinking of it will do you no good. If God designs to set us free, he will do it, in his own time, and way; but think of your bondage to sin and Satan, and do not rest, until you are delivered from it. We cannot be happy if we are ever so free or ever so rich, while we are servants of sin, and slaves to Satan. We must be miserable here, and to all eternity. I will conclude what I have to say with a few words to those negroes who have their liberty. The most of what I have said to those who are slaves may be of use to you, but you have more advantages, on some accounts, if you will improve your freedom, as you may do, than they. You have more time to read God's holy word, and to take care of the salvation of your souls. Let me beg of you to spend your time in this way, or it will be better for you, if you had always been slaves. If you think seriously of the matter, you must conclude, that if you do not use your freedom, to promote the salvation of your souls, it will not be of any lasting good to you. Besides all this, if you are idle, and take to bad courses, you will hurt those of your brethren who are slaves, and do all in your power to prevent their being free. Our great reason that is given by some for not freeing us, I understand is, that we should not know how to take care of ourselves, and should take to bad courses. That we should be lazy and idle, and get drunk and steal. Now all those of you, who follow any bad courses, and who do not take care to get an honest living by your labour and industry, are doing more to prevent our being free, than any body else. Let me beg of you then for the sake of your own good and happiness, in time, and for eternity, and for the sake of your poor brethren, who are still in bondage "to lead quiet and peaceable lives in all Godliness and honesty," and may God bless you, and bring you to his kingdom, for Christ's sake, Amen.

* * *

AN EVENING'S IMPROVEMENT, SHEWING THE NECESSITY OF BEHOLDING THE LAMB OF GOD. TO WHICH IS ADDED A DIALOGUE ENTITLED "THE KIND MASTER AND DUTIFUL SERVANT" (1790)

Master.

1.   Come my servant, follow me,
              According to thy place;
         And surely God will be with thee,
              And send thee heav'nly grace.

Servant.

2.   Dear Master, I will follow thee,
              According to thy word,
         And pray that God may be with me,
              And save thee in the Lord.

Master.

3.   My Servant, lovely is the Lord,
              And blest those servants be,
         That truly love his holy word,
              And thus will follow me.

Servant.

4.   Dear Master, that's my whole delight,
              Thy pleasure for to do;
         As for grace and truth's in sight,
              Thus far I'll surely go.

Master.

5.   My Servant, grace proceeds from God,
        And truth should be with thee;
    Whence e'er you find it in his word,
        Thus far come follow me.

Servant.

6.   Dear Master, now without controul,
        I quickly follow thee;
    And pray that God would bless thy soul,
        His heav'nly place to see.

Master.

7.   My Servant, Heaven is high above,
        Yea, higher than the sky:
    I pray that God would grant his love,
        Come follow me thereby.

Servant.

8.   Dear Master, now I'll follow thee,
        And trust upon the Lord;
    The only safety that I see,
        Is Jesus's holy word.

Master.

9.   My Servant, follow Jesus now,
        Our great victorious King;
    Who governs all both high and low,
        And searches things within.

Servant.

10.   Dear Master, I will follow thee,
        When praying to our King;
    It is the Lamb I plainly see,
        Invites the sinner in.

Master.

11.   My Servant, we are sinners all,
        But follow after grace;

> I pray that God would bless thy soul,
>   And fill thy heart with grace.

Servant.

12.   Dear Master I shall follow then,
            The voice of my great King;
        As standing on some distant land,
            Inviting sinners in.

Master.

13.   My servant we must all appear,
            And follow then our King;
        For sure he'll stand where sinners are,
            To take true converts in.

Servant.

14.   Dear Master, now if Jesus calls,
            And sends his summons in;
        We'll follow saints and angels all,
            And come unto our King.

Master.

15.   My servant now come pray to God,
            Consider well his call;
        Strive to obey his holy word,
            That Christ may love us all.

A Line *on the present* war.

Servant.

16.   Dear Master now it is a time,
            A time of great distress;
        We'll follow after things divine,
            And pray for happiness.

Master.

17.   Then will the happy day appear.
            That virtue shall increase;

Lay up the sword and drop the spear,
And Nations seek for peace.

Servant.

18.   Then shall we see the happy end,
Tho' still in some distress;
That distant foes shall act like friends,
And leave their wickedness.

Master.

19.   We pray that God would give us grace,
And make us humble too;
Let ev'ry Nation seek for peace,
And virtue make a show.

Servant.

20.   Then we shall see the happy day,
That virtue is in power;
Each holy act shall have its sway,
Extend from shore to shore.

Master.

21.   This is the work of God's own hand,
We see by precepts given;
To relieve distress and save the land,
Must be the pow'r of heav'n.

Servant.

22.   Now glory be unto our God,
Let ev'ry nation sing;
Strive to obey his holy word,
That Christ may take them in.

Master.

23.   Where endless joys shall never cease,
Blest Angels constant sing;
The glory of their God increase,
Hallelujahs to their King.

Servant.

24.   Thus the Dialogue shall end,
        Strive to obey the word;
    When ev'ry Nation acts like friends,
        Shall be the sons of God.

25.   Believe me now my Christian friends,
        Believe your friend call'd Hammon:
    You cannot to your God attend,
        And serve the God of Mammon.

26.   If God is pleased by his own hand
        To relieve distresses here;
    And grant a peace throughout the the (*sic*) land,
        'Twill be a happy year.

27.   'Tis God alone can give us peace;
        It's not the pow'r of man:
    When virtuous pow'r shall increase,
        'Twill beautify the land.

28.   Then shall we rejoice and sing
        By pow'r of virtues word,
    Come sweet Jesus, heav'nly King,
        Thou art the Son of God.

29.   When virtue comes in bright array,
        Discovers ev'ry sin;
    We see the dangers of the day,
        And fly unto our King.

30.   Now glory be unto our God,
        All praise be justly given;
    Let ev'ry soul obey his word,
        And seek the joy of heav'n.

* * *

"AN ESSAY ON SLAVERY, WITH JUSTIFICATION TO DIVINE PROVIDENCE, THAT GOD RULES OVER ALL THINGS" (1786)

1
Our forefathers came from Africa
Tost over the raging main
To a Christian shore there for to stay
And not return again.

2
Dark and dismal was the Day
When slavery began
All humble thoughts were put away
Then slaves were made by Man.

3
When God doth please for to permit
That slavery should be
It is our duty to submit
Till Christ shall make us free

4
Come let us join with one consent
With humble hearts and say
For every sin we must repent
And walk in wisdom's way.

5
If we are free we'll pray to God
If we are slaves the same
It's firmly fixt in his [holy] word
Ye shall not pray in vain.

6
Come blessed Jesus in thy Love
And hear thy children cry

And send them smiles now from above
And grant them Liberty.

7

Tis thou alone can make us free
We are thy subjects too
Pray give us grace to bend a knee
The time we stay below.

8

Tis unto thee we look for all
Thou art our only King
Thou hast the power to save the soul
And bring us flocking in.

9

We come as sinners unto thee
We know thou hast the word
Come blessed Jesus make us free
And bring us to our God.

10

Although we are in Slavery
We will pray unto our God
He hath mercy beyond the sky
Tis in his holy word.

11

Come unto me ye humble souls
Although you live in strife
I keep alive and save the soul
And give eternal life.

12

To all that do repent of sin
Be they bond or free
I am their saviour and their king
They must come unto me.

13
Hear the words now of the Lord
The call is loud and certain
We must be judged by his word
Without respect of person.

14
Come let us seek his precepts now
And love his holy word
With humble soul we'll surely bow
And wait the great reward.

15
Although we came from Africa
We look unto our God
To help our hearts to sigh and pray
And Love his holy word.

16
Although we are in slavery
Bound by the yoke of Man
We must always have a single eye
And do the best we can.

17
Come let us join with humble voice
Now on the christian shore
If we will have our only choice
Tis slavery no more.

18
Now [?] let us not repine
And say his wheels are slow
He can fill our hearts with things divine
And give us freedom too.

19

He hath the power all in his hand
And all he doth is right
And if we are tide [*sic*] to the yoke of man
We'll pray with all might.

20

This the state of thousands now
Who are on the christian shore
Forget the Lord to whom we bow
And think of him no more.

21

When shall we hear the joyfull sound
Echo the christian shore
Each humble voice with songs resound
That slavery is no more.

22

Then shall we rejoice and sing
Loud praises to our God
Come sweet Jesus heavenly king
Thee art the son Our Lord.

23

We are thy children blessed Lord
Tho still in slavery
We'll seek thy precepts Love thy word
Untill the day we Die.

24

Come blessed Jesus hear us now
And teach our hearts to pray
And seek the Lord to whom we bow
Before tribunal day.

25
Now glory be unto our God
All praise be justly given
Come seek his precepts love his works
That is the way to Heaven.

Composed by Jupiter Hammon
A Negro Man belonging to Mr John Lloyd
Queens Village on Long Island
November 10th 1786

GEORGE HORTON

Born on a North Carolina tobacco plantation, George Horton (1797–1883) was an enslaved poetic savant who composed poems in his head and performed them in the weekly Chapel Hill market and sold acrostic love poems to University of North Carolina students. The novelist Caroline Lee Whiting Hentz befriended Horton and assisted him in transcribing and publishing his works, including The Hope of Liberty *in 1829. Horton was the first African American person to publish a book in the South. As Horton became more famous, North Carolina citizens and the governor appealed for his freedom, but his enslaver would not comply. Instead, Horton learned to read and write and used the proceeds from his publications to purchase his time from his enslaver over the course of thirty years. During this quasi-sabbatical, Horton wrote full time and took on jobs as a handyman and servant. Horton published* The Poetical Works *in 1845 and* Naked Genius *in 1865. Enslaved for some sixty-eight years, he relocated to Philadelphia, Pennsylvania, after the Civil War.*

"On Liberty and Slavery,"
in *Poems by a Slave*
(1837)

ON LIBERTY AND SLAVERY.

Alas! and am I born for this,
  To wear this slavish chain?
Deprived of all created bliss,
  Through hardship, toil and pain!

How long have I in bondage lain,
   And languished to be free!
Alas! and must I still complain—
   Deprived of liberty.

Oh, Heaven! and is there no relief
   This side the silent grave—
To soothe the pain—to quell the grief
   And anguish of a slave?

Come Liberty, thou cheerful sound,
   Roll through my ravished ears!
Come, let my grief in joys be drowned,
   And drive away my fears.

Say unto foul oppression, Cease:
   Ye tyrants rage no more,
And let the joyful trump of peace,
   Now bid the vassal soar.

Soar on the pinions of that dove
   Which long has cooed for thee,
And breathed her notes from Afric's grove,
   The sound of Liberty.

Oh, Liberty! thou golden prize,
   So often sought by blood—
We crave thy sacred sun to rise,
   The gift of nature's God!

Bid Slavery hide her haggard face,
   And barbarism fly:
I scorn to see the sad disgrace
   In which enslaved I lie.

Dear Liberty! upon thy breast,
   I languish to respire;
And like the Swan unto her nest,
   I'd to thy smiles retire.

Oh, blest asylum—heavenly balm!
   Unto thy boughs I flee—
And in thy shades the storm shall calm,
   With songs of Liberty!

THE SLAVE'S COMPLAINT.

Am I sadly cast aside,
On misfortune's rugged tide?
Will the world my pains deride
        For ever?

Must I dwell in Slavery's night,
And all pleasure take its flight,
Far beyond my feeble sight,
        For ever?

Worst of all, must Hope grow dim,
And withhold her cheering beam?
Rather let me sleep and dream
        For ever!

Something still my heart surveys,
Groping through this dreary maze;
Is it Hope?—then burn and blaze
        For ever!

Leave me not a wretch confined,
Altogether lame and blind—
Unto gross despair consigned,
        For ever!

Heaven! in whom can I confide?
Canst thou not for all provide?
Condescend to be my guide
        For ever:

And when this transient life shall end,
Oh, may some kind, eternal friend

Bid me from servitude ascend,
For ever!

LINES,

On hearing of the intention of a gentleman
to purchase the Poet's freedom.

When on life's ocean first I spread my sail,
I then implored a mild auspicious gale;
And from the slippery strand I took my flight,
And sought the peaceful haven of delight.

Tyrannic storms arose upon my soul,
And dreadful did their mad'ning thunders roll;
The pensive muse was shaken from her sphere,
And hope, it vanish'd in the clouds of fear.

At length a golden sun broke through the gloom,
And from his smiles arose a sweet perfume—
A calm ensued, and birds began to sing,
And lo! the sacred muse resumed her wing.

With frantic joy she chaunted as she flew,
And kiss'd the clement hand that bore her through;
Her envious foes did from her sight retreat,
Or prostrate fall beneath her burning feet.

'Twas like a proselyte, allied to Heaven—
Or rising spirits' boast of sins forgiven,
Whose shout dissolves the adamant away,
Whose melting voice the stubborn rocks obey.

'Twas like the salutation of the dove,
Borne on the zephyr through some lonesome grove,
When Spring returns, and Winter's chill is past,
And vegetation smiles above the blast.

'Twas like the evening of a nuptial pair,
When love pervades the hour of sad despair—
'Twas like fair Helen's sweet return to Troy,
When every Grecian bosom swell'd with joy.

The silent harp which on the osiers hung,
Was then attuned, and manumission sung:
Away by hope the clouds of fear were driven,
And music breathed my gratitude to Heaven.

Hard was the race to reach the distant goal,
The needle oft was shaken from the pole;
In such distress who could forbear to weep?
Toss'd by the headlong billows of the deep!

The tantalizing beams which shone so plain,
Which turned my former pleasures into pain—
Which falsely promised all the joys of fame,
Gave way, and to a more substantial flame.

Some philanthropic souls as from afar,
With pity strove to break the slavish bar;
To whom my floods of gratitude shall roll,
And yield with pleasure to their soft control.

And sure of Providence this work begun—
He shod my feet this rugged race to run;
And in despite of all the swelling tide,
Along the dismal path will prove my guide.

Thus on the dusky verge of deep despair,
Eternal Providence was with me there;
When pleasure seemed to fade on life's gay dawn,
And the last beam of hope was almost gone.

JOHN GREENLEAF WHITTIER

A native of Haverhill, Massachusetts, John Greenleaf Whittier (1807–1892) was a Quaker poet and essayist whose fledgling career as a journalist, poet, and political lobbyist began in earnest after he completed high school. A mentee of the influential abolitionist William Lloyd Garrison, who gave him editorial positions for major publications over the course of his early career, Whittier was a founding member of the American Anti-Slavery Society and editor of the antislavery newspaper Pennsylvania Freeman. *Whittier also founded the Liberty Party (later the Free Soil Party) in 1839, whose tenets called for the persistent, strategic lobbying of lawmakers rather than the more common tactic of appealing to the moral sensibilities of individuals as the most effective manner in which to defeat slavery. Whittier's antislavery agitation, then, was multifaceted and consistent. His poems often effusively celebrated Black and white abolitionists and enslaved rebels, called attention to the institution's cruelties, and lamented the nation's hypocrisies regarding natural rights and liberty.*

Selections from *Poems Written During the Progress of the Abolition Question in the United States, Between the Years 1830 and 1838*

(1837)

TO WILLIAM LLOYD GARRISON.

CHAMPION of those who groan beneath
Oppression's iron hand:

In view of penury, hate and death,
  I see thee fearless stand.
Still bearing up thy lofty brow,
  In the steadfast strength of truth,
In manhood sealing well the vow
  And promise of thy youth.

Go on!—for thou hast chosen well;
  On in the strength of God!
Long as one human heart shall swell
  Beneath the tyrant's rod.
Speak in a slumbering nation's ear,
  As thou hast ever spoken,
Until the dead in sin shall hear—
  The fetter's link be broken!

I love thee with a brother's love,
  I feel my pulses thrill,
To mark thy spirit soar above
  The cloud of human ill.
My heart hath leaped to answer thine,
  And echo back thy words,
As leaps the warrior's at the shine
  And flash of kindred swords!

They tell me thou art rash and vain—
  A searcher after fame—
That thou art striving but to gain
  A long enduring name—
That thou hast nerved the Afric's hand,
  And steeled the Afric's heart,
To shake aloft his vengeful brand,
  And rend his chain apart.

Have I not known thee well, and read
  Thy mighty purpose long!
And watched the trials which have made
  Thy human spirit strong?
And shall the *slanderer's demon breath*

Avail with one like me,
To dim the *sunshine of my faith*,
    And earnest trust in thee?

Go on—the dagger's point may glare
    Amid thy pathway's gloom—
The fate which sternly threatens there,
    Is glorious martyrdom!
Then onward with a *martyr's zeal*—
    Press on to thy reward—
The hour when man shall only kneel,
    Before his Father—God.

TOUSSAINT L'OUVERTURE.

THE moon was up. One general smile
Was resting on the Indian isle—
Mild—pure—ethereal; rock and wood,
In searching sunshine, wild and rude,
Rose, mellowed through the silver gleam,
Soft as the landscape of a dream:
All motionless and dewy wet,
Tree, vine, and flower in shadow met:
The myrtle with its snowy bloom,
Crossing the nightshade's solemn gloom—
The white crecopia's silver rhind
Relieved by deeper green behind—
The orange with its fruit of gold,—
The little paullinia's verdant fold,—
The passion-flower, with symbol holy,
Twining its tendrils long and lowly,—
The rhexias dark, and cassia tall,
And, proudly rising over all,
The kingly palm's imperial stem,
Crowned with its leafy diadem,—
Star-like, beneath whose sombre shade,
The fiery-winged cucullo played!

Yes—lovely was thine aspect, then,
   Fair island of the Western Sea!—
Lavish of beauty, even when
Thy brutes were happier than thy men,
   For *they*, at least, were *free!*
Regardless of thy glorious clime,
   Unmindful of thy soil of flowers,
The toiling negro sighed, that Time
   No faster sped his hours.
For, by the dewy moonlight still,
He fed the weary-turning mill,
Or bent him in the chill morass,
To pluck the long and tangled grass,
And hear above his scar-worn back
The heavy slave-whip's frequent crack;—
While in his heart one evil thought
In solitary madness wrought,—
One baleful fire surviving still,
   The quenching of th' immortal mind—
   One sterner passion of his kind,
Which even fetters could not kill,—
The savage hope, to deal, ere long,
A vengeance bitterer than his wrong!

Hark to that cry!—long, loud and shrill,
From field and forest, rock and hill,
Thrilling and horrible it rung,
   Around, beneath, above;—
The wild beast from his cavern sprung—
   The wild bird from her grove!
Nor fear, nor joy, nor agony
Were mingled in that midnight cry;
But, like the lion's growl of wrath,
When falls that hunter in his path,
Whose barbed arrow, deeply set,
Is rankling in his bosom yet,
It told of hate, full, deep and strong,—
Of vengeance kindling out of wrong;

It was as if the crimes of years—
The agony—the toil—the tears—
The shame and hate, which liken well
Earth's garden to the nether hell,
Had found in Nature's self a tongue,
On which the gathered horror hung;
As if from cliff, and stream, and glen,
Burst, on the startled ears of men,
That voice which rises unto God—
Solemn and stern—the cry of blood!

It ceased—and all was still once more,
Save ocean chafing on his shore—
The sighing of the wind between
The broad banana's leaves of green—
Or, bough by restless plumage shook—
Or, distant brawl of mountain brook.

Brief was the silence.   Once again
    Pealed to the skies that frantic yell—
Glowed on the heavens a fiery stain,
    And flashes rose and fell;
And, painted on the blood-red sky,
Dark, naked arms were tossed on high;
And, round the white man's lordly hall,
    Trode, fierce and free, *the brute he made*,
And those who crept along the wall,
And answered to his lightest call
    With more than spaniel dread.
The creatures of his lawless beck
Were trampling on his very neck!
And, on the night-air, wild and clear,
Rose woman's shriek of more than fear;
For bloodied arms were round her thrown,
And dark cheeks pressed against her own!

Then, injured Afric, for the shame
Of thy own daughters, vengeance came
Full on the scornful hearts of those,

Who mocked thee in thy nameless woes,
And to thy hapless children gave
One choice—pollution, or the grave!

Dark-browed Toussaint!—the storm had risen
    Obedient to his master-call—
The Negro's mind had burst its prison—
    His hand its iron thrall!
Yet where was he, whose fiery zeal
First taught the trampled heart to feel,
Until despair itself grew strong,
And vengeance fed its torch from wrong?
Now—when the thunder-bolt is speeding—
Now—when oppression's heart is bleeding—
Now—when the latent curse of Time
    Is raining down in fire and blood—
That curse, which through long years of crime,
    Had gathered, drop by drop, its flood:
Why strikes he not the foremost one,
Where Murder's sternest deeds are done?

He stood the aged palms beneath,
    That shadowed o'er his humble door,
Listening, with half-suspended breath,
To the wild sounds of fear and death—
    —Toussaint l'Ouverture!
What marvel that his heart beat high!
    The blow for freedom had been given;
And blood had answered to the cry
    Which earth sent up to heaven!
What marvel, that a fierce delight
Smiled grimly o'er his brow of night,
As groan, and shout, and bursting flame,
Told where the midnight tempest came;
With blood and fire along its van,
And death behind!—he was a MAN!

Yes—dark-souled chieftain!—if the light
    Of mild Religion's heavenly ray

Unveiled not to thy mental sight
   The lowlier and the purer way,
In which the Holy Sufferer trod,
   Meekly amidst the sons of crime,—
That calm reliance upon God
   For justice, in his own good time,—
That gentleness, to which belongs
   Forgiveness for its many wrongs;
Even as the primal martyr, kneeling
For mercy on the evil-dealing,—
Let not the favored white man name
Thy stern appeal, with words of blame.
Has *he* not, with the light of heaven
   Broadly around him, made the same—
Yea,—on a thousand war-fields striven,
   And gloried in his open shame?
Kneeling amidst his brothers' blood,
To offer mockery unto God,
As if the High and Holy One
Could smile on deeds of murder done!—
As if a human sacrifice
Were purer in His holy eyes,
Though offered up by Christian hands,
Than the foul rites of Pagan lands!

        *   *   *   *   *

Sternly, amidst his household band,
His carbine grasped within his hand,
   The white man stood, prepared and still,
Waiting the shock of maddened men,
Unchained, and fierce as tigers, when
   The horn winds through their caverned hill.
And one was weeping in his sight,—
   The fairest flower of all the isle,—
The bride who seemed but yesternight
   The image of a smile.
And, clinging to her trembling knee,

Looked up the form of infancy,
With tearful glance in either face,
The secret of its fear to trace.

'Ha—stand, or die!' The white man's eye
 His steady musket gleamed along,
As a tall Negro hastened nigh,
 With fearless step and strong.
'What ho, Toussaint!' A moment more,
His shadow crossed the lighted floor.
'Away,' he shouted; 'fly with me,—
The white man's bark is on the sea;—
Her sails must catch the landward wind,
For sudden vengeance sweeps behind.
Our brethren from their graves have spoken,
The yoke is spurned—the chain is broken;
On all the hills our fires are glowing—
Through all the vales red blood is flowing!
No more the mocking White shall rest
His foot upon the Negro's breast;—
No more, at morn or eve, shall drip
The warm blood from the driver's whip:—
Yet, though Toussaint has vengeance sworn
For all the wrongs his race have borne,—
Though for each drop of Negro blood,
The white man's veins shall pour a flood;
Not all alone the sense of ill
Around his heart is lingering still,
Nor deeper can the white man feel
The generous warmth of grateful zeal.
Friends of the Negro! fly with me—
The path is open to the sea:
Away, for life!'—He spoke, and pressed
The young child to his manly breast,
As, headlong, through the cracking cane,
Down swept the dark insurgent train—
Drunken and grim—with shout and yell
Howled through the dark, like sounds from hell!

Far out, in peace, the white man's sail
Swayed free before the sunrise gale.
Cloud-like that island hung afar,
   Along the bright horizon's verge,
O'er which the curse of servile war
   Rolled its red torrent, surge on surge.
And he—the Negro champion—where
   In the fierce tumult, struggled he?
Go trace him by the fiery glare
Of dwellings in the midnight air—
The yells of triumph and despair—
   The streams that crimson to the sea!

Sleep calmly in thy dungeon-tomb,*
   Beneath Besancon's alien sky,
Dark Haytian!—for the time shall come,—
   Yea, even now is nigh—
When, every where, thy name shall be
Redeemed from *color's infamy;*
And men shall learn to speak of thee,

---

*The reader may, perhaps, call to mind the beautiful sonnet of William Wordsworth, addressed to Toussaint l'Ouverture, during his confinement in France.

   'Toussaint!—thou most unhappy man of men!
      Whether the whistling rustic tends his plough
      Within thy hearing, or thou liest now
   Buried in some deep dungeon's earless den;—
   Oh, miserable chieftain!—where and when
      Wilt thou find patience?—Yet, die not; do thou
      Wear rather in thy bonds a cheerful brow:
   Though fallen thyself never to rise again,
   Live and take comfort. Thou hast left behind
      Powers that will work for thee; air, earth, and skies,—
   There's not a breathing of the common wind
      That will forget thee: thou hast great allies.
   Thy friends are exultations, agonies,
      And love, and man's unconquerable mind.'

As one of earth's great spirits, born
In servitude, and nursed in scorn,
Casting aside the weary weight
And fetters of its low estate,
In that strong majesty of soul,
    Which knows no color, tongue or clime—
Which still hath spurned the base control
    Of tyrants through all time!
For other hands than mine may wreath
The laurel round thy brow of death,
And speak thy praise, as one whose word
A thousand fiery spirits stirred,—
Who crushed his foeman as a worm—
Whose step on human hearts fell firm:—
Be mine the better task to find
A tribute for thy lofty mind,
Amidst whose gloomy vengeance shone
Some milder virtues all thine own,—
Some gleams of feeling pure and warm,
Like sunshine on a sky of storm,—
Proofs that the Negro's heart retains
Some nobleness amidst its chains,—
That kindness to the wronged is never
    Without its excellent reward,—
Holy to human-kind, and ever
    Acceptable to God.

EDWIN F. HATFIELD

Edwin F. Hatfield (1807–1883) was born in Elizabethtown, New Jersey. A writer and minister, Hatfield was commissioned by the executive committee of the American Anti-Slavery Society to compile a volume of hymns to be sold in support of "the holy cause of Emancipation." Included in the thematically organized Freedom's Lyre *are psalms, lyric devotionals, and verses by Hatfield and well-known and unknown sources, many of whom had their works published in other antislavery publications.*

Selections from *Freedom's Lyre; or, Psalms, Hymns, and Sacred Songs for the Slave and His Friends* (1840)

CRIES OF THE SLAVE.

1   **C. M.**

Pleading that God would help, as of old.

1   How long, Most Holy, Just, and True!
              Dost THOU our blood behold?
           Nor rise th' oppressor to subdue,
              As in the days of old?

2   Where is the Pow'r, that led thy seed
              From Egypt's blighted plains,
           Their limbs from cruel bondage freed,
              Their souls from direr chains?

3   Where is the Mighty Arm, that clave
            The waters of the sea,
        And bade the wild unsteady wave
            A wall of safety be?

4   Where is the Hand, that brake the pow'r
            Of proud Assyria's host,
        Went forth at midnight's silent hour,
            And laid their strength in dust?

5   Not shorten'd is thine Arm to save,
            Not clos'd thine Ear to hear;
        Soon for the crush'd and bleeding Slave
            Jehovah will appear.

6   Then Man shall own his strength is weak,
            And God exalted be:
        Our iron bondage he will brake
        AND EV'RY SLAVE SET FREE.
                        Wrongs of Africa.

---

2   **C. M.**

In times of great extremity.—Psalm 102.

1   Hear me, O God! nor hide thy face,
            But answer, lest I die;
        Hast thou not built a throne of grace,
            To hear when sinners cry?

2   My days are wasted like the smoke,
            Dissolving in the air;
         My strength is dried, my heart is broke,
            And sinking in despair.

3   My spirits flag, like with'ring grass,
            Burnt with excessive heat;
        In secret groans my minutes pass,
            And I forget to eat.

4   As on some lonely building's top,
             The sparrow tells her moan;
         Far from the tents of joy and hope,
             I sit and grieve alone.

---

21   8s. & 3s.

                    The slave's complaint.

1   And am I sadly cast aside,
         On dire misfortune's rugged tide,
         And will the world my pains deride
                 Forever?
         Must I still dwell in Slavery's night,
         And ev'ry pleasure take its flight,
         Far—far beyond my feeble sight,
                 Forever?

2   Or, worst of all! must hope grow dim,
         And thus withhold her cheering beam?
         Oh! rather let me sleep and dream
                 Forever!
         Yet leave me not a wretch confin'd,
         Oppress'd, and shackled, lame, and blind,
         To sorrow and despair consign'd
                 Forever!

3   Great God! in whom can I confide?
         Say—canst thou not for all provide?
         Oh! condescend to be my guide
                 Forever!
         And when this transient life shall end,
         May Jesus, my eternal friend,
         Bid me from servitude ascend,
                 Forever!

                                        James Horton.

22   C. M.

                    "And am I born for this?"

1   Alas! and am I born for this—
            To wear this slavish chain?
         Depriv'd of all created bliss,
            Through hardship, toil, and pain!

2   How long have I in bondage lain,
            And languish'd to be free!
         Alas! and must I still complain,
            Depriv'd of liberty?

3   O Heav'n! and is there no relief
            This side the silent grave,
         To sooth the pain, to quell the grief
            And anguish of a slave?

4   Come, Liberty—thou cheerful sound!
            Roll through my ravish'd ears;
         Come let my grief in joy be drown'd,
            And drive away my fears.

5   Say unto foul oppression—Cease!
            Ye tyrants! rage no more;
         And let the joyful trump of peace,
            Now bid the vassal soar.

6   O Liberty—thou golden prize,
            So often sought by blood!
         We crave thy sacred sun to rise—
            The gift of nature's God.

                                        James Horton.

36   C. M.

The little slave's complaint.

1   Who loves the little slave, or cares
     If well or ill I be?
    Is there a living soul, that shares
     A thought or wish for me?

2   I've had no parents since my birth,
     Brothers and sisters—none!
    Oh! what is all this world to me
     When I am only one?

3   I wake, and see the sun arise,
     And all around me gay;
    But nothing I behold is mine,
     No—not the life of day!

4   No—not the very breath I draw,
     These limbs are not my own;
    A master calls me his *by law*,
     My griefs are mine alone.

5   'Tis not for wealth or ease I sigh,
     But few are rich and great;
    Many may be as poor as I,
     But none so desolate.

60   C. M.

The Lord will repay oppressors.—Psalm 94.

1   'Tis sweet, though in affliction's path,
     Thy ways to learn, O Lord!
    Resign'd, through darkest days of wrath,
     To wait thy sure award.

2   For thou wilt not thine own forsake,
           Nor cast away thy saints;
       The throne of judgment thou wilt take,
           And banish their complaints.

3   Canst thou with vile oppressors dwell,
           Who legalize their guilt?
       The helpless sons of want they sell;
           And, ah! what blood they've spilt!

4   Thou, Lord! wilt make thy dreadful wrath
           On their own heads rebound;
       Wilt pour thy vengeance on their path,
           And all their plans confound.

                                     E. F. H.

---

62   C. M. D.

The dying slave.

"I die, and God will surely visit you."—*Gen. 50: 24.*

1   My cruel chain! I mourn not now,
           To wear thy galling link;
       The damps of death are on my brow,
           And fast my pulses sink;
       And when this tortur'd frame shall lie,
           Within the silent grave,
       'Twill little move my soul, that I
           Have liv'd and died a *Slave.*

2   SLAVE! I shall know the name no more—
           Free, as Salvation, free!
       Free, as an angel's wing can soar,
           I shall forever be.
       Adoring at the Throne of Light,
           With freedom's voice I'll sing—
       "Blessing and Honor, Pow'r and Might,
           "To Christ, the Savior, King!"

3   Brethren in bondage! fare ye well!
           Too late—too late for me,
       The promis'd hour, whose voice shall tell,
           That ev'ry slave is FREE.
       And thousands more my grave shall share,
           While Freedom's friends delay,
       Nor drop the fetters that they wear,
           Till they have dropp'd their clay.
                                   Wrongs of Africa.

---

76   C. M.

                 The Guilt of Prejudice.

1   Forgive me, Lord! for in my pride,
           I scorn'd the Ethiop's race;
       And thought they were too darkly dy'd
           To have a brother's place.

2   And when the bondman wept and cried,—
           "Help! Help! thy brother save!"—
       "Peace! wretched one!" I sharp replied:
           "God made thee thus a slave."

3   Thus, from the image of my God,
           The offspring of his breath,
       The object of a Savior's love,
           The purchase of his death.

4   I turned away; and proudly pray'd,
           "I thank thee, God of grace!
       That I of better earth was made,
           Than Ham's accursed race."

5   O Lord! my pride I now confess,
           With shame, before thy feet;
       I'll vanquish all my haughtiness,
           And take the lowest seat.

6 No more the injur'd slave shall pine,
  While none his sorrows move;
 His wounds I'll soothe with oil and wine,
  His aching heart with *love*.

---

78   **C. M.**

Blood upon all the South.

1 Unshelter'd from the burning rays,
  The panting bondman lies,
 Toil and the scourge cut short his days,
  He sinks—he faints—he dies!

2 No Wife's—no Mother's hand is there,
  To close his failing eyes;
 Unsooth'd by Friendship's tender care,
  The wretched bondman dies!

3 He dies—not by the *single* hand,
  That gave the mortal blow—
 His blood is on the guilty *band*,
  Who reckless bade it flow.

4 Ye Masters! rise, and purge the stain,
  A freeman's rights bestow;
 Else God will burst the bondman's chain,
  And fill yourselves with woe.

WILLIAM WELLS BROWN

William Wells Brown (1815–1884) was an abolitionist, lecturer, playwright, and novelist who was born enslaved in Montgomery County, Kentucky. When he was nineteen years old, Brown escaped from slavery and made the free state of Ohio his home for some time before settling in Boston, Massachusetts. A renowned writer, Brown is thought to be the first African American to publish a novel with his Clotel; or, the President's Daughter, *the story of the fictional mixed-race daughters of Thomas Jefferson, whose actual abusive relationship with his wife's half sister and his slave Sally Hemings had long been rumored and was later confirmed. Brown was also the first published African American playwright. On the antislavery lecture circuit, Brown was known for splicing in and/or concluding his powerful oratory by performing antislavery songs. With the passage of the Fugitive Slave Act of 1850, Brown fled the United States for London, where he found safety and solace in his abolitionist friends, two of whom purchased his freedom in 1854. The* Anti-Slavery Harp: A Collection of Songs for Anti-Slavery Meetings *is an anthology of songs and poetic verse that affectively appeals to listeners and singers alike. The works selected here reflect enslaved people's suffering, offer passionate critiques of enslavers, and rally abolitionist-minded individuals to continue their appeals for liberation and equality.*

Selections from *The Anti-Slavery Harp:*
A Collection of Songs for
Anti-Slavery Meetings (1849)

THE LIBERTY BALL.

AIR—Rosin the Bow.

Come all ye true friends of the nation,
    Attend to humanity's call;
Come aid the poor slave's liberation,
    And roll on the liberty ball—
    And roll on the liberty ball—
Come aid the poor slave's liberation,
    And roll on the liberty ball.

The liberty hosts are advancing—
    For freedom to all they declare;
The down-trodden millions are sighing—
    Come break up our gloom of despair.
    Come break up our gloom of despair, &c.

Ye Democrats, come to the rescue,
    And aid on the liberty cause,
And millions will rise up and bless you,
    With heart-cheering songs of applause,
    With heart-cheering songs, &c.

SONG FOR THE TIMES.

I hear the cry of millions, of millions, of millions,
I hear the cry of millions, of millions in bonds;
Oh! set the captive free, set him free, set him free,
Oh! set the captive free from his chains.

I hear the voice of Garrison, of Garrison, of Garrison,
I hear the voice of Garrison, loud pleading for the slave;

Oh! set the captive free, set him free, set him free,
Oh! set the captive free from his chains.

I hear the voice of Phillips, of Phillips, of Phillips,
I hear the voice of Phillips, in strain of eloquence;
Oh! set the captive free, set him free, set him free,
Oh! set the captive free from his chains.

I hear the voice of Foster, of Foster, of Foster,
I hear the voice of Foster, against the priesthood;
Oh! set the captive free, set him free, set him free,
Oh! set the captive free from his chains.

I hear the voice of Pillsbury, of Pillsbury, of Pillsbury,
I hear the voice of Pillsbury, with all his sarcasm;
Oh! set the captive free, set him free, set him free,
Oh! set the captive free from his chains.

I hear the voice of Remond, of Remond, of Remond,
I hear the voice of Remond, on prejudice 'gainst color;
Oh! set the captive free, set him free, set him free,
Oh! set the captive free from his chains.

I hear the voice of Buffum, of Buffum, of Buffum,
I hear the voice of Buffum, with a few more facts;
Oh! set the captive free, set him free, set him free,
Oh! set the captive free from his chains.

I hear the voice of Quincy, of Quincy, of Quincy,
I hear the voice of Quincy, in words of living truth,
Oh! set the captive free, set him free, set him free,
Oh! set the captive free from his chains.

I hear the voice of Walker, of Walker, of Walker,
I hear the voice of Walker, and see his "Branded Hand;"
Oh! set the captive free, set him free, set him free,
Oh! set the captive free from his chains.

I hear the voice of Giddings, of Giddings, of Giddings,
I hear the voice of Giddings, in Congress, for the slave;
Oh! set the captive free, set him free, set him free,
Oh! set the captive free from his chains.

I hear the voice of thousands, of thousands, of thousands,
I hear the voice of thousands, in favor of "Disunion;"
Oh! set the captive free, set him free, set him free,
Oh! set the captive free from his chains.

From Tait's Edinburgh Magazine.

JEFFERSON'S DAUGHTER.

"It is asserted, on the authority of an American newspaper, that the daughter of Thomas Jefferson, late President of the United States, was sold at New Orleans for $1,000."—Morning Chronicle.

Can the blood that at Lexington poured o'er the plain,
   When the sons warred with tyrants their rights to uphold,
Can the tide of Niagara wipe out the stain?
   No! Jefferson's child has been bartered for gold!

Do you boast of your freedom? Peace, babblers—be still;
   Prate not of the goddess who scarce deigns to hear;
Have ye power to unbind? Are ye wanting in will?
   Must the groans of your bondman still torture the ear?

The daughter of Jefferson sold for a slave!
   The child of a freeman for dollars and francs!
The roar of applause, when your orators rave,
   Is lost in the sound of her chain, as it clanks.

Peace, then, ye blasphemers of Liberty's name!
   Though red was the blood by your forefathers spilt,

Still redder your cheeks should be mantled with shame,
  Till the spirit of freedom shall cancel the guilt.

But the brand of the slave is the tint of his skin,
  Though his heart may beat loyal and true underneath;
While the soul of the tyrant is rotten within,
  And his white the mere cloak to the blackness of death.

Are ye deaf to the plaints that each moment arise?
  Is it thus ye forget the mild precepts of Penn,—
Unheeding the clamor that "maddens the skies,"
  As ye trample the rights of your dark fellow-men?

When the incense that glows before Liberty's shrine,
  Is unmixed with the blood of the galled and oppressed,—
O, then, and then only, the boast may be thine,
  That the stripes and stars wave o'er a land of the blest.

SONG OF THE COFFLE GANG.

*This song is said to be sung by Slaves, as they are chained in
gangs, when parting from friends for the far-off South—
children taken from parents, husbands from wives,
and brothers from sisters.*

See these poor souls from Africa,
  Transported to America:
We are stolen and sold to Georgia, will you go along with me?
We are stolen and sold to Georgia, go sound the jubilee.

See wives and husbands sold apart,
  The children's screams!—it breaks my heart;
There's a better day a coming, will you go along with me?
There's a better day a coming, go sound the jubilee.

O, gracious Lord! when shall it be,
  That we poor souls shall all be free?

Lord, break them Slavery powers—will you go along with me?
Lord, break them Slavery powers, go sound the jubilee.

Dear Lord! dear Lord! when Slavery'll cease,
Then we poor souls can have our peace;
There's a better day a coming, will you go along with me?
There's a better day a coming, go sound the jubilee.

LAMENT OF THE FUGITIVE SLAVE.

*"My child, we must soon part to meet no more this side of
the grave. You have ever said that you would not die a slave;
that you would be a freeman. Now try to get your
liberty!"*—W. W. Brown's Narrative.

I've wandered out beneath the moon-lit heaven,
    Lost mother! loved and dear,
To every beam a magic power seems given
    To bring thy spirit near;
For though the breeze of freedom fans my brow,
My soul still turns to thee! oh, where art thou?

Where art thou, mother? I am weary thinking;
    A heritage of pain and woe
Was thine,—beneath it art thou slowly sinking,
    Or hast thou perished long ago?
And doth thy spirit 'mid the quivering leaves above me,
Hover, dear mother, near, to guard and love me?

I murmur at my lot; in the white man's dwelling
    The mother there is found;
Or he may tell where spring buds first are swelling
    Above her lowly mound;
But thou,—lost mother, every trace of thee
In the vast sepulchre of Slavery!

Long years have fled, since sad, faint-hearted,
    I stood on Freedom's shore,

And knew, dear mother, from thee I was parted
    To meet thee never more;
And deemed the tyrant's chain with thee were better
Than stranger hearts and limbs without a fetter.

Yet blessings on thy Roman-mother spirit;
    Could I forget it, then,
The parting scene, and struggle not to inherit
    A freeman's birth-right once again?
O noble words! O holy love which gave
Thee strength to utter them, a poor, heart-broken slave!

Be near me, mother, be thy spirit near me,
    Wherever thou may'st be,
In hours like this bend near that I may hear thee,
    And know that thou art free;
Summoned at length from bondage, toil and pain,
To God's free world, a world without a chain!

THE BIGOT FIRE.

Written on the occasion of George Latimer's imprisonment in Leverett street Jail, Boston.

O kindle not that bigot fire,
    'Twill bring disunion, fear and pain;
'Twill rouse at last the souther's ire,
    And burst our starry land in twain.

Theirs is the high, the noble worth,
    The very soul of chivalry;
Rend not our blood-bought land apart,
    For such a thing as slavery.

This is the language of the North,
    I shame to say it, but 'tis true;
And anti-slavery calls it forth,
    From some proud priests and laymen too.

What! bend forsooth to southern rule?
   What! cringe and crawl to souther's clay,
And be the base, the supple tool,
   Of hell-begotten slavery?

No! Never, while the free air plays
   O'er our rough hills and sunny fountains,
Shall proud New England's sons be *free*,
   And clank their fetters round her mountains.

Go if ye will and grind in dust,
   Dark Afric's poor, degraded child;
Wring from his sinews gold accursed,
   And boast your gospel warm and mild.

While on our mountain tops the pine
   In freedom her green branches wave,
Her sons shall never stoop to bind
   The galling shackle of the slave.

Ye dare demand with haughty tone
   For us to pander to your shame,
To give our brother up alone,
   To feel the lash and wear the chain.

Our brother never shall go back,
   When once he presses our free shore;
Though souther's power with hell to back,
   Comes thundering at our northern door.

No! rather be our starry land
   Into a thousand fragments riven;
Upon our own free hills we'll stand,
   And pour upon the breeze of heaven,
A curse so loud, so stern, so deep,
Shall start ye in your guilty sleep.

FRANCES ELLEN WATKINS HARPER

Born in Baltimore, Maryland, Frances Ellen Watkins Harper (1825–1911) was an abolitionist, suffragist, antislavery essayist and orator, poet, novelist, and teacher. A member of the American Anti-Slavery Society, Harper was an active member of the Pennsylvania Anti-Slavery Society and participated in its major endeavor: the Underground Railroad. In her 1859 essay "Our Greatest Want," Harper proclaimed, "It is no honor to shake hands politically with men who whip women and steal babies." Harper's abolitionist poetry was similarly sharp-witted yet heartrending, drawing sympathy and visceral responses from its readers and hearers. The author of some eighty published poems, some of which are collected in her most popular book, Poems on Miscellaneous Subjects, *Harper is also the author of the well-regarded novel of passing and gendered strife,* Iola Leroy; or, Shadows Uplifted.

Selections from
Poems on Miscellaneous Subjects (1857)

ELIZA HARRIS.

Like a fawn from the arrow, startled and wild,
A woman swept by us, bearing a child;
In her eye was the night of a settled despair,
And her brow was o'ershaded with anguish and care.

She was nearing the river—in reaching the brink,
She heeded no danger, she paused not to think;
For she is a mother—her child is a slave—
And she'll give him his freedom, or find him a grave!

It was a vision to haunt us, that innocent face—
So pale in its aspect, so fair in its grace;
As the tramp of the horse and the bay of the hound,
With the fetters that gall, were trailing the ground!

She was nerv'd by despair, and strengthened by woe,
As she leap'd o'er the chasms that yawn'd from below;
Death howl'd in the tempest, and rav'd in the blast,
But she heard not the sound till the danger was past.

Oh! how shall I speak of my proud country's shame?
Of the stains on her glory, how give them their name?
How say that her banner in mockery waves—
Her "star spangled banner"—o'er millions of slaves?

How say that the lawless may torture and chase
A woman whose crime is the hue of her face?
How the depths of the forest may echo around
With the shrieks of despair, and the bay of the hound?

With her step on the ice, and her arm on her child,
The danger was fearful, the pathway was wild;
But, aided by Heaven, she gained a free shore,
Where the friends of humanity open'd their door.

So fragile and lovely, so fearfully pale,
Like a lily that bends to the breath of the gale,
Save the heave of her breast, and the sway of her hair,
You'd have thought her a statue of fear and despair.

In agony close to her bosom she press'd
The life of her heart, the child of her breast:—
Oh! love from its tenderness gathering might,
Had strengthen'd her soul for the dangers of flight.

But she's free!— yes, free from the land where the slave
From the hand of oppression must rest in the grave;
Where bondage and torture, where scourges and chains
Have plac'd on our banner indelible stains.

The bloodhounds have miss'd the scent of her way;
The hunter is rifled and foil'd of his prey;
Fierce jargon and cursing, with clanking of chains,
Make sounds of strange discord on Liberty's plains.

With the rapture of love and fulness of bliss,
She plac'd on his brow a mother's fond kiss:—
Oh! poverty, danger and death she can brave,
For the child of her love is no longer a slave!

ETHIOPIA.

Yes! Ethiopia yet shall stretch
    Her bleeding hands abroad;
Her cry of agony shall reach
    The burning throne of God.

The tyrant's yoke from off her neck,
    His fetters from her soul,
The mighty hand of God shall break,
    And spurn the base control.

Redeemed from dust and freed from chains,
    Her sons shall lift their eyes;
From cloud-capt hills and verdant plains
    Shall shouts of triumph rise.

Upon her dark, despairing brow,
    Shall play a smile of peace;
For God shall bend unto her wo,
    And bid her sorrows cease.

'Neath sheltering vines and stately palms
    Shall laughing children play,
And aged sires with joyous psalms
    Shall gladden every day.

Secure by night, and blest by day,
　　Shall pass her happy hours;
Nor human tigers hunt for prey
　　Within her peaceful bowers.

Then, Ethiopia! stretch, oh! stretch
　　Thy bleeding hands abroad;
Thy cry of agony shall reach
　　And find redress from God.

THE TENNESSEE HERO.

*"He had heard his comrades plotting to obtain their liberty,
and rather than betray them he received 750 lashes and died."*

He stood before the savage throng,
　　The base and coward crew;
A tameless light flashed from his eye,
　　His heart beat firm and true.

He was the hero of his band,
　　The noblest of them all;
Though fetters galled his weary limbs,
　　His spirit spurned their thrall.

And towered, in its manly might,
　　Above the murderous crew.
Oh! liberty had nerved his heart,
　　And every pulse beat true.

"Now tell us," said the savage troop,
　　"And life thy gain shall be!
Who are the men that plotting, say—
　　'They must and will be free!'"

Oh, could you have seen the hero then,
　　As his lofty soul arose,

And his dauntless eyes defiance flashed
  On his mean and craven foes!

"I know the men who would be free;
  They are the heroes of your land;
But death and torture I defy,
  Ere I betray that band.

And what! oh, what is life to me,
  Beneath your base control?
Nay! do your worst. Ye have no chains
  To bind my free-born soul."

They brought the hateful lash and scourge,
  With murder in each eye.
But a solemn vow was on his lips—
  He had resolved to die.

Yes, rather than betray his trust,
  He'd meet a death of pain;
'T was sweeter far to meet it thus
  Than wear a treason stain!

Like storms of wrath, of hate and pain,
  The blows rained thick and fast;
But the monarch soul kept true
  Till the gates of life were past.

And the martyr spirit fled
  To the throne of God on high,
And showed his gaping wounds
  Before the unslumbering eye.

Children's Literature

Published by the American Anti-Slavery Society beginning in 1837, The American Anti-Slavery Almanac *included astronomical features and weather predictions alongside abolitionist propaganda—speeches, essays, fiction, poetry, and reports of abolitionist activities—about the horrors of slavery and the need for sustained action. The publication's Children's Department presented short-form content about slavery, manners, and respectability to young readers.*

From *The American Anti-Slavery Almanac* for 1837's "Children's Department"
(1837)

CHILDREN'S DEPARTMENT,

A TALK WITH MY YOUNG READERS

"Little children, love one another."
"Despise not one of these little ones."
Fleecy locks and black complexion
Cannot alter nature's claim;
Skins may differ, but affection
Dwells in white and black the same.

Here is a picture of two little sisters. They love each other very much. Slave-holders sometimes tear such little children away from their parents, and sell them to cruel men who will never let them see their mothers while they live. When you see your kind mother smile sweetly upon you, as you are engaged in your sports, or when she gives you the parting kiss, as you go to your quiet bed, O think of the hapless slave mother, who is in constant alarm, lest the kidnapper should seize her darling babe. When you kneel down at night, pray for the helpless slave child, and its trembling mother.

THE AFFECTIONATE SISTER.

There was once a little colored girl in Boston who used often to come into a house in Hancock street, to see if there were any broken victuals left, which she might carry home to her mother and brother. One day when she was in the kitchen, the mistress of the house brought out a little piece of pudding, and told her she had better eat it there. "No I thank you," said she, "I would much rather give my brother half of it than to eat it alone."

TEMPTATION RESISTED.

Communicated by Miss SUSAN PAUL, of Boston.

Jane—What is that the picture of, Miss Paul?

Miss P.—It represents what took place one morning when three little children were coming to my school. The largest child in the picture, an interesting boy about seven years of age, on entering school one day, came to me and said, "Miss Paul, a woman in the street gave Frederick and Amelia (his brother and a little girl who came to school with him) each an apple, but I took them both from them and put them in the cart." "Why did you take them from them?" said I. "Because they did not belong to the woman," said he. "She took them out of a cart that stood in the street, and after she had given them to us she ran away, and I knew she had broken the eighth commandment." I then asked him what it was? "Thou shalt not steal," said he, with earnestness. The children to whom the apples were given being considerably younger than he was, I asked him if they did not cry when he took them from them? "No," said he, "*I told them they were stolen.*" He spoke this as if he thought it a sufficient reason why they should give them up. This was more than I expected from one so young, and I could only clasp him to my bosom, and imprint a kiss on his forehead, breathing a wish that those who scruple not to buy and sell innocent men, women and children, *knowing them to have been stolen*, would learn a lesson from the example of this little colored boy.

In the picture you see the largest boy throwing back the apple given to him, while the others hold apples in their hands.

Slave-holders, and many who are not slave-holders, often tell us we cannot *prove* that it is *wicked* to hold slaves. I guess that if that woman had taken *all* the apples, and every thing else the man had, and *the man himself*, the little boy, and every other honest person would say at once that she was very wicked, and had done a great deal that was forbidden in the eighth commandment.

A MOTHER'S ANGUISH.

CAROLINE What is that woman doing, uncle?

MR. S. She has an axe in her hand, with which she is killing those little children.

CAR. What made her hate them so? What had they done to her?

MR. S. She did n't hate them, my dear.

CAR. I should think she did. What *did* she kill them for?

MR. S. I will tell you. She was a slave. She lived in the state of Missouri, a state seven times as large as Massachusetts, and a thousand miles from here. Those are her own little children, and she loved them very much. When she came home at night, from her day's hard labor, she always hastened to meet her children. It made her feel happy and forget her wretched lot, when she saw them run smiling to meet her, and hold out their little hand to take hold of hers, as you do when your father comes home.

CAR. My mother loves me, too, but she would n't kill me.

MR. S. You ought to thank God that your mother is not a slave. One night when that woman came home, she found that her dear boys had been sold to a man who was going to carry them more than six hundred miles off, to a place where they would have to work under a driver's lash, and where she could never see them again. I cannot tell you how bad she felt. She felt much worse than your mother would, if a stone should fall on you and kill you. The children did not know what was going to be done to them, and they laid down and slept quietly on their bed of straw, clasped in each other's arms.

CAR. Didn't their mother sleep with them?

MR. S. The mother couldn't *sleep* when her children were going to be carried off. The man who bought them, did not think it safe to let her be where she could get at them, to take them away. So they had her *chained* in a shed near the house. As she lay there, and thought of the toil, and stripes and misery her children must endure, she thought she would rather see them both dead and put in the ground. She tried hard to get loose from her chain, and after some time she got it off from her hands and feet. She then took an axe and went to the place where her boys were, and killed them.

CAR. What did the slave-driver do to her, the next morning?

MR. S. She was afraid of his cruelty, and she killed herself.

I cannot tell you how much torment a mother must suffer, before she would kill her own children. You can judge from this what slavery is. The mother, who had tried it, preferred death.

CAR. Is it not wicked to kill?

MR. S. Yes; but this poor woman had not been allowed to read in the Bible, and learn that it was wicked. She did what she thought was best for herself and children.

IMITATION OF MRS. BARBAULD'S SEASONS.—NO. II.

Who is this, with smiling face and rapid step, that is approaching from the east? The shouts of eight hundred thousand ransomed captives announce her approach. Light and truth go before her: peace and plenty follow in her path. In one hand she brings a key to unlock the prison doors: in the other she bears

the open volume of the word of life. All the lovers of mercy rejoice when they see her. A smile of hope lights up the dark face
of the slave. The proud oppressors of their race tremble at her
coming. The whip falls from their feeble grasp. The hard hearts,
which have set at naught the law of God, and defied the thunderbolts of the Almighty, are beginning to soften. They see her
steady progress, and they find it in vain to oppose her. Churches
and schools spring up around her. The ground on which she
treads assumes new verdure and beauty. She builds again 'the
old waste places.' The land which had been gloomy and desolate, becomes 'as a watered garden,' and 'as a spring of water,
whose waters fail not.' Gloomy forebodings, and dismal fears
flee away, when she arrives. Men are no longer troubled with apprehensions of rebellion and revolt. They cease to hear the step
of an assassin in every rustling leaf. Nor do they see threats of
murder and revenge in every colored face. She seats herself in the
'negro's cot and spreads cheerfulness and contentment around
his fireside. Youths and maidens of America, do you see her approaching us? Can you tell me her name?

ARE WE PRODUCING ANY EFFECT
AT THE SOUTH?

A worthy gentleman, who resided some time in North Carolina, relates that he has succeeded in turning the attention of
many persons there to the wickedness of slavery. He mentioned
the case of one young woman, who was heir to his inheritance
of 40 slaves, and who was anxious to give them their liberty.
She commissioned our informant to find places for them at the
North, and promised to send all on as soon as places were
found for them.

But here the despiser of God's image [in a colored man] will
say, 'See how the abolitionists are filling our northern cities
with niggers.' But stop, sir, please to direct your wrath, not
against abolitionists, but against those laws which forbid emancipation at home.

And here, Mr. Gradualist, I should like to say a word to you.

You see by this, that if the slaves are gradually set free, they must leave the place where they are, (and will be likely to go to the north.) that they may not interfere with the slavery which remains. But if they are all set free at once, they may continue where they are.

ELIZA LEE FOLLEN

Eliza Follen (1787–1860) was an abolitionist, editor, and writer of short stories and poetry. An author of numerous traditional children's books on religion, nursery rhymes, and fables, The Liberty Cap *was her most outwardly radical antislavery book, given the directness of its critique of enslavers and their white supremacist sentiments. Antislavery-minded readers appreciated the usefulness of the text for young people, as it quite quickly and convincingly informed readers about how Americans' embrace of and/or silence about slavery, despite its many known and untold terrors, had corrupted far too many citizens' hearts and minds.*

From *The Liberty Cap*
(1846)

AGRIPPA.

In the village of Stockbridge lives a black man by the name of Agrippa Hull, who served in the Revolutionary war. At the close of it he was honorably discharged; in testimony of which he shows a certificate signed by General Washington. He was for some years the servant of General Kosciusko, of whose generous and humane character he speaks with grateful love and admiration.

Agrippa has an uncommonly fine head, and is remarkable for his excellent understanding and good character. By his industry he has become possessed of a valuable farm, which he now, at the age of seventy-six, cultivates himself. He is eminent for his piety, and those who have heard him speak at conference meetings which he is in the habit of attending with his white neighbors, say that in prayer he is distinguished for fervor and eloquence, and for the peculiar originality and richness of his language.

The acuteness and wisdom of his views upon most subjects, and the wit and force of his illustrations, make his conversation so impressive that you remember what he has said, long after you have parted from him. During an interview of perhaps half an hour with him, I was so struck with his remarks that as soon as he left me, I wrote down his very words, as I here transcribe them, without any alteration or embellishment.

When I expressed to Agrippa my opinion upon the subject of prejudice against color, he said,

"When there is a flock of sheep, and some black ones among them, I always think that, if they behave well, they have as good a right to be fed as the white ones. God will not ask what is our color, but what has been our conduct. The Almighty made all colors. If we find fault with the work, we find fault with the workman. His works are all good. A black, ugly bottle may have just as good spirits in it as the cut glass decanter. Not the cover of the book, but what the book contains is the question. Many a good book has dark covers. Which is the worst, the white black man, or the black white man? When a white man says any hard thing to me about my color, I tell him I pity him, but I ask him which is the worst, to be black outside, or in? When a black man is treated ill on account of his color by a white man, and he bears it patiently and only pities him, I think that he has a chance to take a very high place over the white man."

"Once," said Agrippa, "when I was a servant to a gentleman who was very overbearing and haughty, we both went to the same church. One Sunday, a mulatto gentleman, by the name of Haynes, preached. When we came out of meeting, my master said to me, 'Well Agrippa, how do you like nigger preaching?' 'Sir,' I answered, 'he was half black and half white; I liked my half; how did you like yours?'"

Upon the assertion that the slaveholders cannot abolish slavery, Agrippa said, "No one is obliged to do wrong. When the drunkard says he cannot live without spirit, I tell him to take temperate things for a time, and see if he is not better. It is his will that is in fault. There is no necessity to do wrong. God never makes us do wrong."

He put his hand on a little boy's head, and said, "I love children; I love to see them well brought up. It is a good thing to feed the minds of children."

When speaking of the abolitionists, he said, "It will be a great while before the abolitionists can succeed in their purpose; but they will do great good to the black men by inducing them to keep down their bad feelings, because they know that they will have help at last."

"The abolitionists have the great happiness of working for a cause in which they know that they will have God on their side."

In a cause the merit of which depends upon the question whether the black man is a man, no further testimony is needed than the remarks of Agrippa; and what greater encouragement can the abolitionists desire than that contained in his words, "God is on their side"?

HANNAH TOWNSEND AND MARY TOWNSEND

The Anti-Slavery Alphabet *was written by the Quaker sisters Hannah Townsend (1812–?) and Mary Townsend (1814–?), who were members of the Philadelphia Female Anti-Slavery Society, in time for the organization's annual fair in 1846. A primer for children,* The Anti-Slavery Alphabet *introduced youngsters to the injustices and terror inflicted upon enslaved people through alphabetized, rhyming quatrains that could be memorized and recited easily. The Townsends and other abolitionists recognized that the possibility for a future without slavery depended on the antislavery education of children from an early age: "You are very young, 'tis true, / But there's much that you can do. / Even you can plead with men / That they buy not slaves again, / And that those they have may be / Quickly set at liberty."*

From *The Anti-Slavery Alphabet*
(1847)

TO OUR LITTLE READERS.

Listen, little children, all,
Listen to our earnest call:
You are very young, 'tis true,
But there's much that you can do.
Even you can plead with men
That they buy not slaves again,
And that those they have may be
Quickly set at liberty.

They may hearken what *you* say,
Though from *us* they turn away.
Sometimes, when from school you walk,
You can with your playmates talk,
Tell them of the slave child's fate,
Motherless and desolate.
And you can refuse to take
Candy, sweetmeat, pie or cake,
Saying "no"—unless 'tis free—
"The slave shall not work for me."
Thus, dear little children, each
May some useful lesson teach;
Thus each one may help to free
This fair land from slavery.

A

A is an Abolitionist—
   A man who wants to free
The wretched slave—and give to all
   An equal liberty.

B

B is a Brother with a skin
   Of somewhat darker hue,
But in our Heavenly Father's sight,
   He is as dear as you.

C

C is the Cotton-field, to which
   This injured brother's driven,
When, as the white man's *slave*, he toils
   From early morn till even.

D

D is the Driver, cold and stern,
   Who follows, whip in hand,
To punish those who dare to rest,
   Or disobey command.

E

E is the Eagle, soaring high;
   An emblem of the free;
But while we chain our brother man,
   Our type he cannot be.

F

F is the heart-sick Fugitive,
   The slave who runs away,
And travels through the dreary night,
   But hides himself by day.

G

G is the Gong, whose rolling sound,
   Before the morning light,
Calls up the little sleeping slave,
   To labor until night.

H

H is the Hound his master trained,
   And called to scent the track,
Of the unhappy fugitive,
   And bring him trembling back.

I

I is the Infant, from the arms
    Of its fond mother torn,
And, at a public auction, sold
    With horses, cows, and corn.

J

J is the Jail, upon whose floor
    That wretched mother lay,
Until her cruel master came,
    And carried her away.

K

K is the Kidnapper, who stole
    That little child and mother—
Shrieking, it clung around her, but
    He tore them from each other.

L

L is the Lash, that brutally
    He swung around its head,
Threatening that "if it cried again,
    He'd whip it till 'twas dead."

M

M is the Merchant of the north,
    Who buys what slaves produce—
So they are stolen, whipped and worked,
    For his, and for our use.

N

N is the Negro, rambling free
　　In his far distant home,
Delighting 'neath the palm trees' shade
　　And cocoa-nut to roam.

O

O is the Orange tree, that bloomed
　　Beside his cabin door,
When white men stole him from his home
　　To see it never more.

P

P is the Parent, sorrowing,
　　And weeping all alone—
The child he loved to lean upon,
　　His only son, is gone!

Q

Q is the Quarter, where the slave
　　On coarsest food is fed,
And where, with toil and sorrow worn,
　　He seeks his wretched bed.

R

R is the "Rice-swamp, dank and lone,"
　　Where, weary, day by day,
He labors till the fever wastes
　　His strength and life away.

S

S is the Sugar, that the slave
   Is toiling hard to make,
To put into your pie and tea,
   Your candy, and your cake.

T

T is the rank Tobacco plant,
   Raised by slave labor too:
A poisonous and nasty thing,
   For gentlemen to chew.

U

U is for Upper Canada,
   Where the poor slave has found
Rest after all his wanderings,
   For it is British ground!

V

V is the Vessel, in whose dark,
   Noisome, and stifling hold,
Hundreds of Africans are packed,
   Brought o'er the seas, and sold.

W

W is the Whipping post,
   To which the slave is bound,
While on his naked back, the lash
   Makes many a bleeding wound.

X

X is for Xerxes, famed of yore;
   A warrior stern was he
He fought with swords; let truth and love
   Our only weapons be.

Y

Y is for Youth—the time for all
   Bravely to war with sin;
And think not it can ever be
   Too early to begin.

Z

Z is a Zealous man, sincere,
   Faithful, and just, and true;
An earnest pleader for the slave—
   Will you not be so too?

JANE ELIZABETH JONES

Jane Elizabeth Jones (1813–1896) was an abolitionist, suffragist, writer, and editor. A coeditor of the Anti-Slavery Bugle, *Jones gave speeches on the antislavery lecture circuit in the North.* The Young Abolitionists *is framed as a didactic series of conversations between family members about the origins of American slavery, the treatment of enslaved people, and the horror of family separations. In the extract here, a mother and son discuss the plight of enslaved people in comparison to the treatment that white prisoners experienced, leading the mother to proclaim that it would be better to starve to death than be an enslaved person. A prisoner, in her estimation, is at least treated like a person, has rights and decent treatment, and knows that there will be an end to his imprisonment. Enslavement, on the other hand, was a horrific, inherited life sentence for which there was no foreseeable end.*

From *The Young Abolitionists; or, Conversations on Slavery*

(1848)

Chapter IV.

"As you have mentioned the convicts in the State's Prison," said Mrs. Selden to her son, "I would like to show you how much more regard is paid to *their* wants, than to those of the slaves. I have already told you of their miserable huts, and you know there can be none of the comforts of home in such a wretched place."

"When the rain comes in and drives them out," said Charlie, "don't their beds and everything get wet?"

"They have nothing that can properly be called a bed, so many persons say, who have lived in the south, and are well acquainted with their situation. They are generally furnished with one old blanket, and sometimes two. Some have a bundle of straw or a few old rags to lie on, while others sleep on the cold ground. They would consider themselves fortunate indeed could they have such nice beds as the prisoners have.

"I do not wish you to think the situation of the prisoner by any means a pleasant one. Oh! it is dreadful to be shut out from the beautiful world, from all the sources of happiness, almost from the sunlight and the refreshing air of heaven; to be confined in a narrow cell, and never hear the sound of a human voice—as is the case of some prisoners—or be allowed to look upon a human face, save that of the grim keeper who controls the heavy bolt that confines the sufferers in that solitary abode. Oh! the very thought of it makes my blood run cold, and I wonder how human beings ever could have devised such a mode of torture. But when I think of the slave, I see that he is the victim of a system that far exceeds in cruelty any form of punishment ever invented."

"Do tell me how it is, mother; I cannot see," said Charlie, "how slavery can be worse than that."

"Criminals are generally imprisoned," she replied, "for a few years only—the period of the slaves' bondage in the great prison house of oppression ends but with death. The convict, when his term expires, goes out a *free* man. He can return to his home and his friends, if he have any; he can choose his own employment, and pursue his own happiness as it pleases him best. If he has truly repented of his crime, he will, in a great measure, be restored to society, and can enjoy life as well as before. The slave looks forward to no time when *he* shall go out a free man. If he has been separated from his wife and children, he indulges in no pleasing expectation that in a few years or a few months he may return to those he loved so well. There are prisoners who know, that although *they* are shut up in a gloomy cell, their children are enjoying freedom, the care of friends and the comforts of life. The slave feels that *his* children are smarting under the lash, and that they have no kind friend to protect them, and that they are doomed to the deepest degradation and misery. The prisoner is sustained by the expectation of having his freedom again—of being the master of himself. The slave pines under his affliction, his heart fails him, his spirit is broken by the crushing power of slavery, and he lies down in despair, feeling that a night of endless bondage has closed in upon the hopes, the happiness and the liberty of himself and three millions of his race."

"Three millions! mother?" said the astonished boy. "Mr. Gardner told us yesterday there were only about twenty millions of people in the United States;—are three millions of them slaves?"

"It is a mortifying thought, my child, yet it is nevertheless true. When we were in Philadelphia last summer, you were astonished at the multitude of people that were passing up and down the streets and crowding the shops. Had you gone from the Navy Yard to Kensington, from the Delaware to the Schuylkill, and counted all the inhabitants of that great city, you would have had but a small part of the number of slaves. Indeed there are more than twelve times as many of these oppressed and suffering people as you would have found persons in that place. And I believe you could hardly go to any one of these three millions, and ask him if he would be willing to exchange his situation for that of the convict, endure for a few years confinement in a close cell, and then forever after have his freedom, but he would be rejoiced to make the exchange. But let any man go to the convict, and tell him that instead of remaining in the solitary cell a few years, he can be made a slave for life, and then ask him if he would choose the latter: the convict would think him a madman for putting the question."

"But, mother, you said some men were imprisoned for life. Would not such rather be slaves than live always in their cells?"

"I cannot tell how a man would feel under such circumstances; still, I believe even then he would much prefer the prison," said the mother. "In the prison he is sure of comfortable food and clothing, and of not being greatly over-worked. In slavery he is liable to be starved, to go nearly naked, to be compelled to work sixteen or eighteen hours a day. Although a prisoner in close confinement, he is regarded as a man; by the law, he is recognised as a human being; by the people he is spoken of as a member of the human family. In slavery he is looked upon as a brute; he becomes a piece of property; he has an owner who may inflict untold wrongs upon him, and no voice will be raised in opposition. This consideration alone, my child, would induce every man who has any appreciation of his manhood, who has any sense of the dignity of his position as a member of the human race, to choose the convict's cell for life rather than the lot of the American slave!"

"Were I to choose, mistress, I'm sure *I'd* niver be a slave," said Biddy, who had entered the room and heard the foregoing conversation. She had brought with her Phil, her darling pet, whose attention was attracted from his play by the rising spirit of Biddy, which was manifested by her earnest tone. When *she* expressed an opinion, Phil always felt called upon to sustain her. Consequently he informed his mother that he never would be a slave either.

"And," said he, "if the naughty men should come here, Charlie, wouldn't I shoot them with my bow and arrow?"

"Phil don't understand peace principles very well, does he, mother?" asked Charlie.

"No, my dear, he is a little boy and don't know much about any kind of principles. He must not talk of shooting people though, even with his bow and arrow."

"You asked me, Charlie, the other day, if food were cooked for the slaves. Generally it is not, though sometimes one of their number prepares it, but it is always coarse and poor. On many plantations, or farms, as you would call them, they give each full grown slave a peck of corn a week. After working in the hot sun all day, they go home at dark very sad and very weary, thinking how their poor little children have wanted them when they were away; and instead of sitting down to rest and finding a comfortable supper, they have to grind or pound their corn, and bake their hoe-cake, and 'tis often past midnight before this and their other work is done."

"What is hoe-cake?" asked Jenie.

"It is bread made of corn meal and water, and baked before the fire on an old hoe," said the mother, "and quite well satisfied would many of the slaves be with this if they could only get enough of it. It is the testimony of many who have lived in the South, that 'thousands of slaves are pressed with the gnawings of cruel hunger during their whole lives.' Boats on the Mississippi river, when stopping over night, are often boarded by slaves begging for a bone or a bit of bread to satisfy their hunger. They always seem very thankful for these favors, and often a poor crust will call forth a strong expression of gratitude.

"In a conversation I lately had with a friend who had seen much of slavery in his trading voyages on that river, he said, that on one occasion when he was stopping at a plantation landing, a bright little slave boy came on to his boat and begged for something to eat. He gave him some bread and butter. The poor child, delighted with the bountiful gift, looked at him, and with gratitude beaming from his face, said, in his own uneducated dialect, 'When I dies and goes to God, I'll tell him that you gib me dis.' Happy, my dear children, will it be for us all, if, when the poor slave goes into the presence of its Father-God, it shall tell of acts of kindness *we* have done!"

"But, mistress," said Biddy, "the slave sure can't suffer from the hunger-pain as I've seen my own people do at home. Oh! but the like of that I hope niver to see again."

"But then," rejoined Charlie, "they are not hungry all their lives, as some of the slaves are."

"That's true for ye. I've seen many a man who had been well to do, and had always a bit and a sup to give the stranger, who was left without a morsel in his cabin, and, God help him! his children crying for bread, and the darlint wife looking so sad and so sorrowful like, and all bekase the crops failed them, and the pratics they did raise were not fit even for the pig to ate. Sure, I've seen many a sight there that made my heart sore, and at this blessed minit I'm a fearing that hundreds haven't a handful of male in their cabin.

"Ye've a kind heart, master Charles, and I love ye for it, and if ye had seen what I did before I left the ould country, 'twould be after melting itself into tears. The poor little childer were nothing but skin and bone, and went about so silent and so strange like, that it hurt me heart to look at them. They had done crying, and had done asking for bread, for they knew there was none. And oh, but it was hard on the mothers, for the laugh of their darlints that was like a song to them was gone! and they knew that they all must die, and not have even a friend perhaps to carry them to the churchyard. And the fathers too, who had kept up brave hearts as long as they could, when they saw the dead eyes of them they loved, and saw their beautiful boys and girls become so ghostlike they hardly knew them, and they not able to beg a bite for them, or get a stroke of work to do themselves; God save them! but it was hard."

"Biddy!" said Charlie, whose eyes were swimming in tears, "wouldn't these people rather be slaves?"

"That I can't say," replied Biddy, "for when the head is distracted-like, it's hard saying what a man would do if only himself was concerned; but there's not one of them, that I saw, would have been willing to have had a childer made a slave to save *it* from starvation. Sure, but the curse of God would have followed them if they would. And as for meself, I'd rather starve a thousand times, if it be God's will, than to be made a slave by the will of man."

"Biddy is right," said Mrs. Selden, turning to her children; "it is far better to die of starvation than to live in slavery. Besides, if you are in slavery you are liable to die of want as many a poor slave has done. Then you would be as badly off as the Irish in that respect, and subject to a multitude of other evils to which they are strangers."

THE HUNGRY SLAVE BOY.

Oh, will not some massa take pity on me?
    I often am hungry from morning till night,
A bit of good food do I scarce ever see,
    And many a day I get hardly a bite.

What harm can so little a slave boy have done,
    That so sad and so hungry I always must go?
When master calls for me, I'm ready to run
    And do what he bids me as well as I know.

I wish I could get just as much bread and meat
    As the free little boys and and the girls that I see!
Oh, how good it would be to have plenty to eat,
    And how strange it would seem for a slave boy like me!

And mother, she tells me that if when I die,
    I have done as I ought, and have always been good,
I shall live where the folks are all free in the sky,
    And where every body has plenty of food.

                          B.S.J.

KATE BARCLAY

Kate Barclay's collection of short stories, poems, and essays aims to instruct young readers about the horrors of slavery as well as to help them become obedient Christians. The titular story centers on a young white girl's discovery that the nursemaid with whom she has developed a close relationship is missing and will be sold at auction. Minnie May says a prayer and grabs her Bible before running to the auction block in an attempt to rescue her nurse from being sold to a brutal new enslaver. The selections here similarly highlight aspects of slavery that render the lives of the enslaved most unfortunate and precarious. In an essay entitled "The Slave," Barclay makes plain the sentiment that informs her commitment to helping to nurture a new generation of selfless Christian abolitionists, "Dear reader, you cannot imagine how much suffering is endured by the poor blacks . . . O, I do want you to feel for their condition, and, when you pray ask God to bless them."

From *Minnie May;*
with Other Rhymes and Stories
(1856)

CUFFEE.

"When those ladies called here this afternoon, who was it they were talking about? Who was put in chains?"

"It was poor Cuffee, a colored man, who had once been a slave."

"Will you tell me the story now? I did not understand much of it, but I was sorry for poor Cuffee."

"Yes, Anna, I will tell you. Cuffee had lived away at the

south, where the oranges grow, you know. He was a slave there,
and I suppose served his master, or his massa, as he called him,
very faithfully; for one summer he was brought as far north as
the State of Maryland by some of his master's family, who came
there and wanted Cuffee to wait on them. As they were travelling from place to place, Cuffee heard about negroes a little farther to the north being free and living by themselves, or working
for white people and being paid for it; and if they were not well
treated at one place and did not wish to stay, they could leave
and go to another; and as long as they were industrious and behaved well they could make a good living and be happy. Cuffee
began to wonder why he couldn't live in this way as well as any
of them, and not go back to the south and be always a slave,
toiling for nothing and having few comforts. Besides this, he
was likely to be sold at any time to a bad massa who would
treat him very cruelly. He had often seen those on a neighboring plantation beaten for almost nothing. They themselves
often could hardly tell why the whip was laid over their shoulders. He could by some means get away from the family who
owned him and go to the free states where they could not find
him. Then they would go back without him, and then he would
be free, and he would get work as others did and be paid for it.
He thought it all over and over again, and every time he wished
more and more to be free, until one day he said to himself, '*I
will be free!* It is my right, and I will have it.' After a time he
had a good opportunity to get away, and he left his master's
family and travelled off farther and farther north. He could
work, and had no trouble in finding good places where he was
well treated and well paid. So he worked his way along, learned
how people live at the north, and bought him some clothes, and
did just as other free people do. He kept himself very quiet and
out of the way for a long while. But when he thought there was
no danger of being found out and taken back to the south to be
a slave again, he became a waiter at a hotel in the city. He
pleased the landlord, and all liked him very much. He lived
there three or four years and felt quite safe. One day there came
a gentleman to this hotel who watched Cuffee very closely and
asked some questions about him of those in the bar room. The
landlord listened, and began to suspect that this was a southern

gentleman. He feared he was a slaveholder on the lookout for some runaway slave, and he determined to send Cuffee out of the way until he left the house. Quite a number were sitting and standing around, smoking, and talking, and taking their ease, when in came Cuffee, bringing a trunk and an umbrella. He set them down and turned to go out. The landlord stepped to the door to speak with him, and, giving him some general orders, sent him off until he could get an opportunity to tell him what he suspected. The southern gentleman watched the movements, but said nothing, and soon after paid his bill and left the house. The next morning Cuffee was nowhere to be found. No one there knew any thing about him. The landlord hoped he was in some safe place, safe from the slaveholder; but it was not so, as they soon found out. The southern gentleman, who had watched him so closely, had laid claim to him as his slave and had him seized and bound. As soon as it was known there was a great excitement about it, and the friends of freedom tried to rescue him; but they could not do it. The law allowed the man to take him; and nothing could now be done to save him. Poor Cuffee was bound with chains and carried back into slavery again."

"O, that was too bad! I am so sorry for Cuffee! Is that all you know about him?"

"Very nearly all. The last that was known of him by any one at the north was what a blacksmith told about him. He said a man came into his shop one day to get him to fix a pair of handcuffs which did not exactly fit the wrists they were wanted for. The blacksmith would not touch the handcuffs, and said, with some spirit, that he never did such miserable work as that. He looked out at the door, and there sat Cuffee in a wagon, with heavy chains upon him; and he looked as if all courage and hope had gone out of him."

"Poor Cuffee! I fear he will never be free again. His bonds will seem worse than ever now, I am sure. His heart must be almost broken and life but a burden."

THE SALE.

"'Sale at twelve o'clock!' Now, what does it mean?
  Dear mother, do just look at that!
See that girl standing there, with her head bent down,
  By that man in a beaver hat!

"And that one behind, with his hand on her arm,
  Seems pushing or pulling her back:
I wonder if that is a slave being sold;
  She don't look to me very black."

"Yes, Johnny; this is a slave auction you see;
  There's the auctioneer standing up there,
With mallet in hand, crying, 'What will you bid?'
  And the purchasers stand down there.

"How my very heart fills with sadness and grief
  As I think of that poor girl's fate!—
Not a friend to protect or shield her from crime,
  Nor lift from her spirit the weight

"That vile slavery's curse must evermore bind
  On all who are held in its thrall:
Poor delicate, sensitive, heart-bowed quadroon,
  You must bear the rudeness of all.

"You stand on that block to be sold for a sum
  That to you is nothing at all;
The one who bids highest will claim as his own
  Your body, your spirit, your all.

"How sad and how hopeless your young life must be!
  How hard to endure its rough blast!
O, may you but hear of the Savior's kind power,
  And on Jesus your sorrows all cast.

"Then, when this life is o'er and the soul roams free
  In that blessed home above,

'Twill be sweet to bow down in adoring praise
    To the God of infinite love."

THE SLAVE.

Whose heart does not bleed for the wrongs inflicted on Africa's sons? What eye can remain unmoistened at the recital of their woes?

Not a great many years ago, a woman came from one of the Southern States to a town in New England, accompanied by a female slave. She was very ignorant; had never been taught her letters; and was not permitted on the Sabbath to hear the word of God read or explained. A colored man, who heard of her condition, wished very much to set her free; and after one or two ineffectual attempts he succeeded, with the help of a colored woman, in taking her from her cruel mistress. A chaise was in readiness, and the slave was carried about thirty miles from town to an acquaintance of one who had previously engaged the situation. But the poor woman was not contented here: she thought of her husband and children whom she had left at the south, and this made her feel unhappy. Meanwhile her mistress offered individuals fifty dollars and one hundred dollars if they would find and return her: but none made search.

After the slave had been absent two or three weeks, she was so discontented and anxious for her children that she was brought back to town, and, of her own accord, went back to her mistress. "You shall pay dear enough for this when I return," said she; and the poor African was sorry that she had not retained her liberty. But now she could not be set free again; for her mistress watched her very narrowly, and confined her in a chamber a great part of the time she remained in town.

Little children cannot conceive of the wretchedness and the miserable condition of the poor slaves. Many of their owners treat them more like dumb beasts than like human beings. It was so with the mistress of this slave. After she had returned to her with the hope of meeting again her husband and children, even this privilege was denied her; for on the homeward-bound passage *she was sold to a slaveholder in North Carolina.* Ah, then were all her hopes of ever seeing again those whom she loved as life at an end. How must her heart have been rent with agony at the thought! her beloved partner no more to enjoy her company, and her dear children to mourn the loss of a tender and affectionate mother.

Little children, pity the poor slaves—pity them with all your heart. How would you feel to be separated forever from your kind mother—to see her face no more—no more to see her smiling look of approbation—no more to receive the kiss of affection? I ask, how would you feel? Dear reader, you cannot imagine how much suffering is endured by the poor blacks. Husbands are separated from wives, children from parents, brothers from sisters. O, I do want you to feel for their condition, and, when you pray, ask God to bless *them.* Can it be that some of you fret and scold, and disobey your parents and your teachers, when you have so much to enjoy and make you happy? Think of the poor blacks. Do you sometimes say you are cruelly treated when requested to leave your play to do some favor for your parents? Think of the poor blacks. At all times, when you imagine you have reason to be angry, or complain, or disobey your friends, I entreat you to remember the condition of a great many thousands of your fellow-beings who are in slavery—ignorant, unhappy, and miserable.

> I pity the poor little slave,
>   Who labors hard through all the day,
>   And has no one,
>   When day is done,
>   To teach his youthful heart to pray.

> No words of love, no fond embrace,
>   No smiles from parents kind and dear;
>   No tears are shed
>   Around his bed
>   When fevers rage and death is near.

None feel for him when heavy chains
  Are fastened to his tender limb;
      No pitying eyes,
      No sympathies,
  No prayers are raised to Heaven for him.

But I will pity the poor slave,
  And pray that he may soon be free;
      That he at last,
      When days are past,
  In heaven may have his liberty.

ANONYMOUS, JULIA COLMAN, AND MATILDA G. THOMPSON

With a passionate abolitionist plea to young people to reject the evils of slavery, this volume of stories is based on actual people and events. In the opening essay, which is presented here in its entirety along with an extract from the story of an enslaved boy entitled "Little Lewis," the anonymous au-thor emphatically proclaims "a slave is a human being, held and used as property by another human being, and that it is always A SIN AGAINST GOD to thus hold and use a human being as property! . . . Make a solemn vow before the Sav-iour, who loves the slave and slave children as truly as he does you, that you will never hold slaves, never apologize for those who do." The stories work together to evoke sym-pathy by providing children with an accurate, if startling for them, view into slavery's horrors as they are exacted on en-slaved people, particularly children.

From *The Child's Anti-Slavery Book: Containing a Few Words About American Slave Children and Stories of Slave-Life*

(1859)

A FEW WORDS ABOUT AMERICAN SLAVE CHILDREN.

Children, you are free and happy. Kind parents watch over you with loving eyes; patient teachers instruct you from the beauti-ful pages of the printed book; benign laws protect you from violence, and prevent the strong arms of wicked people from hurting you; the blessed Bible is in your hands; when you become men and women you will have full liberty to earn your living, to go, to come, to seek pleasure or profit in any way that you may choose, so long as you do not meddle with the rights of other people; in one word, *you are free children!* Thank God! thank God! my children, for this precious gift. Count it dearer than life. Ask the great God who made you free to teach you to prefer death to the loss of liberty.

But are all the children in America free like you? No, no! I am sorry to tell you that hundreds of thousands of American children are *slaves*. Though born beneath the same sun and on the same soil, with the same natural right to freedom as yourselves, they are nevertheless SLAVES. Alas for them! Their parents cannot train them as they will, for they too have MASTERS. These masters say to them:

"Your children are OURS—OUR PROPERTY! They shall not be taught to read or write; they shall never go to school; they shall not be taught to read the Bible; they must submit to us and not to you; we shall whip them, sell them, and do what else we please with them. They shall never own themselves, never have the right to dispose of themselves, but shall obey us in all things as long as they live!"

"Why do their fathers let these masters have their children? My father wouldn't let anybody have me," I hear one of my little free-spirited readers ask.

Simply, my noble boy, because they can't help it. The masters have banded themselves together, and have made a set of wicked laws by which nearly four millions of men, women, and children are declared to be their personal chattels, or property. So that if one of these slave fathers should refuse to let his child be used as the property of his master, those wicked laws would help the master by inflicting cruel punishments on the parent. Hence the poor slave fathers and mothers are forced to silently witness the cruel wrongs which their helpless children are made to suffer. Violence has been framed into a law, and the poor slave is trodden beneath the feet of the powerful.

"But why did those slaves let their masters bring them into

this state? Why didn't they fight as our forefathers did when they threw off the yoke of England's laws?" inquires a bright-eyed lad who has just risen from the reading of a history of our Revolution.

The slaves were not reduced to their present servile condition in large bodies. When our ancestors settled this country they felt the need of more laborers than they could hire. Then wicked men sailed from England and other parts of Europe to the coast of Africa. Sending their boats ashore filled with armed men, they fell upon the villages of the poor Africans, set fire to their huts, and, while they were filled with fright, seized, hand-cuffed, and dragged them to their boats, and then carried them aboard ship.

This piracy was repeated until the ship was crowded with negro men, women, and children. The poor things were packed like spoons below the deck. Then the ship set sail for the coast of America. I cannot tell you how horribly the poor negroes suffered. Bad air, poor food, close confinement, and cruel treat-ment killed them off by scores. When they died their bodies were pitched into the sea, without pity or remorse.

After a wearisome voyage the survivors, on being carried into some port, were sold to the highest bidder. No regard was paid to their relationship. One man bought a husband, another a wife. The child was taken to one place, the mother to another. Thus they were scattered abroad over the colonies. Fresh loads arrived continually, and thus their numbers increased. Others were born on the soil until now, after the lapse of some two centuries, there are nearly four millions of negro slaves in the country, besides large numbers of colored people who in vari-ous ways have been made free.

You can now see how easy it was for the masters to make the wicked laws by which the slaves are now held in bondage. They began when the slaves were few in number, when they spoke a foreign language, and when they were too few and feeble to offer any resistance to their oppressors, as their masters did to old England when she tried to oppress them.

I want you to remember one great truth regarding slavery, namely, that a slave is a human being, held and used as property by another human being, and that *it is always* A SIN AGAINST GOD *to thus hold and use a human being as property!*

You know it is not a sin to use an ox, a horse, a dog, a squirrel, a house, or an acre of land as property, if it be honestly obtained, because God made these and similar objects to be possessed as property by men. But God did not make *man to be the property of man.* He never gave any man the right to own his neighbor or his neighbor's child.

On the contrary, he made all men to be free and equal, as saith our Declaration of Independence. Hence, every negro child that is born is as free before God as the white child, having precisely the same right to life, liberty, and the pursuit of happiness, as the white child. The law which denies him that right does not destroy it. It may enable the man who claims him as a slave to deprive him of its exercise, but the right itself remains, for the wicked law under which he acts does not and cannot set aside the divine law, by which he is as free as any child that was ever born.

But if God made every man, woman, and child to be free, and not property, then he who uses a human being as property acts contrary to the will of God and SINS! Is it not so, my children?

Yet that is what every slaveholder does. *He uses his slaves as property.* He reckons them as worth so many dollars, just as your father sets a certain money value on his horse, farm, or merchandise. He sells him, gives him away, uses his labor without paying him wages, claims his children as so many more dollars added to his estate, and when he dies wills him to his heirs forever. And this is SIN, my children—a very great sin against God, a high crime against human nature.

Mark what I say! the sin of slavery does not lie merely in whipping, starving, or otherwise ill-treating a human being, but in using him as property; in saying of him as you do of your dog: "He is my property. He is worth so much money to me. I will do what I please with him. I will keep him, use him, sell him, give him away, and keep all he earns, just as I choose."

To say that of a man is sin. You might clothe the man in purple, feed him on manna from heaven, and keep him in a palace of ivory, still, if you used him as your property, you would commit sin!

Children, I want you to shrink from this sin as the Jews did from the fiery serpents. Hate it. Loathe it as you would the leprosy. Make a solemn vow before the Saviour, who loves the slave and slave children as truly as he does you, that you will never hold slaves, never apologize for those who do. As little Hannibal vowed eternal hatred to Rome at the altar of a false god, so do you vow eternal enmity to slavery at the altar of the true and living Jehovah. Let your purpose be, "I will rather beg my bread than live by the unpaid toil of a slave."

To assist you in carrying out that purpose, and to excite your sympathy for poor slave children, the following stories were written. The characters in them are all real, though their true names are not always given. The stories are therefore pictures of actual life, and are worthy of your belief.

*   *   *

LITTLE LEWIS.

"A, B, C," said little Lewis to himself, as he bent eagerly over a ragged primer. "Here's anoder A, an' there's anoder, an' there's anoder C, but I can't find anoder B. Missy Katy said I must find just so many as I can. Dear little Missy Katy! an' wont I be just so good as ever I can, an' learn to read, an' when I get to be a man I'll call myself white folks; for I'm a most as white as Massa Harry is now, when he runs out widout his hat; A, B, C." And so the little fellow ran on, thinking what a fine man he would be when he had learned to read.

Just then he heard a shrill laugh in the distance, and the cry, "Lew! Lew! where's Lew?"

It was Katy's voice, and tucking his book in his bosom, he ran around the house toward her with light feet; for though she was often cross and willful, as only daughters sometimes are, she was the only one of the family that showed him even an occasional kindness. She was, withal, a frolicsome, romping witch, and as he turned the corner, she came scampering along right toward him with three or four white children at her heels, and all the little woolly heads of the establishment, numbering something less than a score.

"Here, Lew!" she said, as she came in sight, "you take the tag and run."

With a quick movement he touched her outstretched hand, and he would have made the others some trouble to catch him, for he was the smartest runner among the children; but as he turned he tripped on a stone, and lay sprawling. "Tag," cried Hal, Katy's cousin, as he placed his feet on the little fellow's back and jumped over him. It was cruel, but what did Hal care for the "little nigger." If he had been at home he would have had some little fear of breaking the child's back, for his father was more careful of his *property* than Uncle Stamford was.

Before Lewis could rise, two or three of the negro boys, who were always too ready to imitate the vices of their masters, had made the boy a stepping stone, and then Dick, his master's eldest son, came down upon him with both knees, and began to cuff him roundly.

"So, you black scamp, you thought you'd run away with the tag, did you!" Just then he perceived the primer that was peeping out of Lewis's shirt bosom. "Ha! what's here?" said he; "a primer, as I live! And what are you doing with this, I'd like to know?"

"Missy Katy give it to me, and she is teaching me my letters out of it. Please, massa, let me have it again," said he, beseechingly, as Dick made a motion as if to throw it away. "I would like to learn how to read."

"You would, would you!" said Dick. "You'd like to read to Tom and Sam, down on a Louisiana plantation, in sugar time, when you'd nothing else to do, I suppose. Ha, ha, ha!" and the young tyrant, giving the boy a vigorous kick or two as he rose, stuffed the book into his own pocket, and walked off.

Poor Lewis! He very well knew the meaning of that taunt, and he did not open his mouth. No threat of a dark closet ever frightened a free child so much as the threat of being sold to a Southern plantation terrifies the slave-child of Kentucky.

Lewis walked slowly toward the kitchen, to see Aunt Sally. It was to her he used to go with all his troubles, and sometimes she scolded, and sometimes she listened. She was very busy dressing the vegetables for dinner, and she looked cross; so the little fellow crept into the chimney corner and said nothing; but he thought all the more, and as he thought, the sad tears rolled down his tawny cheeks.

"What is the matter now, little baby?" was Aunt Sally's tender inquiry.

Lewis commenced his pitiful tale; but as soon as Aunt Sally heard that it was about learning to read, she shut him up with "Good enough for you! What do you want of a book? Readin' isn't for the likes of you; and the less you know of it the better."

This was poor sympathy, and the little fellow, with a half-spiteful feeling, scrambled upon a bench near by, and tumbled out of the window. He alighted on an ash-heap, not a very nice place to be sure, but it was a retired corner, and he often hid away there when he felt sad and wanted to be alone. Here he sat down, and leaning his head against the side of the house, he groaned out, "My mother, O my mother! If you ain't dead, why don't you come to me?"

By degrees he calmed down, and half asleep there in the sunshine, he dreamed of the home that he once had. His mother was a noble woman, so he thought. Nobody else ever looked so kindly into his face; he was sure nobody else ever loved him as she did, and he remembered when she was gay and cheerful, and would go all day singing about her work. And his father, he could just remember him as a very pleasant man that he used to run to meet, sometimes, when he saw him coming home away down the road; but that was long ago. He had not seen him now for years, and he had heard his mother say that his father's master had moved away out of the state and taken him with him, and maybe he would never return. Then Lewis's mother grew sad, and stopped her singing, though she worked as hard as ever, and kept her children all neat and clean.

And those dear brothers and sisters, what had become of them? There was Tom, the eldest, the very best fellow in the world, so Lewis thought. He would sit by the half hour making tops, and whistles, and all sorts of pretty playthings. And Sam, too! he was always so full of fun and singing songs. What a singer he was! and it was right cheerful when Sam would borrow some neighbor's banjo and play to them. But they were all gone; and his sad, sweet-faced, lady-like sister Nelly, too, they were all taken off in one day by one of the ugliest negro-drivers that ever scared a little slave-boy's dreams. And it was while his mother was away from home too. How she did cry and take on when she came back and found them all gone, and she hadn't even the chance to bid them good-by! She said she knew her master sent her off that morning because he was going to sell her children.

Lewis shuddered as he thought of that dreadful night. It was hardly two years ago, and the fearful things he heard then burned into his soul with terrible distinctness. It seemed as if their little cabin was deserted after that, for Tom, and Sam, and Nelly were almost grown up, and the rest were all little ones. The next winter his other sister, Fanny, died; but that wasn't half so sad. She was about twelve years old, and a blithesome, cheerful creature, just as her mother had been. He remembered how his master came to their cabin to comfort them, as he said; but his mother told him plainly that she did not want any such comfort. She wished Nelly was dead too. She wished she had never had any children to grow up and suffer what she had. It was in vain her master tried to soothe her. He talked like a minister, as he was; but she had grown almost raving, and she talked to him as she never dared to do before. She wanted to know why he didn't come to console her when she lost her other children; "three all at once" she said, "and they're ten times worse than dead. You never consoled me then at all. Religion? Pooh! I don't want none of *your* religion."

And now she, too, was gone. She had been gone more than a year. It was said that she was hired out to work in another family; but it wasn't so. They only told her that story to get her away from the children peaceably. She was sold quite a distance away to a very bad man, who used her cruelly.

Ned, who was some two years younger than Lewis, and the only brother he had left, was a wild, careless boy, who raced about among the other children, and did not seem to think much about anything. Lewis often wished he could have somebody to talk with, and he wondered if his mother would ever come back again.

Had he been a poet he might have put his wishes into verses like the following, in which Mrs. Follen has given beautiful expression to the wishes of such a slave boy as Lewis:

THE SLAVE BOY'S WISH.

I wish I was that little bird,
  Up in the bright blue sky,
That sings and flies just where he will,
  And no one asks him why.

I wish I was that little brook,
  That runs so swift along,
Through pretty flowers and shining stones,
  Singing a merry song.

I wish I was that butterfly,
  Without a thought or care,
Sporting my pretty, brilliant wings,
  Like a flower in the air.

I wish I was that wild, wild deer,
  I saw the other day,
Who swifter than an arrow flew,
  Through the forest far away.

I wish I was that little cloud,
  By the gentle south wind driven,
Floating along so free and bright,
  Far, far up into heaven.

I'd rather be a cunning fox,
  And hide me in a cave;
I'd rather be a savage wolf,
  Than what I am—a slave.

My mother calls me her good boy,
   My father calls me brave;
What wicked action have I done,
   That I should be a slave?

I saw my little sister sold,
   So will they do to me;
My heavenly Father, let me die,
   For then I shall be free.

(MRS.) J. D. CHAPLIN

Founded in 1825 in New York City, the American Tract Society reprinted and published religious tracts and short stories, disseminating a range of spiritual propaganda for nearly two centuries. In this antislavery children's story, Mrs. J. D. Chaplin introduces young readers to the orphaned enslaved children Cain and Patsy and teaches, through her depictions of the inhumane ways that enslaved people are treated by atheist and Christian enslavers and proslavery Americans alike, that slavery goes against the will of God.

From *Cain and Patsy; the Gospel Preached to the Poor. A Story of Slave Life*

(1860)

THE SLAVE CHILDREN.

It was a calm, bright sabbath morning. The pine groves whispered softly, and the great river murmured in subdued tones; the rich autumnal flowers sent up their fragrance as incense to heaven; the oriole and mocking bird darted from their downy nests, and took their flight upward, while they warbled their song of praise to the Lord and Father of all. Oh, how beautiful this earth which God hath made and given to us for our dwelling-place! Surely, it speaks forth his omnipotence! For what short of almighty power could call so much beauty into being, and keep it in constant motion? Summer and winter; seedtime and harvest; the sun, the moon, and the stars which he hath made; the mighty seas and lakes and rivers; the hills, the valleys, and the forest; the mighty oak and the tiny flower, are all proofs of the love of our heavenly Father. If angels can gaze from their homes on high, must they not be amazed to see this glorious habitation marred by the sin and ingratitude of man? Earth brings forth enough for all, both man and beast; and yet, through the improvidence of some, and the cruelty of others, want reigns, and misery veils the faces which might otherwise look up, clear and trustingly, to the Giver of all our mercies.

Broad plantations spread out on either side of a noble southern river, and tokens of wealth and refinement met the eye. But it was wealth for the few bought by the poverty of the many; culture for the high at the expense of ignorance for the low; rest for those ever at ease through the burdens of the toil-worn. But God is the Father of all, and the voice of the poorest outcast reaches his ear and moves his pity. He giveth not all his mercies to one, but divideth them as he seeth fit. He may withhold earthly good, and at the same time give blessings which gold can not purchase; so that one who may, like Lazarus at the rich man's gate, be the object of pity or scorn below, will, by and by, be the honored and envied in that land where poverty and oppression are never known.

As we were saying, it was a bright morning of the holy day. Two sable children walked, laughing and talking very gayly, through the stiff stubble of the cornfield, towards the bank of the river. There lay moored what was, in their esteem, more valuable than was Cleopatra's barge to her—an old leaky, flat-bottomed boat, covered with mud outside, and with green slime within. A shout of joy escaped them when they saw it rocking before them, and then commenced a race to see which could first leap into this, to others, most uninviting boat. Their sparkling eyes and ringing laughter told the joy of their simple hearts, as the girl, springing into it with a bound like that of a wild colt, cried out, "Ise beat you, Cain! Ise ahead o' yer dis yer time!"

"Dat's true, Patsy," replied Cain, in a good-natured, patronizing way, "dat's true; you's allers ahead ob eberybody I knows. Der's heaps o' people would gib somethin' for yer quick fingers. Dar, chile, you take in de oars while I onties de boat." Patsy, not at all afraid of soiling her hands, grasped them, mudladen though they were, and, as Cain sprang in, pushed off with vigorous effort from the shore, and they were soon floating down the stream, singing and laughing beneath a huge blue cotton umbrella, an heirloom which had come down to them, nobody knew whence, and through the rents of which the glad sun had free access to their uncovered heads.

THE MASTER.

Years ago, when these poor children were very small, a negro-driver had bought them in Virginia, and brought them away from their mother's grave, to be raised for the cotton-fields of Alabama. They had forgotten almost every thing connected with their early home,—even the face of "mammy" had faded from their memories. But not so her humble teachings. They still repeated at night, from force of habit, a broken prayer, learned at her knee in a lowly cabin; they knew, imperfectly, passages of Scripture and snatches of devotional hymns, and remembered the name of "mighty Jesus." This was all, and their minds were like their brows, dark as midnight.

"Massa was a mighty hard man," and all he cared for was to get the most work possible out of his hands. To accomplish this, he fed and clothed them well, nor would he allow them to be whipped, save when he thought it absolutely necessary. Thus the body grew and prospered, but the soul—alas! "massa" did not believe that man had a soul; so, of course, his own and those of his people were sorely neglected.

He thought that man was like the brutes that perish; that there was no heaven for the holy, no hell for the vile; that all beyond the grave was a long, unknowing sleep. Oh, shocking thought! who would die for ever, and lie in eternal forgetfulness? This is a worse than heathen doctrine.

His plantation was "up river," and at quite a distance from any church or Sunday-school; so his negroes were as much shut out from a knowledge of Christ, and the way of salvation, as were their forefathers in the desert wilds of Africa. Now and then, a new slave would come to the plantation, who, perchance, had lived where the gospel was preached. Then, if a Christian, he would tell of the instruction he had received, and, if of a bold and daring spirit, might propose a meeting by twilight in the canebrake. But these attempts were invariably put an end to by the ungodly master. The thoughtful, if any such there were, buried their fears or hopes for the future, in their own bosoms, communing only with the Judge of the oppressed.

THE TEACHER.

A pale, feeble young man from a northern college had recently come to the neighborhood, hoping to regain health in the genial air of Alabama. A letter from a northern friend introduced him to the owner of Cain and Patsy, who, being fond of society, received him kindly, and soon became greatly interested in the young stranger; and he, being a faithful servant of Christ, resolved that the favor he had found in the eyes of the master, should be turned to some account for the good of the slaves, and for the honor of God. His company was soon found to be necessary to their enjoyment, and he was urged to remain and teach the sons of his hospitable entertainer, for all saw that his qualifications were very rare, and his nature very lovely. The planter was a little surprised that the handsome offer he had made was not eagerly accepted. But an anxious expression passed over the face of the student when pressed to remain. "Is not my offer a very handsome one?" asked the gentleman.

"Yes, far more so than I could have expected," replied the student.

"You told me you were poor, and that you could remain at the South only by your own exertions; why, then, do you hesitate? Have we not treated you like a friend, sir?"

"Yes, like a son," answered the young man, "and the situation you offer me is one for which I have earnestly longed—ay, and for which," he added, solemnly, "I have fervently prayed. Still, I dare not say I will stay with you."

"Why, sir?" proudly returned the planter.

"Because I dare not live in a house where there is no welcome for my Master. I dare not dwell beneath a roof where his name is not acknowledged, nor his blessing sought; where I could not speak of him and his doctrines to the inmates and the servants."

"Oh, ho," cried the planter, jocosely, "if *that's* all, we'll soon manage that. Although I don't believe in these things myself, *I'm very liberal* towards those who do. I let everybody express their own opinions, and claim the same privilege for myself. As to your 'Master and his cause,'" he continued, a smile of scorn playing about his lips, "you may talk about either to any one who will listen to you. But don't annoy me with it; that's all I ask."

"Sir," replied the young man, solemnly, "I see here daily three scores of my fellow-creatures, all of whom I certainly expect to meet again at the judgment-seat of Christ. If I pass them by without speaking of the claim which God has upon them, and of the duty they owe to others, how can I be guiltless? If I *believed* as you do, I should *act* as you do; but do you think that with my belief I could pursue the same course, and be an honest and consistent man?"

"I suppose not," replied the planter, "and I am willing to trust you among my people. I have confidence in you, and do not believe that you will teach them to hate me or rebel against me."

"Far from it," replied the student. "If I might have them together for an hour or two on Sunday, I care not how many whites are present. I should simply teach them the story of the cross, and then their duty to God and to their fellow-creatures; to be sober, honest, faithful, and industrious."

"I don't care how much you teach them of such doctrines, for they need to be taught honesty; such a thievish set as they are! I have, however, said so much against Sunday schools and prayer-meetings, among the blacks, that I should not quite like to have them held on my own premises; but about three miles below, is a man who will welcome you, and give you a place to meet in. I will let some of my people go every Sunday. It shall be as a reward. I will give them a pass, if they work well;" and the rich man looked very wise, as he thought of this new way to get labor out of his people.

OLIVER OPTIC

Writing under the pen name Oliver Optic, William Taylor Adams (1822–1897) was the author of one hundred books, including adventure stories. His books tended to highlight a range of characters, from wholesome to undesirable, the latter of which met the ire of respectable Victorian-era readers and critics. A teacher, schoolmaster, and school board member in Dorchester, Massachusetts, Adams served in the Massachusetts House of Representatives during Reconstruction. Watch and Wait appeared as the third title in Adams's Woodville Stories series; it traces the journey of three enslaved children who had self-liberated themselves from plantation slavery and approached the Grant family for assistance. Interestingly, Adams's preface to the novel indicates that he had been "forced" to acknowledge that the book was not written to support the antislavery cause. Yet he engages in a bit of subversive doublespeak, adding, "As a story of exciting adventure, the writer hopes it will satisfy all his young readers; that they will love the gentle Lily, respect the manly independence of Dan, and smile at the oddities of Cyd; and that the book will confirm and increase their love of liberty and their hatred of tyranny. If the young fugitives were resolute, even to shedding the blood of the slave-hunter, they had forgiving and Christian hearts, in which there was neither malice nor revenge; and in this respect, if in no other, they are worthy exemplars for the young and the old." The extract here includes a set of incidents between Dandy Dan and his young master Archy that led to the fugitive flights of the three youngsters from the Redlawn Plantation.

From *Watch and Wait; or, The Young Fugitives, a Story for Young People* (1864)

Chapter III.

MASTER ARCHY RECEIVES AN UNLUCKY BLOW.

Green Point was a very pleasant place, to which the luxurious occupants of the mansion at Redlawn occasionally resorted to spend a day. The land was studded with a growth of sturdy forest trees. Formerly it had been covered with a thick undergrowth of canes; but these, near the Point, had been cut away, and the place otherwise prepared for the visits of the grand people.

The day was cool and pleasant for that locality, and perhaps the magnificent son and heir of the planter of Redlawn felt that a little sharp exercise would be beneficial to him. He never performed any useful labor; never saddled his own pony, or polished his own boots; never hoed a hill of corn, or dug up a weed in the garden. He had been taught that labor was degrading, and only suited to the condition of the negro.

Master Archy, therefore, never degraded himself. His indolence and his aristocratic principles were in accord with each other. Though he actually suffered for the want of something to do, he was not permitted to demean himself by doing any thing that would develop the resources of the fruitful earth, and add to the comfort of his fellow-beings. I am quite sure, if the young seignior had been compelled to hoe corn, pick cotton, or cut cane for a few hours every day, or even been forced to learn his lessons in geography, grammar, and history, he would have been a better boy, and a happier one.

Idleness is not only the parent of mischief, but it is the fruitful source of human misery. Master Archy, with every thing that ingenuity could devise and wealth purchase to employ his time, was one of the most unhappy young men in the country.

He never knew what to do with himself. He turned coldly from his boats to his pony; then from the pony to the gymnasium; then to the bowling alley; and each in turn was rejected, for it could not furnish the needed recreation.

Master Archy landed at Green Point, and he was fully of the opinion that he could amuse himself for an hour with the boxing gloves. For the want of a white companion of his own age, he had been compelled to practise the manly art of self-defence with his body-servant. Perhaps also there was some advantage in having Dandy for his opponent, for, being a slave, he would not dare to give as good as he received.

Dandy had taken lessons in the art with his young master, and though he was physically and "scientifically" his superior, he was cunning enough to keep on the right side of Master Archy, by letting him have the set-to all his own way. It was no easy matter to play at fisticuffs with the young lord, even with gloves on, for his temper was not particularly mild when he was crossed. If he happened to get a light rap, it made him mad; and in one way or another he was sure to wreak ample vengeance upon the offender. Dandy was therefore obliged to handle his master with extreme care.

Yet Archy had a fantastic manliness in his composition, which enabled him to realize that there was no credit in beating an unresisting opponent. Dandy must do some thing; he must bestow some blows upon his capricious companion, but he had learned that they must be given with the utmost care and discretion. In a word, if he did not hit at all, Master Archy did not like it; and if he hit too hard, or in a susceptible spot, he was mad.

Our readers who are fond of manly sport will readily perceive that Dandy was in the position of the frogs,—that what was fun to Archy was death to him, in a figurative sense. He did not have much fondness for the manly art. He had no moral views on the subject, but he hated the game for its own sake.

With the two pairs of gloves in his hands, Dandy followed his young lord till they came to a smooth piece of ground, under the spreading shade of a gigantic oak. Master Archy then divested himself of his white linen sack, which his attentive valet hung upon the trunk of a tree. He then rolled up his sleeves and put on the gloves. He was assisted in all these preparations by Dandy.

"Come, Dandy, you are not ready," said he, petulantly, when he was fully "mounted" for the occasion.

"I am all ready, sir," replied Dandy, as he slipped on the other pair of gloves.

"No, you are not," snarled Archy, who, for some reason or other, was in unusually bad humor. "Do you think I will box with you while you have your jacket on?"

"I can do very well with my jacket on," replied Dandy, meekly.

"No, you can't. I can whip you in your shirt sleeves. I don't want to take any advantage of you. Off with your jacket, and put yourself in trim."

Dandy obeyed, and in a few moments he was the counterpart, so far as dress was concerned, of his master.

"Now stand up to it like a man, for I'm going to give you a hard one to-day," added Archy, as he flourished with the gloves before his companion.

There was a faint smile upon his countenance as he uttered these words, and Dandy saw signs of unusual energy in his eyes. He evidently intended to do some "big thing," and the sport was therefore more distasteful than ever to the body-servant, whose hands were, in a measure, fettered by his position.

Dandy placed himself in the proper attitude, and went through all the forms incident to the science. At first Master Archy was cool and self-possessed, and his "plungers" and "left-handers" were adroitly parried by the other, who, if his master intended to win a decided triumph on the present occasion, was determined to make him earn his laurels. But Dandy did little more than avoid the blows; he gave none, and received none.

"Come, stand up to it!" shouted Archy, who soon began to be disgusted with these tame proceedings. "Why don't you exert yourself?"

"I do, sir; I have done my best to ward off your blows," replied Dandy.

"I will give you something more to do, then," added Archy, and sprang to his game with redoubled vigor.

As a matter of prudence, Dandy permitted himself to be hit

once on the side of the head. This encouragement was not lost upon Archy, and he increased his efforts, but he could not hit his rival again for some time. After a few moments his "wind" gave out, and operations were suspended. When he had recovered breath enough to speak, he proceeded to declare that Dandy had no spirit, and did not try to make the game exciting.

"I have done my best, sir," replied Dandy.

"No, you haven't. You haven't hit me yet, and you haven't tried to do so."

"Yes, sir, I have."

"Don't contradict me. Now we will try again."

They commenced once more, and immediately Dandy, in order to gratify his master, gave him a pretty smart blow upon the end of his nose. He hoped this would satisfy the grumbler, and bring the sport to a happy termination. As usual, the blow excited the pugnacity of Master Archy; and setting the rules of the art at defiance, he rushed upon his companion with all the impetuosity of his nature.

Dandy simply stood steady, and warded off the blows of his infuriate master; but in spite of his exertions he was hit several times in the breast and face, and even "below the belt," for he did not deem it prudent to give another blow. Archy reared and plunged like an angry steed, till he had exhausted himself; but his temper had not yet spent itself. He sat down upon the ground, and rested himself for a moment, then, throwing away the gloves, proposed to finish the contest with the naked fists.

"I would rather not, Master Archy," replied Dandy, appalled at the idea.

"Throw away your gloves, and come on!" said Archy, brandishing his fists.

"I hope you will excuse me, Master Archy. I don't want to be pounded to a jelly."

This was certainly complimentary, but there was still a burning sensation lingering about the nose of the young planter, where that member had been flattened by his fellow-pugilist.

"No whining; come on!" repeated Archy; and certain malicious thoughts which rankled in his heart were manifest in his eyes.

"If you please, Master Archy, I will keep my gloves on, and you may play without any."

"Do you think I will do that?" sneered Archy. "I am willing to take as good as I send. Off with your gloves!"

"But only consider, sir, if any thing should happen. If I should hit you by accident——"

"Hit, then!" cried Archy, angrily, as he sprang forward, and planted a heavy blow upon the cheek of the body-servant before the latter had time to place himself in the attitude of defence, though he had thrown away his gloves in obedience to the mandate of his master.

For a few moments, Dandy defended himself from the impetuous assault of the young gentleman, who displayed a vigor and energy which he had never before exhibited. The consequences of any "accident" to his master were sufficiently apparent and he maintained his coolness until an unlucky blow on the nose caused that member to bleed, and at the same time produced a sharp and stinging pain.

Dandy had been politic and discreet up to this time, but the sharp pain roused a feeling of resentment in his nature. He had borne all he could, and no longer acting upon the defensive alone, he assumed the aggressive. Both parties were angry now, and for a moment, each did his best, which shortly brought the combat to a disastrous conclusion.

Dandy's arm, which had before been prudentially soft and nerveless, suddenly hardened into solid muscle, and one of his heavy blows came full and square upon the region of Archy's left eye. The young lord of the manor reeled as though a tornado had struck him, and fell heavily upon the ground.

The blow was a hard one, and it fired his southern blood still more. He leaped up, and seizing a large stick which lay upon the ground, he rushed towards his unhappy servant, with the intention of annihilating him upon the spot. Dandy's senses came to him when he saw Archy fall, and he was appalled at the result of the conflict. He had struck the blow upon the impulse of a momentary rage, and he would have given any thing to recall it.

"I didn't mean to do it, Master Archy! Forgive me!" pleaded he, as he retreated to avoid the uplifted club.

Archy was so furious that he could not speak, and Dandy
was compelled to run for his life.

Chapter IV.

DANDY DETERMINES TO WATCH AND WAIT.

Fortunately for Dandy, Master Archy was not as "long-winded"
as some orators of whom we have read, and, unhappily, heard;
and therefore we cannot say to what extent his passion would
have led him on the present occasion. There was no fear of consequences to deter him from smiting his bondman, even unto
death. If he had killed him, though the gentle-hearted might
have frowned or trembled in his presence, there was no law that
could reach him. There was no dread of prison and scaffold to
stay his arm, and what his untamed fury prompted him to do,
he might have done with impunity. Even the statute made for
the protection of the slave from his cruel master, would have
been of no avail, for the want of a white witness to substantiate
the facts.

Dandy ran away. It was all he could do, except defend himself, which might have resulted in further injury to his young
master, and thus involved him deeper than before in the guilt of
striking a blow in his own defence. With no particular purpose
in his mind, except to avoid the blow of the club, he retreated in
the direction which led him away from the point where they
had landed. He ran at his utmost speed for a few moments, for
the impetuosity of his master had wonderfully increased his
fleetness. Master Archy's wind soon gave out, and he was no
longer able to continue the chase. He abandoned the pursuit,
and throwing himself upon the ground, vented his rage in a flood
of tears.

Dandy did not deem it prudent to approach him while in this
mood, and he seated himself on a stump at a point where he
could observe his master's motions. Master Archy was not cruel

or vindictive by nature, and Dandy hoped that a few moments
of rest would restore him to his equilibrium. Archy's faults were
those of his education; they were the offspring of his social position. He had been accustomed to have his own way, except
when his will came in opposition to that of his father, which
was very seldom, for Colonel Raybone was extremely and inju-
diciously indulgent to his children.

It was evident to his body-servant that something had gone
wrong that morning with Master Archy. He had never before
carried his fury to such an extreme. Though he was never reasonable, it was not often that he was so unreasonable as on this
occasion.

Dandy watched him patiently till he thought it was time his
passion had spent itself, and then walked towards him. Archy
discovered the movement before he had advanced many steps;
but without making a demonstration of any kind, he rose from
the ground, and moved off towards the scene of the late encounter. As he passed the spot, he took his coat upon his arm,
and made his way to the Point.

The unhappy servant was troubled and mystified by this conduct; and he was still more bewildered when he saw Archy step
into the boat, and heard him, in sharp tones, order the boatmen
to pull home.

"Dar's Dandy. Isn't he gwine to go home wid us?" said Cyd,
who was even more mystified than the body-servant.

"No questions! Obey my orders, and pull for home," replied
Archy, as he adjusted his shirt sleeves and put on his coat.

When he had arranged his dress, he threw himself upon
the velvet cushions, and took no further notice of Dandy or
the crew. His orders were, of course, obeyed. The bow oarsman
pushed off the boat, and she was headed up the Crosscut. By
this time, poor Dandy, who, notwithstanding the obliquities of
his master's disposition, had a strong regard for him, reached
the shore.

"I am very sorry for what has happened, Master Archy, and
I hope you will forgive me," said he, in humble tones.

The imperious young lord made no reply to this supplicating
petition.

"Please to forgive me!" pleaded Dandy.

"Silence! Don't speak to me again till I give you permission to do so," was the only reply he vouchsafed.

Dandy knew his master well enough to obey, literally, the injunction imposed upon him. Seating himself upon the ground, he watched the receding boat, as the lusty oarsmen drove it rapidly through the water. The events of the morning were calculated to induce earnest and serious reflection. The consequences of the affair were yet to be developed, but Dandy had no strong misgivings. Archy, he hoped and expected, would recover his good nature in a few hours, at the most, and then he would be forgiven, as he had been before.

It is true, he had never before given his master an angry blow; but he had been grievously provoked, and he hoped this would prove a sufficient excuse. Archy had lost his temper, sprung at him with the fury of a tiger, and struck him several severe blows. His face was even now covered with blood, and his nose ached from the flattening it had received. He could not feel that he had done a very wicked deed. He had only defended himself, which is the inborn right of man or boy when unjustly assailed. He had been invited, nay, pressed, to strike the blow which had caused the trouble.

Then he thought of his condition, of the wrongs and insults which had been heaped upon him; and if the few drops of negro blood that flowed in his veins prompted him to patience and submission, the white blood, the Anglo-Saxon inspiration of his nature, which coursed through the same channels, counselled resistance, mad as it might seem. As he thought of his situation, the tears came into his eyes, and he wept bitterly. The future was dark and forbidding, as the past had been joyless and hopeless. They were tears of anger and resentment, rather than of sorrow.

He almost envied the lot of the laborers, who toiled in the cane-fields. Though they were meanly clad and coarsely fed, they were not subjected to the whims and caprices of a wayward boy. They had nothing to fear but the lash of the driver, and this might be avoided by diligence and care. And then, with the tears coursing down his pale cheeks, he realized that the field-hands who labored beneath the eye of the overseer and the driver were better off and happier than he was.

"What can I do!" murmured he, as he rose from the ground, and walked back to the shade of the trees. "If I resist, I shall be whipped; and I cannot endure this life. It is killing me."

"I will run away!" said he, as he sat down upon a stump at some distance from the Point. "Where shall I go?"

He shuddered as he thought of the rifle of the overseer, and the blood-hounds that would follow upon his track. The free states were far, far away, and he might starve and die in the deep swamps which would be his only hiding place. It was too hopeless a remedy to be adopted, and he was obliged to abandon the thought in despair.

"I will watch and wait," said he. "Something will happen one of these days. If I ever go to New Orleans again, I will hide myself in some ship bound to the North. Perhaps Master Archy will travel some time. He may go to Newport, Cape May, or Saratoga, with his father, this season or next, and I shall go with him. I will be patient and submissive—that is what the preacher said we must all do; and if we are in trouble, God will sooner or later take the burden from our weary spirits. I will be patient and submissive, but I will *watch and wait*."

Drama

WILLIAM WELLS BROWN

William Wells Brown's experiences in slavery and the paired relief and uncertainty brought by his fugitive flights certainly informed his play The Escape; or, A Leap for Freedom, *a tale of an enslaved couple who marries secretly and makes their escape when their cruel enslavers use drastic means to prevent them from being together. Brown never staged* The Escape; *instead, he presented portions of the five-act play at antislavery meetings and rallies, giving dramatic readings to much acclaim.*

From *The Escape; or, A Leap for Freedom*
(1858)

Dr. Gaines, *proprietor of the farm at Muddy Creek.*
Rev. John Pinchen, *a clergyman.*
Dick Walker, *a slave speculator.*
Mr. Wildmarsh, *neighbor to Dr. Gaines.*
Major Moore, *a friend of Dr. Gaines.*
Mr. White, *a citizen of Massachusetts.*
Bill Jennings, *a slave speculator.*
Jacob Scragg, *overseer to Dr. Gaines.*
Mrs. Gaines, *wife of Dr. Gaines.*
Mr. and Mrs. Neal, and Daughter, *Quakers, in Ohio.*
Thomas, *Mr. Neal's hired man.*
Glen, *slave of Mr. Hamilton, brother-in-law of Dr. Gaines.*
Cato, Sam, Sampey, Melinda, Dolly, Susan, and Big Sally, *slaves of Dr. Gaines.*
Pete, Ned, and Bill, *slaves.*
Officers, Loungers, Barkeeper, &c.

ACT I.
Scene 1.

—A Sitting-Room.

Mrs. Gaines, *looking at some drawings*—**Sampey,** *a white slave, stands behind the lady's chair.*

Enter **Dr. Gaines, r.**

DR. GAINES.

Well, my dear, my practice is steadily increasing. I forgot to tell you that neighbor Wyman engaged me yesterday as his family physician; and I hope that the fever and ague, which is now taking hold of the people, will give me more patients. I see by the New Orleans papers that the yellow fever is raging there to a fearful extent. Men of my profession are reaping a harvest in that section this year. I would that we could have a touch of the yellow fever here, for I think I could invent a medicine that would cure it. But the yellow fever is a luxury that we medical men in this climate can't expect to enjoy; yet we may hope for the cholera.

MRS. GAINES.

Yes, I would be glad to see it more sickly here, so that your business might prosper. But we are always unfortunate. Every body here seems to be in good health, and I am afraid that they'll keep so. However, we must hope for the best. We must trust in the Lord. Providence may possibly send some disease amongst us for our benefit.

Enter **Cato, r.**

CATO.

Mr. Campbell is at de door, massa.

DR. G.

Ask him in, Cato.

Enter **Mr. Campbell, r.**

DR. G.
Good morning, Mr. Campbell. Be seated.

MR. CAMPBELL.
Good morning, doctor. The same to you, Mrs. Gaines. Fine morning, this.

MRS. G.
Yes, sir; beautiful day.

MR. C.
Well, doctor, I've come to engage you for my family physician. I am tired of Dr. Jones. I've lost another very valuable nigger under his treatment; and, as my old mother used to say, "change of pastures makes fat calves."

DR. G.
I shall be most happy to become your doctor. Of course, you want me to attend to your niggers, as well as to your family?

MR. C.
Certainly, sir. I have twenty-three servants. What will you charge me by the year?

DR. G.
Of course, you'll do as my other patients do, send your servants to me when they are sick, if able to walk?

MR. C.
Oh, Yes; I always do that.

DR. G.
Then I suppose I'll have to lump it, and say $500 per annum.

MR. C.
Well, then, we'll consider that matter settled; and as two of the

boys are sick, I'll send them over. So I'll bid you good day, doctor. I would be glad if you would come over some time, and bring Mrs. Gaines with you.

DR. G.
Yes, I will; and shall be glad if you will pay us a visit, and bring with you Mrs. Campbell. Come over and spend the day.

MR. C.
I will. Good morning, doctor.

[*Exit* **Mr. Campbell, r.**]

DR. G.
There, my dear, what do you think of that? Five hundred dollars more added to our income. That's patronage worth having! And I am glad to get all the negroes I can to doctor, for Cato is becoming very useful to me in the shop. He can bleed, pull teeth, and do almost any thing that the blacks require. He can put up medicine as well as any one. A valuable boy, Cato!

MRS. G.
But why did you ask Mr. Campbell to visit you, and to bring his wife? I am sure I could never consent to associate with her, for I understand that she was the daughter of a tanner. You must remember, my dear, that I was born with a silver spoon in my mouth. The blood of the Wyleys runs in my veins. I am surprised that you should ask him to visit you at all; you should have known better.

DR. G.
Oh, I did not mean for him to visit me. I only invited him for the sake of compliments, and I think he so understood it; for I should be far from wishing you to associate with Mrs. Campbell. I don't forget, my dear, the family you were raised in, nor do I overlook my own family. My father, you know, fought by the side of Washington, and I hope some day to have a handle to my own name. I am certain Providence intended me for something higher

than a medical man. Ah! by-the-by, I had forgotten that I have a couple of patients to visit this morning. I must go at once.

[*Exit* **Dr. Gaines, r.**]
Enter **Hannah, l.**

MRS. G.
Go, Hannah, and tell Dolly to kill a couple of fat pullets, and to put the biscuit to rise. I expect brother Pinchen here this afternoon, and I want every thing in order. Hannah, Hannah, tell Melinda to come here.

[*Exit* **Hannah, l.**]
We mistresses do have a hard time in this world; I don't see why the Lord should have imposed such heavy duties on us poor mortals. Well, it can't last always. I long to leave this wicked world, and go home to glory.

Enter **Melinda.**
I am to have company this afternoon, Melinda. I expect brother Pinchen here, and I want every thing in order. Go and get one of my new caps, with the lace border, and get out my scolloped-bottomed dimity petticoat, and when you go out, tell Hannah to clean the white-handled knives, and see that not a speck is on them; for I want every thing as it should be while brother Pinchen is here.

[*Exit* **Mrs. Gaines, l, Hannah, r.**]

Scene 2.
—Doctor's shop—Cato making pills.

Enter **Dr. Gaines, l.**

DR. G.
Well, Cato, have you made the batch of ointment that I ordered?

CATO.

Yes, massa; I dun made de intment, an' now I is making the bread pills. De tater pills is up on the top shelf.

DR. G.

I am going out to see some patients. If any gentlemen call, tell them I shall be in this afternoon. If any servants come, you attend to them. I expect two of Mr. Campbell's boys over. You see to them. Feel their pulse, look at their tongues, bleed them, and give them each a dose of calomel. Tell them to drink no cold water, and to take nothing but water gruel.

CATO.

Yes, massa I'll tend to 'em.

[*Exit* **Dr. Gaines, l.**]

CATO.

I allers knowed I was a doctor, an' now de ole boss has put me at it, I muss change my coat. Ef any niggers comes in, I wants to look suspectable. Dis jacket don't suit a doctor; I'll change it.

[*Exit* **Cato**—*immediately returning in a long coat.*]

Ah! now I looks like a doctor. Now I can bleed, pull teef, or cut off a leg. Oh! well, well, ef I aint put de pill stuff an' de intment stuff togedder. By golly, dat ole cuss will be mad when he finds it out, won't he? Nebber mind, I'll make it up in pills, and when de flour is on dem, he won't know what's in 'em; an' I'll make some new intment. Ah! yonder comes Mr. Campbell's Pete an' Ned; dems de ones massa sed was comin'. I'll see ef I looks right. [*Goes to the looking-glass and views himself.*]

I em some punkins, ain't I?

[*Knock at the door.*]

Come in.

Enter **Pete** *and* **Ned, r.**

PETE.

Whar is de doctor?

CATO.
Hero I is; don't you see me?

PETE.
But whar is do ole boss?

CATO.
Dat's none you business. I dun tole you dat I is de doctor, an dat's enuff.

NED.
Oh! do tell us whar do doctor is. I is almos dead. Oh me! oh dear me! I is so sick.
[*Horrible faces.*]

PETE.
Yes, do tell us; we don't want to stan here foolin'.

CATO.
I tells you again dat I is de doctor. I larn de trade under massa.

NED.
Oh! well, den, give me somethin' to stop dis pain. Oh dear me! I shall die.
[*He tries to vomit, but can't—ugly faces.*]

CATO.
Let me feel your pulse. Now put out your tongue. You is berry sick. Ef you don't mine, you'll die. Come out in de shed, an' I'll bleed you.

[*Exit all—re-enter.*]

CATO
—Dar, now take dese pills, two in de mornin' and two at night, and ef you don't feel better, double de dose. Now, Mr. Pete, what's de matter wid you?

PETE.
I is got de cole chills, an' has a fever in de night.

CATO.
Come out, an' I'll bleed you.

[*Exit all—re-enter.*]
Now take dese pills, two in de mornin' and two at night, an' ef dey don't help you, double de dose. Ah! I like to forget to feel your pulse and look at your tongue. Put out your tongue. [*Feels his pulse.*]
Yes, I tells by de feel ob your pulse dat I is gib you de right pills.

Enter **Mr.** *Parker's* **Bill,** l.

CATO.
What you come in dat door widout knockin' for?

BILL.
My toof ache so, I didn't tink to knock. Oh, my toof! my toof! Whar is de doctor?

CATO.
Here I is; don't you see me?

BILL.
What! you de doctor, you brack cuss! You looks like a doctor! Oh, my toof! my toof! Whar is de doctor?

CATO.
I tells you I is de doctor. Ef you don't believe me, ax dese men. I can pull your toof in a minnit.

BILL.
Well, den, pull it out. Oh, my toof! how it aches! Oh, my toof! [*Cato gets the rusty turnkeys.*]

CATO.
Now lay down on your back.

BILL.
What for?

CATO.
Dat's de way massa does.

BILL.
Oh, my toof! Well, den, come on.
[*Lies down, Cato gets astraddle of Bill's breast, puts the turn-keys on the wrong tooth, and pulls—Bill kicks, and cries out*]
—Oh, do stop! Oh! oh! oh!
[*Cato pulls the wrong tooth—Bill jumps up.*]

CATO.
Dar, now, I tole you I could pull your toof for you.

BILL.
Oh, dear me! Oh, it aches yet! Oh me! Oh, Lor-e-massy! You dun pull de wrong toof. Drat your skin! ef I don't pay you for this, you brack cuss!
[*They fight, and turn over table, chairs and bench—Pete and Ned look on.*]

Enter **Dr. Gaines,** r.

DR. G.
Why, dear me, what's the matter? What's all this about? I'll teach you a lesson, that I will.
[*The doctor goes at them with his cane.*]

CATO.
Oh, massa! he's to blame, sir. He's to blame. He struck me fuss.

BILL.
No, sir; he's to blame; he pull de wrong toof. Oh, my toof! oh, my toof!

DR. G.
Let me see your tooth. Open your mouth. As I live, you've taken

out the wrong tooth. I am amazed. I'll whip you for this; I'll whip you well. You're a pretty doctor. Now lie down, Bill, and let him take out the right tooth; and if he makes a mistake this time, I'll cowhide him well. Lie down, Bill.
[*Bill lies down, and Cato pulls the tooth.*]
There now, why didn't you do that in the first place?

CATO.
He wouldn't hole still, sir.

BILL.
He lies, sir. I did hole still.

DR. G.
Now go home, boys; go home.

[*Exit* Pete, Ned *and* Bill, l.]

DR. G.
You've made a pretty muss of it, in my absence. Look at the table! Never mind, Cato; I'll whip you well for this conduct of yours to-day. Go to work now, and clear up the office.

[*Exit* Dr. Gaines, r.]

CATO.
Confound dat nigger! I wish he was in Ginny. He bite my finger and scratch my face. But didn't I give it to him? Well, den, I reckon I did.
[*He goes to the mirror, and discovers that his coat is torn— weeps.*]
Oh, dear me! Oh, my coat—my coat is tore! Dat nigger has tore my coat.
[*He gets angry, and rushes about the room frantic.*]
Cuss dat nigger! Ef I could lay my hands on him, I'd tare him all to pieces,—dat I would. An' de ole boss hit me wid his cane after dat nigger tore my coat. By golly, I wants to fight some-body, Ef ole massa should come in now, I'd fight him.
[*Rolls up his sleeves.*]

Let 'em come now, ef dey dare—ole massa, or any body else; I'm
ready for 'em.

Enter **Dr. Gaines,** r.

DR. G.
What's all this noise here?

CATO.
Nuffin', sir; only jess I is puttin' things to rights, as you tole me.
I didn't hear any noise except de rats.

DR. G.
Make haste, and come in; I want you to go to town.

[*Exit* **Dr. Gaines,** r.]

CATO.
By golly, de ole boss like to cotch me dat time, didn't he? But
wasn't I mad? When I is mad, nobody can do nuffin' wid me.
But here's my coat, tore to pieces. Cuss dat nigger!
[*Weeps.*]
Oh, my coat! oh, my coat! I rudder he had broke my head den
to tore my coat. Drat dat nigger! Ef he ever comes here agin, I'll
pull out every toof he's got in his head—dat I will.

[*Exit,* **r.**]

Scene 3.
—A. Room in the Quarters.

Enter **Glen,** l.

GLEN.
How slowly the time passes away. I've been waiting here two
hours, and Melinda has not yet come. What keeps her, I cannot
tell. I waited long and late for her last night, and when she approached, I sprang to my feet, caught her in my arms, pressed

her to my heart, and kissed away the tears from her moistened cheeks. She placed her trembling hand in mine, and said, "Glen, I am yours; I will never be the wife of another." I clasped her to my bosom, and called God to witness that I would ever regard her as my wife. Old Uncle Joseph joined us in holy wedlock by moonlight; that was the only marriage ceremony. I look upon the vow as ever binding on me, for I am sure that a just God will sanction our union in heaven. Still, this man, who claims Melinda as his property, is unwilling for me to marry the woman of my choice, because he wants her himself. But he shall not have her. What he will say when he finds that we are married, I cannot tell; but I am determined to protect my wife or die. Ah! here comes Melinda.

Enter Melinda, r.

I am glad to see you, Melinda. I've been waiting long, and feared you would not come. Ah! in tears again?

MELINDA.
Glen, you are always thinking I am in tears. But what did master say to-day?

GLEN.
He again forbade our union.

MELINDA.
Indeed! Can he be so cruel?

GLEN.
Yes, he can be just so cruel.

MELINDA.
Alas! alas! how unfeeling and heartless! But did you appeal to his generosity?

GLEN.
Yes, I did; I used all the persuasive powers that I was master of, but to no purpose; he was inflexible. He even offered me a new suit of clothes, if I would give you up; and when I told him that

I could not, he said he would flog me to death if I ever spoke to you again.

MELINDA.
And what did you say to him?

GLEN.
I answered, that, while I loved life better than death, even life itself could not tempt me to consent to a separation that would make life an unchanging curse. Oh, I would kill myself, Melinda, if I thought that, for the sake of life, I could consent to your degradation. No, Melinda, I can die, but shall never live to see you the mistress of another man. But, my dear girl, I have a secret to tell you, and no one must know it but you. I will go out and see that no person is within hearing. I will be back soon.

[*Exit* Glen, l.]

MELINDA.
It is often said that the darkest hour of the night precedes the dawn. It is ever thus with the vicissitudes of human suffering. After the soul has reached the lowest depths of despair, and can no deeper plunge amid its rolling, fœtid shades, then the reactionary forces of man's nature begin to operate, resolution takes the place of despondency, energy succeeds instead of apathy, and an upward tendency is felt and exhibited. Men then hope against power, and smile in defiance of despair. I shall never forget when first I saw Glen. It is now more than a year since he came here with his master, Mr. Hamilton. It was a glorious moonlight night in autumn. The wide and fruitful face of nature was silent and buried in repose. The tall trees on the borders of Muddy Creek waved their leafy branches in the breeze, which was wafted from afar, refreshing over hill and vale, over the rippling water, and the waving corn and wheat fields. The starry sky was studded over with a few light, flitting clouds, while the moon, as if rejoicing to witness the meeting of two hearts that should be cemented by the purest love, sailed triumphantly along among the shifting vapors.
Oh, how happy I have been in my acquaintance with Glen!

That he loves me, I do well believe it; that I love him, it is most true. Oh, how I would that those who think the slave incapable of the finer feelings, could only see our hearts, and learn our thoughts,—thoughts that we dare not utter in the presence of our masters! But I fear that Glen will be separated from me, for there is nothing too base and mean for master to do, for the purpose of getting me entirely in his power. But, thanks to Heaven, he does not own Glen, and therefore cannot sell him. Yet he might purchase him from his brother-in-law, so as to send him out of the way. But here comes my husband.

Enter **Glen,** l.

GLEN.
I've been as far as the overseer's house, and all is quiet. Now, Melinda, as you are my wife, I will confide to you a secret. I've long been thinking of making my escape to Canada, and taking you with me. It is true that I don't belong to your master, but he might buy me from Hamilton, and then sell me out of the neighborhood.

MELINDA.
But we could never succeed in the attempt to escape.

GLEN.
We will make the trial, and show that we at least deserve success. There is a slave trader expected here next week, and Dr. Gaines would sell you at once if he knew that we were married. We must get ready and start, and if we can pass the Ohio river, we'll be safe on the road to Canada.

[*Exit,* r.]

Scene 4.
—Dining-Room.

Rev. Mr. Pinchen *giving* **Mrs. Gaines** *an account of his experience as a minister—***Hannah** *clearing away the breakfast table—***Sampey** *standing behind* **Mrs. Gaines'** *chair.*

MRS. GAINES.

Now, do give me more of your experience, brother Pinchen. It always does my soul good to hear religious experience. It draws me nearer and nearer to the Lord's side. I do love to hear good news from God's people.

MR. PINCHEN.

Well, sister Gaines, I've had great opportunities in my time to study the heart of man. I've attended a great many camp-meetings, revival meetings, protracted meetings, and death-bed scenes, and I am satisfied, sister Gaines, that the heart of man is full of sin, and desperately wicked. This is a wicked world, sister Gaines, a wicked world.

MRS. G.

Were you ever in Arkansas, brother Pinchen? I've been told that the people out there are very ungodly.

MR. P.

Oh, yes, sister Gaines. I once spent a year at Little Rock, and preached in all the towns round about there; and I found some hard cases out there, I can tell you. I was once spending a week in a district where there were a great many horse thieves, and one night, somebody stole my pony. Well, I knowed it was no use to make a fuss, so I told brother Tarbox to say nothing about it, and I'd get my horse by preaching God's everlasting gospel; for I had faith in the truth, and knowed that my Savior would not let me lose my pony. So the next Sunday I preached on horse-stealing, and told the brethren to come up in the eve-nin' with their hearts filled with the grace of God. So that night the house was crammed brim full with anxious souls, panting for the bread of life. Brother Bingham opened with prayer, and brother Tarbox followed, and I saw right off that we were gwine to have a blessed time. After I got 'em pretty well warmed up, I jumped on to one of the seats, stretched out my hands, and said, "I know who stole my pony; I've found out; and you are in here tryin' to make people believe that you've got religion; but you ain't got it. And if you don't take my horse back to brother Tarbox's pasture this very night, I'll tell your name right out in meetin' to-morrow night. Take my pony back, you vile and wretched sinner, and come up here and give your heart to God." So the next mornin', I went out to brother Tarbox's pasture, and sure enough, there was my bob-tail pony. Yes, sister Gaines, there he was, safe and sound. Ha, ha, ha.

MRS. G.
Oh, how interesting, and how fortunate for you to get your pony! And what power there is in the gospel! God's children are very lucky. Oh, it is so sweet to sit here and listen to such good news from God's people! You Hannah, what are you standing there listening for, and neglecting your work? Never mind, my lady, I'll whip you well when I am done here. Go at your work this moment, you lazy huzzy! Never mind, I'll whip you well. [*Aside.*]
Come, do go on, brother Pinchen, with your godly conversation. It is so sweet! It draws me nearer and nearer to the Lord's side.

MR. P.
Well, sister Gaines, I've had some mighty queer dreams in my time, that I have. You see, one night I dreamed that I was dead and in heaven, and such a place I never saw before. As soon as I entered the gates of the celestial empire, I saw many old and familiar faces that I had seen before. The first person that I saw was good old Elder Pike, the preacher that first called my attention to religion. The next person I saw was Deacon Billings, my first wife's father, and then I saw a host of godly faces. Why, sister Gaines, you knowed Elder Goosbee, didn't you?

MRS. G.
Why, yes; did you see him there? He married me to my first husband.

MR. P.
Oh, yes, sister Gaines, I saw the old Elder, and he looked for all the world as if he had just come out of a revival meetin'.

MRS. G.
Did you see my first husband there, brother Pinchen?

MR. P.
No, sister Gaines, I didn't see brother Pepper there; but I've no doubt but that brother Pepper was there.

MRS. G.
Well, I don't know; I have my doubts. He was not the happiest man in the world. He was always borrowing trouble about something or another. Still, I saw some happy moments with Mr. Pepper. I was happy when I made his acquaintance, happy during our courtship, happy a while after our marriage, and happy when he died.
[*Weeps.*]

HANNAH.
Massa Pinchen, did you see my ole man Ben up dar in hebben?

MR. P.
No, Hannah; I didn't go amongst the niggers.

MRS. G.
No, of course brother Pinchen didn't go among the blacks. What are you asking questions for? Never mind, my lady, I'll whip you well when I'm done here. I'll skin you from head to foot.
[*Aside.*]
Do go on with your heavenly conversation, brother Pinchen; it does my very soul good. This is indeed a precious moment for me. I do love to hear of Christ and Him crucified.

MR. P.
Well, sister Gaines, I promised sister Daniels that I'd come over and see her this morning, and have a little season of prayer with her, and I suppose I must go. I'll tell you more of my religious experience when I return.

MRS. G.
If you must go, then I'll have to let you; but before you do, I wish to get your advice upon a little matter that concerns Hannah. Last week, Hannah stole a goose, killed it, cooked it, and she and her man Sam had a fine time eating the goose; and her

master and I would never have known a word about it, if it had
not been for Cato, a faithful servant, who told his master. And
then, you see, Hannah had to be severely whipped before she'd
confess that she stole the goose. Next Sabbath is sacrament day,
and I want to know if you think that Hannah is fit to go to the
Lord's supper after stealing the goose.

MR. P.
Well, sister Gaines, that depends on circumstances. If Hannah
has confessed that she stole the goose, and has been sufficiently
whipped, and has begged her master's pardon, and begged your
pardon, and thinks she'll never do the like again, why then I
suppose she can go to the Lord's supper; for
"While the lamp holds out to burn,
The vilest sinner may return."
But she must be sure that she has repented, and won't steal any
more.

MRS. G.
Now, Hannah, do you hear that? For my own part, I don't
think she's fit to go to the Lord's supper, for she had no occasion to steal the goose. We give our niggers plenty of good
wholesome food. They have a full run to the meal tub, meat
once a fortnight, and all the sour milk about the place, and I'm
sure that's enough for any one. I do think that our niggers are
the most ungrateful creatures in the world, that I do. They ag-
gravate my life out of me.

HANNAH.
I know, missis, dat I steal de goose, and massa whip me for it,
und I confess it, and I is sorry for it. But, missis, I is gwine to de
Lord's supper, next Sunday, Kase I ain't agwine to turn my back
on my bressed Lord an' Massa for no old tough goose, dat I ain't.
[*Weeps.*]

MR. P.
Well, sister Gaines, I suppose I must go over and see sister Daniels; she'll be waiting for me.

[*Exit* **Mr. Pinchen, m. d.**]

MRS. G.
Now, Hannah, brother Pinchen is gone, do you get the cowhide and follow me to the cellar, and I'll whip you well for aggravating me as you have to-day. It seems as if I can never sit down to take a little comfort with the Lord, without you crossing me. The devil always puts it into your head to disturb me, just when I am trying to serve the Lord. I've no doubt but that I'll miss going to heaven on your account. But I'll whip you well before I leave this world, that I will. Get the cowhide and follow me to the cellar.

[*Exit* **Mrs. Gaines** *and* **Hannah, r.**]

ACT II.
Scene 1.
—Parlor.
Dr. Gaines *at a table, letters and papers before him.*

Enter **Sampey, l.**

SAMPEY.
Dar's a gemman at de doe, massa, dat wants to see you, seer.

DR. GAINES.
Ask him to walk in, Sampey.

[*Exit* **Sampey, l.**]
Enter **Walker.**

WALKER.
Why, how do you do, Dr. Gaines? I em glad to see you, I'll swear.

DR. G.
How do you do, Mr. Walker? I did not expect to see you up here so soon. What has hurried you?

WALK.

Well, you see, doctor, I comes when I em not expected. The price of niggers is up, and I em gwine to take advantage of the times. Now, doctor, ef you've got any niggers that you wants to sell, I em your man. I am paying the highest price of any body in the market. I pay cash down, and no grumblin'.

DR. G.

I don't know that I want to sell any of my people now. Still, I've got to make up a little money next month, to pay in bank; and another thing, the doctors say that we are likely to have a touch of the cholera this summer, and if that's the case, I suppose I had better turn as many of my slaves into cash as I can.

WALK.

Yes, doctor, that is very true. The cholera is death on slaves, and a thousand dollars in your pocket is a great deal better than a nigger in the field, with cholera at his heels. Why, who is that coming up the lane? It's Mr. Wildmarsh, as I live! Jest the very man I wants to see.

Enter **Mr. Wildmarsh.**

Why, how do you do, Squire? I was jest a thinkin' about you.

WILDMARSH.

How are you, Mr. Walker? and how are you, doctor? I am glad to see you both looking so well. You seem in remarkably good health, doctor?

DR. G.

Yes, Squire, I was never in the enjoyment of better health. I hope you left all well at Licking?

WILD.

Yes, I thank you. And now, Mr. Walker, how goes times with you?

WALK.

Well, you see, Squire, I em in good spirits. The price of niggers is up in the market, and I am lookin' out for bargains; and I was jest intendin' to come over to Lickin' to see you, to see if you had any niggers to sell. But it seems as ef the Lord knowed that I wanted to see you, and directed your steps over here. Now, Squire, ef you've got any niggers you wants to sell, I em your man. I am payin' the highest cash price of any body in the market. Now's your time, Squire.

WILD.
No, I don't think I want to sell any of my slaves now. I sold a very valuable gal to Mr. Haskins last week. I tell you, she was a smart one. I got eighteen hundred dollars for her.

WALK.
Why, Squire, how you do talk! Eighteen hundred dollars for one gal? She must have been a screamer to bring that price. What sort of a lookin' critter was she? I should like to have bought her.

WILD.
She was a little of the smartest gal I've ever raised; that she was.

WALK.
Then she was your own raising, was she?

WILD.
Oh, yes; she was raised on my place, and if I could have kept her three or four years longer, and taken her to the market myself, I am sure I could have sold her for three thousand dollars. But you see, Mr. Walker, my wife got a little jealous, and you know jealousy sets the women's heads a teetering, and so I had to sell the gal. She's got straight hair, blue eyes, prominent features, and is almost white. Haskins will make a spec, and no mistake.

WALK.
Why, Squire, was she that pretty little gal that I saw on your knee the day that your wife was gone, when I was at your place three years ago?

WILD.
Yes, the same.

WALK.

Well, now, Squire, I thought that was your daughter; she looked mightily like you. She was your daughter, wasn't she? You need not be ashamed to own it to me, for I am mum upon such matters.

WILD.

You know, Mr. Walker, that people will talk, and when they talk, they say a great deal; and people did talk, and many said the gal was my daughter; and you know we can't help people's talking. But here comes the Rev. Mr. Pinchen; I didn't know that he was in the neighborhood.

WALK.

It is Mr. Pinchen, as I live; jest the very man I wants to see.

Enter **Mr. Pinchen,** r.

Why, how do you do, Mr. Pinchen? What in the name of Jehu brings you down here to Muddy Creek? Any camp-meetins, revival meetins, death-bed scenes, or any thing else in your line going on down here? How is religion prosperin' now, Mr. Pinchen? I always like to hear about religion.

MR. PIN.

Well, Mr. Walker, the Lord's work is in good condition every where now. I tell you, Mr. Walker, I've been in the gospel ministry these thirteen years, and I am satisfied that the heart of man is full of sin and desperately wicked. This is a wicked world, Mr. Walker, a wicked world, and we ought all of us to have religion. Religion is a good thing to live by, and we all want it when we die. Yes, sir, when the great trumpet blows, we ought to be ready. And a man in your business of buying and selling slaves needs religion more than any body else, for it makes you treat your people as you should. Now, there is Mr. Haskins,—he is a slave-trader, like yourself. Well, I converted him. Before he got religion, he was one of the worst men to his niggers I ever saw; his heart was as hard as stone. But religion has made his heart as soft as a piece of cotton. Before I converted him, he would sell husbands from their wives, and seem to take delight in it; but now he won't sell a man from his wife, if he can get any one to buy both of them together. I tell you, sir, religion has done a wonderful work for him.

WALK.
I know, Mr. Pinchen, that I ought to have religion, and I feel that I am a great sinner; and whenever I get with good pious people like you and the doctor, and Mr. Wildmarsh, it always makes me feel that I am a desperate sinner. I feel it the more, because I've got a religious turn of mind. I know that I would be happier with religion, and the first spare time I get, I am going to try to get it. I'll go to a protracted meeting, and I won't stop till I get religion. Yes, I'll scuffle with the Lord till I gets forgiven. But it always makes me feel bad to talk about religion, so I'll change the subject. Now, doctor, what about them thar niggers you thought you could sell me?

DR. GAINES.
I'll see my wife, Mr. Walker, and if she is willing to part with Hannah, I'll sell you Sam and his wife, Hannah. Ah! here comes my wife; I'll mention it.

Enter **Mrs. Gaines, l.**
Ah! my dear, I am glad you've come. I was just telling Mr Walker, that if you were willing to part with Hannah, I'd sell him Sam and Hannah.

MRS. G.
Now, Dr. Gaines, I am astonished and surprised that you should think of such a thing. You know what trouble I've had in training up Hannah for a house servant, and now that I've got her so that she knows my ways, you want to sell her. Havn't you niggers enough on the plantation to sell, without selling the servants from under my very nose?

DR. G.
Oh, yes, my dear; but I can spare Sam, and I don't like to separate him from his wife, and I thought if you could let Hannah go, I'd sell them both. I don't like to separate husbands from their wives.

MRS. G.
Now, gentlemen, that's just the way with my husband. He thinks more about the welfare and comfort of his slaves, than he does of himself or his family. I am sure you need not feel so bad at the thought of separating Sam from Hannah. They've only been married eight months, and their attachment can't be very strong in that short time. Indeed, I shall be glad if you do sell Sam, for then I'll make Hannah *jump the broomstick* with Cato, and I'll have them both here under my eye. I never will again let one of my house servants marry a field hand—never! For when night comes on, the servants are off to the quarters, and I have to holler and holler enough to split my throat before I can make them hear. And another thing: I want you to sell Melinda. I don't intend to keep that mulatto wench about the house any longer.

DR. GAINES.
My dear, I'll sell any servant from the place to suit you, except Melinda. I can't think of selling her—I can't think of it.

MRS. G.
I tell you that Melinda shall leave this house, or I'll go. There, now you have it. I've had my life tormented out of me by the presence of that yellow wench, and I'll stand it no longer. I know you love her more than you do me, and I'll—I'll—I'll write—write to my father.
[*Weeps.*]

[*Exit* Mrs. Gaines, l.]

WALK.
Why, doctor, your wife's a screamer, ain't she? Ha, ha, ha. Why, doctor, she's got a tongue of her own, ain't she? Why, doctor, it was only last week that I thought of getting a wife myself; but your wife has skeered the idea out of my head. Now, doctor, if you wants to sell the gal, I'll buy her. Husband and wife ought to be on good terms, and your wife won't feel well till the gal is gone. Now, I'll pay you all she's worth, if you wants to sell.

DR. G.
No, Mr. Walker; the girl my wife spoke of is not for sale. My wife does not mean what she says; she's only a little jealous. I'll get brother Pinchen to talk to her, and get her mind turned upon religious matters, and then she'll forget it. She's only a little jealous.

WALK.
I tell you what, doctor, ef you call that a little jealous, I'd like to know what's a heap. I tell you, it will take something more than religion to set your wife right. You had better sell me the gal; I'll pay you cash down, and no grumblin'.

DR. G.
The girl is not for sale, Mr. Walker; but if you want two good, able-bodied servants, I'll sell you Sam and Big Sally. Sam is trustworthy, and Sally is worth her weight in gold for rough usage.

PAULINE ELIZABETH HOPKINS

A journalist, novelist, and playwright, Pauline Elizabeth Hopkins (1859–1930) was born in Portland, Maine, and was raised in Cambridge, Massachusetts. Her interest in the arts was solidified and encouraged when she won a writing prize in high school in an essay contest sponsored by the Congregational Publishing Society of Boston and funded by William Wells Brown. Peculiar Sam, a musical drama about a family who had escaped from slavery, was Hopkins's first well-known work. She went on to write her well-regarded novel Of One Blood; or, The Hidden Self *and a host of other magazine novels in the* Colored American Magazine, *for which she was a board member and shareholder.*

From *Peculiar Sam; or, The Underground Railroad*
(1878)

SAM, [Lucas] *a peculiar fellow (1st Tenor)*
JIM, *overseer (2nd Tenor)*
CAESAR, *station master (Baritone)*
PETE, POMP, *friends to Sam (Tenor, Bass)*
VIRGINIA, *the plantation nightingale (Soprano)*
JUNO, *sister to Sam (Alto)*
MAMMY, *mother to Sam (2nd Soprano)*

ACT I
(Scene, interior of an old cabin. Entrance at back, usual furniture. Time, evening. Unseen chorus sings as curtain rises. At close of chorus, enter SAM, *followed by* JIM, CAESAR,

PETE, *and* POMP, *dressed as field hands.* POMP *with banjo)*

SAM:
Come on boys we'll hab a right smart time hyar, all to our-selves. Mammy and Juno is gone out an' de coast am clar.

PETE:
I say Sam, show de boys dat new step you war
takin' in de fiel' dis mornin'.
(to rest)
Clar, I neber seed a fellar use his feet as dat Sam kan.
(laughter)

SAM:
I allers likes to be 'comidatin' to my frien's. Now Pomp you strike up suthin lively an' de res' ob you gimmens take a turn wid de music till you git kin' o' warmed up, an' soon as you's at de right pitch I'll wade in on de new step.

PETE:
Jes' so sir.
(POMP strikes up lively dance, each takes a turn. SAM beats time and grows more and more excited)

SAM:
(unable to restrain himself longer)
Take kar dar, de spirits a movin' in me, Ise comin'.
(Rest cease dancing, mark time until he drops, exhausted, into a seat)

SAM:
I tell you what gimmens, when I gits off on an ole Virginie, I feels jes like an onthoughtful horse, died I does.

POMP:
(rising)
I tell you boy you's a hi ole dancer, you doesn't kno' your own walloo.

(to rest)
Les all go down to uncle Eph's backyard an' hearse dis new
step. Clar, I jes tingles to get at it.

ALL:
Dat's jes de ting.
(JIM, CAESAR, PETE, and POMP move toward door)

SAM:
I'll meet you dar, soon as I 'sposes ob some tickler bisness lse
got on han'.
(laughter)

PETE:
'Spec' boy you'd better look out for Jim; he's got young Marse
mighty sweet, an' ole times am pas' since old Marse died. I doesn't
like to say it, but Ise might 'fraid you's gwine to lose your gal.

SAM:
(answers PETE with solo)

> One night as the moon was beamin'
> I lay fas' asleep a dreamin';
> That the sun was shinin' bright,
> In the middle of the night
> And the darkies had assembled to have a little fight.
> I woke an' the banjo was soundin'
> An' the bones through the air were boundin';
> How happy I did seem, I was married in a dream,
> In an ole Virginie mudscow floatin down stream.

CHORUS:
(JIM, CAESAR, PETE, and POMP sing)

SAM:
> Din I warn all de niggers not to love her,
> Ef they do it'll cause them to blubber;
> Now git out of my way an' member what I say,
> I'm gwine to marry her myself some very fine day.

ALL:
Kiah! Kiah! Kiah!

PETE:
I 'spec' you will Sam, 'spec' you will.
(Exit JIM, CAESAR, PETE, *and* POMP)

SAM:
Wonder whar all de folks is.
(thoughtfully)
'Pears like to me nuthin's wrong; I feel it inter my bones dat dars gwine to be a disjointin' hyar soon, an' when I gits dose 'pressions dey's neber wrong.

(Enter MAMMY, *excited)*

MAMMY:
(breathing hard)
For de Lor's sake boy do you kno' what dey's gone an' done up to de big house? Dey's gone an married dat dear chile, dat lamb ob a Jinny, to dat rascal ob an oberseer Jim.

SAM:
(excited, grasps her arm)
Mammy, tell me agin! You don't mean it! Tell me dey haint done dat!

MAMMY:
(astonished)
He yar boy, lef' be my arm. You mean to scrunch me to a jelly?
(He drops her arm)
Yes, deys bring dat gal up like a lady; she neber done nuthin' but jes wait on Marse fambly an' now ole Marser's dead dey's gone an' married her, their way to Jim an' de gal can't bar de sight ob him. It's de meanes' thing I eber seed.

SAM:
(dejected)
An' dats' de way they treats dar slabes! An' den they tells

how kin' dey is, an' how satisfied we is, an' den thar dogs an' horses.
(to MAMMY)
Mammy, when am dat time comin' dat you's tol me 'bout eber since I was knee high to a cricket, when am Moses gwine to lead us forsook niggers fro' de Red Sea?
(covers face with arm, and turns away)

MAMMY:
(lays hand on his arm)
Poor boy! Poor Sammy! Chile, I didn't kno' you loved dat gal, but I might a knowed it, I might a knowed it. Don't yer gib up nor lose your spirits, for de Lord am comin' on his mighty chariot, drawn by his big white horse, an' de white folks hyar, am a gwine to tremble. Son Ise been waitin' dese twenty-five year, an' I aint guv up yet.

SAM:
Yes Mammy, but lse bibbed dat gal eber sense we made mud pies, down inter de holler, an' I used to steal milk for her out ob de hog tro.

SAM:
(sorrowfully)
Po' Jinny, po' little gal
(sings)

> Ah! Jinny is a simple chile,
> Wif pretty shinin' curls,
> An' white folks love her best, of all
> The young mulatto girls;
> Tell her to wait a little while,
> Tell her in hope to wait,
> For I will surely break the chain,
> That binds her to the gate.

CHORUS:
(mixed quartet, unseen, sings)

SAM:

> Our old cabin stands upon the stream,
> In old Mississippi state
> And I must quickly hurry on
> An' take po' Jinny from de gate.

> Ole Marser's dead an' I am sold,
> From Mississippi state;
> But I can't leave her here alone,
> To weep beside the gate;
> I cannot tell her we must part,
> Alas! Our cruel fate;
> And so with patient eyes she'll watch
> For me, beside the gate.

CHORUS:
(sings)

SAM:

> T'would be wrong for me to leave her 'lone.
> In Mississippi state;
> But cunning, it will break the chain
> That binds her to the gate;
> So I'll Marser's gol' an' silver get,
> Pray heaven I'm not too late;
> To set my darling Jinny free,
> And take her to the gate.

CHORUS:
(sings)

SAM:

> If you should ever travel to the South.
> To Mississippi state;
> Don't fail to find this cabin out,
> Where Jinny stood at the gate;
> Tell her to wait a little while,
> Tell her in hope to wait;
> For I am he, shall make her free,
> An take her from the gate.

CHORUS:
(sings)
(At close, enter VIRGINIA *and* JUNO, *and* JIM *with bundle)*

JUNO:
Mammy, I jes toted Jinny down hyar, for you to use some salvation wif her; talk 'bout dat gal's bein' sof' and easy. She says she's gwine to run 'way tonight.
(SAM takes VIRGINIA *by one hand,* MAMMY *takes the other,* JUNO *makes circuit around them)*

VIRGINIA:
Yes, Mammy, and Sam, I have come to say good-bye, it's hard to leave the place where I was born, but it is better to do this, than to remain here, and become what they wish me to be. To fulfill this so-called marriage.

JUNO:
Yes, Mammy, orrlies thing they done in de worl' was, Marse he say, "Jim you want to marry Jinny?" Jim he say yes, course Jim say yes. Marse say, "Jinny you want to marry Jim?" Jinny her say no, like to kno' what Jinny want to igernunt ole Jim. Marse say, "You man an' wife, an Lor' hab mussy on you soul." Dat no kin' ob weddin'.

SAM:
Jinny, you isn't 'fraid to trust ol' peculiar Sam, I know, kase you see Ise allers willin' to die fer you. You needn't bid any on us good-bye, kase dis night I' tends to tote you and Mammy and Juno 'way from hyar. Yas, an' I'll neber drop ye till Ise toted you safe inter Canidy.

MAMMY:
(astonished)
Boy what you talkin' 'bout!

JUNO:
Golly mighty jes hyar dat fellar.

SAM:

Yas, we's all gwine to Canidy! Dars been suthin' a growin' an' a growin' inter me, an' it keep sayin', "Run 'way, run away, Sam. Be a man, be a free man." An' Mammy, ef it hadn't been fer you an' de gals I'd been gone long 'go. But Ise prepared myself, in kase ob a 'mergensy.

MAMMY:

Look hyar boy, what has you been a doin'? I doesn't want you to bring no disrace onter me.

SAM:

(looks carefully around)
See hyar.
(They gather around him as he produces slip of paper from his pocket)
Dat's a pass for us to go to camp meetin'. Now all ob you kno's dat dars a lot of fellars roun' hyar runnin' off slabes. Dey runs dem to Canidy, an' all 'long de road, de white 'litioners helps 'em deceitfully, an' dey calls dis, de underground railroad. Ef we kin get 'way from hyar inter te nex' state, we kin reach de fus' station oo de road, an' from dar, they'll take charge on us, an' band us safe in Canidy.

JUNO:

I know whar dat is, dar aint no slabe niggers dar, dey's all tooken care on by Mrs. Queen Victoria, she's de Presidunt ob Canidy.

MAMMY:

You hish up gal, an' laf your brudder talk. Day allers tol' me dat boy was pecoolar, but I neber 'spected it would revelop itself in dis way.

SAM:

Dars a mullato fellar gwine to start a gang up river to-night, an' Ise gwine to be dat fellar, an' you's gwine to be de gang. Ef we kin 'complish dis we's all right, an' we'll say good-bye to the ole plantation.

JUNO:

Sh! Dars somebody comin'.

(runs quickly and seats herself on VIRGINIA'S *bundle. Enter* JIM *as overseer)*

JIM:

I 'spected I'd fin' you hyar Miss Airy but you're my wife now, an' you's got to do as I says. Dars dat hoe cake aint baked for my supper, an' dars my ol' pants wants mendin', an' you's got it to do.

*(*VIRGINIA *shrinks from him.* JIM *follows her.* SAM *follows him)*

You's full o' airs, data what you is, but I'll bring em out o' you, ef I has to tie you up an' gib you a dozen lashes.

(Seizes VIRGINIA *by her arm,* SAM *seizes him by collar jerks him, then releases him)*

SAM:

(shudders with anger)

See hyar, Ise soed you swellin' roun' hyar consid'able, but when you talks 'bout struckin' Jinny, Ise got suthin' to say.

JIM:

You's anoder sassy nigger. But you'e fixed long wif de res' ob you 'culiar coons. Mearse gwine to sell you all down Red riber to-morrer, den I reckon Miss Jinny will have herself. An meantime I don't want any ob your sass.

(Women huddle together)

MAMMY:

(rocking herself to and fro)

Ef old Marse had libed he'd neber 'low it. O Lor', O Lor'!

SAM:

I jes wants you to answer one question, do you 'cider dat Jinny am your wife?

JIM:

Yas sar, an' you's only mad kase she aint yourn.

(cracks his whip at SAM*)*

SAM:
(leaps upon him, seizes whip)
You's a har sar, dats what you is! You crack your whip at me!
(flourishes whip around JIM, *then takes it by butt end as if to strike him with it)*
You say Jinny's your wife agin an' I'll mash you all up, you mean ol' yank nigger.
(Chases JIM *around room with whip.* JIM *tries to take it from him)*

JIM:
Ef you strike me, Marse'll skun you.

SAM:
(contemptuously)
Marser's pet!
(throws whip aside)
Come on, you, you lizard hearted coon, we'll hab a set-to, for Ise boun' to take your sass out on your hide.
(They spar with their fists. Two or three times JIM *butts at* SAM, *but misses him,* SAM *passing over his head in careless manner. Make this set-to as comical as possible)*

JIM:
(glaring at him)
O, ef I only had you tied to the widder!

SAM:
(edging up to JIM*)*
This thing is played out; as for havin' a common nigger talkin' 'bout tyin' me up, I isn't gwine to. I wouldn't be such a 'teriated coon as you is for all de Norf. I want you to know dat the ascendant ob seen a 'structible fambly as I is can lick a dozen sech cantankerferous niggers as you is. You can jes look out now Ise done foolin', Ise gwine to hurt you.
(They stand and glare at each other. JIM *is off guard, and* SAM *rushes at him head first, strikes him in the stomach,* JIM *staggers across room, doubles up)*

JIM:
(howls)
O, Ise gone dead, Ise gone dead.
(Women rush to SAM, to hold him)

SAM:
(rubs his head)
Jingo, dat nigger's stomick am made ob some kind ob cast of iron, I reckon.

MAMMY:
O sonny, sonny, Marse'll kill us all.
(Enter POMP and PETE. PETE with banjo. JIM rises, groaning, limps to door)

JIM:
(to SAM)
Neber min' my fine genman, you'll be sol' down South, an' I'll take de res' ob it out o' Jinny.
(Exit JIM hurriedly, as SAM takes two long strides toward him)

PETE AND POMP:
Why wha's de matter?

JUNO:
Sam's been showin' de oberseer how 'culiar he is, dat's all.

VIRGINIA:
O, let us leave as soon as possible, who can tell what may happen?

SAM:
Dat's jes so Jinny.
(to PETE and POMP)
Boys we's gwine to board de train to-night, am you ready?

PETE:
Lord boy, Ise been ready for de las' year.

POMP:
You kin bet on me, kass my trunk am packed.
(holds up banjo)
An' I allers carries my walables wif me.

SAM:
Well den I'll leave you hyar wif Mammy an' de girls while I goes to reconoyster, an' see if de coas' am clar.
(Exit SAM)
(MAMMY and JUNO pack up bundles. JUNO ties plain handkerchief on her head)

VIRGINIA:
While we are waiting for Sam let's sing again before we leave our old home. For though we leave it in darkness and sorrow, it is still our home.
(She sings solo, others join in quartet. I should think "Home, Sweet Home" well sung by the soprano might be a decided hit. Reenter SAM at close, dressed as gentleman overseer)

JUNO:
(not knowing him)
See hyar Marsc, you's in de wrong place. De big house am up ce road dar.

SAM:
(flourising whip)
Why, don't you know me?

ALL:
Am dat you Sam?

MAMMY:
Why, honey, I hardly know'd my own chile.

JUNO:
What a peccoliar fellar you is! Look jes like a gemman.

SAM:
Am you ready? Now is our safest time.
(They pick up their bundles. Start for door, turn as they reach it and form tableau in door around VIRGINIA *and* MAMMY*)*

MAMMY:
(weeping)
Good-bye ole home, de place whar my chillern war born, an' my ole man am buried. Ise ole now, I may neber see you 'gin, but my chillern's gwine, an' I'm boun' to go too. So Good-bye ole home.
(Chorus. Curtain)

ACT II
Scene 1
(Time, night. Front of an old hut in the woods. Enter SAM, VIRGINIA, MAMMY, JUNO, PETE, *and* POMP. *Sing several choruses)*

CAESAR:
(opens window as they finish)
Whar in de name ob de Lor' did all you stray coons drap down from? Ef you don't go 'way from hyar mislestin' 'spectible people, I'll set de dogs onter you, so you'd better git.
(Closes window)

SAM:
(pounds at the door)
Ol' man, ol' man, open de do', it's de delegation from down de riber, don't be 'feard, its' only me, peculiar Sam.

CAESAR:
(opens window slowly)
Aint you gone yet? You needn't tell me you's 'cular Sam, you's one ob dem tricksy m'latter fellars, dat's what you is.

SAM:
'Deed it are me uncle, don't you 'member how I was to come hyar by the 'the undergroun'—

CAESAR:
(interrupts him)
You's bin 'tirely mistook, kase dar aint no underhan' nuthin'
hyar, done moved up Norf long 'go.

SAM:
Now look hyar uncle dar aint no use bein' uppish, kase de black
clouds am risin'.

CAESAR:
(astonished)
Wha', wha' dat you say? Finish dat now, say de res' ob it.

JUNO:
Say uncle, aint you got a 'possum leg in dar, Ise mos' starved?

MAMMY:
You gal hish.

SAM:
Uncle dar aint nuthin' in de worl' dat tastes so sweet as a good
ole ash cake.

CAESAR:
(excited)
Dats de word! dats to word! ash cake am de word!! How you
tink I gwine to kno' you, comin hyar all dressed up dat a way.

MAMMY:
(peers at CAESAR from, under her hand)
'Pears like to me Ise seed you befo'; aint you Caesar dat used to
lib down on de ol' 'Nolin plantation?

CAESAR:
Who dat? In course Ise Caesar.
(looks at her earnestly)
Why Mammy, dat aint you am it? Jes wait til I comes down dar
an' takes a look at you.

(disappears from window, reenters from door. MAMMY *and* CAESAR *laugh and shake hands heartily)*

MAMMY:
Why ol' man thought you war dead an' gone dese ten year!

CAESAR:
Why ol' 'ooman, Ise mighty glad to see you, you's lookin' jes as han'som' as eny gal.
(still shake hands)
Why whar's you all gwine?

SAM:
We're trablin' to Canidy. 'Deed uncle dey is gittin' so hi on des plantations dat a fellar's got to run 'way ef he's got eny 'spectible feelin's 'tall.

CAESAR:
Well children, Ise glad you's foun' de ol' man, an' hope you'll 'scuse my 'seption, but de slabe holders am layin' fer de 'litioners an' I doesn't dar to breaf hard knowin' dat Ise in charge ob one ob dese stations.

SAM:
I tell you uncle Ise jes b'ginnin' te feel mysel', an' ef eny man puts his han' onter me to stop me dar's gwine te be trubble, kase Ise foo'ld long nuff. Ef youll jes gib Mammy an' de gals a chance to take breaf an' den put us onto de next station you'll 'lieve my min'; fer we's had a hard time, de white folks am arter us an' we's been almos' kotched, an' we haint got long to stay hyar.

CHORUS:
"Steal Away"

CAESAR:
(at close)
Well son, you stay an' take keer ob de house, while I tote de folks to de car; den I'll come back fer you.

SAM:

All right uncle, an' ef eny body cames, I reckon I can gib dem all de defamation dey wants. Now you jez han' ober dat dressum gown an' dat cap an' I'll reguise mysel' inter them.
(places wig and moustache in his pocket, exchanges his coat and hat for CAESAR'S)

CAESAR:
(dons SAM'S hat and coat)
'Member honey dat de black clouds is risin' an' ash cake am de words.
(all, save SAM, exit singing)

SAM:
(calls to VIRGINIA)
Don't git scared Jinny I'll meet you by me by. Now I reckon I'll make a reconoyster, an' den turn in an' take some sleep.
(yawns, looks arounds carefully, yawns again. Disappears in hut. Enter JIM)

JIM:
I kno' dey mus' hab come dis way, I'm moz' sho' dis am one ob dem stations. Wonder ef dat do' am fastened.
(tries door, it does not yield, knocks, no answer)
Playin' 'possum.
(knocks louder, no answer)
Wonder ef dar aint no one hyar sho' nuff.
(knocks again)

SAM:
(faintly, as if half asleep)
Who dar? Wha's de matter?

JIM:
(still pounding)
Ol' man you'd better come down hyar, I wants to see you on a very reportant matter.

SAM:
(appears at window with lighted candle, disguised voice)
What you mean comin' hyar in sech a blunderous manner? Ef
you don't go 'way fro' dat do', I'll, I'll, I'll spill suthin' on you,
'deed I will.

JIM:
(as SAM turns to go away)
See hyar uncle, you kno's me, you kno's oberseer Jim; Ise only
come to ax you a few questions.

SAM:
Well, what you want no how? Kase Ise a gemman ob bisness, I
hires my time, I does.

JIM:
I doesn't mean no defense uncle, but you sees some ob my nigs
is runned away, an' I wants to kno' had you hyard ob dem eny
whar?

SAM:
(in scolding voice)
What you doin' lettin' your slabes run 'way? What kin' oberseer is you losin' nigs, an' den runnin' all ober creation an' ebry
whar else lookin' fer em. No I haint seed 'em, I jes haint.

JIM:
See hyar uncle, dars a 'ward out for dem fellars, an' ef you'll gib
me eny reformation, I'll 'garve some o' it fer you.

SAM:
Has you got eny idee whar dey is?

JIM:
O yas, Marse gib me a hunded dollar; an' I foller de trail up
from de plantation, an' jes as I get hyar I lose it. But I reckon de
'litioners am running dem off. But we'll ketch 'em sho. Has you
seed enythig' on 'em?

SAM:
Come to think ob it I did see some stray coons 'roun'. But Lot', my 'mcmbance am so bad.

JIM:
(excited)
You mus' 'member uncle, whar'd dey go, wha'd dey look like?

SAM:
'Clar, it are clean gone from me. My membance am so bad.

JIM:
See hyar uncle, ef you'll tell me anythin' 'bout dem fellars, I'll gib you . . .
(thoughtfully)
I'll gib you fifty cents.

SAM:
Wha's fifty cents side ob a hunded dollars? No, I don't 'member nuthin'.

JIM:
Ef you'll 'member anythin' 'bout dem pussons uncle, I'll gib you, yas I'll gib you dollar.

SAM:
'Pears like dar was a tall coon wif de crowd I see, but I isn't sho.

JIM:
Yas! Yas! Dem's em! An' a singin' gal, say dar war a singin' gal, an' I gib you . . .
(pauses)
I'll gib you two whole dollars.

SAM:
Lor' child 'taint no use axing on me, kase I jes don' kno' wesfer I 'member dat tickler gal or not.

JIM:
Ef you'll jes say she war dar, kase I know'd you seed her, I'll gib you free dollars, dat's all de change Ise got.

SAM:
Lay de money onter de do' sill dar, den I'll see ef I can 'member any mo'!
(JIM *lays money down*)
I reckon de singin' gal war wif dem fellars, reckon you'll fin' her sho nuff, when you kotch 'em.

JIM:
Whar'd dey go? Which way'd dey go?

SAM:
Down de road a piece, dar's a empty house, an' I reckon deys done gone dar.

JIM:
How'd you get at dat house?

SAM:
Reckon you'd better take de railroad track on yer right an' de woods onto your lef' an' foller dat paf till you gits to a blasted juniper tree, an' when you git to dat tree you turn ober it, an' foller dat puf till you gits to de house. Ef you don't fin' it, you kin come back an' go 'roun' de tother way.

JIM:
(ready to start)
How long's dey been gone?

SAM:
'Deed it might a bin a hour 'go, an' it might a bin fourteen hour 'go; an' den agin it might a bin longer, an' it mightent a bin so long, it war some whar 'roun' dar. My membance has 'clipses wery bad, but I reckun dat's about de time dey whar hyar.
(SAM *disappears from window*)

JIM:
Dat fellar aint foolin' me eny, I hasn't got fer to go to fin' dem coons; I'll kotch him.
(disappears. Enter SAM *from door)*

SAM:
(chuckles)
Hope dat fellar'll fin' dat house.
(laughs)
Don't blive dars any sech place on de face ob de earth.
(picks up money)
Dis money come in right smart, it'll be mighty handy up dar in Canidy. 'Clar I wishes I could git dat hunded dollars.
(enter JIM, *as ghost, groans.* SAM *turns, startled, and stands shaking in terror)*
Who, who'd you want to see sar? Kase dar aint nobody to home, I don't lib hyar mysel' Ise jes keepin' house till de fambly 'turns.
(ghost groans, extends right arm, moves slowly toward SAM, *who retreats, followed by ghost, step for step)*
O Marse debbil, jes 'low me to satisfy you dat I isn't de fellar you's lookin fer, 'deed I aint, he's done gone 'way five long year 'go.
(ghost draws nearer)
I neber done nuthin' to nobody. I allers says my prayers ebery night, 'deed I does.
(ghost places his hand on SAM. SAM *falls on his knees)*
I'll 'fess, I'll 'fess.
(his eyes fall on ghost's feet. SAM *rises to his feet with mouth open in astonishment. Aside)*
I know dem feet! 'Course I knows dem feet!
(looks at them again)
Dem's de same pair o' feet. I know dey is, kase dem feet neber growed on no oder fellar but Jim, in de worl'.
(to ghost)
Playin' ghos' am you? Well reckon I'll make you de sickes' ghos' in 'Merica, 'fore I'm done wif you.
(ghost turns to run. SAM *grapples with him. Overcomes him and has arms behind him)*

Gwine to leab me war you? When you kno's how Mammy an'
de gals will 'mire to see a ghos'.
(helps JIM *to his feet)*
You's a pretty lookin' ghos', aint you? You's a disrace to de prefe-
shun. Now I wants you to hand out dat hunded dollar Marse guv
you.

JIM:
(feebly)
It's in my pants pocket.
*(SAM takes out pocket book, opens it disclosing bills. Forgets
ghost, sits down on stage floor, begins to count, chuckling to
himself)*

SAM:
Dars a five, an' a ten, an' a one, an' a twenty . . .
*(JIM meantime steals along stage to entrance, stumbles in his
dress, making noise. SAM stops counting, looks up, produces
pistol, which he points at ghost)*
Come back hyar sar, ef you moves dat karkass o' yourn de lengf
of a 'possum's tail, I'll make a sho nuff ghos' ob you.

JIM:
For de Lor's sake Sam don't shoot, Ise only playin' wif you.

SAM:
(rising)
Well I isn't playin', an' ef you tries to git 'way I'll shoot you.
'Taint no harm to shoot ghosts, an' dis pistol got a piece ob sil-
ber in it, so you see Ise a peculiar fellar to play wif. Recken I'd
better shoot you anyway, don't b'lieve anythin' else will 'bieve
my feelin's.

JIM:
See hyar Sam you wouldn't hurt an unabled fellar would you?
(Enter CAESAR)

CAESAR:
For de good Marser's sake boy, what is you doin', wha's dat
you got?

SAM:
Dis am a ghos' uncle, dat Ise captivated. He comed powlin'
roun' hyar, tryin to do mischief, an' Ise been promisin' him to
make a truly ghos' ob him.

CAESAR:
(examines JIM *curiously. To* SAM*)*
Ghos' hey! 'Pears like to me dat dis am oberseer Jim.

SAM:
Dis am dat very same ole snake.

CAESAR:
Well chile, I reckon de ol' man'll hab to tot himself to Canidy
'long wif you. It's been gittin' woserer an' woserer, an' now dis
fellar has foun' me out, de ol' man'll hab to go.

SAM:
Den de sooner we's gone, de better. Ise glad you's gwine uncle.
Won't we be happy when we all "git on board."

CHORUS:
"Gospel Trail."
*(CAESAR disappears and returns with bundle, while SAM
strikes up song and is answered by unseen chorus. They take
JIM between them and exit)*

THE DAWN OF
FREEDOM

FREDERICK DOUGLASS

Perhaps the most prominent abolitionist, essayist, and ora-
tor, Frederick Douglass (1818–1895) was born in slavery in
Maryland. Douglass *chronicled his fugitive escape from*
slavery in Narrative of the Life of Frederick Douglass: An
American Slave, *which was a bestseller and first in a series*
of autobiographies by Douglass. Douglass delivered speeches
across the US North, Ireland, and England, and was a mem-
ber of a range of antislavery societies over the course of his
many years of abolitionist activism. A proponent of civil
rights and liberty for all, Douglass was the editor of the
North Star *newspaper and* Frederick Douglass' Paper. *Dur-*
ing the Civil War, Douglass was asked to give a speech be-
fore the Women's National Loyal League at the Cooper
Institute in New York. Anticipating postbellum debates
over the cause of the War Between the States, Douglass
makes plain that slavery was the cause and that though the
battles had dragged on for many years with a tremendous
amount of bloodshed, "We are writing the statutes of eter-
nal justice and liberty in the blood of the worst of tyrants as
a warning to all aftercomers. We should rejoice that there
was normal life and health enough in us to stand in our
appointed place, and do this great service for mankind."
Douglass called for the total abolition of slavery, full, unre-
stricted civil rights for Black Americans in the North and
the South, the eradication of prejudice and racial intimida-
tion, and for a future America that is united and lives up to
the most democratic of its founding principles.

From "The Mission of the War" (1864)

We are now wading into the third year of conflict with a fierce
and sanguinary rebellion, one which, at the beginning of it, we

were hopefully assured by one of our most sagacious and trusted political prophets would be ended in less than ninety days; a rebellion which, in its worst features, stands alone among rebellions a solitary and ghastly horror, without a parallel in the history of any nation, ancient or modern; a rebellion inspired by no love of liberty and by no hatred of oppression, as most other rebellions have been, and therefore utterly indefensible upon any moral or social grounds; a rebellion which openly and shamelessly sets at defiance the world's judgment of right and wrong, appeals from light to darkness, from intelligence to ignorance, from the ever-increasing prospects and blessings of a high and glorious civilization to the cold and withering blasts of a naked barbarism; a rebellion which even at this unfinished stage of it counts the number of its slain not by thousands nor by tens of thousands, but by hundreds of thousands; a rebellion which in the destruction of human life and property has rivaled the earthquake, the whirlwind and the pestilence that waketh in darkness and wasteth at noonday. It has planted agony at a million hearthstones, thronged our streets with the weeds of mourning, filled our land with mere stumps of men, ridged our soil with two hundred thousand rudely formed graves and mantled it all over with the shadow of death. A rebellion which, while it has arrested the wheels of peaceful industry and checked the flow of commerce, has piled up a debt heavier than a mountain of gold to weigh down the necks of our children's children. There is no end to the mischief wrought. It has brought ruin at home, contempt abroad, has cooled our friends, heated our enemies and endangered our existence as nation.

Now, for what is all this desolation, ruin, shame, suffering and sorrow? Can anybody want the answer? Can anybody be ignorant of the answer? It has been given a thousand times from this and other platforms. We all know it is slavery. Less than a half a million of Southern slaveholders—holding in bondage four million slaves—finding themselves outvoted in the effort to get possession of the United States government, in order to serve the interests of slavery, have madly resorted to the sword—have undertaken to accomplish by bullets what they failed to accomplish by ballots. That is the answer.

It is worthy of remark that secession was an afterthought with the rebels. Their aim was higher; secession was only their second choice. Who was going to fight for slavery in the Union? It was not separation, but subversion. It was not Richmond, but Washington. It was not the Confederate rag, but the glorious Star-Spangled Banner.

Whence came the guilty ambition equal to this atrocious crime. A peculiar education was necessary to this bold wickedness. Here all is plain again. Slavery—the peculiar institution— is aptly fitted to produce just such patriots, who first plunder and then seek to destroy their country. A system which rewards labor with stripes and chains, which robs the slave of his manhood and the master of all just consideration for the rights of his fellow man—has prepared the characters, male and female, the figure in this rebellion—and for all its cold-blooded and hellish atrocities. In all the most horrid details of torture, starvation and murder in the treatment of our prisoners, I behold the features of the monster in whose presence I was born, and that is slavery. From no sources less foul and wicked could such a rebellion come. I need not dwell here. The country knows the story by heart. But I am one of those who think this rebellion— inaugurated and carried on for a cause so unspeakably guilty and distinguished by barbarities which would extort a cry of shame from the painted savage—is quite enough for the whole lifetime of any one nation, though the lifetime should cover the space of a thousand years. We ought not to want a repetition of it. Looking at the matter from no higher ground than patriotism—the American considerations of justice, liberty, progress and civilization—the American people should resolve that this shall be the last slaveholding rebellion that shall ever curse this continent. Let the War cost more or cost little, let it be long or short, the work now begun should suffer no pause, no abatement, until it is done and done forever.

I know that many are appalled and disappointed by the apparently interminable character of this war. I am neither appalled nor disappointed without pretending to any higher wisdom than other men. I knew well enough and often said it: once let the North and South confront each other on the battlefield, and slavery and freedom be the inspiring motives of the respective sections, the contest will be fierce, long and sanguinary. Governor Seymour charges us with prolonging the war, and I say the longer the better if it must be so in order to put an end to the hell-black cause out of which the rebellion has risen.

Say not that I am indifferent to the horrors and hardships of the war. I am not indifferent. In common with the American people generally, I feel the prolongation of the war a heavy calamity, private as well as public. There are vacant space at my hearthstone which I shall rejoice to see filled again by the boys who once occupied them, but which cannot be thus filled while the war lasts, for they have enlisted "during the war."

But even from the length of this struggle, we who mourn over it may well enough draw some consolation when we reflect upon the vastness and grandeur of its mission. The world has witnessed many wars—and history records and perpetuates their memory—but the world has not seen a nobler and grander war than that which the loyal people of this country are now waging against the slaveholding rebels. The blow we strike is not merely to free a country or continent, but the whole world, from slavery; for when slavery fails here, it will fall everywhere. We have no business to mourn over our mission. We are writing the statutes of eternal justice and liberty in the blood of the worst of tyrants as a warning to all aftercomers. We should rejoice that there was normal life and health enough in us to stand in our appointed place, and do this great service for mankind.

It is true that the war seems long. But this very slow progress is an essential element of its effectiveness. Like the slow convalescence of some patients the fault is less chargeable to the medicine than to the deep-seated character of the disease. We were in a very low condition before the remedy was applied. The whole head was sick and the whole heart faint. Dr. Buchanan and his Democratic friends had given us up and were preparing to celebrate the nation's funeral. We had been drugged nearly to death by proslavery compromises. A radical change was needed in our whole system. Nothing is better calculated to effect the desired change than the slow, steady and certain progress of the war.

I know that his view of the case is not very consoling to the peace Democracy. I was not sent and am not come to console this breach of our political church. They regard this grand moral revolution I the mind and heart of the nation as the most distressing attribute of the war, and howl over it like certain characters of whom we read—who thought themselves tormented before their time.

Upon the whole, I like their mode of characterizing the war. They charge that it is no longer conducted upon constitutional principles. The same was said by Breckinridge and Vallandigham. They charge that it is not waged to establish the Union as it was. The same idea has occurred to Jefferson Davis. They charge that his is a war for the subjugation of the South. In a word, that is, an Abolition war.

For one, I am not careful to deny this charge. But it is instructive to observe how this charge is brought and how it is met. Both warn us of danger. Why is this war fiercely denounced as an Abolition war? I answer, because the nation has long bitterly hated Abolition and the enemies of the war confidently rely upon this hatred to serve the ends of treason. Why do the loyal people deny the charge? I answer, because they know that Abolition, though now a vast power, is still odious. Both the charge and the denial tell how the people hate and despise the only measure that can save the country.

An Abolition war! Well, let us thank the Democracy for teaching us this word. The charge in a comprehensive sense is most true, and it is a pity that it is true, but it would be a vast pity if it were not true. Would that it were more true than it is. When our government and people shall bravely avow this to be an Abolition war, then the country will be safe. Then our work will be fairly mapped out. Then the uplifted arm of the nation will swing unfettered to its work, and the spirit and power of the rebellion will be broken. Had slavery been abolished in the Border States at the very beginning of the war, as it ought to have been—had it been abolished in Missouri, as it would have been but for Presidential interference—there would now be no rebellion in the Southern states, for, instead of having to watch these Border States, as they have done, our armies would have marched in overpowering numbers directly upon the rebels and overwhelmed them. I now hold that a sacred regard for truth, as well as sound policy, makes it our duty to own and avow before heaven and earth that this war is, and of right ought to be, and Abolition War.

The abolition of slavery is the comprehensive and logical object of war, for it includes everything else which the struggle involves. It is a war for the Union, a war for the Constitution, I admit; but it is logically such a war only in the sense that the greater includes the lesser. Slavery has proved itself the strong man of our national house. In every rebel state it proved itself stronger than the Union, stronger than the Constitution, and stronger than the Republican institutions can become possible. An Abolition war, therefore, includes Union, Constitution, Republican institutions, and all else that goes to make up the greatness and glory of our common country. On the other hand, exclude Abolition, and you exclude all else for which you are fighting.

The position of the Democratic party in relation to the war ought to surprise nobody. It is consistent with the history of the party for thirty years. Slavery, and only slavery, has been its recognized master during all the time. It early won for itself the title of being the natural ally of the South and of slavery. It has always been for peace or against peace, for war and against war, precisely as dictated by slavery. Ask why it was for the Florida War, and it answers, slavery. Ask why it was for the Mexican War, and it answers, slavery. Ask why it was for the annexation of Texas, and it answers, slavery. Ask why it was opposed to habeas corpus when a Negro was the applicant, and it answers slavery. Ask why it is now in favor of the habeas corpus, when rebels and traitors are the applicants for its benefits, and it answers, slavery. Ask why it was for mobbing down freedom of speech a few years ago, when that freedom was claimed by the Abolitionists, and it answers, slavery. Ask why it now asserts freedom of speech, when sympathizers with traitors claim that freedom, and again slavery is the answer. Ask why it denied the right of a state to protect itself against possible abuses of the fugitive Slave Bill, and you have the same old answer. Ask why it now asserts the sovereignty of the states separately as against the states united, and again slavery is the answer. Ask why it was opposed to giving persons claimed as fugitive slaves a jury trial before returning them to slavery; ask why it is now in favor of giving jury trial to traitors before sending them to the forts for safekeeping; ask why it was for war at the beginning of the Rebellion; ask why it has attempted to embarrass and hinder the loyal government at every step of its progress, and you have but one answer, slavery.

The fact is, the party in question—I say nothing of individual men who were once members of it—has had but one vital and animating principle for thirty years, and that has been the same old horrible and hell-born principle of Negro slavery.

It has now assumed a saintly character. Its members would receive the benediction due to peacemakers. At one time they would stop bloodshed at the South by inaugurating bloody revolution at the North. The livery of peace is a beautiful livery, but in this case it is a stolen livery and sits badly on the wearer. These new apostles of peace call themselves Peace Democrats, and boast that they belong to the only party which can restore the country to peace. I neither dispute their title nor the pretensions founded upon it. The best that can be said of the peacemaking ability of this class of men is their bitterest condemnation. It consists in their known treachery to the loyal government. They have but to cross the rebel lines to be hailed by the traitors as countrymen, clansmen, kinsmen, and brothers beloved in a common conspiracy. But, fellow-citizens, I have far less solicitude about the position and the influence of this party than I have about that of the great loyal party of the country. We have much less to fear from the bold and shameless wickedness of the one than from the timid and short-sighted policy of the other.

I know we have recently gained a great political victory; but it remains to be seen whether we shall wisely avail ourselves of its manifest advantages. There is danger that, like some of our Generals in the field, who, after soundly whipping the foe, generously allow him time to retreat in order, reorganize his forces, and intrench himself in a new and stronger position, where it will require more power and skill to dislodge him than was required to vanquish him in the first instance. The game is now in our hands. We can put an end to this disloyal party by putting an end to Slavery. While the Democratic party is in existence as an organization, we are in danger of a slaveholding peace, and of Rebel rule. There is but one way to avert this calamity, and that is destroy Slavery and enfranchise the black man while we have the power. While there is a vestige of Slavery remaining, it will unite the South with itself, and carry with it the Democracy of the North. The South united and the North divided, we shall be hereafter as heretofore, firmly held under the heels of Slavery.

Here is a part of the platform of principles upon which it seems to me every loyal man should take his stand at this hour:

First: That this war, which we are compelled to wage against slaveholding rebels and traitors, at untold cost of blood and treasure, shall be, and of right ought to be, an Abolition war.

Secondly: That we, the loyal people of the North and of the whole country, while determined to make this a short and final war, will offer no peace, accept no peace, consent to no peace, which shall not be to all intents and purposes an Abolition peace.

Thirdly: That we regard the whole colored population of the country, in the loyal as well as in the disloyal states, as our countrymen—valuable in peace as laborers, valuable in war as soldiers—entitled to all the rights, protection, and opportunities for achieving distinction enjoyed by any other class of our countrymen.

Fourthly: Believing that the white race has nothing to fear from fair competition with the black race, and that the freedom and elevation of one race are not to be purchased or in any manner rightfully subserved by the disfranchisement of another, we shall favor immediate and unconditional emancipation in all the states, invest the black man everywhere with the right to vote and to be voted for, and remove all discriminations against his rights on account of his color, whether as a citizen or as a soldier.

Ladies and gentlemen, there was a time when I hoped that events unaided by discussion would couple this rebellion and slavery in a common grave. But, as I have before intimated, the facts do still fall short of our hopes. The question as to what shall be done with slavery—and especially what shall be done with the Negro—threaten to remain open questions for some time yet.

It is true we have the Proclamation of January 1863. It was a vast and glorious step in the right direction. But unhappily, excellent as that paper is—and much as it has accomplished temporarily—it settles nothing. It is still open to decision by courts, canons and Congresses. I have applauded that paper and do now applaud it, as a wide measure—while I detest the motive and principle upon which it is based. By it the holding and flogging of Negroes is the exclusive luxury of loyal men.

Our chief danger lies in the absence of all moral feeling in the utterances of our rulers. In his letter to Mr. Greeley the President told the country virtually that the abolition or non-abolition of slavery was a matter of indifference to him. He would save the Union with slavery or without slavery. In his last Message he shows the same moral indifference, by saying as he does say that he had hoped that the rebellion could be put down without the abolition of slavery.

When the late Stephen A. Douglas uttered the sentiment that he did not care whether slavery were voted up or voted down in the territories, we thought him lost to all genuine feeling on the subject, and no man more than Mr. Lincoln denounced that sentiment as unworthy of the lips of any American statesman. But today, after nearly three years of a slaveholding rebellion, Douglas wanted popular sovereignty; Mr. Lincoln wants the Union. Now did a warm heart and a high moral feeling control the utterance of the President, he would welcome, with joy unspeakable and full of glory, the opportunity afforded by the rebellion to free the country form the matchless crime and infamy. But policy, policy, everlasting policy, has robbed our statesmanship of all soul-moving utterances.

The great misfortune is and has been during all the progress of this war, that the government and loyal people have not understood and accepted its true mission. Hence we have been floundering in the depths of dead issues. Endeavoring to impose old and worn-out condition upon new relations—putting new wines into old bottles, new cloth into old garments and thus making the rent worse then before.

Had we been wise we should have recognized the war at the outset as at once the signal and the necessity for a new order of social and political relations among the whole people. We could, like the ancients, discern the face of the sky, but not the signs of the times. Hence we have been talking of the importance of carrying on the war within the limits of a Constitution broken down by the very people in whose behalf the Constitution is pleaded! Hence we have from the first been deluding ourselves with the miserable dream that the old Union can be revived in the states where it has been abolished.

Now, we of the North have seen many strange things and may see many more; but that old Union, whose canonized bones we saw hearse in death and inurned under the frowning battlements of Sumter, we shall never see again while the world standeth. The issue before us is a living issue. We are not fighting for the dead past, but for the living present and the glorious future. We are not fighting for the old Union, nor for anything like it, but for that which is ten thousand times more important; and that thing, crisply rendered, is national unity. Both sections have tried union. It has failed.

The lesson for the statesmen at his hour is to discover and apply some principle of government which shall produce unity of sentiment, unity of idea, unity of object. Union without unity is, as we have seen, body without soul, marriage without love, a barrel without hoops, which falls at the first touch.

The statesmen of the South understood this matter earlier and better than the statesmen of the North. The dissolution of the Union on the old bases of compromise was plainly foreseen and predicted thirty years ago. Mr. Calhoun, and not Mr. Seward, is the original author of the doctrine of the irrepressible conflict. The South is logical and consistent. Under the teachings of their great leader they admit into their form of government no disturbing force. They have based their confederacy squarely on their cornerstone. Their two great all-commanding ideas are, first, that slavery is right, and second, that the slaveholders are a superior order or class. Around these two ideas their manners, morals, politics, religion and laws revolve. Slavery being right, all that is inconsistent with its entire security is necessarily wrong, and of course ought to be put down. There is no flaw in their logic.

They first endeavored to make the federal government stand upon their accursed cornerstone; and we but barely escaped, as well you know, that calamity. Fugitive-slave laws, slavery-extension laws, and Dred Scott decisions were among the steps to get the nation squarely upon the cornerstone now chosen by the Confederate states. The loyal North is less definite in regard to the necessity of principles of national unity. Yet, unconsciously to ourselves, and against our own protestations, we are in reality, like the South, fighting for national unity—a unity of which the great principles of liberty and equality, and not slavery and class superiority, are the cornerstone.

Long before this rude and terrible war came to tell us of a broken Constitution and a dead Union, the better portion of the loyal people had outlived and outgrown what they had been taught to believe were the requirements of the old Union. We had come to detest the principle by which slavery had a strong representation in Congress. We had come to abhor the idea of being called upon to suppress slave insurrections. We had come to be ashamed of slave hunting, and being made the watchdogs of slaveholders, who were too proud to scent out and hunt down their slaves for themselves. We had so far outlived the old Union four years ago that we thought the little finger of the hero of Harpers Ferry of more value to the world struggling liberty than all the first families of old Virginia put together.

What business, then, have we to be pouring out our treasure and shedding our best blood like water for that old worn-out, dead and buried Union, which had already become a calamity and a curse? The fact is, we are not fighting for any such thing, and we ought to come out under our own true colors, and let the South and the whole world know that we don't want and will not have anything analogous to the old Union.

What we now want is a country—a free country—a country not saddened by the footprints of a single slave—and nowhere cursed by the presence of a slaveholder. We want a country which shall not brand the Declaration of Independence as a lie. We want a country whose fundamental institutions we can proudly defend before the highest intelligence and civilization of the age. Hitherto we have opposed European scorn of our slavery with a blush of shame as our best defense. We now want a country in which the obligations of patriotism shall not conflict with fidelity to justice and liberty. We want a country, and are fighting for a country, which shall be free from sectional political parties—free from sectional religious dominations—free from sectional benevolent associations—free from every kind and description of sect, party, and combination of a sectional character. We want a country where men may assemble from any part of it, without prejudice to their interests or peril to their persons.

CHARLOTTE FORTEN

Charlotte Forten (1837–1914) was an abolitionist, educa-
tor, and poet. She was born and raised in Philadelphia,
Pennsylvania, in a prominent abolitionist family that as-
sisted fugitives from slavery in their passage to freedom.
Forten was well-known in antislavery circles in the North
and was a member of the Salem Female Anti-Slavery Soci-
ety in Massachusetts. During the Civil War, Forten was
among the first Black teachers to travel to the Lowcountry
region of South Carolina to assist with the Port Royal Ex-
periment on the sea islands. The selection here is an extract
of her experiences—a catalog of memories that she penned
in a diary and subsequently published in the Atlantic
Monthly *in 1864. Forten describes the range of challenges*
faced, and celebrates the determination with which the
newly freed South Carolinians worked to educate them-
selves and step into their new lives.

From *Life on the Sea Islands* (1864)

A few days before Christmas, we were delighted at receiving a
beautiful Christmas Hymn from Whittier, written by request,
especially for our children. They learned it very easily, and enjoyed singing it. We showed them the writer's picture, and told
them he was a very good friend of theirs, who felt the deepest
interest in them, and had written this hymn expressly for them
to sing,—which made them very proud and happy. Early Christmas morning, we were wakened by the people knocking at the
doors and windows, and shouting, "Merry Christmas!" After
distributing some little presents among them, we went to the
church, which had been decorated with holly, pine, cassena,
mistletoe, and the hanging moss, and had a very Christmas-like
look. The children of our school assembled there, and we gave

them the nice, comfortable clothing, and the picture-books, which had been kindly sent by some Philadelphia ladies. There were at least a hundred and fifty children present. It was very pleasant to see their happy, expectant little faces. To them, it was a wonderful Christmas-Day,—such as they had never dreamed of before. There was cheerful sunshine without, lighting up the beautiful moss-drapery of the oaks, and looking in joyously through the open windows; and there were bright faces and glad hearts within. The long, dark night of the Past, with all its sorrows and its fears, was forgotten; and for the Future,—the eyes of these freed children see no clouds in it. It is full of sunlight, they think, and they trust in it, perfectly.

After the distribution of the gifts, the children were addressed by some of the gentlemen present. They then sang Whittier's Hymn, the "John Brown" song, and several of their own hymns, among them a very singular one, commencing,—

> "I wonder where my mudder gone;
> Sing, O graveyard!
> Graveyard ought to know me;
> Ring, Jerusalem!
> Grass grow in de graveyard;
> Sing, O graveyard!
> Graveyard ought to know me;
> Ring, Jerusalem!"

They improvise many more words as they sing. It is one of the strangest, most mournful things I ever heard. It is impossible to give any idea of the deep pathos of the refrain,—

> "Sing, O graveyard!"

In this, and many other hymns, the words seem to have but little meaning; but the tones,—a whole lifetime of despairing sadness is concentrated in them. They sing, also, "Jehovyah, Hallelujah," which we like particularly:—

> "De foxes hab holes,
> An' de birdies hab nes',

But de Son ob Man he hab not where
To lay de weary head.
Chorus.
"Jehovyah, Hallelujah! De Lord He will purvide!
Jehovyah, Hallelujah! De Lord He will purvide!"

They repeat the words many times. "De foxes hab holes," and the succeeding lines, are sung in the most touching, mournful tones; and then the chorus—"Jehovyah, Hallelujah"—swells forth triumphantly, in glad contrast.

Christmas night, the children came in and had several grand shouts. They were too happy to keep still.

"Oh, Miss, all I want to do is to sing and shout!" said our little pet, Amaretta. And sing and shout she did, to her heart's content.

She read nicely, and was very fond of books. The tiniest children are delighted to get a book in their hands. Many of them already know their letters. The parents are eager to have them learn. They sometimes said to me,—

"Do, Miss, let de chil'en learn eberyting dey can. We nebber hab no chance to learn nuttin', but we wants de chil'en to learn."

They are willing to make many sacrifices that their children may attend school. One old woman, who had a large family of children and grandchildren, came regularly to school in the winter, and took her seat among the little ones. She was at least sixty years old. Another woman—who had one of the best faces I ever saw—came daily, and brought her baby in her arms. It happened to be one of the best babies in the world, a perfect little "model of deportment," and allowed its mother to pursue her studies without interruption.

While taking charge of the store, one day, one of the men who came in told me a story which interested me much. He was a carpenter, living on this island, and just before the capture of Port Royal had been taken by his master to the mainland,— "the Main," as the people call it,—to assist in building some houses which were to shelter the families of the Rebels in case the "Yankees" should come. The master afterward sent him back to the island, providing him with a pass, to bring away a boat and some of the people. On his arrival he found that the Union troops were in possession, and determined to remain here with his family instead of returning to his master. Some of his fellow-servants, who had been left on "the Main," hearing that the Federal troops had come, resolved to make their escape to the islands. They found a boat of their master's, out of which a piece six feet square had been cut. In the night they went to the boat, which had been sunk in a creek near the house, measured the hole, and, after several nights' work in the woods, made a piece large enough to fit in. They then mended and sank it again, as they had found it. The next night five of them embarked. They had a perilous journey, often passing quite near the ene-my's boats. They travelled at night, and in the day ran close up to the shore out of sight. Sometimes they could hear the hounds, which had been sent in pursuit of them, baying in the woods. Their provisions gave out, and they were nearly exhausted. At last they succeeded in passing all the enemy's boats, and reached one of our gun-boats in safety. They were taken on board and kindly cared for, and then sent to this island, where their fami-lies, who had no hope of ever seeing them again, welcomed them with great rejoicing.

We were also told the story of two girls, one about ten, the other fifteen, who, having been taken by their master up into the country, on the mainland, at the time of the capture of the islands, determined to try to escape to their parents, who had been left on this island. They stole away at night, and travelled through woods and swamps for two days, without eating. Sometimes their strength gave out, and they would sink down, thinking they could go no farther; but they had brave little hearts, and got up again and struggled on, till at last they reached Port-Royal Ferry, in a state of utter exhaustion. They were seen there by a boat-load of people who were also making their escape. The boat was too full to take them in; but the peo-ple, on reaching this island, told the children's father of their whereabouts, and he immediately took a boat, and hastened to the ferry. The poor little creatures were almost wild with joy when they saw him. When they were brought to their mother, she fell down "jes' as if she was dead,"—so our informant ex-pressed it,—overpowered with joy on beholding the "lost who were found."

New-Year's-Day—Emancipation-Day—was a glorious one to
us. The morning was quite cold, the coldest we had experienced; but we were determined to go to the celebration at Camp
Saxton,—the camp of the First Regiment South-Carolina Volunteers,—whither the General and Colonel Higginson had bid-
den us, on this, "the greatest day in the nation's history." We
enjoyed perfectly the exciting scene on board the Flora. There
was an eager, wondering crowd of the freed people in their
holiday-attire, with the gayest of head-handkerchiefs, the whitest of aprons, and the happiest of faces. The band was playing,
the flags streaming, everybody talking merrily and feeling
strangely happy. The sun shone brightly, the very waves seemed
to partake of the universal gayety, and danced and sparkled
more joyously than ever before. Long before we reached Camp
Saxton we could see the beautiful grove, and the ruins of the
old Huguenot fort near it. Some companies of the First Regiment were drawn up in line under the trees, near the landing,
to receive us. A fine, soldierly-looking set of men; their brilliant
dress against the trees (they were then wearing red pantaloons)
invested them with a semi-barbaric splendor. It was my good
fortune to find among the officers an old friend,—and what it
was to meet a friend from the North, in our isolated Southern
life, no one can imagine who has not experienced the pleasure.
Letters were an unspeakable luxury,—we hungered for them,
we could never get enough; but to meet old friends,—that was
"too much, too much," as the people here say, when they are
very much in earnest. Our friend took us over the camp, and
showed us all the arrangements. Everything looked clean and
comfortable, much neater, we were told, than in most of the
white camps. An officer told us that he had never seen a regiment in which the men were so honest. "In many other camps,"
said he, "the colonel and the rest of us would find it necessary
to place a guard before our tents. We never do it here. They are
left entirely unguarded. Yet nothing has ever been touched."
We were glad to know that. It is a remarkable fact, when we
consider that these men have all their lives been slaves; and we
know what the teachings of Slavery are.

The celebration took place in the beautiful grove of live-oaks
adjoining the camp. It was the largest grove we had seen. I wish

it were possible to describe fitly the scene which met our eyes as we sat upon the stand, and looked down on the crowd before us. There were the black soldiers in their blue coats and scarlet pantaloons, the officers of this and other regiments in their handsome uniforms, and crowds of lookers-on,—men, women, and children, of every complexion, grouped in various attitudes under the moss-hung trees. The faces of all wore a happy, interested look. The exercises commenced with a prayer by the chaplain of the regiment. An ode, written for the occasion by Professor Zachos, was read by him, and then sung. Colonel Higginson then introduced Dr. Brisbane, who read the President's Proclamation, which was enthusiastically cheered. Rev. Mr. French presented to the Colonel two very elegant flags, a gift to the regiment from the Church of the Puritans, accompanying them by an appropriate and enthusiastic speech. At its conclusion, before Colonel Higginson could reply, and while he still stood holding the flags in his hand, some of the colored people, of their own accord, commenced singing, "My Country, 'tis of thee." It was a touching and beautiful incident, and sent a thrill through all our hearts. The Colonel was deeply moved by it. He said that that reply was far more effective than any speech he could make. But he did make one of those stirring speeches which are "half battles." All hearts swelled with emotion as we listened to his glorious words,—"stirring the soul like the sound of a trumpet."

His soldiers are warmly attached to him, and he evidently feels towards them all as if they were his children. The people speak of him as "the officer who never leaves his regiment for pleasure," but devotes himself, with all his rich gifts of mind and heart, to their interests. It is not strange that his judicious kindness, ready sympathy, and rare fascination of manner should attach them to him strongly. He is one's ideal of an officer. There is in him much of the grand, knightly spirit of the olden time,—scorn of all that is mean and ignoble, pity for the weak, chivalrous devotion to the cause of the oppressed.

General Saxton spoke also, and was received with great enthusiasm. Throughout the morning, repeated cheers were given for him by the regiment, and joined in heartily by all the people. They know him to be one of the best and noblest men in the world. His Proclamation for Emancipation-Day we thought, if possible, even more beautiful than the Thanksgiving Proclamation.

At the close of Colonel Higginson's speech he presented the flags to the color-bearers, Sergeant Rivers and Sergeant Sutton, with an earnest charge, to which they made appropriate replies. We were particularly pleased with Robert Sutton, who is a man of great natural intelligence, and whose remarks were simple, eloquent, and forcible.

Mrs. Gage also uttered some earnest words; and then the regiment sang "John Brown" with much spirit. After the meeting we saw the dress-parade, a brilliant and beautiful sight. An officer told us that the men went through the drill remarkably well,—that the ease and rapidity with which they learned the movements were wonderful. To us it seemed strange as a miracle,—this black regiment, the first mustered into the service of the United States, doing itself honor in the sight of the officers of other regiments, many of whom, doubtless, "came to scoff." The men afterwards had a great feast, ten oxen having been roasted whole for their especial benefit.

We went to the landing, intending to take the next boat for Beaufort; but finding it very much crowded, waited for another. It was the softest, loveliest moonlight; we seated ourselves on the ruined wall of the old fort; and when the boat had got a short distance from the shore the band in it commenced playing "Sweet Home." The moonlight on the water, the perfect stillness around, the wildness and solitude of the ruins, all seemed to give new pathos to that ever dear and beautiful old song. It came very near to all of us,—strangers in that strange Southern land. After a while we retired to one of the tents,—for the night-air, as usual, grew dangerously damp,—and, sitting around the bright wood-fire, enjoyed the brilliant and entertaining conversation. Very unwilling were we to go home; for, besides the attractive society, we knew that the soldiers were to have grand shouts and a general jubilee that night. But the Flora was coming, and we were obliged to say a reluctant farewell to Camp Saxton and the hospitable dwellers therein, and hasten to the landing. We promenaded the deck of the steamer, sang patriotic songs, and agreed that moonlight and water had never looked so beautiful as on that night. At Beaufort we took the row-boat for St. Helena; and the boatmen, as they rowed, sang some of their sweetest, wildest hymns. It was a fitting close to such a day. Our hearts were filled with an exceeding great gladness; for, although the Government had left much undone, we knew that Freedom was surely born in our land that day. It seemed too glorious a good to realize,—this beginning of the great work we had so longed and prayed for.

L. and I had one day an interesting visit to a plantation about six miles from ours. The house is beautifully situated in the midst of noble pine-trees, on the banks of a large creek. The place was owned by a very wealthy Rebel family, and is one of the pleasantest and healthiest on the island. The vicinity of the pines makes it quite healthy. There were a hundred and fifty people on it,—one hundred of whom had come from Edisto Island at the time of its evacuation by our troops. There were not houses enough to accommodate them, and they had to take shelter in barns, out-houses, or any other place they could find. They afterwards built rude dwellings for themselves, which did not, however, afford them much protection in bad weather. The superintendent told us that they were well-behaved and industrious. One old woman interested us greatly. Her name was Daphne; she was probably more than a hundred years old; had had fifty grandchildren, sixty-five great-grandchildren, and three great-great-grandchildren. Entirely blind, she yet seemed very cheerful and happy. She told us that she was brought with her parents from Africa at the time of the Revolution. A bright, happy old face was hers, and she retained her faculties remarkably well. Fifteen of the people had escaped from the mainland in the previous spring. They were pursued, and one of them was overtaken by his master in the swamps. A fierce grapple ensued,—the master on horseback, the man on foot. The former drew a pistol and shot his slave through the arm, shattering it dreadfully. Still, the heroic man fought desperately, and at last succeeded in unhorsing his master, and beating him until he was senseless. He then made his escape, and joined the rest of the party.

One of the most interesting sights we saw was a baptism among the people. On one Sunday there were a hundred and fifty baptized in the creek near the church. They looked very picturesque in their white aprons and bright frocks and handkerchiefs. As they marched in procession down to the river's edge, and during the ceremony, the spectators, with whom the banks were crowded, sang glad, triumphant songs. The freed people on this island are all Baptists.

We were much disappointed in the Southern climate. We found it much colder than we had expected,—quite cold enough for as thick winter clothing as one would wear at the North. The houses, heated only by open fires, were never comfortably warm. In the floor of our sitting-room there was a large crack through which we could see the ground beneath; and through this and the crevices of the numerous doors and windows the wind came chillingly. The church in which we taught school was particularly damp and cold. There was no chimney, and we could have no fire at all. Near the close of the winter a stove came for us, but it could not be made to draw; we were nearly suffocated with smoke, and gave it up in despair. We got so thoroughly chilled and benumbed within, that for several days we had school out-of-doors, where it was much warmer. Our school-room was a pleasant one,—for ceiling the blue sky above, for walls the grand old oaks with their beautiful moss drapery, but the dampness of the ground made it unsafe for us to continue the experiment.

At a later period, during a few days' visit to some friends living on the Milne Plantation, then the head-quarters of the First South-Carolina, which was on picket-duty at Port-Royal Ferry, we had an opportunity of seeing something of Port-Royal Island. We had pleasant rides through the pine barrens. Indeed, riding on horseback was our chief recreation at the South, and we enjoyed it thoroughly. The "Secesh" horses, though small, poor, and mean-looking, when compared with ours, are generally excellent for the saddle, well-trained and very easy. I remember particularly one ride that we had while on Port-Royal Island. We visited the Barnwell Plantation, one of the finest places on the island. It is situated on Broad River. The grounds are extensive, and are filled with magnificent live-oaks, magnolias, and other trees. We saw one noble old oak, said to be the largest on these islands. Some of the branches have been cut off, but the remaining ones cover an area of more than a hundred feet in circumference. We rode to a point whence the Rebels on the opposite side of the river are sometimes to be seen. But they were not visible that day; and we were disappointed in our long-cherished hope of seeing a "real live Rebel." On leaving the plantation, we rode through a long avenue of oaks,—the moss-hung branches forming a perfect arch over our heads,— and then for miles through the pine barrens. There was an Italian softness in the April air. Only a low, faint murmur—hardly "the slow song of the sea"—could be heard among the pines. The ground was thickly carpeted with ferns of a vivid green. We found large violets, purple and white, and azaleas of a deeper pink and heavier fragrance than ours. It was leaving Paradise, to emerge from the beautiful woods upon the public road,—the shell-road which runs from Beaufort to the Ferry. Then we entered a by-way leading to the plantation, where we found the Cherokee rose in all its glory. The hedges were white with it; it canopied the trees, and hung from their branches its long sprays of snowy blossoms and dark, shining leaves, forming perfect arches, and bowers which seemed fitting places for fairies to dwell in. How it gladdened our eyes and hearts! It was as if all the dark shadows that have so long hung over this Southern land had flitted away, and, in this garment of purest white, it shone forth transfigured, beautified, forevermore.

On returning to the house, we were met by the exciting news that the Rebels were bringing up pontoon-bridges, and were expected to attempt crossing over near the Ferry, which was only two or three miles from us. Couriers came in every few moments with various reports. A superintendent whose plantation was very near the Ferry had been watching through his glass the movements on the opposite side, and reported that the Rebels were gathering in large force, and evidently preparing for some kind of demonstration. A messenger was despatched to Beaufort for reinforcements, and for some time we were in a state of expectancy, not entirely without excitement, but entirely without fear. The officers evidently enjoyed the prospect of a fight. One of them assured me that I should have the pleasure of seeing a Rebel shell during the afternoon. It was proposed that the women should be sent into Beaufort in an ambulance; against which ignoble treatment we indignantly protested, and declared our intention of remaining at our post, if the Colonel would consent; and finally, to our great joy, the best of colonels did consent that we should remain, as he considered it quite safe for us to do so. Soon a light battery arrived, and during the evening a brisk firing was kept up. We could hear the explosion of the shells. It was quite like being in the war; and as the firing was principally on our side, and the enemy was getting the worst of it, we rather enjoyed it. For a little while the Colonel read to us, in his spirited way, some of the stirring "Lays of the Old Cavaliers." It was just the time to appreciate them thoroughly, and he was of all men the fittest person to read them. But soon came a courier, "in hot haste," to make report of the doings without, and the reading was at an end. In the midst of the firing, Mrs. D. and I went to bed, and slept soundly until morning. We learned afterward that the Rebels had not intended to cross over, but were attempting to take the guns off one of our boats, which they had sunk a few days previous. The timely arrival of the battery from Beaufort prevented them from accomplishing their purpose.

In April we left Oaklands, which had always been considered a particularly unhealthy place during the summer, and came to "Seaside," a plantation on another and healthier part of the island. The place contains nearly a hundred people. The house is large and comparatively comfortable. Notwithstanding the name, we have not even a distant glimpse of the sea, although we can sometimes hear its roar. At low tide there is not a drop of water to be seen,—only dreary stretches of marshland, reminding us of the sad outlook of Mariana in the Moated Grange,—"The level waste and rounding gray."

But at night we have generally a good sea-breeze, and during the hottest weather the air is purer and more invigorating than in many parts of the island.

On this, as on several other large plantations, there is a "Praise-House," which is the special property of the people. Even in the old days of Slavery, they were allowed to hold meetings here; and they still keep up the custom. They assemble on several nights of the week, and on Sunday afternoons. First, they hold what is called the "Praise-Meeting," which consists of singing, praying, and preaching. We have heard some of the old negro preachers make prayers that were really beautiful and touching. In these meetings they sing only the church-hymns which the Northern ministers have taught them, and which are far less suited to their voices than their own. At the close of the Praise-Meeting they all shake hands with each other in the most solemn manner. Afterward, as a kind of appendix, they have a grand "shout," during which they sing their own hymns. Maurice, an old blind man, leads the singing. He has a remarkable voice, and sings with the greatest enthusiasm. The first shout that we witnessed in the Praise-House impressed us very much. The large, gloomy room, with its blackened walls,—the wild, whirling dance of the shouters,—the crowd of dark, eager faces gathered around,—the figure of the old blind man, whose excitement could hardly be controlled, and whose attitude and gestures while singing were very fine,—and over all, the red glare of the burning pine-knot, which shed a circle of light around it, but only seemed to deepen and darken the shadows in the other parts of the room,—these all formed a wild, strange, and deeply impressive picture, not soon to be forgotten.

Maurice's especial favorite is one of the grandest hymns that we have yet heard:—

> "De tallest tree in Paradise
> De Christian calls de Tree ob Life,
> An' I hope dat trumpet blow me home
> To my New Jerusalem.
> Chorus.
> "Blow, Gabriel! trumpet, blow louder, louder!
> An' I hope dat trumpet blow me home
> To my New Jerusalem!
> "Paul and Silas jail-bound
> Sing God's praise both night and day,
> An' I hope dat trumpet blow me home
> To my New Jerusalem.
> Chorus.
> "Blow, Gabriel! trumpet, blow louder, louder!
> An' I hope dat trumpet blow me home
> To my New Jerusalem!"

The chorus has a glad, triumphal sound, and in singing it the voice of old Maurice rings out in wonderfully clear, trumpet-like tones. His blindness was caused by a blow on the head from a loaded whip. He was struck by his master in a fit of anger. "I feel great distress when I become blind," said Maurice; "but den I went to seek de Lord; and eber since I know I see in de next world, I always hab great satisfaction." We are told that the master was not a "hard man" except when in a passion, and then he seems to have been very cruel.

One of the women on the place, Old Bess, bears on her limbs many marks of the whip. Some of the scars are three and four inches long. She was used principally as a house-servant. She says, "Ebery time I lay de table I put cow-skin on one end, an' I git beatin' and thumpin' all de time. Hab all kinds o' work to do, and sich a gang [of children] to look after! One person couldn't git along wid so much work, so it go wrong, and den I git beatin'."

But the cruelty of Bess's master sinks into insignificance, when compared with the far-famed wickedness of another slave-holder, known all over the island as "Old Joe Eddings." There seem to have been no bounds to his cruelty and licentiousness; and the people tell tales of him which make one shudder. We were once asking some questions about him of an old, half-witted woman, a former slave of his. The look of horror and loathing which overspread her face was perfectly indescribable, as, with upraised hands, she exclaimed, "What! Old Joe Eddings? Lord, Missus, he second to none in de world but de Debil!" She had, indeed, good cause to detest him; for, some years before, her daughter, a young black girl, maddened by his persecutions, had thrown herself into the creek and been drowned, after having been severely beaten for refusing to degrade herself. Outraged, despised, and black, she yet preferred death to dishonor. But these are things too heart-sickening to dwell upon. God alone knows how many hundreds of plantations, all over the South, might furnish a similar record.

SUSIE KING TAYLOR

Susie King Taylor (1848–1912) was born enslaved near Savannah, Georgia. When she was fourteen years old, Taylor's uncle led her to Union-occupied territory on the Georgia sea islands. As the Civil War raged on, Taylor served the First South Carolina Volunteers (Union)/Thirty-third United States Colored Infantry Regiment as a nurse and laundress. Taylor also taught students from the newly freed Black population in the freedmen's schools before returning to Savannah to serve as an educator. Her memoir centers mainly on military life in the midst of war, with early reflections on her family and concluding remarks on the ways that racism and segregationist policies render Black life in her contemporary moment increasingly precarious and frustrating.

From *Reminiscences of My Life in Camp with the 33d United States Colored Troops Late 1st S.C. Volunteers*
(1902)

A BRIEF SKETCH OF MY ANCESTORS

My great-great-grandmother was 120 years old when she died. She had seven children, and five of her boys were in the Revolutionary War. She was from Virginia, and was half Indian. She was so old she had to be held in the sun to help restore or prolong her vitality.

My great-grandmother, one of her daughters, named Susanna, was married to Peter Simons, and was one hundred years old when she died, from a stroke of paralysis in Savannah. She was the mother of twenty-four children, twenty-three being girls. She was one of the noted midwives of her day. In

1820 my grandmother was born, and named after her grandmother, Dolly, and in 1833 she married Fortune Lambert Reed.
Two children blessed their union, James and Hagar Ann. James
died at the age of twelve years.

My mother was born in 1834. She married Raymond Baker
in 1847. Nine children were born to them, three dying in infancy. I was the first born. I was born on the Grest Farm (which
was on an island known as Isle of Wight), Liberty County,
about thirty-five miles from Savannah, Ga., on August 6, 1848,
my mother being waitress for the Grest family. I have often
been told by mother of the care Mrs. Grest took of me. She was
very fond of me, and I remember when my brother and I were
small children, and Mr. Grest would go away on business, Mrs.
Grest would place us at the foot of her bed to sleep and keep her
company. Sometimes he would return home earlier than he had
expected to; then she would put us on the floor.

When I was about seven years old, Mr. Grest allowed my
grandmother to take my brother and me to live with her in Savannah. There were no railroad connections in those days between this place and Savannah; all travel was by stagecoaches.
I remember, as if it were yesterday, the coach which ran in from
Savannah, with its driver, whose beard nearly reached his
knees. His name was Shakespeare, and often I would go to the
stable where he kept his horses, on Barnard Street in front of
the old Arsenal, just to look at his wonderful beard.

My grandmother went every three months to see my mother.
She would hire a wagon to carry bacon, tobacco, flour, molasses, and sugar. These she would trade with people in the neighboring places, for eggs, chickens, or cash, if they had it. These,
in turn, she carried back to the city market, where she had a
customer who sold them for her. The profit from these, together
with laundry work and care of some bachelors' rooms, made a
good living for her.

The hardest blow to her was the failure of the Freedmen's
Savings Bank in Savannah, for in that bank she had placed her
savings, about three thousand dollars, the result of her hard
labor and self-denial before the war, and which, by dint of
shrewdness and care, she kept together all through the war. She
felt it more keenly, coming as it did in her old age, when her life

was too far spent to begin anew; but she took a practical view of the matter, for she said, "I will leave it all in God's hand. If the Yankees did take all our money, they freed my race; God will take care of us."

In 1888 she wrote me here (Boston), asking me to visit her, as she was getting very feeble and wanted to see me once before she passed away. I made up my mind to leave at once, but about the time I planned to go, in March, a fearful blizzard swept our country, and travel was at a standstill for nearly two weeks; but March 15 I left on the first through steamer from New York, en route for the South, where I again saw my grandmother, and we felt thankful that we were spared to meet each other once more. This was the last time I saw her, for in May, 1889, she died.

MY CHILDHOOD

I was born under the slave law in Georgia, in 1848, and was brought up by my grandmother in Savannah. There were three of us with her, my younger sister and brother. My brother and I being the two eldest, we were sent to a friend of my grandmother, Mrs. Woodhouse, a widow, to learn to read and write. She was a free woman and lived on Bay Lane, between Habersham and Price streets, about half a mile from my house. We went every day about nine o'clock, with our books wrapped in paper to prevent the police or white persons from seeing them. We went in, one at a time, through the gate, into the yard to the L kitchen, which was the schoolroom. She had twenty-five or thirty children whom she taught, assisted by her daughter, Mary Jane. The neighbors would see us going in sometimes, but they supposed we were there learning trades, as it was the custom to give children a trade of some kind. After school we left the same way we entered, one by one, when we would go to a square, about a block from the school, and wait for each other. We would gather laurel leaves and pop them on our hands, on our way home. I remained at her school for two years or more, when I was sent to a Mrs. Mary Beasley, where I continued until May, 1860, when she told my grandmother she had taught me all she knew, and grandmother had better get some one else who could teach me more, so I stopped my studies for a while.

I had a white playmate about this time, named Katie O'Connor, who lived on the next corner of the street from my house, and who attended a convent. One day she told me, if I would promise not to tell her father, she would give me some lessons. On my promise not to do so, and getting her mother's consent, she gave me lessons about four months, every evening. At the end of this time she was put into the convent permanently, and I have never seen her since.

A month after this, James Blouis, our landlord's son, was attending the High School, and was very fond of grandmother, so she asked him to give me a few lessons, which he did until the middle of 1861, when the Savannah Volunteer Guards, to which he and his brother belonged, were ordered to the front under General Barton. In the first battle of Manassas, his brother Eugene was killed, and James deserted over to the Union side, and at the close of the war went to Washington, D. C., where he has since resided.

I often wrote passes for my grandmother, for all colored persons, free or slaves, were compelled to have a pass; free colored people having a guardian in place of a master. These passes were good until 10 or 10.30 P.M. for one night or every night for one month. The pass read as follows:—

> SAVANNAH, GA., March 1st, 1860.
> *Pass the bearer—from 9 to 10.30. P.M.*
>   VALENTINE GREST.

Every person had to have this pass, for at nine o'clock each night a bell was rung, and any colored persons found on the street after this hour were arrested by the watchman, and put in the guard-house until next morning, when their owners would pay their fines and release them. I knew a number of persons who went out at any time at night and were never arrested, as the watchman knew them so well he never stopped them, and seldom asked to see their passes, only stopping them long enough, sometimes, to say "Howdy," and then telling them to go along.

About this time I had been reading so much about the "Yankees" I was very anxious to see them. The whites would tell their colored people not to go to the Yankees, for they would harness them to carts and make them pull the carts around, in place of horses. I asked grandmother, one day, if this was true. She replied, "Certainly not!" that the white people did not want slaves to go over to the Yankees, and told them these things to frighten them. "Don't you see those signs pasted about the streets? one reading, 'I am a rattlesnake; if you touch me I will strike!' Another reads, 'I am a wild-cat! Beware,' etc. These are warnings to the North; so don't mind what the white people say." I wanted to see these wonderful "Yankees" so much, as I heard my parents say the Yankee was going to set all the slaves free. Oh, how those people prayed for freedom! I remember, one night, my grandmother went out into the suburbs of the city to a church meeting, and they were fervently singing this old hymn,—

"Yes, we all shall be free,
Yes, we all shall be free,
Yes, we all shall be free,
When the Lord shall appear,"

—when the police came in and arrested all who were there, saying they were planning freedom, and sang "the Lord," in place of "Yankee," to blind any one who might be listening. Grandmother never forgot that night, although she did not stay in the guard-house, as she sent to her guardian, who came at once for her; but this was the last meeting she ever attended out of the city proper.

On April 1, 1862, about the time the Union soldiers were firing on Fort Pulaski, I was sent out into the country to my mother. I remember what a roar and din the guns made. They jarred the earth for miles. The fort was at last taken by them. Two days after the taking of Fort Pulaski, my uncle took his family of seven and myself to St. Catherine Island. We landed under the protection of the Union fleet, and remained there two weeks, when about thirty of us were taken aboard the gunboat P—, to be transferred to St. Simon's Island; and at last, to my unbounded joy, I saw the "Yankee."

After we were all settled aboard and started on our journey, Captain Whitmore, commanding the boat, asked me where I was from. I told him Savannah, Ga. He asked if I could read; I said, "Yes!" "Can you write?" he next asked. "Yes, I can do that also," I replied, and as if he had some doubts of my answers he handed me a book and a pencil and told me to write my name and where I was from. I did this; when he wanted to know if I could sew. On hearing I could, he asked me to hem some napkins for him. He was surprised at my accomplishments (for they were such in those days), for he said he did not know there were any negroes in the South able to read or write. He said, "You seem to be so different from the other colored people who came from the same place you did." "No!" I replied, "the only difference is, they were reared in the country and I in the city, as was a man from Darien, Ga., named Edward King." That seemed to satisfy him, and we had no further conversation that day on the subject.

In the afternoon the captain spied a boat in the distance, and as it drew nearer he noticed it had a white flag hoisted, but before it had reached the Putumoka he ordered all passengers between decks, so we could not be seen, for he thought they might be spies. The boat finally drew alongside of our boat, and had Mr. Edward Donegall on board, who wanted his two servants, Nick and Judith. He wanted these, as they were his own children. Our captain told him he knew nothing of them, which was true, for at the time they were on St. Simon's, and not, as their father supposed, on our boat. After the boat left, we were allowed to come up on deck again.

ON ST. SIMON'S ISLAND

1862

Next morning we arrived at St. Simon's, and the captain told Commodore Goldsborough about this affair, and his reply was, "Captain Whitmore, you should not have allowed them to return; you should have kept them." After I had been on St. Simon's about three days, Commodore Goldsborough heard of me, and came to Gaston Bluff to see me. I found him very cordial. He said Captain Whitmore had spoken to him of me, and that he was pleased to hear of my being so capable, etc., and wished me to take charge of a school for the children on the island. I told him I would gladly do so, if I could have some books. He said I should have them, and in a week or two I received two large boxes of books and testaments from the North. I had about forty children to teach, beside a number of adults who came to me nights, all of them so eager to learn to read, to read above anything else. Chaplain French, of Boston, would come to the school, sometimes, and lecture to the pupils on Boston and the North.

About the first of June we were told that there was going to be a settlement of the war. Those who were on the Union side would remain free, and those in bondage were to work three days for their masters and three for themselves. It was a gloomy time for us all, and we were to be sent to Liberia. Chaplain French asked me would I rather go back to Savannah or go to Liberia. I told him the latter place by all means. We did not know when this would be, but we were prepared in case this settlement should be reached. However, the Confederates would not agree to the arrangement, or else it was one of the many rumors flying about at the time, as we heard nothing further of the matter. There were a number of settlements on this island of St. Simon's, just like little villages, and we would go from one to the other on business, to call, or only for a walk.

One Sunday, two men, Adam Miller and Daniel Spaulding, were chased by some rebels as they were coming from Hope Place (which was between the Beach and Gaston Bluff), but the latter were unable to catch them. When they reached the Beach and told this, all the men on the place, about ninety, armed themselves, and next day (Monday), with Charles O'Neal as their leader, skirmished the island for the "rebs." In a short while they discovered them in the woods, hidden behind a large log, among the thick underbrush. Charles O'Neal was the first to see them, and he was killed; also John Brown, and their bodies were never found. Charles O'Neal was an uncle of Edward King, who later was my husband and a sergeant in Co. E., U. S. I. Another man was shot, but not found for three days. On Tuesday, the second day, Captain Trowbridge and some soldiers landed, and assisted the skirmishers. Word having been sent by the mail-boat Uncas to Hilton Head, later in the day Commodore Goldsborough, who was in command of the naval station, landed about three hundred marines, and joined the others to oust the rebels. On Wednesday, John Baker, the man shot on Monday, was found in a terrible condition by Henry Batchlott, who carried him to the Beach, where he was attended by the surgeon. He told us how, after being shot, he lay quiet for a day. On the second day he managed to reach some wild grapes growing near him. These he ate, to satisfy his hunger and intense thirst, then he crawled slowly, every movement causing agony, until he got to the side of the road. He lived only three months after they found him.

On the second day of the skirmish the troops captured a boat which they knew the Confederates had used to land in, and having this in their possession, the "rebs" could not return; so pickets were stationed all around the island. There was an old man, Henry Capers, who had been left on one of the places by his old master, Mr. Hazzard, as he was too old to carry away. These rebels went to his house in the night, and he hid them up in the loft. On Tuesday all hands went to this man's house with a determination to burn it down, but Henry Batchlott pleaded with the men to spare it. The rebels were in hiding, still, waiting a chance to get off the island. They searched his house, but neglected to go up into the loft, and in so doing missed the rebels concealed there. Late in the night Henry Capers gave them his boat to escape in, and they got off all right. This old man was allowed by the men in charge of the island to cut grass for his horse, and to have a boat to carry this grass to his home, and so they were not detected, our men thinking it was Capers using the boat. After Commodore Goldsborough left the island, Commodore Judon sent the old man over to the mainland and would not allow him to remain on the island.

There were about six hundred men, women, and children on St. Simon's, the women and children being in the majority, and we were afraid to go very far from our own quarters in the daytime, and at night even to go out of the house for a long time, although the men were on the watch all the time; for there were not any soldiers on the island, only the marines who were on the gunboats along the coast. The rebels, knowing this, could steal by them under cover of the night, and getting on the island would capture any persons venturing out alone and carry them to the mainland. Several of the men disappeared, and as they were never heard from we came to the conclusion they had been carried off in this way.

The latter part of August, 1862, Captain C. T. Trowbridge, with his brother John and Lieutenant Walker, came to St. Simon's Island from Hilton Head, by order of General Hunter, to get all the men possible to finish filling his regiment which he had organized in March, 1862. He had heard of the skirmish on this island, and was very much pleased at the bravery shown by these men. He found me at Gaston Bluff teaching my little school, and was much interested in it. When I knew him better I found him to be a thorough gentleman and a staunch friend to my race.

Captain Trowbridge remained with us until October, when the order was received to evacuate, and so we boarded the Ben-De-Ford, a transport, for Beaufort, S. C. When we arrived in Beaufort, Captain Trowbridge and the men he had enlisted went to camp at Old Fort, which they named "Camp Saxton." I was enrolled as laundress.

The first suits worn by the boys were red coats and pants, which they disliked very much, for, they said, "The rebels see us, miles away."

The first colored troops did not receive any pay for eighteen months, and the men had to depend wholly on what they received from the commissary, established by General Saxton. A great many of these men had large families, and as they had no money to give them, their wives were obliged to support themselves and children by washing for the officers of the gunboats and the soldiers, and making cakes and pies which they sold to the boys in camp. Finally, in 1863, the government decided to give them half pay, but the men would not accept this. They wanted "full pay" or nothing. They preferred rather to give their services to the state, which they did until 1864, when the government granted them full pay, with all the back pay due.

I remember hearing Captain Heasley telling his company,

one day, "Boys, stand up for your full pay! I am with you, and so are all the officers." This captain was from Pennsylvania, and was a very good man; all the men liked him. N. G. Parker, our first lieutenant, was from Massachusetts. H. A. Beach was from New York. He was very delicate, and had to resign in 1864 on account of ill health.

I had a number of relatives in this regiment, —several uncles, some cousins, and a husband in Company E, and a number of cousins in other companies. Major Strong, of this regiment, started home on a furlough, but the vessel he was aboard was lost, and he never reached his home. He was one of the best officers we had. After his death, Captain C. T. Trowbridge was promoted major, August, 1863, and filled Major Strong's place until December, 1864, when he was promoted lieutenant-colonel, which he remained until he was mustered out, February 6, 1866.

In February, 1863, several cases of varioloid broke out among the boys, which caused some anxiety in camp. Edward Davis, of Company E (the company I was with), had it very badly. He was put into a tent apart from the rest of the men, and only the doctor and camp steward, James Cummings, were allowed to see or attend him; but I went to see this man every day and nursed him. The last thing at night, I always went in to see that he was comfortable, but in spite of the good care and attention he received, he succumbed to the disease.

I was not in the least afraid of the small-pox. I had been vaccinated, and I drank sassafras tea constantly, which kept my blood purged and prevented me from contracting this dread scourge, and no one need fear getting it if they will only keep their blood in good condition with this sassafras tea, and take it before going where the patient is.

CAMP SAXTON—
PROCLAMATION AND BARBECUE

1863

On the first of January, 1863, we held services for the purpose of listening to the reading of President Lincoln's proclamation by Dr. W. H. Brisbane, and the presentation of two beautiful stands of colors, one from a lady in Connecticut, and the other from Rev. Mr. Cheever. The Presentation speech was made by Chaplain French. It was a glorious day for us all, and we enjoyed every minute of it, and as a fitting close and the crowning event of this occasion we had a grand barbecue. A number of oxen were roasted whole, and we had a fine feast. Although not served as tastily or correctly as it would have been at home, yet it was enjoyed with keen appetites and relish. The soldiers had a good time. They sang or shouted "Hurrah!" all through the camp, and seemed overflowing with fun and frolic until taps were sounded, when many, no doubt, dreamt of this memorable day.

I had rather an amusing experience; that is, it seems amusing now, as I look back, but at the time it occurred it was a most serious one to me.

When our regiment left Beaufort for Seabrooke, I left some of my things with a neighbor who lived outside of the camp. After I had been at Seabrooke about a week, I decided to return to Camp Saxton and get them. So one morning, with Mary Shaw, a friend who was in the company at that time, I started off. There was no way for us to get to Beaufort other than to walk, except we rode on the commissary wagon. This we did, and reached Beaufort about one o'clock. We then had more than two miles to walk before reaching our old camp, and expected to be able to accomplish this and return in time to meet the wagon again by three o'clock that afternoon, and so be taken back. We failed to do this, however, for when we got to Beaufort the wagon was gone. We did not know what to do. I did not wish to remain overnight, neither did my friend, although we might easily have stayed, as both had relatives in the town.

It was in the springtime, and the days were long, and as the sun looked so bright, we concluded to walk back, thinking we should reach camp before dark. So off we started on our ten-mile tramp. We had not gone many miles, however, before we were all tired out and began to regret our undertaking. The sun was getting low, and we grew more frightened, fearful of meeting some animal or of treading on a snake on our way. We did not meet a person, and we were frightened almost to death. Our feet were so sore we could hardly walk. Finally we took off our shoes and tried walking in our stocking feet, but this made them worse. We had gone about six miles when night overtook us. There we were, nothing around us but dense woods, and as there was no house or any place to stop at, there was nothing for us to do but continue on. We were afraid to speak to each other.

Meantime at the camp, seeing no signs of us by dusk, they concluded we had decided to remain over until next day, and so had no idea of our plight. Imagine their surprise when we reached camp about eleven P.M. The guard challenged us, "Who comes there?" My answer was, "A friend without a countersign." He approached and saw who it was, reported, and we were admitted into the lines. They had the joke on us that night, and for a long time after would tease us; and sometimes some of the men who were on guard that night would call us deserters. They used to laugh at us, but we joined with them too, especially when we would tell them our experience on our way to camp. I did not undertake that trip again, as there was no way of getting in or out except one took the provision wagon, and there was not much dependence to be put in that returning to camp. Perhaps the driver would say one hour and he might be there earlier or later. Of course it was not his fault, as it depended when the order was filled at the Commissary Department; therefore I did not go any more until the regiment was ordered to our new camp, which was named after our hero, Colonel Shaw, who at that time was at Beaufort with his regiment, the 54th Massachusetts.

I taught a great many of the comrades in Company E to read and write, when they were off duty. Nearly all were anxious to learn. My husband taught some also when it was convenient for him. I was very happy to know my efforts were successful in camp, and also felt grateful for the appreciation of my services. I gave my services willingly for four years and three months without receiving a dollar. I was glad, however, to be allowed to go with the regiment, to care for the sick and afflicted comrades.

FRANCES ELLEN WATKINS HARPER

After slavery ended, Frances Ellen Watkins Harper (1825–1911) became the superintendent of the Colored Sections of the Philadelphia and Pennsylvania Women's Christian Temperance Unions and helped cofound the National Association of Colored Women in 1896. Harper continued writing poetry, essays, and speeches to agitate for equality. In 1866, Harper was invited to speak before the Eleventh National Women's Rights Convention in New York City, a stage she shared with the prominent suffragists Elizabeth Cady Stanton and Susan B. Anthony.

"We Are All Bound Up Together"
(1866)

I feel I am something of a novice upon this platform. Born of a race whose inheritance has been outrage and wrong, most of my life had been spent in battling against those wrongs. But I did not feel as keenly as others, that I had these rights, in common with other women, which are now demanded. About two years ago, I stood within the shadows of my home. A great sorrow had fallen upon my life. My husband had died suddenly, leaving me a widow, with four children, one my own, and the others stepchildren. I tried to keep my children together. But my husband died in debt; and before he had been in his grave three months, the administrator had swept the very milk-crocks and wash tubs from my hands. I was a farmer's wife and made butter for the Columbus market; but what could I do, when they had swept all away? They left me one thing-and that was a looking glass! Had I died instead of my husband, how different would have been the result! By this time he would have had another wife, it is likely; and no administrator would have gone into his house, broken up his home, and sold his bed, and taken away his means of support.

I took my children in my arms, and went out to seek my living. While I was gone, a neighbor to whom I had once lent five dollars, went before a magistrate and Swore that he believed I was a non-resident, and laid an attachment on my very bed. And I went back to Ohio with my orphan children in my arms, without a single feather bed in this wide world, that was not in the custody of the law. I say, then, that justice is not fulfilled so long as woman is unequal before the law.

We are all bound up together in one great bundle of humanity, and society cannot trample on the weakest and feeblest of its members without receiving the curse in its own soul. You tried that in the case of the Negro. You pressed him down for two centuries; and in so doing you crippled the moral strength and paralyzed the spiritual energies of the white men of the country. When the hands of the black were fettered, white men were deprived of the liberty of speech and the freedom of the press. Society cannot afford to neglect the enlightenment of any class of its members. At the South, the legislation of the country was in behalf of the rich slaveholders, while the poor white man was neglected. What is the consequence today? From that very class of neglected poor white men, comes the man who stands to-day, with his hand upon the helm of the nation. He fails to catch the watchword of the hour, and throws himself, the incarnation of meanness, across the pathway of the nation. My objection to Andrew Johnson is not that he has been a poor white man; my objection is that he keeps "poor whits" all the way through. That is the trouble with him.

This grand and glorious revolution which has commenced, will fail to reach its climax of success, until throughout the length and brea[d]th of the American Republic, the nation shall be so color-blind, as to know no man by the color of his skin or the curl of his hair. It will then have no privileged class, trampling upon and outraging the unprivileged classes, but will be then one great privileged nation, whose privilege will be to produce the loftiest manhood and womanhood that humanity can attain.

I do not believe that giving the woman the ballot is immediately going to cure all the ills of life. I do not believe that white women are dew-drops just exhaled from the skies. I think that like men they may be divided into three classes, the good, the bad, and the indifferent. The good would vote according to their convictions and principles; the bad, as dictated by preju[d]ice or malice; and the indifferent will vote on the strongest side of the question, with the winning party.

You white women speak here of rights. I speak of wrongs. I, as a colored woman, have had in this country an education which has made me feel as if I were in the situation of Ishmael, my hand against every man, and every man's hand against me. Let me go to-morrow morning and take my seat in one of your street cars—I do not know that they will do it in New York, but they will in Philadelphia—and the conductor will put up his hand and stop the car rather than let me ride.

Going from Washington to Baltimore this Spring, they put me in the smoking car. Aye, in the capital of the nation, where the black man consecrated himself to the nation's defence, faithful when the white man was faithless, they put me in the smoking car! They did it once; but the next time they tried it, they failed; for I would not go in. I felt the fight in me; but I don't want to have to fight all the time. Today I am puzzled where to make my home. I would like to make it in Philadelphia, near my own friends and relations. But if I want to ride in the streets of Philadelphia, they send me to ride on the platform with the driver. Have women nothing to do with this? Not long since, a colored woman took her seat in an Eleventh Street car in Philadelphia, and the conductor stopped the car, and told the rest of the passengers to get out, and left the car with her in it alone, when they took it back to the station. One day I took my seat in a car, and the conductor came to me and told me to take another seat. I just screamed "murder." The man said if I was black I ought to behave myself. I knew that if he was white he was not behaving himself. Are there not wrongs to be righted?

In advocating the cause of the colored man, since the Dred Scott decision, I have sometimes said I thought the nation had touched bottom. But let me tell you there is a depth of infamy lower than that. It is when the nation, standing upon the threshold of a great peril, reached out its hands to a feebler race, and asked that race to help it, and when the peril was over, said, You are good enough for soldiers, but not good enough for citizens. . . .

We have a woman in our country who has received the name of "Moses," not by lying about it, but by acting it out-a woman who has gone down into the Egypt of slavery and brought out hundreds of our people into liberty. The last time I saw that woman, her hands were swollen. That woman who had led one of Montgomery's most successful expeditions, who was brave enough and secretive enough to act as a scout for the American army, had her hands all swollen from a conflict with a brutal conductor, who undertook to eject her from her place. That woman, whose courage and bravery won a recognition from our army and from every black man in the land, is excluded from every thoroughfare of travel. Talk of giving women the ballot-box? Go on. It is a normal school, and the white women of this country need it. While there exists this brutal element in society which tramples upon the feeble and treads down the weak, I tell you that if there is any class of people who need to be lifted out of their airy nothings and selfishness, it is the white women of America.

HENRY McNEAL TURNER

An African Methodist Episcopal (AME) minister and bishop, Henry McNeal Turner (1834–1914) was born free in Newberry, South Carolina. In 1858, Turner's family fled South Carolina for St. Louis, Missouri, as the Fugitive Slave Act of 1850 had the unwitting effect of encouraging kidnappers to snatch and sell free Black people into slavery. Turner continued his education to become an ordained AME minister, and he was later appointed the first Black chaplain of the United States Colored Troops during the Civil War. He went on to serve in the Georgia House of Representatives during Reconstruction. On September 3, 1868, Turner gave a fiery speech before the assembly, as he was disgusted by the white Democratic legislators' refusal to seat the "Original 33," the first Black members of Georgia's General Assembly, on the grounds that the state constitution did not explicitly guarantee Black people the right to hold office. The following year, the Georgia Supreme Court affirmed the Black lawmakers' rights, and they were reinstated for the second session.

"I Claim the Rights of a Man"
(1868)

Mr. Speaker: Before proceeding to argue this question upon its intrinsic merits, I wish the members of this House to understand the position that I take. I hold that I am a member of this body. Therefore, sir, I shall neither fawn nor cringe before any party, nor stoop to beg them for my rights. Some of my colored fellow members, in the course of their remarks, took occasion to appeal to the sympathies of members on the opposite side, and to eulogize their character for magnanimity. It reminds me very much, sir, of slaves begging under the lash. I am here to demand my rights and to hurl thunderbolts at the men who would dare to cross the threshold of my manhood. There is an old aphorism which says, "fight the devil with fire," and if I should observe the rule in this instance, I wish gentlemen to understand that it is but fighting them with their own weapon.

The scene presented in this House, today, is one unparalleled in the history of the world. From this day, back to the day when God breathed the breath of life into Adam, no analogy for it can be found. Never, in the history of the world, has a man been arraigned before a body clothed with legislative, judicial or executive functions, charged with the offense of being a darker hue than his fellow men. I know that questions have been before the courts of this country, and of other countries, involving topics not altogether dissimilar to that which is being discussed here today. But, sir, never in the history of the great nations of this world never before has a man been arraigned, charged with an offense committed by the God of Heaven Himself. Cases may be found where men have been deprived of their rights for crimes and misdemeanors; but it has remained for the state of Georgia, in the very heart of the nineteenth century, to call a man before the bar, and there charge him with an act for which he is no more responsible than for the head which he carries upon his shoulders. The Anglo Saxon race, sir, is a most surprising one. No man has ever been more deceived in that race than I have been for the last three weeks. I was not aware that there was in the character of that race so much cowardice or so much pusillanimity. The treachery which has been exhibited in it by gentlemen belonging to that race has shaken my confidence in it more than anything that has come under my observation from the day of my birth.

What is the question at issue? Why, sir, this Assembly, today, is discussing and deliberating on a judgment; there is not a Cherub that sits around God's eternal throne today that would not tremble even were an order issued by the Supreme God Himself to come down here and sit in judgment on my manhood. Gentlemen may look at this question in whatever light they choose, and with just as much indifference as they may think proper to assume, but I tell you, sir, that this is a question which will not die today. This event shall be remembered by

posterity for ages yet to come, and while the sun shall continue
to climb the hills of heaven.

Whose legislature is this? Is it a white man's legislature, or is
it a black man's legislature? Who voted for a constitutional convention, in obedience to the mandate of the Congress of the
United States? Who first rallied around the standard of Reconstruction? Who set the ball of loyalty rolling in the state of
Georgia? And whose voice was heard on the hills and in the valleys of this state? It was the voice of the brawny armed Negro,
with the few humanitarian hearted white men who came to our
assistance. I claim the honor, sir, of having been the instrument
of convincing hundreds yea, thousands of white men, that to reconstruct under the measures of the United States Congress was
the safest and the best course for the interest of the state.

Let us look at some facts in connection with this matter. Did
half the white men of Georgia vote for this legislature? Did not
the great bulk of them fight, with all their strength, the Constitution under which we are acting? And did they not fight against
the organization of this legislature? And further, sir, did they
not vote against it? Yes, sir! And there are persons in this legislature today who are ready to spit their poison in my face, while
they themselves opposed, with all their power, the ratification
of this Constitution. They question my right to a seat in this
body, to represent the people whose legal votes elected me. This
objection, sir, is an unheard of monopoly of power. No analogy
can be found for it, except it be the case of a man who should
go into my house, take possession of my wife and children, and
then tell me to walk out. I stand very much in the position of a
criminal before your bar, because I dare to be the exponent of
the views of those who sent me here. Or, in other words, we are
told that if black men want to speak, they must speak through
white trumpets; if black men want their sentiments expressed,
they must be adulterated and sent through white messengers,
who will quibble and equivocate and evade as rapidly as the
pendulum of a clock. If this be not done, then the black men
have committed an outrage, and their representatives must be
denied the right to represent their constituents.

The great question, sir, is this: Am I a man? If I am such, I
claim the rights of a man. Am I not a man because I happen to

be of a darker hue than honorable gentlemen around me? Let me see whether I am or not. I want to convince the House today that I am entitled to my seat here. A certain gentleman has argued that the Negro was a mere development similar to the orangoutang or chimpanzee, but it so happens that, when a Negro is examined, physiologically, phrenologically and anatomically, and I may say, physiognomically, he is found to be the same as persons of different color. I would like to ask any gentleman on this floor, where is the analogy? Do you find me a quadruped, or do you find me a man? Do you find three bones less in my back than in that of the white man? Do you find fewer organs in the brain? If you know nothing of this, I do; for I have helped to dissect fifty men, black and white, and I assert that by the time you take off the mucous pigment the color of the skin you cannot, to save your life, distinguish between the black man and the white. Am I a man? Have I a soul to save, as you have? Am I susceptible of eternal development, as you are? Can I learn all the arts and sciences that you can? Has it ever been demonstrated in the history of the world? Have black men ever exhibited bravery as white men have done? Have they ever been in the professions? Have they not as good articulative organs as you? Some people argue that there is a very close similarity between the larynx of the Negro and that of the orangoutang. Why, sir, there is not so much similarity between them as there is between the larynx of the man and that of the dog, and this fact I dare any member of this House to dispute. God saw fit to vary everything in nature. There are no two men alike no two voices alike no two trees alike. God has weaved and tissued variety and versatility throughout the boundless space of his creation. Because God saw fit to make some red, and some white, and some black, and some brown, are we to sit here in judgment upon what God has seen fit to do? As well might one play with the thunderbolts of heaven as with that creature that bears God's image God's photograph.

The question is asked, "What is it that the Negro race has done?" Well, Mr. Speaker, all I have to say upon the subject is this: If we are the class of people that we are generally represented to be, I hold that we are a very great people. It is generally considered that we are the children of Canaan, and the curse of a father rests upon our heads, and has rested, all through history. Sir, I deny that the curse of Noah had anything to do with the Negro. We are not the Children of Canaan; and if we are, sir, where should we stand? Let us look a little into history. Melchizedek was a Canaanite; all the Phoenicians all those inventors of the arts and sciences were the posterity of Canaan; but, sir, the Negro is not. We are the children of Cush, and Canaan's curse has nothing whatever to do with the Negro. If we belong to that race, Ham belonged to it, under whose instructions Napoleon Bonaparte studied military tactics. If we belong to that race, Saint Augustine belonged to it. Who was it that laid the foundation of the great Reformation? Martin Luther, who lit the light of gospel truth alight that will never go out until the sun shall rise to set no more; and, long ere then, Democratic principles will have found their level in the regions of Pluto and of Prosperpine. . . .

The honorable gentleman from Whitfield (Mr. Shumate), when arguing this question, a day or two ago, put forth the proposition that to be a representative was not to be an officer "it was a privilege that citizens had a right to enjoy." These are his words. It was not an office; it was a "privilege." Every gentleman here knows that he denied that to be a representative was to be an officer. Now, he is recognized as a leader of the Democratic party in this House, and generally cooks victuals for them to eat; makes that remarkable declaration, and how are you, gentlemen on the other side of the House, because I am an officer, when one of your great lights says that I am not an officer? If you deny my right the right of my constituents to have representation here because it is a "privilege," then, sir, I will show you that I have as many privileges as the whitest man on this floor. If I am not permitted to occupy a seat here, for the purpose of representing my constituents, I want to know how white men can be permitted to do so. How can a white man represent a colored constituency, if a colored man cannot do it? The great argument is: "Oh, we have inherited" this, that and the other. Now, I want gentlemen to come down to cool, common sense. Is the created greater than the Creator? Is man greater than God? It is very strange, if a white man can occupy on this floor a seat created by colored votes, and a black man

cannot do it. Why, gentlemen, it is the most shortsighted reasoning in the world. A man can see better than that with half
an eye; and even if he had no eye at all, he could forge one, as
the Cyclops did, or punch one with his finger, which would enable him to see through that.

It is said that Congress never gave us the right to hold office.
I want to know, sir, if the Reconstruction measures did not base
their action on the ground that no distinction should be made
on account of race, color or previous condition? Was not that
the grand fulcrum on which they rested? And did not every re-
constructed state have to reconstruct on the idea that no discrimination, in any sense of the term, should be made? There is
not a man here who will dare say No. If Congress has simply
given me a merely sufficient civil and political rights to make
me a mere political slave for Democrats, or anybody else giving
them the opportunity of jumping on my back in order to leap
into political power I do not thank Congress for it. Never, so
help me God, shall I be a political slave. I am not now speaking
for those colored men who sit with me in this House, nor do I
say that they endorse my sentiments, but assisting Mr. Lincoln
to take me out of servile slavery did not intend to put me and
my race into political slavery. If they did, let them take away my
ballot I do not want it, and shall not have it. I don't want to be
a mere tool of that sort. I have been a slave long enough already.

I tell you what I would be willing to do: I am willing that the
question should be submitted to Congress for an explanation as
to what was meant in the passage of their Reconstruction measures, and of the Constitutional Amendment. Let the Democratic Party in this House pass a resolution giving this subject
that direction, and I shall be content. I dare you, gentlemen, to
do it. Come up to the question openly, whether it meant that
the Negro might hold office, or whether it meant that he should
merely have the right to vote. If you are honest men, you will do
it. If, however, you will not do that, I would make another
proposition: Call together, again, the convention that framed
the constitution under which we are acting; let them take a vote
upon the subject, and I am willing to abide by their decision . . .

These colored men, who are unable to express themselves with
all the clearness and dignity and force of rhetorical eloquence,

are laughed at in derision by the Democracy of the country. It reminds me very much of the man who looked at himself in a mirror and, imagining that he was addressing another person, exclaimed: "My God, how ugly you are!" These gentlemen do not consider for a moment the dreadful hardships which these people have endured, and especially those who in any way endeavored to acquire an education. For myself, sir, I was raised in the cotton field of South Carolina, and in order to prepare myself for usefulness, as well to myself as to my race, I determined to devote my spare hours to study. When the overseer retired at night to his comfortable couch, I sat and read and thought and studied, until I heard him blow his horn in the morning. He frequently told me, with an oath, that if he discovered me attempting to learn, that he would whip me to death, and I have no doubt he would have done so, if he had found an opportunity. I prayed to Almighty God to assist me, and He did, and I thank Him with my whole heart and soul . . .

So far as I am personally concerned, no man in Georgia has been more conservative than I. "Anything to please the white folks" has been my motto; and so closely have I adhered to that course, that many among my own party have classed me as a Democrat. One of the leaders of the Republican party in Georgia has not been at all favorable to me for some time back, because he believed that I was too "conservative" for a Republican. I can assure you, however, Mr. Speaker, that I have had quite enough, and to spare, of such "conservatism" . . .

But, Mr. Speaker, I do not regard this movement as a thrust at me. It is a thrust at the Bible a thrust at the God of the Universe, for making a man and not finishing him; it is simply calling the Great Jehovah a fool. Why, sir, though we are not white, we have accomplished much. We have pioneered civilization here; we have built up your country; we have worked in your fields and garnered your harvests for two hundred and fifty years! And what do we ask of you in return? Do we ask you for compensation for the sweat our fathers bore for you for the tears you have caused, and the hearts you have broken, and the lives you have curtailed, and the blood you have spilled? Do we ask retaliation? We ask it not. We are willing to let the dead past bury its dead; but we ask you, now for our rights. You have all the elements of superiority upon your side; you have our money and your own; you have our education and your own; and you have our land and your own too. We, who number hundreds of thousands in Georgia, including our wives and families, with not a foot of land to call our own strangers in the land of our birth; without money, without education, without aid, without a roof to cover us while we live, nor sufficient clay to cover us when we die! It is extraordinary that a race such as yours, professing gallantry and chivalry and education and superiority, living in a land where ringing chimes call child and sire to the church of God a land where Bibles are read and Gospel truths are spoken, and where courts of justice are presumed to exist; it is extraordinary that, with all these advantages on your side, you can make war upon the poor defenseless black man. You know we have no money, no railroads, no telegraphs, no advantages of any sort, and yet all manner of injustice is placed upon us. You know that the black people of this country acknowledge you as their superiors, by virtue of your education and advantages . . .

You may expel us, gentlemen, but I firmly believe that you will some day repent it. The black man cannot protect a country, if the country doesn't protect him; and if, tomorrow, a war should arise, I would not raise a musket to defend a country where my manhood is denied. The fashionable way in Georgia, when hard work is to be done, is for the white man to sit at his ease while the black man does the work; but, sir, I will say this much to the colored men of Georgia, as, if I should be killed in this campaign, I may have no opportunity of telling them at any other time: Never lift a finger nor raise a hand in defense of Georgia, until Georgia acknowledges that you are men and invests you with the rights pertaining to manhood. Pay your taxes, however, obey all orders from your employers, take good counsel from friends, work faithfully, earn an honest living, and show, by your conduct, that you can be good citizens.

Go on with your oppressions. Babylon fell. Where is Greece? Where is Nineveh? And where is Rome, the Mistress Empire of the world? Why is it that she stands, today, in broken fragments throughout Europe? Because oppression killed her. Every act that we commit is like a bounding ball. If you curse a man, that

curse rebounds upon you; and when you bless a man, the blessing returns to you; and when you oppress a man, the oppression also will rebound. Where have you ever heard of four
millions of freemen being governed by laws, and yet have no
hand in their making? Search the records of the world, and you
will find no example. "Governments derive their just powers
from the consent of the governed." How dare you to make laws
by which to try me and my wife and children, and deny me a
voice in the making of these laws? I know you can establish a
monarchy, an autocracy, an oligarchy, or any other kind of oc-
racy that you please; and that you can declare whom you please
to be sovereign; but tell me, sir, how you can clothe me with
more power than another, where all are sovereigns alike? How
can you say you have a republican form of government, when
you make such distinction and enact such proscriptive laws?

Gentlemen talk a good deal about the Negroes "building no
monuments." I can tell the gentlemen one thing: that is, that we
could have built monuments of fire while the war was in progress. We could have fired your woods, your barns and fences,
and called you home. Did we do it? No, sir! And God grant that
the Negro may never do it, or do anything else that would destroy the good opinion of his friends. No epithet is sufficiently
opprobrious for us now. I saw, sir, that we have built a monument of docility, of obedience, of respect, and of self control,
that will endure longer than the Pyramids of Egypt.

We are a persecuted people. Luther was persecuted; Galileo
was persecuted; good men in all nations have been persecuted;
but the persecutors have been handed down to posterity with
shame and ignominy. If you pass this bill, you will never get
Congress to pardon or enfranchise another rebel in your lives.
You are going to fix an everlasting disfranchisement upon Mr.
Toombs and the other leading men of Georgia. You may think
you are doing yourselves honor by expelling us from this House;
but when we go, we will do as Wickliffe and as Latimer did.
We will light a torch of truth that will never be extinguished
the impression that will run through the country, as people picture in their mind's eye these poor black men, in all parts of this
Southern country, pleading for their rights. When you expel us,
you make us forever your political foes, and you will never find

a black man to vote a Democratic ticket again; for, so help me God, I will go through all the length and breadth of the land, where a man of my race is to be found, and advise him to beware of the Democratic party. Justice is the great doctrine taught in the Bible. God's Eternal justice is founded upon Truth, and the man who steps from justice steps from 'Ruth, and cannot make his principles to prevail.

I have now, Mr. Speaker, said all that my physical condition will allow me to say. Weak and ill, though I am, I could not sit passively here and see the sacred rights of my race destroyed at one blow. We are in a position somewhat similar to that of the famous "Light Brigade," of which Tennyson says, they had

Cannon to right of them, Cannon to left of them, Cannon in front of them, Volleyed and thundered.

I hope that our poor, downtrodden race may act well and wisely through this period of trial, and that they will exercise patience and discretion under all circumstances.

You may expel us, gentlemen, by your votes, today; but, while you do it, remember that there is a just God in Heaven, whose All-Seeing Eye beholds alike the acts of the oppressor and the oppressed, and who, despite the machinations of the wicked, never fails to vindicate the cause of Justice, and the sanctity of His own handiwork.

CONGRESSMAN RICHARD HARVEY CAIN

Richard Harvey Cain (1825–1887) was born in Greenbrier County, Virginia, and raised in Ohio. He was an abolitionist, minister, and member of the House of Representatives from South Carolina. Cain was appointed a missionary for the African Methodist Episcopal Church in South Carolina and went on to serve at the historic Emanuel AME Church in Charleston after the Civil War. Cain founded the South Carolina Leader *newspaper in 1866, which attracted thousands of converts to the AME Church as well as political constituents who were heartened by Cain's plans for Black upward mobility and land ownership. Cain had a storied, if frustrating, political career in South Carolina, his beliefs becoming increasingly radical as white supremacist groups tormented Black South Carolinians, and white politicians openly espoused racist views and behaviors. In this speech from an 1874 congressional debate, Cain methodically and passionately addresses the positions held by resistant white lawmakers who found civil rights legislation unnecessary. Exhausted from corruption in South Carolina politics and the rollback of the rights afforded to Black people after Reconstruction ended in 1877, Cain dedicated the remainder of his life to the AME Church.*

From "All We Ask Is Equal Laws, Equal Legislation, and Equal Rights"
(1874)

Sir, social equality is a right which every man, every woman, and every class of persons have within their own control. They have a right to form their own acquaintances, to establish their own social relationships. Its establishment and regulation is not within the province of legislation. No laws enacted by legislators can compel social equality. Now, what is it we desire? What we desire is this: inasmuch as we have been raised to the dignity, to the honor, to the position of our manhood, we ask that the laws of this country should guarantee all the rights and immunities belonging to that proud position, to be enforced all over this broad land.

Sir, the gentleman states that in the State of North Carolina the colored people enjoy all their rights as far as the highways are concerned; that in the hotels, and in the railroad cars, and in the various public places of resort, they have all the rights and all the immunities accorded to any other class of citizens of the United States. Now, it may not have come under his observation, but it has under mine, that such really is not the case; and the reason why I know and feel it more than he does is because my face is painted black and his is painted white. We who have the color—I may say the objectionable color–know and feel all this. A few days ago, in passing from South Carolina to this city, I entered a place of public resort where hungry men are fed, but I did not dare–I could not without trouble–sit down to the table. I could not sit down at Wilmington or at Weldon without entering into a contest, which I did not desire to do. My colleague, the gentleman who so eloquently spoke on this subject the other day, [Mr. ELLIOTT,] a few months ago entered a restaurant at Wilmington and sat down to be served, and while there a gentleman stepped up to him and said, "You cannot eat here." All the other gentlemen upon the railroad as passengers were eating there; he had only twenty minutes, and was compelled to leave the restaurant or have a fight for it. He showed fight, however, and got his dinner; but he has never been back there since. Coming here last week I felt we did not desire to draw revolvers and present the bold front of warriors, and therefore we ordered our dinners to be brought into the cars, but even there we found the existence of this feeling; for, although we had paid a dollar a piece for our meals, to be brought by the servants into the cars, still there was objection on the part of the railroad people to our eating our meals in the cars, because they said we were putting on airs. They refused us in the restaurant, and then did not desire that we should eat our meals in the cars, although we paid for them. Yet this was in the noble State of North Carolina.

Mr. Speaker, the colored men of the south do not want the adoption of any force measure. No; they do not want anything by force. All they ask is that you will give them, by statutory enactment under the fundamental law, the right to enjoy precisely the same privileges accorded to every other class of citizens.

The gentleman, moreover, has told us that if we pass this civil-rights bill we will thereby rob the colored men of the South of the friendship of the whites. Now, I am at a loss to see how the friendship of our white friends can be lost to us by simply saying we should be permitted to enjoy the rights enjoyed by other citizens. I have a higher opinion of the friendship of the southern men than to suppose any such thing. I know them too well. I know their friendship will not be lost by the passage of this bill. For eight years I have been in South Carolina, and I have found this to be the fact, that the higher class, comprising gentlemen of learning and refinement, are less opposed to this measure than are those who do not occupy so high a position in the social scale.

Sir, I think that there will be no difficulty. But I do think this, that there will be more trouble if we do not have those rights. I regard it important, therefore, that we should make the law so strong that no man can infringe those rights.

But, says the gentleman from North Carolina, some ambitious colored man will, when this law is passed, enter a hotel or railroad car, and thus create disturbance. If it be his right, then there is no vaulting ambition in his enjoying that right. And if he can pay for his seat in a first-class car or his room in a hotel, I see no objection to his enjoying it. But the gentleman says more. He cited, on the school question, the evidence of South Carolina, and says the South Carolina University has been destroyed by virtue of bringing into contact the white students with the colored. I think not. It is true that a small number of students left the institution, but the institution still remains. The buildings are there as erect as ever; the faculty are there as attentive to their duties as ever they were; the students are coming in as they did before. It is true, sir, that there is a mixture of students now; that there are colored and white students of law and medicine sitting side by side; it is true, sir, that the prejudice of some of the professors was so strong that it drove them out of the institution; but the philanthropy and good sense of others were such that they remained; and thus we have still the institution going on, and because some students have left, it cannot be reasonably argued that the usefulness of the institution has been destroyed. The University of South Carolina has not been destroyed.

But the gentleman says more. The colored man cannot stand, he says, where this antagonism exists, and he deprecates the idea of antagonizing the races. The gentleman says there is no antagonism on his part. I think there is no antagonism so far as the country is concerned. So far as my observation extends, it goes to prove this: that there is a general acceptance upon the part of the larger and better class of the whites of the South of the situation, and that they regard the education and the development of the colored people as essential to their welfare, and the peace, happiness, and prosperity of the whole country. Many of them, including the best minds of the South are earnestly engaged in seeking to make this great system of education permanent in all the States. I do not believe, therefore, that it is possible there can be such an antagonism. Why, sir, in Massachusetts there is no such antagonism. There the colored and the white children go to school side by side. In Rhode Island there is not that antagonism. There they are educated side by side in the high schools. In New York, in the highest schools, are to be found, of late, colored men and colored women. Even old democratic New York does not refuse to give the colored people their rights, and there is no antagonism. A few days ago, when in New York, I made it my business to find out what was the position of matters therein this respect. I ascertained that there are, I think, seven colored ladies in the highest school in New York, and I believe they stand No. 1 in their class, side by side with members of the best and most refined families of the citizens of New York, and without any objection to their presence.

I cannot understand how it is that our southern friends, or a certain class of them, always bring back this old ghost of prejudice and of antagonism. There was a time, not very far distant in the past, when this antagonism was not recognized, when a feeling of fraternization between the white and the colored races existed, that made them kindred to each other. But since our emancipation, since liberty has come, and only since—only since we have stood up clothed in our manhood, only since we have proceeded to take hold and help advance the civilization of this nation—it is only since then that this bugbear is brought up against us again. Sir, the progress of the age demands that the colored man of this country shall be lifted by law into the enjoyment of every right, and that every appliance which is accorded to the German, to the Irishman, to the Englishman, and every foreigner, shall be given to him; and I shall give some reasons why I demand this in the name of justice.

For two hundred years the colored men of this nation have assisted in building up its commercial interests. There are in this country nearly five million of us, and for a space of two hundred and forty-seven years we have been hewers of wood and drawers of water; but we have been with you in promoting all the interests of the country. My distinguished colleague, who defended the civil rights of our race, the other day on this floor, set this forth so clearly that I need not dwell upon it at this time.

I propose to state just this: that we have been identified with the interests of this country from its very foundation. The cotton crop of this country has been raised and its rice-fields have been tilled by the hands of our race. All along as the march of progress, as the march of commerce, as the development of your resources has been widening and expanding and spreading, as your vessels have gone on every sea, with the stars and stripes waving over them, and carried your commerce everywhere, there the black man's labor has gone to enrich your country and to augment the grandeur of your nationality. This was done in the time of slavery. And, if for the space of time I have noted, we have been hewers of wood and drawers of water; if we have made your cotton fields blossom as the rose; if we have made your rice fields wave with luxuriant harvests; if we have made your corn fields rejoice; if we have sweated and toiled to build up the prosperity of the whole country by the productions of our labor, I submit, now that the war has made a change, now that we are free—I submit to the nation whether it is not fair and right that we should come in and enjoy to the fullest extent our freedom and liberty.

A word now as to the question of education. Sir, I know that, indeed, some of our republican friends are even a little weak on the school clause of this bill; but, sir, the education of the race, the education of the nation, is paramount to all other considerations. I regard it important, therefore, that the colored people should take place in the educational march in this nation, and I would suggest that there should be no discrimination. It is against discrimination in this particular that we complain.

Sir, if you look over the reports of superintendents of schools in the several States, you will find, I think, evidences sufficient to warrant Congress in passing the civil-rights bill as it now stands. The report of the commissioner of education of California shows that, under the operation of law and of prejudice, the colored children of that State are practically excluded from schooling. Here is a case where a large class of children are growing up in our midst in a state of ignorance and semi-barbarism. Take the report of the superintendent of education of Indiana, and you will find that while efforts have been made in some places to educate the colored children, yet the prejudice is so great that it debars the colored children from enjoying all the rights which they ought to enjoy under the law. In Illinois, too, the superintendent of education makes this statement: that, while the law guarantees education to every child, yet such are the operations among the school trustees that they almost ignore, in some places, the education of colored children.

All we ask is that you, the legislators of the nation, shall pass a law so strong and so powerful that no one shall be able to elude it and destroy our rights under the Constitution and laws of our country. That is all we ask.

But, Mr. Speaker, the gentleman from North Carolina [Mr. VANCE] asks that the colored man shall place himself in an attitude to receive his rights. I ask, what attitude can we assume? We have tilled your soil, and during the rude shock of the war, until our hour came, we were docile during that long, dark night, waiting patiently the coming day. In the Southern States during that war our men and women stood behind their masters; they tilled the soil, and there were no insurrections in all the broad lands of the South; the wives and daughters of the slaveholders were as sacred then as they were before; and the history of the war does not record a single event, a single instance, in which the colored people were unfaithful, even in slavery; nor does the history of the war record the fact that on the other side, on the side of the Union, there were any colored men who were not willing at all times to give their lives for their country. Sir, upon both sides we waited patiently. I was a student at Wilberforce University, in Ohio, when the tocsin of war was sounded, when Fort Sumter was fired upon, and I never shall forget the thrill that ran through my soul when I thought of the coming consequences of that shot. There were one hundred and fifteen of us, students at that university, who, anxious to vindicate the stars and stripes, made up a company, and offered our services to the governor of Ohio; and, sir, we were told that it was a white man's war and that the negro had nothing to do with it. Sir, we returned—docile, patient, waiting, casting our eyes to the heavens whence help always comes. We knew that there would come a period in the history of this nation when our strong black arms would be needed. We waited patiently; we waited until Massachusetts, through her noble governor, sounded the alarm, and we hastened then to hear the summons and obey it.

Sir, as I before remarked, we were peaceful on both sides. When the call was made on the side of the Union we were ready; when the call was made for us to obey orders on the other side, in the confederacy, we humbly performed our tasks, and waited patiently. But, sir, the time came when we were called for; and I ask, who can say that when that call was made, the colored man did not respond as readily and as rapidly as did any other class of your citizens? Sir, I need not speak of the history of this bloody war. It will carry down to coming generations the valor of our soldiers on the battlefield. Fort Wagner will stand forever as a monument of that valor, and until Vicksburg shall be wiped from the galaxy of battles in the great contest for human liberty that valor will be recognized.

And for what, Mr. Speaker and gentleman, was the great war made? The gentleman from North Carolina [Mr. VANCE] announced before he sat down, in answer to an interrogatory by a gentleman on this side of the House, that they went into the war conscientiously before God. So be it. Then we simply come and plead conscientiously before God that these are our rights, and we want them. We plead conscientiously before God, believing that these are our rights by inheritance, and by the inexorable decree of Almighty God.

We believe in the Declaration of Independence, that all men are born free and equal, and are endowed by their Creator with certain inalienable rights, among which are life, liberty, and the pursuit of happiness. And we further believe that to secure those rights governments are instituted. And we further believe that when governments cease to subserve those ends the people should change them.

I have been astonished at the course which gentlemen on the other side have taken in discussing this bill. They plant themselves right behind the Constitution and declare that the rights of the State ought not to be invaded. Now, if you will take the history of the war of the rebellion, as published by the Clerk of this House, you will see that in 1860 the whole country, each side, was earnest in seeking to make such amendments to the Constitution as would forever secure slavery and keep the Union together under the circumstances. The resolutions passed, and the sentiments expressed in speeches at that time, if examined by gentlemen, will be found to bear out all that I have indicated. It was felt in 1860 that anything that would keep the "wayward sisters" from going astray was desirable. They were then ready and willing to make any amendments.

And now, when the civil rights of our race are hanging upon the issue, they on the other side are not willing to concede to us such amendments as will guarantee them; indeed, they seek to impair the force of existing amendments to the Constitution of the United States, which would carry out the purpose.

I think it is proper and just that the civil-rights bill should be passed. Some think it would be better to modify it, to strike out the school clause, or to so modify it that some of the State constitutions should not be infringed. I regard it essential to us and the people of this country that we should be secured in this if in nothing else. I cannot regard that our rights will be secured until the jury-box and the school-room, those great palladiums of our liberty, shall have been opened to us. Then we will be willing to take our chances with other men.

We do not want any discriminations to be made. If discriminations are made in regard to schools, then there will be accomplished just what we are fighting against. If you say that the schools in the State of Georgia, for instance, shall be allowed to discriminate against colored people, then you will have discriminations made against us. We do not want any discriminations. I do not ask any legislation for the colored people of this country that is not applied to the white people. All that we ask is equal laws, equal legislation, and equal rights throughout the length and breadth of this land.

The gentleman from North Carolina [Mr. VANCE] also says that the colored men should not come here begging at the doors of Congress for their rights. I agree with him. I want to say that we do not come here begging for our rights. We come here clothed in the garb of American citizenship. We come demanding our rights in the name of justice. We come, with no arrogance on our part, asking that this great nation, which laid the foundations of civilization and progress more deeply and more securely than any other nation on the face of the earth, guarantee us protection from outrage. We come here, five millions of people—more than composed this whole nation when it had its great tea-party in Boston Harbor, and demanded its rights at the point of the bayonet—asking that unjust discriminations against us be forbidden. We come here in the name of justice, equity, and law, in the name of our children, in the name of our country, petitioning for our rights.

Our rights will yet be accorded to us, I believe, from the feeling that has been exhibited on this floor of the growing sentiment of the country. Rapid as the weaver's shuttle, swift as the lightning's flash, such progress is being made that our rights will be accorded to us ere long. I believe the nation is perfectly willing to accord this measure of justice, if only those who represent the people here would say the word. Let it be proclaimed that henceforth all the children of this land shall be free; that the stars and stripes, waving over all, shall secure to every one equal rights, and the nation will say "amen."

Let the civil-rights bill be passed this day, and five million black men, women, and children, all over the land, will begin a new song of rejoicing, and the thirty-five millions of noble hearted Anglo-Saxons will join in the shout of joy. Thus will the great mission be fulfilled of giving to all the people equal rights.

Inasmuch as we have toiled with you in building up this nation; inasmuch as we have suffered side by side with you in the war; inasmuch as we have together passed through affliction and pestilence, let there be now a fulfillment of the sublime thought of our father—let all men enjoy equal liberty and equal rights.

In this hour, when you are about to put the cap-stone on the mighty structure of government, I ask you to grant us this measure, because it is right. Grant this, and we shall go home with our hearts filled with gladness. I want to "shake hands over the bloody chasm." The gentleman from North Carolina has said that he desires to have forever buried the memory of the recent war. I agree with him. Representing a South Carolina constituency, I desire to bury forever the tomahawk. I have voted in this House with a free heart to declare universal amnesty. Inasmuch as general amnesty has been proclaimed, I would hardly have expected there would be any objection on this floor to the civil-rights bill, giving to all men the equal rights of citizens. There should be no more contest. Amnesty and civil rights should go together. Gentlemen on the other side will admit that we have been faithful; and now, when we propose to bury the hatchet, let us shake hands upon this measure of justice; and if heretofore we have been enemies, let us be friends now and forever.

Our wives and our children have high hopes and aspirations; their longings for manhood and womanhood are equal to those of any other race. The same sentiment of patriotism and of gratitude, the same spirit of national pride that animates the hearts of other citizens, animates theirs. In the name of the dead soldiers of our race, whose bodies lie at Petersburg and on other battle-fields of the South; in the name of the widows and orphans they have left behind; in the name of the widows of the confederate soldiers who fell upon the same fields, I conjure you let this righteous act be done. I appeal to you in the name of God and humanity to give us our rights, for we ask nothing more.

LUCY E. PARSONS

Lucy E. Parsons (1851–1942) was a radical African American anarchist who was born enslaved in Texas. Along with her husband, Albert (1848–1887), she began labor organizing and participating in a wide range of activism to protect workers, women, and people of color. Parsons wrote for the Socialist *newspaper and the* Alarm *in Chicago, Illinois, and helped found the International Working People's Association. In 1886, Albert was arrested and executed by hanging after being found guilty of conspiracy to commit the Haymarket Square bombing, during which a police officer perished. Parsons continued her political agitation after her husband's death, adding her commitment to anti-lynching campaigns and her work to identify and defeat instances of Black peonage in the South. In 1886, her powerful speech "I Am an Anarchist" was published in the* Kansas City Journal.

"I Am an Anarchist"

(1886)

I am an anarchist. I suppose you came here, the most of you, to see what I, a real, live anarchist looked like. I suppose some of you expected to see me with a bomb in one hand and a flaming torch in the other, but are disappointed in seeing neither. If such has been your ideas regarding an anarchist, you deserved to be disappointed. Anarchists are peaceable, law abiding people. What do anarchists mean when they speak of anarchy? Webster gives the term two definitions, chaos and the state of being without political rule. We cling to the latter definition. Our enemies hold that we believe only in the former.

Do you wonder why there are anarchists in this country, in this great land of liberty, as you love to call it? Go to New York. Go through the byways and alleys of that great city. Count the

myriads starving; count the multiplied thousands who are homeless; number those who work harder than slaves and live on less
and have fewer comforts than the meanest slaves. You will be
dumbfounded by your discoveries, you who have paid no attention to these poor, save as objects of charity and commiseration.
They are not objects of charity, they are the victims of the rank
injustice that permeates the system of government, and of political economy that holds sway from the Atlantic to the Pacific. Its
oppression, the misery it causes, the wretchedness it gives birth
to, are found to a greater extent in New York than elsewhere. In
New York, where not many days ago two governments united in
unveiling a statue of liberty, where a hundred bands played that
hymn of liberty, "The Marseillaise." But almost its equal is
found among the miners of the West, who dwell in squalor and
wear rags, that the capitalists, who control the earth that should
be free to all, may add still further to their millions! Oh, there
are plenty of reasons for the existence of anarchists.

But in Chicago they do not think anarchists have any right to
exist at all. They want to hang them there, lawfully or unlaw-
fully. You have heard of a certain Haymarket meeting. You have
heard of a bomb. You have heard of arrests and of succeeding
arrests effected by detectives. Those detectives! There is a set of
men nay, beasts for you! Pinkerton detectives! They would do
anything. I feel sure capitalists wanted a man to throw that bomb
at the Haymarket meeting and have the anarchists blamed for it.
Pinkerton could have accomplished it for him. You have heard a
great deal about bombs. You have heard that the anarchists said
lots about dynamite. You have been told that Lingg made bombs.
He violated no law. Dynamite bombs can kill, can murder, so
can Gatling guns. Suppose that bomb had been thrown by an
anarchist. The constitution says there are certain inalienable
rights, among which are a free press, free speech and free assem-
blage. The citizens of this great land are given by the constitution
the right to repel the unlawful invasion of those rights. The meeting at Haymarket square was a peaceable meeting. Suppose,
when an anarchist saw the police arrive on the scene, with murder in their eyes, determined to break up that meeting, suppose
he had thrown that bomb; he would have violated no law. That
will be the verdict of your children. Had I been there, had I seen

those murderous police approach, had I heard that insolent command to disperse, had I heard Fielden say, "Captain, this is a peaceable meeting," had I seen the liberties of my countrymen trodden under foot, I would have flung the bomb myself. I would have violated no law, but would have upheld the constitution.

If the anarchists had planned to destroy the city of Chicago and to massacre the police, why was it they had only two or three bombs in hand? Such was not their intention. It was a peaceable meeting. Carter Harrison, the mayor of Chicago, was there. He said it was a quiet meeting. He told Bonfield [Captain John Bonfield, Commander of Desplaines Police Station] to send the police to their different beats. I do not stand here to gloat over the murder of those policemen. I despise murder. But when a ball from the revolver of a policeman kills it is as much murder as when death results from a bomb.

The police rushed upon that meeting as it was about to disperse. Mr. Simonson talked to Bonfield about the meeting. Bonfield said he wanted to do the anarchists up. Parsons went to the meeting. He took his wife, two ladies and his two children along. Toward the close of the meeting, he said, "I believe it is going to rain. Let us adjourn to Zeph's hall." Fielden said he was about through with his speech and would close it at once. The people were beginning to scatter about, a thousand of the more enthusiastic still lingered in spite of the rain. Parsons, and those who accompanied him started for home. They had gone as far as the Desplaine's street police station when they saw the police start at a double quick. Parsons stopped to see what was the trouble. Those 200 policemen rushed on to do the anarchists up. Then we went on. I was in Zeph's hall when I heard that terrible detonation. It was heard around the world. Tyrants trembled and felt there was something wrong.

The discovery of dynamite and its use by anarchists is a repetition of history. When gun powder was discovered, the feudal system was at the height of its power. Its discovery and use made the middle classes. Its first discharge sounded the death knell of the feudal system. The bomb at Chicago sounded the downfall of the wage system of the nineteenth century. Why? Because I know no intelligent people will submit to despotism. The first means the diffusion of power. I tell no man to use it.

But it was the achievement of science, not of anarchy, and would do for the masses. I suppose the press will say I belched forth treason. If I have violated any law, arrest me, give me a trial, and the proper punishment, but let the next anarchist that comes along ventilate his views without hindrance.

Well, the bomb exploded, the arrests were made and then came that great judicial farce, beginning on June 21. The jury was impaneled. Is there a Knight of Labor here? Then know that a Knight of Labor was not considered competent enough to serve on that jury. "Are you a Knight of Labor?" "Have you any sympathy with labor organizations?" were the questions asked each talisman. If an affirmative answer was given, the talisman was bounced. It was not are you a Mason, a Knight Templar? O, no! [Great applause.] I see you read the signs of the times by that expression. Hangman Gary, miscalled judge, ruled that if a man was prejudiced against the defendants, it did not incapacitate him for serving on the jury. For such a man, said Hangman Gary, would pay closer attention to the law and evidence and would be more apt to render a verdict for the defense. Is there a lawyer here? If there is he knows such a ruling is without precedent and contrary to all law, reason or common sense.

In the heat of patriotism the American citizen sometimes drops a tear for the nihilist of Russia. They say the nihilist can't get justice, that he is condemned without trial. How much more should he weep for his next door neighbor, the anarchist, who is given the form of trial upon such a ruling.

There were "squealers" introduced as witnesses for the prosecution. There were three of them. Each and every one was compelled to admit they had been purchased and intimidated by the prosecution. Yet Hangman Gary held their evidence as competent. It came out in the trial that the Haymarket meeting was the result of no plot, but was caused in this wise. The day before the wage slaves in McCormick's factory had struck for eight hours labor, McCormick, from his luxurious office, with one stroke of the pen by his idle, be ringed fingers, turned 4,000 men out of employment. Some gathered and stoned the factory. Therefore they were anarchists, said the press. But anarchists are not fools; only fools stone buildings. The police were sent out and they killed six wage slaves. You didn't know that. The capitalistic press kept it quiet, but it made a great fuss over the killing of some policemen. Then these crazy anarchists, as they are called, thought a meeting ought to be held to consider the killing of six brethren and to discuss the eight hour movement. The meeting was held. It was peaceable. When Bonfield ordered the police to charge those peaceable anarchists, he hauled down the American flag and should have been shot on the spot.

While the judicial farce was going on the red and black flags were brought into court, to prove that the anarchists threw the bomb. They were placed on the walls and hung there, awful specters before the jury. What does the black flag mean? When a cable gram says it was carried through the streets of a European city it means that the people are suffering—that the men are out of work, the women starving, the children barefooted. But, you say, that is in Europe. How about America? The *Chicago Tribune* said there were 30,000 men in that city with nothing to do. Another authority said there were 10,000 barefooted children in mid winter. The police said hundreds had no place to sleep or warm. Then President Cleveland issued his Thanksgiving proclamation and the anarchists formed in procession and carried the black flag to show that these thousands had nothing for which to return thanks. When the Board of Trade, that gambling den, was dedicated by means of a banquet, $30 a plate, again the black flag was carried, to signify that there were thousands who couldn't enjoy a 2 cent meal.

But the red flag, the horrible red flag, what does that mean? Not that the streets should run with gore, but that the same red blood courses through the veins of the whole human race. It meant the brotherhood of man. When the red flag floats over the world the idle shall be called to work. There will be an end of prostitution for women, of slavery for man, of hunger for children.

Liberty has been named anarchy. If this verdict is carried out it will be the death knell of America's liberty. You and your children will be slaves. You will have liberty if you can pay for it. If this verdict is carried out, place the flag of our country at half mast and write on every fold "shame." Let our flag be trailed in the dust. Let the children of workingmen place laurels to the brow of these modern heroes, for they committed no crime. Break the two fold yoke. Bread is freedom and freedom is bread.

At the close of slavery, newly freed Black people often went in search of long-lost relatives and friends who had been sold away or otherwise could not be located. Several Christian publications printed "Lost Friends" notices, which listed the last-known names and locations of the persons whom the petitioners were in search of as well as the longing that sorrowful petitioners possessed for reunion. Decades later, these formerly enslaved people were still in search of their loved ones, a testament to the fact that even the brutal horrors of slavery could not break the bonds of affection or loyalty between family members and chosen kin. Printed here are select Lost Friends notices that were published in the 1880s and 1890s by the Southwestern Christian Advocate, *a New Orleans–based newspaper.*

Lost Friends Advertisements from the *Southwestern Christian Advocate*
(1880s–1890s)

APRIL 15, 1880

[NOTE.—We receive many letters asking for information about lost friends. All such letters will be published in this column. We make no charge for publishing these letters from subscribers to the SOUTHWESTERN. All others will please enclose fifty cents to pay for publishing the notices. Pastors will please read the requests published below from their pulpits, and report any case where friends are brought together by means of letters in the SOUTHWESTERN.]

DEAR EDITOR—I desire information of my mother, sisters and brothers. Mother belonged to Wm Taller. Father was Drury. Mother married John Semmen. When last heard from she was living in St. Joseph, Mo. I was then living with the family of Oscar Newton, Summit, Miss. Address me at Lavernia, Texas.

MRS. KATY REESE.

NOVEMBER 18, 1880

[We make no charge for publishing these letters from subscribers. All others will be charged fifty cents. Pastors will please read the requests published below from their pulpits, and report any case where friends are brought together by means of letters in the SOUTHWESTERN.]

MR. EDITOR—I wish to inquire for my friends, named Adline Baily and Tommy Kingsbury. The first belonged to the old widow White that lived at Buck Snort, Miss., and they went from Mississippi, up on the Pigeon Roost plank road, and stayed there three years, and Tommy went from there to Hernando, Miss., and Ned White sold Tommy to Kingsbury, and he brought him to Texas in 1858. Adeline Baily was sold to John Baily, and she lived at Senatobia, Miss., and after she left there the second year of the war she went to Texas. I don't know what county. Their father was Allen White; now goes by the name of Allen Tally. Their mother was named Eliza White; now goes by Eliza Tally. They were separated from Tommy in Hernando, Miss., and were seperated from Adeline on the Pigeon Roost, Plank Road, Shelby county, Tennessee. Eliza had only four children, Phillis belonged to Lewis White at Buck Snort, De Soto county, Miss., Adline was the next and Tommy. Rosana the oldest is dead. Address me Springfield, Conway county, Ark., Box 32.

W. D. DAVIS.

JANUARY 20, 1881

[We make no charge for publishing these letters from subscribers. All others will be charged fifty cents. Pastors will
please read the requests published below from their pulpits,
and report any case where friends are brought together by
means of letters in the SOUTHWESTERN.]

DEAR EDITOR—I wish to inquire for my son. I left him
in Montgomery, Ala., in 1865 with my owner, William Bel-
fort. His name is Henry Mason and my name is Elvira
Strued, and the last time I heard of him he was in Kansas.
His father's name was Edward Strued. Please address me at
Benton, Miss., in care of Rev. J. C. Clemons.

MAY 19, 1881

DEAR EDITOR—I desire information of my brothers and
sisters whom I left near Perryville, Mercer Co., Ky., in 1828. I
and my brother Cip, and Mary, were owned by Peter Lyster. I
was sold to Capt. R. A. Hinckley, and was carried to Mississippi, and from there to Sabine county, Texas. Brother Cip and
Sister Mary were sold to John Leddywich, of Mercer county.

JESSY LYSTER.
Milam, Sabine Co., Texas.

NOVEMBER 17, 1881

MR. EDITOR—I write to inquire for my son and daughter.
His name is John Batis Botlow. Her name Elisabeth Botlow.
Our master was Pierre Botlow. Our home was on Bayou De-
glaise, Avoyelles Parish, La., near St. Marks. Left my son in
Vicksburg, and daughter in Frenier. My mistress name An-
cine Laura Botlow. my youngest daughter and the one I have
with me Sylvinia Botlow, my name Maria Botlow but now
Mary Brown. My owners were French. I live near Monroe,
La., Ouachita parish.

MAY 14, 1885

MR. EDITOR—I wish to inquire for my son, Daniel Nathaniel Johnson. He used to belong to Dr. Monette, of Washington, Adams county, Miss. My name is Millie Johnson; his
father's name is Gabriel Johnson. We have another son
whose name is Willis Johnson, who left at the same time, but
has returned, saying that he left Daniel in Nashville. Any information concerning him will be gladly received by Millie
Johnson.

SEPTEMBER 23, 1886

[We make no charge for publishing these letters from subscribers. All others will be charged fifty cents. Pastors will
please read the requests published below from their pulpits,
and report any case where friends are brought together by
means of letters in the SOUTHWESTERN.]

MR. EDITOR—I desire to find my people, whom I left 51
years ago in Owen county, Virginia. I have neither seen or
heard of them since. My mother was named Bettie Callie.
Father lived with Mr. Thomas Nelson and mother with Mr.
Chickams. I had one brother and four sisters, as follows:
James Callie, Lucy, Edney, Sarah, and Susan. My grandmother and father were named Lewis and Susan and they
belonged to the Thompson estate. I am very anxious to learn
whether any of them still live, and if so, where. Address
Melton Napper, Ooltewah, James county, Tenn.

DECEMBER 16, 1886

MR. EDITOR—I have found out where my brother Emanuel and Stephen are by the help of the SOUTHWESTERN. So
please to make another inquiry for my sister Pinnie and her
husband Robin; Robert is his name, but they call him Robin;
their eldest sons are named Stephen and Richard, and girls

are Mame, Emmer and Caloline. I haven't called half of her childrens' names, as I cannot remember them; I have four names of cousins: Edmond, Comadore, Hudson, Nelson, all of them use to belong to Joe Green, who lived near Montgomery, Ala., and I have got one brother and sister I have not found yet. Brother Stephen told me that they were sold in New Orleans and was sold together, names are Frank and Mrry. Our first owner was Louis Toliver. I was born in Georgia, and when Louis Toliver moved to Mississippi I was 7 or 8 years old, and when I left there I went up to the plantation that was called the Monroe Place with Nick Toliver, my young master, and was sold to Morgan Smith in Alabams, and he died in the summer about the year 1860, and about the last of November 1860 I was moved to Louisiana by Frank Smith, and I pray God they may see this. Any information as to her whereabouts will be gladly received. Address Valentine Toliver, Shreveport, La.

JUNE 28, 1888

MR. EDITOR—My father's name was Rich, but was called Bob. He was a free colored man. My mother's name was Mary Ann McMullen. There were seven children of us: Mary Jane, General, Louisa, Millie, Andrew, Lucinda and Sammie. I think we were separated from mother and father at Alexandria, La., bought by a man named Dempsey, who was killed shortly after in Alexandria. My father was off at the time that we were taken away. He went off with a herd of cattle. I also had an uncle by the name of Joe, and one by the name Sam Gandy, who was at the time a Methodist preacher. I am the oldest of the children. Any one that will give me any information about the above named persons will be so thankfully received. Please address me at Waco, Tex., in care of Rev. J. T. Gibbons, box 65. Mrs. Mary Jane Randolph.

JULY 19, 1888

MR. EDITOR—I desire to inquire for the mother of Mrs. Adeline Allison. Her name was Adeline Sheels. Her mother's name was Hannah Sheely. She was taken from Nashville, Tenn., two years before the war by traders to Louisiana, and she wrote to Nashville, Tenn., ten years ago, but the letter was not received. Any information will be gladly received. Address Rev. R. A. Fletcher, Union City, Tenn.

AUGUST 9, 1888

DEAR EDITOR—I wish to find my son who left me the third year after surrender. He went from Tehula, Miss., to Alabama; to what part I cannot say. I used to belong to Jeff Poole. My son had, when he left, five sisters, viz: Louisiana, Masourria, Sophronia, Mary and Laura, and four brothers, viz: Tom Fletcher, Sam Moore and Hamilton Wright. His father's name was Peter Moore and his name was Peter Moore, Jr. He left a wife by name of Chloe on Col. Johnson's place near Tehula. Henry I. Richmond is his stepfather and was when he left. Any information about him will speak peace to a troubled mother. Address me in care of Rev. G. W. Beamon, Howard, Miss.

MARY J. RICHMOND.

AUGUST 23, 1888

DEAR EDITOR—Will you please inquire for my people. My mother was Katie Holmes; she lived in Georgia in 1846. I was stolen from her in 1841, by Sam McCrary. My mother belonged to Bob McDonald. The last I heard from her she was in Jasper, Texas, Tyler Co., she belonged to Jim Delaney. I have two sisters who were with my mother, Amy Ann Holmes and Mary Jane Holmes. I also had three sisters who were brought to Texas, and one brother; Harriet, Rachel and Mary and Dennis Ragen. He stopped in Victoria, Texas. I have also another brother and sister, Hannah and Abraham, who was a twin to Rachel. Amy Ann and Dennis were twins also. The last I heard from them they were on Red River in Texas. I had a brother named January, married to Betsey. The last I heard of them they were in Jasper, Texas. The four that were brought to Victoria were owned by Wyatt Hanks. Mary Jane was left with John Hanks, and was married at that time to John Teel. Dan died three miles from Cuero, Tex. Brother Dennis died in Victoria. When Harriet left Victoria she had a daughter named Katie, after her mother. Address any information at Wharton, Tex.

LAURA BROWN.

APRIL 18, 1889

[We make no charge for publishing these letters from subscribers. All others will be charged fifty cents. Pastors will please read the requests published below from their pulpits, and report any case where friends are brought together by means of letters in the SOUTHWESTERN.]

DEAR EDITOR: I wish to inquire for my children, one son and daughter. My son was Clabron Partlo, daughter, Caroline Hale. Clabron was owned by a Mr. Dempie Pattlo, who lived near Ashville, Ala. Caroline was owned by a Mr. Morton Hale, who lived near Centre, Cherokee County, Ala. I belonged to a Mr. Sam Eckcles in Cherokee County, Ala. Any information will be gladly received. Address me at Kosciusko, Miss.

CLABRON KEGTON.

JUNE 27, 1889

MR. EDITOR: I wish to inquire for my dear mother and father whom I left in Virginia when I was sold at ten years old.

My name at that time was Roe Burter Anna King George Thomas. My father's name was Louis Taylor and mother was Elizabeth Taylor. My brothers were Robert Taylor, Jack Taylor and James Taylor. Sisters were Lina Taylor and Sally Taylor. My master's name was Mr. Wm. Quall. My father belonged to Mr. Dick Wartha, son of J. Taylor. The last time I was with my people, they were living in Virginia near Stern's Postoffice I was sold at Bowling Green, Va., at ten years old. My master had been married three times before I was sold, and all three of his wives were buried in the garden. My dear mother and father, do you remember what you said to me when I was sold? You told me if you never saw me in this life you wanted to meet me in heaven. I am married now and have six children. My husband is named Geo. Quinn. I go by the name of Anna Quinn. Any information will be gladly received. In care of Rev. W. R. M. Gatewood, Akerman, Miss.

FEBRUARY 28, 1895

[We make no charge for publishing these letters from yearly subscribers. Others will be charged 50 cents. Pastors will please read the requests published below from their pulpits, and report any case where friends are brought together by means of letters in the SOUTHWESTERN.]

I wish to make some inquiry for my relatives. I was born in Tuscumba, Franklin county, Alabama, July 4, 1833. Manda Boney was mother's name. She moved back to Alabama three years before the civil war. I am her oldest son. I have not heard from her but once since she left Texas. If living, she is about 80 years of age. She was the mother of ten children. Address Thomas Winston, Montgomery, Texas.

Bibliography

Camp, Stephanie M. H. *Closer to Freedom: Enslaved Women and Everyday Resistance in the Plantation South.* Chapel Hill: University of North Carolina Press, 2004.

Douglass, Frederick. "West India Emancipation." In *Two Speeches; One on West India Emancipation, Delivered at Canandaigua, Aug. 4th, and the Other on the Dred Scott Decision, Delivered in New York, on the Occasion of the Anniversary of the American Abolition Society, May, 1857, 3–24.* Rochester, NY: C. P. Dewey, 1857.

Equiano, Olaudah. *The Interesting Narrative of the Life of Olaudah Equiano, or Gustavus Vassa, the African / Written by Himself.* New York: W. Durell, 1791.

Schomburg, Arthur A. "The Negro Digs Up His Past." *Survey Graphic* (March 1925): 670–72.

Sinha, Manisha. *The Slave's Cause: A History of Abolition.* New Haven, CT: Yale University Press, 2017.

Smallwood, Stephanie. *Saltwater Slavery: A Middle Passage from Africa to American Diaspora.* Cambridge, MA: Harvard University Press, 2008.

Stanton, Lucy. "A Plea for the Oppressed." *Oberlin Evangelist*, December 17, 1850.

Trans-Atlantic Slave Trade Database. https://www.slavevoyages.org. Accessed July 30, 2020.

Walker, David. *Walker's Appeal, in Four Articles; Together with a Preamble, to the Coloured Citizens of the World, but in Particular, and Very Expressly, to Those of the United States of America, Written in Boston, State of Massachusetts, September 28, 1829.* 3rd ed. Boston: David Walker, 1830.

ALSO AVAILABLE

THE PORTABLE NINETEENTH-CENTURY AFRICAN AMERICAN WOMEN WRITERS
Edited with an Introduction by Hollis Robbins and Henry Louis Gates, Jr.
General Editor: Henry Louis Gates, Jr.

THE PORTABLE FREDERICK DOUGLASS
Frederick Douglass
Edited with an Introduction and Notes by John Stauffer and Henry Louis Gates, Jr.

THE LIGHT OF TRUTH
Writings of an Anti-Lynching Crusader
Ida B. Wells
Edited with an Introduction and Notes by Mia Bay
General Editor: Henry Louis Gates, Jr.

NARRATIVE OF THE LIFE OF FREDERICK DOUGLASS, AN AMERICAN SLAVE
Frederick Douglass
Edited with an Introduction by Ira Dworkin

TWELVE YEARS A SLAVE
Solomon Northup
Foreword by Steve McQueen
Introduction by Ira Berlin
Afterword by Henry Louis Gates, Jr.
General Editor: Henry Louis Gates, Jr.

THE INTERESTING NARRATIVE AND OTHER WRITINGS
Revised Edition
Olaudah Equiano
Introduction by Vincent Carretta

 PENGUIN CLASSICS

Ready to find your next great classic? Let us help. Visit prh.com/penguinclassics